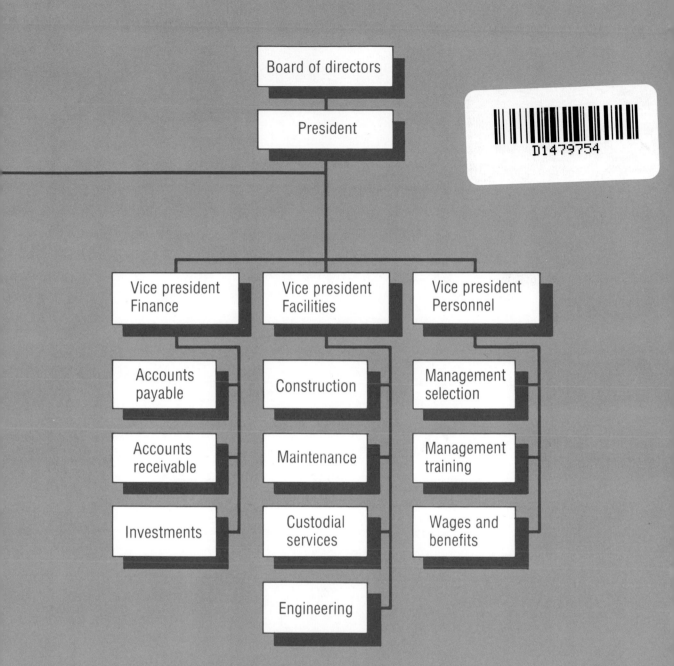

Peter's Pan Pizza, Inc.
Before the Merger

Industrial/Organizational Psychology SCIENCE AND PRACTICE

Industrial/Organizational Psychology SCIENCE AND PRACTICE

Frank E. Saal
Patrick A. Knight
Kansas State University

Brooks/Cole Publishing Company
Pacific Grove, California

Brooks/Cole Publishing Company
A Division of Wadsworth, Inc.

Printed in the United States of America

10 9 8 7 6 5 4 3 2

Library of Congress Cataloging-in-Publication Data
Saal, Frank E. [date]
    Industrial/organizational psychology.

    Bibliography: p.
    Includes index.
    1. Psychology, Industrial. I. Knight, Patrick A.,
            . II. Title.
HF5548.8.S225   1987   158.7   87-21824
ISBN 0-534-08214-9

Sponsoring Editor: C. DEBORAH LAUGHTON
Project Development Editor: JOHN BERGEZ
Marketing Representative: JONELLE C. CALON
Editorial Assistants: MONIQUE ETIENNE AND AMY MAYFIELD
Production Editor: PENELOPE SKY
Production Assistant: DOROTHY BELL
Permissions Editor: CARLINE HAGA
Interior and Cover Design: VERNON T. BOES
Art Coordinator: LISA TORRI
Interior Illustration: PRECISION GRAPHICS
Typesetting: OMEGATYPE TYPOGRAPHY, INC., CHAMPAIGN, ILLINOIS
Printing and Binding: THE MAPLE–VAIL BOOK MANUFACTURING GROUP, MANCHESTER, PENNSYLVANIA

To Cathie and Diane, our wives;
and to our children:
Kiersten, Kaele, and Kevin;
Malachi and Mikeile.

PREFACE

Most college students have already participated in the paid work force, either by holding down summer jobs or by working full time. Almost all of them will join that work force in the not-too-distant future. The field of industrial/organizational (I/O) psychology focuses on women's and men's work behavior, and is therefore relevant to every student, regardless of major field of study, curriculum, or career aspirations. You might expect, then, that students would find any textbook devoted to I/O psychology to be inherently interesting. Unfortunately, this is just not so.

Discussions with many of our students have convinced us that I/O psychology textbooks typically suffer from one or more of three serious ailments: (1) prose that is either highly sophisticated and laden with technical jargon, or far too simplistic for a post-secondary school audience; (2) discussions that overemphasize some aspects of I/O psychology and treat other aspects too lightly, and that fail to integrate the many issues and concerns that make up the field; and (3) presentations that are dry and overly abstract because they fail to take advantage of the obviously applied nature of the discipline. Our decision to write this book evolved from our conviction that these pitfalls are not inevitable, from our enthusiasm for and fascination with a field that addresses problems that concern every working woman and man, and from our desire to describe it in a way that allows students to share our enthusiasm and fascination.

PEDAGOGICAL FEATURES

Terminology and Prose Style

Most of our readers will be undergraduate or beginning graduate students in courses offered by psychology departments or business schools. Some will have taken several other psychology courses, and perhaps a statistics course or two, and some will not. Given this diversity, we have tried not to presume any specialized knowledge or expertise. When we introduce new terms or ideas, we either define them extensively in the text, or provide a definition in the running glossary that appears on the same page as the new term or concept. Our prose is purposefully informal. This style reflects our belief that readability need not be sacrificed to academically sound scholarship, and that a text can be readable without trivializing the research and theory that it describes.

We also make a concerted effort to avoid using sexist language. We believe this is particularly important because I/O psychology has historically been one of the notorious male bastions within the field of psychology. Happily, "the times they are a'changin.' " As more and more women enter graduate programs in I/O psychology, our field is becoming more representative of the population at large. Our balanced use of masculine and feminine proper names and personal pronouns is specifically intended to support this constructive trend.

Balance and Integration

Although in the first half of the book we examine material that is traditionally considered to be "personnel psychology," and in the latter half we focus on topics associated with "organizational psychology," we have refrained from dividing the book into two explicitly separate sections. More significantly, we frequently point out how the material under discussion ties in with material that appears elsewhere in the book. Throughout, we emphasize how the various subjects that constitute I/O psychology fit together. Finally, the two halves of the book are approximately equal in length. This balance reflects our belief that each set of topics contains valuable contributions to our current understanding of people's behavior at work.

Application

We are most excited by our effort to avoid the abstraction common to I/O textbooks. The most widely used strategies for illustrating the applied nature of I/O psychology have been to interrupt each chapter with a box or two containing brief descriptions of workaday applications, or to append a relevant case study to the end of each chapter (or to completely ignore the issue!). Our solution is to create a fictional organization, Peter's Pan Pizza, Inc., with an industrial/organizational psychologist, Dr. Jennilyn A. MacKeven, on staff.

Each chapter begins with a memo that describes a specific problem or issue confronting our make-believe company. Throughout the chapter we examine our topic in terms of how it might (or might not) contribute to our I/O psychologist's efforts to respond to that situation. For example, in the chapter on work motivation our discussion is related to a manager's observation that a group of employees don't seem to be expending an appropriate amount of effort on their jobs. Motivation theories and relevant empirical research results are presented and analyzed with regard to how they might shed some light on the problem, and the kinds of solutions they might suggest.

At the conclusion of each chapter is a memo from Dr. MacKeven, responding to the memo that opened the chapter. She describes her thoughts about the current problem or issue, and offers tentative plans for solving that problem or clarifying the issue, using an approach drawn from the contents of the chapter. Dr. MacKeven's response, of course, is only one of many alternatives that an I/O psychologist might choose. At the very least, her decision can serve as a jumping-off point for further discussion of the chapter's content, and for presentation and discussion of other possible responses. After each closing memo is a list of review or "thought" questions that assist in summarizing the chapter's content and inspire further discussion and analysis of Dr. MacKeven's resolution of the problem at hand. The overall structure of the book thus brings the subject matter of I/O psychology to life, and shows its relevance to the everyday concerns of working women and men.

Our strategy also has the advantage of providing an element of continuity throughout the text. As readers progress through the chapters, they learn more and more about our fictional company. In each chapter we can present new material quickly and efficiently, without having to acquaint the reader with new organizational contexts, situations, and personnel. As readers come to know our I/O psychologist better, and perhaps empathize with her as she tackles challenging tasks, we hope that their interest in I/O psychology will become more personal, and that their appreciation of the exciting and relevant nature of the field will grow accordingly.

ACKNOWLEDGMENTS

Frank E. Saal

Although this textbook bears our names, we could neither have undertaken nor completed this project without the efforts of a number of other individuals. Professor Joseph M. Madden at Rensselaer Polytechnic Institute in Troy, New York, inspired me with his enthusiasm and love for the field of I/O psychology, and instilled an appreciation for excellence that continues to serve as a guiding beacon. Professor Frank J. Landy at Pennsylvania State University taught me the meaning of professional commitment, and convinced me that there is precious little that cannot be accomplished if one works hard enough (with the possible exception of playing a decent game of tennis!). Professors James L. Farr and Charles N. Cofer (then at Penn State) provided examples of patience, friendship, and scholarship, and the late Don Trumbo rescued a struggling graduate student on many an occasion. Professor E. Jerry Phares, my department head at Kansas State University, was a constant source of encouragement and much-needed advice from the very beginning of this project. So was my coauthor Pat, whose knowledge of the field, writing skills, dependability, and good humor are largely responsible for the modicum of sanity that is still mine.

Closer to home, I wish to express my love and gratitude to my wife Cathie, whose constructive criticism of every word of every draft was invaluable, whose support and understanding made it possible for me to devote so many hours to this project, and whose love makes my life worth living. And to my children, Kiersten, Kaele, and Kevin, who brighten my days, and who were willing to share their Daddy with the demands of this project, my thanks and love.

Patrick A. Knight

I would like to thank Professor Neal Schmitt at Michigan State University, who introduced me to the field of I/O psychology, and whose guidance and encouragement helped focus my career aspirations. Professor Howard M. Weiss at Purdue University, through dedication to sound research, thorough scholarship, and good humor, demonstrated that I/O psychology is a dynamic, responsive science, and that it is the responsibility of those in the field to define its boundaries. These lessons have served to keep my day-to-day work fresh and exciting, and I thank him especially for that. I also wish to thank the other faculty at Purdue, especially Professors Daniel R. Ilgen (now at Michigan State), Ernest J. McCormick, and Kay Deaux, whose excellent teaching and counsel were invaluable during my graduate school days. Also invaluable was the support and camaraderie of my 23 fellow members of the Purdue Association of Graduate Students in Industrial Psychology (PAGSIP). It is difficult to imagine not having been part of PAGSIP.

I strongly echo my coauthor's appreciation for the support given to us throughout this project by E. Jerry Phares. I also offer my personal thanks to Skip Saal himself. Although we shared writing responsibilities equally, this book was his brainchild and vision, and he attended to all of the pesky administrative details that popped up on a regular basis. I owe you one, Skip.

Finally, I want to express my thanks and love to my wife Diane, whose love and patience have been a sustaining force for years, and who put up with more than she could have ever expected while this book was being written; and to my sons Malachi and Mikeile, who have also learned to be patient, and of whom I am very proud.

Both of us express our appreciation to the many people at Brooks/Cole who transformed our ideas and our manuscript into the book you now hold in your hands. Jonelle C. Calon originally brought us to the attention of Brooks/Cole, and creatively borrowed a name for our fictional company from the first author's favorite childhood story. John Bergez and Jody Larson edited the first drafts of several of our chapters in ways that were both instructive and encouraging. Carline Haga helped us obtain permission to draw from the work of others in preparing this text, and Lisa Torri coordinated much of the art work. Designer Vernon Boes created the crisp and functional look of the text and cover. Penelope Sky ran the anchor lap in our race to the final deadline by carefully coordinating the many stages of production.

The manuscript was reviewed by Milton Davis, Portland State University; William Deeds, Moravian College; Patrick James Devine, Kennesaw College; Dan Farrell, Western Michigan University; Donald L. Grant, University of Georgia at Athens; Kenneth Heilman, University of Wisconsin at Eau Claire; Charles Hulin, University of Illinois at Champaign; Leon Meggison, Mobile College; John E. Nangle, Western Michigan University; James S. Phillips, University of Houston; Loriann Roberson, New York University; and Walter Vernon, Illinois State University, Normal.

In a class by herself is our editor, C. Deborah Laughton, who had the vision to see the merits of this project from the very beginning, the ability to convince us that Brooks/Cole was the company to publish it, the patience to stick with us as early deadlines came and went with no sign of a preliminary manuscript, and the courage to come to Manhattan, Kansas, in the middle of November to ensure that the final deadline for producing a revised manuscript would be treated with more respect. To C. Deborah, and to all who made this project possible, our heartfelt thanks.

FRANK E. SAAL
PATRICK A. KNIGHT

A WORD TO THE READER

Welcome to the field of industrial/organizational (I/O) psychology! We hope you will find our way of describing and presenting our subject both interesting and informative. As you will see, we have adopted a unique approach in our efforts to emphasize the relevance and potential for application that characterize the discipline. The cornerstone of our strategy is a fictional organization, Peter's Pan Pizza, Inc., which we use both as a context and as a source of continuity that should facilitate your understanding of the material. We refer you to the Preface for a more detailed discussion of our approach.

As you read the memo at the end of each chapter, in which the I/O psychologist at Peter's Pan Pizza describes her tentative plan for solving the problem posed in the chapter's opening memo, remember that Dr. MacKeven's decision is only one of several that might be made after mastering the material presented in the chapter. One way to assess your understanding of that material is to constructively criticize our I/O psychologist's plan, and to suggest one or more alternative approaches to solving the problem(s) at hand. We also urge you to attend to the "thought" or review questions at the end of each chapter. If you can answer them thoroughly and accurately, the chances are good that you have gained a satisfactory understanding of the material in that chapter. They will also help you to identify gaps in your knowledge that can be eliminated with further study and review.

Because some of our readers will have a greater number of psychology and statistics courses under their belts than others, we have tried to presume no specialized knowledge or expertise on your part. When we introduce a new word or concept, we either define it clearly right in the text itself, or we provide you with a clear definition in a running glossary on the same page that contains the new idea. Reviewing your knowledge of those new terms and concepts can also be a diagnostic exercise and a guide for further study.

One of our goals has been to emphasize the high degree of integration that can (and should) be inherent in the varied topics that make up I/O psychology. Although those topics are separated into chapters for purposes of clarity and organization, you should resist the temptation to consider them as relatively independent issues and concerns. Instead, we urge you to see how they fit together. To help you in this endeavor, we have included frequent cross-references throughout the text to material that appears either earlier or later in the book. We encourage you to pursue those references, especially those that allude to topics that you have already studied, so that you might appreciate the overall integration of I/O psychology's subject matter.

An additional piece of advice is in order before you begin. Because more people work in service industries than in traditional manufacturing and production jobs, we decided to locate our imaginary company within the service sector. As you proceed through the text, you should remain sensitive to instances when our choice of this specific industry might influence the ways in which the subject matter could be applied. In most cases, however, we are confident that focusing your attention on a particular type of industry should not detract from your appreciation of how I/O psychology can contribute to greater productivity and stronger feelings of satisfaction among the men and women whose labor fuels our economy.

Enjoy yourself!

BRIEF CONTENTS

CONTENTS

CHAPTER 2
An Organization, an I/O Psychologist, and Her Methods and Procedures   27

CHAPTER 3
Job-Performance Criteria   64

CHAPTER 4
Measurement and Evaluation of Work Performance   96

CHAPTER 6
Personnel Decision-Making Systems   178

CHAPTER 7
Personnel Training   216

CHAPTER 11
Labor Unions   374

CHAPTER 12
Organizations and Behavior   404

CHAPTER 13
Organizational Change   444

CHAPTER 1

Description and History of I/O Psychology

Learning Points

After studying this chapter, you should

- understand what psychology is, and how it relates to "common sense"
- know the difference between licensing and certification, and the advantages and disadvantages of each
- be able to describe the content and scope of industrial and organizational (I/O) psychology
- know how World Wars I and II contributed to the development of I/O psychology
- be able to explain the purpose, the results, and the significance of the Hawthorne studies
- be able to describe I/O psychology's development since the conclusion of World War II
- be prepared to speculate on the future of I/O psychology as a science and a profession

PSYCHOLOGY AND PSYCHOLOGISTS

We will begin our study of I/O psychology with a brief look at its parent discipline, general psychology, and those who research, teach, and practice it. We will continue with a more in-depth description of I/O psychology and psychologists, and provide an overview of some of the more significant events in the history of the field. Most of us are better able to understand and appreciate something when we can view it in an appropriate context. This remains true whether that "something" is an idea, another person's behavior, or a field of study.

Definition and Description of Psychology

The word "psychology" evolved from the Greek *psychē,* which originally signified the soul, the spirit, and the source of all vitality (Denmark, 1980). Although Wilhelm Wundt is commonly acknowledged as the "father" of the discipline, Russo and O'Connell (1980) reminded us of some of psychology's "foremothers'" contributions. The word "psychology" aptly described the subject matter of Wundt's research (attention, feelings, and other mental processes), as well as his primary methodological technique, **introspection,** which required people to "look inward" into their own minds.

Today psychology is typically defined as the scientific study of behavior. In this context, "behavior" can include the mental processes that fascinated Wundt, as well as the readily observable actions and responses that captured the attention of John B. Watson and B. F. Skinner, two noted **behaviorists.** As Mueller (1979) pointed out, the kinds of measurements one makes (objective behavioral observations or subjective introspective reports) do *not* define a discipline. Instead, a discipline is defined by the questions that it asks. Studying behavior does not mean that we have abandoned people's minds, thoughts, consciousness, or awareness.

An interesting issue is the relationship between the science and practice of psychology and "common sense." Gordon, Kleiman, and Hanie (1978) described common sense as "a homespun awareness resulting from everyday experience, as opposed to knowledge acquired from formal training in a technical philosophy" (p. 894). They suggested that the development of human common sense must have had important survival value to the species. Blum and Naylor (1968) were quite clear on the nature of this relationship: " . . . the term *psychology* is not synonymous with 'common sense.' Often when 'common sense' is applied, the conclusions are incorrect because of insufficient information or a confusion of cause and effect" (p. 1). After acknowledging that "commonsense psychology" may suffice in some situations, Zimbardo (1979) warned that "it can also at times lead . . . to false conclusions and ineffective actions . . . [perhaps] because of faulty assumptions about human nature, cultural and personal biases and prejudices, poorly controlled observations, or an uncritical acceptance of information provided by your senses, by so-called authorities, or by the mass media" (pp. 4–5).

Joynson (1974) disagreed, claiming that the layperson's conclusions are often based on long and varied experience, while psychological research "typically operates over short periods of time, in very restricted environments, and on narrow segments of behavior" (p. 9). Gordon et al. (1978) acknowledged that the results of psychological research are not always readily accepted if they contradict commonly held beliefs.

Our own position on this issue recognizes some truth in all these viewpoints. As we define it, human psychology is the study of individuals' behavior (thoughts, feelings, and consciousness, as well as observable actions) using one or more of a variety of techniques capable of producing information that is verifiable and replicable. Common sense is derived from people's everyday experiences that may or may not be verifiable in any scientific sense. When these two approaches to understanding human behavior lead to similar conclusions, we can have more confidence in those conclusions than either approach by itself could have provided. When they lead to contradictory conclusions, we should neither disparage the layperson's understanding nor reject the legitimacy of the psychologist's results. Rather, the psychologist should reexamine her **hypotheses** and procedures, and further explore this particular aspect of the layperson's self-understanding (Joynson, 1974); the layperson should critically examine his commonsense conclusions for the presence of faulty assumptions or personal and cultural biases (Zimbardo, 1979). Thus, the science and application of psychology and everyday common sense can each benefit from the insights of the other, whether those insights are congruent or wildly discrepant. Neither has a monopoly on truth.

Specialization   Like so many other fields of study (medicine may be the most visible example), psychology has become increasingly specialized in recent years. Perhaps the best indication of this trend is the fact that the American Psychological Association (APA) currently includes 40 separate divisions, each emphasizing a different aspect of the field.

Given the incredible diversity of interests and areas of expertise reflected in these 40 divisions, two observations are worth noting. First, as Muchinsky (1983) so eloquently stated, the idea that every psychologist "is a shrink, has a black couch, [and] likes to discover what makes people tick" (p. 3), commonly held by everyday people, is indeed a misconception. Although some of the divisions have a decidedly "clinical" flavor, most do not. Second, industrial and organizational psychologists tend to be concentrated in a very different subset of divisions than their clinically oriented colleagues. Although Division 14, the Society for Industrial and Organizational Psychology, claims the largest number of psychol-

---

introspection: the process of examining one's own consciousness or mental processes, focusing exclusively on sensations while ignoring the meanings commonly associated with those sensations

behaviorists: those who advocate the study of observable animal or human behaviors, and the relationships between those behaviors and observable environmental conditions

hypotheses: tentative assumptions, guesses, or hunches that often guide the research process

ogists interested in work-related topics, those specialists are also found in divisions that focus on military, engineering, and consumer psychology. Thus, specialization has not only influenced the field of psychology as a whole, but has also affected the subfield of I/O psychology, a topic to which we shall return shortly.

Psychologists' Education and Employment

Although most psychologists, like other individuals who work in psychological fields, have completed one or more graduate programs beyond the bachelor's degree, a few job opportunities exist for those with B.S. or B.A. degrees, and even for those holding two-year associate degrees. Master's degree programs typically take one or two years to complete, and often require the student to write a thesis based on a research project, and/or to obtain practical experience. Those with the M.S. or M.A. degree are usually supervised by psychologists with doctoral degrees, and can be found in a variety of work settings, including "teaching in two-year colleges . . . doing [laboratory] research in fields such as human factors, engineering psychology, industrial psychology, and human performance technology . . . [or working in] public and private treatment facilities and in school settings" (*Careers in Psychology*, 1980, pp. 20–21).

Most doctoral programs require four or more years beyond the bachelor's degree to complete. Requirements often include completion of a master's degree program, successful performance on rigorous written and oral examinations, preparation of a dissertation that represents an original research contribution to the field of psychology, and sometimes an internship (supervised on-the-job training) in a professional specialty (clinical, counseling, industrial, and so on). Those holding the doctor of philosophy (Ph.D.) degree in psychology have the widest range of job opportunities; these include teaching at the college or university level, providing therapy or counseling, offering private consultation to a variety of individuals and organizations, and conducting and publishing original psychological research. A recent innovation at the doctoral level is the doctor of psychology (Psy.D.) degree. Whereas the emphasis of the Ph.D. is on research, those who earn the Psy.D. concentrate more on practical experience and application. An original research contribution is usually not required.

The best source of information on graduate programs in psychology is a publication entitled *Graduate Study in Psychology*, published and revised annually by the APA. Program descriptions include the type(s) and specialty area(s) of degrees offered, minimum entrance requirements, numbers of degrees granted in recent years, and miscellaneous facts about the institutions. Students considering graduate study in psychology will find this book an invaluable resource.

As we indicated earlier, psychologists with advanced degrees are distributed among a variety of different employment settings. Colleges and universities are the primary employers of psychologists, followed by hospitals, clinics, and nonprofit organizations. Government, private business and industry, and self-employment—contexts in which I/O psychologists are highly visible—are also major employment sites.

Professional associations National organizations for psychologists include the APA, the Canadian Psychological Association, the British Psychological Association, and so forth. The APA, in addition to serving as the "mother" organization for the 40 divisions mentioned earlier, holds an annual convention at which members present their latest research, theory, and applications. The APA also publishes a variety of professional journals devoted to several of the major subdisciplines. According to Rubin-Rabson (1982) women constitute approximately 30 percent of the APA's membership. Many psychologists also belong to one or more regional associations, including the Midwestern, Eastern, New England, Southeastern, Western, and Southwestern Psychological Associations. Like the APA, these organizations hold annual conventions for the dissemination of timely ideas and empirical findings.

Psychologists also hold memberships in a wide assortment of other professional associations. In the United States these include state psychological associations, the Psychonomic Society, the Cognitive Science Society, the American Nurses' Association, and many others. International associations to which psychologists belong and contribute include the International Association for Cross-Cultural Psychology, the International Society of Political Psychology, the International Congress of Hypnosis and Psychosomatic Medicine, and the International Society for the Prevention of Child Abuse and Neglect, just to mention a few.

LICENSING AND CERTIFICATION

All 50 states regulate the practice of professional psychology by law. Shimberg (1981) reported that approximately 800 occupations in the United States are regulated by state governments (including nurses, barbers, pharmacists, physicians, horseshoers, and lightning rod installers), and so psychologists have not been singled out for special attention or harassment.

Licensing is the process whereby a government agency officially grants a person permission to engage in a particular occupation. Such permission is granted when the agency determines that the individual has attained the minimal degree of competency necessary to ensure that the health, safety, and welfare of the public will be reasonably well protected. Licensing usually specifies a "scope of practice" that defines what the person may do. It is illegal, then, for unlicensed individuals to engage in those activities. This is the more restrictive form of regulation.

Certification, on the other hand, is simply a form of "title control." This allows employers and the public to identify practitioners who have met a standard that is usually set well above the minimal level required for licensing. This form of regulation does not prohibit uncertified persons from practicing their occupations, however. It merely forbids them to use a particular title, such as "psychologist" (Shimberg, 1981).

Danish and Smyer (1981) and Locke (1982a) have criticized licensing requirements. According to Danish and Smyer, requiring helping professionals such as psychologists to obtain a license (often by demanding that they pass a written multiple-choice examination) does little to guarantee practitioners' competence. In addition, licensing procedures have several undesirable, albeit unintended consequences, such as increased cost of services, uneven public accessibility, restricted job mobility, and restricted innovation and self-direction of graduate study. Locke agreed, but suggested that these authors had ignored two even more fundamental problems: (1) that no government agency is capable of setting rational licensing standards that balance the potential harm versus benefits of state regulation in any morally justifiable way; and (2) that licensing is a blatant violation of individual rights, prohibiting free trade between consenting adults. Locke advocated consideration of noncoercive alternatives to licensing, such as private certification, competition for professional reputation, education of the public, and strict enforcement of antifraud legislation.

As Danish and Smyer (1981) acknowledged, it is very difficult to discuss licensing and its effects in a detached, unemotional manner, as several vital interests are involved. These include concern for the future of psychology (both the science and the profession), concern for the consumer and the community, and concern for individual psychologists' livelihoods. Although we recognize the shortcomings of current licensing procedures so eloquently described by these and other writers, we believe that the potential benefits outweigh the costs. Elimination of legal restrictions would leave the public completely vulnerable to charlatans and quacks of all types who are sufficiently glib to pass themselves off as qualified professionals. The public would suffer, as would the profession of psychology.

This is not to say, of course, that existing regulations need no improvement. Some professions require those who apply for a license to pass rigorous **performance tests** in addition to the standard paper-and-pencil exams; dentistry is a notable example. Others have recognized the need for periodic reexamination, peer review, audits of records, and/or continuing education as prerequisites for license renewal. Such innovations render licensing regulations more effective protection for the public and the various professions, including psychology.

I/O PSYCHOLOGY AND I/O PSYCHOLOGISTS

As we did with the field of psychology as a whole, we will now describe the discipline of I/O psychology, and continue by looking at the men and women who pursue that profession.

Definition and Description of I/O Psychology

More than a half century ago, Viteles (1932) described the field of industrial psychology as the "study of human behavior, with the view of guarding against . . . waste in the form of individual maladjustment and of industrial inefficiency." He added, "In formulating a program of industrial psychology the maximum *efficiency* of the individual in industry and his optimum *adjustment* are looked upon as complementary facets of a single objective" (p. 4). A review of other, more recent authors' definitions of the field reveals the extent to which Viteles' description has stood the test of time, despite the dramatic social and technological changes that have occurred in the intervening years.

In the preface to the first edition of his textbook, Tiffin (1942) insisted that the applications of industrial psychology were not limited to the selection and placement of employees, but that the field was also concerned with improving the quality of merit ratings, reducing accidents, solving visual problems, increasing inspection accuracy, improving training methods, and measuring and improving employee morale. Ten years later, Gray (1952) was a bit less specific when he described industrial psychology as the "study of certain factors which affect workers in the procedure of processing materials," and as being concerned with "the human factor in industry" (p. 3).

During the next decade, Gilmer (1966) stipulated that industrial psychology "is concerned with four relationships of man [sic] as he functions in industry. It is interested in relations between person and person, between person and group, between person and object; and it is interested in problems of the inner man himself" (p. 11). Shortly thereafter, Blum and Naylor (1968) defined industrial psychology as "simply the application or extension of psychological facts and principles to the problems concerning human beings operating within the context of business and industry" (p. 4), a description almost as broad as Gray's (1952).

In the 1970s, McCormick and Tiffin (1974), in the sixth edition of Tiffin's (1942) original volume, stated that "the *raison d'être* of industrial psychology is the existence of human problems in organizations, and its objective is to somehow provide the basis for resolving these problems or, more realistically, for minimizing them" (p. 4). It was during this decade that the nature of the field began to expand beyond the confines of traditional industrial psychology to include organizational issues and concerns such as job satisfaction, motivation, and leadership. In 1970, Division 14 of the APA changed its name to Industrial and Organizational Psychology. One year later, Korman (1971) published his text entitled *Industrial and Organizational Psychology*; to the best of our knowledge, this was the first textbook to explicitly recognize the organizational aspects of industrial psychology in its title.

More recently, Schultz (1982) offered a sweeping definition of industrial psychology very similar to Gray's (1952) and Blum and Naylor's (1968): "the application of the methods, facts, and principles of the science of human behavior to people at work" (p. 7). This can be compared with Guion's (1965a) more specific definition of I/O psychology as "the scientific study of the relationship between man [sic] and the world at work: the study of the adjustment

---

performance tests: examinations that require people to do something rather than merely to say or to write something

people make to the places they go, the people they meet, and the things they do in the process of making a living" (p. 817).

Earlier we defined human psychology as the study of individuals' behavior using techniques capable of producing verifiable, replicable information. Extrapolating from that definition, and considering the ideas of Viteles (1932) and those who followed him, we offer this two-part definition of I/O psychology: It is (1) the *study* of the behavior, thoughts, and feelings of women and men as they adjust to the people, objects, and surroundings they encounter in the workplace; and (2) the *use* of that information to maximize the economic and psychological well-being of all employees—female and male, white and black, labor and management, and so on. This two-part definition highlights the dichotomy between the *science* of I/O psychology, which searches for new knowledge, and the *practice* of I/O psychology, which applies that knowledge for the benefit of the organization and all its members. Although many I/O psychologists operate as both scientists and practitioners, the relationship between these two aspects of the field has not always been one of harmony and mutual respect.

Meltzer and Stagner (1980) observed that "pure" researchers have traditionally been seen as occupying the highest positions in the status hierarchy among psychologists. Bruce Moore (1962), who was awarded the first Ph.D. degree in industrial psychology in 1921, quoted an unnamed "eminent psychologist's" remark from 1919: "Now that the war is over, psychologists ought to be getting back to the *real* science of psychology." In 1936, the continuing tension between "pure" and "applied" psychologists in the APA led to the founding of the American Association of Applied Psychology.

Such bickering was misguided and counterproductive. The two factions need each other. Although the prospect didn't excite him, even Wundt was aware of the practical implications of some of his work. Attempts to apply the results of "pure" research have often provided valuable insights into the theoretical nature of a research problem, and many research procedures developed entirely in response to theoretical curiosity have turned out to be surprisingly practical.

As we suggested earlier, I/O psychology has not been immune to the trend of increased specialization (over and above the "pure" versus "applied" dichotomy just discussed). Muchinsky (1983) listed six different subspecialties:

1. *Personnel psychology* examines the important role of individual differences in selecting and placing employees, in appraising the level of employees' work performance, and in training recently hired as well as veteran employees to improve various aspects of their job-related behavior.
2. *Organizational behavior* studies the impact of group and other social influences on role-related behaviors, on personal feelings of motivation and commitment, and on communication within the organizational setting.
3. *Organizational development* concerns planned changes within organizations that can involve people, work procedures, job design and technology, and the structure of organizational relationships.

4. *Industrial relations* concerns the interactions between and among employees and employers, and often involves organized labor unions.
5. *Vocational and career counseling* examines the nature of rewarding and satisfying career paths in the context of individuals' different patterns of interests and abilities.
6. *Engineering psychology* generally focuses on the design of tools, equipment, and work environments with an eye toward maximizing the effectiveness of women and men as they operate in human–machine systems.

Several authors have included a seventh subspecialty, *consumer psychology*, in their discussion of I/O psychology (McCormick & Tiffin, 1974; Schultz, 1982). Concerned with such issues as purchasing behavior, brand loyalty, advertising effectiveness and packaging, consumer psychology has, in the eyes of many, "increasingly split off from the major trends and movements of the field [of I/O psychology]" (Korman, 1971, p. 13).

For the purpose of surveying the field of I/O psychology, we believe the most useful distinctions are between the subfields of personnel psychology, organizational psychology (including organizational development and industrial relations), and engineering psychology. Subsequent chapters will therefore focus on these three areas. Chapters in the personnel psychology section of the book will examine recruiting, selecting and placing employees, measuring workers' job-performance levels, and training both experienced and inexperienced workers. The organizational psychology section includes chapters devoted to work motivation, job satisfaction, leadership, labor unions and union–management relations, and organizational structure, behavior, and change. The final chapter in the text focuses on the work environment, and includes a brief discussion of engineering psychology, the interface between human beings and the tools and equipment they use at work.

I/O Psychologists' Education and Employment

Most I/O psychologists have completed one or more graduate programs in their chosen specialties. Master's and doctoral degrees in I/O psychology can now be earned at a wide variety of colleges, universities, and professional schools. These programs are described in *Graduate Training Programs in Industrial/Organizational Psychology and Organizational Behavior*, published by the Society for Industrial and Organizational Psychology (1986).

Another source of information is a study by Greenberg, Thomas, Dossett, Robinson, DeMeuse, and Pendergrass (1981), who asked 429 members of the Society (APA Division 14) to evaluate 39 different schools that offer the Ph.D. in I/O psychology. Based on the information provided by the 122 individuals who responded, the ten programs with the highest average ratings were those in which (1) the faculty members and graduates were widely known and had strong reputations; (2) the curriculum emphasized quantitative methods, an experimental orientation, and personnel selection and training; and (3) a variety of research tools were readily accessible.

I/O psychologists are currently employed in many different work settings. Business and industry employ the largest numbers, followed in turn by colleges, universities, consulting firms, and governmental agencies. They hold titles that range from "professor" to "manager" to "researcher" to "private consultant."

Professional associations   As we said earlier, many I/O psychologists are members of the APA, especially Division 14, as well as one or more of the regional psychological associations. In addition, I/O psychologists also belong and contribute to more specialized groups such as the International Association of Applied Psychology, the Academy of Management, the International Personnel Management Association, the New England Society of Applied Psychologists, and the Southeastern Industrial/Organizational Psychological Association, just to name a few.

A relatively recent innovation is the annual Industrial/Organizational and Organizational Behavior Graduate Student Convention. This event is designed to provide graduate students in these related fields with a forum in which to exchange information and ideas in a more supportive environment than might otherwise be found at national and regional conventions.

HISTORICAL OBSERVATIONS ABOUT WORK AND I/O PSYCHOLOGY

In the chapters to follow, this text will introduce you to the field of I/O psychology as it exists and is practiced today. As you'll see, it is currently a complex, diversified discipline, dealing with many different aspects of human behavior as it relates to the workplace.

We stated earlier that seeing something in context invariably leads to better understanding and deeper appreciation. We therefore devote the next several pages to some brief observations of some events and accomplishments that have played important roles in the evolution of I/O psychology.

Perspectives on the Nature of Human Work

Viteles (1932) viewed industrial psychology as being concerned with people's efficiency and their adjustment in the workplace. Each of these concerns is influenced by the meaning(s) people attach to their labors. Drawing heavily on Tilgher (1930), Lofquist and Dawis (1969) concluded, for example, that work had at least three basic meanings prior to the Industrial Revolution. First, work was viewed as a necessary evil, a hard, painful, and burdensome exercise. This perspective has both religious and sociological origins. The ancient Hebrews saw work as a way of atoning for people's sins, including the "original sin" that resulted in Adam's and Eve's eviction from the Garden of Eden. Ancient philosophers thought of work as drudgery doled out by the gods (Heneman, 1973), and classical Greek writings specify that all work in the city-states of Sparta and Athens was done by slaves, serfs, and other noncitizens. As Neff (1968) observed, "it is easy to see how Greek thought developed the conception that work is inherently servile and degrading" (p. 61).

A second perspective saw work as an instrumental activity, as a means for achieving ends, especially religious ends. For early Christians, work was a way to express charity to one's neighbors. In his prescriptions for monks' behavior, St. Benedict stated that labor, both manual and intellectual, was a religious duty (Neff, 1968). While regarding work as a duty, others believed that one should not work to acquire goods or property, but only to provide sustenance. The Protestant Reformation added a variation to this theme. According to Martin Luther, perfectly performing the work involved in one's occupation or profession was the best way to serve God. Calvin went even further, declaring that "work alone sufficed to curb the evil bent of man" (Lofquist & Dawis, 1969, p. 8). The Protestant Reformation was a powerful force in promoting the idea that work was ennobling.

The third perspective viewed work as an intrinsically good activity because it represents the creative act of human beings. For Renaissance thinkers and artists such as Leonardo da Vinci, work was a way to master nature, to move "away from the animal and nearer to the divine" (Lofquist & Dawis, 1969, p. 8). From this perspective, work is truly valued for its own sake.

Heneman (1973) contended that the Industrial Revolution stripped human work once and for all of its religious connotations. With the advent of the machine, work began to have important implications for people's search for personal identity (Lofquist & Dawis, 1969). According to these authors, the growth of automation in contemporary society has increased the likelihood that work will dehumanize men and women and reduce them to the status of "machine-tenders." Neff (1968) agreed that technological advances have stripped heavy manual labor of much of the value it once enjoyed:

> The enormous pace of industrialization . . . has brought about . . . a major shift in the evaluation placed on different *kinds* of work. While it is still more virtuous to work than to be idle, people are now evaluated in accordance with a very elaborate occupational hierarchy. . . . Certain kinds of work are "better" than others (p. 68).

Although brief, this description of the way in which the meanings of human work have evolved suggests the dramatic changes that have characterized our view of this basic human activity. It is a safe bet that such changes will continue (Dunnette, 1973).

Snapshots from I/O Psychology's Past

As you will see, the history of "modern" I/O psychology is short. It is therefore impossible to draw parallels between our field and the various perspectives on human work we just described. It is not only possible, however, but imperative that the field of I/O psychology be viewed in the context of *today's* perception of the meaning of work. Further, as the meaning we attach to work continues to evolve, so must the field of I/O psychology.

BEFORE WORLD WAR I

Stagner (1982) suggested that the origins of industrial psychology can be traced all the way back to biblical times, when Gideon used a simple performance test to select prospective soldiers. DuBois (1970) described a program for assessing individual differences in occupational proficiency that was used in China approximately 4000 years ago. By the time we reach the Han Dynasty (206 B.C. to 220 A.D.) "written examinations had been introduced for civil servants working in such areas as geography, agriculture, civil law, and military affairs" (Minton & Schneider, 1980, p. 5). These authors also acknowledged the ancient Greeks' recognition of the importance of individual differences in work performance. Plato's *Republic* emphasized that the ideal state was one in which individuals were assigned to perform those tasks for which they were best suited, and advocated the use of an aptitude test for identifying those most qualified to pursue military careers.

Following the Greek and Roman periods, concern with the differences between people waned. This trend reached its extreme during the Middle Ages, when the individual in European society was perceived as inseparable from the group to which he or she belonged (Williams, 1961). As Fromm (1941) said, "a person was identical with his role in society; he *was* a peasant, an artisan, [or] a knight, and not *an individual* who *happened* to have this or that occupation" (pp. 41–42). This perspective didn't change until the time of the Renaissance. The emergence of capitalism, based on individual economic initiative, and the Protestant Reformation, which displaced the central authority of the church, rekindled the belief that each person is a separate entity, and must be treated as such.

"Modern" industrial psychology is commonly believed to have emerged around the beginning of the twentieth century. Bryan and Harter (1897) offered a description of how professional telegraphers developed their skills in sending and receiving Morse code. Shortly thereafter, Bryan (1904) encouraged the APA to conduct research on "concrete activities and functions as they appear in everyday life." Muchinsky (1983) reported the following interesting footnote to Bryan's work:

> The term *industrial psychology* was used apparently for the first time in Bryan's 1904 article. Ironically, it appeared in print only as a typographical error. Bryan . . . was quoting a sentence he had written five years earlier . . . in which he spoke of the need for more research in individual psychology. Instead, Bryan wrote *industrial* psychology and did not catch his mistake (p. 12).

Some of the earliest landmark contributions to the emerging field of industrial psychology came from the work of Frederick Taylor, Walter Dill Scott, and Hugo Münsterberg. Taylor (1911) was concerned with such issues as violent strikes, labor turnover, disciplinary problems in factories, group influences on work behavior such as work restrictions, and unmotivated workers (Nord, 1982; Stagner, 1982). Along with other industrial engineers such as Lillian and Frank Gilbreth, Taylor redesigned jobs, developed training programs, and used selection methods to increase the efficiency of workers. In his well-known book *Principles of Scientific*

Management, he advocated scientific design of work methods and procedures so as to maximize efficiency, systematic selection of employees who could be trained to use those work methods and procedures, and cooperation between management and workers in sharing the responsibility for designing and accomplishing work.

Scott, who like Münsterberg had trained in Germany under Wundt, also developed a variety of interests throughout his professional career. He addressed himself to the use of suggestion and argument as a means of influencing people, and attempted to maximize human efficiency by promoting competition, loyalty, concentration, and imitation. He also devoted some attention to human motivation, distinguishing between "selfish" and "selfless" motives (Stagner, 1982). Scott is probably best known for his application of psychology to advertising; his *Theory of Advertising* and *Psychology of Advertising* were published in 1903 and 1908, respectively.

Münsterberg, who came to Harvard University at the invitation of the noted American psychologist William James, was interested in the selection of workers, the design of work stations, and the application of psychology to sales. According to Stagner (1982), Münsterberg's book *Psychology and Industrial Efficiency,* which was published in 1913, laid the foundation for research in the areas of personnel selection and training. In perhaps his best-known study, he analyzed the job of streetcar motorman and developed a selection test for a local Boston company. Although some consider Münsterberg to be *the* "father" of industrial psychology, his support of the German cause in World War I greatly reduced his influence.

During the period prior to America's entry into World War I, then, we can identify two major roots that nourished the growing field of industrial psychology. First, there was the influence of industrial engineers, whose work often relied upon traditional experimental psychology to supply generalizations about human capabilities and limitations. This approach was based on the assumption of universal laws of behavior, which led Taylor and his colleagues to conduct **time and motion studies** in their efforts to discover the *one best way* to design and perform jobs. Second, we have described the impact of differential psychology, which emphasizes the differences that exist between and among individuals. Münsterberg's work on the selection of employees was predicated on the uniqueness of each job applicant.

Moore (1962) believed that the history of industrial psychology began with an argument between Wilhelm Wundt and James McKeen Cattell, who had also studied with Wundt, on the importance of universal laws of the mind versus individual differences in the functioning of those laws. These two perspectives led to two different approaches to the collection and analysis of data.

The methodology of experimental psychology is based on presumed relationships between a set of circumstances or stimulus conditions manipulated or controlled by the experimenter and particular behaviors of interest. Any individual differences among subjects exposed to the same conditions are attributed to errors

---

time and motion studies: investigations designed to determine the best combinations of actions or behaviors for accomplishing specific tasks, as well as the time necessary for performing those tasks

such as carelessness or chance. In contrast, differential psychologists usually do not manipulate any variables. Rather, they measure naturally occurring variables and use certain statistical procedures designed to assess the degree of relationship among those variables. Although the debate between these two camps has often been acrimonious, the trend today is toward simultaneously considering the roles of individual differences and experimental manipulations in attempting to understand complex human behaviors (Cronbach, 1957, 1975; Owens, 1968). Contemporary I/O psychology is one of the best examples of this integration.

WORLD WAR I

Ghoulish as it sounds, the field of industrial psychology benefited enormously from global armed conflicts. Korman (1971) went so far as to proclaim that "it took World War I to start the first great growth of industrial psychology in this country" (pp. 3–4). Although they recognized that tests had been used to make decisions about people for centuries, Dunnette and Borman (1979) claimed that the modern era of personnel selection began on April 6, 1917, when the United States declared war on Germany. When America entered the war, the U.S. Army was confronted with an immense task. In a reasonably short period of time, decisions had to be made about how to effectively utilize the tremendous pool of manpower that became available through enlistments and the military draft. Who should be trained for advanced, technically skilled jobs, and who should be handed a rifle? Who should attend officer candidate school, and who should remain in the enlisted ranks?

In answering these questions, Robert Yerkes and other psychologists involved in the war effort proceeded from the assumption that "the major differences between those who could perform difficult jobs and those who could not was intelligence" (Korman, 1971, p. 4). Unfortunately, the only known instrument for assessing human intelligence, other than those used by Galton and Cattell that equated people's mental skills with the speed of their reaction times and their ability to discriminate among various sensory stimuli, was a measure that had been developed in France by Alfred Binet. Binet's test, devised at the request of the French Minister of Education, was designed to identify those children who could not be expected to benefit from a newly instituted system of public education because of inadequate mental abilities. What was unfortunate was that this test was an **individual test;** it could only be administered to one individual at a time, and it required one examiner for each examinee. Since time was crucial, these were serious problems.

The solution came to be known as the Army Alpha, a paper-and-pencil measure of intelligence that assessed approximately the same mental skills as Binet's test, and that could be administered to a large number of people at the same time by a single examiner or proctor. Wisely, Yerkes and his colleagues realized that a number of recruits were obtaining low scores on the Alpha *not* because of low levels of intelligence, but because of inadequate verbal (especially reading) skills. As a result, a second test (the Army Beta) that relied less on verbal skills and more on performance of other intellectually demanding tasks was developed.

Within two years, Yerkes (who was most instrumental in getting psychology into the war), Walter Bingham, and other members of the APA had tested more than 1.5 million men, written job specifications, constructed job-knowledge tests, developed officer-rating forms, and initiated training and psychological counseling programs. According to Dunnette and Borman (1979), "this marked the beginning of large-scale use of tests and other systematic methods to aid personnel decisions in the world of work" (p. 478).

There can be little doubt that the intelligence-testing program for selecting and placing World War I recruits was *perceived* to be highly successful. In Korman's (1971) words, "Army Alpha was so successful in achieving the goals set for it that this achievement probably stands as the major single reason for the increase in the use of psychology by U.S. industry after World War I" (p. 4). More recently, however, some disagreement on this point has surfaced.

Muchinsky (1983) pointed out that the Adjutant General's office did not issue its final order giving complete authority to the testing program until August 1918, just three months prior to the signing of the Armistice and the end of World War I. Thus, although almost 1.75 million people were ultimately tested, actual use of the test results was minimal. Samelson (1977) offered additional evidence that the intelligence tests developed and administered during this period were not nearly as effective as many reports indicated. Nevertheless, the authority and recognition that accrued to psychologists because of these tests provided a powerful shot in the arm to the discipline of psychology in general, and to industrial psychology in particular. With respect to the growth of the field, the perception was far more important than whatever the reality may have been.

Scott was also active during World War I. Working with the Committee on Classification of Personnel attached to the Adjutant General's office, Scott's contributions to classifying and placing enlisted soldiers in specialized situations, to developing officers' performance ratings for making promotion decisions, and to preparing descriptions of duties and qualifications for more than 500 jobs were deemed so successful that he was later awarded the Distinguished Service Medal (Korman, 1971).

Although it had nothing directly to do with World War I, another event occurred during this period that would have a substantial impact on the field of industrial (and later, I/O) psychology. In 1917, the first issue of the *Journal of Applied Psychology* was published. Today, almost three-quarters of a century later, many I/O psychologists recognize this periodical as one of the primary vehicles for disseminating their ideas and the results of their research.

BETWEEN WORLD WARS I AND II

As suggested above, industrial psychology emerged from World War I with a reputation as a useful personnel management tool. Since the testing program instituted during the war was perceived as successful, it isn't surprising that

---

individual test: an examination that is administered to people one at a time, and that requires one examiner for each person tested

managers in private and public organizations seized on the possibility of effectively using tests to select new employees from among all those applying for civilian postwar jobs. Among the more tangible expressions of this trend were the psychological research bureaus that emerged with the goal of harnessing industrial psychology's perceived power to solve practical problems. Bingham organized the Bureau of Salesmanship Research at the Carnegie Institute of Technology, which focused on the selection, classification, and development of sales personnel, as well as clerical and executive personnel. In 1921, Cattell established the Psychological Corporation for the purpose of promoting the useful application of psychology. Originally an information clearinghouse and source of reference checks for anyone about to hire a psychologist, the Psychological Corporation today is one of the nation's primary sources of psychological tests.

Fame is fleeting, however. During the latter half of the 1920s, many managers became increasingly disenchanted with industrial psychology. Korman (1971) cited three reasons why the field's image became tarnished:

1. Many of the tests being used to make selection decisions were simply not effective; those who were hired on the basis of test scores were performing their jobs no better than those who were hired without the aid of tests.
2. Many managers recognized that the ability tests being used totally ignored such factors as motivation and personality, factors they deemed important in predicting performance on a wide variety of jobs.
3. Many managers had been attracted to industrial psychology because they saw it as a means to make trade unions less attractive to workers. The growth of unions abated during the relatively affluent 1920s, however, so that industrial psychology became less relevant for these managers.

A number of other events that occurred between the wars deserve mention. The 1930s saw the publication of the first *Dictionary of Occupational Titles (DOT)*, a mammoth document commissioned by the U.S. Department of Labor that described characteristics of jobs and the traits and abilities deemed necessary for satisfactorily performing them. The *DOT*, currently in its fourth revision (1977), is still widely used by employment counselors, trainers, and many other professionals. Other more-or-less isolated developments included the publication of Viteles' influential books *Industrial Psychology* (1932) and *The Science of Work* (1934), and Joseph Tiffin's arrival at Purdue University in 1938, where he established what was to become the largest graduate program in industrial psychology. We should also mention the emigration to the U.S. and elsewhere of eminent social scientists who were escaping the gathering storm of Hitler's Nazi Germany.

Of course, we cannot overlook the tremendous impact of the Great Depression of the 1930s on the ways in which men and women viewed their work. It is impossible to fully understand the development of research and theory pertaining to job satisfaction, work motivation, and union–management relations, among other subareas of I/O psychology, without appreciating the role of this unparalleled economic disaster. Thousands of people lost their jobs, and there were no unemployment or welfare programs in place to cushion the blows.

However, the single event during this time period that had the greatest impact on the development of I/O psychology began during the 1920s at the Hawthorne plant of the Western Electric Company just outside of Chicago. In what came to be known as the "Hawthorne studies," several researchers from Harvard University (none of whom were industrial psychologists by training) began a collaborative effort with Western Electric in 1924 for the purpose of establishing the relationship between different levels of lighting, or illumination, and optimal working efficiency. To everyone's surprise, no clear relationship emerged. Productivity seemed to increase, or at least remain at a satisfactory level, whether illumination was increased, decreased, or allowed to remain at a constant level. Clearly, factors other than illumination seemed to be affecting productivity. These apparently bizarre results led to a series of several other major studies designed to clarify matters.

As originally described in Roethlisberger and Dickson's (1939) and Whitehead's (1938) research reports, and more recently summarized by Sonnenfeld (1982), the Hawthorne studies suggested that

- Individual work behavior is rarely a pure consequence of simple cause and effect, but is rather determined by a complex set of factors.
- Work groups develop their own **norms** that mediate between individuals' needs and the demands of the work setting.
- The social structures of these work groups are influenced by job-related symbols of prestige and power.
- Individuals' unique needs and satisfactions can only be understood in the context of their personal lives.
- Awareness of workers' sentiments and their inclusion in the decision-making process can reduce their resistance to change.
- The workplace must be seen as a social system, and not merely a production system.

In view of conclusions such as these, it is easy to see why many writers point to the Hawthorne studies as the beginning of the "human relations movement" in industry (Bass & Barrett, 1981)—the point of departure that eventually resulted in the name of the field being changed to industrial *and organizational* psychology.

One particular aspect of the Hawthorne results has seemed to take on a life of its own, the **Hawthorne effect.** Recall that workers' productivity in the first of the Hawthorne studies sometimes increased as soon as the researchers began to adjust the lighting. The Hawthorne effect, which Bass and Barrett (1981) equated

---

norms: expectations or standards of behavior that are shared by the members of a group

Hawthorne effect: change(s) in behavior attributable to the perceived novelty of a situation; behavior usually reverts to its original form as the novelty of the situation wears off with the passage of time

with the **"placebo effect,"** suggests that the workers' performance improved simply because of the novelty of the situation. Given the often-oppressive atmosphere that existed in many factories at that time, it was indeed unusual for workers to perceive any evidence that supervisors cared about their working conditions (Locke, 1982b). This change in behavior following the onset of some novel treatment, because of the novelty and not because of the treatment per se, is the Hawthorne effect. Of course, behavior often returns to its original level after the novelty of the new situation has worn off.

After almost a half-century of debate, it is clear that the Hawthorne studies do *not* represent examples of perfect field research. Based on their statistical analyses, for example, Franke and Kaul (1978) suggested that more than 90 percent of the improvement in the Hawthorne workers' performance could be explained by such factors as improved raw materials, increased supervisory discipline, and workers' anxiety about being laid off. More recently, we have witnessed a spirited debate concerning the relevance of Marxism to a proper interpretation and understanding of the Hawthorne results (Bramel & Friend, 1981, 1982; Feldman, 1982; Friend & Bramel, 1982; Locke, 1982b; Parsons, 1982; Sonnenfeld, 1982; Toch, 1982; Vogel, 1982).

These arguments aside, there can be little doubt that workers have derived a great deal of benefit from the Hawthorne studies. According to Sonnenfeld (1982), who recently interviewed four of the participants in the original relay assembly test room studies, "the many rebuttals to the same critical charges, the views of the participants, the decades of supportive research, and the plainly observable results of Japanese management practices indicate that the value and validity of the Hawthorne findings is no longer a point of intellectually legitimate contention" (p. 1399).

This was brought out at a symposium that took place on November 10 through 13, 1974, in Oakbrook, Illinois, to commemorate the occasion of the 50th anniversary of the original Hawthorne studies. *Man and Work in Society,* the proceedings of that meeting, is described by its editors as a compilation of "views of a varied group of contemporary authorities on some of the topics rooted in the [Hawthorne] Studies—topics which continue to have wide implications for today and for the future" (Cass & Zimmer, 1975).

WORLD WAR II

Industrial psychologists were far better prepared to contribute to America's preparation for and participation in World War II. This time the U.S. Army took the initiative and approached the psychologists first. During World War I, the emphasis was largely on selection and placement. Although these issues were also addressed in World War II, industrial psychologists became heavily involved in a variety of other projects, too.

Development of the Army General Classification Test (AGCT), a **group test** for separating new recruits into a few basic categories according to their presumed ability to learn various military duties and responsibilities, was the major accomplishment in the area of personnel selection and placement. Along with the AGCT, the advisory committee chaired by Bingham contributed tests designed to measure trade proficiencies and other aptitudes, and potential to successfully complete officer training.

Major advances occurred, too, in the realm of personnel training, especially the training of pilots to operate the variety of increasingly complex war planes being designed and produced by American industry. **Simulators,** along with actual airplane cockpits, were the sites for many of the engineering psychologists' important contributions. With an eye toward making pilots' jobs easier and safer, cockpits were redesigned and standardized across different types of aircraft, and equipment and instruments were modified to maximize effective communication between pilots and their planes. The substantial impetus given to the field of engineering psychology during World War II is reflected today in the important roles these psychologists play in our current space programs.

A major contribution of a different sort emerged from a project undertaken by the U.S. Office of Strategic Services (OSS). Given the nature of this agency's mission, which included espionage, sabotage, and other highly demanding and dangerous tasks, the OSS was interested in assessing candidates' abilities to withstand and effectively function under high levels of stress. Toward this end, psychologists designed a series of situational stress tests (Murray & MacKinnon, 1946). These tests, which usually took place over several consecutive days, placed candidates for OSS duty in extremely stressful, often impossible situations, where failure was often preordained. Small teams of observers kept close watch on the candidates' performance, paying particular attention to their emotional stability and their ability to tolerate frustration. This general approach has evolved today into what we call **assessment centers,** pioneered in the civilian sector by American Telephone and Telegraph (Finkle, 1976).

One final World War II phenomenon that merits our consideration is "Rosie the Riveter." With millions of American men in uniform, there was insufficient manpower to keep American industries running at the peak capacities necessary to support the Allied war efforts. As a result, women were encouraged to join the work force and "pick up the slack." They responded by the thousands. Within a few months, women could be found welding in shipyards, packing artillery shells in ammunition plants, and performing a host of distinctly "unladylike" tasks, including riveting (thus the nickname) the aluminum skins onto combat aircraft. After the war, most of these women relinquished their relatively high-paying, challenging jobs to the men who came home from Europe

---

placebo effect: improvement in a person's medical or psychological condition resulting from the attention they receive rather than from any specific medication or therapy

group test: an examination that can be administered simultaneously to many individuals by a single examiner or proctor; examinees usually read the questions and respond in writing

simulators: facsimiles or representations of actual, "real-life" machines or equipment

assessment centers: standardized sets of experiences that place people in simulated job situations so that their behaviors and performance under a variety of conditions can be evaluated

and the Pacific; they returned to their homes as full-time spouses, mothers, and homemakers, or took more menial jobs for less pay. Nevertheless, their accomplishments should have debunked the myth that women cannot perform certain kinds of jobs. We will return to this theme of sex-typed tasks and occupations several times in the remainder of this book.

SINCE WORLD WAR II

Korman (1971) described the decade immediately following the end of World War II as a period of growth and prosperity for the field of industrial psychology. Among the encouraging signs between 1945 and 1955, he emphasized

- a marked increase in the number of specialized graduate programs in industrial psychology
- a similar increase in the number of interdisciplinary research centers devoted to industrial problems
- inclusion of a Division of Industrial Psychology in a newly reorganized APA
- ever-increasing numbers of industrial psychologists who were gaining employment with private companies and government agencies
- establishment of a new professional journal in 1948, *Personnel Psychology*, to assist the *Journal of Applied Psychology* in its task of disseminating research results and theory pertinent to industrial psychology

Nevertheless, Korman (1971) also observed that the late 1950s and early 1960s "saw industrial psychology come under as concentrated a series of attacks from as wide a variety of sources as have probably been made on any area of professional and/or scientific activity" (p. 10). Among these criticisms were that

- Industrial psychology had forfeited its status as a science by developing tools and techniques specifically designed to help personnel managers do their jobs, thereby becoming a technical assistant to management.
- The tools and techniques used by industrial psychologists were hopelessly outdated and based on assumptions about the workplace that were no longer valid (the overwhelmingly male, blue-collar work force was rapidly becoming a thing of the past).
- Industrial psychologists permitted fads and popular ideas of the moment to dominate their activities and recommendations.

In Korman's view, these criticisms were fortunate because they were accurate, and because the self-examination that ensued has firmly established the field of I/O psychology as both a theoretical and an applied discipline, and placed it "on a much firmer footing, both scientifically and professionally," than ever before.

Much of the specialization within I/O psychology that we described earlier has evolved since the conclusion of World War II. This "splintering effect" is reflected in the three major subareas of I/O psychology: personnel psychology, organizational psychology, and engineering psychology. Further evidence of increased specialization is the *Handbook of Industrial and Organizational Psychology* edited by Dunnette (1976). This 37-chapter tome is the most comprehensive description of the field of I/O psychology ever provided.

Any discussion of I/O psychology during the years since World War II would be incomplete if it neglected to mention an event that has literally transformed the entire subarea of personnel psychology: the passage of the Civil Rights Act in 1964. This legislation made it expressly illegal to discriminate against certain groups of individuals (including blacks, women, Asian Americans, Hispanic Americans, and several others) in such diverse realms as housing, education, and employment. Title VII of the Civil Rights Act created the Equal Employment Opportunity Commission (EEOC), charged with the responsibility to investigate claims of discrimination in employment, and to eliminate such discrimination wherever it occurs.

This legislation imposes a set of guidelines that require *any* technique (paper-and-pencil tests, interviews, application blanks, and so forth) used to select or promote workers to be job-related. That is, job applicants may be legally rejected (or hired) using these procedures *only* if the organization can demonstrate that applicants' performance on those procedures is systematically related to how well they will perform on the job, if they are given the opportunity to do so. Personnel psychologists must now not only develop techniques that are useful for selecting and promoting employees, but they must also limit themselves to procedures that do not discriminate against the groups that are specifically covered.

Many members of these groups, believing themselves to be victims of discrimination, have filed lawsuits under Title VII. As a result, I/O psychologists have recently found themselves in the previously unfamiliar position of having to provide testimony in courts of law regarding the validity of particular selection tests and techniques. In earlier periods, I/O psychologists had to satisfy only the manager(s) who engaged their services. Today's practitioners must satisfy the U.S. Congress (by way of the judicial system) as well.

THE FUTURE?

We claim no expertise at reading palms or tea leaves. Yet there is something to be said for cautious attempts to anticipate the future of any enterprise, for such anticipation can sometimes allow us to help shape the future, rather than being resigned merely to react to whatever the future brings. The following comments are a sample of some I/O psychologists' thoughts about what the future will be, or at least should be, like.

Stagner (1982) offered one of the more detailed views of I/O psychology's future. Among his predictions:

- High-technology jobs will demand a greater emphasis on **cognitive** variables during the personnel selection process.

---

cognitive: pertaining to all the various forms of mental experiences (perceiving, remembering, judging, reasoning, imagining, and so on) or thought processes

- Personality variables, such as tolerance for stress, will also become more important for predicting job success.
- Assessment centers will play a larger role in selecting and evaluating workers.
- I/O psychologists will be expected to function more often as counselors.
- The **"face validity"** of our measuring instruments will become more important.
- Continued efforts to satisfy EEOC requirements will be made.

He also speculated about the need to redesign jobs by enlisting the aid of the workers who know the jobs best, in order to make those jobs more **intrinsically motivating,** and suggested that unions will play an increasingly important role in the 1990s.

Nord (1980) agreed that future I/O psychologists will need to pay more attention to labor unions and their influence on people's work behavior. Recent declines in unions' strength (see Chapter 11), however, suggest that Stagner and Nord may have been "off the mark" with this prediction. Nord (1982) also stressed the importance of considering I/O psychology's future in the context of whatever political and economic processes may prevail in the years to come. More specifically, he stressed that

- I/O psychologists must consider their political and economic assumptions, and whose specific interests are being served by their work.
- "Bottom-line" financial data will be less adequate as a guide for management than has typically been assumed; and measures of quality, efficiency, waste, and the value of human resources will be in greater demand.
- The changing nature of the work force will necessitate different forms of organizational control; the continuing pattern of trying to reconcile routine work and rigid controls with our generally liberal value system will result in the adoption of more and more fads.

In her presidential address to the Society for Industrial and Organizational Psychology, Tenopyr (1981) focused on the current national concern with productivity. In her opinion, I/O psychology can only contribute to greater productivity if it

- Carefully defines productivity, so that working individuals or groups are relevant factors.
- Narrows the gap between the statistics I/O psychologists use to analyze individuals' behaviors and those used by economists to analyze the behavior of larger groups and broader societal phenomena.
- Designs both long- and short-term research and carefully evaluated action programs that address productivity in a broad, integrated fashion.
- Makes itself heard by organizational and governmental policy makers.

- Improves its level of communication, both between and among researchers and practitioners within the field, and with scholars and professionals in other disciplines as well.

A number of writers have stressed the need for I/O psychology researchers and practitioners to increase their levels of cooperation and communication (Meltzer & Stagner, 1980; Nord, 1980; Ronen, 1980). Strasser and Bateman (1984) suggested that better cooperation could increase the likelihood of procuring research sites, monetary grants, consulting opportunities, and greater responsiveness from organizational participants in training and development seminars and workshops. Alluisi and Morgan (1976) predicted greater cooperation between researchers and implementers within the area of engineering psychology. On a more cautionary note, however, Gordon et al. (1978) warned against **"dustbowl empiricism,"** and the tendency to conduct research *only* because of its usefulness to practitioners.

Without doubt, the future holds many challenges for I/O psychology. Many obstacles and pitfalls, both conceptual and practical, loom ahead of us. Yet, our potential to contribute to Viteles' (1932) original goals—to promote the efficiency and adjustment of women and men as they strive to meet their various needs in the workplace—is sufficiently great to spur I/O psychologists onward. As Campbell (1982) affirmed in his "farewell editorial" after nine years of close association with the *Journal of Applied Psychology*, we deal with societal issues of fundamental importance.

THE PLAN OF THIS BOOK

Earlier in this chapter we described how we have organized the content of I/O psychology throughout the remainder of this text. While this is a fairly typical order for presenting the topics that the field comprises, our approach is a bit more unusual. The rest of the text is structured in such a way as to emphasize the relevance and applicability of I/O psychology to common concerns of organizations and the men and women who work for them. The next chapter begins with a description of a fictional organization that is sufficiently detailed to serve as a realistic context in which you can understand and appreciate the

---

face validity: the property of "looking like" or giving the appearance of measuring whatever is intended to be measured; a typing test, for example, "looks like" it measures typing skills

intrinsic motivation: the tendency to expend effort on a task because of the enjoyment, fun, or challenge inherent in performing the task

"dustbowl empiricism": the process of researching and documenting relationships between variables with little or no concern for the logical or theoretical underpinnings of those relationships material that follows. We will also describe a professional I/O psychologist who is on the staff of that hypothetical company. We will then use our organization and its I/O psychologist to inject some life into the discussions that follow.

Beginning with Chapter 3, each chapter opens with a memo addressed to our I/O psychologist by one or more organization members, describing their perceptions of a specific issue or problem that is currently undermining the organization's effectiveness. The subject of each memo pertains to the area of I/O psychology that is discussed in the chapter to follow. The heart of each chapter then presents relevant theory and research, paying particular attention to the ways in which that information might be used by the staff I/O psychologist to address the problem(s) posed in the introductory memo. Each chapter then closes with a return memo from the I/O psychologist that describes her suggestions and specific recommendations for solving, or at least minimizing, the problem(s). In this way, we hope to highlight for you the potential of I/O psychology to address problems and concerns that you (and anyone else who ever works for a living) can realistically expect to encounter in the workplace. Of course, the specific problems described in the memos introducing each chapter represent only a small sample of the concerns that commonly plague organizations and their employees. Therefore, we provide a series of "thought questions" at the end of each chapter that are intended to stimulate your thinking about how the material in the chapter might be used to address other difficulties that could reasonably be expected to arise.

CHAPTER SUMMARY

Psychology is the scientific study of people's observable behaviors and actions, as well as their thoughts, feelings, and other mental processes that cannot be directly observed. By focusing on the behaviors and mental processes of women and men as they function in the workplace, industrial and organizational (I/O) psychology strives to maximize both the economic well-being of organizations and the personal well-being of employees. Most I/O psychologists hold one or more graduate degrees, and many are licensed or certified by state agencies.

I/O psychology emerged as a recognizable subdiscipline during the early 1900s with Münsterberg's work on personnel selection, Taylor's notion of scientific management, and Scott's contributions to advertising. World Wars I and II stimulated dramatic growth in the areas of personnel testing and machine/equipment design, respectively, while the Hawthorne studies drew attention to the role of "human relations" in the workplace. More recently, a greater concern with organized labor unions, a willingness to revise assumptions and techniques, and other responses to well-aimed criticisms have supplemented these historical developments to yield a science and profession that is capable of promoting economic and personal well-being.

REVIEW QUESTIONS AND EXERCISES

1. Imagine that you have decided to pursue a career in I/O psychology. Write a letter to a close friend or relative explaining the potential challenges, rewards, and frustrations of such a career.
2. What are the major lessons to be learned from the Hawthorne studies?
3. How would you describe the "meaning of work" today?
4. Trace the evolution of I/O psychology, and speculate on how the field might be different today if the United States had not participated in World Wars I and II.
5. How will I/O psychology have changed by the time your children or nieces and nephews are in college?

CHAPTER 2

An Organization, an I/O Psychologist, and Her Methods and Procedures

Learning Points

After studying this chapter, you should

- be familiar enough with our hypothetical organization and its staff I/O psychologist to describe the organization's structure and goals, as well as the psychologist's graduate preparation and her role in the organization
- be able to describe the scientific method, and to explain how it is both a boon and a burden to I/O psychologists
- know four different ways that I/O psychologists use numbers to measure behavior
- be able to explain the complementary strengths and weaknesses of experimental and observational, and of laboratory and field research strategies
- know the difference between descriptive statistics and inferential statistics, and how descriptive statistics can be used to either describe or to misrepresent empirical data
- be able to explain the difference between the statistical and practical significance of research findings
- know what a correlation coefficient does and does not reveal about the relationship between two variables
- understand the basic challenges and benefits of meta-analysis, cross-cultural research, and ethical principles for research and practice in I/O psychology.

THE ORGANIZATION: PETER'S PAN PIZZA, INC.

We will begin this chapter with a description of Peter's Pan Pizza, Inc. (PPP), the hypothetical organization that will serve as the context for our subsequent discussions of I/O psychology. We will also introduce you to Dr. Jennilyn MacKeven, who is PPP's "in-house" I/O psychologist. The major portion of the chapter, however, is devoted to descriptions of some of the basic research methods and statistical procedures that I/O psychologists depend on to accomplish their work. Finally, we will conclude this chapter by acquainting you with some of the ethical considerations that affect their work.

Peter's Pan Pizza is a nationwide chain of restaurants that serve pizzas as well as a variety of other Italian specialties at reasonable, competitive prices. The company's headquarters is located in Suardell Springs, Colorado. Approximately one-third of the organization's 527 retail operations are owned by the parent company; the other two-thirds are owned and operated under franchising arrangements by more-or-less independent entrepreneurs.

Figure 2.1 is an organizational chart that depicts the company's structure, division of responsibilities, and chain of command. As you can see, the president of Peter's Pan Pizza, who reports directly to the board of directors, exercises organizational control through a senior vice president in charge of operations, and three other vice presidents responsible for finance, facilities, and personnel. The senior vice president for operations directly supervises four additional vice presidents responsible for purchasing, marketing, distribution, and retail operations. All these executives, like their subordinate department managers and staffs, operate out of the home office in Suardell Springs.

Three additional departments that provide a variety of professional services for Peter's Pan Pizza personnel are also located in the home office. These include the legal department, the data-processing section, and the human resources department. Although the individuals who run these departments report directly to the president, their primary function is to serve as "internal consultants" to all company personnel.

The company's resident I/O psychologist is in charge of the human resources department, and holds the title of Human-Resources Coordinator. The core of this department consists of the coordinator, who has a Ph.D. degree, one other professional psychologist with master's level training, and two psychological technicians with bachelor's degrees in psychology. At any given time, there are also usually one or two graduate or undergraduate students serving internships within the department.

At present, the concerns of the human resources department and its coordinator center on three basic issues. First, and most general, there is a strong commitment to utilize behavioral science theory and research in constructive ways to contribute to the economic viability of the organization and to the personal and professional welfare of all its employees. Second, Peter's Pan Pizza is seriously committed to its status as an equal opportunity employer. As a result, the human resources department has been charged with the

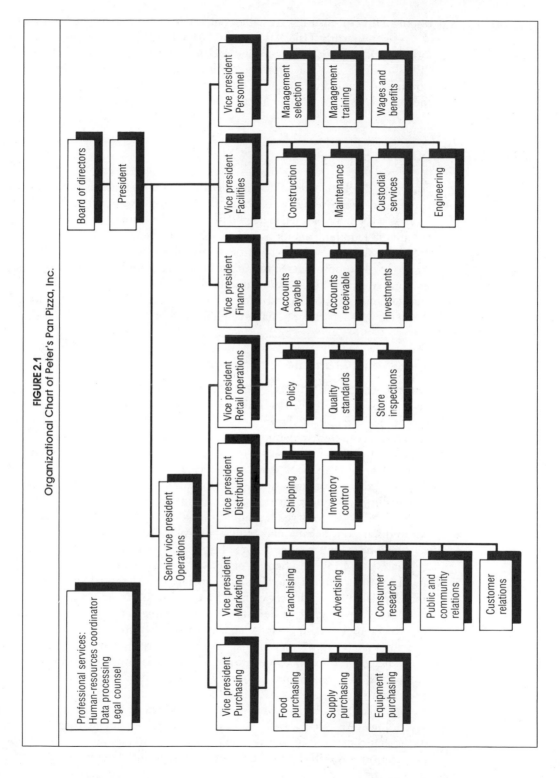

FIGURE 2.1
Organizational Chart of Peter's Pan Pizza, Inc.

responsibility of ensuring that the company's personnel policies and practices are consistent with Title VII of the 1964 Civil Rights Act, which expressly forbids racial, ethnic, religious, and sex discrimination in the workplace. Third, PPP is in the process of acquiring a smaller company that produces and distributes frozen foods, including pizza. The human resources department has been studying the possible psychological and organizational implications of that purchase.

THE I/O PSYCHOLOGIST

Four years ago Peter's Pan Pizza hired Dr. Jennilyn A. MacKeven to serve as the company's human-resources coordinator. Dr. MacKeven's academic credentials include a bachelor of science degree from a small liberal arts college, where she completed requirements for a dual major in business and psychology; a master of science degree in psychology from a large Midwestern state university; and a doctor of philosophy degree from that same large university. Her major field of doctoral study was industrial/organizational psychology, and she had a secondary area of concentration in statistics. She also served a six-month internship in the personnel department of a large public utility.

Overview of Dr. MacKeven's Graduate Preparation

Typical of many Ph.D. I/O psychologists, Dr. MacKeven's graduate training can be conveniently described as falling into four categories: I/O psychology, general psychology, supporting disciplines such as business and computer science, and research procedures (including methodology and statistical analysis). The basic content of her graduate courses in I/O psychology is described throughout the remainder of this textbook, and can be seen at a glance in the Table of Contents. Specific graduate courses included Work Motivation, Personnel Training, Leadership, Personnel Selection and Performance Appraisal, and Organizational Psychology. Most followed a seminar format that permitted a great deal of in-depth discussion, debate, and analysis of issues.

Among the more general psychology courses that appear on Dr. MacKeven's graduate transcript are Theories of Personality, Social Psychology, Motivation and Learning, Perception, Human Learning and Memory, Physiological Psychology, and Philosophy of Science. In an effort to extend her area of expertise into other fields that either support or complement I/O psychology, Dr. MacKeven took formal graduate course work in her university's departments of computer science, sociology, management, industrial engineering, and statistics.

The remainder of her graduate preparation falls into the category of research procedures and techniques for analyzing empirical data. With only a few exceptions, these courses in Research Methodology, Psychological Measurement, and Psychological Statistics were offered within the department of psychology. An overview of the basic research, measurement, and statistical issues that constitute an indispensable part of a contemporary I/O psychologist's preparation and skills forms the major section of this chapter.

METHODOLOGICAL ISSUES

Most graduate programs in I/O psychology, including Dr. MacKeven's, teach their students the "researcher–practitioner model" of professional behavior. This approach acknowledges that it is impossible for anyone to learn everything in just four or five years of graduate study. Instead, such programs place a heavy emphasis on teaching students how to go about discovering solutions to the many and varied organizational problems they are bound to encounter. Typically, students learn to solve such problems by using the **scientific method.** Howell and Dipboye (1986) described the scientific method as "a set of attitudes and some general rules for gathering information . . . all of which are aimed at maximizing the objectivity of reported findings" (p. 2). They observed that a scientific explanation relies upon "empirical fact rather than speculation, [on] objective data rather than opinion, faith, anecdote, or pure logic" (p. 2). Wexley and Yukl (1984) cited eight essential characteristics of the scientific approach; these are presented in the following list:

1. *Self-correcting:* There are built-in checks all along the way to obtaining scientific knowledge.
2. *Empirical:* Perceptions, beliefs, and attitudes are carefully checked against objective reality.
3. *Open to public inspection:* Procedures can be replicated (repeated) and results tested by other qualified researchers.
4. *Objective and statistical:* Data collection is not biased, and a certain level of confidence can be placed in the results obtained.
5. *Controlled and systematic:* Scientists try to systematically rule out alternative explanations for the results they obtain.
6. *Generates theories:* Conceptual frameworks for organizing and explaining empirical observations also direct future research and suggest new hypotheses.
7. *Tests hypotheses:* Tentative propositions about the relationships among various phenomena are evaluated in the light of empirical observations.
8. *Aims to explain, understand, predict, and change:* Only through explanation and understanding can I/O psychologists hope to solve organizational problems efficiently and appropriately.

SOURCE: Adapted from *Organizational Behavior and Personnel Psychology,* by K. N. Wexley and G. A. Yukl. Copyright 1984 by Richard D. Irwin, Inc. Reprinted by permission.

While no one can reasonably deny the usefulness of the scientific approach in many fields, Boehm (1980) recently suggested that I/O psychologists' applied research efforts would yield a great deal more progress if they acknowledged that the traditional scientific method frequently does not fit the realities encountered in actual organizational settings. Figure 2.2 depicts both the traditional scientific

---

scientific method: an approach to generating new knowledge that involves recognizing and defining a problem, collecting data through observation and/or experiment, and formulating and testing hypotheses

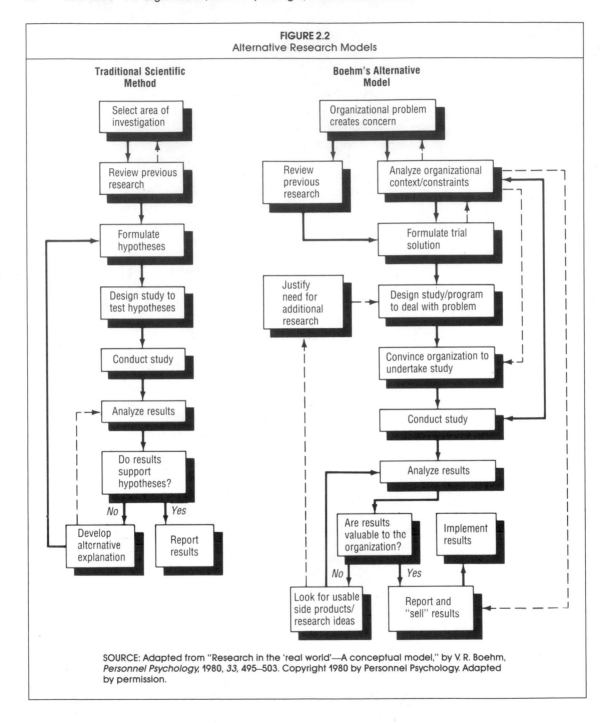

FIGURE 2.2
Alternative Research Models

SOURCE: Adapted from "Research in the 'real world'—A conceptual model," by V. R. Boehm, *Personnel Psychology,* 1980, *33,* 495–503. Copyright 1980 by Personnel Psychology. Adapted by permission.

method (on the left) and Boehm's alternative model of the research process within organizations (on the right). According to Boehm, her alternative model involves a greater number of processes, such as "analyzing organizational contexts and restraints"; contains more numerous and more complex interactions among the processes; and emphasizes an organization's need to solve a current or anticipated performance problem (p. 497).

Because of I/O psychology's single-minded allegiance to the traditional scientific method, Boehm (1980) contended that the field's progress has been limited in four specific ways: (1) The scientific community has ignored a lot of "real-world" research because it is deemed methodologically flawed; (2) organizations have ignored a great deal of academic (traditional) research because it fails to fit the practitioner's reality and because it is impractical; (3) organizational research has been limited to those areas and problems that conform to the assumptions and requirements of the traditional scientific model, whereas crucial topics such as the relationship between organizational staffing procedures and employees' productivity and satisfaction have been avoided because such research is scientifically "messy"; and (4) positive features of conducting real-world research in organizational settings have gone unrecognized.

Boehm (1980) concluded that the traditional scientific method and her alternative approach to organizational research are complementary with respect to their basic orientations, their topics of inquiry, their experimental designs, their use of samples, and their interpretations of results. Her closing remarks say it best:

> Organizations do not exist primarily as research laboratories for behavioral scientists. If this basic fact of life is recognized and [an alternative model] . . . is accepted as being equally legitimate as the [traditional scientific] model . . . , there are exciting possibilities for the advancement of I/O psychology. . . . If, however, I/O psychologists continue to adhere solely to a model based on the ideal, in which organizational realities are viewed solely as problems to be circumvented, stagnation of the field is a strong possibility, and widening of the communications gap between academic and organizational I/O psychologists a virtual certainty (pp. 502–503).

Dr. MacKeven's methodological orientation is basically an **eclectic** one. Although she recognizes the value of the traditional (scientific method) model of research, she is also aware of its limitations. Further, she recognizes that psychological research is not as unbiased and value-free as Wexley and Yukl's (1984) list of "essential" characteristics suggests it should be. The cultural and professional values that provide the context for individual psychologists' research can (and do) influence the questions they set out to answer and the manner in which they collect and analyze information.

The scientific method, then, is best thought of as an ideal, a demanding standard that should guide the research of I/O psychologists who wish to rid their work of avoidable biases and unnecessary subjectivity. It should not, however, be

---

eclectic: making use of what appear to be the best aspects of various methods, procedures, or theories

an altar on which they sacrifice any and all research endeavors that do not (and perhaps cannot) conform to that demanding standard.

Psychological Measurement

According to Young (1984), we generate measurements by using rules to assign numbers to attributes of things or events we observe. These attributes may be qualitative (differing in kind) or quantitative (differing in amount). The numbers we assign to attributes of things or events, however, cannot always be interpreted in the same fashion. Stevens (1951) identified four different kinds of measurement scales that correspond to four different ways that numbers can be used to convey information about things or events; these will be briefly described below.

At the most basic level, numbers can be used simply to name or identify. The numbers on athletes' uniforms serve this purpose, as do the numbers 1, 2, and 3 when they are used to code the religious affiliations of Protestants, Catholics, and Jews, respectively. It is apparent that numbers used in this way convey *none* of the information we typically expect them to communicate. Number 4 on a baseball team is not necessarily twice as valuable to the team as number 2, nor only half as valuable as number 8. Catholics (if coded "2" for computer purposes) are not assumed to be twice as religious as Protestants (coded "1"), nor any less devout than Jews (coded "3"). When numbers are used this way, serving no other purpose than to name or identify a person or event, they reflect what Stevens called a *nominal* scale of measurement.

We use numbers somewhat differently when we rank or order a set of people, events, or things along some continuum or dimension. For instance, when a supervisor at Peter's Pan Pizza rank-orders her workers according to the quality of their work, and she ranks Ms. Smith as "1," Mr. Jones as "2," and Ms. Kelly as "3," she has done more than use numbers merely to name or identify her subordinates. She has used numbers to convey her opinion that Smith is a better worker than Jones, who in turn is a better worker than Kelly. When numbers are used in this way, describing which persons or events have more or less of some attribute or quality than other persons or events, they reflect an *ordinal* scale of measurement.

Although the supervisor's rankings in the example above tell us that Smith is better than Jones, who is better than Kelly, they do not tell us *how much* better Smith is than Jones, or by *how much* Kelly is inferior to Jones. Smith could be enormously superior to Jones, who is only slightly better than Kelly; or Smith could be only marginally better than Jones, who is far superior to Kelly. Ordinal measures, then, tell us nothing about the intervals that separate people, events, or things on a given continuum.

The numbers etched on a Fahrenheit or a Celsius thermometer eliminate much of this ambiguity. The amount of additional heat required to raise the temperature from 10° to 15° is the same as the amount required to raise the temperature from 15° to 20°. This is true because successive numbers on the Fahrenheit and Celsius scales are designed to reflect equal amounts of difference in temperature. When numbers are used this way, when the intervals between successive numbers are assumed to be equal, they reflect an *interval* scale of measurement.

Compared with nominal-scale measurements, interval-scale numbers convey almost all of the information you typically expect from numbers. The only unusual property of interval-scale numbers is that zero (0) cannot be interpreted to mean a complete absence or lack of whatever attribute is being measured. Think again about the Fahrenheit or Celsius scales; zero (0) degrees does not mean that there is a complete and total absence of any heat or thermal energy in the atmosphere. In this case, zero (0) is simply a number that lies halfway between -1 and $+1$. The most important implication of this situation is that we cannot properly claim that a day when the temperature reaches a high of 4° is twice as warm as the next day when the temperature rises only to 2°. The amount of heat in the air on the first day is not twice as great as the amount on the second day.

Comparing the weights of objects, however, is another matter entirely. In this case we can quite properly claim that an object that weighs 4 kilograms is twice as heavy as an object that weighs 2 kilograms. We can do so because an "object" that weighs zero (0) kilograms has a complete absence of weight. When numbers are used in this fashion, when the intervals between successive numerals reflect equal differences in whatever is being measured, *and* when the number zero (0) reflects a complete absence of whatever attribute is being measured, those numbers reflect a *ratio* scale of measurement.

You can see that as we move from nominal measures through ordinal, interval, and finally to ratio measures, we introduce new properties with each new scale. Kaplan and Saccuzzo (1982) referred to these incremental pieces of information as magnitude, equal intervals, and absolute zero.

I/O psychologists may use any or all four of these measurement scales in the process of doing their research. As suggested above, Dr. MacKeven might use nominal measures to code different religious preferences, as well as different organizations, departments, or occupations. In addition to supervisors' rank-orderings of their subordinates' work performance, Dr. MacKeven might use ordinal measures to indicate the relative difficulties of a variety of tasks. When she uses questionnaire data to assess workers' levels of job satisfaction, or test scores to indicate workers' levels of motivation or intelligence, Dr. MacKeven usually assumes that she is dealing with interval measures. Finally, when she evaluates workers' performance by counting the numbers of objects they produce or the dollar value of the sales they generate, she is using a ratio measurement scale.

At the same time that he introduced the distinction between these four types of measurement scales, Stevens (1951) initiated a controversy by suggesting that the measurement scale one uses determines the kinds of statistical analyses that are suitable and appropriate. Specifically, Stevens indicated that nominal and ordinal scale measures require **nonparametric** statistical procedures, while

---

nonparametric: A property of some statistical procedures that tend to be less potent because their usefulness does not depend on any limiting assumptions

interval and ratio scale measures allow the use of **parametric** procedures (Gaito, 1980). Contemporary supporters of this position include Townsend and Ashby (1984), who stated that measurement should be "a process of assigning numbers to objects in such a way that interesting qualitative empirical relations among the objects are reflected in the numbers themselves as well as in important properties of the number system" (p. 394). They claimed that if inappropriate statistical procedures are used, these relations are altered and the results of the analyses become meaningless.

Others have insisted that psychological meaning is not a statistical matter, and that the type of measurement scale used has little relevance to the question of which statistical procedures should be used (Gaito, 1980). Lord (1953) may have been the bluntest advocate of this position when he proclaimed that "the numbers [used in statistical analyses] do not know where they came from" (p. 751).

Resolution of this conflict is not presently in sight. Although it is clearly inappropriate to perform most statistical procedures when numbers have only nominal measurement-scale properties, issues concerning ordinal, interval, and ratio scales are not so easily resolved. Pending such resolution, Dr. MacKeven must contend with a certain amount of uncertainty and ambiguity regarding the "proper" statistical procedures for analyzing her data.

Research Strategies

Many different approaches are available to I/O psychologists who wish to implement the researcher–practitioner model. One way to illustrate this variety is to distinguish between experimental research strategies and observational procedures. A second way is to distinguish between research that is conducted in a laboratory and research that is conducted outside of a laboratory (usually referred to as "the field").

EXPERIMENTAL VS. OBSERVATIONAL PROCEDURES

The hallmark of experimentation is control. Typically the researcher systematically manipulates certain conditions and then obtains measurements to determine whether those manipulations had any influence on a second set of conditions. At Peter's Pan Pizza, Dr. MacKeven might allow one group of workers to set their own performance goals, while "arbitrarily" imposing the same goals on a second group of workers, and see whether the two groups' subsequent job-performance levels show any differences. Whatever the researcher manipulates, self-set vs. imposed work goals in this example, is usually referred to as an independent variable. The set of circumstances subsequently assessed for the purpose of identifying any changes, the two groups' levels of work performance in this example, is referred to as the dependent variable.

If the *only* difference between the two work groups in our example was that one group was permitted to set their own goals while the other group had their goals imposed upon them, Dr. MacKeven would be able to logically defend the conclusion that any discrepancies in the groups' subsequent performance levels was due to, or was caused by, this difference. Herein lies the major strength of experimental research procedures: If all other conditions are strictly controlled, so that the two groups are identical in every way except for their status on the independent variable, any subsequent differences in the dependent variable must be attributable to that independent variable. Put another way, actual differences in the groups' levels of performance *must* have been caused by the differences in the independent variable, since the two groups were exactly the same in every other respect.

Unfortunately, such strict control of all other conditions is usually very difficult if not impossible to obtain. The workers in one of the groups in our example may have had higher levels of intelligence (on the average), or more work experience, or easier tasks to perform than the members of the other group. If any or all of these differences existed (in addition to the difference in the way performance goals were set), the difference in the groups' levels of performance might have been due to any one (or a combination) of them, and not to the different manner in which the groups' goals were assigned. These other possibilities (differences in intelligence, experience, or task difficulty in this example) are usually referred to as confounding or contaminating variables.

Experimentation, then, is potentially a very powerful research strategy, since it allows us to draw conclusions about what variables or conditions are influencing other variables or conditions that are important to the organization. In order to take advantage of this aspect of the experimental strategy, however, I/O psychologists like Dr. MacKeven must strive to control as many potential contaminating variables as possible.

One way to achieve this control is to use a process known as random assignment—where every worker chosen to participate in the study has an equal chance of being placed in either of the groups—to create different groups of workers (experimental "subjects"), who will experience different levels of the independent variable. Since workers are assigned to groups in a completely *un*systematic way (by flipping a coin, for example: "heads" you go to Group A, "tails" you go to Group B), there is no reason to suspect that the workers in one group will be any more or less intelligent or experienced than the workers in another group. In fact, there is every reason to expect that the average levels of intelligence and experience in the groups will be essentially the same.

A second option for Dr. MacKeven as she tries to control anticipated contaminating variables is to match the workers who are assigned to the groups. For example, she might assemble the groups such that each group has the same ratio of women to men, the same ratio of "more experienced" to "less experienced" workers, the same ratio of "more intelligent" to "less intelligent" workers, and so forth. Once again, the groups would be similar in every way

---

parametric: a property of other statistical procedures that tend to be more powerful because they depend on limiting assumptions about how data are collected and distributed

except for the independent variable, so that any subsequent differences in the groups' performance levels can reasonably be attributed to the independent variable.

Either of these tactics can successfully eliminate the influences of contaminating variables from experimental research. Use of matched groups, however, requires that the researcher anticipate *all* potential contaminants. Obviously, this can be an incredibly difficult if not impossible task. The random-assignment approach, although it makes no such demands on the researcher, is effective only when the groups are sufficiently large that one could reasonably expect similar levels of potentially confounding variables to be present in each.

Observational research procedures are much simpler to implement, since the researcher makes no effort to manipulate or control anything. One simply observes and records (measures) the circumstances or variables of interest, and then uses one or more statistical procedures to determine whether or not any relationship exists between those variables. Because the **correlation coefficient** is the statistic used most often to assess such a relationship, the observational approach is sometimes called correlational research.

Since no manipulation is involved (and therefore the distinction between independent and dependent variables becomes meaningless), the observational research strategy can be very convenient and cost-effective, especially when a very large number of observations must be made. This strategy can also be very useful when it would be clearly unethical for a researcher to manipulate a particular variable. For example, suppose Dr. MacKeven was interested in the relationship between the quality of an employee's marriage and the level of his or her job performance. While it would be unethical to manipulate a worker's marital relationship, it would generally not be deemed unethical to ask employees to respond to questionnaires that yield a numerical index of marital satisfaction (obnoxious, perhaps, but not unethical). Those observations could then be compared with employees' levels of job performance to determine whether or not the two variables are related in any way.

Whereas convenience, cost-effectiveness, and avoidance of some ethical problems represent the "good news" associated with observational research, there is, as you might suspect, some "bad news," too. In this case, the bad news is that observational (correlational) research strategies do *not* allow the researcher

THE SMALL SOCIETY, reprinted with special permission of King Features Syndicate, Inc.

to draw any cause-and-effect conclusions about the variables under study. Since nothing is manipulated or controlled, there is no way to ascertain which variable is a "cause" and which is an "effect," or even if there is any causal relationship at all.

In the example cited above, suppose that Dr. MacKeven determined that workers who have happy marriages tend to receive higher performance ratings from their supervisors than do workers who are less satisfied with their spouses. What's the cause and what's the effect? It may be that a happy marriage causes workers to perform better at work (perhaps because they can concentrate on their work), while an unhappy marriage causes workers to perform poorly (because they are distracted, angry, or hurt). Alternatively, workers' happy marriages may result from their good work performance (perhaps better work performance translates into more pay, which contributes to a happier marriage), while unhappy marriages may be caused by poor work performance (fear of being fired may result in anxiety and, perhaps, abusive behavior at home). As if this were not sufficiently confusing, a third alternative is possible. Perhaps both variables, marital satisfaction and level of job performance, are being caused by a third variable that hasn't even been measured. In this case, perhaps workers' interpersonal skills are responsible for both the state of their marriages (better interpersonal skills allowing for more communication, which can improve the quality of a marriage) and their job-performance levels (especially if the job in question involves communicating with others).

Fortunately, the experimental and observational research strategies have complementary strengths and weaknesses. Dr. MacKeven might use the observational approach to gather data from all of the employees at Peter's Pan Pizza to see whether any relationship exists between two variables of interest, such as job performance and job satisfaction. If those data suggest that a relationship does exist, she could then conduct a controlled experiment to determine which variable (if either) is the cause and which the effect.

On the other hand, Dr. MacKeven might discover in the course of an experiment with two groups of workers that friendly behavior on the part of a supervisor tends to result in better work performance than does formal or unfriendly behavior. She might then conduct an observational (correlational) study to investigate whether this relationship also exists in all of the other work groups that make up Peter's Pan Pizza. In both of these cases, you can see how experimental and observational research strategies can be used in combination to supply more comprehensive and more satisfying answers to research questions than either approach could provide when used by itself.

LABORATORY VS. FIELD RESEARCH

This distinction refers to the setting in which research is conducted. An investigation that is conducted in a setting specifically created for the purpose of doing such research is typically referred to as a "lab study." Of course, the

---

correlation coefficient: a statistic that indicates the manner or direction and the extent to which two variables are linearly related to each other

"laboratory" for an I/O psychologist may consist of nothing more than a room containing a table and a few chairs (or an entirely empty room, for that matter). A field study is an investigation that takes place in a setting that has not been designed for the purpose of conducting research. The "field" for I/O psychologists is usually an actual workplace or organization where the emphasis is on producing a product or providing a service, and not on providing data for psychological research.

REVIEW AND INTEGRATION OF RESEARCH STRATEGIES

There is no necessary or implicit relationship between the type of research procedure one uses (experimental or observational) and the setting in which one implements that procedure (the laboratory or the field). One can manipulate and control variables in a lab or in the field, and one may simply record observations either in the field or in the lab. Nevertheless, just as experimental and observational procedures have complementary strengths and weaknesses, so do laboratory and field settings, and those complementary characteristics are not always independent of one another.

Since the laboratory is defined as a setting the researcher creates for the express purpose of conducting an investigation, it should come as no surprise that the I/O psychologist who wishes to exercise precise control over her independent (and contaminating) variables will usually be freer to do so in the lab than in the field. Alternatively, a researcher who wishes to take advantage of the observational procedure's capability of handling large amounts of information about a great many people will be able to gain access to a large sample more quickly and conveniently in the field.

A long-standing debate among I/O psychologists (and other applied social scientists) concerns the belief that field settings, because they are "natural" and not contrived, automatically permit the researcher to generalize his or her findings to a greater extent than do laboratory settings, which are by definition more artificial. Generalization, in this context, involves making inferences about larger groups of people, perhaps in different settings, from the particular behaviors emitted by particular individuals in a specific setting. Can other people in other settings be expected to behave in a similar fashion? A number of recent contributions to the I/O literature suggest that this debate is far from over. Dipboye and Flanagan (1979) surveyed a number of I/O psychology journals and concluded that field research has dealt with a rather narrow subset of settings, subjects (individuals), and behaviors, and that the inherent **external validity** (generalizability) of field research is a myth. While laboratory studies were no better, neither were they any worse. In a subsequent article (Flanagan & Dipboye, 1981), these same authors concluded that (1) laboratory research in I/O psychology is *not* rare, (2) applied researchers (such as Dr. MacKeven) do *not* primarily publish field research, and (3) field research does *not* tend to be more "applied" than lab research.

In their critique of Dipboye and Flanagan (1979), Bass and Firestone (1980) urged that we not confuse generalizability with representativeness, which refers to the *similarity* of the people, setting, and behaviors that we study to the people, settings, and behaviors about whom or which we would like to make inferences. Lack of representativeness does not rule out the possibility of generalizing, nor does it guarantee generalizability. Berkowitz and Donnerstein (1982) agreed, pointing out that it is the meaning that experimental subjects assign to their behaviors and their surroundings that determines the generalizability of an experiment's results, more than the **demographic** representativeness of those subjects or the surface realism of the experimental setting.

Pursuing a related point, Berkowitz and Donnerstein (1982) concluded that a number of published attacks on laboratory experiments reveal a serious misunderstanding of just why such research is conducted. Mook (1983) agreed, stating that laboratory research is best used to inquire about what *can* occur, not about the probability that a particular event or set of events actually *will* occur in a particular population of individuals. Among the specific things that can be accomplished in the laboratory, Mook included the following: (1) We can ask whether something can happen, rather than whether it typically does happen; (2) we can specify something that *ought to* happen in the lab, and test a theory or model in terms of whether our prediction is borne out; and (3) we can test the power of a phenomenon by demonstrating that it happens even under unnatural conditions that might be expected to preclude it.

EXAMPLES OF SPECIFIC TECHNIQUES

To summarize, Dr. MacKeven's research can be either experimental or observational, and she can conduct it either in the "field" (that is, within the normal ongoing operations of Peter's Pan Pizza) or in a "laboratory" (perhaps a small suite of rooms physically separated from other company offices and facilities). Although a lengthy and comprehensive list of alternative research techniques is beyond the scope of this text, it is appropriate at this point to provide you with a few examples of specific research strategies that Dr. MacKeven might use as she strives to serve the interests of PPP and its employees.

1. A laboratory experiment   In our earlier discussion of experimental and observational research procedures, we briefly described an experiment that Dr. MacKeven might conduct to determine the relationship (if any) between a work group's job performance and the manner in which the group's work goals had been determined (either by the group itself, or more or less arbitrarily by a supervisor or an experimenter). A typical laboratory experiment would be a situation where Dr. MacKeven formed her groups by randomly selecting workers from all departments and divisions of Peter's Pan Pizza, where she carefully manipulated the manner in which the group's goals were set, where she obtained relatively precise measures of the groups' performance levels, and where she did

---

external validity: a property of research results that are applicable or can be generalized to settings and situations other than those in which the results were generated

demographic: pertaining to various descriptive human characteristics such as age, sex, race, and so forth

all this away from the actual workplace (most likely in her suite of laboratory rooms).

2. A *field experiment*   Dr. MacKeven might attempt to answer the same research question by collecting data from employees right at their workstations as they are doing their jobs. A typical field experiment would be a situation where Dr. MacKeven formed her groups by assigning employees that were matched with respect to sex, age, experience, and so on to two or more *newly created* work groups (assuming, of course, that she was able to provide those workers and their managers with a reasonable rationale for assembling these new work groups), where she manipulated as carefully as possible the manner in which each group's goals were set, where she obtained measures of each group's work performance that were as accurate as possible, and where she did all this while the groups were engaged in actual work tasks in their regular work environments.

You can see that a field experiment confronts the researcher with formidable problems as she tries to exercise the control necessary for making causal inferences about the results of the experiment. Dr. MacKeven may therefore resort to field experiments only when her *primary* concern is generalizing her results to the workers' regular work behaviors and environments. When she is only interested in the *possibility* of a causal relationship between two or more variables, a field experiment would not be worth the additional effort.

3. A *field study*   Like a field experiment, a field study takes place in the regular work environment. It is not an experiment, however, because the researcher exercises little or no control over the variables of interest; instead, it is an observational procedure. Dr. MacKeven might try to answer her research question by collecting work-performance data, as well as information about the processes by which work goals were assigned, from two or more *existing* work groups within Peter's Pan Pizza. She could then use correlational analyses to see if any relationship existed between these two variables. Although this observational procedure is much simpler than either of the experimental strategies discussed above, total lack of control over the variables makes it impossible to draw any causal inferences about the results. Any variable, measured or unmeasured, might be the cause or the effect in any relationship that emerges.

4. A *survey*   A second observational strategy that Dr. MacKeven might use to answer her question about the relationship between the goal-assignment process and groups' levels of work performance is the survey. A typical survey involves asking employees questions about the variables of interest: How do you prefer to have your work goals determined? Do you tend to work harder when you can set your own goals? How has your most/least effective supervisor gone about setting your work goals? Employees' responses to such questions, asked either orally in an interview format or in writing in a questionnaire format, are then analyzed to provide information about the research question of interest. Once again, the simplicity and convenience of this procedure are obvious. It is equally obvious, however, that no causal relationships can be inferred from the ways in which workers answer such questions, and that workers' responses to questions may or may not accurately reflect their behaviors or beliefs.

5. A simulation study   A fifth research technique merits our attention, even though it is usually a special case of one of the other four procedures we have already described. A typical simulation involves creating an artificial work environment that is as similar to the actual work environment as possible. This approach usually amounts to a laboratory experiment, although it is conceivable that a field experiment might also be based on simulation. The work environment that is approximated can be physical or technological, as in the case of a flight simulator which recreates the surroundings found in an airplane cockpit, or interpersonal, as when participants in an experiment are asked to role-play or pretend that they hold particular organizational positions or face particular sets of circumstances. The researcher can exercise a great deal of control over independent and potentially contaminating variables, and can create devices for precisely measuring people's behaviors. Since generalizing to the actual work environment is usually one of, if not *the* primary reason for doing a simulation study, a perceived lack of realism can still be a problem, however. Even though recent innovations in computer technology have rendered some simulators incredibly realistic (airplane cockpits and supertanker control rooms, for example), the research participants still know that they will not *really* cause millions of dollars in damages and perhaps kill themselves if they "fly" the simulator into the side of a mountain.

SUMMARY

Realizing that the strengths and weaknesses of these procedures and techniques tend to complement each other, Dr. MacKeven strives to combine them in ways that provide the most useful and appropriate answers to her research questions, as efficiently and conveniently as possible. For example, she might begin her investigation of the possible relationship between work groups' performance and the manner in which their goals were assigned by administering a survey questionnaire to all, or to a representative sample, of Peter's Pan Pizza employees. That survey information may point to a small number of existing work groups that have very different perspectives on goal-setting. By conducting a field study of those groups, she may learn that different levels of performance do seem to be related to different procedures for setting goals. She might then conduct a series of laboratory studies to investigate some specific hypotheses regarding exactly which aspects of goal assignment are responsible for which aspects of the groups' work performance (quantity, quality, and so on).

Statistical Analyses

After using one or more of the specific research techniques described above to obtain psychological data, Dr. MacKeven must use certain arithmetic procedures to determine exactly what those data are saying about the specific research questions that were asked. Those arithmetic procedures are called statistics, or statistical analyses. This is not a statistics textbook, and so we have no intention of torturing you with complex laws of probability or arcane statistical formulas. We intend only to acquaint (or reacquaint) you with those concepts and formulas that are necessary to help you become an informed consumer of psychological research in general and, more specifically, the I/O psychology research results that comprise much of the rest of this textbook.

A useful distinction to make as we begin our brief sojourn in the world of statistics is between descriptive and inferential statistics. Descriptive statistics are used to summarize or to describe data. Descriptive statistics also serve as the raw material for inferential statistics, which help us to decide whether the data obtained from a given **sample** of individuals can be generalized to a larger **population** of individuals.

DESCRIPTIVE STATISTICS

After collecting data from a sample of people on a particular variable, an I/O psychologist's next task is to interpret those numbers. Suppose that Dr. MacKeven obtained a single index of job performance for each of the 15 custodians who work at the home office of Peter's Pan Pizza in Suardell Springs. Suppose, further, that this index is a number on a 7-point scale, where "7" indicates outstanding performance and "1" indicates totally unsatisfactory performance. (We'll wait until Chapter 4 to explain why this would not be a particularly good measure of job performance.) These performance scores for each custodian appear in Table 2.1.

Even though we have presented data for only 15 individuals, it is somewhat difficult to get a feel for how well or poorly the custodians as a group are performing their jobs just by looking at Table 2.1. Imagine how difficult it would be to look at a table showing the performance data for all 527 restaurant managers throughout the nation, and to be able to make any sense of it! Here is where descriptive statistics can play a useful role.

TABLE 2.1 Custodians' Job-Performance Scores

Name	Score
Adams, Kermit	4
Baker, Cindy	5
Cato, Amy	2
Davis, Ken	3
Ellis, Tom	4
Faber, Greg	6
Gray, Kathy	5
Houts, Vicky	3
Innes, Ray	6
Jones, Russ	4
Keck, Ruby	7
Lang, Jill	1
Martin, Debbie	3
Nash, Rick	5
Odle, Steve	4

The data in Table 2.1 are presented in a more interpretable fashion in Figure 2.3. This bar graph, or histogram, shows the number of individuals who obtained each of the seven possible scores on our measure of custodians' performance. This is one way to depict the distribution of performance scores.

The two most commonly used types of descriptive statistics also describe such distributions of scores. These are indices of central tendency, which provide information about the "center" or "middle" of a distribution of scores, and indices of dispersion or variability, which describe the extent to which the scores in a distribution are spread out around that middle or central score. With or without a histogram, these descriptive statistics facilitate interpretation of data distributions.

The three indices of central tendency that are typically used to identify the center of a distribution of scores are the mean, the median, and the mode. A mean is simply the arithmetic average of all the scores, obtained by adding up the scores and dividing that sum by the number of scores in the distribution. The mean performance score for our custodians is

$$\frac{\Sigma X}{N} = \frac{62}{15} = 4.133$$

where Σ (uppercase Greek sigma) indicates summation or addition, X indicates the scores to be summed, and N indicates the number of scores to be summed.

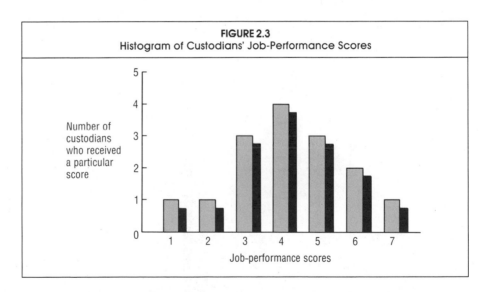

FIGURE 2.3
Histogram of Custodians' Job-Performance Scores

Number of custodians who received a particular score

Job-performance scores

sample: a group of people, selected for research purposes, whose demographic characteristics and status/scores on various independent and dependent variables can be directly measured

population: a group of people that is usually of indefinite or infinite size, about which researchers attempt to draw inferences or conclusions based on data collected from known samples

The mean is the most frequently used index of central tendency, partly because its meaning is easy to understand, and partly because it is more useful as "raw material" for subsequent calculations of inferential statistics. For our sample of custodians, you can see that the mean of 4.133 is a fairly representative index of central tendency by locating it on the histogram in Figure 2.3.

There are times, however, when the mean is *not* a particularly representative index of central tendency. Suppose that instead of the performance scores depicted in Table 2.1, eight of the custodians had received scores of "7" while the remaining seven all received scores of "1." The histogram for this modified distribution of performance scores is shown in Figure 2.4. The mean in this case is 63/15 = 4.2, almost identical to the mean of the scores displayed in Table 2.1 and Figure 2.3. In this case, however, this is a rather misleading index of central tendency; the average score is not really representative of *any* of the scores in the distribution.

A more useful index of central tendency in cases such as this is the mode, which is defined as the most frequently occurring score in a distribution. Strictly speaking, of course, it is also somewhat misleading to report that the mode in this case is "7," since that doesn't represent the other scores in the distribution very well. In this case, the most appropriate way to describe the central tendency of these scores is to say that the distribution is bimodal, that it has two modes, one at "7" and a second at "1."

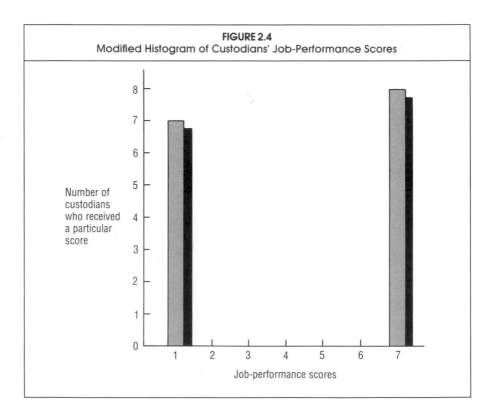

FIGURE 2.4
Modified Histogram of Custodians' Job-Performance Scores

Number of custodians who received a particular score

Job-performance scores

Another situation where the mean is not the best index of central tendency is presented in Figure 2.5. In this case, 11 of the custodians received scores of either "1" or "2," while the remaining 4 received scores of "7." The mean in this case would be 46/15 = 3.067. You can see once again that this is a somewhat misleading representation of the distribution, since none of the custodians received a score of "3."

In cases such as this, where there are a few **outliers** that cause the mean to fall above or below most of the scores in the distribution, the most informative index of central tendency is usually the median. The median score is that value which divides the top half of the distribution of scores from the bottom half; it's "2" in this case, a number that is certainly more representative of the majority of our custodians whose performance scores fell at the lower end of the distribution.

The mean, mode, and median, then, are three alternative descriptive statistics for representing the center or middle of a distribution of scores. None is necessarily the "right" or "wrong" index to use in a given situation. However, as our examples suggest, there are times when one of these indices of central tendency is perhaps more representative, or less misleading, than the others. We should add, too, that the most appropriate index of central tendency may also be determined by the type of measurement scale that is used (Stevens, 1951). The

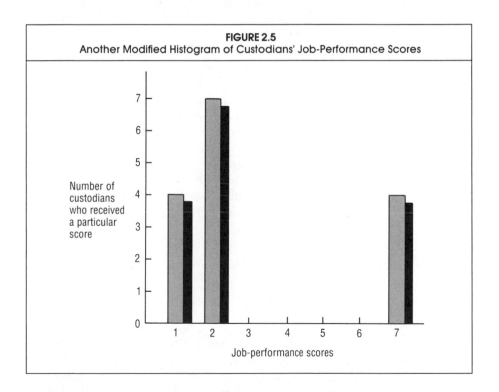

FIGURE 2.5
Another Modified Histogram of Custodians' Job-Performance Scores

Number of custodians who received a particular score

Job-performance scores

---

outliers: unusual, aberrant, or atypical scores that are markedly higher/larger or lower/smaller than the main body of more-or-less contiguous scores

mean, since it depends on division, is appropriate for ratio and, usually, interval measures, but the idea of an "average religious preference" (when this variable is measured using nominal scale numbers) makes less sense. The mode is more understandable as a measure of central tendency when dealing with nominal data; it is not gibberish to speak of a modal, or most common, religious preference among a sample of individuals.

No matter how appropriate an index of central tendency may be, however, it is not sufficient to unambiguously describe a distribution of numerical data. Look at the distributions in Figure 2.6. Although the means of the two distributions are identical, these distributions are very dissimilar in the extent to which the data are spread out around that mean. A second type of descriptive statistic is an index of dispersion or variability, which provides this missing piece of information. We will describe two indices of dispersion below, the range and the standard deviation. We will also acquaint you with the concept of variance, which makes it easier to understand the standard deviation.

The range of a distribution of numbers is typically defined as the difference or numerical "distance" between the largest and the smallest scores. Look again at Table 2.1. Those scores range from a high of "7" to a low of "1." The difference between these two scores is equal to $7 - 1 = 6$. Yet you can see that there are *seven* different scores in this distribution, "1" through "7." Thus, to actually calculate the range of a distribution of numbers, we subtract the smallest number from the largest, and then add 1. The range of the scores in Table 2.1, then, is equal to $(7 - 1) + 1 = 7$.

Just as the mean can be heavily (overly?) influenced by one or two extremely large or small values, making the median a more appropriate index of central tendency, the range can be similarly affected by an outlier or two. For example, suppose that all 15 custodians in our prior example had received scores of "6" or "7," except for Greg Faber, who received a score of "1." The range would be equal to $(7 - 1) + 1 = 7$, but you can see that this is a somewhat misleading description of the dispersion of numbers in this distribution, since 14 of the 15 values were separated at most by a single point on the scale. Although it isn't used very often, the **interquartile range** overcomes this difficulty.

A much more commonly used index of dispersion in I/O psychology is the standard deviation. In order to understand this index, however, it is wise to begin by examining a related index, variance. A formula for calculating the variance of a distribution, usually symbolized as s^2, is

$$s^2 = \frac{\Sigma(X - M)^2}{N}$$

where Σ indicates summation, X refers to the individual scores in the distribution, M is the mean of the scores in the distribution, and N is the number of scores in the distribution. In other words, variance is equal to the average squared difference between each of the scores in a distribution and the mean of those scores. If you think about it, this "makes sense" as an index of the extent to which scores are spread out around the mean. Closely clustered scores, where the differences

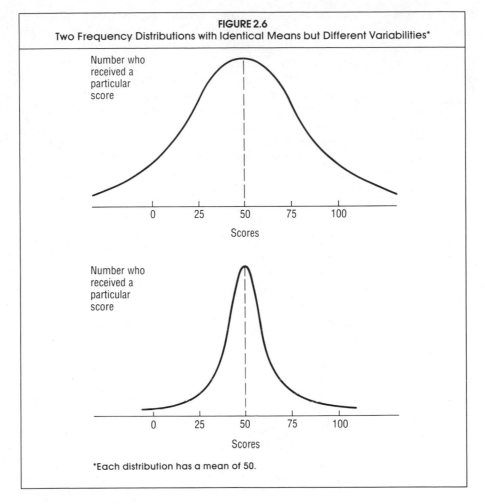

FIGURE 2.6
Two Frequency Distributions with Identical Means but Different Variabilities*

Number who received a particular score

Scores

Number who received a particular score

Scores

*Each distribution has a mean of 50.

between the mean and each score are relatively small, yield a relatively small variance; loosely clustered scores, where the differences are greater, yield a relatively large variance.

Since the mean of the scores in Table 2.1 is 4.133, the variance of those scores is calculated as follows:

$$s^2 = \frac{[(4 - 4.133)^2 + (5 - 4.133)^2 + \ldots + (4 - 4.133)^2]}{15}$$

$$= \frac{[.018 + .752 + \ldots + .018]}{15}$$

$$= 1.783$$

interquartile range: the difference or numerical "distance" between the score that separates the top one-fourth of a frequency distribution from the bottom three-fourths (75th percentile) and the score that separates the bottom one-fourth of that distribution from the top three-fourths (25th percentile)

Now that you understand variance, you are well on your way to understanding the standard deviation, since the standard deviation is simply the square root of the variance. Thus, the standard deviation of the custodians' job-performance scores is equal to the square root of 1.783, or 1.335.

The standard deviation is an extremely useful index of dispersion. If the distribution of scores is **normal,** or bell-shaped, as shown in Figure 2.7, the standard deviation provides information about the percentages of scores that lie within given distances from the mean. Also, the standard deviation enables us to meaningfully compare scores from two or more normal distributions. As you can see in Figure 2.8, Mr. Smith's scores of 30 on Test A and 36 on Test B are less impressive overall than Mr. Jones' scores of 36 on Test A and 30 on Test B, since the standard deviations for Tests A and B are quite different, 2 points and 10 points, respectively. If we did not know these standard deviations, we would have no reason to consider Smith's and Jones' combined scores on Tests A and B to be anything other than equivalent.

Not all distributions are normal, or bell-shaped, however; sometimes they look like those in Figure 2.9. The distributions in Figure 2.9*a* and 2.9*b* are **skewed.** Figure 2.9*a*, where there is a preponderance of high scores, is negatively skewed; we might expect such a distribution if we obtained intelligence-test scores from all the college graduates working at Peter's Pan Pizza, Inc. Figure 2.9*b*, where there is a preponderance of low scores, is positively skewed; we might expect such a distribution if we measured the annual incomes of the women and men who deliver pizzas from the franchises to the homes of PPP's customers.

The distributions in Figure 2.9*c* and 2.9*d* also depart from normality, but in a different way. These distributions reflect kurtosis, or the extent to which a distribution is flatter or more peaked than a normal distribution. Figure 2.9*c* shows **leptokurtosis;** a supervisor who rates almost all her workers as "average"

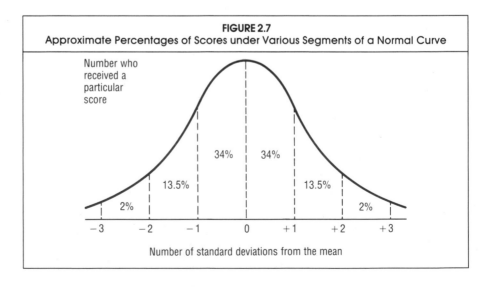

FIGURE 2.7
Approximate Percentages of Scores under Various Segments of a Normal Curve

Number who received a particular score

34%   34%

13.5%   13.5%

2%   2%

−3   −2   −1   0   +1   +2   +3

Number of standard deviations from the mean

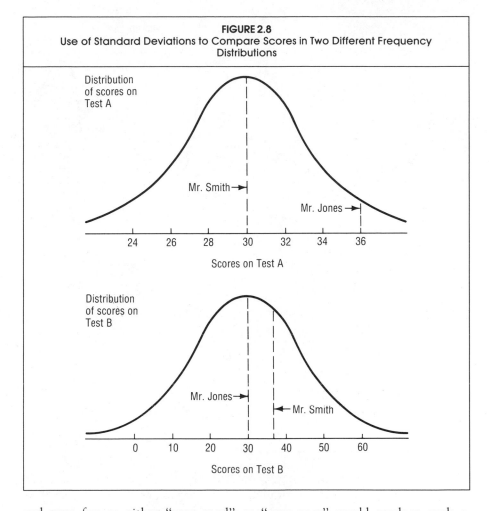

FIGURE 2.8
Use of Standard Deviations to Compare Scores in Two Different Frequency Distributions

Distribution of scores on Test A

Mr. Smith→|

Mr. Jones→|

24   26   28   30   32   34   36

Scores on Test A

Distribution of scores on Test B

Mr. Jones→|

|←Mr. Smith

0   10   20   30   40   50   60

Scores on Test B

and very few as either "very good" or "very poor" would produce such a distribution. Figure 2.9*d* depicts **platykurtosis;** supervisors who intentionally rate approximately equal proportions of their workers as "very poor," "below average," "average," "above average," and "very good" produce distributions that look like this.

normal distribution: a frequency distribution of scores that is symmetrical and bell-shaped; although it is mathematically defined, it closely approximates the way in which many human characteristics (height, weight, intelligence, and so on) are distributed

skewed: property of frequency distributions that have a preponderance of either high (negatively skewed) or low (positively skewed) scores, and are neither bell-shaped nor symmetrical

leptokurtosis: property of frequency distributions that are higher and narrower (than a normal distribution) in the middle range of scores

platykurtosis: property of frequency distributions that are lower and broader or flatter (than a normal distribution) in the middle range of scores

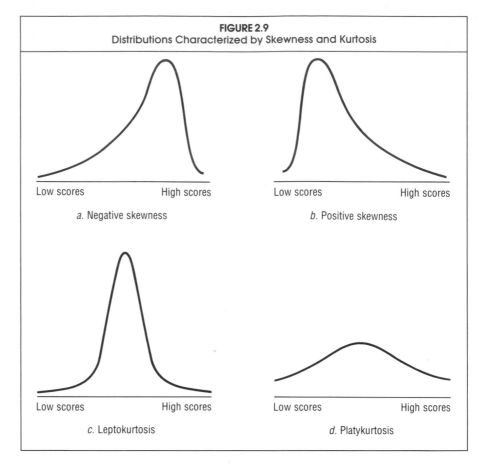

FIGURE 2.9
Distributions Characterized by Skewness and Kurtosis

a. Negative skewness

b. Positive skewness

c. Leptokurtosis

d. Platykurtosis

Since none of the distributions in Figure 2.9 is normal, the standard deviation is of limited or no use in helping us put a particular score in proper perspective. You can see that the percentages of cases that fall between the mean and plus or minus a given number of standard deviations will be very different from those shown in Figure 2.8.

INFERENTIAL STATISTICS

As we said earlier, we use inferential statistics to help us make decisions about the extent to which our research results, which are almost always based on a limited sample of individuals or observations, can legitimately be generalized to larger populations of individuals who did not provide data for our research. Since this is *not* a statistics text, we shall offer only very brief descriptions of some of the more commonly used inferential statistics. Our goal is to provide you with enough information to appreciate some of the analytic procedures used to generate the research described throughout the remainder of this text. Because one particular statistic, the correlation coefficient, has played such an important role in I/O psychology, especially within the subarea of personnel psychology, we shall examine it in a bit more detail.

Among the inferential statistics most commonly used in I/O psychology research are the chi-square test, the *t*-test, analysis of variance and its associated *F*-test, and the correlation coefficient. Chi-square, which can be used with nominal data, tells the researcher whether obtained frequencies of observations could reasonably have been obtained due to chance. For example, suppose Dr. MacKeven discovered that 5 women and 12 men had been promoted to managerial positions during the past year, and she wondered whether women were being victimized by discrimination. By comparing those numbers with the numbers of females and males that could have been expected to receive promotions if no discrimination were occurring (that is, by chance), she could satisfy her curiosity. Perhaps only 15 women had been eligible for promotion, while 36 men had been similarly eligible. In this case, since one-third of each group received promotions, there is no convincing evidence of discrimination. Alternatively, suppose that 13 males and 13 females had been eligible for promotion; now the observed frequencies (12 and 5, respectively) paint a different picture. The chi-square test is a systematic procedure for answering questions such as this.

The *t*-test is a procedure for determining whether two mean scores are "really" different from each other, or whether a given mean is "really" different from zero (0) or some other number, when the sample size is relatively small, usually less than 30 (Wright, 1976). If Dr. MacKeven wanted to compare men's and women's job-satisfaction scores, a *t*-test would be the appropriate statistic to use in the event that she was unable or unwilling to collect data from a large group of workers.

Analysis of variance (ANOVA) is a procedure for comparing the mean values of a dependent variable for two or more groups of individuals, when each group has been exposed to a different level of one or more independent variables. Factorial research designs, where two or more independent variables are measured or manipulated and each level of each independent variable is systematically paired with each level of every other independent variable, are also typically analyzed using ANOVA. The logic of this procedure is to compare the variance of the dependent variable *across different levels* of the independent variable with the variance of the dependent variable *within given levels* of the independent variable. If the *F*-test reveals that the "between-level" variance exceeds the "within-level" variance by a predetermined amount, we conclude that the independent variable did indeed have an effect on the dependent variable.

Suppose that Dr. MacKeven wanted to compare the job-satisfaction scores of employees in all seven of Peter's Pan Pizza's departments (see Figure 2.1). ANOVA would be the appropriate statistical procedure to use. Or, if she were interested in simultaneously assessing the combined and independent effects of department membership (one independent variable) and sex (a second independent variable) on job satisfaction (the dependent variable), a "two-way factorial" ANOVA would allow her to do this. Interestingly, ANOVA only began to appear in psychological journals during the late 1930s, "yet by 1952 it was fully established as the most frequently used technique in experimental research" (Rucci & Tweney, 1980).

STATISTICAL SIGNIFICANCE

An important concept for understanding any inferential statistic is the idea of statistical significance. A statistically significant research result is one that is sufficiently unique or distinctive that it is unrealistic to attribute it to chance or random errors or fluctuations in the data-gathering procedures. For example, Dr. MacKeven might hypothesize that the men who work for Peter's Pan Pizza are more satisfied with their work than the women, perhaps because the women are more heavily burdened with other, nonwork roles (mother, cook, laundress, nurse, and so on). Most likely, she would obtain measures of job satisfaction from some of the men and some of the women (samples), and then compare the two groups' mean satisfaction scores using a t-test or an F-test. Since it is extremely unlikely that the two means will be *exactly* identical, Dr. MacKeven must decide how large a difference between them is great enough to conclude that it reflects a "real" difference. She makes this decision by appealing to the concept of statistical significance.

Two additional comments about statistical significance are relevant here. First, a researcher never *proves* or *disproves* a hypothesis. Instead, data are collected and, through inferential statistics, the researcher makes a probability statement about the likelihood that the hypothesis is true or false. Second, the statistical significance of a finding must be distinguished from its *practical* significance, or the extent to which a given result can (or should, in the context of policy-making) make any *meaningful* difference in people's daily activities. Although a statistically significant finding may always be of theoretical importance, that finding may reflect such a small effect that it could (or should) almost never be used to explain people's behavior or to formulate policy for governing their activities. For example, it is entirely possible for the difference between men's and women's job-satisfaction scores to be statistically significant (*not* due to chance), but for that difference to be too small for Dr. MacKeven or anyone else to worry about it, or to spend time and money trying to eliminate it. Once a statistically significant result emerges from a research study, there are a variety of procedures for determining the practical importance of that finding. Although a statistically significant finding may turn out to have little or no practical significance, a research result should *never* be judged practically significant *unless* it is also statistically significant.

CORRELATION COEFFICIENT

The correlation coefficient is perhaps the most widely used statistic in all of I/O psychology, and certainly within the subarea of personnel psychology. Formally known as the Pearson product–moment correlation coefficient (for Karl Pearson, who originally derived it), and symbolized r, it is used to assess the extent to which two variables are associated with each other. A computational formula for the correlation coefficient is as follows:

$$r = \frac{N\Sigma XY - \Sigma X\Sigma Y}{\sqrt{[N\Sigma X^2 - (\Sigma X)^2][N\Sigma Y^2 - (\Sigma Y)^2]}}$$

where X and Y are the two variables whose interrelationship is of interest, and N is the number of pairs of observations or measures on X and Y available.

The computed value of r can range form -1.00 through zero (0.00) to $+1.00$. A positive algebraic sign suggests a "direct" relationship between the two variables: As the value of one of the variables increases, so does the other. This situation is depicted by the **scattergrams** in Figures 2.10*a* and 2.10*b*. A negative algebraic sign suggests an "inverse" relationship: As the value of one variable increases, the value of the other decreases. Figures 2.10*c* and 2.10*d* depict this situation.

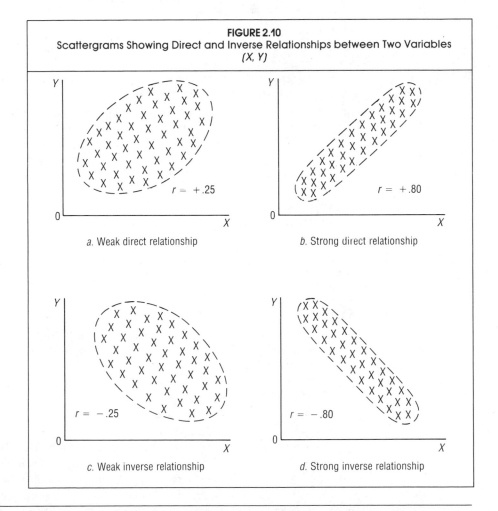

FIGURE 2.10
Scattergrams Showing Direct and Inverse Relationships between Two Variables
(X, Y)

$r = +.25$
a. Weak direct relationship

$r = +.80$
b. Strong direct relationship

$r = -.25$
c. Weak inverse relationship

$r = -.80$
d. Strong inverse relationship

scattergrams: graphic plots, for a given sample, of pairs of observations on two variables using two coordinate axes *(X,Y)*

A value of zero (0.00) suggests that there is no **linear relationship** between the two variables of interest. Figure 2.11*a* presents a scatter diagram where *r* = 0.00 and where there is no apparent relationship *of any kind* between the two variables. The scattergram in Figure 2.11*b* also depicts a situation where *r* = 0.00; in this case, however, it is clear that the two variables *are* related, but in a nonlinear (or curvilinear) fashion. This illustrates a very important property of the correlation coefficient: It reflects only *linear* relationships between two variables, and tells us nothing about any nonlinear relationships that might exist.

A second important property of the correlation coefficient, and one that we mentioned briefly during our discussion of research strategies, is that it says nothing about causality. Although two variables may be very highly correlated (positively or negatively, since the algebraic sign refers only to the direction of the relationship, and not to its magnitude), we cannot say that either of them is responsible for the other. Variable A may cause changes in Variable B, Variable B may cause changes in Variable A, or an unmeasured variable may cause changes in both Variables A and B. As you will recall from our earlier discussion, causality is best determined through experimental research strategies, although recent innovations in correlational procedures, such as **cross-lagged correlations,** offer some potential for "teasing" causal conclusions out of correlational analyses (Randolph, 1981; Rogosa, 1980).

As we said, *r* is widely used in I/O psychology. When Dr. MacKeven is interested in assessing the **reliability,** or consistency of her measures, she will often calculate *r* and refer to it as a "reliability coefficient." Similarly, you will learn that when she is interested in assessing the extent to which job applicants' subsequent job-performance levels can be predicted from their scores on tests taken before they are hired, she will calculate a correlation coefficient to describe the linear relationship between test scores (Variable A) and subsequent job-performance scores (Variable B), and refer to it as a "validity coefficient." Your acquaintance with the Pearson product–moment correlation coefficient has only just begun.

SO WHAT?

At this point, you may be wondering why we have tormented you with all this statistical information. Although some of our students might have a second opinion, we are not sadistic. We have spent time on these topics because understanding them will help you to appreciate the procedures that have yielded the research findings discussed throughout the remainder of this text, and because the methodological rigor with which a research study is conducted can have a direct impact on the results of that study.

Terpstra (1981) illustrated this point with a systematic examination of 52 research studies published in the *Journal of Applied Behavioral Science* between 1965 and 1980 that described the application of organizational-intervention procedures in various settings. He reported an inverse relationship between the degree of methodological rigor used to evaluate each study's results and the degree of success reported for the intervention procedure used. Specifically, as

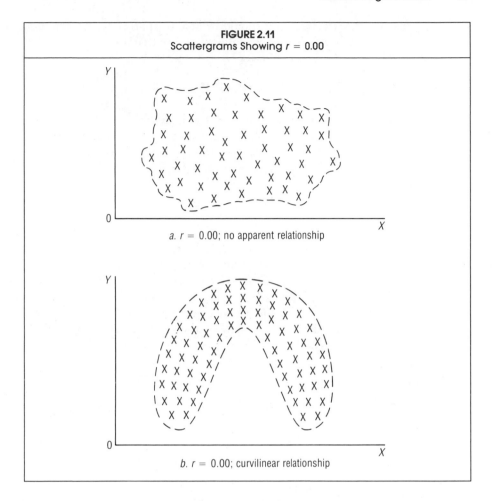

FIGURE 2.11
Scattergrams Showing *r* = 0.00

a. r = 0.00; no apparent relationship

b. r = 0.00; curvilinear relationship

methodological rigor (including sampling strategy and size, use of control groups and random assignment of subjects to groups, measurement strategy, and whether a level of statistical significance was reported) *increased,* the likelihood that the researcher would report a positive or beneficial effect of the intervention strategy *decreased.* Although Bass (1983) has offered some alternative explanations for these results (see Chapter 13), the importance of sound methodology to the science and practice of I/O psychology cannot be denied. As a student of I/O

linear relationship: an association between two variables that produces a scattergram that resembles a straight line

cross-lagged correlations: correlations where each variable is measured on at least two separate occasions, and causal inferences are drawn based on the logic that a "later" event could not possibly cause an "earlier" event

reliability: consistency of measurement, either across a time interval, across different measuring instruments, or within a given measuring instrument (across the multiple items that comprise a single test, for example)

psychology, you should be able to appreciate the differences between research procedures that are solid and those that are not.

CURRENT METHODOLOGICAL CONCERNS

Along with all the topics we have discussed so far, I/O psychologists today (including, of course, our own Dr. MacKeven) are becoming increasingly concerned with two methodological issues we have yet to mention: meta-analytic procedures and cross-cultural research.

Meta-Analysis

Many psychologists are appropriately interested in integrating the findings of large numbers of research studies that focus on the same topics, and drawing more general conclusions about those topics based on the wealth of information available in professional research journals. One of the periodicals published by the APA, *Psychological Bulletin,* is in fact largely devoted to review articles that attempt to do just that. These potential "integraters" and "generalizers" have typically read as much of the relevant material as they could obtain, and, through some highly subjective and completely idiosyncratic cognitive procedures, drawn some sort of general conclusions that seemed to make sense.

Recently, however, a number of people have proposed systematic, mathematical procedures for combining and comparing the results of different studies conducted by different researchers (Glass, 1976; Rosenthal, 1978; Walberg & Haertel, 1980). Many of these procedures rely on some of the descriptive statistics (means, variances) that we have discussed. In the context of I/O psychology, these meta-analytic studies have dealt with leadership (Strube & Garcia, 1981; Vecchio, 1983), job classification (Cornelius, Schmidt, & Carron, 1984), and most notably, personnel selection (Hunter & Hunter, 1984; Schmidt & Hunter, 1984; Schmitt, Gooding, Noe, & Kirsch, 1984). It is in the area of personnel selection that we will discuss meta-analysis in more detail under the heading of "validity generalization" (see Chapter 6).

Cross-Cultural Research

A second issue that is receiving increased attention from I/O (and other) psychologists comes from the realization that psychological research and practice transcend national, ethnic, and cultural boundaries. Once we acknowledge that a person's surroundings can have important effects on his or her behavior, it seems rather obvious that the culture in which that person lives and works should not be ignored. It should be equally obvious, given the wide diversity of cultures that coexist on this planet, that the research findings of I/O psychologists in the United States or Canada should not automatically be considered useful, or even relevant, in such very different cultures as those found in other parts of North America or Europe, not to mention those found in South America, Asia, and Africa. In fact, the vast cultural diversities that exist within given countries (Anglophiles and Francophiles in Canada, for example) dictate caution even when we are trying to generalize within national borders.

A number of cross-cultural articles have appeared in *The Industrial-Organizational Psychologist (TIP)*, the quarterly newsletter published by Division 14 of the APA. Examples include Dorfman and Howell's (1984) look at production sharing in Mexico, Summers' (1984) discussion of I/O psychology in Cairo (Egypt), Sekimoto's (1983) examination of performance appraisal in Japan, and Wilpert's (1983) and Dachler's (1983) descriptions of I/O psychology in Germany and Switzerland, respectively.

Although Peter's Pan Pizza, Inc., has yet to venture into the world of multinational corporations, Dr. MacKeven is certainly not excused from her responsibility to remain aware of cross-cultural issues. Who knows what the future will bring? Of more immediate concern, PPP has 527 retail operations scattered throughout the United States. The men and women employed in those restaurants represent a variety of races and ethnic groups who bring to their work a broad diversity of backgrounds and cultural experiences. If Dr. MacKeven is to be effective in her quest to promote the economic and psychological welfare of PPP and all its employees, she cannot ignore that diversity.

The remainder of this chapter is a discussion of the ethical considerations that influence research and practice in I/O psychology. Although we present this information in a chapter that is primarily concerned with research and methodological issues, you must remember that I/O psychologists who practice their profession in consulting firms or single organizations (like Peter's Pan Pizza) have no less of an obligation to abide by certain ethical standards than their research-oriented colleagues.

ETHICAL CONSIDERATIONS

The word "ethics" is derived from the Greek *ēthos,* meaning character, custom, or usage (Reese & Fremouw, 1984). All I/O psychologists who belong to the APA, as well as many who do not, subscribe to two sets of guidelines that were recently revised and published in the *American Psychologist.*

The first of these documents, entitled "Ethical Principles of Psychologists" (1981), lists ten principles that are intended to guide the research and practice of all psychologists. They are reproduced below. As you can see, most of these principles are directly applicable to research and practice in I/O psychology:

1. *Responsibility:* Psychologists are expected to maintain the highest professional standards, to take responsibility for the consequences of their acts, and to ensure that their services are used appropriately.

2. *Competence:* Psychologists keep abreast of current scientific and professional information, and recognize the limitations of their competence and their techniques. They provide only those services for which their training and experience qualify them.

3. *Moral and legal standards:* While recognizing the personal nature of such standards, psychologists are expected to be sensitive to community standards and to the possible impact of their behaviors on the public's trust in psychologists and on psychologists' ability to fulfill their professional responsibilities.

4. *Public statements:* Announcements or advertisements by psychologists should serve to assist the public in making informed judgments and choices. Professional qualifications and affiliations must be accurately described, and the limits and uncertainties associated with one's services should be specified.

5. *Confidentiality:* Psychologists reveal information about people obtained in the course of their work only with the consent of the person involved or that person's legal representative, except in those *very unusual* circumstances when failure to do so would result in an obvious danger to that person or to others.

6. *Welfare of the consumer:* Consumers of psychologists' services should be fully informed as to the purpose and nature of procedures, be they evaluative, educational, therapeutic, or training-oriented in design. Psychologists also acknowledge that clients, students, or participants in research procedures have complete freedom of choice with respect to their participation or withdrawal.

7. *Professional relationships:* Psychologists respect the needs, special competencies, and obligations of their colleagues in psychology and other professions, as well as the prerogatives and obligations of the institutions and organizations with which they are associated.

8. *Assessment techniques:* Psychologists promote clients' welfare and best interests when developing and using psychological assessment techniques by guarding against the misuse of results, by maintaining appropriate test security, and by respecting the client's right to know the results, the interpretations, and the bases for any conclusions or recommendations.

9. *Research with human participants:* Psychologists respect the dignity and welfare of their research participants, as well as federal and state regulations and professional standards governing the conduct of research with human beings.

10. *Care and use of animals:* Psychologists ensure the welfare of animals used for research purposes, and treat them humanely. They recognize that, laws and regulations notwithstanding, an animal's immediate protection is determined by the researcher's conscience and standards. (This is the only one of the ten principles that is not immediately applicable to the work of I/O psychologists.)

SOURCE: Ethical principles of psychologists, *American Psychologist, 36,* 1981, 630–633, Copyright 1981 by the American Psychological Association. Reprinted by permission.

The second document, entitled "Speciality Guidelines for the Delivery of Services by Industrial/Organizational Psychologists" (1981), which supplements the *Standards for Providers of Psychological Services* adopted by the APA in 1974 and revised in 1977, directly addresses the concerns of our subdiscipline. After carefully defining the background requirements of a fully qualified I/O psychologist, as well as the nature of I/O psychological services, this document lists and elaborates on three guidelines designed for professional self-regulation and protection of the public interest:

Guideline 1: Providers   I/O psychologists keep up to date on scientific and professional developments, limit their practice to demonstrated areas of competence, and strive to develop innovative procedures and theory within their discipline.

Guideline 2: Professional considerations   This guideline speaks to the issues of protecting the user of one's services, and to planning organizational goals. With regard to the first of these, I/O psychologists support the legal and civil rights of those who use their services, they abide by relevant APA policies, and they keep informed of relevant statutes, regulations, and legal precedents established by federal, state, and local governmental groups. With respect to the second issue, I/O psychologists state explicitly what can and cannot be reasonably expected from their services, they do not try to gain any competitive advantage through the use of privileged information, they carefully coordinate their activities with those of other professionals involved in the same project, and they systematically protect the confidentiality of their records.

Guideline 3: Accountability   Guided primarily by the principle of promoting human welfare, I/O psychologists' services should be subjected to periodic, systematic, and effective evaluations.

A growing body of literature attests to the fact that psychologists are genuinely concerned about implementing these principles and guidelines. Thoughtful treatments of the ethics of testing and assessment (London & Bray, 1980; Messick, 1980), as well as empirical investigations of perceived invasions of privacy (Fusilier & Hoyer, 1980; Stone, Gueutal, Gardner, & McClure, 1983; Tolchinsky, McCuddy, Adams, Ganster, Woodman, & Fromkin, 1981), are appearing with notable consistency.

Ronan (1980) focused the ethical spotlight on psychologists' participation in managers' attempts to control the work force, and suggested that such activities can have serious "anti-union aspects" (p. 1151). He recommended that I/O psychologists seek the following assurances: (1) that psychological interventions are not intended as anti-union activities, (2) that workers will be fully informed as to the nature of interventions and their implications, (3) that resulting economic benefits will be shared on at least an equal basis with the workers, and (4) that any given worker can opt out of an "experiment" or research procedure without prejudice.

Recognizing that the ethical norms underlying I/O psychologists' activities can sometimes come into conflict, Mirvis and Seashore (1979, 1980) exhorted us to confront such conflicts openly and honestly, and to develop *specific* guidelines in concert with *specific* clients in the context of *specific* projects. Walter and Pinder (1980), however, expressed some reservations about "negotiating" ethical principles with clients, and asserted that certain minimum standards (including freedom, privacy, esteem, and realistic expectations) must always be met. In the "best of all worlds," we would agree. Given the complexities of organizational research and practice, however, we tend to concur with Mirvis and Seashore. Developing ethical guidelines within a specific professional relationship is more applicable to the ethical dilemmas encountered by I/O psychologists than is "blindly" imposing the psychologist's (or anyone else's) absolute standards on the client or organization.

Dr. MacKeven's position as a full-time employee of a single organization confers both ethical advantages and disadvantages. Because she works only within the organizational context of Peter's Pan Pizza, she can develop ("negotiate," if you will) a fairly stable set of expectations with her employer. This is in marked contrast to the circumstances surrounding her colleagues who work for private consulting firms, or who are affiliated with colleges or universities and engage in private consulting activities. Since they provide their services to a wide variety of clients, these I/O psychologists must be ever vigilant concerning their allegiance to the minimum standards emphasized by Walter and Pinder (1980), and the applicability of those (and other) ethical principles to particular organizational settings and clients.

On the other hand, Dr. MacKeven's long-term relationship with a single organization can lead to conflict between her professional loyalties and ethics and her organizational loyalties. Because their professional relationships are more transient, her consultant colleagues are less likely to have to wrestle with conflicts of this type. Nevertheless, no matter what the particular circumstances surrounding an I/O psychologist's professional activities, the duty to integrate ethical principles and guidelines with sound research and practice comes with the territory. Ethical considerations do not supplement good research and practice, but are instead an integral part of these activities.

CHAPTER SUMMARY

Peter's Pan Pizza, Inc., is a hypothetical organization that consists of a headquarters, or home office, and 527 restaurants scattered throughout the U.S. Dr. J. A. MacKeven, who holds a Ph.D. in I/O psychology, is the company's human-resources coordinator. We will rely on Dr. MacKeven and her organization to illustrate the "real-world" applicability and limitations of the field of I/O psychology.

While pledging allegiance to the scientific method, effective I/O psychology researchers must often be flexible in their approach. They use either experimental or observational research strategies, and sometimes both, to generate measures of behavior that may have nominal, ordinal, interval, or ratio scale properties. Whether they collect data in the laboratory or in "the field," I/O researchers use descriptive statistics to summarize those data, and inferential statistics to draw inferences from known samples to larger populations. The most widely used descriptive statistics are indices of central tendency (mean, mode, median) and variability or dispersion (range, standard deviation). The correlation coefficient, which indicates the direction and magnitude of a linear relationship between two variables, is another pervasive statistic. Although statistical significance is no guarantee of practical significance, the latter is impossible without the former. Contemporary challenges to the I/O psychology research process include meta-analysis, cross-cultural studies, and ethical principles designed to protect the dignity and welfare of the men and women whose behavior is the focus of that research.

REVIEW QUESTIONS AND EXERCISES

1. Why might an organization hesitate to hire an I/O psychologist whose academic training has not been supplemented by off-campus field research and experience?
2. When is zero (0) not zero (0) in psychological measurement?
3. Design a research strategy to investigate the relationship between college professors' teaching styles and their effectiveness as instructors. Explain the rationales for each of your choices/decisions.
4. Describe three different ways to "lie with statistics."
5. Is it ethical for an I/O psychologist to collect data on workers' behaviors if the workers are not aware that they are "participating" in a research project?

CHAPTER 3

Job-Performance Criteria

Learning Points

After studying this chapter, you should

- understand what a criterion is, and be able to describe the crucial role of criteria in I/O psychology

- be able to describe the "ultimate criterion" for assessing performance on your current or most recent job, and to evaluate the characteristics and quality of the actual criteria that are/were used to evaluate your job performance

- be able to distinguish among single, multiple, and composite criteria, between proximal and distal criteria, and between "hard" and "soft" criteria

- be familiar with the kinds of information that can emerge from a job analysis, and be able to describe three or more specific job-analysis techniques

- understand the logical sequence whereby job-analysis information is transformed into job-performance criteria

- be able to explain the impact of the Civil Rights Act of 1964 and the Equal Pay Act of 1963 on the role of job analysis in the criterion-development process

- know what job evaluation is, and how it depends on job analysis

- understand the concept of comparable worth, and be able to explain why it is so controversial

INTEROFFICE MEMO

TO: J. A. MacKeven, Human—Resources Coordinator

FROM: Agnes Creighton, Vice President for Personnel

As you know, Peter's Pan Pizza has been experiencing unacceptably high rates of turnover among our restaurant managers in the last four or five years. Since this unfortunate situation clearly falls within my area of responsibility, I asked the directors of the three departments that report to me (James Schiftner in management selection, Florence Landis in management training, and Andrew LeGette in wages and benefits) to study the situation from their own perspectives, and to make appropriate recommendations to me.

Careful study of their recommendations revealed a single underlying theme. All three expressed various degrees of dissatisfaction with our current job description for the position of restaurant manager. After examining our files, I can understand their concern. At present, we have a single job description that is supposedly appropriate for all our restaurant managers, and that document hasn't been updated since 1975.

The simple fact (as I see it, at least) is that <u>we</u> <u>do</u> <u>not</u> <u>have</u> <u>an</u> <u>up-to-date</u> <u>description</u> <u>of</u> <u>exactly</u> <u>what</u> <u>these</u> <u>men</u> <u>and</u> <u>women</u> <u>are</u> <u>supposed</u> <u>to be doing.</u> Without this kind of information, <u>we</u> <u>cannot</u> <u>be</u> <u>certain</u> <u>about</u> <u>who</u> <u>is</u> <u>doing</u> <u>their</u> <u>job</u> <u>well</u> <u>and</u> <u>who</u> <u>isn't.</u> This makes it extremely difficult to select, train, and appropriately compensate these employees. How can we know that we are selecting, training, and paying these people properly without knowing exactly what a successful/effective restaurant manager is supposed to do? Our failure in any or all of these three areas could be contributing to our problem with voluntary turnover.

Any assistance that you can provide will be greatly appreciated.

Dr. MacKeven probably winced when she read Ms. Creighton's memo. In her brief description of her directors' perspectives on Peter's Pan Pizza's turnover problem (too many restaurant managers voluntarily quitting their jobs), the vice president for personnel put her finger on what many I/O psychologists consider to be "the curse" of their profession: the criterion problem. Although I/O psychologists have no monopoly on this problem, it is an especially crucial and challenging obstacle to Dr. MacKeven and her colleagues. As you will see throughout the remainder of this text, I/O psychologists are constantly wrestling with the notion of adequate criteria, whether they are designing systems to select, train, or evaluate employees, or trying to identify optimal leadership styles or ways to (re)design jobs.

Typical dictionary definitions describe a criterion (the singular form; the plural is *criteria*) as a rule or a standard that enables people to make judgments. For I/O psychologists, it is a "measure for judging the effectiveness of persons, organizations, treatments, or predictors of behavior" (Smith, 1976, p. 745). Just as we use a yardstick as a criterion for judging a person's height, I/O psychologists need similar "yardsticks" to measure such important variables as the adequacy of workers' job performance, the extent to which they are satisfied with their work situation, or the success of extensive programs to train employees or to redesign their jobs. The choice of which "yardstick" to use is a crucial one. The consequences of inappropriately measuring workers' levels of job performance can be disastrous for everyone concerned. (Of course, the consequences of measuring people's heights with a 39-inch yardstick can also be disastrous, especially if they're being fitted for suits of armor!)

In her memo to Dr. MacKeven, Ms. Creighton referred to the problem of excessive turnover among the men and women who manage Peter's Pan Pizza's restaurants. As you will learn later in this chapter, turnover is an example of a criterion for assessing workers' job performance; we assume that employees who remain on the job are making more valuable contributions to the organization than workers who voluntarily quit their jobs. Unfortunately, as far as Ms. Creighton's subordinates (especially the director of management selection and the director of management training) are concerned, turnover is not a very useful or informative criterion. Although the turnover rate serves to bring a potential organizational problem to their attention, it doesn't provide a clue as to how it can be reduced or eliminated, or even whether it *should* be eliminated. If these directors are to meet their responsibilities, they must know more about what constitutes an effective, successful restaurant manager. What does "success" mean in this situation, beyond the idea of simply remaining on the job? A satisfactory answer to this question can be obtained only through a direct confrontation with "the criterion problem."

This chapter will acquaint you with a variety of issues and procedures that I/O psychologists confront and use as they try to develop helpful criteria for individuals and organizations. We will describe important characteristics of criteria, as well as a sample of some commonly used techniques for developing criteria. Finally, we will consider some of the contemporary challenges to I/O psychology that have arisen from recent governmental legislation concerned directly or indirectly with the criterion-development process. Throughout the chapter, we will periodically refer back to Ms. Creighton's memo, and highlight the implications of the material for Dr. MacKeven's task.

SCOPE AND CHARACTERISTICS OF CRITERIA

Before turning our attention to the procedures for developing organizationally relevant criteria, it is important to recognize that a number of choices must be made that will determine the characteristics of the criteria that are eventually developed. Any suggestions that Dr. MacKeven might make to the vice president for personnel without carefully considering these issues would constitute nothing more than a "shotgun approach" to the problem that may or may not prove effective.

Criteria for What?

As we suggested earlier, I/O psychologists concern themselves with criteria for a variety of important organizational variables. Depending on the question at hand, "yardsticks" may be needed to determine the effectiveness of workers' job performance, the effectiveness of particular programs for employee training or organizational development, or the effectiveness of a systematic program for redesigning jobs. In the interest of clarity, and because of its relevance to the concerns raised in Ms. Creighton's memo, we will limit our discussion to one particular class of criteria: job-performance criteria.

Much of personnel psychology depends on our ability to develop adequate standards for making judgments about employees' job performance. We cannot design adequate performance appraisal instruments (rating scales, etc.) unless we know precisely what we want to measure. The director of management selection cannot possibly choose or design procedures for selecting successful managers until he is able to describe exactly what a successful manager does on the job. The director of management training cannot determine whether a given training program is effective, or even necessary, unless she is able to satisfactorily define managerial effectiveness. Finally, the director of wages and benefits has no way of knowing whether his salary plan is appropriate unless he has some specific ideas about what constitutes a worthy contribution to the organization. Each of these directors requires adequate job-performance criteria in order to meet their responsibilities.

The Ultimate Criterion

A useful conceptual aid for I/O psychologists who are asked to develop job-performance criteria is the idea of an ultimate criterion. Thorndike (1949) described the ultimate criterion as "the complete final goal of a particular type of selection or training . . . stated in very broad terms . . . that are often not susceptible to practical quantitative evaluation," and suggested that a "really complete ultimate criterion is multiple and complex in almost every case. . . . [It] is ultimate in the sense that we cannot look beyond it for any higher or further standard in terms of which to judge the outcome of a particular personnel program" (p. 121). You can think of it as the most comprehensive and error-free "yardstick" or standard imaginable for assessing the quality of a worker's job performance, a standard that ignores nothing of importance and includes nothing that is irrelevant.

If the ultimate criterion is an abstraction that can never be measured, you might wonder how it can be a useful concept. It is useful to the extent that it provides Dr. MacKeven with a frame of reference in which to evaluate the *actual* criteria of job performance that she eventually develops. In effect, it is an abstract, ideal standard against which to compare actual, measurable criteria.

Figure 3.1 should clarify this point. The top circle represents Dr. MacKeven's idea of the ultimate criterion, in this case an all-inclusive yet error-free standard for assessing the job performance of Peter's Pan Pizza's restaurant managers. The bottom circle represents whatever actual criterion measures she decides to use (such as performance ratings and monthly profit/loss ratio). Ideally, she would like the two circles to overlap perfectly. Unfortunately, this never occurs. Thus, her goal is to arrive at the best description of the ultimate criterion that she can imagine, and then to develop criterion measures that she can actually use that come as close as possible to "perfectly overlapping" that ultimate criterion.

The extent to which she succeeds is reflected in that portion of Figure 3.1 where the two circles overlap. This is known as criterion relevance, or the degree to which an actual criterion captures portions of the ultimate criterion. That portion of the ultimate criterion that is *not* contained in the actual criterion chosen for use is known as criterion deficiency. Finally, that portion of the actual criterion that does not overlap the ultimate criterion is known as criterion contamination. In trying to maximize criterion relevance, Dr. MacKeven strives to minimize both criterion deficiency and criterion contamination.

For example, as components of the ultimate criterion for a restaurant manager's performance, Dr. MacKeven might point to highly satisfied customers who return again and again, and who recommend Peter's Pan Pizza to their friends and relatives, who then return again and again. She might also point to a food-service operation that never fails to comply with legislation governing both food preparation and employment conditions. Finally, she will probably point to a restaurant that makes a profit each month. You can see how difficult it might be to actually measure some of these components of the ultimate criterion. Nevertheless, this ideal can assist Dr. MacKeven in assessing the adequacy of any given criterion of job performance that she actually decides to use.

The vice president for personnel referred in her memo to a high rate of turnover among restaurant managers. As we indicated, this is potentially an actual criterion of job performance. Let's see how it compares to the ultimate criterion. Does the fact that a manager quits tell us anything about satisfied

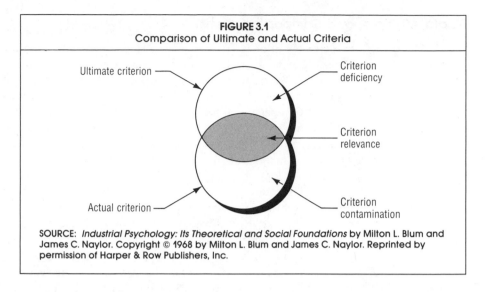

FIGURE 3.1
Comparison of Ultimate and Actual Criteria

Ultimate criterion

Criterion deficiency

Criterion relevance

Actual criterion

Criterion contamination

SOURCE: *Industrial Psychology: Its Theoretical and Social Foundations* by Milton L. Blum and James C. Naylor. Copyright © 1968 by Milton L. Blum and James C. Naylor. Reprinted by permission of Harper & Row Publishers, Inc.

customers returning again and again, or recommending that manager's restaurant to their friends and relatives? Probably not. Does his or her voluntary termination of employment say anything about compliance with governmental laws and statutes? Again, probably not. Both of these suggest a level of criterion deficiency, instances where the actual criterion (turnover) ignores portions of the ultimate criterion.

Finally, does quitting one's job have any effect on the profitability of a manager's restaurant? In this case, the answer is probably "yes," for it will cost time and money to recruit, select, and train a new restaurant manager, and the personnel change may have a negative impact on the job performance of those restaurant employees who remain. The actual criterion of turnover, then, does have some criterion relevance.

What about criterion contamination? The actual criterion of voluntary turnover is contaminated to the extent that it reflects situations or factors that have absolutely nothing to do with the ultimate criterion. For example, turnover is known to be influenced by the current unemployment rate: when unemployment is high and jobs are scarce, workers are more reluctant to abandon their jobs in the hope of obtaining better ones. The turnover that prompted Ms. Creighton's memo may simply reflect favorable economic conditions and a low level of unemployment, factors that are not directly related to the ultimate criterion of restaurant managers' job performance. This is criterion contamination.

Now that you understand criterion relevance, deficiency, and contamination, you are in a position to appreciate some of the decisions that I/O psychologists must make as they set out to develop actual criteria for evaluating workers' job performance. Many of these decisions concern the number of actual criteria to use, when those criterion measures are to be used, and the relative subjectivity of the actual criteria that are to be used.

Single, Multiple, and Composite Criteria

It is very tempting to try to identify a single measure that can serve as the actual criterion of job performance. Such an index could minimize the time and expense associated with criterion assessment. Unfortunately, the search for such a single criterion is almost always doomed to failure. In today's society, it is difficult to imagine a job that is so uncomplicated that the job holder's performance can be described adequately with a single measure. At the very least, everyone's work can be described in terms of both quantity and quality, which may or may not bear any relationship to each other. The position of restaurant manager at Peter's Pan Pizza is certainly too complex to be captured by a single index, since it involves making a profit, training employees, promoting customer relations, and so on. After all, the proposed ultimate criterion had at least three or four distinguishable components. We should therefore abandon the vain hope of identifying a single criterion for anyone's job performance.

What we cannot dispense with, however, is the recurring need to *be able* to describe a worker's job performance with a single index. As we indicated earlier, a major purpose for developing job-performance criteria is to assess the level of individuals' or groups' work performance so that we can make personnel decisions about promotion, transfer, or dismissal on the basis of merit. Consider promotion. Often there are several employees who are eligible and more-or-less qualified for a single, available promotion. Regardless of whatever mental gymnastics precede the decision, all the eligible workers must ultimately be placed in some sort of rank order that reflects their overall merit, so that the "best" person can be identified and promoted. Fortunately, we can derive a necessary single index of merit without relying on a hopelessly deficient (and, most likely, a contaminated) single job-performance criterion.

The solution is to acknowledge the complexity of jobs by collecting several different measurements that, when considered in combination, approximate the ultimate criterion as closely as possible. Such multiple criteria can be used to "fill in" the ultimate criterion like pieces of a jigsaw puzzle. Possible multiple criteria for the job of restaurant manager might include: (1) ratings from customers regarding the quality of the food and service received; (2) the number of customers who patronize the restaurant after hearing high praise from friends and relatives; (3) the number of violations of federal and local government codes; (4) the establishment's profit/loss ratio (including, perhaps, the costs of the personnel work necessitated by voluntary turnover); (5) ratings from nearby homeowners regarding the restaurant's level of social responsibility (for example, their perceptions of trash-disposal procedures, or the extent to which the restaurant sponsors local children's athletic teams); and so forth. Multiple measures of job performance are, of course, essential for providing employees with specific feedback about their performance, so that they can correct their deficiencies and maintain or improve performance that is already satisfactory or even exemplary. In this context, a single criterion of job performance would be almost worthless.

Multiple criterion measures, so useful for feedback purposes, can then be combined to meet those situations (such as making promotion decisions) that demand a single index of each employee's performance. That is, composite criteria can be formed by simply adding all the multiple criteria together. Alternatively, they can be created by weighting each of the multiple criteria in a way that reflects their relative importance or contribution to the ultimate criterion, and then summing them. Unfortunately, the "correct" weights to be applied to various multiple criteria are not always obvious.

The decision whether multiple criteria should *ever* be combined to form a composite criterion, or whether they should always be considered separately, has generated some disagreement among I/O psychologists. Some have maintained that multiple measures can only be combined to form a meaningful composite when the individual criteria are highly intercorrelated (Dunnette, 1963). Others have argued that multiple criteria *are* all related in one way or another to an organization's economic viability, and that they can therefore be meaningfully combined regardless of their actual levels of intercorrelation (Brogden & Taylor, 1950).

We agree with Schmidt and Kaplan (1971), among others, who asserted that the use of multiple versus composite criteria should be guided primarily by the manner in which the criteria are to be used. As we stated earlier, personnel decisions involving selection, promotion, transfer, demotion, and dismissal all require that each individual be described by a single number. Because we dismissed the idea of a single criterion as hopelessly simplistic, these personnel decisions can only be made with the aid of a composite criterion. On the other hand, when we are interested in generating information that we can share with individual employees to help them improve poor performance and maintain satisfactory or outstanding performance, multiple criteria are necessary. Being informed that one is a "5" on a 7-point scale of overall effectiveness provides a conscientious worker with few clues about how to improve.

The implications for Dr. MacKeven are clear. Because the directors of management selection, management training, and wages and benefits all pointed to the inadequacy of the existing job description (which, after all, is supposed to contain reasonably detailed statements about the different tasks that make up the job of restaurant manager), it will be necessary to consider *all* the components of this particular job. She must therefore think in terms of multiple criteria. Of course, this does not preclude the use of a composite criterion when the situation demands it, since the multiple criteria will be available for constructing such an index.

Proximal and Distal Criteria

Dr. MacKeven must also consider the time span she wishes to address with whatever job-performance criteria she develops for Peter's Pan Pizza's restaurant managers. In the words of Blum and Naylor (1968): "When should one obtain his [sic] criterion data? At what moment in time is our criterion 'ripe'?" (p. 182).

Once again, the answers to questions like these will be determined, at least in part, by the way(s) in which the criterion data are to be used. The director of management training may wish to assess the effectiveness of her training program(s) for restaurant managers as soon as possible, in order to avoid continued expenditure of money and time on ineffective programs. Alternatively, the director of management selection may prefer to delay such assessment until he can be relatively certain that the restaurant managers that were hired have had adequate time to demonstrate their (in)competence on the job.

Unfortunately, these timing decisions are not always quite so straightforward. Although the director of management training may wish to obtain relatively **proximal** criterion measures for reasons of cost and efficiency, she may share her colleague's concern that restaurant managers should be given adequate time to demonstrate their skills, and thereby the effectiveness of a given training program. Similarly, the director of management selection may prefer more **distal** criterion measures so as to avoid abandoning or embracing a particular selection strategy too hastily; he may also, however, share his colleague's concern with expense and efficiency. The decision whether one's criteria should be proximal or distal, or both, can only be made after careful consideration of the purpose(s) for collecting those measures.

This discussion of proximal and distal criteria suggests another characteristic of job-performance criteria that has received some attention in the I/O psychology literature. The performance criteria for any given job may change with the passage of time, and criterion-development efforts must take this possible lack of stability into account (Bass, 1962; Fleishman & Fruchter, 1960: Ghiselli & Haire, 1960). Offering an opposing viewpoint, Barrett, Caldwell, and Alexander (1985) suggested that concerns about the possibly dynamic nature of criteria have been overemphasized. They examined three definitions of dynamic criteria: (1) a change over time in the average *level* of group performance; (2) changes in *validity coefficients* that describe relationships between specific selection tests and subsequent criterion measures; and (3) changes in the relationships *among multiple criteria* over time. Based on their review of all the issues of *Journal of Applied Psychology* published between 1917 and 1984, and *Personnel Psychology* published between 1948 and 1984, and their critical analysis of the concept itself, Barrett et al. concluded that "dynamic criteria are rare phenomena" (p. 41).

Because Division 14 of the APA (1980) has stated that "predictability [of job performance] may diminish over long time spans as a result of changes in abilities and skills required, changes in the job itself, . . . and related factors" (p. 9), and because Bass and Barrett (1981) agreed that "criteria of success may or may not be stable over time" (p. 253), the case regarding dynamic criteria is still unresolved. Consequently, as Dr. MacKeven sets out to develop criteria for the performance of restaurant managers, she must not ignore the possibility that a successful retail restaurant operation two or five or ten years from now may be very different from a successful operation today. Although some things will probably never change (customers' preference for friendly and attentive service, for example), other things such as relevant governmental regulations very probably will.

"Hard" and "Soft" Criteria

A final issue that Dr. MacKeven must confront as she contemplates the development of performance criteria for restaurant managers concerns the relative objectivity or subjectivity of those standards of performance. Smith (1976) characterized criteria as "hard" or "soft," depending on how heavily they rely on human judgments. "Hard" criteria are those that can be obtained from some sort of record; that is, those that can be objectively counted and are not the product of someone's judgment. Examples include the number of units produced during a specified time interval, the number or dollar value of items sold, an employee's salary, the number of promotions a worker receives during a certain period of time, the number of years (or months, or weeks) an employee remains with the company, the number of accidents a worker has, and recorded instances of absenteeism or tardiness.

"Soft" criteria are the product of human judgment. They typically take the form of one person's ratings of another person's job performance; the worker's immediate supervisor is usually asked to provide these ratings. Other potential raters are an employee's peers (those at the same level of the organizational hierarchy), subordinates, or even the worker him/herself. Dr. MacKeven could also solicit the opinions of Peter's Pan Pizza's customers.

Summary

As you can see, both "hard" and "soft" criteria are potentially appropriate for assessing restaurant managers' job performance. Similarly, both proximal and distal criteria may serve as useful "yardsticks." As she develops actual performance criteria for these employees, Dr. MacKeven should consider multiple measures that vary along these two dimensions. Whether the criteria she actually develops are more proximal than distal, or more "hard" than "soft," or vice versa, her choices should be guided by the goal of maximizing criterion relevance and minimizing criterion deficiency and contamination (Figure 3.1).

DEVELOPING JOB-PERFORMANCE CRITERIA

Development of useful job-performance criteria properly begins with a careful job analysis. Our discussion therefore begins with an overview of this extremely important process, and continues with more detailed examinations of several widely used job-analytic techniques. We will then describe some of the issues that must be considered as an I/O psychologist transforms job-analytic data into actual job-performance criteria, and conclude the chapter with a brief description of some of the more recent governmental regulations that pertain to the use of job-analysis information.

---

proximal: nearby or close in time, order, or space; next to
distal: further away in time, order, or space

You will see that job analysis can be a tedious, time-consuming task, and that it can be very tempting to take shortcuts when developing job-performance criteria. Guion's (1961) tongue-in-cheek description of a psychologist who gives in to that temptation is reproduced here:

1. The psychologist has a hunch (or insight!) that a problem exists and that he [sic] can help solve it.
2. He reads a vague, ambiguous description of the job.
3. From these faint stimuli, he formulates a fuzzy concept of an ultimate criterion.
4. Being a practical psychologist, he may then formulate a combination of several variables which will give him—as nearly as he can guess—a single, composite measure of "satisfactoriness."
5. He judges the relevance of his measure: the extent to which it is neither deficient nor contaminated.
6. He may judge the relative importance of each of the elements in his composite and assign some varying amount of weight to each.
7. He then finds that the ideas required for his carefully built composite are not available in the company files, nor is there any immediate prospect of having such records reliably kept.
8. Therefore, he will then select "the best available criterion." Typically, this will be a rating, and the criterion problem, if not resolved, can at least be overlooked for the rest of the research.

SOURCE: Adapted by permission from "Criterion Measurement and Personnel Judgment," by R. M. Guion, *Personnel Psychology*, 1961, *14*, 141–149.

In the unlikely event that Dr. MacKeven were to follow this person's example, she should expect her "work" to contribute little or nothing to resolving the concerns of Ms. Creighton, the vice president for personnel.

Job Analysis

Simply stated, job analysis refers to one or more procedures designed to collect information about jobs. Among the kinds of information sought during job analysis, McCormick (1976) listed the following:

- work activities, including both individual behaviors and job outcomes
- machines, tools, equipment, and work aids used
- job-related tangibles and intangibles, such as materials processed and knowledge applied, respectively
- standards of work performance
- job context
- personnel requirements, such as education, experience, aptitudes, and so forth

The first item on McCormick's (1976) list—work activities, both individual behaviors and work outcomes—suggests an important distinction between two different but related kinds of job information. First, every job in any organization should exist solely because that job makes a meaningful contribution to the organization's overall goals, whether those goals entail producing a product (pizza!), providing a service (selling it!), or both. Job-analysis procedures designed to assess these intended outcomes or job results, as well as the conditions under which those results are obtained, are known as job-oriented approaches.

Although job-oriented information is essential, it isn't enough just to know the goals or purposes of a job. We must also learn about the behaviors or activities that are required of the men and women who hold that job, as they go about accomplishing those end results. Procedures designed to assess workers' behaviors or activities on their jobs are known as worker-oriented approaches to job analysis.

Both kinds of job-analysis information are needed. It does an I/O psychologist little good to know the specific behaviors demanded by a given job unless she knows the purposes of those behaviors, as well as the physical and psychological conditions under which those behaviors occur. Similarly, an I/O psychologist who collects job-analysis information for the purpose of developing behavior-based performance appraisal measures or a new personnel training program cannot be satisfied with the knowledge of why a given job exists. He must identify the specific behaviors demanded by the job, so that he can appropriately evaluate or train employees.

Lopez, Kesselman, and Lopez (1981) suggested a third approach to job analysis that complements the job- and worker-oriented approaches. Advocating a trait-oriented job-analysis technique called Threshold Trait Analysis, they described a procedure that determines "whether or not a **trait** is relevant [to a given job] and, if relevant, the level of the trait required for acceptable job performance" (p. 486). Lopez et al. characterized this trait-oriented approach as a way "to link a **taxonomy** of job functions with a taxonomy of human behaviors required to acceptably perform these same job functions" (p. 499).

These three approaches to job analysis, when used in combination, can provide an I/O psychologist with all the information necessary to carry out the entire range of personnel functions (selection, training, performance evaluation, etc.). Job-oriented procedures describe the reasons for a job's existence and the conditions under which a job's purpose is fulfilled. Worker-oriented procedures describe the actual behaviors required of the job incumbent in order to accomplish the intended end result. Trait-oriented procedures describe the human characteristics that are prerequisite to performing those behaviors or activities. As she plans her job analysis of the restaurant manager position, Dr. MacKeven should select a combination of procedures that will yield all three kinds of information.

---

trait: a psychological characteristic that tends to be relatively stable across different situations (shyness, honesty, diligence, and so on)

taxonomy: a classificaton of people, objects, behaviors, or events into categories on the basis of specified similarities and differences

OVERVIEW OF JOB-ANALYSIS METHODS

Whether she seeks job- or worker- or trait-oriented information, Dr. MacKeven will be able to choose from among a variety of techniques for collecting her data. Citing Morsh (1964), Blum and Naylor (1968) listed nine different techniques for gathering job-analysis information:

- questionnaires, where workers answer written questions about their jobs
- checklists, where workers simply indicate whether or not their jobs include any or all of a list of possible tasks
- individual interviews, where workers are presented with oral questions about their jobs
- group interviews, where several workers are questioned simultaneously
- diaries, where workers are asked to record their daily work activities
- technical conferences, where "experts" (usually those who supervise the job in question) meet in order to identify all the aspects of the job
- critical incidents, where workers and/or "experts" are asked to describe aspects of the job in question that are crucial to either success or failure
- observation interviews, where workers are interviewed right at their work stations by the job analyst, who also observes them going about their daily activities
- work participation, where the job analyst actually performs the job in question

Even this list is by no means exhaustive. Nevertheless, each of these methods, as well as any others that you might imagine, can be categorized under one or more of the following headings: (1) asking, (2) observing, or (3) doing. As a rule, the more sources of information one taps, the more complete and accurate the job analysis. In most cases, job analysts restrict themselves to asking or observing, or a combination of the two. Having the job analyst assume the role of the worker can be impractical, illegal, or just downright dangerous!

Even if she limits herself to one or both of the first two methods, Dr. MacKeven should not lose sight of some of the problems inherent in conducting job analyses by observing workers or asking them questions about their jobs. Asking questions assumes that the job holder has the necessary verbal skills to understand and respond to those questions. This may not always be the case. Even if it is, workers' responses may or may not be accurate or truthful. Some employees may sincerely wish to answer the job analyst's questions accurately, but may unintentionally provide inaccurate information because of ignorance or simple oversight. Other workers may be threatened by job analysts, perceiving them as "efficiency experts" bent on making people work harder and longer for the same pay, and may therefore intentionally supply incorrect information that portrays workers in a more favorable light.

Nor is observation without its drawbacks. Most of us act differently when we know that someone is "looking over our shoulder." Additionally, job analysts don't always know just what to look for, and so a quick movement that is rarely repeated may not be noted, even though it may be crucial to job success. Of course, many work behaviors such as thinking, making decisions, planning, and other cognitive activities performed by a variety of workers (including restaurant managers) simply do not lend themselves to observation.

Since Dr. MacKeven is concerned with the position of restaurant manager, she can probably expect to encounter women and men with adequate verbal skills. Some of these individuals may be suspicious of her intentions, however, or they may behave differently simply as a function of "being under a microscope." Any steps that she or the organization can take to minimize these potential problems (such as including representative restaurant managers in the planning stages of the project, or keeping them completely informed throughout all phases of the project) will be effort well spent.

EXAMPLES OF SPECIFIC JOB-ANALYSIS TECHNIQUES

Job analysts can choose specific techniques from among a number of options. Those discussed here are offered neither as an exhaustive nor even as a representative sample of available techniques. Instead, they are included because they are widely used in applied settings, because they have been the focus of a substantial amount of empirical research, or because they represent relatively new approaches to job analysis.

Functional job analysis (FJA) is an approach that the United States Employment Service adopted; it is reflected in the *Dictionary of Occupational Titles (DOT)* (U.S. Department of Labor, 1977), a document that has emerged as one of the primary sources of information about jobs. As described by Olson, Fine, Myers, and Jennings (1981), FJA

> begins by examining the purpose and goals of the work . . . [and then] determine[s], step by step, what must be done to accomplish it. Two types of information are derived . . . (a) what gets done (. . . procedures/methods and processes with which the worker is engaged as he/she performs a task), and (b) how the worker does it (. . . the physical, mental, and interpersonal involvement of the worker as he/she carries out procedures and processes). . . . It provides explicit terminology for getting at and understanding what workers do to accomplish the objectives of an organization (p. 352).

You can see that FJA yields both job-oriented (what gets done) and worker-oriented (how it gets done) information. The job analyst obtains that information through one or more of the "asking" or "observing" techniques we listed earlier.

FJA analyzes every job in terms of the extent to which it requires workers to deal with data (information), people (co-workers, supervisors, subordinates, customers, and so on), and things (objects). The *DOT* describes jobs according to their levels of complexity in each of these three domains. These levels are arranged in hierarchies, based on the assumption that a job that demands a more complex level of interaction with data, people, or things will also require the worker to perform all of the less complex functions in the respective hierarchies. Those three hierarchies of worker functions are presented in Table 3.1. Some of the definitions of specific functions or levels within each hierarchy follow:

DATA

0 *Synthesizing:* Integrating analyses of data to discover facts and/or develop knowledge concepts or interpretations.

1 *Coordinating:* Determining time, place, and sequence of operations or actions to be taken on the basis of analysis of data; executing determination and/or reporting on events.

6 *Comparing:* Judging the readily observable functional, structural, or compositional characteristics (whether similar to or divergent from obvious standards) of data, people, or things.

PEOPLE

0 *Mentoring:* Dealing with individuals in terms of their total personality in order to advise, counsel, and/or guide them with regard to problems that may be resolved by legal, scientific, clinical, spiritual, and/or other professional principles.

3 *Supervising:* Determining or interpreting work procedures for a group of workers, assigning specific duties to them, maintaining harmonious relations among them, and promoting efficiency. A variety of responsibilities is involved in this function.

8 *Taking instructions; helping:* Helping applies to "nonlearning" helpers. No variety of responsibility is involved in this function.

THINGS

0 *Setting up:* Adjusting machines or equipment by replacing or altering tools, jigs, fixtures, and attachments to prepare them to perform their functions, change their performance, or restore their proper functioning if they break down. Workers who set up one or a number of machines for other workers or who set up and personally operate a variety of machines are included here.

7 *Handling:* Using body members, hand tools, and/or special devices to work, move, or carry objects or materials. Involves little or no latitude for judgment with regard to attainment of standards or in selecting appropriate tool, object, or material.

SOURCE: U.S. Department of Labor, Employment and Training Administration. (1977). *Dictionary of occupational titles* (4th ed.). Washington, D.C.: U.S. Government Printing Office.

The information listed in the *DOT* under the heading of "Manager, Fast Food Services," which corresponds reasonably well with the position of restaurant manager for Peter's Pan Pizza, is presented here:

185.137-010 MANAGER, FAST FOOD SERVICES

Manages franchised or independent fast food or wholesale prepared food establishment: Directs, coordinates, and participates in preparation of, and cooking, wrapping, or packing types of food served or prepared by establishment, collecting of monies from in-house or take-out customers, or assembling food orders for wholesale customers. Coordinates activities of workers engaged in keeping business records, collecting and paying accounts, ordering or purchasing supplies, and delivery of foodstuffs to wholesale or retail customers. Interviews, hires, and trains personnel.

TABLE 3.1 Hierarchies of Worker Functions

Data	People	Things
0 Synthesizing	0 Mentoring	0 Setting up
1 Coordinating	1 Negotiating	1 Precision working
2 Analyzing	2 Instructing	2 Operating–controlling
3 Compiling	3 Supervising	3 Driving–operating
4 Computing	4 Diverting	4 Manipulating
5 Copying	5 Persuading	5 Tending
6 Comparing	6 Speaking–signaling	6 Feeding–offbearing
	7 Serving	7 Handling
	8 Taking instructions–helping	

Note: Smaller numbers (toward the top of each column) indicate more complex functions, which are generally assumed to include all functions in that column of lesser complexity (larger numbers). McCormick and Ilgen (1985), however, claimed that "there are instances in which the implied hierarchical relationships are limited, imprecise, reversed, or nonexistent" (pp. 45–46); they advised caution in interpreting these levels too rigidly.

SOURCE: U.S. Department of Labor, Employment and Training Administration. (1977). *Dictionary of occupational titles* (4th ed.). Washington, D.C.: U.S. Government Printing Office.

May contact prospective wholesale customers, such as mobile food vendors, vending machine operators, bar and tavern owners, and institutional personnel, to promote sale of prepared foods, such as doughnuts, sandwiches, and specialty food items. May establish delivery routes and schedules for supplying wholesale customers. Workers are usually classified according to type or name of franchised establishment or type of prepared foodstuff retailed or wholesaled.

SOURCE: U.S. Department of Labor, Employment and Training Administration. (1977). *Dictionary of occupational titles* (4th ed.). Washington, D.C.: U.S. Government Printing Office.

The *DOT* lists a nine-digit code number for each job. The first three digits identify a particular job group. The numbers 185 for the fast food manager indicate that this job belongs to the group of Wholesale and Retail Trade Managers and Officials. The middle three digits describe the job's level of complexity with respect to data, people, and things, respectively. The numbers 137 for this position indicate that this job requires "coordinating" data, "supervising" people, and "handling" things (see the list above that defines worker functions). The final three digits reflect the alphabetical order of the job titles within given six-digit code groups. If a six-digit code applies only to a single job title, the numbers 010 are always assigned as the final three digits (as in the *DOT* job description for the fast food manager).

Although FJA is an intuitively appealing technique, in that it yields both job- and worker-oriented information, a recent study by Cain and Green (1983) advised job analysts to exercise caution when using it, or when relying on FJA-based ratings in the *DOT*. Specifically, these authors investigated the extent to which a group of job analysts agreed with each other when rating the levels of involvement with data, people, and things demanded by a wide variety of different jobs. Agreement among 42 job analysts with respect to data and people was high;

agreement regarding things, however, was less impressive. Their recommendation that job analysts should use the ratings available in the *DOT* only in an informed and selective way seems to be a wise one.

A second job-analysis technique that has been widely used and studied is the *Position Analysis Questionnaire (PAQ)* developed by McCormick, Jeanneret, and Mecham (1972). Basically a worker-oriented approach, the PAQ consists of 194 different job elements or statements describing human behaviors that could be demanded by any given job. These job elements are organized into six different categories or divisions: (1) information input, (2) mental processes, (3) work output, (4) relationships with other persons, (5) job context, and (6) other job characteristics. A central question that underlies each category, and the major subheadings included within each category, are presented in the following outline.

1. *Information input:* Where and how does a worker get the information to be used in performing the job?
   1.1 Sources of job information
       1.1.1. Visual sources of job information
       1.1.2. Nonvisual sources of job information
   1.2. Sensory and perceptual processes
   1.3. Estimation activities
2. *Mental processes:* What reasoning, decision-making, planning, and information-processing activities does the job involve?
   2.1. Decision making, reasoning, and planning/scheduling
   2.2. Information-processing activities
   2.3. Use of learned information
3. *Work output:* What physical activity does the worker perform, and what tools or other devices are used?
   3.1. Use of devices and equipment
       3.1.1. Hand-held tools or instruments
       3.1.2. Other hand-held devices
       3.1.3. Stationary devices
       3.1.4. Control devices (on equipment)
       3.1.5. Transportation and mobile equipment
   3.2. Manual activities
   3.3. Activities of the entire body
   3.4. Level of physical exertion
   3.5. Body positions/postures
   3.6. Manipulation/coordination activities
4. *Relationships with other persons:* What relationships with other people are required to perform the job?
   4.1. Communications
       4.1.1. Oral (speaking)
       4.1.2. Written
       4.1.3. Other communications
   4.2. Miscellaneous interpersonal relationships
   4.3. Amount of job-required personal contact

4.4. Types of job-required personal contact

4.5. Supervision and coordination

    4.5.1. Supervision/direction given

    4.5.2. Other organizational activities

    4.5.3. Supervision received

5. *Job context:* What are the physical and social contexts in which the work is performed?

  5.1. Physical working conditions

    5.1.1. Outdoor environment

    5.1.2. Indoor temperatures

    5.1.3. Other physical working conditions

  5.2. Physical hazards

  5.3. Personal and social aspects

6. *Other job characteristics:* What activities, conditions, or characteristics other than those already described are relevant to the job?

  6.1. Apparel worn

  6.2. Licensing

  6.3. Work schedule

    6.3.1. Continuity of work

    6.3.2. Regularity of working hours

    6.3.3. Day–night schedule

  6.4. Job demands

  6.5. Responsibility

  6.6. Job structure

  6.7. Criticality of position

  6.8. Pay/income

SOURCE: E. J. McCormick, P. R. Jeanneret, and R. C. Mecham, *Position Analysis Questionnaire,* copyright © 1969 by Purdue Research Foundation, West Lafayette, Indiana 47907. Reprinted with permission.

The PAQ is intended to be used as a guide for a highly structured oral interview. That is, the job analyst reads each of the 194 items to the job incumbent, listens carefully to the worker's responses, asks any clarifying questions deemed necessary, and then mentally integrates the information obtained and chooses the appropriate response on the rating scale that applies to each particular item or job element. Depending on the item or question, rating scales may address (1) *extent of use,* with responses ranging from "nominal" or "very infrequently" to "very substantial"; (2) *importance* to the job, ranging from "very minor" to "extreme"; (3) *amount of time,* ranging from "less than one-tenth of the time" to "almost continually"; and (4) *possibility of occurrence,* ranging from "no possibility" to "high." In addition, there are a limited number of statements that require special rating scales or response codes. A page from the PAQ that contains the final item from the mental-processes section (#49—an item that requires a special rating scale) and the first five items from the work-output section (#50 through #54), each of which is answered using the "importance-to-this-job" rating scale, is reproduced in Figure 3.2.

FIGURE 3.2
Sample Page from the PAQ

Mental Processes and Work Output

49 |S_| Using mathematics (indicate, using the code below, the highest level of mathematics required by the job)

— *Code*   *Level of Mathematics*

N   Does not apply
1   Simple basic (counting, addition and subtraction of 2-digit numbers or less)
2   Basic (addition and subtraction of numbers of 3 digits or more, multiplication, division, etc.)
3   Intermediate (calculations and concepts involving fractions, decimals, percentages, etc.)
4   Advanced (algebraic, geometric, trigonometric, and statistical concepts, techniques, and procedures, usually applied in standard practical situations)
5   Very advanced (advanced mathematical and statistical theory, concepts, and techniques, for example, calculus, topology, vector analysis, factor analysis, probability theory, etc.)

3 WORK OUTPUT

3.1 Use of Devices and Equipment

3.1.1 Hand-held Tools or Instruments

Consider in this category those devices which are used to move or modify workpieces, materials, products, or objects. Do *not* consider measuring devices here.

Code	*Importance to this Job (I)*
N	Does not apply
1	Very minor
2	Low
3	Average
4	High
5	Extreme

Manually powered

50 |I_| Precision tools/instruments (that is, tools or instruments powered by the *user* to perform *very accurate* or *precise* operations, for example, the use of engraver's tools, watchmaker's tools, surgical instruments, etc.)

51 |I_| Nonprecision tools/instruments (tools or instruments powered by the *user* to perform operations *not* requiring *great* accuracy or precision, for example, hammers, wrenches, trowels, knives, scissors, chisels, putty knives, strainers, hand grease guns, etc.; do *not* include long-handle tools here)

52 |I_| Long-handle tools (hoes, rakes, shovels, picks, axes, brooms, mops, etc.)

53 |I_| Handling devices/tools (tongs, ladles, dippers, forceps, etc., used for moving or handling objects and materials; do *not* include here protective gear such as asbestos gloves, etc.)

Powered (manually controlled or directed devices using an energy source such as electricity, compressed air, fuel, hydraulic fluid, etc., in which the component part which accomplishes the modification is hand-held, such as dentist drills, welding equipment, etc., as well as devices small enough to be entirely hand-held)

54 |I_| Precision tools/instruments (hand-held powered tools or instruments used to perform operations requiring *great* accuracy or precision, such as dentist drills, soldering irons, welding equipment, saws, etc., used for *especially accurate* or *fine* work)

SOURCE: E. J. McCormick, P. R. Jeanneret, and R. C. Mecham, *Position Analysis Questionnaire,* copyright © 1969 by Purdue Research Foundation, West Lafayette, Indiana 47907. Reprinted with permission.

Perhaps the PAQ's greatest strength is its applicability to many different kinds of jobs. This is especially important if one of the job analyst's goals is to meaningfully compare several dissimilar jobs. Job evaluation, the process of applying dollar values to jobs for the purpose of determining appropriate salaries (which we discuss later in this chapter), is one instance when such comparisons become necessary. In cases like this, the value of being able to assess two or more different jobs using the same "yardstick" is obvious. Of course, the price one pays for this luxury of being able to "compare apples and oranges" is a possible reduction in the specificity with which any particular job can be described. (Recall the job-specific functional language that FJA encourages.)

The PAQ has been the focus of a great deal of job-analysis research, and is also the technique used by many researchers in their investigations of other related topics. McCormick et al. (1972) reported average reliability coefficients that reflected agreement between pairs of individuals who had analyzed the same job using the PAQ; these correlations were quite high, ranging from .74 to .89. Similarly, Smith and Hakel's (1979) data suggested that workers, their supervisors, trained job analysts, and students all provided similar information about job content when using the PAQ. Although a more recent study disputed Smith and Hakel's contention that students are capable of reproducing the PAQ-generated job analyses of professional job analysts (Cornelius, DeNisi, & Blencoe, 1984), this study did not undermine the value of the PAQ when it is used by properly trained analysts. The trend that has emerged from most PAQ research is that interrater agreement tends to be relatively low at the level of individual items, but to improve dramatically when responses are analyzed at the level of job dimensions or major PAQ categories (information input, mental processes, and so on; Jones, Main, Butler, & Johnson, 1982).

Arvey, Davis, McGowen, & Dipboye (1982) investigated whether job analyses based on the PAQ would be distorted as a function of the social behavior (friendliness, for example) of the job incumbent, or as a function of the degree to which the job was described as being interesting or uninteresting. Their data indicated that irrelevant comments or behaviors on the part of the job incumbent had no effect on the results of the job analyses. Other research has suggested that PAQ ratings can also be reliably and meaningfully derived from existing **narrative job descriptions** (Jones et al., 1982). In a different vein, Shaw and Riskind (1983) reported evidence indicating "a fairly strong relationship among the job dimension scores of the PAQ and several indices of the stresses experienced by incumbents on those jobs" (p. 259). This study suggests that jobs characterized by greater demands in the areas of information input, mental processes, relationships with other persons, and so forth, are potentially more stressful for the men and women who hold those jobs. The PAQ is a widely used and potentially very informative technique for analyzing jobs.

---

narrative job descriptions: written, comprehensive descriptions of the duties and responsibilities associated with all jobs in an organization that share a common job title

Less optimistically, Dunnette and Borman (1979) claimed that "the PAQ, in its present form, is too difficult . . . and unwieldy for broad use" (p. 485). Pointing to some of the moderately low indices of interrater agreement that have appeared in the literature, Tenopyr and Oeltjen (1982) suggested that the PAQ scales should be **standardized,** perhaps by developing more specific verbal anchors for the rating scales (extent of use, amount of time, etc.). Similarly, Cornelius et al. (1984) suggested that "the PAQ may not be equally appropriate for all jobs," and that it may be "more suited for use with blue collar manufacturing jobs, than with professional, managerial, or some technical jobs" (p. 463). Finally, Ash and Edgell (1975) investigated the level of reading ability demanded by the PAQ, and reported that it required reading skills somewhere between high school and college graduate level. (Look again at Figure 3.2, and see if you agree.) This finding highlights the important role of the job analyst, who may have to "translate" PAQ items into more understandable language for workers with less highly developed verbal skills.

The *critical-incidents technique,* which focuses on specific behaviors deemed critical or crucial to successful (or unsuccessful) job performance (Flanagan, 1954), is a third approach to job analysis. "Job experts" (usually the job holders or their supervisors) are asked, either individually or in groups, to provide anecdotes or examples of things that they have either done or neglected to do (or witnessed, in the case of supervisors) that had a profound impact on the quality of the work. That is, they are asked to supply critical, work-related incidents. After collecting as many of these as possible, the job analyst typically eliminates redundancies and, usually with the assistance of the job experts, organizes the remaining incidents into meaningful categories or job dimensions. These categories and their associated critical incidents, both good and bad, reflect composites of the essential elements of the job being analyzed.

Robinson (1981) described a very similar approach to job analysis that "focuses on job objectives and goals as a basis for generating task statements . . . which avoid both extreme generality" (such as "Supervises restaurant operations") and specificity (such as "Inserts key into lock when opening for business")" (p. 78). He listed the following steps:

1. Convene a panel of experts
2. Ask the panel to identify the broad, all-encompassing objectives that an ideal job incumbent should meet
3. Ask the panel to list all of the specific behaviors necessary for meeting each of the broad objectives
4. From among these, ask the panel to identify "critical tasks," tasks that are extremely crucial to the job because of their frequency, their importance, or the cost associated with making an error
5. Determine the extent to which the experts agree on the relative importance of the major dimensions of the job

Since most of the empirical research concerning critical incidents has been done for the purpose of developing performance appraisal instruments, we shall reserve our detailed comments on this procedure for Chapter 4. Suffice it to say that critical-incidents approaches to job analysis, which can be described as both job-oriented (broad objectives of the job) and worker-oriented (specific behaviors necessary for reaching those broad objectives), and which permit a more job-specific analysis than the PAQ, seem to be very useful, especially in situations where there are relatively few job incumbents (Robinson, 1981).

Although these three job-analytic techniques (FJA, PAQ, and critical incidents) have received most of the research attention, there are several other promising approaches that deserve at least a brief mention. Hogan, Ogden, Gebhardt, and Fleishman (1980) demonstrated that college students' ratings of the physical effort required to perform a sample of tasks were highly related to the actual metabolic costs associated with performing those tasks. They concluded that "diverse tasks can be ranked and grouped according to common levels of physical demands, without the need for actual physiological and **ergonomic** assessments" (p. 679).

Banks, Jackson, Stafford, and Warr (1983) presented data suggesting the usefulness of the Job Components Inventory (JCI) for analyzing jobs that require only a limited amount of skill. They reported significant agreement between supervisors and job holders who used the JCI, and support for the contention that the JCI is capable of differentiating among different jobs. The JCI assesses five different kinds of requirements: (1) tools and equipment, (2) perceptual and physical requirements, (3) mathematical requirements, (4) communication requirements, and (5) decision making and responsibility.

The Occupational Analysis Inventory (OAI) is a structured job-analysis questionnaire that contains 617 "work elements" (descriptions of work activities and conditions) for rating jobs and occupations. These work elements are also organized into five major divisions: (1) information received, (2) mental activities, (3) work behavior, (4) work goals, and (5) work context. As you can see, the OAI is not unlike the PAQ in adopting an information-processing approach, viewing the task performer as "an agent who transforms information and materials into prescribed outcomes" (Cunningham, Boese, Neeb, & Pass, 1983, p. 234). According to these authors, who described the OAI as more "job-oriented" than the PAQ, each of the 617 work elements is rated by the job analyst on one of four scales: significance, extent, applicability, or a special scale specifically designed for a particular element. (Again, you can see the similarity to the PAQ.) Based on their study of OAI ratings obtained from 12 job analysts and 21 psychology graduate students for 1414 different jobs, they concluded that OAI job-related factors "would seem the logical choice for describing concrete activities and conditions as they exist in jobs" (p. 247).

---

standardized: a measuring instrument is standardized when it is carefully constructed and administered (under constant conditions) to large samples of people that are representative of the population(s) of interest, for the purpose of establishing norms

ergonomic: pertaining to the amount of work done through muscular exertion

Recent work with the JCI and the OAI notwithstanding, Zedeck and Cascio (1984) observed in their recent review of the literature that "a **plethora** of new job analytical procedures has not recently emerged . . . [and that this was] encouraging since many of the previously developed methodologies were accepted uncritically" (p. 466). These reviewers went on to call for comparative research on the validity, accuracy, and usefulness of some of the better-known and more widely used job-analytic techniques. The final paragraphs of this section are devoted to brief descriptions of some of the evaluative research that addresses Zedeck and Cascio's concerns.

COMPARISONS OF JOB-ANALYSIS TECHNIQUES

Levine and his colleagues provided some of the most comprehensive comparisons of various job-analysis techniques (Levine, Ash, & Bennett, 1980; Levine, Ash, Hall, & Sistrunk, 1983). Focusing their attention on the relative **utility** of each technique for personnel selection purposes, Levine et al. (1980) asked 64 personnel selection specialists to compare the following four procedures: critical incidents, the PAQ, task analysis (part of FJA), and job elements. Primoff (1975) described the job-elements procedure as one that requires the job analyst to judge the importance of 55 different elements that might be required by any given job, such as keenness of vision, public contacts, works rapidly, and so forth. Their results suggested that the critical-incidents technique is considerably more costly than either the PAQ or job elements, but that the critical-incidents approach yields job analyses that are judged to be of higher quality by occupational experts. Further, the critical-incidents method was favored by the personnel selection specialists "for providing adequate information to develop performance measures" (p. 529). The PAQ, on the other hand, was viewed less favorably "for highlighting general job areas as well as specific job components, for providing adequate information to develop performance measures, and for establishing **content validity**" (p. 529). Nevertheless, after examining a large number of different comparisons, these authors were surprised to find that perceived meaningful differences between different job-analysis procedures were relatively rare.

In a more recent study, Levine et al. (1983) asked 93 experienced job analysts to evaluate the quality and practicality of seven different job-analysis techniques: critical incidents, the PAQ, job elements, ability requirements (Fleishman, 1975), FJA, a task-inventory procedure (Christal, 1974), and Threshold Traits Analysis (Lopez et al., 1981). For organizational purposes such as writing job descriptions, classifying jobs, job evaluation, and job design, the task-inventory approach and FJA were consistently rated as most effective. The PAQ was also deemed useful for job-evaluation and classification purposes. In terms of practicality, the PAQ and the task-inventory approach received consistently high ratings, while critical incidents and job elements tended to receive lower ratings. Not surprisingly, these job analysts generally preferred various combinations of techniques over single methods used alone. Frequently chosen combinations included (1) the PAQ and task inventories, (2) critical incidents and FJA, (3) critical incidents and the PAQ, and (4) critical incidents, task inventories, and FJA. As you have learned, these combinations involve techniques that have complementary strengths and weaknesses in terms of cost, job specificity, and so forth.

Cornelius and Lyness (1980) reported that global or overall judgments of job requirements, as well as "decomposed" (more specific and detailed) judgments that were statistically combined, yielded job-analysis information that was typically higher in quality than did decomposed judgments that subjects were asked to "combine in their heads." This latter strategy probably overloaded the subjects (96 workers from four different organizations) with more information than they could reasonably be expected to handle "mentally."

Similarly, Sackett, Cornelius, and Carron (1981) advocated the use of global judgments of job similarity as a quicker, less expensive approach to classifying different jobs. They acknowledged, however, that it is "not clear that the global judgment approach could stand alone from a legal perspective" (p. 802). (See the final section of this chapter.)

Based on data collected from 1282 field agency managers (all males) from 50 different life insurance companies distributed across the United States and Canada, Schneider and Mitchel (1980) concluded that "a job analysis tailored to a specific position should be available to characterize the behavioral richness of a position" (p. 805), and that such behavioral specificity is necessary for justifying human resource practices, according to current government guidelines.

Clearly, the available data suggest that there is no "one best way" to do a job analysis. The most effective technique, or combination of techniques, can only be identified in the context of a specific purpose or need for the job-analysis information. Because the memo from the vice president for personnel suggested the need for a basic job description of the restaurant manager position, and hinted at the possibility that the selection, training, and appraisal of these employees may have to be reexamined as well, Dr. MacKeven would be wise to choose a combination of techniques that can provide both job- and worker-oriented information about the position in question. Functional job analysis (FJA), with its focus on specific tasks for accomplishing specific end results, and the Position Analysis Questionnaire (PAQ), perhaps followed by a limited critical-incidents analysis to ensure that nothing crucial has been overlooked, would provide her with a wealth of information to facilitate the writing of job descriptions, as well as a review of personnel selection, training, and performance appraisal procedures, if such a review is necessary.

---

plethora: an excess or overabundance

utility: usefulness, especially when taking such factors as monetary costs and time requirements into consideration

content validity: the extent to which a measurement captures all or a representative sample of whatever is intended to be measured; one of the approaches to validity specifically recognized by the EEOC *Guidelines*

Translating Job-Analysis Results into Performance Criteria

Following the implementation of whatever job-analysis procedures Dr. Mac-Keven decides to adopt, she will face the very important task of developing actual "yardsticks" to measure workers' levels of effectiveness on the job elements or components that emerged from the job analyses. This is a crucial step in the criterion-development process. The actual measurement of performance effectiveness is known as performance appraisal, which we discuss in detail in Chapter 4. For the present, we will concern ourselves only with some of the basic considerations that should guide the transformation of job-analysis information into useful job-performance criteria.

Identifying job-performance criteria involves *operationally* defining levels of work effectiveness. An operational definition is nothing more than a measurement procedure that is accepted as a definition of whatever is being measured. Thus, if the job analysis reveals that interpersonal skills are an important component of the restaurant manager's job, and if Dr. MacKeven develops a questionnaire that solicits customers' opinions of restaurant managers' interpersonal skills, that questionnaire becomes an operational definition of restaurant managers' interpersonal skills. Although any given operational definition may or may not conform to your *conceptual* definition of what constitutes interpersonal skills, at least we can all agree on the meaning of this job component as it is used to assess restaurant managers' effectiveness. This is the primary reason that scientists of all specialties and persuasions rely heavily on operational definitions of the variables they study. Such definitions reduce ambiguity and promote understanding, which are major goals of any scientific or professional undertaking.

Although the number of actual performance criteria that could be identified for any given job is potentially unlimited, the basic sources of information about job performance are more finite. In fact, there are only three such data sources. They are usually referred to as "productivity" data, "personnel" data, and "judgmental" data. Productivity and personnel data tend to yield "hard" criteria, while judgmental data produce "soft" criteria (Smith, 1976).

Productivity data are pieces of information that reflect some readily quantifiable aspect of job performance. Examples include the number of units produced by workers during a specified interval of time, or the volume of merchandise sold (either in units or in dollars). For Peter's Pan Pizza's restaurant managers, productivity data might include monthly sales volume, numbers of pizzas sold, or any other countable index of performance that is consistent with the results of the job analysis.

Personnel data are also countable pieces of information that reflect a worker's performance. Unlike productivity data, however, personnel data are more indirect measures of performance. They can usually be found in employees' personnel files (thus the label "personnel" data). Examples include the numbers of times a worker is absent or tardy, the number of accidents a worker has, or the numbers of letters of reprimand or commendation that are addressed to a worker during a given time interval. For our restaurant managers, personnel data might include rates of absenteeism, numbers of customer complaints and commendations, or the results of periodic inspections by store inspectors from Peter's Pan Pizza's retail operations division or by governmental agencies such as the board of health. Once again, of course, the relevance of such information should be directly traceable to the results of the job analysis.

Unlike the first two categories of information, judgmental data are not directly countable. They are, in fact, often used precisely because quantifiable pieces of information are either unavailable, inappropriate, or inadequate. As the name implies, judgmental data are generated by other individuals who provide their opinions of the quality of an employee's work. Ratings of a person's work performance using some kind of rating scale, and placing individuals in some sort of rank order according to the quality of their work, are the two most common varieties of judgmental data. Peter's Pan Pizza's restaurant managers could be rated by their customers, by their subordinates (cooks, waitresses and waiters), or by their superiors at corporate headquarters.

Each of these types or sources of work-performance information is discussed in much greater detail in the next chapter. Our intention here is simply to acquaint you with the different sources of information that are potentially available and merit consideration during the criterion-development process.

NECESSARY CRITERION CHARACTERISTICS

Regardless of the exact nature of the performance criteria that are developed from job-analysis information, or the eventual source of work-performance data, the criterion measures that are chosen must have three important properties: They must be reliable, they must be valid, and they must be practical. Since these concepts are also discussed in greater detail later on, we will be content to (re)introduce you to them now. As we stated in Chapter 2, reliability refers to the consistency with which something is measured. If we are interested in measuring a quantity that we believe remains fairly constant over reasonable intervals of time, it is very important that the measurements we generate also remain constant. Consider the following "weighty" example.

For most of us, weight remains fairly stable over short periods of time. Imagine hopping on your bathroom scales the first thing in the morning, and watching the dial climb to 125 pounds. You brush your teeth, wash your face, and then get back on the scales. To your astonishment, the dial registers 142 pounds! Since you know you didn't eat *that* much pizza at dinner the previous evening, you step down, take a deep breath, and warily sneak back onto the scales (for the third time in five minutes). Now it reads 115 pounds. Which do you believe?

This silly little example demonstrates the drawbacks of an unreliable measuring instrument. In this case, of course, you would probably have some idea of what your "true weight" actually is, so you wouldn't be completely baffled (and you'd suspect that it's time to invest in new bathroom scales). An I/O psychologist who attempts to measure employees' levels of work performance, however, is not in a similarly advantageous position. Dr. MacKeven probably has no idea what any given employee's "true" level of work effectiveness is.

Further, because performance measures are usually administered only once during an evaluation period, and *not* several times in the course of just a few minutes, she has to "trust" that the measure she obtains the first time *would be obtained again* if she took the trouble to reassess performance. Such trust is well placed only in reliable measures.

Important as reliability is, however, it isn't enough. Job-performance criteria (along with every other measurement) must be valid, too. Validity refers to the extent to which a measuring instrument measures whatever it is designed to measure. Your bathroom scales are constructed to assess your weight, and not some other personal characteristic such as your intelligence, your charm, or your sense of humor. If your scales do, in fact, provide readings that reflect weight but none of these other variables, then they are a source of valid measures. Returning to our I/O psychologist's search for job-performance measures, any criteria and related measures must provide an index of work effectiveness, and not some other variable such as satisfaction with the job, or the extent to which the worker and the supervisor are social friends outside the workplace.

Sometimes validity can be equated with accuracy. It is, for example, quite possible for your bathroom scales to be very reliable, yet hopelessly inaccurate, and therefore invalid. If your "true weight" is 125 pounds, but your scales *consistently* read 134 pounds, those scales are providing measures that are reliable but not valid. Similarly, if a supervisor *consistently* reports that an employee is performing at an outstanding level (perhaps because they *are* social friends), when in fact that worker's effectiveness is only average, this would be another example of a measurement that is reliable but invalid. Thus, we say that reliability is necessary for good measurement, but that it is not sufficient by itself to guarantee high-quality measurement.

In addition to the **psychometric** properties of reliability and validity, work-performance criterion measures must also be practical. I/O psychology is, after all, an applied science (and profession). Workers' performance must be assessed reliably and validly, to be sure; but it must also be measured in such a way that the assessment procedure does not seriously disrupt ongoing work activities. Dr. MacKeven would not be very popular with the vice president for personnel if she developed a reliable and valid measure of work performance that required *three days* of each supervisor's time to complete. Nor would Ms. Creighton award her I/O psychologist any medals if the suggested measurement technique was outrageously expensive. Finally, performance criteria that are eventually adopted must be acceptable to those individuals who are asked to use them. It is not very practical to waste people's time with measuring devices that they neither like nor trust, for they can be counted on to resist and subvert the performance-measurement process in one way or another, and thereby undermine the usefulness of any data that are obtained.

Since the early 1960s, I/O psychologists' concerns with job analysis and the development of work-performance criteria have received a "shot in the arm" from federal and state laws that are designed to protect workers from various forms of discrimination. The last section of this chapter deals with some of these important pieces of legislation.

Governmental Regulations and Criterion Development

Among the many pieces of legislation that have affected I/O psychologists, two have had particularly strong implications for the criterion-development process. These are the Civil Rights Act of 1964, and the Equal Pay Act of 1963. We will briefly discuss each of these.

Title VII of the Civil Rights Act (1964) established the Equal Employment Opportunity Commission (EEOC) which, after years of competing and collaborating with other federal agencies charged with similar responsibilities (the Department of Labor, the Office of Federal Contract Compliance, etc.), eventually developed the *Uniform Guidelines on Employee Selection Procedures* (*Federal Register*, 1978). This document spells out detailed standards and procedures that are designed to prohibit discrimination in employment on the basis of race, color, religion, sex, or national origin; it is currently administered and enforced by the EEOC.

Although we will refer to the *Guidelines* in greater detail during our discussions of personnel selection procedures in Chapters 5 and 6, it is important to note here that the enactment of this document did more to legitimize and emphasize the role of job analysis in personnel procedures than any other event. It accomplished this by declaring that any measuring instrument used to make decisions about people's employment status (selection tests, interviews, performance-appraisal techniques, etc.) *must generate information that is job-related.* The only way to demonstrate that the data obtained from such procedures are, in fact, job-related is to compare them with a detailed description of exactly what a given job entails—the results of a careful job analysis.

As a result of the Civil Rights Act (1964) and the ensuing EEOC *Guidelines,* the lazy approach to criterion development described earlier in this chapter is likely to render an organization defenseless to charges of illegal discrimination. Thompson and Thompson (1982) summarized some of the job-analysis procedures that have been accepted and some that have been rejected by various courts of law since 1971. Those found to be acceptable typically relied on critical incidents and/or detailed task identification. Many of those that were rejected seemed to be based on some of the shortcuts that Guion (1961) ridiculed so eloquently.

The Equal Pay Act (1963), which amended the Fair Labor Standards Act of 1938, stipulates that men and women who are employed by the same company must receive the same pay if their jobs demand equal levels of skill, responsibility, and effort, and if their working conditions are the same. Also administered by the EEOC, this legislation prohibits sex discrimination in pay, except in certain unusual cases. Once again, the only defensible way to demonstrate that two or more jobs require or involve equal (or unequal) skills, responsibility, effort, and working conditions is to begin with careful job analyses of the positions in question.

---

psychometric: pertaining to the technical or statistical aspects of psychological measurement; reliability and validity are psychometric properties of measurements

The process of assigning monetary value to the job components or elements that are identified through job analysis is known as job evaluation. Almost all of the job-evaluation methods currently in use are variations of one or more of four basic procedures: (1) ranking, (2) classification, (3) factor comparison, and (4) point systems (Snelgar, 1983).

The ranking method is the simplest approach. Job evaluators are asked only to rank-order the jobs in an organization according to some global concept of each job's relative worth or value to the organization. Classification involves placing all the jobs in an organization into a predetermined taxonomy of grades or classes. The U.S. Government's "GS system" for evaluating civil service jobs is perhaps the best-known example of such a taxonomy.

The factor-comparison method, originated by Benge, Burk, and Hay (1941), is a very complex procedure that involves identifying "key" or "landmark" jobs within an organization. These are jobs that are well known and that are presently being compensated at a rate that is generally deemed appropriate. Key jobs are examined to determine the extent to which they depend on several job factors (mental requirements, physical requirements, responsibility, etc.), and the existing pay for each of those jobs is then apportioned or "assigned" to those job factors according to the relative importance of each factor to each job. Other jobs in the organization are then examined to determine the importance of the same job factors, and those other jobs are then "fit into" a job-comparison scale that uses the key jobs (and their known and accepted rates of pay) as anchors. Nash and Carroll (1975) acknowledged that the factor-comparison procedure "is so complex that it is virtually impossible to explain to an ordinary aggrieved employee who wants to know why his [sic] job is not being paid more" (pp. 131–132).

Point systems involve assigning points to various levels of skill, knowledge, responsibility, working conditions, and other important job elements, and then summing the points to obtain a total for each job. This approach is widely used and has been the focus of much research (Doverspike & Barrett, 1984; Doverspike, Carlisi, Barrett, & Alexander, 1983; Gomez-Mejia, Page, & Tornow, 1982; Sigelman, Milward, & Shepard, 1982; Taber, Beehr, & Walsh, 1985). Regardless of which job-evaluation technique an organization chooses to implement, the important thing to remember is that they all depend on information that can be reliably obtained only through careful job analyses.

COMPARABLE WORTH

Closely related to the job-evaluation process is the concept of comparable worth, which is currently generating a great deal of controversy. The basic thrust of comparable-worth policies is that men and women who hold *different* jobs in an organization (or, on a broader scale, in a society) should nevertheless receive the same pay if their jobs make equal or "comparable" contributions to attaining the organization's (society's) goals. The cases of *Lemons* v. *City of Denver* (1980), in which female nurses compared their worth to that of higher-paid male plumbers, and *Christensen* v. *State of Iowa* (1977), where female clerical workers compared their worth to physical plant workers, are typical of the lawsuits that have been initiated by comparable-worth advocates. Although relevant articles are beginning to appear in the professional and scientific literature (Madigan, 1985; Schwab & Wichern, 1983), we must confess to some skepticism that the comparable-worth debate will ever be resolved to everyone's satisfaction. Recent decisions and reversals in several state court systems attest to the confusion that prevails.

Madigan (1985) went to the heart of the issue when he observed that "comparable worth . . . requires measurement of a predefined job worth construct" (p. 137), and that defining this construct is a purely *subjective, judgmental* undertaking. There are no magic formulas for equating nurses with plumbers. One's perspective on their relative worths to their organizations or to society will depend, among other things, on whether one is currently suffering from a ruptured disk or a ruptured sewer line!

The same reservations apply to the entire job-evaluation process. It will remain a question of judgment, not fact. Nevertheless, some of the subjectivity and arbitrariness can be minimized if job-evaluation judgments are based on the results of sound job analyses. At least the job elements about which we are making subjective judgments will be "out on the table" for everyone who is concerned to see.

CHAPTER SUMMARY

Job-performance criteria are standards for evaluating the quality of employees' work behaviors. Most people's jobs are sufficiently complex that several different criteria are necessary for complete and informative evaluations. These multiple criteria can be combined to form a composite job-performance criterion when personnel decisions must be based on objective, countable events or on subjective human judgments. In any case, they must be practical, reliable, and valid.

Valid job-performance criteria reflect all aspects of an employee's job while ignoring everything that is not part of that job. That is, they maximize criterion relevance while minimizing criterion deficiency and contamination. Development of valid criteria, therefore, requires detailed knowledge of what employees do on their jobs, the purpose(s) for which they do those things, and the conditions under which they do them. This detailed knowledge is acquired through a process known as job analysis.

Regardless of whether we use functional job analysis, the Position Analysis Questionnaire, the critical-incidents technique, or a combination of these and perhaps other procedures, most job analyses boil down to asking workers to describe their jobs and/or observing them while they do their work. Since the passage of the Civil Rights Act (1964) and the Equal Pay Act (1963), the logical necessity of doing job analyses on the way to developing job-performance criteria has been reinforced by legal prescriptions.

INTEROFFICE MEMO
TO: Agnes Creighton, Vice President for Personnel
FROM: J. A. MacKeven, Human–Resources Coordinator

My own review of our files has convinced me that you and your depart—
ment directors have identified a serious deficiency in our personnel
documents and system. The existing job description for the position
of restaurant manager is so vague and so outdated that it is essen—
tially useless. I have therefore devised the following tentative
''game plan'' to correct this deficiency.

First, we must conduct a detailed analysis of the restaurant manager
position. This will necessitate a series of meetings with executives
and managers in retail operations, as well as with a representative
sample of our 527 restaurant managers. These people are in the best
positions to tell us what restaurant managers are supposed to be
accomplishing, how they're supposed to be accomplishing these things,
and what sorts of personal traits or characteristics facilitate the
necessary behaviors. I anticipate using Position Analysis Question—
naires, functional job analysis, and the critical—incidents approach
to obtain this needed information.

Armed with this information, we can then develop specific standards or
criteria for evaluating restaurant managers' job performance. These
criteria will, in turn, allow your subordinate directors to implement
rational policies and procedures for selecting, training, and paying
these very important members of our organization.

Let me know if you have any questions or suggestions concerning my
proposed plan. I will keep you informed of my progress.

REVIEW QUESTIONS AND EXERCISES

1. What is your evaluation of Dr. MacKeven's return memo to the vice president of personnel? What are its strengths? What are its weaknesses?

2. What do you think of Dr. MacKeven's choice of job-analysis techniques? Would you add or delete any? Why?

3. How should Dr. MacKeven use the other members of the human resources department (one masters-level psychologist, two psychological technicians, and two college interns) to effectively and efficiently administer the job-analysis techniques you recommended in response to Question 2? Provide rationales for your suggestions.

4. Assume that the job-analysis process resulted in the *DOT* listing for "Manager, Fast Food Services" given earlier in the chapter.

    • How many (multiple) criteria do you think would be necessary to provide a comprehensive evaluation of restaurant managers' job peformance? List them.

    • Which of those criteria seem to be more proximal to being hired as a restaurant manager? Which seem to be more distal? Explain your answers.

    • Which appear to be "hard" criteria? Which appear to be "soft"? Explain your answers.

5. What is comparable worth? How is the comparable worth of two or more jobs (or the lack of it) determined?

CHAPTER 4

Measurement and Evaluation of Work Performance

Learning Points

After studying this chapter, you should

- understand the relationship between criterion development and performance appraisal
- know the three purposes of performance appraisal, and the kind(s) of performance data that each purpose requires
- be able to explain why "objective" performance data are not objective, and why "personnel" data are thought to be shallow
- be able to explain why a majority of organizations rely on judgmental performance data as a last resort
- be able to describe the similarities and differences that characterize three different procedures for comparing workers' job performance
- know the advantages and disadvantages associated with supervisory ratings, peer ratings, and self-ratings
- be able to describe six different rating scale formats, and explain how each format facilitates or inhibits ambiguity in performance ratings
- be able to define leniency/severity, central-tendency, and halo "errors," to explain the conditions under which they may not be errors at all, and to describe how they undermine the three purposes of performance appraisal
- be able to describe the "process approach" to understanding performance ratings, and to offer a rationale for the current popularity of that approach
- be familiar with some of the obstacles that confront organizations when they try to implement a performance appraisal system

INTEROFFICE MEMO
TO: J. A. MacKeven, Human—Resources Coordinator
FROM: Ellen Dieckman, Director of Advertising

Last Friday, literally minutes before the 5:00 p.m. deadline, I sub—
mitted performance—evaluation ratings for each of the employees in
the Advertising Department to your office. Every six months—each time
we must complete these performance appraisals—I experience the same
set of misgivings. Consequently, I procrastinate until the very last
minute. Informal discussions with other directors, managers, and
supervisors have convinced me that I am not alone in harboring these
concerns. It therefore seems appropriate to share my reservations
about our performance appraisal system with you and your staff.

As you know, our system requires us to use 5—point rating scales (1 =
unsatisfactory; 3 = average; 5 = excellent) to evaluate each of our
employees on several aspects of their jobs. Here in Advertising,
these job dimensions include such things as job knowledge, judgment,
initiative, and productivity. While I am satisfied with the appropri—
ateness of evaluating these aspects of my employees' work performance
(since they evolved directly from the job analyses you conducted for
us), I am <u>not</u> satisfied with our current procedures. Specifically, the
rating scales seem to be too subjective on one hand, and too restric—
tive on the other. That is, I am concerned that the ratings I assign
my subordinates may be biased, either consciously or unconsciously,
or simply unfair. At the same time, I am frustrated by the expecta—
tion that I am to make a single mark on each rating scale that is
supposed to capture and reflect the breadth and depth of each employ—
ee's performance in that area. Unfavorable comments about our evalua—
tion system from my employees during their individual performance—
review (feedback) sessions have done nothing to assuage my
discomfort.

I would greatly appreciate your input and assistance.

Ms. Dieckman's memo addresses one of the most common sources of anxiety among employees at all levels of organizational hierarchies. Neither managers nor the employees they supervise relish the prospect of performance appraisal. Those whose work is being evaluated face the possibility of failing to "measure up," which can lead to such unpleasant outcomes as lowered self-esteem, reduced or withheld salary increments, or even dismissal. On the other side of the desk, many managers are uncomfortable with the idea of "playing God" by judging other human beings, especially when the consequences of their judgments can be serious. Similar reservations about the performance appraisal process pervade the entire spectrum of industrial and service organizations, from steel mills and automobile assembly plants to hospitals and (as Ms. Dieckman's memo indicates) food service industries.

This chapter focuses on the issues that confront I/O psychologists or managers as they develop and implement performance appraisal systems in their organizations. We begin by explaining the purposes of performance appraisal (why, after all, do we subject managers and their employees to this particular form of torture?), and continue with a description of the various kinds of information potentially available to those who must evaluate others' job performance. We shall emphasize the role of human judgments in the performance appraisal process. Finally, we address some of the questions and challenges that are inherent in implementing a useful performance appraisal system and integrating it into an organization's personnel system: Who should evaluate whom? How often? How can appraisals be used for the maximum benefit of the organization and its people? Of course, we will allude to Ms. Dieckman's memo throughout the chapter, and will emphasize the relevance of our discussion to the advertising director's concerns.

You should strive to appreciate the relationship between the material in this chapter and the information we presented in Chapter 3. The previous chapter described processes for analyzing jobs and developing criteria of job performance; it focused on *jobs,* with little or no concern for the individuals who hold those jobs. This chapter concentrates on the *workers,* on evaluating the levels of skill, ability, and performance that individual women and men display on their jobs. This distinction, however, should not distort your perception of the logical and intimate relationship between these two chapters. Evaluating workers' performance presumes knowledge of what they are supposed to be doing and accomplishing. Performance appraisal involves using the criteria ("yardsticks") developed through job analyses to assess workers' contributions to organizational goals.

PURPOSES OF PERFORMANCE APPRAISAL

Landy and Farr (1983) organized the many different uses of performance appraisal information into three basic categories: (1) making administrative decisions involving pay raises, promotions or demotions, transfers, or even dismissals about employees; (2) providing employees with feedback concerning their individual strengths and weaknesses on the job; and (3) conducting personnel research that benefits the organization and establishes or maintains compliance with EEOC regulations. We will briefly examine each of these purposes.

Administrative Personnel Decisions

It is obviously in any organization's best interests to recognize and reward those employees who perform their jobs well. Behavior that is reinforced or rewarded is much more likely to be repeated than behavior that is either ignored or punished (Skinner, 1953). Organizations are also likely to benefit when more competent employees are assigned to more difficult and demanding tasks, when less competent workers are given less crucial tasks, and when incompetent workers are dismissed. In each case, the organization must be able to distinguish between satisfactory and even exemplary employees, and marginal or unsatisfactory workers. "Merit-based" decisions presume knowledge of merit, which is assessed through performance appraisal.

Employee Feedback

It is unrealistic to expect employees to improve in areas where their job performance is weak, and to maintain or continue to improve on performance that is already satisfactory, in the absence of information concerning their strengths and weaknesses. Imagine trying to improve your archery skills if you were not allowed to see the spots on the target where your arrows struck (assuming they struck the target at all). You would, quite literally, be shooting blind!

Although the importance of accurate and detailed performance information to workers at Peter's Pan Pizza may not be quite so obvious, the same principle applies. Advertising specialists in Ms. Dieckman's department cannot know whether their publicity campaigns are effective unless they receive feedback concerning changes in sales volume or the public image of their products and services.

Personnel Research

Since the passage of the Civil Rights Act in 1964, and especially since the EEOC *Guidelines* were adopted in 1978, performance appraisal information has become increasingly important to organizations in their quest to comply with federal and local statutes concerning employee-selection procedures. Identification of procedures and techniques for hiring or promoting employees who will perform their work well presumes the capability to distinguish between good and poor job performance.

Of course, many organizations conduct research simply to improve their human resource systems. Hiring people who can perform their job successfully and rejecting those who cannot, in addition to complying with the law, serves to maximize an organization's overall level of performance, and thus its profits.

Summary

As you have seen, performance appraisals can contribute to an organization's well-being in several different ways. Unfortunately, these three uses of appraisals require different kinds of performance measures.

Recall our discussion of multiple and composite criteria in Chapter 3. Performance-based administrative decisions ultimately require a single or (preferably) a composite measure; promotions, differential salary adjustments, transfers, and selective training assignments require comparisons among all eligible employees. Such composite measures need only have ordinal scale properties, so that eligible workers can be rank-ordered. Useful performance feedback, however, requires multiple measures that preferably have interval-scale and even ratio-scale properties. Workers' efforts to improve upon weaknesses and maintain strengths are not enhanced when they are informed that their "overall performance" is (un)satisfactory. Nor is it particularly helpful to know that one is the "second-best" employee in the department, without knowing what level of performance that rank represents. Personnel research can require composite and/or multiple indices of job performance, depending on the specific question(s) under investigation.

These reasons for collecting job-performance information suggest two properties that must characterize appraisal data. First, those data must distinguish or discriminate among employees based on their different levels of job performance. Merit-based decisions become impossible when performance data show no differences in employees' levels of job performance. If everyone is "average," or even if everyone is "outstanding," who should be promoted? Second, performance data should be free of systematic bias. Feedback that consistently misrepresents workers' performance levels will be of no use to those who wish to eliminate their deficiencies. As we describe the various kinds of job-performance information (in the next section), we will point out the degree to which each satisfies these two important requirements. A "between-the-lines" reading of Ms. Dieckman's opening memo suggests that Peter's Pan Pizza's current performance appraisal system may produce data that satisfies neither requirement.

VARIETIES OF JOB-PERFORMANCE DATA

A popular taxonomy separates job-performance data into three categories: (1) objective, (2) personnel, and (3) judgmental. Although we will examine each of these in turn, we will concentrate on the third kind of data, those based on human judgments.

Objective Performance Data

This category of job-performance information is typically labeled "objective" because it includes indices of work performance that can be counted. Countable measures of job performance include the number of units or items produced during a specified time interval, the amount of time required to complete a specified set of tasks, or the dollar value of goods produced or services rendered. Table 4.1 contains a list of objective performance measures that emerged from Landy and Farr's (1983) comprehensive review.

Being directly countable constitutes the major advantage associated with these measures. Regardless of the counter's personal likes or dislikes, careful tallies of workers' outputs should yield the same results. In this sense, then, these data are unbiased.

Unfortunately, there are other ways in which such data *can* be biased or contaminated by irrelevant factors. First, the decision to use one objective index instead of another is hardly objective. For example, Ms. Dieckman could count the number of ads each of her subordinates placed in the mass media (radio, TV, etc.) during a specified time interval. Alternatively, she could count the number of formal advertising campaign proposals each employee makes to upper management. These are only two of the possibilities. In all likelihood, employees' levels of performance would not remain constant across these two (or more) different "objective" indices.

Second, many countable measures of job performance are influenced by factors beyond the workers' control. Compared with their colleagues who prepare ads for radio broadcasts, those in Ms. Dieckman's department who work with television stations will be limited in the number of ads they can run at a given overall cost. If the focus is on the number of potential customers reached, however, those working with national TV networks will have a marked

TABLE 4.1 Examples of Objective Job-Performance Measures

Job title	Measure
Typist	Lines per week
Forester	Cords (of wood) cut
Keypuncher	Number of characters; number of errors
Service representative	Errors in processing customer orders
Toll collector	Dollar accuracy/axle accuracy
Clerk	Errors per 100 documents checked; number of documents processed
Wood harvester	Number of cords delivered
Tree planter	Bags of tree seedlings planted
Skateboard maker	Number produced; number rejected
Sewing machine operator	Minutes per operation
Logger	Weight of wood legally hauled
Dentist	Errors in reading radiographs
Open hearth foreman	Time between "taps"
Inspector	Errors detected in finished product
Tool/die maker	Dies produced
Helicopter pilot	Deviations from proper instrument readings
Bank teller	Number of shortages; number of overages
Air traffic controller	Speed of movement of aircraft through the system; correction of pilot error; errors in positioning aircraft for final approach; errors in aircraft separation

SOURCE: Adapted from *The Measurement of Work Performance: Methods, Theory, and Applications*, by F. J. Landy and J. L. Farr. Copyright 1983 by Academic Press. Reprinted by permission.

advantage. As you may have surmised, it is quite possible to combine these two objective indices of performance into a single measure—number of potential customers reached per dollar spent—that is relatively free of extraneous influences. Once again, however, the ability to recognize and the decision to use such combinations of measures can hardly be construed as objective processes.

A third problem associated with objective performance measures concerns their reliability or consistency over time. What can we conclude about a particular advertiser's effectiveness on the basis of a single ad, or even on the basis of a single advertising campaign? What can we say about a worker's performance based on a single day's or a single week's output? After all, people have "good" days/weeks and "bad" days/weeks. This problem can be relieved somewhat if we obtain objective measures of performance over longer intervals of time, thereby allowing employees' good days and bad days to balance out. Based on their study of sewing machine operators, and folders and packers, in a large textile company, Rambo, Chomiak, and Price (1983) reported that average hourly output rates over a *three-and-one-half-year* period were about as consistent as scores typically obtained on standard psychological tests. These findings suggest that the time intervals necessary to achieve acceptable levels of reliability may be quite long.

Two additional weaknesses of objective performance measures are that they are not available or appropriate for a great many jobs, and that they are just "too objective" for many people's tastes. How, for example, should Ms. Dieckman go about objectively measuring the job performance of her subordinate managers? What should she count? This is a serious problem when trying to assess the performance of employees whose organizational contributions do not readily translate into "things" that are easily or appropriately counted.

Finally, objective indices of performance are sometimes criticized precisely because they are *too* objective. They do not allow appraisers to include sufficient detail or qualitative evidence in their evaluations. How well, after all, can one or two numbers represent the intricacies and subtleties associated with many jobs? This is a particularly interesting objection, since objective performance data are usually sought precisely *because* they are relatively invulnerable to such subjective, qualitative influences.

Personnel Performance Data

This category of performance data includes information that is often available in employees' personnel folders. Instances of tardiness or absenteeism, job-related accidents, grievances, letters of reprimand or commendation, and turnover (when one's job performance simply "stops") are common examples of this kind of performance information. Like objective data, personnel performance data can be counted. Once again, this property represents the major advantage associated with using these data. Regardless of the counter's biases, prejudices, or predispositions, careful counts should produce the same accurate results. Unlike objective data, however, personnel data are *indirect* measures of job performance; a certain amount of inference is required. For example, we infer that a worker who is absent from the workplace is less effective on the job than one who is present. We assume that an employee who quits his job makes less of a contribution to the organization than one who remains. We often accept management's characterization of a worker who files grievances as a "troublemaker."

The fact that such inferences are not always warranted constitutes one of the major drawbacks of personnel performance data. Many jobs, for example, do not actually require a worker's physical presence at the workplace. Artists, copy writers, and those in Peter's Pan Pizza's advertising department who devise creative ad campaigns (not to mention some textbook authors) may do some of their best work at home, away from the distractions and annoyances common to many office environments. In the same vein, accidents that are caused by unavoidably dangerous working conditions should not automatically be construed as poor job performance on the part of the "victim."

Workers who quit their jobs may not always harm the organization by doing so. O'Connor, Peters, Pooyan, Weekley, Frank, and Erenkrantz (1984) studied 731 convenience store managers, and reported a significant *negative* correlation ($r = -.20; p < .001$) between these managers' job performance and turnover; the direction of the relationship indicates that it was the *poorer* performers who quit their jobs. Jacofsky (1984) summarized a review of 18 different studies and reported an inverse (negative) relationship between performance and turnover in 8 studies, no relationship in 5 studies, and a positive relationship (where the better performers quit) in only 5 studies. External factors such as job-market conditions and the health of the economy were at least partially responsible for these inconsistent results (Bhagat, McQuaid, Lindholm, & Segovis, 1985; Wells & Muchinsky, 1985). Boudreau and his colleagues also discussed the concept of "functional turnover," referring to a situation where a highly paid employee quits and is replaced by an equally competent worker who does not demand such a high salary (Boudreau, 1983a; Boudreau & Berger, 1985). This concept also applies when a marginally competent worker leaves and is replaced by a better-performing individual, or whenever an employee's resignation or departure improves the organization in any way.

Finally, a worker who files grievances should not automatically be "pigeonholed" as a troublemaker or a bad employee. He or she may, in fact, be a more conscientious and devoted organizational citizen than one who does nothing to improve unsatisfactory situations.

A second problem associated with the use of personnel performance data concerns the choice of operational definitions. When, for instance, is a worker classified as "late"? Five minutes after the starting whistle? Ten minutes? Half an hour? Of course, one is technically "late" within seconds after work is scheduled to begin, but the important question is, "When does it *really* matter?"

Gaudet (1963) identified 41 different indices of absence. Is the job performance of an employee who is absent a total of 26 days over a one-year period because of two extended absences (of 8 and 18 days, for example) the same as that of another worker who is absent every other Monday during that same one-year period? Under what conditions is an absence to be considered "excused"? Is the distinction between excused and unexcused absences even relevant? After all, workers whose presence is required at the workplace cannot contribute to the organization when they are absent, regardless of whether they are in the hospital for appendicitis or out on the golf course!

A third difficulty with personnel data is their relative lack of availability. Most workers *never* have work-related accidents, *never* file grievances, and *never* receive letters of reprimand or commendation. Such skewed distributions of performance data make it very difficult to discriminate among the majority of workers in terms of their job-performance levels.

Fourth, personnel data are similar to objective data in that they are vulnerable to charges of unreliability and "sterility" (or the inability to capture the richness of people's job performance). Gordon and Miller (1984) suggested that "the reliability of [individual] grievance filing behavior is probably low" (p. 125). Hackett and Guion (1985) examined three different indices of absenteeism, and reported that "all three indices are quite unreliable" (p. 346). As with objective data, however, the reliability of personnel data can be improved by taking measurements over longer periods of time. The perception of sterility, or lack of valuable information, is based on the idea that the number of days a worker is tardy or absent, the number of accidents experienced or grievances filed, and whether a worker leaves the organization or remains on the job are rather "shallow," uninformative indices of performance. These data simply do not capture the rich, qualitative details that underlie the numbers.

You may have noticed that, as with objective data, we seem to be talking out of both sides of our mouths at the same time. We use personnel data because they are countable and relatively free of personal biases, but we criticize them for being too simplistic and psychologically sterile. It is precisely because of the perceived inadequacies of countable performance measures that most organizations turn to the third category of performance data. Typically referred to as "judgmental" measures, these indices permit (and often demand) the rich, qualitative subjectivity that is unavailable in objective measures. It is to these overtly *non*objective measures of job performance that we now turn.

Judgmental Performance Data

Unlike objective or personnel data, judgmental data are usually not obtained by counting things. Instead, they represent one person's judgment or opinion about the work performance of another person. Since no one except the "judge" can have direct access to the cognitive processes that produce these judgments, they are (by definition) subjective. There is, therefore, no such thing as an "objective judgment." While there is no question that some judgments are freer of various biases and prejudices than others, even those judgments that are uncontaminated by obvious racial or sex biases or by other rating errors are still decidedly subjective. This property is, after all, the primary reason for the popularity of judgmental performance measures. They afford the appraiser the opportunity and often impart the responsibility to elaborate on, and potentially clarify, more uninformative indices of work performance.

Most judgmental performance data result from one of two different procedures: ratings or direct employee comparisons. Ratings typically require one person (the rater) to record judgments about the performance of another person (the ratee) using an instrument that describes various standards of excellence (a rating scale). The rater compares the ratee's job performance with the various standards, and indicates which of those standards most accurately describes that performance. The standards may reflect absolute levels of performance or accomplishment, with no reference to other individuals, or they may use other employees' levels of job performance as reference points. These two kinds of scales are known as criterion-referenced and norm-referenced measures, respectively. Employee comparison procedures, by their very nature, are norm-referenced. The next two sections of this chapter are devoted to discussions of these two kinds of judgmental performance measures.

EMPLOYEE-COMPARISON PROCEDURES

Employee-comparison procedures yield judgmental performance data with ordinal-scale properties (see Chapter 2). They tell us which employees are deemed better or worse than others, but they reveal nothing about *how much* better or worse any given employee performs. We examine three comparison procedures: paired comparisons, rankings, and forced distributions.

Paired Comparisons

In its simplest form, this procedure requires the "judge" to consider every possible pair of workers to be evaluated, and to indicate, for each pair, the employee whose performance is better. Indices of individuals' relative standings among their co-workers (that is, "rankings") can then be obtained by determining the number of times each employee was judged to be superior. This procedure has a certain intuitive appeal. Its use is limited, however, because of two potential difficulties.

First, as the number of workers to be evaluated increases, the total number of possible pairs of those workers becomes dramatically larger. Given N employees, the number of possible pairs is determined according to the following formula:

$$\frac{N(N - 1)}{2}$$

As few as 10 employees necessitates 45 comparisons; with 50 employees, 1225 comparisons must be made! Fortunately, there is some evidence that comparable results can be obtained when the appraiser is required to judge only a selected half of all the possible comparisons (McCormick & Bachus, 1952; McCormick & Roberts, 1952).

The second possible problem with paired comparisons is a violation of logic known as intransitivity. For example, if Ms. Jones is judged superior to Mr. Smith, and Smith is deemed superior to Ms. Adams, then logic dictates that Jones should be judged superior to Adams. Unfortunately, this does not always occur, especially when comparisons are based on "overall job performance" and the perceived differences between Jones', Smith's, and Adams' levels of performance are small (Tversky, 1969). (Recall that ordinal measures reveal nothing about the "size" of the differences between measurements.) Modified paired-comparison procedures that focus on specific aspects of job performance, and that permit "ties" when two workers are thought to be essentially the same on any of those aspects, hold some promise for reducing intransitivity problems.

Rankings

Sometimes appraisers are asked directly to list all of their employees in order of their relative merit, without going through the paired-comparison procedure. Because each employee is evaluated only once on each aspect of job performance, the possibility of intransitivity is eliminated. Rankings, however, are not without their own problems.

As with paired comparisons, ranking can become an unwieldy task when the number of people to be evaluated is large. This often leads to unreliability. Think of the last time you tried to rank ten or more things. While you probably had no trouble identifying your two or three "most favorite" and your two or three "least favorite" items, it was probably very difficult to assign specific ranks to those items that fell somewhere in the middle of your list. In fact, you may have assigned ranks "4" through "7" in an almost arbitrary way. If you had been asked to reproduce those ranks several days later, whatever had been ranked "4" could just as easily be ranked "6" or "7" the second time around.

If Ms. Dieckman were ranking her subordinate managers, and only the top four were going to receive salary increases, you can see how this lack of reliability could translate into a very serious problem. Permitting ties, where two or more workers are assigned the same rank, may at least partially mitigate this problem (although the power of rankings to distinguish among employees on the basis of their performance is also reduced). Using a modified procedure known as alternation ranking, where the appraiser alternates between identifying the "best" and "worst" performers from an ever-shrinking list, may also provide some relief. Most appraisers still experience some uneasiness, however, as they work their way further and further into the "middle of the pack."

A second dubious quality that rankings share with other employee-comparison procedures is an unavoidable consequence of using norm-referenced measures. The fact that Ms. Jones may emerge as the top-ranked employee in a given section of the advertising department conveys no specific information about her level of performance with respect to some absolute scale of performance quality. Stated another way, Ms. Jones simply may be the "best of a bad lot." Similarly, being ranked last among a group of employees does not necessarily reflect an unsatisfactory level of performance. All the workers may be outstanding performers; some may just be more "outstanding" than others.

Forced Distributions

This comparison procedure is really nothing more than a modified ranking where ties are not only permitted, but required. The "judge" is typically asked to place employees in groups or categories that represent relatively higher and lower levels of performance. The percentages or proportions of the workers to be placed in the given categories are specified, thereby forcing the appraiser to "distribute" employees among the various levels of performance in a specified manner.

For example, the appraiser might be asked to place workers in categories such that 10 percent end up in the top ("best") category, 20 percent in the second-highest category, 40 percent in the middle category, 20 percent in the next-to-lowest category, and 10 percent in the lowest ("worst") category. This would approximate a normal distribution (see Chapter 2). Alternatively, the judge might be instructed simply to place one-fifth of the workers in each of the five categories; this would produce a "rectangular" distribution.

While forced distributions relieve some of the anxiety that can result from making more-or-less arbitrary decisions about people in the "middle of the pack," they do not completely eliminate this problem. Assigning a person to the middle or to the second-highest of five categories can still boil down to flipping a coin, yet the consequences of that placement may be anything but trivial. Forcing an appraiser to place specified proportions of her workers in the "lowest" (or "highest") category may also create frustration if she is very pleased (or displeased) with most or all of her subordinates' job performance.

Summary

There is both "good news" and "bad news" when we look at how employee-comparison procedures contribute to the two major purposes of performance appraisal. The good news is that these procedures *do* discriminate among employees, especially the paired-comparison and ranking procedures. Permitting ties or placing people into a limited number of categories reduces the level of discrimination obtained. Employee-comparison procedures, then, may be particularly useful for generating job-performance data to be used in making merit-based administrative decisions (promotions, raises, etc.). In fact, as we suggested earlier, such decisions ultimately *require* us to transform performance data into ordinal measures.

The bad news is that these procedures generate very little useful information that can be passed on to employees as feedback. The knowledge that you are first, last, or somewhere in the middle of a group of workers doesn't tell you much about how to remain at the top, or how to improve your performance. Constructive feedback requires some sort of criterion-referenced information, such as the objective or personnel data discussed earlier, or job-performance ratings, which we examine in detail in the next section.

Because they are undeniably subjective, and they can easily be seen as too restrictive ("forced" distributions!), it is unlikely that employee-comparison procedures hold much promise for allaying the two basic concerns Ms. Dieckman expressed in her memo. Although they are also patently subjective, some of the performance rating procedures described below impose fewer restrictions on those who must evaluate others' job performance.

PERFORMANCE RATINGS

Ratings are judgmental data produced when one person compares his or her perceptions of another person's job performance with various criteria or standards of excellence. These standards are usually displayed on a scale that the rater uses to record his or her judgments. Because workers' performance is compared to external standards of quality rather than to other workers' performance, ratings are usually classified as criterion-referenced measures. Ratings are the most widely used of all the available procedures for appraising job performance (Guion, 1965b; Landy, 1985).

Our discussion of ratings is divided into four sections. First, we address the question of who should rate whose performance. Second, we describe a variety of rating scale formats, and point out the relative advantages and disadvantages associated with each. Next, we examine the standards or criteria that are used to assess the quality and usefulness of the judgmental data generated with these various formats, and summarize the research evidence that speaks to the question of which scale format (if any) is superior. Finally, we present a theoretical model of rating behavior, and explain how this model reflects the recent changes in the ways we study job-performance ratings.

Who Should Rate Whom?

Ratings (as well as the employee-comparison procedures discussed earlier) can be obtained from a variety of different sources. These include workers' immediate supervisors, their peers or co-workers, the workers themselves, and their clients and customers if their work involves direct contact with the public. The situation in Ms. Dieckman's advertising department, where immediate supervisors provide the ratings, is the most common (Landy & Farr, 1983). Nevertheless, co-workers' ratings and self-ratings can also provide very useful information.

PEER RATINGS

Kane and Lawler (1978) reviewed the peer-assessment literature, and concluded that co-workers are capable of providing reliable and valid job-performance information. Peer *ratings,* however, tend to be less reliable and valid than peer *nominations,* which require employees to identify and categorize their "best" and/or their "worst" group(s) of co-workers. Nevertheless, the available evidence and common sense suggest that co-workers have access to unique information about each other's job performance.

Peer appraisals are therefore especially useful when performance is assessed for the purpose of providing detailed and accurate feedback to workers (Kane & Lawler, 1978). If, on the other hand, appraisals are to be used to make administrative personnel decisions, lack of trust combined with a competitive system (where, for example, many workers vie for a limited number of promotions or raises) can render peer assessments less appropriate and less acceptable (Brief, 1980).

SELF-RATINGS

As you might suspect, self-ratings are also inappropriate for making administrative personnel decisions (Levine, 1980; Meyer, 1980; Thornton, 1980). Asking employees to rate their own performance can be very useful, however, when those self-ratings are used during a one-on-one feedback session involving a worker and his or her supervisor (Bassett & Meyer, 1968; Meyer, Kay, & French, 1965). Having evaluated their own performance, workers are better prepared to discuss that performance and to request specific kinds of feedback, and perhaps assistance, from their supervisor.

Steel and Ovalle (1984) developed a procedure called "Feedback Based Self-Appraisal" that encourages workers to base their self-ratings *exclusively* on the formal or informal feedback they have already received from their supervisor. These authors expressed their hope that this "frame of reference [will] reduce the ambiguity in the rating situation [and] decrease the likelihood that raters will resort to improper responses" (p. 681).

COMPARISONS OF RATINGS FROM DIFFERENT SOURCES

The research literature contains a number of studies that compared ratings obtained from immediate supervisors with those obtained from peers or co-workers. Supervisors' ratings tend to be less favorable than peers' ratings (Rothaus, Morton, & Hanson, 1965; Springer, 1953; Zedeck, Imparato, Krausz, & Oleno, 1974). There is some disagreement, however, concerning the relative levels of agreement among these two types of raters. Klieger and Mosel (1953) and Springer (1953) reported greater agreement among supervisors, but Gordon and Medlund (1965) found more consistency among co-workers. Although Booker and Miller (1966) reported agreement *between* supervisors' and peers' ratings, other authors have emphasized that differences between these two groups of judges/raters are to be expected, since each typically has access to very different aspects of workers' job performance (Borman, 1974; Landy, Farr, Saal, & Freytag, 1976; Zedeck et al., 1974).

The most common finding when supervisors' ratings and self-ratings are compared is quite predictable: Self-ratings tend to be more favorable (Kirchner, 1965; Parker, Taylor, Barrett, & Martens, 1959; Steel & Ovalle, 1984). Even here, however, there is some conflicting evidence (Heneman, 1974). Kirchner and Parker et al. also reported moderate levels of agreement *between* supervisors' and self-ratings.

More recently, comparative studies have focused on *several* different kinds of raters. Lawler (1967) and Klimoski and London (1974) compared supervisors', peers', and self-appraisals; Mount (1984) compared supervisors', subordinates', and self-ratings; and Tsui (1984) looked at yet a third combination (supervisors', peers', and subordinates' ratings). The value of these studies is their ability to document the relative properties and characteristics of judgmental data obtained from a variety of different sources, enabling Dr. MacKeven and others to use them in the most appropriate ways. These studies should *not* be construed as a search for the "best" source of judgments. In most cases, the expression "the more, the merrier" applies. Judgmental data obtained from many different sources are more likely to yield information that can be used effectively and appropriately in a variety of different situations, from making fair and profitable personnel decisions to providing accurate and timely performance information during constructive and nonthreatening feedback sessions.

Rating Scale Formats

Rating scales have been around for a long time. Although Sir Francis Galton is commonly credited with introducing rating scales as psychological measuring devices (Garrett & Schneck, 1933), Ellson and Ellson (1953) reported that Robert Owen, who in 1825 founded an experimental community at New Harmony, Indiana, was using "highly developed" psychological rating scales to assess children's capabilities "when Galton was a child." Landy and Farr (1983) credited Donald Paterson with introducing the "graphic" rating scale to psychologists in 1922.

GRAPHIC RATING SCALES

Guion (1965b) presented a variety of different graphic rating scales, several of which are reproduced in Figure 4.1. These examples reflect three dimensions, along which the quality of graphic rating scales can vary: (1) the ambiguity of the aspects or *dimensions* of job performance to be rated, (2) the ambiguity of the *meaning* of a given rater's *response* on the scale, and (3) the ambiguity of the rater's *intended response*.

Look at examples *f* and especially *i* in Figure 4.1. The performance dimension to be rated ("Quality") is relatively well defined. Compare these to examples *a*, *b*, *e*, and *g*, which are devoid of any explanatory information concerning the meaning of "quality of work."

Now look at examples *c* and especially *h*. These include anchors or benchmarks at various points along the scales that convey the meanings associated with various rating responses. Compare these to examples *a*, *b*, and especially *e*, which offer few or no clues to the meanings of specific locations on the scales.

Finally, look at examples *g* and especially *f*. These permit the rater to make a response that is relatively (or completely) unambiguous; there can be little or no doubt about where the rater intended to mark the scales. Now compare these to examples *a*, *b*, *c*, and *d*. What, exactly, does the rater's check mark in example *b* mean? A rating of "3"? or "4"? or "3.5"?

You can use these three dimensions of rating scale quality to evaluate each of the scale formats discussed in this section. Formats that provide specific definitions of the dimensions of job performance to be rated, that provide descriptive and informative anchors or benchmarks at various points along the scales, and that reduce the likelihood of misinterpreting the rater's responses,

FIGURE 4.1
Examples of Graphic Rating Scales

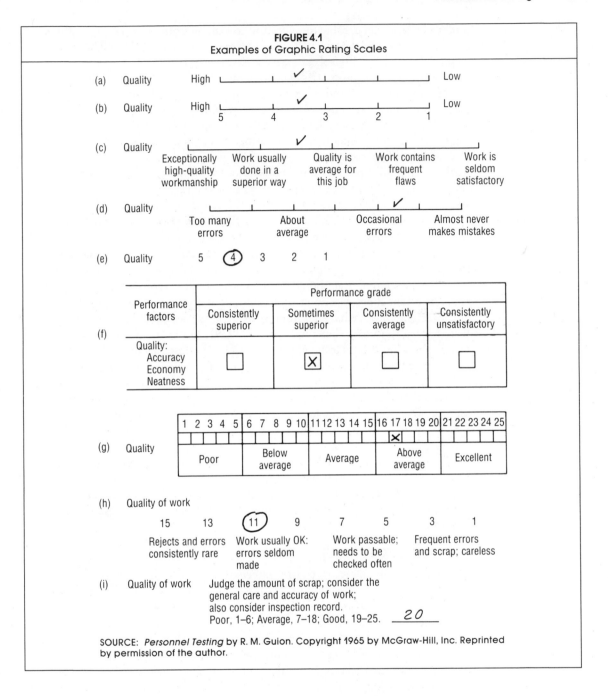

SOURCE: *Personnel Testing* by R. M. Guion. Copyright 1965 by McGraw-Hill, Inc. Reprinted by permission of the author.

tend to be more acceptable to raters and to yield performance data that are more accurate and useful (Barrett, Taylor, Parker & Martens, 1958; Bendig, 1952a, 1952b, 1953; Maas, 1965; Peters & McCormick, 1966).

Other desirable properties of graphic rating scales include an optimal number of response options, and an emphasis on job *behaviors* rather than abstract personality *traits*. A series of studies by Bendig (1952a, 1952b, 1953, 1954a, 1954b) and others (Finn, 1972; Jenkins & Taber, 1977; Lissitz & Green, 1975) suggests that the optimal number of rating options lies somewhere between 5 and 9. Fewer than 5 prevents raters from making judgments as fine as they would like, while more than 9 reduces the reliability of the ratings. Of course, any anchors that are attached to those rating options should be developed in a nonarbitrary, systematic fashion (Barnes & Landy, 1979; Landy & Guion, 1970; Rotter & Tinkleman, 1970; Wells & Smith, 1960). Banks and Roberson (1985) suggested that those who develop rating scales should assume the role of "test developers," who must pay particularly close attention to selecting, analyzing, scoring, and interpreting alternative responses/ratings. (We will discuss "tests" in Chapter 5.)

The question of *what* should be rated has yet to be resolved. Kavanagh (1971) concluded that there was no justification for eliminating either personality traits or observable job behaviors from consideration as potential rating targets. Brumback (1972) and Kane and Lawler (1979), however, suggested that performance appraisal should avoid personality traits (honesty, emotional stability, and so on), and that raters should instead focus on observable job behaviors (instances of lying, "shouting matches," and so on). Kane and Lawler claimed that personality traits serve only to facilitate or impair job performance, and that they are not aspects of job performance in and of themselves. Recognizing that many raters rely on traits to help them predict how a person will behave in a given situation, Landy and Farr (1983) proposed a compromise that would permit "dimension labels [to] be trait names whereas the dimension definitions and scale anchors may be task and behavior oriented" (p. 87).

Researchers have developed a number of alternative scale formats in their quest to improve upon traditional graphic scale ratings. It is to these that we now turn our attention.

FORCED-CHOICE RATING SCALES

The U.S. Army developed this alternative in the late 1940s because of dissatisfaction with the graphic rating scales then in use (Travers, 1951). According to Berkshire and Highland (1953), the soundest and most widely used forced-choice scale presents the rater with four examples of possible employee behaviors, all of which are examples of either positive or negative job performance. The rater must select those two examples of positive (or negative) behavior that, in the rater's opinion, most accurately describe the ratee's job performance. Raters are "forced" to choose from among alternatives that seem to be equally positive (or negative). The key is that, based on prior background research, only two of the four alternatives actually discriminate between satisfactory and unsatisfactory workers; the other two alternatives "sound good" (or "bad"), but are not empirically related to job performance. Each ratee's overall evaluation is usually derived by summing the number of *discriminating* alternatives selected by the rater.

Because raters are not informed about which alternatives actually discriminate between satisfactory and unsatisfactory job performance and which do not, their ratees' overall evaluations remain unknown to them (Zavala, 1965). Many raters resent being "kept in the dark," and therefore resist using forced-choice rating scales (Berkshire & Highland, 1953). In addition, the rather general, nonspecific nature of these overall evaluations is not very helpful in providing employees with useful feedback. Thus, elaborate efforts to overcome raters' resistance to using these scales may just not be warranted, unless the ratings are to be used exclusively for making administrative personnel decisions.

CHECKLISTS

In its simplest form, a checklist presents a rater with a list of items that describe a variety of possible work behaviors and/or personality traits, and asks the rater to indicate ("check") those items that are applicable to the worker being evaluated. Overall evaluations can then be determined by summing the number of positive items checked. Sometimes the total number of negative or undesirable items that have been checked is subtracted from the number of positive items checked.

Summated checklists are a variation on this format. The rater is typically instructed to use a five-item scale to indicate his or her level of (dis)agreement concerning the extent to which *each* of a series of items accurately describes the job performance of the worker being rated. Unlike simple checklists, these require the rater to respond to each item. Once again, overall evaluations are determined by summing the number of positive or desirable items that the rater agreed were descriptive of the ratee, as well as the number of negative or undesirable items that the rater believed were *not* descriptive.

BEHAVIORAL OBSERVATION SCALES

A recent variation on the summated checklist procedure, behavioral observation scales (BOS), presents raters with a list of job-performance-related behaviors, and asks them to indicate *how often* they have observed the ratee engaging in those behaviors (Latham & Wexley, 1977). Raters typically choose from among several "percentage of the time" options, such as 0–19, 20–39, 40–59, 60–79, or 80–100 percent of the time.

Latham, Fay, and Saari (1979) demonstrated that BOS evaluations need not be limited to general, overall assessments. In addition, Latham and Wexley (1981) suggested that BOS present a rating task that is simpler than those demanded by other rating scale formats, although Murphy, Martin, and Garcia (1982) disputed this claim. Because BOS are a relatively recent innovation, any firm conclusions regarding their utility, or the quality of the judgmental data they generate, would be premature. We must await further research.

Like the two rating scale formats yet to be discussed, BOS owe a debt to Flanagan's (1954) concept of "critical incidents." As we said in Chapter 3, these are behaviors or events that play a crucial role in a worker's success or failure on the job.

BEHAVIORALLY ANCHORED RATING SCALES

Originally developed by Smith and Kendall (1963), behaviorally anchored rating scales (BARS) have arguably generated more empirical research than any other scale format, or any other component of the performance appraisal process. They developed BARS in an effort to reduce or eliminate some of the sources of ambiguity in rating scales that Guion (1965b) has described (Figure 4.1). Specifically, examples of actual or possible job behaviors "are intended as anchors to define levels of the characteristic [being rated], and the operational definitions of the dimension being rated" (Smith & Kendall, 1963, p. 150). Misinterpretations of raters' responses are minimized by asking them to supplement each of their ratings with written notes (placed right on the scales) that describe ratees' work behaviors that they have actually observed. One of Smith and Kendall's original BARS is reproduced in Figure 4.2.

BARS have been developed for a wide variety of jobs (teachers, police officers, nurses, engineers, etc.). They are typically designed to be used by ratees' supervisors, but BARS can also be used for peer ratings (Landy et al., 1976). Several researchers have suggested modifications of Smith and Kendall's (1963) original developmental procedures (Campbell, Dunnette, Arvey, & Hellervik, 1973; Carroll & Schneier, 1982), as well as changes in the actual format of the scale (Landy & Farr, 1975). Some BARS openly ask for raters' *expectations* concerning ratees' job performance, recognizing that it is very unlikely that the specific anchors on any given scale will exactly correspond to any given rater's unique observations. The anchors attached to this variation of the BARS format usually begin with the phrase "Could be expected to . . . ," and they are usually referred to as behavioral expectation scales (BES).

Those who have used indices of rating quality (discussed in the next section) to compare BARS to other rating scale formats have arrived at something of a consensus: The empirical evidence does *not* lead to the conclusion that BARS are superior to other scale formats (Kingstrom & Bass, 1981; see also Jacobs, Kafry, & Zedeck, 1980, and Schwab, Heneman, & DeCotiis, 1975). Nevertheless, these reviewers also agreed that BARS should not necessarily be abandoned, primarily because of what Blood (1974) referred to as the desirable "spin-offs" of the developmental procedures. Landy and Farr's (1983) summary of those procedures is presented in Table 4.2.

Study of this table should suggest to you some of the positive spin-offs Blood (1974) identified. The most important of these appears to be the intensive participation of those who will use the scales (the raters) and those whose job performance will be evaluated (the ratees). Such participation often makes BARS more acceptable to both parties. You can also see in Table 4.2, especially in the first three steps, that developing BARS entails an intensive job analysis using Flanagan's (1954) critical-incident methodology.

In addition, BARS generate judgmental performance data that are sufficiently quantitative to facilitate personnel decision making, and sufficiently specific to

FIGURE 4.2
A Behaviorally Anchored Rating Scale

Skill in Human Relationships (with patients, families, and coworkers) — behaves in a manner appropriate to the situation and individuals involved.

Even when there is considerable emotional self-involvement, behavior with others is so skillful and insightful that it not only smooths but often prevents difficult emotional and social situations; this implies the ability to recognize the subtle as well as the more obvious components of basic emotional reactions in self and others (e.g., anxiety, fear, frustration, anger, etc.).

2.00

This nurse could be expected, whenever possible, to sit down and talk with a terminal-cancer patient who is considered to be "demanding."

1.75

If two aides asked this nurse, acting as team leader, if they could exchange assignments because of rapport problems with the patients assigned, would expect this nurse to discuss the problem with the aides and make certain changes which would be satisfying to them.

If this nurse were admitting a patient who talks rapidly and continuously of her symptoms and past medical history, could be expected to look interested and listen.

1.50

If this nurse were assigned for the first time to a patient who insists upon having her treatment done in a certain order, could be expected to do as the patient wishes without making an issue about it.

1.25

If emotional self-involvement is minimal, behavior with others is such that it does not complicate difficult emotional and social situations; this implies the ability to recognize the more obvious components of basic emotional reactions in self and others.

1.00

If the husband of a woman, who is postoperative and in good condition, asks about his wife, this nurse could be expected to reply as follows: "Her condition is good."

0.75

If a convalescent patient complained about the service in the hospital, this nurse would be likely to tell the patient that the hospital is short of nurses and the needs of the sickest patients have to be met first.

If this nurse were assigned to care for a terminal-cancer patient, in a two-bed room, who is depressed and uncommunicative, could be expected to carry on a conversation with the other patient while giving care to the terminal-cancer patient.

0.50

In the presence of a woman who is crying because her husband is dangerously ill, this nurse would be expected to tell the woman not to cry.

If this nurse were told by an ambulatory patient that a patient in the ward was having difficulty in breathing, could be expected to tell the ambulatory patient that his help in caring for the patients was not needed.

0.25

Behavior with others is such that it tends to complicate or create difficult emotional or social situations; this implies an inability to recognize even the obvious basic emotional reactions of self and others.

0.00

SOURCE: *A method for rating the proficiency of the hospital general staff nurse: Manual of directions.* Copyright 1964 by the National League for Nursing. Research and Studies Service, New York. Reprinted by permission.

TABLE 4.2 Procedures for Developing BARS

Identification and definition of performance dimensions	Group A of job experts identifies all important dimensions of performance for job in question. They also define conceptually each performance dimension and define high, average, and low performance on each dimension.
Generation of behavior examples	Group B of job experts gives examples of good, average, and poor job behaviors for each performance dimension. (Examples are edited by personnel researchers to reduce redundancy and to place each example in the expectation format.)
Retranslation and allocation	Group C of job experts is presented with a randomized list of behavioral examples and a list of the performance dimensions. They each independently allocate or classify each behavioral example to the performance dimension that it best represents. (A behavioral example is eliminated by the personnel researcher unless a large majority [e.g., 70 percent] of the group assigns it to the same performance dimension.)
Scaling	Group D of job experts evaluates the behavioral examples meeting the allocation criterion in the previous step in terms of the effectiveness of the performance described.
Scale-anchor selection	Personnel researcher computes the mean and standard deviation of the ratings given to each behavioral example in the scaling step. Examples are selected as anchors for each performance dimension such that items have mean values that provide anchors for the entire performance scale (from low to high) and that items have relatively small standard deviations.

SOURCE: Adapted from *The measurement of work performance: Methods, theory, and applications*, by F. J. Landy and J. L. Farr. Copyright 1983 by Academic Press. Reprinted by permission.

contribute to the performance-feedback process. For these reasons, neither Jacobs et al. (1980) nor Kingstrom and Bass (1981) were willing to conclude that the time, money, and effort that go into the development of BARS are wasted. Neither are we.

MIXED STANDARD RATING SCALES

Developed by Blanz in his doctoral dissertation, and refined by Blanz and Ghiselli (1972), mixed standard scales (MSS) also rely on critical behaviors as anchors, and bear a resemblance to summated checklists. The developmental process is very similar to that for BARS, up to the point when the BARS anchors are "attached" to the scales. More specifically, job experts (usually incumbents, supervisors, etc.) generate an exhaustive list of work dimensions, as well as specific examples of job behaviors that are thought to reflect those dimensions. Through scaling techniques similar to those described for BARS (see Table 4.2), three specific examples of work behavior are selected for each dimension. One of these describes excellent job performance, one describes average performance, and the third describes poor job performance.

At this point, however, rather than "attaching" these examples as anchors to performance-dimension scales, and then asking raters to check the appropriate scale value, those examples of excellent, average, and poor work behavior are listed in a random order, with the job dimensions being neither labeled nor defined. (That is, job dimensions do not appear on the scales at all.) For example, if the scale-development procedure yielded nine job dimensions, the MSS would consist of a randomized list of 27 work behaviors (three for each dimension) and *no* dimension labels or definitions. The rater's task is to indicate, for each example of work behavior, whether the ratee's job performance is better than, worse than, or at about the same level as the example. Raters provide no numerical ratings. An example follows of a mixed standard scale that was developed for police patrol officers (Saal & Landy, 1977).

EXAMPLE OF A MIXED STANDARD SCALE

+ = patrolman is better than this statement

0 = this statement fits the patrolman

− = patrolman is worse than this statement

STATEMENT	RATING
1. Could be expected to only polish his leather and clean his pistol immediately prior to a personnel inspection.	1. Dem–M _____
2. Could be expected to misinform the public on legal matters through lack of knowledge.	2. JK–L _____
3. Could be expected to seldom gripe about departmental procedures.	3. Att–M _____
4. Could be expected to never have to ask others about points of law.	4. JK–M _____
5. Could be expected to report for duty with his hair uncombed, with an obvious hangover, and with beer on his breath.	5. Dem–L _____
6. Could be expected to take the time to carefully answer a rookie's questions.	6. RwO–H _____
7. Could be expected to be considered "one of the boys" on his watch or shift.	7. RwO–M _____
8. Could be expected to refrain from writing tickets for traffic violations which occur at a particular intersection which is unusually confusing to motorists.	8. Ju–M _____
9. Could be expected to work to keep himself in top shape even though he's 45 years old.	9. Dem–H _____
10. Could be expected to consider law enforcement a career, not just a job.	10. Att–H _____
11. Could be expected to follow correct procedures for evidence preservation at the scene of a crime.	11. JK–H _____
12. Could be expected to call for assistance and clear the area of bystanders before confronting a barricaded, heavily armed suspect.	12. Ju–H _____

13. Could be expected to turn in reports which are neat, accurate, and well written.

13. <u>Comm–H</u>

14. Could be expected to use racially toned language in front of minority group members.

14. <u>RwO–L</u>

15. Could be expected to make a special effort to find the majority of burglaries on his beat before the owners open their stores for business by carefully inspecting for signs of possible break-ins.

15. <u>In–H</u>

16. Could be expected to continue to write a traffic violation when he hears a report of a nearby robbery in progress.

16. <u>Ju–L</u>

17. Could be expected to talk so fast over the radio he is unintelligible.

17. <u>Comm–L</u>

18. Could be expected to never have to be asked to repeat himself over the radio.

18. <u>Comm–M</u>

19. Could be expected to "crack up" in tense situations and threaten to shoot other officers.

19. <u>Dep–L</u>

20. Could be expected to remain cool under any circumstances.

20. <u>Dep–H</u>

21. Could be expected to rely on his supervisor to make important decisions for him.

21. <u>In–L</u>

22. Could be expected to use up a small number of sick days each year.

22. <u>Dep–M</u>

23. Could be expected to fail to correct his own deficiencies without prompting from others.

23. <u>In–M</u>

24. Could be expected to "go out of his way" to defy departmental regulations

24. <u>Att–L</u>

Note: Entries in the "Rating" column, which of course do not appear when the MSS is actually used, indicate the job-performance dimension and the level of performance represented by each behavioral example. Dem = demeanor; JK = job knowledge; Att = attitude; RwO = relations with others; Ju = judgment; Comm = communication; In = initiative; Dep = dependability. H = an example of good job performance; M = an example of moderate or average job performance; L = an example of poor job performance.

Two different scoring schemes are currently available for transforming raters' "better than," "worse than," or "the same as" judgments into numerical ratings. Blanz and Ghiselli's (1972) original scoring system contains some omissions and some logical inconsistencies (Saal & Landy, 1977). Saal (1979) suggested a complete scoring system that eliminates most of those inconsistencies. Both scoring schemes appear in Table 4.3.

Although MSS have received only a fraction of the research attention that has been lavished on BARS, several studies have compared MSS to other scale formats (Arvey & Hoyle, 1974; Dickinson & Zellinger, 1980; Saal & Landy, 1977). The results are "mixed" (sorry!), reflecting neither clear superiority nor inferiority with respect to various criteria of rating quality.

TABLE 4.3 Original and Revised Systems for Scoring Mixed Standard Scale Response Combinations

No.	Response combination[a] Superior behavior	Average behavior	Inferior behavior	Numerical ratings Original	Revised[b]
1	+	+	+	7	7
2	+	+	0	7	6
3	+	+	−	7	5
4	+	0	+	4	6
5	+	0	0	3	5
6	+	0	−	4	4
7	+	−	+	3	5
8	+	−	0	2	4
9	+	−	−	1	3
10	0	+	+	6	6
11	0	+	0	6	5
12	0	+	−	6	4
13	0	0	+	omitted	5
14	0	0	0	4	4
15	0	0	−	4	3
16	0	−	+	5	4
17	0	−	0	2	3
18	0	−	−	1	2
19	−	+	+	5	5
20	−	+	0	5	4
21	−	+	−	5	3
22	−	0	+	4	4
23	−	0	0	omitted	3
24	−	0	−	3	2
25	−	−	+	3	3
26	−	−	0	2	2
27	−	−	−	1	1

[a] + indicates "ratee is better than this behavior"; 0 indicates "ratee is the same as this behavior"; − indicates "ratee is worse than this behavior."
[b] Revised numerical ratings were derived as follows: numerical equivalent of response to superior behavior (+ = 8, 0 = 7, − = 6) + numerical equivalent of response to average behavior (+ = 5, 0 = 4, − = 3) + numerical equivalent of response to inferior behavior (+ = 2, 0 = 1, − = 0) − 8.
SOURCE: "Mixed standard rating scale: A consistent system for numerically coding inconsistent response combinations," by F. E. Saal, *Journal of Applied Psychology*, 1979, 64, 422–428. Copyright 1979 by the American Psychological Association. Reprinted by permission of the author.

More recently, Barnes-Farrell and Weiss (1984) examined the procedures used to generate the examples of excellent, average, and poor work performance that constitute MSS. They concluded that at least one of the problems associated with this scale format (logical-inconsistency errors, where a rater says, for example, that a ratee is "better than" the example of excellent job performance, but "worse than" the example of average or poor performance *within the same job dimension*) "is not one which can be primarily attributed to individual differences in raters or ratees [as Blanz & Ghiselli (1972) originally proposed], but is more likely associated with the instrument and the way raters respond to a mixed standard scale format" (p. 313). Because such logical inconsistencies (which are another example of the intransitivity problem discussed earlier) detract from the utility of MSS if they reflect a flaw in the scale format instead of revealing something diagnostic about the rater, the ratee, or the job dimension in question, this is not an encouraging conclusion.

The evidence supporting the use of MSS, then, is far from overwhelming. As we just said, Barnes-Farrell and Weiss (1984) questioned the usefulness of the format for diagnosing problematic raters, ratees, or job dimensions, and empirical comparisons do not reflect any consistent psychometric advantages associated with MSS ratings. In addition, as was the case with forced-choice ratings, MSS have been known to generate hostility among raters because they are kept uninformed about the ultimate numerical ratings that are assigned to ratees based on their judgments. Like BARS, however, MSS may be useful because of the job analyses and the employee participation required during their development.

SUMMARY

Ms. Dieckman's memo to Dr. MacKeven described her lack of satisfaction with the subjectivity and the restrictiveness of the rating scales that are currently part of Peter's Pan Pizza's performance appraisal system. We hope it is clear to you that *none* of the rating scale formats discussed here will eliminate the so-called problem of subjectivity. Dr. MacKeven will need to educate the advertising director (and probably many other managers, too) concerning the advantages associated with subjective rating scales, and the reasons for using them either instead of, or along with, other more objective indices of job performance.

Choice of format may, however, serve to reduce or eliminate some of the concerns about restrictiveness. BARS may hold some promise here, especially if raters are encouraged to supplement or elaborate on their ratings by describing specific instances of ratees' relevant work behaviors right on the rating scales. Of course, even the plainest graphic rating scale could be improved in a similar fashion. What is important is that the 5-point scales with ambiguous anchors ("unsatisfactory," "below average," and so on) that Peter's Pan Pizza currently uses can be improved by making those anchors more descriptive of actual work behaviors, and by allowing or encouraging raters to supplement ratings with their own specific observations. This would make the ratings more informative, and therefore more useful for feedback purposes. Any of the behaviorally based rating scale formats (BOS, BARS, MSS) could contribute to such improvements.

Rating the Ratings: Psychometric Indices of Quality

As we mentioned in our discussion of forced-choice ratings and MSS, it is important that a rating scale format be acceptable to those who will use it. Acceptability may be influenced by such factors as cost, time required to develop and use the scales, and the "hidden-scoring-system" problem discussed earlier.

Along with these concerns, judgmental data in the form of ratings must meet certain psychometric criteria if those data are to be useful for distinguishing among workers on the basis of their job performance, and for providing employees with constructive, specific feedback. This section deals with several rating "errors" that undermine the quality and usefulness of rating data. These errors do not include such things as random rating errors (inadvertently marking the wrong place on a rating scale, for example) or such overt prejudices as age-, race- or sex-related biases. (These problems can often be identified through a close inspection of the pattern of a given judge's ratings.) Instead, our focus here is on biases that tend to influence the distributions of raters' ratings, either across several job dimensions for a single ratee, or across a number of different ratees.

LENIENCY AND SEVERITY

Some raters consistently give ratees evaluations that are better or worse than the ratees' actual job performance warrants. These tendencies are known as "leniency" and "severity errors," respectively (Saal, Downey, & Lahey, 1980). Although raters are not always aware of these biases, some of the reasons for their existence are not hard to understand.

A rater may exaggerate the quality of ratees' performance because of (1) a desire to be liked; (2) a desire to avoid hostility on the part of ratees, particularly during any subsequent performance-feedback sessions; (3) a fear that other raters will exaggerate the performance of their ratees, who will then have an unfair advantage when promotions or pay raises become available; (4) a perception that it will reflect positively on the rater's own capabilities; and (5) abnormally low standards of excellence, just to name a few reasons. On the other hand, a rater may consistently underestimate the quality of others' performance for a variety of reasons, including (1) a perception that employees who receive high ratings may eventually compete for the rater's job; (2) a wish to "motivate" employees by giving them "room for improvement"; and (3) unusually high, and perhaps unreasonable, standards of excellence.

Whatever the dynamics that underlie leniency or severity errors, the implications for the purposes of performance appraisal are unfortunate. If all or most ratees are rated high (or low), that restriction in the range of ratings makes it very difficult for anyone who must discriminate among employees for the purposes of promotion, training, or pay raises. And, because lenient (or severe) ratings are, by definition, higher (lower) than they should be, any subsequent performance feedback based on those ratings will be inaccurate. Overly lenient feedback may result in complacent ratees, whereas overly severe feedback can be extremely discouraging.

CENTRAL TENDENCY

This is another instance where the rater restricts the range of assigned ratings. Instead of uniformly rating people too high or too low, however, the rater in this case rates all or most of the ratees somewhere "in the middle" of the rating scale, or "about average." Again, this is not always done consciously, and some of the reasons for its occurrence are not difficult to understand.

Sometimes raters are unwilling to "stick their necks out" and commit themselves to very high or very low ratings because they haven't been able to carefully observe ratees' job performance. This may be due either to the rater's own inadequacies (poor observation skills, perhaps, or just plain laziness) or to the nature of the ratees' jobs. For some jobs, such as store inspector in Peter's Pan Pizza's retail operations department or truck driver in the shipping department (see Figure 2.1), where the work takes the employee far away from his or her immediate supervisor, observation may be extremely impractical, or even impossible. In such cases, raters sometimes believe "average" ratings to be "safe," or least likely to "raise any eyebrows" and thereby focus unwanted attention on their (uninformed) ratings.

Sometimes the rating scale being used actually *encourages* central-tendency error by asking raters to justify either very high or very low ratings with written explanations of the specific work behaviors that merited those extreme ratings. Although Ms. Dieckman and her colleagues might jump at such an opportunity, many raters are either too lazy or too uninformed to provide that kind of documentation.

Regardless of the cause(s), central-tendency errors undermine a performance appraisal system in the same way that leniency and severity errors do. Discrimination is impaired, since most or all employees receive "about average" ratings, and feedback is inaccurate to the extent that ratees' performance is under- or overestimated.

HALO

Halo error is defined as "a rater's failure to discriminate among conceptually distinct and potentially independent aspects of a ratee's behavior" (Saal et al., 1980, p. 415). Unlike leniency, severity, and central-tendency errors, which reflect raters' *general tendencies* to consistently assign ratings to *several ratees* that are either too high, too low, or in the middle of the scale, respectively, halo error can be limited to *specific rater–ratee pairs*.

A rater's inability to distinguish between different dimensions of a ratee's job performance can result from a number of factors, operating either singly or in combination. Latham, Wexley, and Pursell (1975) described a "first-impression error," which you have probably already experienced yourself. If an employee makes a notably good or bad first impression on the rater, subsequent ratings on a variety of different dimensions (that may or may not have anything to do with the first impression) may be unduly influenced by that overall impression or aura. (This is where halo error got its name.) If the first impression is a good one, the halo hovering over the ratee's head may prevent the rater from seeing anything other than outstanding job performance. If the general impression is negative, the rater may subsequently see only inadequate performance, regardless of the quality of the ratee's actual performance on distinguishably different job dimensions.

A second possible explanation for halo error is based on the idea that one aspect of a worker's performance can be so remarkable that it overrides other performance dimensions where the employee is not quite so unique. It isn't uncommon for a rater to infer that any employee whose behavior is so extreme (good or bad) in a particular domain of job performance *must be* similarly "outstanding" in the other domains or dimensions of performance. Consequently, this rater assigns uniformly high (or low) ratings to that ratee on all job dimensions. Both of these explanations for halo error become even more feasible when, for whatever reason, a rater doesn't have all the necessary information at his or her disposal to provide accurate ratings on all the job dimensions.

A third possibility is that a rater may simply not understand the difference between two (or more) job dimensions, and he or she therefore assigns ratees similar ratings on those aspects of job performance. In this case, however, halo error will not be limited to specific rater–ratee pairs, but will characterize all of the ratings generated by that particular rater.

Nevertheless, because halo error *can* be limited to specific rater–ratee dyads, it need not produce a restriction in the range of ratings assigned to a number of ratees in the same way that leniency, severity, and central-tendency errors do. Since some ratees may receive uniformly high ratings while others receive uniformly low or uniformly "average" ratings from the same rater, distinguishing among workers for the purpose of making personnel decisions need not be a problem. Of course, if the distinctions among employees are based on *erroneous* global impressions, they will not lead to decisions that are in the best interests of the organization. More predictable is the damage halo error inflicts when ratings are used to provide workers with feedback concerning their levels of job performance. Since few of us are uniformly good or bad at all aspects of our jobs, consistently high or low ratings will be inaccurate, thereby undermining the effectiveness of the feedback process. (We will soon return to this all-important issue of accuracy.)

RELIABILITY

Although not a rating "error" in the same sense as leniency, severity, central tendency, and halo, lack of reliability can also undermine the quality and usefulness of rating data. As you will recall from Chapter 2, reliability refers to the consistency with which something is measured. If Ms. Dieckman assigns a certain set of ratings to one of her subordinates today, Dr. MacKeven would like to be able to assume that those ratings would be identical, or at least very similar, if she (Dieckman) were asked to rerate that same subordinate tomorrow. We cannot assess the reliability of her ratings in this way, of course, because it is impractical to do so (completing just *one* set of ratings can be very time-consuming), and because Ms. Dieckman would surely remember the ratings she assigned the day before and simply reproduce them from memory. In this latter case, we wouldn't be obtaining two independent measures of that subordinate's performance.

For these reasons, reliability of ratings is typically assessed by asking two or more individuals who are familiar with a given worker's performance to provide independent ratings of that performance. To the extent that these raters tend to agree with each other, we can have more confidence in the reliability of those ratings. This is usually referred to as interrater reliability. If the raters do not agree in their assessments of a given ratee's or, more commonly, a given group of ratees' performance, we often conclude that those ratings lack reliability. Since we discussed the implications of unreliable measures in Chapter 2, we won't repeat them here, other than to reemphasize the point that unreliable ratings are essentially useless for making personnel decisions or for providing employees with constructive feedback.

OPERATIONAL DEFINITIONS OF RATING QUALITY

It isn't enough for I/O psychologists to conceptually define reliability or the rating errors that we just discussed. Dr. MacKeven must also operationally define these indices of rating quality if she wants to use them to help raters generate judgmental data that contribute to the purposes of performance appraisal. Unfortunately, a bewildering array of different operational definitions has appeared in the literature, *and they do not all lead to the same conclusions.*

Based on their review of relevant studies published in three widely read I/O psychology journals (*Journal of Applied Psychology, Personnel Psychology,* and *Organizational Behavior and Human Performance*), Saal et al. (1980) identified three different operational definitions for leniency/severity, four for central tendency, four for halo, and five for interrater reliability. We have listed them all in Table 4.4. They then asked police sergeants to use both graphic rating scales and MSS to evaluate the performance of their subordinate patrol officers, and reported that "reliance on one operational definition [sometimes] produced results diametrically opposed to those that . . . emerged with a different quantification strategy" (p. 421).

This is a rather unsettling result, for it suggests that much of the research literature that has compared indices of rating quality for two or more rating scale formats should be "taken with a grain of salt." The frequency with which different researchers used different operational definitions of these indices of rating quality may at least partially explain the inconsistent results that have appeared in the journals. Recall that no rating scale format consistently emerged as superior to any of the others.

These operational definitions for assessing the quality of rating data suffer from one additional, very serious shortcoming. Simply stated, none of them directly addresses the issue of *accuracy* in ratings. We find a rater who gives all

TABLE 4.4 Different Operational Definitions of Rating Quality Criteria

Rating quality criterion	Operational definitions
Leniency or severity	Mean dimension ratings
	Rater main effect (in an ANOVA)
	Skewness
Central tendency	Mean dimension ratings
	Ratee main effect (in an ANOVA)
	Standard deviations
	Kurtosis
Halo	Rater × ratee interaction (ANOVA)
	Standard deviations
	Dimension intercorrelations
	Principal components analysis (a complex, multivariate statistical procedure)
Interrater reliability	Ratee main effect (ANOVA)
	Rater × ratee interaction (ANOVA)
	Standard deviations
	Pearson product–moment correlations
	Intraclass correlations (basically an ANOVA procedure)

SOURCE: Adapted from "Rating the ratings: Assessing the psychometric quality of rating data," by F. E. Saal, R. G. Downey, and M. A. Lahey, *Psychological Bulletin*, 1980, 88, 413–428. Copyright 1980 by the American Psychological Association. Reprinted by permission of the authors.

her subordinates very high ratings, for example, and accuse her of being too lenient. We see a particular ratee who receives uniformly high or low ratings and assume that halo error is operating. We observe that two raters disagree about the performance level of an employee and conclude that their ratings are unreliable. These inferences may or may not be warranted.

In the case of suspected leniency, might we not *expect* employees who have been carefully selected and well trained to perform their jobs in an exceptional manner? Uniformly high ratings would then be quite accurate, and not a symptom of leniency error. Might we not also expect *some* workers to be uniformly good at all or most aspects of their jobs? What appears to be halo error might really be no error at all. And finally, why should we insist that two or more raters *must* agree about the performance of a specified set of employees? Discrepancies are entirely predictable, since different raters have probably observed the ratees under different sets of circumstances. Furthermore, multiple raters are very likely to have different perspectives concerning which aspects of employees' job performance are important and which are more peripheral, and those different viewpoints are very likely to influence their respective ratings (Freeberg, 1969). Two (or more) raters who disagree, then, could still both be "right."

Several researchers have begun to address the issue of accuracy. Borman (1975, 1979) emphasized that interrater reliability and the absence of leniency, severity, central-tendency, and halo error are no guarantee of accurate ratings. Pulakos (1984), in fact, reported *no* relationship between accuracy of ratings and halo or leniency. Findings such as this also call into question the meaning and value of many published studies that have relied on these indices of rating quality as criteria for comparing rating scale formats.

Much of the research literature that describes training programs to improve the quality of raters' judgments is subject to the same reservations, since most studies relied on indices of halo, leniency, and interrater reliability as criteria of success (Bernardin, 1978; Bernardin & Walter, 1977; Brown, 1968; Ivancevich, 1979; Latham et al., 1975). In fact, Bernardin and Pence (1980) presented data suggesting that reductions in psychometric rating errors may be associated with *reductions* in rating accuracy. Seen in this light, the inconsistent and inconclusive results of many rater-training studies are not as perplexing as they might otherwise appear (Smith, 1986). More recent investigations of rater-training programs have recognized the importance of accuracy as *the* crucial criterion of success or failure (McIntyre, Smith, & Hassett, 1984; Pulakos, 1984).

SUMMARY

What emerges, then, is the rather discouraging conclusion that much of the research that has compared rating scale formats or rater-training programs has relied on criteria that do not consistently reflect what should be our major concern—accuracy. Until we develop criteria for assessing the quality of judgmental data that are characterized by less deficiency (and contamination), there is little or no point in continuing to search for the "best" rating scale format or the "best" program for training raters.

An alternative approach to the study of ratings focuses on the *processes* involved when one person uses a rating scale to record his or her judgments of another's behavior. In the irreverent words of Landy and Farr (1983): "It appears likely that greater progress in understanding performance judgments will come from research on the rating process than from a continued search for the 'Holy Format' " (p. 90). We shall now describe two models that reflect this approach, and present examples of empirical research that offer support for these models.

Process Models of Performance Rating

After an extensive review of performance rating literature published since 1950 (see Wherry, 1950, for a review of earlier studies), Landy and Farr (1980) offered what they described as a relatively "refined, coherent, **catholic** representation of the system of performance rating" (p. 94). Their model is presented in Figure 4.3.

Several processes are contained in this model. First and foremost, there are the rater's cognitive processes. These include the observation of ratees' job performance, as well as the storage, retrieval, and judgment of that information.

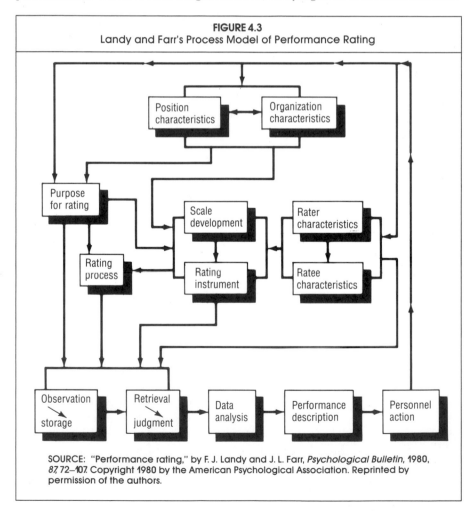

FIGURE 4.3
Landy and Farr's Process Model of Performance Rating

SOURCE: "Performance rating," by F. J. Landy and J. L. Farr, *Psychological Bulletin*, 1980, *87,* 72–107. Copyright 1980 by the American Psychological Association. Reprinted by permission of the authors.

Studies of raters' cognitive styles (Cardy & Kehoe, 1984; Lahey & Saal, 1981; Lord, 1985; Nathan & Lord, 1983), memory processes (Larson, Lingle, & Scerbo, 1984; Murphy, Balzer, Lockhart, & Eisenman, 1985; Phillips, 1984), and judgmental inferences (Nathan & Alexander, 1985) support the role of raters' cognitive processes in the overall performance rating system.

A second set of processes includes the organization's administrative procedures that influence performance ratings. These include the procedures used to develop rating scales, the actual rating instruments or scale formats used, and the determination of who should rate whom. The characteristics of those who occupy the roles of rater and ratee also play an important part in the rating system. For example, Kraiger and Ford's (1985) meta-analysis of race effects in performance ratings confirmed that "both black and white raters gave significantly higher ratings to members of their own race" (p. 60).

Research by Mobley (1982), Wexley and Pulakos (1982), and Peters, O'Connor, Weekley, Pooyan, Frank, and Erenkrantz (1984) failed to uncover a similar interaction involving sex. Instead, both male and female raters tended to give higher ratings to male ratees than to female ratees. Heilman and Stopeck (1985) reported an interesting twist on this pro-male rating bias. Whereas physical attractiveness was an advantage for women who held *nonmanagerial* positions, it was a distinct disadvantage for female managers. Men's ratings were unaffected by their physical appearance. According to Landy and Farr (1983), "much of the research concerned with ratee gender is supportive of the hypothesis that the gender stereotype of the occupation (i.e., whether a particular job is typically perceived as masculine or feminine) interacts with the gender of the ratee" (p. 132).

A pro-male bias also seems to govern the **attributions** raters make when they attempt to understand the causes of workers' performance. Whereas a man's good performance is usually attributed to his ability, similar performance by a woman is often attributed to good luck, to an easy task, or (at best!) to an unusual amount of effort. These systematically different attributions can lead to sex-based discrimination in personnel decisions (promotions, for example), since ability is believed to be a relatively stable, and therefore predictable, personal characteristic, while effort and luck are seen as more unstable, and therefore less dependable (Weiner, Frieze, Kukla, Reed, Rest, & Rosenbaum, 1972).

Landy and Farr's (1980) model also acknowledges the importance of the context in which ratings are generated. Such factors as organizational size and the characteristics of the ratee's position (level in the hierarchy, blue- vs. white-collar, and so on) define this context, as does the purpose for which the ratings are generated. McIntyre et al. (1984) reported data that support the general conclusion that ratings generated strictly for research purposes tend to be more severe than ratings generated for the purpose of making administrative decisions. This finding is typically explained by appealing to raters' compassion and desire

---

catholic: all inclusive, of general interest or value

attributions: inferences or conclusions about the causes and effects of behavior or events

to avoid negatively influencing their subordinates' organizational rewards (such as pay). Williams, DeNisi, Blencoe, & Cafferty (1985) suggested, however, that "the purpose and outcome of an appraisal decision [that is, its context] may serve a cognitive function in addition to the motivational function usually proposed" (p. 334). That is, raters who know that their ratings are to be used for administrative purposes may actually observe, categorize, and remember subordinates' work behaviors differently than raters who have been assured that their ratings will be used solely for research (or, perhaps, feedback) purposes.

DeNisi, Cafferty, and Meglino (1984) proposed an alternative model of performance rating that emphasizes a cognitive view of the process. A flow diagram of their model appears in Figure 4.4

Less comprehensive than Landy and Farr (1980), DeNisi et al. (1984) focused most of their attention on the "rater as an active seeker of the information required to complete evaluations" (p. 362). They also considered the purposes for which appraisals are conducted, the nature of the rating instrument, and time pressures that may affect the rater. Of particular value to future researchers, DeNisi et al. offered 28 specific hypotheses concerning the interrelationships among these factors.

Because their model is rather complex, and because space limitations preclude a full discussion of their hypotheses, we urge you to consult the authors' original article for a complete description of their work. In any event, you should be aware that Landy and Farr (1980) are not alone in their pursuit of a process model to facilitate our understanding of performance ratings.

SUMMARY

Whether subsequent research ultimately confirms and elaborates on these process models, or refutes them, they represent invaluable contributions in our quest to understand subjective job-performance appraisals. They are rich sources of hypotheses, and they offer guidance to Dr. MacKeven, Ms. Dieckman, and others who must wrestle with the challenges of developing and implementing performance appraisal systems that accomplish their purposes fairly and efficiently.

Dr. MacKeven would, therefore, be wise to rely on either or both of these models as she revises Peter's Pan Pizza's performance appraisal system, and explains to Ms. Dieckman and other raters in the organization their respective roles in that system. Open recognition of the observation and cognitive skills (storage, retrieval, etc.) that the system demands, accompanied by systematic

PEANUTS, © 1979 United Feature Syndicate, Inc.

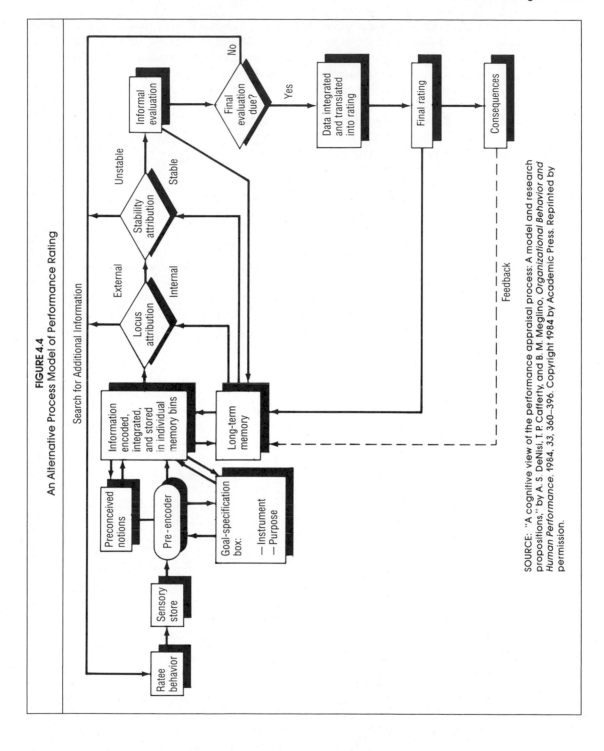

FIGURE 4.4
An Alternative Process Model of Performance Rating

SOURCE: "A cognitive view of the performance appraisal process: A model and research propositions," by A. S. DeNisi, T. P. Cafferty, and B. M. Meglino, *Organizational Behavior and Human Performance,* 1984, 33, 360–396. Copyright 1984 by Academic Press. Reprinted by permission.

training to develop those skills (see Chapter 7), may go a long way toward alleviating Ms. Dieckman's and her colleagues' discomforts with the dangers of bias. Modifying the rating scale format, and allowing raters to elaborate on the meanings of the ratings they assign (changes designed to take advantage of and reflect the complex cognitive demands of performance rating) should reduce their feelings of constraint and restriction.

These suggestions lead us to the final section of this chapter, where we discuss some of the obstacles that litter the path of those who must implement a performance appraisal system.

PUTTING A PERFORMANCE APPRAISAL SYSTEM TO WORK

Among the challenges Dr. MacKeven will face as she attempts to integrate a performance appraisal system into Peter's Pan Pizza's personnel procedures are the following: (1) clarifying the respective roles of managers and workers; (2) determining the frequency with which employees' performance should be formally appraised; (3) actually using performance data to make administrative decisions, and to provide feedback, effectively and efficiently; and (4) obeying the laws of the land.

Employees' Roles in Implementing a System

Any performance appraisal system will yield more reliable and accurate performance data when that system is accepted and used willingly, if not enthusiastically, by all those who are affected by it, from hourly workers to the chief executive officer. The support of upper-level managers is crucial to the system's credibility. It is they who must provide supervisors and anyone else who rates performance with adequate time to complete their appraisals, and they must reward raters for providing accurate assessments of workers' performance. Rank-and-file workers won't take feedback seriously, nor will they believe that personnel decisions are being made fairly, unless they respect the system.

As we suggested earlier, such support and respect are often facilitated when employees from all levels of the organizational hierarchy are permitted and encouraged to participate in developing and implementing a performance appraisal system. Banks and Murphy (1985) reminded us not to ignore raters' *willingness* and *motivation* to provide accurate ratings, in our enthusiasm to develop models of cognitive (unemotional) processes.

Frequency of Formal Appraisals

Although there are no hard-and-fast rules, *formal* performance appraisals should probably be conducted every six months or so. Annual appraisals place excessive demands on the cognitive abilities (especially memory) of raters, and allow employees to go too long without any formal notification of where they stand. Asking supervisors to provide formal evaluations of their subordinates' performance any more frequently than every six months is probably "too much of a good thing." The demands on raters' time may generate resistance, which can translate into unreliable or inaccurate performance measures. As Chhokar and Wallin (1984) put it, "more may not always be better" (p. 529).

Informal appraisals are another matter entirely. Supervisors should provide their workers with feedback about their job performance as soon as possible after observing the performance. This allows corrections to be timely, and serves to remind workers that their supervisors are paying attention to their work behaviors. Larson's (1984) model of the informal feedback process emphasizes the dynamic nature of these interactions. A safe assumption is that any worker whose *formal* performance appraisal comes as a surprise, pleasant or unpleasant, is working for a supervisor whose own job performance in this domain is unsatisfactory.

Effective Use of Performance Data

We have discussed at some length the need for performance measures to be reliable and accurate if they are to contribute to effective and profitable personnel decisions. Although providing workers with constructive feedback also depends on reliable and accurate information, something else is required: a one-to-one performance feedback interview that doesn't sabotage the entire performance appraisal system. This face-to-face session can render performance appraisal either a very useful management tool, or an unmitigated disaster.

JOB-PERFORMANCE FEEDBACK

A sizable body of research and theory pertaining to feedback exists in the literature. Consistent with the recent emphasis on processes, Ilgen, Fisher, and Taylor (1979) devised a process model of feedback that is reproduced in Figure 4.5. As you can see, this model focuses on how feedback affects the workers who receive it.

Much recent research reflects the influence of this model. Stone, Gueutal, and McIntosh (1984) reported a positive relationship between raters' expertise and the perceived accuracy of their feedback. Others have addressed the recipient's desire to respond to feedback. Silverman and Wexley (1984) found that those who had participated in (BARS) scale development had more positive reactions to the feedback process, and were more motivated to improve their performance. Jacoby, Mazursky, Troutman, and Kuss (1984) identified circumstances under which even accurate feedback tends to be ignored. Specifically, better performers were more likely to ignore feedback that was merely descriptive, having no predictive or explanatory value. Matsui, Okada, and Inoshita (1983) went as far as to suggest that "feedback improve[s] performance *only* [italics added] through its influence on the subject's intention to work" (p. 114).

Ashford and Cummings (1983) also stressed the recipients' active role in the feedback process, describing them as seekers of information who strive to "negotiat[e] their organizational environments in the pursuit of valued goals" (p. 370). More recently, Herold and Parsons (1985) developed the Job-Feedback Survey specifically for addressing the feedback environment in work organizations. All of these efforts fit nicely into Ilgen et al.'s (1979) model. Although much remains to be learned, research in this area is progressing well.

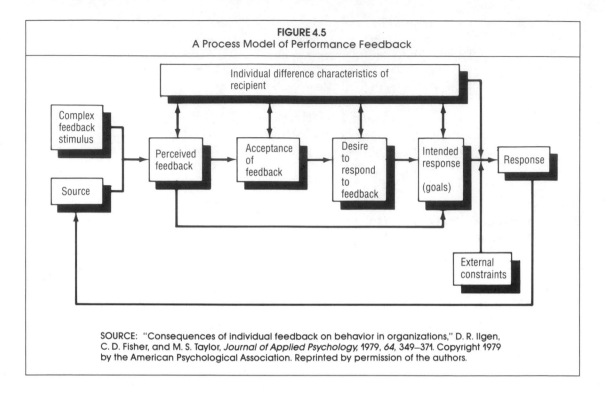

FIGURE 4.5
A Process Model of Performance Feedback

SOURCE: "Consequences of individual feedback on behavior in organizations," D. R. Ilgen, C. D. Fisher, and M. S. Taylor, *Journal of Applied Psychology,* 1979, *64,* 349–371. Copyright 1979 by the American Psychological Association. Reprinted by permission of the authors.

UTILITY OF PERFORMANCE APPRAISAL

In their desire to justify every expenditure, managers can be expected to ask about the utility of any personnel procedure. Utility implies a comparison of the economic advantages and disadvantages associated with a given procedure.

I/O psychologists' initial concerns with utility emerged in the context of personnel selection (hiring), so we will discuss this concept more fully in Chapter 6. More recently, however, Landy, Farr, and Jacobs (1982) extended these economic concerns to performance appraisal. Landy and Farr (1983) predicted that "utility calculation will become a standard tool . . . in the years to come [and that] this will help strengthen the bond between research and practice" (p. 274). Because establishing and fortifying that bond is crucial to the continued growth of I/O psychology, we hope they're right.

There can, of course, be little doubt that a convincing utility analysis of the cost/benefit ratio of Peter's Pan Pizza's performance appraisal system will be of great interest to Ms. Dieckman, as well as to other managers and executives. Dr. MacKeven's assurances regarding the inherent subjectivity of performance ratings, as well as any changes she makes in the performance appraisal system, will surely be better received if they are accompanied by a "dollars-and-cents" analysis of the system's value to the organization.

Legal Concerns

Title VII of the Civil Rights Act (1964) stipulated that personnel decisions must be based on job-related factors, and not on such personal characteristics as race, sex, or ethnic background. The EEOC, charged with enforcing Title VII, devoted most of its initial attention to the personnel selection process, since that seemed to be where the most blatant examples of illegal discrimination were taking place (see Chapters 5 and 6).

Nevertheless, if performance data are used to make such personnel decisions as promotion, demotion, transfer, or dismissal, there is no question that these data are also subject to Title VII restrictions (Bernardin & Beatty, 1984). After all, promoting a person is nothing more than a form of "selection," where the pool of applicants is located within rather than outside of the organization. Seen in this light, the need for performance measures to be based on careful job analyses becomes obvious. How better to demonstrate the job-relatedeness of performance appraisal data?

CHAPTER SUMMARY

Performance appraisals are conducted for the purposes of making merit-based personnel decisions, providing employees with constructive feedback concerning their job performance, and generating criterion data that can be used in an organization's human resources research projects. In order to contribute to these goals, performance data must distinguish "good" workers from "bad" ones, and must convey information about multiple aspects of workers' job performance that is accurate and unbiased.

Objective and personnel performance data share the desirable property of being countable, but both are also vulnerable to contaminating factors that are beyond workers' control. Because these kinds of data are often unavailable, or thought to be inappropriate, most organizations rely on judgmental data to assess employees' performance. Ranking methods, including paired comparisons and forced distributions, do a reasonable job of discriminating among "better" and "poorer" performers (at least at the extremes), but are less useful for feedback purposes. Ratings, which can come from supervisors, peers, or even the workers themselves, and which can be based on a variety of scale formats, are more likely to provide useful feedback information, assuming that they are not contaminated by leniency/severity, central-tendency, or halo errors. Because of the confusion that still surrounds the operational definitions of these errors, recent performance appraisal research has shifted its focus to rating accuracy and the cognitive factors that influence the rating process.

Several process models of rating behavior are now available. Their primary contribution is to focus our attention on such cognitive processes as observation, memory and integration of information, and judgment. This emphasis may not only facilitate productive research, but may also lead to more effective procedures for designing performance appraisal systems and implementing them in organizations.

INTEROFFICE MEMO

TO: Ellen Dieckman, Director of Advertising

FROM: Jennilyn MacKeven, Human—Resources Coordinator

I understand your concerns with our present performance appraisal system and rating scales. I have been stewing about them for some time now, and your memo prompted me to ''get the ball rolling'' to make some necessary changes. Here's my tentative plan:

Beginning with your department, my staff and I will conduct a series of workshops with <u>all</u> your employees, managers, and workers. At these workshops, we will

1. inform people about the basic reasons for conducting perfor—mance appraisals
2. acquaint them with the kinds of performance data that are potentially available (paying particular attention to the rationales for ''falling back on'' judgmental data), and the variety of available judgmental procedures and rating scale formats
3. distribute the job analyses and descriptions for the positions in the Advertising Department (the ones we completed about a year ago), and solicit their ideas and preferences concerning the ''best'' kinds of job—performance data for capturing the criteria that evolved from those job analyses

With this information at our disposal, my staff and I will design some performance appraisal instruments and procedures that reflect your employees' ideas and preferences as much as possible, while not sacrificing basic psychometric necessities (reliability, validity, etc.). We shall then conduct a second series of workshops that will give your people an opportunity to help us ''fine tune'' the new instrument(s) and procedures, and give us the opportunity to provide them with some training (especially the managers/supervisors) in how to use and implement our new performance appraisal tools.

Finally, I shall analyze the performance data that are generated by these new procedures over a one—year period. We should be able to detect employees' (dis)satisfaction with the system, as well as any unexpected psychometric problems.

What do you think?

REVIEW QUESTIONS AND EXERCISES

1. What do you think of Dr. MacKeven's plan?
2. What are the advantages and disadvantages of so much employee participation?
3. Should supervisors/managers and their subordinates attend the same workshops? Why (not)?
4. What kind(s) of performance data would you advocate including in the advertising department's performance appraisal system? Why?
5. What kind(s) of performance data would you recommend excluding from that system? Why?
6. What should Dr. MacKeven "look for" during the one-year follow-up period?
7. How can Dr. MacKeven use a process model of performance appraisal as she carries out the steps described in her memo to the advertising director? Do you anticipate any dangers of relying on such a model?

CHAPTER 5

Predictors of Job Performance

Learning Points

After studying this chapter, you should

- know the classical definition of test reliability, based on the concept of "true score"

- be able to explain why we must be satisfied with estimating the reliability of our measuring instruments, and to describe three different methods for deriving such estimates

- understand how various characteristics of a test, of the people taking the test, and of the testing environment can influence our estimates of a test's reliability

- know what validity is, and be able to describe three different ways to analyze the validity of test scores

- be familiar with the validities of scores on various paper–and–pencil tests (of intelligence, motivation, and personality) for predicting job performance

- be able to describe the validities of biographical data, personal interviews, work samples and situational exercises, letters of recommendation, and assessment centers for predicting job performance

INTEROFFICE MEMO

TO: Jennilyn A. MacKeven, Human-Resources Coordinator

FROM: James Schiftner, Director of Management Selection

Most of the current managers at Peter's Pan Pizza began their employment with us at lower, nonsupervisory levels, and have "come up
through the ranks" of the organization. My efforts and attention as
Director of Management Selection have been primarily focused on identifying potential managerial talent among our current employees.
While we have certainly experienced our share of difficulties as a
result of this "promotion-from-within" policy (placing managers in
the sometimes awkward position of exercising authority over their
former colleagues, friends, and co-workers, for example), the overall
results have proven to be generally satisfactory.

Considering that "track record," I believe it would be foolish to
totally abandon this policy and strategy for staffing Peter's Pan Pizza's managerial ranks. Nevertheless, I am also convinced that relying
almost exclusively on a "promotion-from-within" policy is a self-
defeating approach to management selection—an approach that will
ultimately lead to complacency and stagnation. In today's rapidly
changing business environment (and given the rumors going around
about PPP's purchasing a frozen-food company), this could prove to be
fatal.

I therefore intend to develop a set of procedures for identifying and
selecting managerial talent that can be effective when applied either
to our current employees or to men and women from outside of Peter's
Pan Pizza (recent MBAs, managers in other organizations, etc.). I
would appreciate any help you can provide me in the areas of (1)
recruitment strategies, (2) specific selection tests or instruments,
(3) overall management-selection strategy, and (4) relevant legal
considerations.

You may recall from Chapter 1 that organizations have shared Mr. Schiftner's concern with personnel selection for a very long time. Ancient Chinese and Classical Greeks developed procedures for selecting civil servants and soldiers, respectively, thousands of years ago. More recently, the City of Boston contributed to the growth of I/O psychology in America in the early 1900s when it asked Hugo Münsterberg to design a system for selecting streetcar motormen. Since that time, the complexity of the personnel selection process has increased manyfold, due in no small way to rapidly changing technologies and to the dramatically altered social, political, and legal contexts in which organizations exist and operate.

Because personnel selection has become so complicated, we devote two chapters to descriptions and discussions of the relevant issues. In this first chapter, we will concentrate on specific selection instruments or tests. Following our discussion of reliability and validity, crucial measurement concepts that underlie the effectiveness of any selection device, we will describe a variety of instruments and procedures that are currently being used to predict people's job performance, and thereby make personnel selection decisions. We will continue our examination of selection issues in Chapter 6, by placing specific selection instruments and procedures into the context of potentially effective personnel selection *systems*. This will involve a look at recruiting (identifying a pool of job applicants from among whom new employees can be selected), at ways to improve selection decisions by combining and integrating information gleaned from several specific selection instruments, at utility concepts (relative costs and benefits of selection systems), and at legal considerations and issues that bear on the personnel selection process. As always, we will anchor our discussions with specific references to the memos that begin each chapter.

PSYCHOMETRIC ISSUES

Psychometric issues are those that pertain to psychological measurement (Guilford, 1954). As you learned in Chapter 2, to measure is to assign numbers to objects or events according to certain rules. Recall that Stevens (1946) distinguished among four different sets of such rules in his descriptions of nominal, ordinal, interval, and ratio scales.

The basic assumption that underlies the personnel selection process is that the women and men who apply for jobs differ with respect to certain skills and abilities, and that these differences may be associated with or predictive of different levels of job performance. The first step in developing any selection system, then, is to develop measuring instruments ("selection tests") capable of reflecting those individual differences, and thereby discriminating among potentially successful and unsuccessful employees. As we stated in Chapter 3, useful measurements are characterized by both reliability and validity. It is to these central psychometric concepts that we now turn our attention.

Reliability

Reliability refers to the consistency with which something is measured. If our measurements are to be useful, the numbers we generate must be as consistent or stable as the **construct** or variable that they are being used to describe. Another way to say this is that reliable measures are relatively free of errors or mistakes that are random or without any discernible pattern.[1]

This leads us to the formal definition of reliability (Ghiselli, 1964; Nunnally, 1978): A measurement is reliable to the extent that the variance in a set of observed scores is related to the variance in the "true scores" of the people, objects, or events being measured, and not to random-error variance. More precisely, reliability is indicated by the ratio of true-score variance to observed-score variance (Aiken, 1979; Allen & Yen, 1979; Lemke & Wiersma, 1976). In order for you to understand this formal definition, and how it is related to the idea of consistency, you must understand the concepts of true scores, random-error scores, and observed scores. Let's examine them now.

Whenever we measure something, the number we get and record is the "observed" score. If you measure your height with a yardstick and get 5'8", or you measure your algebra skills with a final examination and get 86 out of 100 points, those numbers are your observed scores. They are sometimes called "total" scores, because they are assumed to be determined by the sum of two subscores, your true score on each variable (height or algebra skills) and random-error scores. For the sake of consistency, we shall continue to refer to these "total" scores as observed scores.

A true score is the measurement we would obtain and record if our measuring instrument (and the measurer) were *perfect*—completely free of any error. Few of us would question the notion that we each have an actual, precise height, and that if we measure carefully enough, we can determine what that height is. If you asked ten of your friends to independently measure your height using the same yardstick, however, you would invariably discover that not everyone would record the same observed score. Some may get 5'8" (which we'll assume, for the moment, is your true height), while others may record scores as low as 5'7" or as high as 5'9", or anything in between. That is, there will be some variance in the observed scores. Now, if each of your ten friends measured your height within a period of five minutes, you could be fairly certain that your actual height, your true score, did not vary during such a short time interval. Because your true score remained constant while the observed scores varied, we attribute that variance to the effects

[1]Nonrandom errors, which are systematic or patterned, also undermine useful measurement, but the problem is not one of reliability. By definition, systematic errors display some consistency, and therefore some reliability. The problem in such cases is one of validity, which we shall discuss next.

---

construct: an abstract concept that cannot be directly observed or measured, but must be inferred from more directly observable events; hunger, intelligence, and motivation are examples of constructs

of random error. Each of your friends made a small error as they assessed your height (except, of course, those who arrived at an observed score of 5′8″ exactly). Some of these errors resulted in overestimates, while some led to underestimates. This shows a certain lack of reliability. If each of your friends had recorded observed scores of 5′8″, there would have been *no* variance in the observed scores; because your true score *should have been the same* each time it was measured, those measures would have reflected perfect reliability.

The same ideas apply when we assess a sample of several (or many) individuals. For example, you could obtain measures of 250 people's heights. The observed score for each person would be the sum of each individual's true height and a greater or lesser amount of random error. The variance in their observed scores (across all 250 people, each of whom was measured only once) is equal to the variance in their true scores (we can expect that not everyone will be the same height) plus the variance in the error scores that "contaminate" their observed scores. If each person's height had been measured without any random error, then the variance in the observed scores would be equal to the variance in the true scores, and the measure would be perfectly reliable.

The same principles apply to students' scores on algebra tests, and to applicants' scores on any selection tests they may take in the process of applying for a job. In order for those test scores to be useful, they must reflect applicants' true scores on whatever construct is being measured (algebra skills, intelligence, communication skills, and so on), and be relatively free of the influences of random error. That is, they must be reliable.

With some notable exceptions (Lumsden, 1976), this classical psychometric definition of reliability is widely accepted. At this point, with your understanding of true, random-error, and observed scores, you should be able to see how this definition speaks to the issue of consistency. Unfortunately, a major difficulty associated with this psychometric definition of reliability is that true scores are abstractions that *cannot be directly measured.* The implication of this for I/O psychologists is that it is therefore impossible to *directly* assess the reliability of a measurement, because it is impossible to *directly* calculate the ratio of true-score variance to observed-score variance.

SHOE, reprinted by permission: Tribune Media Services.

Because it is essential to know how reliable a measurement is before using it to select or reject individual job applicants, and because direct calculation of true-score–to–observed-score ratios is impossible, I/O psychologists must be satisfied with *estimating* the reliability of their measures. Although there are a variety of ways to do this, each relies on the concept of correlation and a form of the correlation coefficient (r). We will describe the three most common methods for estimating reliability: the test–retest method, the equivalent-forms method, and the internal-consistency method. As you will see, each method estimates reliability from a different perspective.

TEST–RETEST

Perhaps the easiest of the three approaches to understand, the test–retest method estimates the reliability of a measuring instrument by administering the "test"[2] to a sample of individuals at Time 1, and then at a later Time 2, administering the *same test* to the *same group of individuals.* The correlation coefficient that describes the linear relationship between individuals' scores on the same test taken at two different times is interpreted as the estimate of reliability, and is referred to as a reliability coefficient. To the extent that this index approaches its upper limit of + 1.00, individuals who scored high or low on the test the first time it was administered also tended to score high or low, respectively, the second time. That is, there is evidence of some consistency in people's scores. In this case, the reliability coefficient reflects consistency in scores over a period of time, the interval between the two administrations of the test.

Consistency over time is an especially important property of test scores that are to be used to predict job applicants' levels of job performance months, or even years, after they have been hired. The major obstacle to using this highly relevant approach to estimating reliability is determining the proper interval of time that should separate the two administrations of the test. If it is too short, people will remember how they responded the first time, and simply reproduce those responses the second time. The desire to appear consistent, or just "plain old laziness," can prompt people to rely on their memories, rather than taking the test again "as if they had never seen it before." To the extent that this occurs, the correlation between the two sets of scores reflects memory, and not the consistency with which the test is capable of assessing some other important construct (such as intelligence or communication skills).

If, on the other hand, the interval between the two administrations of the test is too long, individuals' true scores on whatever construct is being measured may change. While we wouldn't expect dramatic changes in adults' levels of intelligence over a six-month interval, we would *not* be surprised to find that people's communication skills changed extensively during that time. In this latter case, a small reliability coefficient could reflect such true-score changes, rather than a lack of reliability in the measuring instrument.

[2]For purposes of convenience, we will refer to measuring instruments in general as "tests" from now on, even though many selection devices, such as interviews and application blanks, bear little resemblance to a traditional test or examination.

As you can see, choosing the proper time interval can be a challenge. Those using the test–retest method to estimate the reliability of a selection test must be able to describe the nature of the construct they wish to measure, and then identify a period of time that is not so long that people's true scores can be expected to change, but not so short that individuals will remember exactly how they responded the first time, and simply reproduce those responses from memory the second time.

EQUIVALENT FORMS

A second method for estimating reliability requires *two different tests* that measure the same construct. Both tests are consecutively administered to the *same sample* of individuals, and the correlation coefficient that describes the linear relationship between their scores on the two tests is interpreted as the estimate of reliability. As this reliability coefficient approaches +1.00, it indicates that people who score high on one of the tests also tend to score high on the other, while those who obtain low scores on the first test also score low on the other. The assumption in this case, as before, is that individuals' more-or-less constant true scores constitute a large proportion of their observed scores on both tests. Smaller reliability coefficients suggest less consistency in people's scores on the two different tests. In this case, then, reliability refers to consistency across separate measuring instruments that are designed to measure the same construct.

This method for estimating reliability tends to be used less frequently than the test–retest approach. Equivalent (sometimes referred to as "parallel") forms of tests must meet certain rigorous statistical criteria (equal means, equal variances, equal correlations with other measures, and so on), but experience shows that it is very difficult to create two or more tests that actually do so. The basic challenge inherent in creating equivalent forms is devising two or more tests that actually measure the same construct in the same way. To the extent that we fall short of this goal, correlations between scores on "equivalent" tests tend to underestimate the reliability with which a given construct can be measured, since the observed scores used to calculate the reliability coefficient reflect true scores on nonidentical constructs. Given these difficulties, you can see why this is not a particularly popular method for estimating reliability, in spite of the fact that "classical psychometric theory is based on the conception of exactly parallel [equivalent] measures" (Guion & Ironson, 1983).

INTERNAL CONSISTENCY

The third method for estimating the reliability of test scores requires only that *a single test* be administered to *a single sample* of people, on *a single occasion*. The test items are subsequently partitioned to form two "subtests," and correlations are computed between individuals' scores on those subtests. Correlations that approach +1.00 indicate that people who did well on one portion of the overall test also did well on the other portion of the test, while people who performed poorly on one subgroup of items also did relatively poorly on the other subgroup of items. Once again, this is evidence of consistency, but this time it is consistency *within* a given measuring instrument—"internal" consistency. Because this is the most convenient method for estimating reliability, requiring only one test, one sample of people, and one administration of the test, it isn't surprising that it is the most commonly reported method in the empirical research literature.

There are several ways to estimate the internal consistency of a test. Perhaps the simplest is the split-half estimate, where the test items are divided into two groups to form two subtests, and individuals' scores on one half of the items are correlated with their scores on the other half of the items. If we have a test with 100 items, the most obvious strategy is to correlate people's subtotal scores on items 1 through 50 with their subtotal scores on items 51 through 100. This is *not* an advisable strategy, however, for at least two reasons.

First, some people may perform worse on the second 50 items because of fatigue. Because everyone in the sample would not succumb to fatigue in the same way at the same time, this would result in a smaller split-half correlation, which would (erroneously) suggest a lack of internal consistency among the items on the test. Second, some tests are designed so that the earlier items are relatively easier to answer correctly, while the later items become progressively more difficult to answer correctly. Such "power tests," then, do not measure the same thing in the same way throughout; correlating scores on the first 50 items with scores on the second 50 items would be expected to yield lower estimates of internal consistency. Other tests, known as "speed tests," contain relatively simple items throughout, but the people taking the test are allowed only a limited amount of time to complete all the items. If everyone manages to answer the first 50 items, but individuals vary in how many of the second group of 50 items they had time to answer, we would again expect a lower correlation between these two subtest scores.

You may already have realized that the solution to both of these dilemmas involves creating the subtests in a different way. The most common procedure is to obtain subscores based on all of the even-numbered items (2, 4, 6, and so forth) and correlate them with subscores based on all of the odd-numbered items (1, 3, 5, 7, and so on). Any effects of fatigue (or of boredom, or of power- or speed-test characteristics) will be evenly distributed across both sets of subscores; that is, they will be controlled. The resulting internal-consistency reliability coefficient will then reflect only internal consistency. This method is known as an "odd–even, split-half" estimate of reliability.

There are, of course, many different ways to divide a test in half for the purpose of estimating internal consistency, and any given division is arbitrary. One could avoid the problem of arbitrariness by averaging the reliability coefficients obtained from *all* of the possible ways that a test could be divided in half. Unfortunately, as Aiken (1979) pointed out, this would be very time consuming, even with the aid of a computer: A test with only 50 items would require the calculation and averaging of 1225 split-half reliability coefficients!

Several psychometricians developed shortcuts for obtaining estimates of these average split-half correlations (Cronbach, 1951; Hoyt, 1941; Kuder & Richardson, 1937). Kuder and Richardson developed more than 20 different formulas for obtaining such estimates under a variety of different conditions. Their most popular formula (KR-20), which is appropriate when items vary in relative difficulty levels, is known as coefficient alpha (Cronbach, 1951). Perusal of the empirical literature reveals that coefficient alpha is by far the most commonly reported estimate of internal-consistency reliability.

Two additional considerations are important when we use an internal-consistency method to estimate reliability. First, any correlation based on split-half subscores will be an underestimate of a (whole) test's reliability, because reliability estimates are influenced by the number of items that a test comprises. Split-half estimates for a 100-item test actually reflect the reliability of 50-item subtests. Because we would actually plan to use the (entire) 100-item test for personnel selection purposes, the estimate based on 50-item subtests must be corrected. The Spearman–Brown prophecy formula is typically used for this purpose:

$$r' = \frac{Kr}{1 + (K-1)r}, \text{ where}$$

$r' = $ the corrected split-half reliability coefficient
$r = $ the uncorrected split-half reliability coefficient
$K = $ the factor by which the subtests must be increased to equal the length of the actual test that is to be used ($K = 2$, for split-half estimates, since the uncorrected correlation is based on subtests that are one-half the length of the whole test that is to be used)

An algebraic manipulation of the formula shown above can also be used to estimate the increase in internal-consistency reliability that can be expected if the number of test items is increased by a given factor (K), *or* to estimate the factor by which the number of test items must be increased in order to obtain a test with a given corrected reliability (r'). The latter case is illustrated by the following example:

Suppose that Dr. MacKeven had a 35-item test with a reliability of $r = .52$. Algebraically manipulating the Spearman–Brown formula to "solve for" K yields the following equation:

$$K = \frac{(r' - rr')}{(r - rr')}$$

If she wished to obtain a "corrected" reliability coefficient of $r = .80$, she could solve this equation to learn that $K \approx 3.7$. Thus, Dr. MacKeven would have to increase her 35-item test by a factor of 3.7, to include almost 130 items, in order to have an internal-consistency reliability of .80. Of course, she would need to determine the feasibility of developing an additional 95 items to add to her test.

The second important consideration when using internal-consistency estimates of reliability concerns the content of the test items. Remember, this method for estimating reliability focuses on consistency within a single measuring instrument, rather than consistency over time or across different tests. It is an appropriate estimate of reliability, then, only when a test measures a single construct or variable. If a test is instead multidimensional—that is, if it assesses individuals on two or more different aspects of ability, personality, or motivation, and if those multiple aspects are *not* perfectly correlated—we would *expect* the internal consistency of that test to be lower than it would be if the test measured only a single construct. This is just another way of saying that internal-consistency estimates of reliability are appropriate only when all the test items measure the same thing. Dr. MacKeven's task (in the hypothetical example described above) of coming up with 95 additional items *that measure the same construct* may therefore be a very challenging one. It is therefore important for her to reassess the internal-consistency reliability of her revised, expanded test.

By now you should appreciate the importance of test reliability, and the advantages and disadvantages associated with the different methods for estimating this psychometric property. Before discussing validity, we want to acquaint you with some of the factors that can influence the size of reliability coefficients, and that can therefore influence and potentially mislead those who strive to develop reliable personnel selection instruments.

Factors That Influence Reliability Estimates

Among the factors that can affect the magnitude of reliability estimates are the estimation method used, the characteristics of the items that make up the test, the characteristics of the sample of individuals whose test scores are used to estimate reliability, and the environment or context in which the test is administered.

ESTIMATION METHOD

We just described the three basic methods for estimating test reliability using correlation coefficients (or averages thereof). Coefficient alpha and corrected split-half internal-consistency estimates are best interpreted as upper limits or ceilings of reliability (Nunnally, 1978). Equivalent-forms estimates, on the other hand, tend to be too low to the extent that the two forms actually measure different constructs (Ghiselli, 1964); such estimates are therefore best interpreted as lower limits of reliability. Test–retest estimates tend to fall somewhere in between these two extremes, depending on the appropriateness of the time interval that separates the two administrations of the test. Because it is so difficult to determine the proper interval for a test–retest estimate, however, Nunnally (1978) recommended avoiding that method for reliability estimation. He contended that "coefficient alpha provides a good estimate of reliability in most situations" (p. 230). As we indicated earlier, examination of the empirical literature (in the *Journal of Applied Psychology, Personnel Psychology,* and the *Academy of Management Journal,* for example) suggests that many researchers concur with Nunnally.

As we describe the following categories of factors that are known to influence reliability estimates, remember that more reliable measurements are those that predominantly reflect individuals' true scores on whatever construct is being measured and that are relatively free of random error. A good way to understand these factors is in terms of how they permit or preclude the influence of random error.

CHARACTERISTICS OF TESTS

First, we already know that increasing the number of items that a test consists of will increase the reliability of the scores, provided, of course, that all of the items assess the same thing. If, for example, Mr. Schiftner were interested in measuring a managerial candidate's spelling ability, he wouldn't ask her to spell only one or two words. After all, he might just happen to choose words (items) that the candidate just doesn't know. A person is not necessarily a poor speller just because she can't spell "chrysanthemum" correctly! He could be more confident that a candidate was a poor speller (has a low true score on spelling ability) if she misspelled 35 out of 40 words tested. In this case, the candidate probably had a much better opportunity to display her true spelling ability; and her low observed score (5 words correct) is less likely to be attributable to random error (word selection, loss of concentration, and so forth).

Two additional factors influence the relationship between test length and reliability. The first reflects a "law of diminishing returns." As more and more items are added to a test, the attendant increases in reliability grow smaller and smaller (Lemke & Wiersma, 1976). The second is really an extension of the first: If the test becomes so long that the people taking it grow bored or fatigued (or fall asleep!), the additional items will not add to the reliability of the observed scores.

Other test-related factors include the order in which relatively easy and difficult items are presented, the appropriateness of the test's overall level of difficulty, the diversity of the items' content, and the extent to which the items' format precludes or facilitates correct guessing in the absence of any relevant knowledge or skill. We will briefly discuss each of these factors.

Tests typically begin with relatively easy items, and then progress to more difficult items. This sequence allows those taking the test to "build up their confidence" before encountering the difficult items, and thereby increases the likelihood that their test performance will reflect their actual abilities (their true scores). If, on the other hand, they encounter difficult items at the very beginning of the test, they may become discouraged or anxious. Either of these emotional reactions may result in incorrect answers on later, easier test items—items that the individual could answer correctly when in a more "positive" frame of mind. In this way, the serial order of easy and difficult items can introduce random error into individuals' observed test scores.

Entire tests that are either much too easy or much too difficult for the people being examined also yield observed scores that will appear relatively unreliable. In each case, the distribution of observed scores tends to be highly skewed, and the variance is restricted; everyone does either very well or very poorly. Because reliability estimates depend on correlation coefficients, and because correlation coefficients reflect the related *variance* in two measures, such restricted variance serves to deflate the size of the computed reliability coefficient. Similarly, tests that are uniformly too easy or too difficult do not give individuals an opportunity to demonstrate their true scores on the constructs being measured.

Diversity of item content operates in a similar way. It does not matter that a test consists of many items, if every item addresses exactly the same thing. Imagine a "ten-question" arithmetic test that contains the following four items:

$$7 + 4 = ? \qquad \begin{array}{r} 7 \\ +4 \\ \hline ? \end{array} \qquad \begin{array}{r} 4 \\ +7 \\ \hline ? \end{array}$$

$$4 + 7 = ?$$

Would that really be a ten-item test, or would it be only a seven-item test? After all, four of the items measure the same "piece of knowledge," and anyone who answers one of these four items correctly (incorrectly) will probably answer the other three items correctly (incorrectly). You can see that individuals' observed scores will be influenced by this lack of item diversity, and this will undermine the reliability of those observed test scores. Additionally, circumstances such as this often deprive people of an adequate opportunity to demonstrate their true scores.

Finally, test items that make it easier for individuals to guess the correct answers in the absence of any relevant knowledge tend to yield less reliable observed scores, since correct guesses are nothing more than random error that inflates a person's observed score relative to his or her true score. True–false questions are most vulnerable to correct guessing, since the probability of answering any item correctly by chance alone is equal to .5. Multiple-choice tests with four or five alternative answers reduce the probability of correct guessing to .25 or .2, respectively (although people who are "test-wise" can often increase this probability, as we will explain momentarily). Questions that ask individuals to "fill in the blanks" reduce the likelihood of correct guesses even more, and therefore contribute to more reliable test scores. (Of course, the subjectivity of the "system" used to score such open-ended responses can undermine the reliability of those observed test scores.)

CHARACTERISTICS OF PEOPLE TAKING THE TEST

We have already alluded to one of these factors, the "test-wiseness" or prior test-taking experience of the individuals taking the test. This is perhaps most relevant for multiple-choice items. It is "common knowledge" among many test-wise students that the correct answer to a multiple-choice question is likely to be (1) alternative *b* or *c*, rather than either *a* or *d*; (2) the alternative that contains the largest number of words; (3) alternatives such as "all (none) of the above"; and so forth. Additionally, correct answers to later questions are often contained in earlier questions. Regardless of which of these pieces of common knowledge is operating, its effect (if it "works") is to reduce the reliability of observed test scores by introducing random error.

People's attitudes toward taking a test can also influence the reliability of their observed scores. Individuals who are highly motivated to perform well on a test will obtain scores that better reflect their true scores than will individuals who don't care whether they do well or not (assuming, of course, that they are not *so* highly motivated that they can't concentrate, or become distracted or overly anxious). As a rule, people's observed scores will usually be less reliable when they are ill than when they are feeling well. Those who take a test voluntarily may demonstrate their true scores more reliably than those who are forced to take the test (by a supervisor, for example).

A final factor in this category is the variance in the true scores of those individuals who take the test. As you might have predicted by now, a very homogeneous sample of test-takers will generate observed scores characterized by relatively little variance, which in turn will inhibit the size of any calculated reliability coefficient. By definition, heterogeneous samples will generate observed scores with greater variance, which will translate into larger reliability coefficients.

CHARACTERISTICS OF THE TESTING ENVIRONMENT

The environment or context in which people take a test can introduce random error into their observed scores. Physical surroundings that promote concentration tend to increase the reliability of observed test scores. These include relative quiet, comfortable temperature and humidity, enough illumination, absence of pollutants, and so forth. Those who administer and score the test can also contribute to reliability by creating the proper atmosphere, morale, and motivation among the test-takers, by providing instructions in a way that is understandable and consistent, and by scoring the test according to a more "objective" set of criteria.

Validity

As we stated earlier, reliability is a necessary psychometric property, but it isn't sufficient in itself to guarantee useful measurement. It isn't enough that a selection test measures some aspect of applicants' qualifications consistently; that test must measure the qualifications that the I/O psychologist (or manager, or whoever is making the selection decisions) *intends* to measure. Consistently measuring some irrelevant quality or characteristic of job applicants is of no use to anyone. Tests must measure whatever is intended to be measured if they are to play a useful role in the decision-making process. This property is known as validity.

Just as there are several ways to estimate the reliability of test scores, so too are there several ways to analyze the validity of measurements. Before describing them, however, we want to reemphasize a point that was clearly stated in the APA's *Standards for Educational and Psychological Testing* (1985) and in Division 14's *Principles for the Validation and Use of Personnel Selection Procedures* (APA, 1980). Lawshe (1985) put it well: "It is not tests which are valid or invalid, but, rather, inferences [that are drawn] from test scores" that are valid or invalid.

Suppose, for example, that Dr. MacKeven administers a "test of managerial motivation" to a group of prospective managers. Lawshe's point is that it is incorrect to refer to the validity or invalidity of those applicants' test scores. It is, instead, the *inferences* or the *conclusions* that Dr. MacKeven (or Mr. Schiftner, or whoever uses those test scores to make predictions about applicants' future job performance) draws on the basis of those test scores that are valid or invalid.

The distinction is important, since a validity-analysis strategy should be chosen according to the kind(s) of inferences one wishes to make, or conclusions one wishes to draw about job applicants on the basis of their test scores. Now let's take a look at several different kinds of inferences that Dr. MacKeven may wish to make on the basis of managerial applicants' test scores, and the different validity-analysis strategies that she may adopt.

CONTENT-VALIDITY ANALYSIS

Lawshe (1985) advocated this strategy when we wish to make inferences about "the extent to which a [job] candidate currently possesses (*a*) a relatively simple proficiency that is a component of the job or (*b*) knowledge required to perform the job (thus, to evaluate a present competence)." Content-validity analysis is "a logical procedure that determines the extent to which the behavior elicited by the test is the same as or similar to that required by the job or some portion of the job" (p. 237).

For example, drawing inferences about a typist's future job performance from scores obtained on a typing test can be supported on the basis of a content-validity analysis. In this case, the behavior required to do well on the test is extremely similar, if not identical, to the behavior required to perform well on the job. Unfortunately, the job of manager at Peter's Pan Pizza (or any other organization) entails behaviors that are far more abstract (planning, deciding, and so on) than typing or performing some other concrete, readily observable task. As a result, content-validity analysis is less likely to satisfy Dr. MacKeven's and Mr. Schiftner's needs than one or more of the other approaches to validity analysis (Sackett & Dreher, 1982, 1984).

As you may have inferred from Lawshe's (1985) description, content-validity analysis is usually a judgmental rather than a statistical procedure. Nevertheless, several quantitative approaches are available (Distephano, Pryer, & Erffmeyer, 1983; Faley & Sundstrom, 1985; Lawshe, 1975). An example of these is Lawshe's Content Validity Ratio (CVR) for a single test item:

$$CVR = (n_e - N/2)/(N/2), \text{ where}$$

n_e = the number of judges (usually job experts) who say that the knowledge or skill tested by an item is "essential" to job performance

N = the total number of judges queried

A Content Validity Index (CVI), which is computed for an entire test, is the average of the CVR values for all of the items that the test comprises. As you can see from the formula above, the CVR has a negative algebraic sign when fewer than half the judges say that the knowledge or skill tapped by a test item is essential to job performance. If more than half the judges say it is essential, the CVR has a positive sign; CVR = + 1.00 when *all* the judges say that a test item taps a knowledge or skill that is essential to job performance. Although it is less sophisticated than many of the statistics I/O psychologists use, the CVR does introduce some quantification into content-validity analysis.

Tenopyr (1977) and others suggested an important distinction between content validation and other forms of validity analysis. She claimed that content-validity analysis is more appropriate for making inferences about the *construction* of tests than for making inferences about the *meaning* of applicants' scores on those tests. The idea is that a test should be constructed in such a way that it includes all or a representative sample of all the behaviors that one is interested in assessing. In the context of personnel selection, those behaviors include the tasks that constitute the job for which the applicant is applying.

As you can see, the role of content-validity analysis in assessing the psychometric quality of personnel selection tests is a matter of some debate. Those who would apply the strategy only to an assessment of how well the content of a test samples the kinds of situations or behaviors being examined are opposed by those who think that content-validity analysis can address the validity of inferences, based on test scores, about subsequent job behaviors. What *does* seem clear is that those who would use content-validity analysis to legitimize predictions about applicants' subsequent job-performance levels should limit themselves to situations where both the behaviors on the test and the behaviors on the job are relatively simple and *directly observable*.

Since Dr. MacKeven must identify personnel selection tests that can discriminate between applicants who have the requisite knowledge, skills, and abilities to become competent managers and those who do not, and since most of that knowledge and those skills and abilities (planning, deciding, organizing, and so forth) are highly abstract and *not* directly observable, she might limit her use of content-validity analysis to making inferences about test construction. The quality of her inferences about applicants' future job performance, based on their test scores, may be better assessed using one or both of the other approaches to validity analysis: criterion-related or construct-validity analysis.

CRITERION-RELATED VALIDITY ANALYSIS

This approach is indicated "if the purpose is to infer how well a candidate will perform on the . . . job (thus, to predict future behavior). . . . We determine the mathematical relationship between test scores and some numerical index of job success" (Lawshe, 1985, p. 237). The emphasis here is squarely on prediction. The mathematical relationship between selection-test scores and a numerical index of job performance is usually expressed in the form of a correlation coefficient (r), which is referred to in this context as a validity coefficient.

Criterion-related validity analysis, then, requires at least two measures for each applicant: a selection-test score and a job-performance score. There are two different ways to obtain these scores. The first, known as "predictive-validity" analysis, involves obtaining test scores from *actual job applicants,* selecting some applicants for the available jobs according to some strategy that has nothing to do with their test scores[3], obtaining quantitative measures of job performance for those who are hired (after a reasonable time interval), and then calculating the validity coefficient that describes the relationship between these employees' selection-test scores and subsequent job-performance scores. The second strategy, known as "concurrent-validity" analysis, is much more convenient. In this case, the selection test being considered is administered to *current employees* (rather than to applicants); job-performance scores for those workers are simultaneously ("concurrently") obtained from their personnel files or from their supervisors, and the validity coefficient is calculated. Unfortunately, the convenience of this second strategy does not come without a price. More encouraging is the fact that these two approaches to criterion-related validity analysis have strengths and weaknesses that tend to complement each other.

The major strength of predictive-validity analysis is that it examines the validity of inferences under conditions that are very similar to those under which the selection test will actually be used. That is, selection-test scores are obtained from actual job applicants, who are genuinely interested in gaining employment, and those scores are then examined at a later time to determine how well they predict hired applicants' job performance. If the applicants who were hired were indeed selected in a way that had nothing to do with their obtained selection-test scores, we can reasonably expect to find some variance in those selection-test scores. That is, there should be little or no restriction in the range of the selection-test scores that are used to calculate the validity coefficient. Such restrictions, if they are present, tend to limit the magnitude of the calculated validity coefficient.

Unfortunately, predictive-validity analysis suffers from two major flaws. First, not many employers are willing to take the trouble to administer a selection test to applicants and then *ignore* those applicants' scores when making their hiring decisions. Second, this approach to assessing criterion-related validity takes time. After some of the applicants are hired, a time interval that is long enough to allow the new employees to learn their jobs and to demonstrate their abilities must be permitted to elapse (the criterion should be a relatively distal one). Because of these two drawbacks, many managers and I/O psychologists rely on the second approach to criterion-related validity analysis, concurrent analysis.

Unlike the predictive approach, concurrent-validity analysis entails no lengthy time interval. Job incumbents complete the selection test being considered for use at the very same time that measures of their job performance are obtained or extracted from their records. A second reason that the concurrent approach is usually more acceptable to managers and executives is that it does not require them to ignore anybody's test score. You have, however, probably deduced some of the costs associated with this convenience and acceptability.

[3]Usually an organization will continue to rely on whatever selection instruments or procedures are currently in use while the criterion-related validity of a new instrument is being studied.

The primary drawback of the concurrent approach is that the people who generate scores on the selection test under investigation, and whose job performance is concurrently assessed, may not be very representative of the population of people from which actual job applicants will emerge. These job incumbents have already been selected in one way or another, and have already gained certain levels of experience in their respective jobs. If the strategy used to select them was in any way related to their scores on the selection test under investigation, the range of their scores on the "new" selection test will be restricted, as we described above. People who would have scored low on the test under consideration would not have been hired, and would therefore not be available to participate in the concurrent-validity analysis. Further, incumbents' job experience may somehow influence their scores on the selection test under consideration. Because actual job applicants would not have the benefit of such experience, the concurrent-analysis results may not generalize to the applicant population.

As you may have guessed, the use of predictive- versus concurrent-validity analysis has generated some debate among I/O psychologists. Barrett, Phillips, and Alexander (1981) claimed that the conceptual distinction between predictive and concurrent approaches has been exaggerated, and that any differences have a minimal impact on the magnitude of the validity coefficient. Similarly, Kleiman and Faley (1985) affirmed that "well conducted concurrent studies can provide useful estimates of predictive validity" (p. 817). Guion and Cranny (1982), however, appealed to both conceptual and practical considerations in their assertion that the different validity designs are neither equivalent nor interchangeable.

We should point out that the problem of range restriction inherent in the concurrent approach is not an insurmountable one. Many researchers have described and advocated statistical corrections for the effects of range restriction on a validity coefficient (Lee, Miller, & Graham, 1982; Linn, Harnisch, & Dunbar, 1981; Olson & Becker, 1983; Sackett, & Wade, 1983). Nevertheless, in her review of criterion-related validity studies published in the *Journal of Applied Psychology* and *Personnel Psychology* between 1960 and 1979, Boehm (1982) reported a (statistically nonsignificant) tendency for I/O psychologists to use predictive designs.

Boehm's (1982) review of published criterion-related validity analyses also revealed the following trends:

- a significant *decrease* in the number of articles that even report the results of validity studies
- those that are published tend to focus on individuals and jobs at higher occupational and organizational levels, such as managerial and professional positions
- the sizes of reported validity coefficients are not very impressive (the mean of the validity coefficients from 176 studies was only $r = +.219$), and their magnitude has not changed much over the years

Schmitt, Gooding, Noe, and Kirsch's (1984) meta-analytic review of 99 criterion-related validity studies published in the same two journals between 1964 and 1982 corroborated Boehm's findings; they reported an average overall validity of only $r = +.28$.

These relatively small validity coefficients, which indicate that selection-test scores are explaining only 4 to 6 percent of the variance in workers' job-performance scores, have prompted a number of researchers to investigate alternative strategies for assessing criterion-related validity. These include validity generalization, synthetic-validity analysis, and the use of moderator and suppressor variables, all of which are discussed in Chapter 6.

Dr. MacKeven will most likely have to rely on some form of criterion-related validity analysis as she responds to Mr. Schiftner's request for help in selecting men and women who will succeed as managers in Peter's Pan Pizza, Inc. Fortunately, she may not find herself in the position of having to choose between the predictive and concurrent approaches to empirical validity analysis; she may be able to use both. Specifically, she may be able to administer whatever selection tests or devices she considers appropriate to *all* (or a representative sample of all) nonmanagerial employees, and then wait until a sufficient number of them have been promoted "from within the ranks," and assess their subsequent job-performance scores. Naturally, this will take some time. In the meantime, she can administer the selection tests to be validated to men and women who currently hold managerial positions in PPP's hierarchy, and concurrently obtain these managers' job-performance scores. In any case, there can be little doubt that Dr. MacKeven will rely on criterion-related validity analysis to investigate the predictive power of the inferences she makes about people's success as managers, based on their scores on one or more selection tests.

CONSTRUCT-VALIDITY ANALYSIS

A third approach is indicated "if we wish to infer the degree to which the candidate currently possesses a trait or other characteristic . . . critical to job performance." Construct-validity analysis "must demonstrate that the attribute (*a*) is required by or inherent in the job and (*b*) is measured by the . . . test" (Lawshe, 1985, p. 237)

The apparent similarity between construct- and content-validity analyses has led to some confusion (Tenopyr, 1977). The key to understanding the distinction lies in the nature of the variable that we are trying to measure. Construct-validity analysis is appropriate when we wish to assess *hypothetical* or *abstract traits* or *psychological constructs* that are believed to underlie more concrete, observable forms of behavior. Intelligence and motivation are two "everyday" examples of constructs that help us to explain a wide variety of work-related behaviors. Content-validity analysis, on the other hand, is appropriate if we wish to assess relatively *simple skills* or knowledge necessary for satisfactory job performance. Typing skills and knowledge of word-processing procedures are two examples of skills or knowledge that can be more-or-less directly observed and understood, without appealing to abstract, hypothetical, and unobservable constructs or traits.

We do not mean to imply, of course, that psychological constructs are completely irrelevant to typing skills. Tenopyr (1977) correctly asserted that *all* inferences about test scores or any other behavior are ultimately based on one or more underlying constructs. Typing skills and performance are certainly influenced by manual dexterity, by visual acuity, and by intelligence and motivation, all of which can be thought of as constructs. The point is, however, that we do not *need* to appeal to these abstractions in order to see how performance on a typing test is relevant to ultimate performance as a typist, and so content-validity analysis is usually deemed sufficient. Making inferences about the relevance of performance on intelligence or motivation tests for understanding a person's performance as a manager, however, requires a much greater "logical leap"; construct-validity analysis aids us in making that leap.

There are a variety of ways to conduct a construct-validity analysis. Our review of recent literature turned up four different approaches: (1) constructing a nomological network (Friedman, 1983; Kopelman, Greenhaus, & Connolly, 1983); (2) examining a multitrait–multimethod matrix (Campbell & Fiske, 1959; Neidig & Neidig, 1984); (3) performing a **factor analysis** (Neidig & Neidig, 1984; Sackett & Dreher, 1982); and (4) relying on latent trait theories (Maxwell & Delaney, 1985). Embretson (Whitely) (1983) described an approach to construct-validity analysis that she called "construct modeling"; it incorporates both a nomological network and an attempt to identify theoretical mechanisms such as information-processing strategies that underlie a person's item responses. Because nomological networks and multitrait–multimethod matrices tend to be the more common approaches to construct-validity analysis, we will describe these in a bit more detail. We will also acquaint you with latent trait theory, since it is currently generating some interest in the literature.

A nomological network is a "fabric" of empirical, statistical relationships between individuals' scores on the test being investigated and their scores on other variables. Based on our conceptual definition of the construct we are trying to measure (intelligence, for example), we can predict how people who score high or low on our "intelligence" test *should* perform on certain other tests or tasks. We might expect, for instance, that people who obtain high scores on our (so-called) intelligence test should also (1) earn higher grades in school, (2) read more books during a specified time interval (say, one year), (3) score higher on other tests that are *known* to measure intelligence (such as the Wechsler or Stanford–Binet tests), and (4) be first-born or "only" children. Each of these predictions is based either on common sense or on the results of considerable amounts of empirical research.

In order to use the nomological-network approach to construct-validity analysis, we must obtain scores on the test being considered (our "intelligence" test) from a given sample of people, as well as their scores on the other variables involved in the predicted relationships described above. If the correlation coefficients between scores on our "intelligence" test and each of the other variables are in the predicted directions, we will have established a nomological network that supports the construct validity of the test under investigation. That is, if people who score higher on our test *do* earn higher grades, *do* read more books, *do* score higher on other well-known intelligence tests, and *do* tend to be first-born or only children, we will have reason to believe that all these measures are tapping the same underlying construct (intelligence). Alternatively, if any one or more of these correlations is in a direction opposite to that which we predicted, or is not significantly different from zero (0), we would have reason to doubt that our test actually measures the construct we intended it to measure. Examples of two nomological networks, one that supports the construct validity of scores obtained on our "intelligence" test and one that fails to provide such support, are depicted in Figure 5.1.

The multitrait–multimethod approach to construct validity can be thought of as an extension of a nomological network. It is an attempt to demonstrate not only that test scores correlate highly with other variables with which they *should* theoretically correlate, but also that the test scores do *not* correlate significantly with variables from which they should *differ.* Campbell and Fiske (1959) referred to the first of these conditions as convergent validity, and to the second as discriminant validity.

An example of a multitrait–multimethod matrix appears in Figure 5.2. Such a matrix contains the correlations between scores obtained on three ostensibly different variables, traits, or constructs (A = intelligence, B = motivation, and C = manual dexterity, for example), each of which has been measured in three different ways (Method 1 = supervisor's rating, Method 2 = peer's rating, and Method 3 = self-rating, for example; Lawler, 1967).

The three diagonals of boldface numbers reflect convergent validity; these are correlations between particular traits or constructs measured in different ways (monotrait–heteromethod correlations). The correlations in the solid triangles reflect the relationships between different traits or constructs measured using the same method (heterotrait–monomethod correlations). Those in the "broken" triangles reflect the relationships between different traits or constructs measured using different methods (heterotrait–heteromethod correlations). These latter two groups of correlations speak to discriminant validity. The correlations in parentheses along the main diagonal of the matrix are reliability coefficients (monotrait–monomethod correlations).

Evidence of satisfactory construct validity consists of convergent-validity coefficients that are larger than the correlations (in the triangles) that reflect discriminant validity. That is, we can be more confident that we are measuring a given construct when the correlation between two different measures of that construct exceeds the correlations between two different constructs measured in either the same way or in different ways. As you can see, the evidence in Figure 5.2 is somewhat mixed.

---

factor analysis: a complex statistical procedure used to reduce a large number of variables to a smaller, more manageable number, by identifying more basic constructs or patterns of correlations that underlie those variables

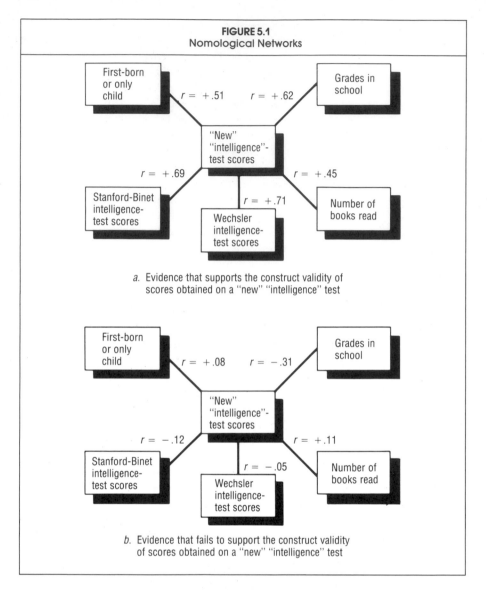

FIGURE 5.1
Nomological Networks

a. Evidence that supports the construct validity of scores obtained on a "new" "intelligence" test

b. Evidence that fails to support the construct validity of scores obtained on a "new" "intelligence" test

While the (boldfaced) convergent-validity coefficients are uniformly larger than the correlations between different traits measured by different methods (in broken triangles), they are not consistently or notably larger than the correlations between different traits measured by the same method (in the solid triangles). These data, then, suggest *some* construct validity, but also a troubling level of "common-method variance," where a given method of measurement fails to distinguish between ostensibly different constructs or traits.

Latent trait theory is sometimes referred to as Item Response Theory (IRT) because it is capable of addressing whatever is measured *by individual test items*, as well as what is measured by tests in their entirety (Maxwell & Delaney, 1985).

FIGURE 5.2
Hypothetical Multitrait–Multimethod Matrix

Traits	Method 1			Method 2			Method 3		
	A_1	B_1	C_1	A_2	B_2	C_2	A_3	B_3	C_3
Method 1 A_1	(.89)								
B_1	.51	(.89)							
C_1	.38	.37	(.76)						
Method 2 A_2	**.57**	.22	.09	(.93)					
B_2	.22	**.57**	.10	.68	(.94)				
C_2	.11	.11	**.46**	.59	.58	(.84)			
Method 3 A_3	**.56**	.22	.11	**.67**	.42	.33	(.94)		
B_3	.23	**.58**	.12	.43	**.66**	.34	.67	(.92)	
C_3	.11	.11	**.45**	.34	.32	**.58**	.58	.60	(.85)

Note. Letters *A, B, C* refer to traits, subscripts 1, 2, 3 to methods. Validity coefficients (monotrait–heteromethod) are the three diagonal sets of boldface numbers; reliability coefficients (monotrait–monomethod) are the numbers in parentheses along principal diagonals. Solid triangles enclose heterotrait–monomethod correlations; broken triangles enclose heterotrait–heteromethod correlations.

SOURCE: "Convergent and Discriminant Validation by the Multitrait–Multimethod Matrix," by D. T. Campbell and D. W. Fiske, *Psychological Bulletin*, 1959, *56,* 81–105. Copyright 1959 by the American Psychological Association. Reprinted by permission.

Although there are a number of such theories, they all "share a common perspective, [in that] they assume that the probability of an observable response or behavior [on a test] is related to the individual's standing on an underlying latent characteristic [or construct]" (Hulin, Drasgow, & Parsons, 1983, p. 14).

Guion and Ironson (1983) described some of the problems associated with classical psychological measurement theory. These include dependence on specific samples of subjects, difficulties associated with obtaining equivalent or parallel test forms, and lack of concern with *patterns* of item responses on a given test (after all, the same observed test score can be obtained in a variety of different ways). They then described some of the basic theoretical concepts, as well as several computer programs, that are available to I/O psychologists who wish to use the latent trait approach to determine what particular tests (and test items) are measuring. Although these authors also acknowledged some of the drawbacks to latent trait analysis (including the need for larger samples, increased cost and complexity, and inappropriateness in a number of situations), they concluded that it "has enough advantages over classical psychometric theory to make it worth considering . . . as a promising addition to the repertoire of measurement methods in [I/O] psychology" (p. 84).

Given the important role of construct validity in the measurement process, we certainly agree that latent trait theory (or IRT) is worthy of very serious consideration, as well as careful empirical and theoretical evaluation. Only time will tell whether these more complex, item-specific approaches to construct validity will replace or supplement those based on classical psychometric assumptions, or whether they will be relegated to the pages of esoteric journals and psychometric texts.

Dr. MacKeven's need to conduct a construct-validity analysis will depend on the nature of the selection test(s) she identifies in her efforts to respond to Mr. Schiftner's memo. If she chooses well-known, widely used tests, the construct validity of which is already well established, it will probably be unnecessary for her to repeat those analyses and "reinvent the wheel." On the other hand, if she decides to develop new tests to satisfy the director of management selection, there will be a greater need for construct-validity analyses. Criterion-related validity analysis of new tests in the absence of construct-validity analysis leaves one open to the charge of "dustbowl empiricism," or documenting relationships between and among variables without any understanding of the nature (the "hows" and "whys") of those relationships.

SUMMARY

If a personnel selection test or device is to be useful, it must generate scores that are reliable, and from which valid inferences can be made. Just as there are several ways to assess reliability, so too are there several ways to assess validity. If we wish to make inferences about the items that make up a test, or about relatively simple and directly observable skills or behaviors that are obviously important to successful job performance, then content-validity analysis may be appropriate. If we wish to predict applicants' future behaviors on the job (in the event that they are hired), then criterion-related validity analysis is appropriate. Finally, if we wish to make inferences about relatively complex and abstract psychological constructs (or latent traits) that are critical to job performance, then construct-validity analysis is necessary.

Now that you know about the important psychometric properties of any personnel selection instrument, we can turn our attention to the variety of measures and procedures that have been used to make decisions about whether or not individual women and men should be selected for particular jobs. Up to this point, we have generically referred to selection "tests." Some of the selection instruments available to Dr. MacKeven, however, bear little or no resemblance to traditional paper–and–pencil tests. Nevertheless, their psychometric properties are no less important. During our discussion of a variety of these selection instruments in the second half of this chapter, we will present some evidence of their reliability and validity (or lack thereof), and we will assess each one's potential usefulness to Dr. MacKeven as she strives to create a system for selecting successful managers for Peter's Pan Pizza, Inc.

PERSONNEL-SELECTION PROCEDURES

As we have already implied, Dr. MacKeven will be able to choose from among a wide variety of personnel selection procedures and instruments. These include traditional paper–and–pencil tests, a variety of performance tests (work samples, situational exercises), application blanks, interviews, letters of recommendation, performance appraisals (especially peer assessments), and formal assessment centers. You've probably had some first-hand experience with one or more of these.

Paper–and–Pencil Tests

There are literally hundreds of different kinds of paper–and–pencil tests that have been used to generate potentially useful information about job applicants for making personnel selection decisions. One scheme for categorizing these tests focuses on whether the test can be administered to a group of people all at the same time ("group" tests), or whether it must be administered to one person at a time ("individual" tests; Kaplan & Saccuzzo, 1982). A second distinction is between "speed" tests and "power" tests. We have discussed these distinctions in earlier sections of this textbook.

If we look instead at test content, or the variables or constructs that different paper–and–pencil tests are designed to measure, the diversity of available tests becomes apparent. Guion (1965b) used the following taxonomy: (1) measures of general intellectual ability, (2) measures of specific intellectual abilities, (3) measures of motivational variables, and (4) measures of personality variables. We shall adopt his taxonomy as we describe some of these measures for you.

INTELLIGENCE TESTS

General intelligence measures include the Wechsler Adult Intelligence Scale—Revised, the Wonderlic Personnel Test, the Miller Analogies Test (which is required for admission to some graduate programs), as well as some nonverbal tests. Ghiselli and Brown (1955) concluded that these general intelligence tests tend to be better predictors of performance in training programs than performance on the job. They also suggested that such tests are especially appropriate for selecting managerial and sales personnel. (They reported an average validity coefficient for managerial proficiency of $r = +.37$.)

Schmidt and Hunter's (1977) more recent discussions of validity generalization (which we consider in Chapter 6) suggest that .37 is an underestimate of the true average validity coefficient. Hunter and Hunter's (1984) meta-analysis led them to conclude that if "general cognitive ability alone is used as a predictor, the average validity *across all jobs* [italics added] is .54 for a training success criterion and .45 for a job proficiency criterion" (p. 81). Although the precise magnitude of validity coefficients based on measures of general intellectual ability is open to debate, the available evidence strongly suggests that such measures are potentially useful, especially in situations such as Dr. MacKeven's, where one is interested in predicting job performance as a manager.

More specific measures of intellectual ability include tests of clerical aptitude, spatial relations, creativity, and judgment. Multi-attribute test batteries such as the Differential Aptitude Test (DAT), which assesses verbal reasoning, numerical ability, abstract reasoning, space relations, mechanical reasoning, and clerical speed and accuracy, and the General Aptitude Test Battery (GATB), developed by the United States Employment Service, yield measures on a variety of specific cognitive skills. If the specific intellectual abilities assessed are congruent with the requirements of the job(s) in question, the encouraging conclusions about tests of general cognitive ability may also apply to these more specific measures.

MOTIVATION TESTS

Among the motivational measures that may be particularly useful to Dr. MacKeven are those designed to assess people's desire to manage the activities of others. Miner and his colleagues have demonstrated the validity of the Miner Sentence Completion Scale for identifying individuals who eventually attain higher levels of responsibility and authority within organizational hierarchies (Berman & Miner, 1985). He has also used his approach to examine managerial potential among minorities, especially blacks, and among women (Miner, 1977a). Gough (1984) developed a Managerial Potential Scale for the California Psychological Inventory (CPI) that significantly predicted performance ratings for 143 military officers ($r = +.20$).

McClelland and others have extended the original work on achievement, affiliation, and power motivation (McClelland, Atkinson, Clark, & Lowell, 1953; Atkinson, 1958). McClelland and Boyatzis' (1982) study of 237 managers revealed that those (in nontechnical managerial positions) who were characterized by the "leadership motive pattern" (LMP) obtained higher levels of promotion after 8 and 16 years than did those with different patterns of motives. The LMP did *not* predict performance for technical managers with engineering responsibilities, however. Cornelius and Lane (1984) reported similar results, based on their study of people who managed second-language instruction centers. Although LMP predicted managerial success for those with broader supervisory responsibilities, it was not a valid predictor for those with more specific (administrative and public relations) responsibilities. Interestingly, the LMP in both of these studies involved moderate–to–high need for power, and low need for affiliation, but it did not depend on need for achievement.

Stahl (1983), however, reported somewhat different results. He operationalized high managerial motivation as high scores on both need for power and need for achievement, and found that "those who scored high in managerial motivation had higher managerial performance than others, had a higher managerial promotion rate than others, [and] . . . were more likely to be managers than blue collar workers" (p. 775). Although the exact nature of the motive pattern or patterns that predict successful managerial performance is still open to question, it seems clear that motivation scores obtained from certain paper–and–pencil procedures hold some promise as valid predictors of managerial performance.

Other motivational measures include a number of interest inventories, such as the Strong–Campbell Interest Inventory and the Kuder Occupational Interest Survey. Although these measures may have some value for predicting the kinds of occupations people eventually pursue, and the amount of satisfaction they experience in those occupations, they were not intended to predict level of job performance or success. Because their primary usefulness lies in the area of career counseling, we will not discuss them any further here.

PERSONALITY TESTS

This group of measures includes the Minnesota Multiphasic Personality Inventory (MMPI), which was designed to assess certain psychopathologies (and has recently been revised); the CPI, which focuses on "normal" behavior, and which Gough (1984) used to develop his Managerial Potential Scale; and various instruments designed to measure temperament, values, and other assorted personality factors. Guion's (1965b) summary of the validity of these measures was not very enthusiastic: They "have generally been developed for clinical and counseling purposes rather than selection, they are too subjective, and the evidence of their value is too weak" (p. 352). More recent research has failed to overrule this general conclusion.

Nevertheless, research in this area continues. Johnson, Messé, and Crano (1984) developed the Work Opinion Questionnaire to predict job performance among low-income workers. Gough (1985) has now developed a Work Orientation Scale for the CPI, which assesses self-discipline, dedication to obligations, and adherence to rules. Hogan, Hogan, and Busch (1984) have examined a measure of service orientation, which refers to a disposition to be helpful, thoughtful, considerate, and cooperative. And Drory (1982) has even come up with a measure of truck drivers' proneness to boredom. Although it is much too soon to be optimistic, especially considering the unimpressive history of personality measures as predictors of job performance, these authors were moderately hopeful that their measures may someday contribute to the personnel selection process.

Sackett and Harris (1984) reviewed the research on paper–and–pencil measures of honesty (operationalized as the absence of employee theft in the workplace), and concluded that "compelling evidence of the validity of honesty tests has yet to be produced" (p. 241). Keinan, Friedland, Yitzhaky, and Moran (1981) reported that their personality tests added nothing to the prediction of performance. At best, then, the status of paper–and–pencil personality tests as predictors of job performance seems to be questionable.

SUMMARY

Based on the available research evidence, Dr. MacKeven would probably be wise to limit the use of paper–and–pencil tests for predicting managerial success to certain measures of intelligence, and to certain instruments specifically designed to assess individuals' motivation to manage others. Complete updates on most of these potentially useful tests are available in Oscar K. Buros' exhaustive reference books *Tests in Print II* (1974) and *The Eighth Mental*

Measurements Yearbook (1978). Fortunately, Dr. MacKeven has several other personnel selection procedures at her disposal.

Biographical Information

Biographical information, or what we will refer to as "biodata," includes demographic data and information about a person's past life and work experiences. Demographic data include such things as age, sex, race, amount of formal education, and marital status. Experiential data include information about how many and what kinds of jobs an individual has had, how one spends one's leisure hours, whether one has served in the military, and so forth. Most organizations collect biodata by asking job applicants to complete an application blank, and/or to submit resumés describing their backgrounds and their relevant work experiences. Some biographical information that is particularly sensitive in the context of the EEOC's guidelines (race, religious preference, number of children, etc.) might not be solicited until after individuals have been hired (see Chapter 6). If such information *is* collected prior to the hiring decision, the organization must not use it to make that decision; in fact, the organization should do everything reasonable and prudent to avoid even *giving the appearance* of using such information as a basis for hiring some applicants and rejecting others.

Most major reviews and discussions in the literature have been encouraging about the reliability and validity of biodata for predicting job performance (Hakel, 1986; Owens, 1976; Tenopyr & Oeltjen, 1982; Zedeck & Cascio, 1984). Hunter and Hunter (1984), in their review of alternative predictors of job performance, described reviews by Dunnette (1972) and by Reilly and Chao (1982) indicating that *only biodata* yield validity coefficients ($r = +.34$ and $+.38$, respectively) that are high enough to compare with those associated with ability (intelligence) tests. Vineberg and Joyner's (1982) review of military studies also endorsed biodata as valid predictors of job performance, although they reported validity coefficients ranging only from $r = +.20$ to $+.29$.

Hunter and Hunter (1984) did caution, however, that the validity of biodata, when used to make actual performance predictions, may be lower than the validity reported in research journals, for a variety of reasons. For one thing, the scoring keys used to transform application-blank information into biodata tend to be highly specific to particular organizations, and to specific criterion measures within those organizations. Meritt-Haston and Wexley (1983), in their review of the validity and legality of educational job requirements, concurred with the latter reservation: Validity "evidence suggests . . . a moderate relationship between educational achievements and job performance but the results vary depending on how job performance is measured" (p. 750). They reported average validity coefficients of $r = +.27$, $+.23$, and $+.15$, for criteria of tenure, promotions, and performance ratings, respectively.

Biodata keys also tend to become less valid over time (Davis, 1984; Eberhardt & Muchinsky, 1984). Further, the empirical process of developing scoring keys is vulnerable to "mass capitalization on chance," or random errors, because of the relatively small sample sizes typically used in such research (Hunter & Hunter, 1984). Mitchell and Klimoski (1982), who used an empirically based scoring system, reported a significant amount of "shrinkage" in the size of the validity coefficients they obtained after removing the influence of chance or random error. Nevertheless, those validity coefficients remained significantly greater than similar coefficients based on a more "rational" scoring key.[4]

Hough (1984) and some of her colleagues (Hough, Keys, & Dunnette, 1983; Pannone, 1984) have applied the principle of behavioral consistency ("the best predictor of future behavior is relevant past behavior") to soliciting and scoring experiential data. Her "accomplishment-record method" yields self-reports of accomplishments that pertain to very relevant, behavioral job dimensions. These reports can be reliably rated ($r = .82$); they appear to be unrelated to traditional psychological measures such as aptitude tests, grades, honors, and so forth; but they do correlate ($r = .25$) with measures of job performance. Hough's (1984) study of 329 attorneys suggested that the accomplishment-record method is fair, and that it predicts performance equally well for minorities and nonminorities and for men and women.

Hough et al. (1983) pointed out that the accomplishment record "capture[s], in an objectively scorable way, the types of information usually gathered and interpreted via more subjective personnel procedures such as application blanks (background information), interviews (interests, opinions, and previous accomplishments), and reference checks (accomplishments)" (p. 274). They also stressed that applicants' accomplishment records can only be scored and interpreted meaningfully in the context of a complete and accurate job analysis (see Chapter 3). Finally, and of particular interest to Dr. MacKeven as she addresses herself to Mr. Schiftner's memo, these authors recognized that this method "also possesses merit as a means of systematically and objectively evaluating the professional accomplishments of employment candidates who have worked in other organizations since obtaining their professional training" (p. 275).

One of Heilman's (1984) recent studies led her to conclude that highly relevant job information, such as the data that can be obtained via the accomplishment-record method of biodata collection, can weaken the damaging effects of negative stereotypical attributes commonly ascribed to female job applicants. Thus, this approach may help to reduce sex discrimination during the personnel selection process.

SUMMARY

Biodata are vulnerable to a number of scoring-related problems (Hunter & Hunter, 1984), as well as to "inflation bias," where applicants fraudulently claim to have observed or performed actual or bogus job-related tasks (Anderson, Warner, & Spencer, 1984). Further, some recent studies of biodata have either failed to confirm their validity, or demonstrated only weak relationships between certain pieces of biodata and job-performance criteria (Turnage & Muchinsky, 1984; Wakabayashi & Graen, 1984; Wells & Muchinsky, 1985). Nevertheless,

[4]A "rational" scoring key is one in which specific pieces of biographical information are used to predict performance criteria based on logic, theory, or "common sense." An "empirically based" scoring key is one in which specific pieces of information are assigned predictive value solely on the basis of their demonstrated ability to predict performance criteria for a specific sample of individuals.

most reviewers have pointed to the relative superiority of biodata for predicting subsequent job performance. Recent work with the accomplishment-record method for assessing and evaluating biodata has tended to support these reviewers' conclusions.[5]

It would therefore seem to be highly appropriate for Dr. MacKeven to consider supplementing applicants' scores on ability and motivation tests with scores derived from biodata, especially scores based on the accomplishment-record method for collecting and evaluating experiential biodata. A third major personnel selection procedure that merits our I/O psychologist's attention is the personal interview, which we shall examine now.

Interviews

Interviews can take a variety of forms, but they all share one thing in common. They constitute an opportunity for a job applicant and an organizational representative to interact face–to–face. You have probably participated in one or more interviews already. You may realize, therefore, that these personal encounters can be either informative or uninformative, comfortable or anxiety-provoking, useful or useless, depending on how the interview is conducted and the goals that the organization tries to accomplish through this personnel selection procedure.

As we just implied, there are several different ways to conduct a selection interview. Probably the most basic distinction is that between structured and unstructured interviews. A structured interview is one where the interviewer asks the applicant a preplanned series of questions. Because all applicants are asked to respond to the same basic set of questions, the interviewer (and the organization) can make direct comparisons between different applicants' responses, and thereby arrive at a more informed decision about whom to hire. Unstructured interviews, the kind that you have probably experienced, are more freewheeling affairs, where the interviewer asks whatever questions come to mind. Because there is no guarantee that all applicants will be asked to respond to the same questions, the interviewer is usually put in the uncomfortable position of having to "compare apples and oranges" when it comes to making selection decisions.

As you may have already surmised, structured interviews lend themselves much more readily to the validation process. With a known, foreordained content, structured interviews more closely resemble paper–and–pencil tests, in that all applicants respond to the same set of questions. The validity of interviewers' inferences, based on applicants' responses to particular questions (items), can be determined by any of the three validity analyses discussed earlier in this chapter.

Unstructured interviews, however, present a more formidable challenge to the validation process. Because there is no set content, content-validity analysis

---

[5]Although the behavioral-consistency method did not emerge as superior to other methods for evaluating training and experience in Ash and Levine's (1985) recent comparative study, their "quasi-validity" coefficients were based on peer nominations of who would make the best supervisors if promoted, rather than on actual, more traditional job-performance criteria.

is out of the question. Because different applicants respond to different questions in a more–or–less random and unpredictable order, unstructured interviews typically do not yield the kind of data required for reliability analyses, or for criterion-related or construct-validity analyses. About the only piece of data that can be analyzed is the interviewer's overall prediction about the ultimate job success of each applicant. Although there is no question that some interviewers are able to consistently make more valid predictions than others (Landy, 1976; Zedeck, Tziner, & Middlestadt, 1983), even those relatively valid predictions will have a rather "hollow ring" to them, since the content and substance that contribute to them are variable, and remain essentially unknown and undocumented.

Recent comparisons of unstructured interviews and a specific kind of structured interview, the patterned behavior-description interview, have illustrated the superiority of this structured approach. Based on critical incidents that "suggest specific occasions in the applicant's experiences that are predictive of future job behavior" (Orpen, 1985, p. 774), these structured interviews have generated valid predictions of both dollar value of sales and supervisors' ratings of life insurance salesmen. Earlier, Janz (1982) reported similar findings for teaching assistants. The validity of patterned interviews for predicting students' ratings of teaching assistants' performance was .54; the corresponding coefficient for unstructured interviews was .07. Interestingly, Orpen's data revealed no differences in test–retest reliability between the structured and the unstructured interviews ($r \doteq .70$ for both), while Janz' structured-interview data were *less* reliable than the unstructured data ($r = .46$ and .71, respectively).

Other ways in which interviews can be classified depend on the number of interviewers and the amount of stress that is intentionally created during the interview session. Many organizations have two or more interviewers present for each session (see Landy, 1976, for example). Sometimes either a single interviewer or the multiple interviewers purposely try to make an applicant anxious by creating a stressful interview environment. Such "stress interviews" can occasionally be justified through a content-validity analysis, when the job in question necessarily involves high levels of interpersonal stress (such as the job of a municipal police patrol officer).

PUBLISHED LITERATURE REVIEWS

Published reviews of empirical research on the selection interview have appeared periodically in the professional literature. Most of them are not encouraging with respect to the reliability or the validity of this personnel selection procedure. In the first comprehensive review of this literature, Wagner (1949) reported a median reliability coefficient of .27. He encouraged the use of patterned or structured interviews, and recommended that the information collected through interviews be combined in statistical rather than in "clinical" or subjective ways.

Mayfield (1964) reviewed the literature published after Wagner's (1949) commentary, and reported that interview research was still generating relatively low reliability and validity coefficients. He concurred with his predecessor in advocating the structured-interview format. Ulrich and Trumbo's (1965) review, published only six months later, reinforced Mayfield's conclusions. In addition, these reviewers recommended that the interview should concentrate on assessing applicants' interpersonal-relations skills and their levels of work motivation, and leave the assessment of other traits and skills to other, more appropriate selection instruments.

Wright (1969) and Schmitt (1976) reviewed research that investigated the decision-making processes inherent in the selection interview. As summarized by Arvey and Campion (1982), Wright and Schmitt arrived at the following conclusions:

1. Interviewers make their final decision about an applicant early in the interview session, often within the first four minutes.
2. Interviewers are more influenced by negative information about an applicant than by positive or flattering information.
3. Interviewers often have stereotypes of "the ideal successful job applicant," against which actual applicants are compared.
4. Interviewers make better (more reliable) decisions when they are better informed about the nature of the job(s) to be filled.
5. Interviewers differ in the ways they interpret pieces of information, and in the ways they use that information in making final decisions about applicants.
6. Interviewers use nonverbal as well as verbal cues in arriving at decisions about applicants.
7. The race and gender of both the interviewer and the applicant can influence the interviewer's decision.
8. Less experienced interviewers tend to be vulnerable to a "contrast effect," whereby an "average" applicant will be evaluated inordinately high or low if the person interviewed immediately before was unusually unqualified or unusually qualified, respectively.
9. Structured interviews are superior to unstructured interviews.

SOURCE: Adapted from "The Employment Interview: A Summary and Review of Recent Research," by R. D. Arvey and J. E. Campion, *Personnel Psychology*, 1982, 35, 281–322. Copyright 1982 by Personnel Psychology, Inc. Reprinted by permission.

Arvey and Campion's own generalizations, extracted from more recent research, are presented next:

1. Panel interviews may improve the reliability and validity of interview data.
2. Interview questions should be derived directly from job analyses or from other appropriate job-related information.
3. More recent studies are more methodologically sophisticated in their attempts to reproduce more realistic stimulus and response conditions.
4. Interviewers are still influenced by contrast effects and by primacy and recency effects, where information that emerges very early or very late in the interview, respectively, makes a greater impression than information that emerges "in the middle" of the interview; they are also influenced by first impressions and by personal feelings and biases.

5. Applicants' nonverbal behaviors (gestures, eye contact, and so on) affect interviewers' decisions.

SOURCE: Adapted from "The Employment Interview: A Summary and Review of Recent Research," by R. D. Arvey and J. E. Campion, *Personnel Psychology,* 1982, *35,* 281–322. Copyright 1982 by Personnel Psychology, Inc. Reprinted by permission.

In an earlier review, Arvey (1979) focused on the role of various biases in the employment interview. These included prejudices based on race, sex, age, and physical handicap. His conclusions are presented here:

1. Women are usually evaluated less favorably than equally qualified men, especially if the job in question is a traditionally "masculine" one (such as manager, for example).
2. There is little evidence that race is associated with the favorability or unfavorability of interviewers' decisions.
3. Applicants' ages play an important role in interviewers' decisions, which generally favor younger applicants.
4. Handicapped applicants receive lower hiring recommendations than able-bodied applicants, but the handicapped are typically given credit for higher levels of work motivation.

SOURCE: Adapted from "Unfair Discrimination in the Employment Interview: Legal and Psychological Aspects," by R. D. Arvey. *Psychological Bulletin,* 1979, *86,* 736–765. Copyright 1979 by the American Psychological Association. Reprinted by permission.

EXAMPLES OF RECENT RESEARCH

Many recent empirical investigations of the selection interview have addressed and elaborated on the conclusions that emerged from the earlier reviews just described. Some of the evidence supports those conclusions, while some of the data refute them. Sackett (1982) and McDonald and Hakel (1985), for example, examined the hypothesis that interviewers tend to make up their minds during the first few minutes of an interview, and then spend the remaining time trying to generate information from the applicant that confirms their earlier impression. Neither study found any support for this hypothesis, especially among experienced interviewers.

Several studies have continued to document the impact of the sex of the interviewer and the applicant on the outcome of the selection interview, however. James, Campbell, and Lovegrove (1984) found that three experienced police officers who interviewed 150 male and 129 female applicants over a six-month interval displayed systematically different policies for evaluating the two sexes. Parsons and Liden (1984) examined interviews of 517 applicants for seasonal jobs at a large amusement park, and discovered that female applicants received higher ratings than male applicants on nonverbal behaviors and on overall qualifications. Finally, Baron (1983) reported that female interviewers gave higher ratings to male or female applicants who wore a popular brand of cologne or perfume, respectively, while male interviewers gave lower ratings to more fragrant applicants. (This line of research "nose" no bounds!)

Other researchers have pursued the relationships between nonverbal behaviors and interview outcomes. Gifford, Ng, and Wilkinson (1985) found that applicants' social skills were more accurately inferred from an interview than other personal abilities or traits, and that those social skills were transmitted via three specific nonverbal behaviors or cues: (1) the amount of time the applicant spent talking, (2) the formality of the applicant's clothing, and (3) the rate at which the applicant made physical gestures (hand movements, for example). Forsythe, Drake, and Cox (1985) also studied the influence of applicants' dress, and found that female applicants who dressed in a more "masculine" fashion (within an "acceptable range") received more positive hiring recommendations when applying for managerial positions. The size of the effect, however, was quite small.

In a similar vein, Rasmussen (1984) reported that nonverbal behavior had a sizable impact on interview outcome *only* when applicants had comparable job-relevant credentials, and when they displayed very similar behavior during the interview. Under those conditions, more exaggerated nonverbal behaviors made strong applicants look even better, and weak applicants look even worse. Sterrett (1978), on the other hand, found no effects of body language or dress on interview data generated by 100 male and 60 female personnel managers and department heads in the insurance industry.

Other recent miscellaneous findings include the following:

- Judges who are held more accountable and responsible for the results of their decisions tend to produce descriptions of target persons (applicants) that more reliably reflect those persons' actual characteristics (Rozelle & Baxter, 1981).
- Interviewers' judgments based on specific and relevant job dimensions are superior to judgments based on more general, all-inclusive dimensions (Osburn, Timmreck, & Bigby, 1981).
- The criterion-related validity of interview data still tends to be relatively low (Hunter & Hunter, 1984; Latham & Saari, 1984).

SUMMARY

Despite the fact that the reliability and validity of interview data continue to be lower than we might wish, and despite some preliminary evidence that information generated on a group-administered questionnaire may predict certain aspects of performance just as well as interview data (Tubiana & Ben-Shakhar, 1982), Arvey and Campion (1982) confessed that they knew of only one organization that hired applicants "sight unseen," without any form of personal interview. They suggested four possible explanations for this persistence; we have listed them here:

1. The interview *is "really" valid* for making inferences about applicants' sociability and verbal skills, and perhaps their work motivation, but our psychometric models and statistical procedures are not sufficiently sensitive to detect this validity.
2. The interview *may not be valid*, but it retains its popularity because of one or more of the following practical considerations:

a. There are not enough applicants to warrant more expensive and more elaborate selection procedures.
b. An erroneous assumption that the EEOC *Guidelines* do not apply to "unscored" interviews is made.
c. It furnishes an opportunity to answer applicants' questions and to provide them with realistic sets of expectations about the available job(s).

3. The interview *is not valid*, but interviewers remain confident about their judgments, partially, at least, because they usually receive little or no feedback about the quality of their hiring decisions.
4. The interview *is not valid*, but it accomplishes other purposes very well, such as "selling" the applicant on the job, and creating good public relations in the surrounding community.

SOURCE: Adapted from "The Employment Interview: A Summary and Review of Recent Research," by R. D. Arvey and J. E. Campion, *Personnel Psychology*, 1982, *35*, 281–322. Copyright 1982 by Personnel Psychology, Inc. Reprinted by permission.

Regardless of which of these is/are operating, Mr. Schiftner will probably question Dr. MacKeven's sanity (among other things) if she suggests a set of procedures for identifying and selecting managers that does not include some form of personal interview. It will therefore be necessary for her to review the relevant research literature, and to supplement whatever paper–and–pencil tests and biodata forms she decides to use with selection interviews that generate maximally reliable and valid data. Those interviews should have limited and realistic goals, such as evaluating *only* applicants' interpersonal and communication skills; they should be structured or patterned, based on job-analysis data for managerial positions; and they should minimize or eliminate the harmful effects of personal biases, as well as more–or–less predictable phenomena such as contrast, primacy, and recency effects.

Situational Exercises and Other Miscellaneous Predictors

Other available selection procedures that Dr. MacKeven may consider include work samples, situational exercises, letters of recommendation, and peer assessments.

WORK SAMPLES

Up to this point we have described selection tests that rely on procedures that bear little or no resemblance to the actual work tasks that people are being hired to perform (paper–and–pencil tests, interviews, and so on). Work samples are more direct, in that they present applicants with an opportunity to demonstrate their ability to perform small, manageable segments of actual job tasks or duties. Prediction requires little or no inference, so that content-validity analysis may be appropriate. In a criterion-related validity analysis, Campion (1972) designed a work sample for mechanics, and reported a validity coefficient of .46 with an overall mechanical-ability criterion. According to Hunter and Hunter's (1984) review, validity coefficients of this magnitude are typical for work-sample predictors.

A disadvantage of work samples as predictors of job performance is the time and expense often required to administer them. Because they tend to be individual tests, work samples usually require one examiner per applicant. Necessary equipment may also be costly, and may require substantial amounts of time to "set up" or prepare. A second problem with work samples is that they tend to focus on what applicants are capable of doing at the time they are being considered for a job, and ignore their potential to acquire important job skills through formal training programs or on-the-job experience.

Siegel's (1983) research suggested that "miniature job training" may represent at least a partial solution to the second problem. According to Siegel, "the job seeker is trained to perform a sample of tasks involved in the job for which he [sic] is an applicant and, immediately following the training, his ability to perform these tasks is measured." The rationale for miniature job training is that "a person who can demonstrate the ability to learn and perform on a job sample will be able to learn and perform on the total job" (p. 42).

SITUATIONAL EXERCISES

Unlike work samples, which are more–or–less exact replicas of job segments, situational exercises are approximations to segments or components of jobs. For professional and especially for managerial jobs, the Leaderless Group Discussion (Bass, 1954) and the In-Basket Test (Frederiksen, 1968) are among the more popular situational exercises. For jobs that require manual labor or other physical activities, tests of strength or other physical capabilities may be appropriate situational exercises.

The Leaderless Group Discussion brings a small group of applicants together, and requires that they talk about a topic that is usually job-related in some way. No other structure or directions are provided, no rules or procedures are imposed, and no leader is appointed. The point of the exercise is to see who emerges as a group leader, who addresses the social and emotional needs of group members, who imposes structure or organization on the group's discussion and activities, and how these individuals accomplish these things. Typical validity coefficients that describe the relationship between observers' ratings of these outcomes and subsequent managerial-performance criteria (salary progress, for example) seldom exceed .40.

The In-Basket Test requires an applicant to actually work his or her way through an "in-basket" filled with memos, telephone messages, short reports, and other documents that might demand a manager's attention. Observers record the order or priority applicants assign to the various tasks, and the way(s) in which they dispose of those tasks (making telephone calls, writing letters, convening meetings, and so forth). Although an In-Basket Test may require several hours to complete, applicants' scores tend to be somewhat predictive of their future performance as managers.

Validity analyses of strength tests and tests of other physical abilities or characteristics have produced less consistent results. Reilly, Zedeck, and Tenopyr

(1979) reported tests of body density, balance, and static strength that yielded valid scores for predicting safe job performance among telephone line workers. Arnold, Rauschenberger, Soubel, and Guion (1982) found that a single measure of static arm strength (an arm dynamometer) significantly predicted performance on a variety of tasks performed by both male and female steelworkers. Hogan and Fleishman (1979) offered evidence that personnel specialists are capable of providing reliable and valid judgments of the physical effort demanded by a variety of occupational tasks, thereby suggesting the possibility that actual physical assessment may not be necessary.

Hogan's (1985) more recent data are less encouraging, however. Her evaluation of the validity of five well-known physical-fitness batteries for predicting attrition among U.S. Navy divers during fitness training revealed that these batteries were "less effective predictors of performance in a physical conditioning training program than originally expected" (p. 223). Campion (1983) concluded his recent review of this literature with the following cautionary statement: " . . . although the relationship between maximum performance physical ability measures and maximum performance job samples seems to be strong, the relationship between physical ability measures and typical on-the-job performance has not been established" (pp. 545–546).

Several researchers have gone beyond traditional tests of physical strength to assess the validity of other, more unusual situational measures for predicting job performance. Sturgis, Pulling, and Vaillancourt (1981) measured individuals' sensitivity to glare, and reported sufficient individual differences to justify further research that may help to establish minimum standards for night driving (truck drivers, bus drivers, and so on). Rafaeli and Klimoski (1983) used expert graphologists in their effort to predict job-performance criteria for real estate sales associates. Predictions based on samples of their handwriting showed no evidence of validity. Finally, Olian (1984) discussed the possibility of using genetic factors to screen applicants for employment in work sites where some individuals may be susceptible to the negative effects of chemical and other pollutants. We may have *only begun* to explore the potential of situational tests.

LETTERS OF RECOMMENDATION

Other people's opinions of applicants' qualifications, job-related abilities, and experience constitute another category of potential measures that Dr. MacKeven might consider using to help Mr. Schiftner select successful managers for Peter's Pan Pizza. Although they can be solicited over the telephone, recommendations are usually conveyed in writing. You may already have been in a position where you had to ask a teacher, professor, or former boss to write a letter recommending you for admission to an academic institution or for a new job.

Although many organizations use letters of recommendation as they select some candidates and reject others, the available research evidence doesn't support the popularity of this device. Bias is almost built into the procedure. Who in her right mind would ask a person to write such a letter unless she was quite certain that the writer would convey favorable information and impressions, and a positive recommendation?

Baxter, Brock, Hill, and Rozelle (1981) examined letters of recommendation for 40 graduate school applicants, and found that the letters contained "a pattern of nondiscriminative, nonconsensual, and nondifferentiating descriptions" (p. 296). In other words, letter writers generally failed to discriminate among several different applicants; they also typically failed to agree on the important characteristics possessed by individual applicants. This pattern does not bode well for the validity of these measures. Hunter and Hunter's (1984) meta-analyses revealed average validities ranging between .16 and .27.

Shaffer and Tomarelli (1981) studied the unintended consequences of the Buckley Amendment (Family Educational Rights and Privacy Act, 1974), which permits postsecondary students to request either "open" letters of recommendation (from individuals who know that their comments will be accessible to the student) or "confidential" letters (from individuals who know that their comments will not be shared with the student). These researchers discovered that the people who made the selection decisions tended to favor applicants who had requested confidential letters from their sponsors. Presumably, they concluded that "open" letters would be even more positively biased than is typically the case.

Knouse (1983) examined the impact of three different factors on the perceived favorability of letters of recommendation. He found that letters describing specific examples of applicants' qualifications were reviewed more favorably, and made the writer appear more credible. Although a single negative statement in the letter tended to deflate several perceptions of the applicant's ability, such a statement, *when combined with specific examples of an applicant's strong points*, rendered an applicant "most hireable." Nevertheless, Knouse cautioned that "the influence of unfavorable statements is still unclear," and that "whether unfavorable statements add realism to the letter or condemn the recommendee with a 'kiss of death' remains [a topic] for future research" (p. 340).

SELF- AND PEER RATINGS

Others have examined the validity of self- and peer ratings of job-related skills, abilities, and characteristics. Reilly and Chao's (1982) review reported "some" validity for self-assessments, although the danger of "inflation bias" in self-ratings has been well documented (Anderson et al., 1984). Mabe and West's (1982) review of 55 studies that compared self-evaluations of abilities with more objective measures of performance revealed a "low mean validity coefficient" of .29 (p. 280).

Evidence concerning the validity of peer ratings has been considerably more encouraging. Kane and Lawler (1978) reported validity coefficients of .49, .49, and .36 for criteria based on promotions, supervisors' ratings, and training success, respectively (Hunter & Hunter, 1984). Peer ratings have emerged as particularly useful predictors of future job performance in military settings.

SUMMARY

Based on the available evidence, Dr. MacKeven should consider a number of situational exercises, especially those that assess problem-solving abilities, such as the Leaderless Group Discussion and the In-Basket Test. She might also consider soliciting recommendations from former peers and supervisors. Work samples, tests of physical strength or other physical capacities, as well as self-assessments, will probably prove to be less useful to her as she responds to Mr. Schiftner's request.

We have reserved the final few pages of this chapter for a brief discussion of a personnel selection procedure that will allow Dr. MacKeven and Mr. Schiftner to collect a variety of potentially valid data from applicants under controlled sets of conditions, in reasonable amounts of time. This procedure, known as an "assessment center," is a promising approach to identifying potentially successful managers.

Assessment Centers

Finkle (1976) described assessment centers as "group-oriented, standardized series of activities which provide a basis for judgments or predictions of human behaviors believed or known to be relevant to work performed in an organizational setting" (p. 861). He also listed four central or defining characteristics of this approach to personnel selection: (1) Applicants or candidates are assessed or evaluated in groups, (2) by groups of assessors, (3) using a variety of different measurement or selection techniques, (4) to determine their (the candidates') suitability for managerial positions.

Originally used by the Office of Strategic Services (the OSS was the forerunner of the Central Intelligence Agency) during World War II to identify people who were suitable for espionage activities, assessment centers were subsequently developed by American Telegraph & Telephone (AT&T), Standard Oil of Ohio, IBM, Sears, General Electric, and J. C. Penney, among other organizations, to assist in identifying women and men who were more likely to succeed as managers.

Included among the multiple measurement techniques typically used in assessment centers are

- objective paper–and–pencil tests
- **projective tests,** such as sentence-completion tests and the **Thematic Apperception Test** (McClelland, Atkinson, Clark, & Lowell, 1953; Murray, 1938)
- interviews
- peers' (other candidates') ratings
- and especially situational exercises, such as in-basket tests and leaderless group discussions (Borman, 1982; Finkle, 1976; Turnage & Muchinsky, 1982; Tziner & Dolan, 1982)

---

projective tests: sets of ambiguous questions or exercises that have no definite meaning and no obviously "correct" or "incorrect" answers; individuals therefore project their own personalities (motives, feelings, and so on) into their interpretations of, and answers to, the ambiguous test items

Thematic Apperception Test: a projective test that asks individuals to tell or to write stories in response to a series of ambiguous, nondescript pictures

Groups of assessors observe candidates' performance on these exercises, and typically arrive at a consensus of opinion concerning the managerial potential of each candidate. Sackett and Wilson (1982) suggested that a simple mechanical (statistical) decision rule can often substitute for the more laborious and time-consuming process of achieving consensus.

Although the research literature does contain an occasional discouraging word (Sackett & Dreher, 1982; Turnage & Muchinsky, 1984), most published studies support the validity of assessors' judgments. Borman (1982) and Tziner and Dolan (1982) reported validity coefficients of approximately .50 for assessors' predictions of the training performance of military recruiters and female military officers, respectively. This is only slightly more impressive than the validities (r = .43) that emerged from reviews by Cohen, Moses, and Byham (1974) and Hunter and Hunter (1984). Ritchie and Moses (1983) reported that assessment-center ratings were significantly related to female managers' career progress seven years following assessment, and that the skills these women required for success were no different than those required by successful male managers.

Several researchers have suggested that these apparently positive results are largely attributable to the fact that most of these validity studies used candidates' subsequent promotion rates as the criterion. The implication is that assessment-center ratings are not nearly as valid when the criterion is some other form of job-performance measure (Hunter & Hunter, 1984; Klimoski & Strickland, 1977). London and Stumpf's (1983) research is a recent example of a study that examined the validity of assessment center ratings for predicting managerial promotions. Turnage and Muchinsky (1984) reported assessment center ratings that predicted promotability, but not traditional job-performance ratings.

Although these authors' reservations are not without foundation, a recent study by Schmitt, Noe, Meritt, and Fitzgerald (1984) found that assessment-center ratings of school administrators *did* predict their subsequent performance ratings from their supervisors, their teachers, and their support staff. Their data suggest that assessment center ratings may indeed go well beyond capturing a given organization's promotion policy, and may instead reflect important job-related constructs.

Some of the more recent research on assessment centers has focused on the role of the assessors: how they go about arriving at a consensus, whether it is actually necessary to do so, and so forth. As we mentioned earlier, Sackett and Wilson (1982) suggested that a simple, mechanical decision rule can predict (be used in place of) consensus ratings approximately 95 percent of the time. Borman's (1982) data led him to conclude that assessors need *not* be trained behavioral scientists in order to be effective. In fact, there is evidence that managers who serve as assessors improve their proficiency in acquiring, evaluating, and communicating information about people (Lorenzo, 1984). Russell (1985) was able to document both formal and informal methods used by assessors to arrive at overall assessment ratings, while Borman, Eaton, Bryan, and Rosse (1983) reported an encouraging level of consistency in the validities associated with different assessors' judgments. On a less positive note, Turnage and Muchinsky (1982) concluded that assessment center ratings provide little useful information beyond what can be obtained from more global ratings of candidates' potentials.

SUMMARY

Given the definite managerial orientation of assessment centers, their comprehensiveness in utilizing a variety of different personnel selection procedures, and their apparent validity, there is no question that Dr. MacKeven should consider this multiprocedural approach as she sets out to respond to Mr. Schiftner's request for help in selecting new managers for Peter's Pan Pizza.

CHAPTER SUMMARY

Any useful selection test must be both reliable and valid. Reliability, which decreases as test scores are influenced by random error, can be estimated by the test–retest, the equivalent forms, or the internal-consistency method; each has its own strengths and weaknesses. Test-score reliability can be affected by anything that admits random error: characteristics of the test (number and diversity of items, format and serial order of items, and so on), characteristics of the sample of people taking the test ("test-wiseness," attitudes and motivation, and so forth), and characteristics of the testing environment (the test administrator or proctor, temperature, illumination, noise, and so on). Validity of test scores can be analyzed in three different ways, depending on the nature of the inferences one wishes to make on the basis of the scores. These include content, criterion-related, and construct-validity analyses.

Personnel selection tests that are widely used and that have been the focus of I/O psychologists' research include various paper–and–pencil tests of intelligence, motivation, and personality (creativity, honesty, psychopathology, and so forth). Of these, tests of intellectual abilities and motivation to manage other people have the highest validities for predicting job performance. Biographical information, especially relevant work experience, also seems to be reasonably predictive. Evidence concerning personal interviews is less encouraging, unless the interview is structured and the interviewer concentrates on assessing a limited number of applicants' characteristics (interpersonal communication skills, for example). Work samples and situational exercises can yield valid predictions if they are carefully designed in accordance with appropriate job-analysis data. Letters of recommendation tend to be far less useful than their popularity would indicate. A particularly promising approach for selecting managers is the assessment center, where applicants take a variety of tests and participate in numerous exercises under the close scrutiny of observers, who then convene to arrive at consensus predictions for each applicant.

INTEROFFICE MEMO
TO: Jim Schiftner, Director of Management Selection
FROM: Jenni MacKeven, Human—Resources Coordinator

I've given your memo a lot of thought, Jim, and I think you're wise not to limit yourself to the confines of PPP in your search for effective managers. Let me concentrate for the moment on specific selection tests and procedures. (We can discuss recruitment and overall selection strategies, as well as relevant legal issues, at a later date.)

As I understand your current procedures, you rely on a combination of personal recommendations, interviews, and a ''quick—and—dirty'' test of intelligence to identify potentially successful managers from among PPP's nonmanagerial ranks. Although you alluded to a good ''track record,'' I am aware of only one or two small studies that have examined the validity of your selection process. Based on the available research evidence (as well as the evolving legal climate), I think we should take a close look at your current selection instruments, and design some ''full—blown'' studies to examine the validity of the inferences being drawn from those instruments. At the same time, I want to discuss with you the possibility of revising your current instruments (structuring your interviews a bit more, for example), and incorporating some new ones into your managerial selection procedures.

Let me know when your schedule will allow us to ''get our heads together'' on this.

REVIEW QUESTIONS AND EXERCISES

1. What will Dr. MacKeven recommend to Mr. Schiftner regarding his reliance on personal recommendations? Why?

2. Based on your knowledge of relevant research, draw up a set of specific recommendations for Mr. Schiftner concerning his continued use of personal interviews.

3. From what you know about Peter's Pan Pizza, Inc., so far, what kind(s) of validity analysis will be appropriate, and what kind(s) will not, when Dr. MacKeven and Mr. Schiftner meet to design their validity studies? What would you recommend? Why?

4. What kind(s) of selection instruments will Dr. MacKeven suggest for possible inclusion in Mr. Schiftner's selection procedures? What sorts of tests should be excluded? Explain your answers.

5. How should Dr. MacKeven and Mr. Schiftner estimate the reliability of whatever selection tests they decide to examine? Describe the various factors that may influence the magnitudes of their reliability estimates.

CHAPTER 6

Personnel Decision-Making Systems

Learning Points

After studying this chapter, you should

- understand the recruiting options available to organizations, and be able to explain how recruiting can violate Title VII of the Civil Rights Act (1964)

- know the "pros" and "cons" of realistic job previews

- be able to construct individual and organizational expectancy charts (given the necessary data, of course), and to interpret them for someone (your roommate, perhaps) who has never heard of I/O psychology

- be able to describe the strengths and weaknesses of regression approaches and multiple-cutoff approaches to personnel selection

- understand the ways in which moderator and suppressor variables, as well as synthetic validity and validity generalization, can contribute to an effective personnel selection system

- be able to explain the concept of utility, and how it is related to validity

- know the meaning of "adverse impact," and how it is determined

- be able to explain and defend your position on the EEOC *Guidelines* and affirmative action policies and programs

INTEROFFICE MEMO
TO: Jennilyn A. MacKeven, Human-Resources Coordinator
FROM: T. J. Smith, Legal Counsel

Jim Schiftner in Management Selection showed me a copy of his memo to you that described his plan to develop a set of procedures for iden-tifying and selecting men and women with potential to succeed as man-agers at Peter's Pan Pizza. Based on our telephone conversation of last week, I understand you are planning to evaluate the validity of paper-and-pencil measures of intelligence and managerial motivation, biographical information, a structured interview designed to assess interpersonal communication skills, and some situational exercises (In-Basket Test, Leaderless Group Discussion) as possible components of a managerial selection system, and that you are entertaining the possibility of collecting these data in the context of an ''assess-ment-center'' situation.

My purpose today is to remind you of the legal context in which such a selection system must operate. The <u>Uniform Guidelines on Employee Selection Procedures</u>, adopted by the Equal Employment Opportunity Commission in order to facilitate organizations' compliance with Title VII of the 1964 Civil Rights Act, places particular emphasis on protecting certain groups (such as blacks and women) from adverse impact by stressing the need for job analyses. Any selection system you develop, as well as any other personnel decisions you recommend (recruiting, promoting, and so on), must comply with these <u>Guidelines</u>.

If I can be of any assistance to you or to Mr. Schiftner in your efforts to improve our system for selecting managers, please don't hesitate to call on me.

Mr. Smith's memo reflects a basic fact of organizational life. The passage of the Civil Rights Act in 1964 dramatically altered the personnel and human-resource functions in organizations. No longer is it sufficient just to select, recruit, promote, or dismiss people in ways that satisfy upper-level management. The EEOC *Guidelines* (1978) now stipulate that it is also necessary to make these personnel decisions in ways that avoid discrimination, either intentional or unintentional, against anyone on the basis of their race, sex, or ethnic-group membership.

In this chapter we shall continue our discussion of the personnel selection process by examining recruitment and some of the other procedures available to Dr. MacKeven and Mr. Schiftner as they try to combine and integrate the information they obtain from applicants using the various selection instruments (predictors) described in the previous chapter and mentioned in Mr. Smith's memo. We shall also describe the concept of utility for determining the relative costs and benefits associated with a particular selection system. Finally, we shall describe in some detail the EEOC *Guidelines* (1978) and the legal requirements they impose on organizations to make personnel decisions in a fair and unbiased way. As you will see, the Civil Rights Act (1964) made the already difficult job of personnel selection even more challenging.

RECRUITING

Recruiting refers to organizational procedures that are designed to identify potentially suitable job applicants, and to entice them to apply for the available jobs. Because this is the first extraorganizational step in the personnel selection process, it is also the first point at which an organization must be careful not to illegally discriminate against women, blacks, or any of the other groups of people protected by the EEOC *Guidelines* (1978).

There are a number of different ways in which an organization can inform potential applicants of existing job opportunities. These include personal communications from organization members (such as "college interviews," where a recruiter visits a university or college to interview potential job candidates), written notices posted in and around the organization, employment agencies, announcements in the mass media (usually newspapers, but radio and television are also possibilities), and friends or relatives who are familiar with the organization. As long as an organization uses enough of these different recruiting sources to reach all or a representative sample of all those who are qualified to apply for given jobs, there is little or no danger of illegal discrimination. The size and geographic limits of a potential applicant population are determined by such factors as the amount of prior training that is required to perform a job effectively, and the likelihood that applicants will be willing to relocate in order to accept a given position in the company. If an organization selectively uses only certain recruiting sources (sources that systematically exclude certain protected groups of people from learning about the available jobs), that organization is vulnerable to prosecution under Title VII of the Civil Rights Act (1964). Examples of such selective recruiting strategies include newspaper "want ads" that specify "Man

Wanted" or "Woman Wanted," or radio announcements that are limited to stations or broadcast times that selectively reach certain groups of people and, by implication, selectively bypass certain other groups of people.

Although there is not exactly an abundance of empirical research on recruiting in the I/O psychology literature, a small number of studies have investigated the relative effectiveness of some of the recruiting sources listed above, as well as the impact(s) of various recruiter behaviors, and the effect(s) of informing potential job applicants about specific aspects, attributes, or characteristics of the available jobs.

The available data on the effectiveness of different recruiting sources are mixed. While Swaroff, Barclay, and Bass (1985) reported that different recruiting sources or "vehicles" (newspaper ads, employee referrals, and so forth) were *not* related to subsequent levels of employee productivity or length of time on the job among technical salespersons, Caldwell and Spivey (1983) found that informal recruiting sources (employee referrals) led to longer job tenure among white store clerks, while more formal procedures (employment agencies) led to greater tenure among black clerks. Taylor and Schmidt (1983) suggested that different recruiting sources are differentially effective because they reach individuals from different applicant populations, whose attendance, time on the job, and performance are likely to be systematically different. If these different applicant populations include one or more of the groups protected by the EEOC, an organization would be wise to use as many different recruiting sources as possible.

Turning to the effects of different recruiter behaviors, Powell (1984) examined the impact of a variety of recruiter behaviors and practices (including answering applicants' questions, showing interest in applicants, being familiar with applicants' backgrounds, and so on), and found that they did *not* affect the likelihood that college graduates would accept a given job offer. Rynes and Miller (1983) suggested that job applicants interpret a recruiter's behavior as a signal regarding their chances of receiving a job offer. It's reasonable to assume that encouragement from a recruiter might lead to more positive applicant behaviors, which in turn may lead to additional encouragement from the recruiter, and ultimately to a job offer. Of course, the opposite "downward spiral" could also ensue. Except for the results of one of Rynes and Miller's studies, however, there is little evidence to support the hypothesis that recruiters' behaviors directly affect the perceived desirability of given jobs.

More in line with your expectations, perhaps, is the substantial empirical evidence that job characteristics *do* influence the perceived desirability of jobs, as well as the likelihood of applicants saying that they would accept given jobs if they were offered. Powell (1984) reported that properties of the jobs themselves (variety of activities, opportunity to use abilities, and so forth), as well as compensation and security factors (salary, fringe benefits) and work environment (company location and reputation), all influenced the probability that college graduates would accept given job offers. Rynes and Miller (1983) affirmed that job attributes (salaries, career paths) do influence the perceived desirability of jobs. Although Posner (1981) identified some notable differences in students', faculty members', and corporate recruiters' perceptions of the desirability of various job factors (and the relative importance of various applicant characteristics, too) his study was based on the assumption that these job factors are important determinants of the outcome of recruiting exercises.

A relatively recent innovation designed to provide job applicants with specific and accurate information about available jobs is known as the realistic job preview (RJP). Before concluding our discussion of recruiting, we'll bring you up-to-date on research conducted to assess the role of RJPs in effectively recruiting new organization members.

Realistic Job Previews

We began our discussion of recruiting by acknowledging that one of the purposes of this procedure was to "sell" the organization and its available job(s) to promising prospective applicants. In their efforts to realize this goal, organizations have often been guilty of not only "putting their best foot forward," but also of "painting an overly rosy picture" of a particular job, the tasks that it comprises, and the physical and social environments in which it is performed. Subsequent high rates of voluntary turnover have sometimes been attributed to the unrealistic expectations of new organization members.

A realistic job preview (RJP) is a direct effort on the part of an organization to make certain that job applicants accept any forthcoming job offers "with their eyes wide open." It is designed not only to avoid giving applicants unrealistic ideas about what a given job entails, but also to overcome or negate unrealistic expectations that applicants may already have developed courtesy of fictional literature, television programs, or other sources of less-than-accurate information.

Quite a bit of empirical research has investigated the ability of RJPs to accomplish these aims. Reilly, Brown, Blood, and Malatesta (1981) found that RJPs, whether presented on film or conducted in the form of actual job visits, had *no* effect on telephone-service representatives' rate of job acceptance, their level of job commitment, the extent to which they reported that their job expectations were or were not met, and most importantly, their level of turnover. Similarly, Zaharia and Baumeister (1981) reported that both written and videotaped RJPs produced statistically *non*significant changes in turnover rates among basic-care staff in a residential facility for retarded individuals. Guzzo, Jette, and Katzell's (1985) recent meta-analysis of 98 different studies led them to the similarly unencouraging conclusion that the average impact of job previews on workers' productivity was *not* statistically significant.

On the brighter side, Dean and Wanous' (1984) field experiment with bank tellers compared the effectiveness of two different types of RJPs, one very specific and one a bit more general, with a control condition in which subjects received no RJP. Although they uncovered no differences in tellers' initial attitudes, levels of job performance, or overall survival rates on the job, these researchers did report that both forms of RJPs influenced the rate at which new employees left their jobs. Specifically, those tellers who had received either a specific or a general RJP were more likely to quit *sooner* (during an initial three-week training program), which limited the amount of time and organizational resources that were "wasted" on these short-term employees.

Colarelli (1984) also worked with bank tellers, and reported that RJPs provided by incumbent employees reduced turnover among newly hired tellers more than written brochures or no RJP. His data, however, did not support the hypothesis that self-selection and increased commitment would help to explain the effectiveness of those personal RJPs. Premack and Wanous' (1985) meta-analysis of 21 experiments led them to conclude that RJPs *did* tend to increase self-selection during the hiring process, as well as employees' organizational commitment, job satisfaction, performance, and job survival. Their review also indicated that audiovisual RJPs may be superior to those presented in the form of written booklets.

Although Premack and Wanous (1985) concluded that there was little or no evidence that personal or situational variables had any effect on the influence of RJPs, McEvoy and Cascio's (1985) meta-analysis of 20 relevant experiments tended to support the earlier suggestion of Reilly et al. (1981) that task complexity may influence the effects of RJPs. Specifically, RJPs may be more effective at reducing turnover among people who are hired for more complex jobs. Nevertheless, McEvoy and Cascio's review revealed that RJPs were only about half as effective as job-enrichment programs (where jobs are redesigned to be more challenging and personally rewarding; see Chapter 13) for reducing employee turnover.

If, at this point, you are totally confused about the effectiveness of RJPs, you have plenty of company. What seems to be a logical, intuitively appealing procedure for reducing employees' unrealistic job expectations, and thereby reducing their voluntary turnover, has received mixed support (at best) in the empirical research literature. Although it is much too soon to abandon RJPs, Dr. MacKeven and other organizational researchers and practitioners should be "realistic" about the potential of this procedure for reducing employee turnover and improving workers' performance.

Summary

Because Mr. Schiftner's memo (at the beginning of Chapter 5) specifically referred to tapping sources outside of, as well as within, the organizational boundaries of Peter's Pan Pizza, recruiting must occupy a central place in Dr. MacKeven's eventual response. Her recruiting procedures must be sufficiently broad to bring managerial job openings to the attention of all possible candidates, as this will both increase the likelihood of finding the best women and men for the jobs, and minimize the possibility that PPP will violate EEOC guidelines on nondiscrimination. This can be accomplished by using as many different recruiting sources or vehicles as possible. Because managerial jobs tend to be rather complex, Dr. MacKeven might also entertain the idea of including some form of RJP in the recruitment process. Personal communications from incumbent managers or audiovisual materials will probably be more effective than written brochures.

Following recruitment and the administration of the various predictors (selection instruments) described in the previous chapter, Dr. MacKeven's new task will be to identify a strategy or set of procedures for integrating all the information that is generated for each applicant, in a way that facilitates decisions to hire or to reject. We shall now describe some of the decision-making strategies that are available to her.

PERSONNEL DECISION-MAKING STRATEGIES

Having generated the necessary information to conduct one or more of the validity analyses described in the previous chapter, Dr. MacKeven can choose from among a variety of procedures for using those data to help her make hiring (or other personnel) decisions. These procedures range from constructing relatively simple expectancy charts or tables, to considerably more complex strategies such as deriving multiple regression equations, searching for useful moderator and suppressor variables, or taking a more analytic approach that focuses on separate job components rather than on jobs in their entirety. This section includes descriptions of each of these approaches to decision making, along with some others and a relatively new approach known as validity generalization.

Expectancy Charts

An expectancy chart usually takes the form of a bar graph (histogram) that depicts the probabilities of successful job performance given certain scores on one or more predictors or selection instruments (tests, interviews, and so forth). There are two different, yet related, types of information.

An example of an *individual* expectancy chart appears in Figure 6.1. It depicts, for a given sample of applicants or job incumbents (depending on whether a predictive or concurrent criterion-related validity study was done), the probabilities of *individuals* performing successfully on the job when their selection-test scores fall into specified ranges. This particular individual expectancy chart reflects a positive validity coefficient: Individuals who score higher on the predictor are more likely to be successful employees.

The same empirical predictor and criterion data can be summarized in a different way. Figure 6.2 shows an *organizational* or *institutional* expectancy chart, which shows the different percentages of successful employees that an organization can expect when all of those hired have certain minimum scores on the selection test. When an organization is in the favorable position of having many more applicants than there are jobs to be filled, it has the luxury of being "choosy" by hiring only those men and women with the highest probabilities of job success, thereby maximizing the percentage of new hires that will succeed. Alternatively, when there are not as many applicants for the available jobs, the organization may have to "settle for" individuals with lower individual probabilities of job success, thereby lowering the overall percentage of new hires that

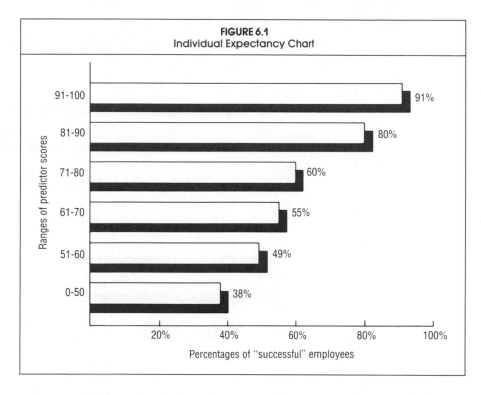

FIGURE 6.1
Individual Expectancy Chart

will succeed. The ratio of job applicants to job openings is known as the hiring rate, a concept we will discuss in more detail later on when we consider the utility or usefulness of a given personnel selection system.

As we implied above, expectancy charts are perhaps the simplest, most straightforward way to describe the relationship between individuals' scores on one or more predictors and their subsequent levels of job performance. Because they do not depend on psychological or statistical **jargon,** and because they require no statistical expertise beyond the concept of percentage or proportion, such charts are very useful for describing one of the outcomes of a selection procedure: the percentage of successful employees that can be anticipated. Expectancy charts reveal nothing, however, about the magnitude of job-performance improvement, or the cost-effectiveness associated with a given personnel selection system. More complex procedures are required to generate those types of information.

Regression Analysis and Equations

Regression analysis is a statistical procedure that is based on, and is a direct extension of, the correlation coefficient (r). Recall from Chapter 5 that a

---

jargon: technical language used by certain groups or academic specialties; facilitates communication within the group, but is relatively unintelligible to others

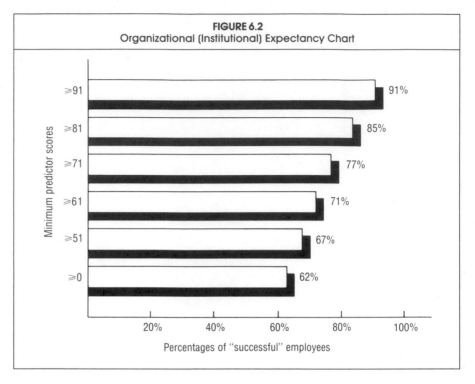

FIGURE 6.2
Organizational (Institutional) Expectancy Chart

criterion-related validity coefficient describes the size and direction (direct or inverse) of the linear relationship between scores on a given predictor and scores on a criterion of job performance. (More precisely, r^2, the square of the validity coefficient, represents the percentage of variance in the criterion scores that can be predicted from scores on the selection instrument.) The validity coefficient itself, however, does not tell us *how* to use the selection-test scores to make predictions about job performance.

In order to make these predictions, we must transform the correlation (validity) coefficient into a regression equation, the simplest of which is the generic equation for a straight line:

$$\hat{Y} = a + bX, \text{ where}$$

$\hat{Y}$ = the predicted criterion (job-performance) score
a = the constant numerical value that depicts where the regression line crosses or intercepts the ordinate (the vertical Y axis on a set of coordinate axes)
X = the observed score on the predictor (selection test)
b = the constant numerical value that describes the slope of the regression line (the number of units of change in the criterion score that is associated with one unit of change in the predictor score)

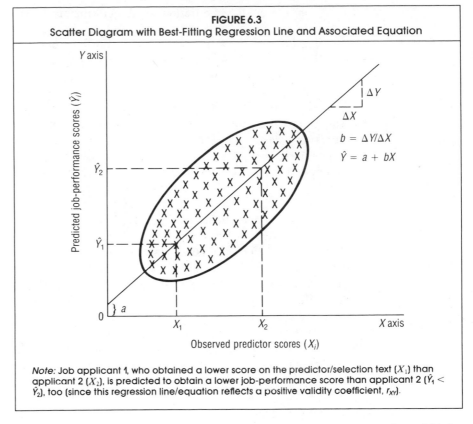

FIGURE 6.3
Scatter Diagram with Best-Fitting Regression Line and Associated Equation

Note: Job applicant 1, who obtained a lower score on the predictor/selection text (X_1) than applicant 2 (X_2), is predicted to obtain a lower job-performance score than applicant 2 ($\hat{Y}_1 < \hat{Y}_2$), too (since this regression line/equation reflects a positive validity coefficient, r_{XY}).

Although the mathematical procedures for deriving the constants (a and b) for a given set of predictor and criterion scores are too complex to describe here, you should know that they are designed to *minimize* the distance between the straight line described by the regression equation and each of the data points that make up the scatter diagram of those predictor and criterion scores (see Chapter 2). (You can consult Pedhazur, 1982, or a variety of other statistical texts for complete descriptions of the procedures for deriving regression equations.) Figure 6.3 depicts a scatter diagram for a set of predictor and criterion scores, as well as the regression line that describes those joint scores, and the equation that describes that straight line.

The equation shown above is known as a "simple" regression equation, because it is based only on a set of scores from a single predictor. If we generate two or more sets of scores, based on two or more predictors (or selection tests), we can derive a "multiple" regression equation that simultaneously uses information from all of the multiple predictors to make predictions about people's job performance scores. An example of a multiple regression equation looks like this:

$$\hat{Y} = a + b_1 X_1 + b_2 X_2 + b_3 X_3, \text{ where}$$

$\hat{Y}$ = the predicted criterion or job-performance score

a = the constant "Y-intercept"

b_1, b_2, and b_3 = the constant regression coefficients that reflect the relationships between scores on the three predictors (X_1, X_2, and X_3) and scores on the job-performance criterion

When two or more predictors are used to derive a multiple regression equation, the overall relationship between those multiple predictors and the criterion is described by the multiple correlation coefficient (R). Except that its algebraic sign is always positive, R is interpreted just like its "simple" counterpart, r. The percentage of variance in the criterion that can be explained or predicted on the basis of the multiple selection-test scores is given by R^2.

Although predictions about individuals' performance based on regression equations are mathematically precise, and although they tend to be more accurate in the long run than more subjective or "clinical" predictions (Meehl, 1954, 1957, 1965), the mathematical procedures that underlie that precision and accuracy are quite complex. As a result, it is a far greater challenge for Dr. MacKeven to explain the meaning of regression equations to Mr. Schiftner (or any other manager who is less statistically sophisticated) than it is to explain expectancy charts.

Like expectancy charts, however, regression equations can only be derived from more-or-less complete sets of predictor and criterion scores *from a given sample* of job applicants or incumbents, such as would be obtained in the course of a predictive- or concurrent-validity study. Remember that any sample's scores will be less than perfectly reliable. The mathematical procedures for deriving a regression equation do *not* distinguish between the true-score and the error-score components of observed predictor and criterion scores. (You may need to review our discussion of true, random-error, and observed scores in Chapter 5.) The value of R^2 associated with a regression equation derived from any given sample, therefore, almost always overestimates the size of the true predictor–criterion relationship. Adding insult to injury, the size of R^2 is also inflated when the number of predictors (selection tests) in an equation is large relative to the number of individuals who make up the sample used to generate the equation. Fortunately, there are two ways to correct for the inflation inherent in sample-specific regression equations.

One approach is to apply what is known as a "shrinkage" formula to the obtained value of R^2:

$$R^2_s = 1 - (1 - R^2)\,[(N - 1)/(N - k)], \text{ where}$$

R^2_s = the "corrected" estimate of the percentage of criterion variance explained by the predictors

R^2 = the uncorrected squared multiple correlation coefficient computed for a given sample of N job applicants or incumbents using k different predictors or selection tests

Inflation bias, and therefore shrinkage, is greatest when the size of the sample used to derive the equation is small relative to the number of predictors in the equation. In the extreme case where $N = k$, the uncorrected value of R^2 will always be equal to 1.00. A typical "rule of thumb" that minimizes shrinkage is to have at least 10 observations, cases, or subjects, for each predictor in the equation. Thus, if a regression equation is based on three selection tests (predictors), there should be at least 30 applicants or job incumbents in the sample whose data are used to derive that equation.

A second method for eliminating sample-specific inflation bias involves a set of procedures collectively known as cross-validation. One of the most common cross-validation strategies involves the following steps:

1. Divide the sample of job applicants or incumbents into two subsamples: a "primary" sample that consists of a randomly selected two-thirds of the entire sample, and a "hold-out" sample that consists of the remaining one-third of the original sample.
2. Derive a regression equation using only the data obtained from the primary sample. (The original sample should be sufficiently large so that the necessary N-to-k ratio described above is at least 10-to-1 in the primary sample.)
3. Use the regression equation derived from the primary sample to obtain a predicted criterion score for each member of the hold-out sample by entering the hold-out individuals' predictor scores into the equation derived from the primary sample's data.
4. Compute the correlation coefficient (r) that describes the linear relationship between the hold-out sample's actual criterion scores and the criterion scores that the primary sample's regression equation predicted for them.

A large, positive correlation indicates that the regression coefficients (b_x) and the constant (a) derived from the primary sample's data did a good job of predicting the hold-out sample's criterion scores, and that the regression equation is therefore *not* overly contaminated by large random-error scores. A small or negative correlation indicates that the equation derived from the primary sample *is* contaminated with error, and is therefore not representative of other samples of applicants or job incumbents.

Murphy (1983, 1984) recently argued that, unless the primary and hold-out samples are *independently* drawn from the population of job applicants or incumbents (as opposed to being formed by simply partitioning a single sample of people into two smaller subsamples), the more costly and time-consuming cross-validation procedures have no clearcut advantages over the simpler, quicker, and less expensive shrinkage formula estimates. Unless Dr. MacKeven has the resources to conduct a truly multisample cross-validation study (and she might!), she should probably heed Murphy's advice.

Another characteristic of multiple regression equations can be either an advantage or a disadvantage, depending on the specific predictors and criterion under consideration. Multiple regression equations are "compensatory" procedures for making selection or other personnel decisions. This means that individual applicants can still be judged acceptable, even though one or more of their predictor scores is *very* low, if other predictor scores are sufficiently high to compensate for the low score(s). An example should help to explain this property of multiple regression equations.

Suppose that Dr. MacKeven uses applicants' scores on an intelligence test, on a motivation-to-manage test, and on a structured interview, as three predictors of job performance as a Peter's Pan Pizza manager. Suppose further that two applicants' combined predictor scores generate identical predictions of their ultimate success as managers. Although their predicted criterion scores are the same, their individual predictor scores may have been very different. Applicant 1 may have scored at slightly above average levels on all three predictors, leading to a prediction of satisfactory managerial performance. Applicant 2, on the other hand, may have generated an average interview score, an exceptionally high intelligence score, and a low motivation-to-manage score. Since this second applicant's predicted managerial performance could be just as high as the first applicant's, it is clear that the multiple regression approach to personnel selection is allowing the second applicant's extremely high intelligence score to compensate for his decidedly lackluster motivation-to-manage score.

This compensatory property of multiple regression equations may be an advantage, if Mr. Schiftner believes that high intelligence *can* indeed compensate for lower levels of motivation. Alternatively, if he believes that no amount of intelligence can compensate for low levels of motivation, the compensatory nature of multiple regression equations becomes a disadvantage or weakness inherent in the procedure.

Imagine, instead, that Dr. MacKeven had been asked to select a pilot for Peter's Pan Pizza's corporate jet airplane, and that two of the multiple predictors were intelligence scores and corrected visual acuity (eyesight) scores. Would you feel comfortable flying with a pilot who had an **IQ** of 175, but who couldn't see the broad side of a barn (from the inside!)? Probably not.

You can understand, then, that Dr. MacKeven's and Mr. Schiftner's assessment of the compensatory nature of multiple regression selection strategies will depend heavily on the specific predictors that are included in any eventual equation. In the event that they deem it inappropriate that high scores on some predictors should be allowed to compensate for low scores on others, they may choose to use an alternative decision-making strategy. The most common alternative is known as the "multiple cutoff" approach.

Multiple Cutoff Selection Strategies

Multiple cutoff selection strategies are designed for those instances when it is inappropriate, unacceptable, and/or dangerous to permit a job applicant's extremely high score on one or more predictors to compensate for an extremely low score on other predictors. In such cases, the personnel selection specialist can identify minimum "cutoff scores" on each of the predictors, and those applicants who are hired must obtain *at least* those minimum scores on each respective predictor or selection test. Under these conditions, a job applicant who scores below the minimum cutoff point on any predictor is automatically eliminated from further consideration, regardless of how high he or she scores on the other selection tests.

The major obstacle to implementing a multiple cutoff selection strategy is setting the minimum cutoff scores in a way that facilitates valid prediction of job performance without discriminating against people who actually could perform the job satisfactorily, if given the opportunity to do so. That is, there must be either logical or empirical evidence to support the use of any particular cutoff score on a given selection test; those scores cannot be set arbitrarily. Sometimes an expectancy chart, such as those we discussed earlier, can provide empirical evidence to support the use of a particular cutoff score.

MULTIPLE HURDLE STRATEGIES

When an organization uses two or more selection tests or predictors in its personnel selection system, those multiple predictors often require greater or lesser amounts of money and time to purchase, administer, and score. If the hiring rate is favorable from the organization's perspective—that is, if there are many applicants for every open position—then a variation of the multiple cutoff strategy can be used to take advantage of these different costs.

Known as multiple hurdle strategies (in recognition of the fact that a hurdler on a track team must negotiate one hurdle at a time in order to reach the finish line), these approaches use the multiple predictors or selection tests as successive "hurdles" that job applicants must "clear" in order to receive a job offer. Of course, the order in which particular hurdles are laid out for a track star is irrelevant, since all of the hurdles are identical. The situation can be very different for multiple predictors of job performance, however.

The purpose of multiple hurdle selection strategies is to identify applicants with the greatest probability of succeeding on the job in the most efficient and least expensive way. The basic idea is to administer the least expensive and least time-consuming selection test to the entire sample of job applicants, and to eliminate those whose scores do not surpass the minimum cutoff score for that predictor. The next most expensive and/or time-consuming predictor is then administered to the smaller group of applicants who survived the first hurdle, and those whose scores fall below the minimum score for that second predictor are then eliminated from further consideration. This "weeding out" process continues, as relatively more expensive and more time-consuming selection tests are administered to smaller and smaller groups of applicants, until only a very few applicants remain for each available job. Only these "survivors" are given the opportunity to take the most costly or time-consuming selection

---

IQ: intelligence quotient, which reflects a person's relative score on a standard intelligence test compared with the scores of others; by definition, the mean IQ score = 100, and 1 standard deviation is usually 15 or 16 points

tests. Final hiring decisions are then made on the basis of applicants' scores on these final hurdles.

Suppose, for example, that Dr. MacKeven and Mr. Schiftner agree to use an application blank for collecting biographical data, paper–and–pencil tests for measuring motivation to manage and intelligence, a structured personal interview for assessing interpersonal-communication skills, and a two-day assessment center as predictors of performance as a Peter's Pan Pizza manager. A useful multiple hurdle strategy might arrange these selection devices in the following serial order: (1) the application blank, (2) the paper–and–pencil tests, (3) the structured interview, and (4) the two-day set of assessment center exercises. This is the order that would be least expensive and most time-efficient.

We should point out here that the compensatory multiple regression approach and the noncompensatory multiple cutoff and multiple hurdle approaches for making personnel decisions are not necessarily antagonistic or mutually exclusive. That is, they can be effectively combined to take maximum advantage of each procedure's relative strengths. Dr. MacKeven might identify minimum cutoff points for any or all of the selection tests that she includes in her selection system, in order to eliminate applicants who are clearly unacceptable. She could then use the remaining applicants either to derive a multiple regression equation to be used with subsequent samples of applicants (assuming successful cross-validation or application of the shrinkage formula), or simply take the surviving applicants' predictor scores and "plug them into" an existing regression equation. Often the best answer to questions that take the form of "Which is the best technique/approach/procedure/etc.?" is "None is best; they are best used in combination."

Efforts to Improve Prediction of Job Performance

Although I/O psychologists have continually tried to improve the predictive validity of various selection instruments since the early 20th century, when Hugo Münsterberg helped the City of Boston select streetcar motormen, our success has been limited. A number of critical reviews of the validity literature have confirmed the discouraging conclusion that our predictive validity coefficients rarely exceed a value of .50, and more typically fall at or below a value of .35 (Ghiselli, 1956, 1966, 1973; Hull, 1928). Although even such modest validity coefficients may possess substantial utility under certain conditions (see our discussion of utility below), these findings suggest that we rarely explain more than 25 percent of the variance in job performance with our predictor scores, and that we typically explain less than 10 percent of that variance.

In response to these unimpressive findings, a number of researchers and theoreticians have devised approaches with some potential to render our predictions of job performance more valid and accurate. In the following sections, we shall acquaint you with several of these efforts, including the search for moderator variables and suppressor variables, and the investigation of a more analytic approach to validation that focuses on predicting performance on specific components of jobs, rather than predicting overall job performance.

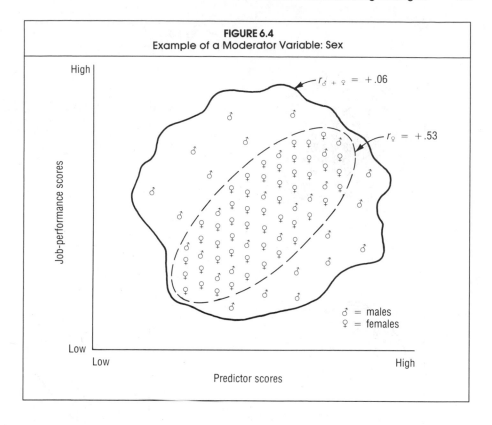

FIGURE 6.4
Example of a Moderator Variable: Sex

MODERATOR VARIABLES

Moderator variables reflect the assumption that some individuals are more predictable than other individuals under specific circumstances. Given a certain set of predictors (selection test scores) and an associated set of criterion scores (job performance) for a given group of individuals, Dr. MacKeven may be able to identify some additional variable that will allow her to distinguish between those people whose predictor scores actually predict their job-performance levels, and those people whose performance levels are not so predictable (given *that* set of predictors). Such a variable is known as a "moderator variable."

An example might help to illustrate this concept. The scatter diagram in Figure 6.4 enclosed in the solid line represents the joint predictor and criterion scores for an entire sample of job applicants. As you may have guessed from its shape, which is approximately circular, the validity coefficient associated with this scattergram would be quite small, say $r = +.06$. Suppose, however, that the portion of this scattergram that is enclosed within the dashed or broken line represents the joint predictor and criterion scores for an identifiable subsample of the entire sample of applicants—only the women, for example. The elongated shape of this subsample's scattergram suggests a more substantial relationship between predictor and criterion scores, say $r = +.53$. In this example, where criterion-related validity is different for men and women, applicants' sex is operating as a moderator variable.

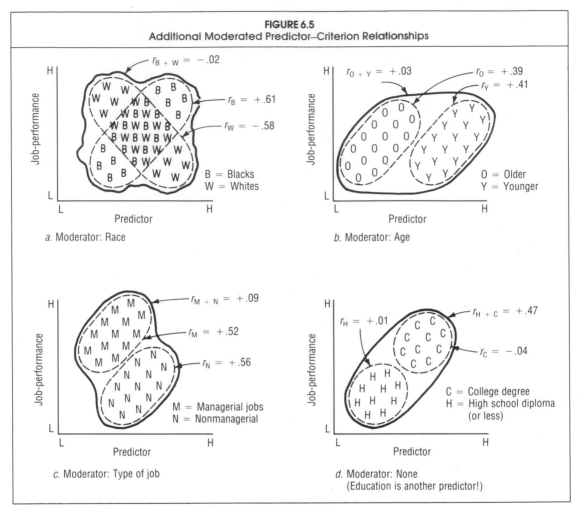

FIGURE 6.5
Additional Moderated Predictor–Criterion Relationships

a. Moderator: Race

b. Moderator: Age

c. Moderator: Type of job

d. Moderator: None
(Education is another predictor!)

Moderator variables can take many different forms other than that depicted in Figure 6.4. A few examples of the variety of moderated predictor–criterion relationships that are conceivable are shown in Figures 6.5a, 6.5b, and 6.5c. Bartlett and O'Leary (1969) provided a number of such examples. In each of these cases, the I/O psychologist who restricts her inspection of the scatter diagram or the correlation coefficient to the entire sample's data will come away with an inaccurate, and possibly illegal, interpretation of those data. (Figure 6.5d, of course, suggests an altogether different possibility.)

According to James and Brett (1984), moderator variables have the following characteristics:

1. They are uncorrelated, or show minimum covariation, with either the predictor or the criterion variables. In the example shown in Figure 6.4, neither men nor women outscored each other as a group on either the predictor or the criterion.

2. They reflect a significant "interaction" with the predictor variable. Referring again to Figure 6.4, knowing *either* an applicant's score on the predictor *or* an applicant's sex tells us nothing about that applicant's job performance, but knowing *both* of these things allows us to predict job performance for the "predictable" group (women, in this example), and to refrain from making predictions for the "unpredictable" group (men). In Figure 6.5b, knowing *both* an applicant's age and his or her score on the predictor allows us to use the selection test one way for "older" applicants (a lower cutoff score?) and another way for "younger" applicants (a higher cutoff score?).

3. They do *not* imply any causal relationships. Figure 6.4 does not suggest that being a woman "causes" one to be more predictable under these circumstances, or causes men to be less predictable. They just *are*.

There are several different methods for identifying potential moderator variables. First, a researcher may simply have a "hunch" or hypothesis, based either on past experience or on "common sense," that the job-performance scores for one group of applicants may be more or less predictable than another group's scores. Second, the personnel researcher may be aware of a theory or model that suggests one or more potential moderator variables for a given combination of predictor and criterion measures.

Third, an I/O psychologist like Dr. MacKeven can engage in a "fishing expedition" by examining a scatter diagram through a process known as "quadrant analysis" (Hobert & Dunnette, 1967). If you look at the scattergram in Figure 6.6, you will see that the cutoff points that separate those applicants who are hired from those who are rejected (on the X axis), and those who are successful on the job from those who are not (on the Y axis), divide the joint data points into four groups, or quadrants. Those people whose data points are in either the upper-right or the lower-left quadrants are designated as "hits." On the basis of their selection test scores, we would predict that they would succeed or fail on the job, respectively, and, in fact, if given the opportunity to perform the job, they do. Those individuals in the upper-left and lower-right quadrants, however, are "misses." Those in the upper left are known as "false negatives," because their low predictor scores suggest that they would fail on the job, but if given the opportunity, they succeed. Those in the lower right are known as "false positives," because their higher predictor scores suggest they can succeed on the job, but if hired, they fail.

In its simplest form, quadrant analysis involves separating the "hits" from the "misses," and examining other variables (demographic, biographical, situational) to determine whether there are any systematic differences between the more and less predictable groups. Of course, in the event that a potential moderator variable emerges, a procedure similar to cross-validation is necessary in order to maximize the likelihood that the moderated predictor–criterion relationship generalizes to other samples of people.

Ghiselli (1956) suggested a similar, but simpler, approach to identifying moderator variables. If you look once again at the scatter diagram in Figure 6.3,

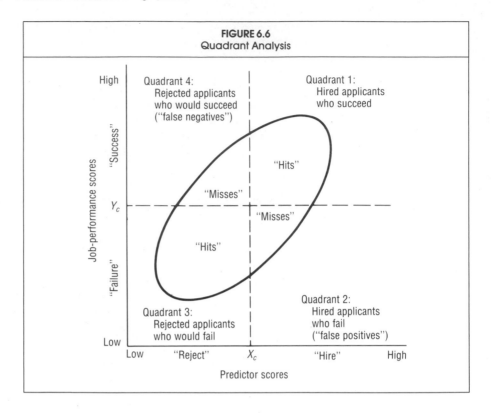

FIGURE 6.6
Quadrant Analysis

you will notice that some of the joint data points lie extremely close to the "best fitting" straight line, while other data points lie at greater distances from that line. If we drew two lines parallel to that regression line, one above it and the other below it, we would separate those individuals who are "more predictable" (whose data points lie closer to the line) from those who are "less predictable" (whose data points lie farther away from the regression line). We could then examine other variables to see whether these two subgroups of people differ in any systematic way(s).

Although the specifics of the argument are very complex, you should know that there is considerable controversy in the literature concerning the "appropriate" statistical analyses for investigating possible moderator variables. One camp advocates a form of regression analysis (Stone & Hollenbeck, 1984), while other researchers are decidedly less enthralled with this procedure (Arnold, 1982; Blood & Mullet, 1977). Perhaps the most useful contribution to this dispute is Arnold's (1984) recognition that researchers should avoid being overly dependent on a single statistical technique, but should instead adapt their analytical procedures to provide answers that are most appropriate considering the questions being asked.

Some recent empirical evidence suggests that identifying moderator variables may indeed contribute to more accurate, more valid predictions of job performance. Gutenberg, Arvey, Osburn, and Jeanneret (1983) found that the extent to which a job was characterized by decision-making or information-processing dimensions tended to moderate the validities of general intelligence, verbal ability, and numerical ability test scores (from the GATB). They also reported that the validities of finger- and manual-dexterity test scores for predicting performance on 111 diverse jobs (engineers, clerks, salespeople, machine operators) were moderated by the presence or absence of manual job dimensions.

Working with U.S. Coast Guard Academy cadets, Barnes, Potter, and Fiedler (1983) reported that the existence of interpersonal stress tended to moderate the validity of intellectual ability test scores (from the Scholastic Aptitude Test, or SAT) for predicting performance (grades) in an academic setting. Validity coefficients for freshmen and sophomores were .66 under low-stress conditions, but only .37 under high-stress conditions. In a similar vein, Peters, Fisher, and O'Connor's (1982) study revealed that the relationship between performance on a clerical task and certain individual difference variables (relevant experiences and abilities) was moderated by the extent to which the experimental situation *permitted* greater or lesser amounts of variability in task performance. Not surprisingly, when performance was situationally restricted, validity coefficients were smaller.

As you may have noticed, each of these studies involved situational rather than individual or demographic moderator variables. In a study that is very relevant to the current concerns with fairness and discrimination in employment, Heilman and Herlihy (1984) documented the role of an individual moderator variable. Their data suggested that a woman's perceptions about whether other women had been hired because of their job-related skills, *or* because the company needed more women on its payroll to avoid the appearance of discrimination, tended to moderate the relationship between the proportion of females who held a particular job and the level of interest that other women expressed in obtaining that job. Specifically, women were more interested in obtaining jobs held predominantly by other women *only* when they perceived that those women had been hired on the basis of merit, and *not* simply because they were women.

Although the identification of moderator variables will not solve all our validity problems, the available evidence suggests that higher validity coefficients can result when entire samples of people are divided into subgroups that are relatively more or less predictable, either on the basis of personal or situational variables. It would therefore be unwise for Dr. MacKeven to dismiss the possibility of identifying such moderator variables as she develops a set of valid procedures for selecting Peter's Pan Pizza managers.

SUPPRESSOR VARIABLES

A suppressor variable also improves our ability to predict criterion scores, even though it is completely unrelated to the criterion variable. Because it is uncorrelated with the criterion, a suppressor variable cannot add to the absolute amount of criterion variance explained by one or more predictors. Instead, a suppressor improves the efficiency and accuracy of our predictions by allowing us to ignore variance in the predictor scores that is *not* correlated with criterion score variance.

Figure 6.7 may help to explain how a suppressor variable works. The diagram in the top of the figure (Figure 6.7a) depicts criterion score variance and predictor score variance, and the overlap (or validity, or criterion relevance) that exists between these two variances. As you can see, a substantial portion of predictor score variance is completely unrelated to criterion score variance, and therefore constitutes a source of erroneous predictions. In the middle of the

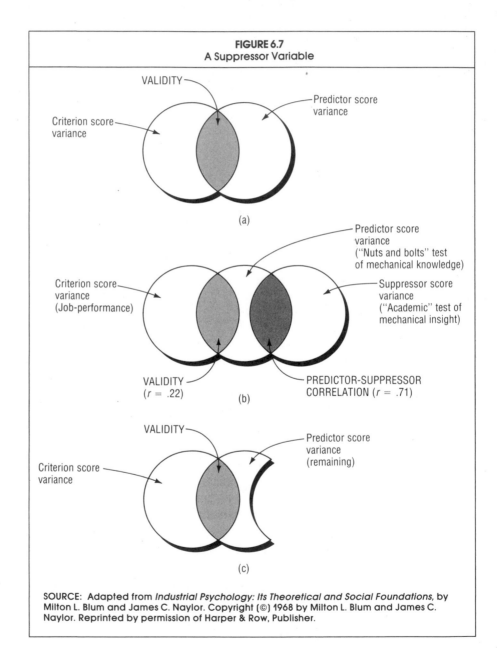

FIGURE 6.7
A Suppressor Variable

SOURCE: Adapted from *Industrial Psychology: Its Theoretical and Social Foundations,* by Milton L. Blum and James C. Naylor. Copyright (©) 1968 by Milton L. Blum and James C. Naylor. Reprinted by permission of Harper & Row, Publisher.

figure (Figure 6.7*b*), we have added a suppressor variable, which shares an appreciable amount of variance with the predictor, but is totally unrelated to the criterion. By subtracting, or "partialing out," that portion of the predictor variance that is unrelated to the criterion variance (this is usually accomplished via multiple regression procedures), we are left with a much smaller amount of predictor variance that is unrelated to the criterion and can therefore lead to erroneous or invalid predictions of criterion scores (see Figure 6.7*c*). Although the absolute amount of criterion variance that is explained remains the same, the *proportion* of remaining predictor variance that is shared with the criterion variance is larger. Increasing the magnitude of this proportion serves to increase the size of R^2 associated with the multiple regression equation that includes the predictors *and* the suppressor variable.

Unfortunately, our success in identifying suppressor variables has not matched our success in locating useful moderator variables. Suppressors are, in fact, quite rare. Sorenson's (1966) study of mechanics is one exception to this disappointing generalization. In this study, scores on a very practical, "nuts–and–bolts" test of mechanical knowledge predicted a performance criterion of industrial mechanics' performance with a reasonable degree of validity ($r = +.22$). A second, more academically oriented test of mechanical insight was completely unrelated to this criterion measure, but was very highly correlated with the "nuts–and–bolts" test of mechanical skills ($r = +.71$). When this second, "academic" test was included in the regression equation, Sorenson was able to make predictions about mechanics' job performance that were uncontaminated by their verbal skills, or their abstract "book-learning" that was totally unrelated to performance.

Although it would be foolish to rule out the possibility of finding similar suppressor variables that would improve the prediction of successful managerial performance, there isn't much cause for optimism. Dr. MacKeven might use her time more wisely by exploring the possibilities inherent in a more analytic approach to empirical validation known as "synthetic validity."

SYNTHETIC VALIDITY

The basic idea that underlies synthetic validity is that it may be easier to find valid predictors of *specific components* of job performance than it is to find a valid predictor of *overall* job performance. Synthetic validation (also known as job-component validation), then, involves identifying separate valid predictors for each important component of a job, and then building, or "synthesizing," valid predictions of overall job performance by combining the predictors of components in some systematic way.

In order to explore this possibility, Dr. MacKeven must be able to describe all (or many) jobs in the organization using the same set of job dimensions. Job-analytic techniques and procedures, such as functional job analysis (which describes all jobs in terms of their greater or lesser involvement with people, data, and things), or the PAQ (which uses a small number of information-processing dimensions to describe jobs), are particularly appropriate in this context. By using either of these job-analysis procedures (see Chapter 3), she can derive a matrix like the one that appears in Figure 6.8, where an *X* appearing at the intersection

FIGURE 6.8
Synthetic Validity Matrix

"General" job dimensions

Jobs in the organization

	1	2	3	4	5	6	7	8	9	10	11
A			X		X			X	X		X
B	X		X	X			X			X	
C	X	X			X	X		X		X	
D		X		X	X		X				
E	X				X		X	X		X	X
⋮	⋮	⋮	⋮	⋮	⋮	⋮	⋮	⋮	⋮	⋮	⋮
N		X	X			X	X	X		X	

of a particular job and a specific job dimension simply indicates that that dimension is an important component of that job.

Given the job-analytic information conveyed in Figure 6.8, and one or more selection devices for making valid predictions about performance on each of the 11 separate dimensions, Dr. MacKeven could use a synthesis, or combination, of the predictors for dimensions 3, 5, 8, 9, and 11 for predicting overall job performance on Job A. She would use a combination of the predictors for dimensions 1, 3, 4, 7, and 10 for predicting overall performance on Job B, and so forth.

An important advantage of the synthetic validation approach, beyond the logical expectation that it should be easier to predict more specific kinds of performance, is that the actual validity analyses can be conducted with a much smaller total number of job applicants or incumbents than are required for a traditional criterion-related validity analysis. Whether she uses predictive or concurrent validation, Dr. MacKeven would not have to wait until a sufficient number of people became available in each individual job to proceed. Because she is now concerned primarily with finding valid predictors of separate job components, she can use people in each and every job for which a given component or dimension is important when conducting the analyses.

For example, referring again to Figure 6.8, a validity analysis for a predictor of Job Dimension 1 could utilize individuals in Jobs B, C, and E; the analysis for a predictor of Job Dimension 2 could use individuals in Jobs C, D, and N; and so forth. This logistical difference can be a terrific advantage, especially in smaller organizations and in organizations with low turnover rates, where it takes a long time to amass a sufficient number of applicants for, or incumbents in, a single job to conduct a traditional criterion-related validity analysis.

After tracing its origins and historical development back to Lawshe (1952) and Balma (1959), Mossholder and Arvey (1984) described the two predominant approaches for assessing synthetic validity. The first of these relies on the J-coefficient, which in turn depends on subjective *estimates* of the relationships between certain job components or dimensions and both selection test performance and job performance. The second, known as the Job Component Model, focuses on the centrality of certain PAQ dimensions, and either selection test scores or criterion-related validity coefficients. Both approaches are quite complex.

There is some disagreement concerning which of these two approaches comes closest to satisfying the validation requirements specified in the EEOC *Guidelines* (1978). Mecham, Jeanneret, and McCormick (1983) argued that the Job Component Model is better, because it identifies selection tests that actually distinguish between successful and unsuccessful jobholders (Mossholder & Arvey, 1984). Trattner (1982), however, argued in favor of the J-coefficient because it breaks jobs down into specific knowledge, skills, and ability components.

Although synthetic validity may eventually play an important role in improving the personnel selection process, the available research evidence has only demonstrated the concept's feasibility (Mossholder & Arvey, 1984). Much remains to be done before we can speak to the actual usefulness, or utility, of synthetic validity for making personnel selection decisions. Since Dr. MacKeven has a potentially very large sample of managerial applicants or incumbents at her disposal, she will probably not be forced to adopt a synthetic validity analysis on logistical grounds. This does not rule out the possibility, however, that she may decide that trying to predict specific components of managers' jobs at Peter's Pan Pizza will be substantially easier than trying to predict overall managerial performance.

Schmidt and Hunter (1980) suggested quite a different approach for dealing with, or overcoming, the small validity coefficients that have emerged from traditional criterion-related validity analyses. Referred to in the literature as "validity generalization," their ideas, and those of their supporters and detractors, represent one of the "cutting edges" of personnel selection research.

VALIDITY GENERALIZATION

A form of meta-analysis (see Chapter 2), the goal of validity generalization is to be able to apply the results of a validity analysis conducted in one organizational setting to other, similar settings and sets of circumstances. Although the EEOC *Guidelines* allow for the possibility of an organization appealing to validity studies that were conducted elsewhere to justify their own use of particular selection instruments, any company that does so must be prepared to demonstrate that the jobs for which the selection tests are being used are similar (through appropriate job analyses), and that the tests are fair for each race, sex, and ethnic group that makes up the organization's labor market. Implicit in the *Guidelines*, however, is the "situational-specificity hypothesis," the assumption that one or more of a variety of individual or situational variables may moderate the validity coefficient that describes the relationship between scores on a given test or selection instrument and performance on a particular job. In essence, the *Guidelines* direct employers to demonstrate that no such moderator variables are likely to be operating.

A superficial review of the empirical literature seems to confirm the existence of such moderator variables, for the validity coefficients reported for given selection tests and given job performance measures have *not* been very consistent. That is, it is not unusual for a specific selection test to predict managers' performance well in some studies, but very poorly or not at all in others. Schmidt and Hunter (1980) contend, however, that most, if not all, of this variation is attributable *not* to individual or situational moderator variables, but rather to a number of **statistical artifacts** and other factors that have no actual bearing on the "true" magnitude of a given predictor–criterion validity coefficient. These artifacts and other influences include the following:

- differences between studies in criterion reliability
- differences between studies in selection-test reliability
- differences between studies in the range restriction associated with relevant variables
- sampling error due to small sample sizes
- differences between studies in the amounts and kinds of criterion contamination and deficiency
- computational and typographical errors in written/published reports and articles
- differences in factor structure (based on factor analyses) between ostensibly similar tests

The general procedure that is typically used to support the idea of validity generalization (and thereby to refute the situational specificity hypothesis) involves a variety of statistical procedures to eliminate or explain the inconsistencies (variance) in a set of validity coefficients that can be attributed to the artifacts and influences listed above. More specifically, the rule–of–thumb that has evolved is to conclude that the situational specificity hypothesis *has* been refuted when 75 percent of that variance (in validity coefficients) can be explained in terms of the first four artifacts or influences. It is then assumed that the other three influences (which are extremely difficult or impossible to assess accurately) account for a sizable portion of the remaining variance in reported validity coefficients, and that the "true" validity coefficient for a given predictor–criterion combination is equal to the average of all the validity coefficients reported for that predictor–criterion pair.

The concept of validity generalization has generated vast amounts of both computer-simulated (Callender & Osburn, 1981) and empirical (Schmidt, Hunter, & Pearlman, 1981) research, and no small amount of controversy. Recent empirical studies have focused on jobs in the petroleum industry (Schmidt, Hunter, & Caplan, 1981), in the life insurance industry (Brown, 1981), and on stenographers (Schmidt & Hunter, 1984). These studies examined validity generalization for a number of different selection instruments, including biographical inventories

(Brown, 1981) and paper–and–pencil tests of various cognitive or intellectual abilities (Schmidt, Ocasio, Hillery, & Hunter, 1985).

The controversies surrounding validity generalization are focused, first, on the merits of meta-analytic procedures in general, and second, on the optimal procedures for conducting validity generalization analyses. Several authors have described a variety of problems inherent in meta-analysis (Bullock & Svyantek, 1985) and validity generalization research (Burke, 1984). These difficulties include the following:

- unavailability of relevant studies
- inadequate documentation of data-coding procedures used in relevant studies
- imprecision in defining the content domain of relevant studies
- inadequate descriptions of the characteristics of relevant studies

Nevertheless, Burke's belief that these problems do *not* represent insurmountable obstacles to progress in the area of validity generalization represents something of a consensus.

Opinions regarding the best or optimal procedures for conducting validity generalization analyses show fewer signs of moving toward consensus. The longest running debate is between Schmidt and Hunter and their colleagues (Hunter, Schmidt, & Pearlman, 1982; Schmidt, Hunter, & Pearlman, 1982) and Callender and Osburn and their allies (Callender & Osburn, 1981, 1982; Callender, Osburn, Greener, & Ashworth, 1982; Obsurn, Callender, Greener, & Ashworth, 1983). Although the practical implications are often trivial, this debate concerns the appropriate equations for estimating one of the necessary parameters in validity generalization research—the variance of "true" predictor–criterion validities. Raju and Burke (1983) recently joined the fray by suggesting two new procedures for studying and evaluating the merits of validity generalization.

A somewhat broader perspective appeared in *Personnel Psychology*, which published a lengthy report that summarized most of the key criticisms of validity generalization and then included advocates' responses to those criticisms and related questions (Sackett, Schmitt, Tenopyr, Kehoe, & Zedeck, 1985; Schmidt, Hunter, Pearlman, & Hirsh, 1985). Although this document neglects to provide practitioners with some important specific recommendations for implementing the validity generalization concept, Dr. MacKeven will certainly want to review it if she entertains the possibility of adapting validity generalization principles to Peter's Pan Pizza, Inc.

UTILITY OF A PERSONNEL SELECTION SYSTEM

Although the concept of utility is not new (Brogden, 1949; Cronbach & Gleser, 1965), it is only in recent years that the professional literature has begun to

---

statistical artifacts: numerical results that reflect the properties of the statistical procedure used, rather than the empirical data being analyzed

reflect the concerns of I/O psychologists and others who recognize that statistical significance is no guarantee that one or more predictors will make a useful, practical contribution to an organization's personnel selection system. In a capitalist economy, this "useful contribution" usually means increasing productivity or profits and/or decreasing costs. In its most basic sense, then, the utility of any personnel or human-resources system can be expressed as the difference between what that system contributes to an organization and what it costs (Cronshaw & Alexander, 1985).

Utility concepts have been applied to a number of different personnel systems, including training and other "intervention" programs (Schmidt, Hunter, & Pearlman, 1982), recruitment (Boudreau & Rynes, 1985), and performance appraisal (Landy, Farr, & Jacobs, 1982). Nevertheless, the primary focus of utility has always been, and remains, the personnel selection process.

Before we show you an example of a modern utility formula and describe some of the earlier efforts to capture this very important property of a selection system, a "picture [may well be] worth a thousand words." If you look at Figure 6.9, where we have once again depicted traditional scatter diagrams reflecting two positive correlations between a predictor and criterion, you will see some of the factors that determine just how useful a predictor–criterion relationship might be.

First, the utility of any predictor–criterion relationship will increase as the *reliability and quality of the criterion* measure (of job performance) increases. Trying to predict an unreliable criterion measure is impossible, and trying to predict an irrelevant criterion is an exercise in futility. Second, the utility of a predictor–criterion relationship will increase as the *reliability of the predictor* increases. No measure can be expected to predict any other measure better than it "predicts" itself.

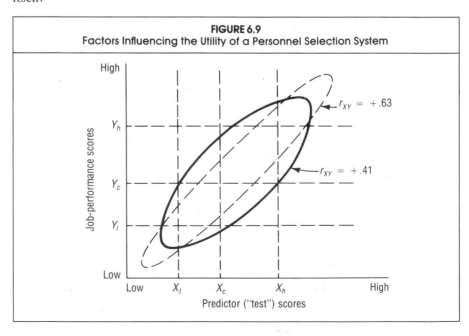

FIGURE 6.9
Factors Influencing the Utility of a Personnel Selection System

Third, assuming that the utility of a selection system is directly related to the ratio of "hits" to "misses" (see Figure 6.6) that it generates, that utility will increase as the *size of the criterion-related validity coefficient* increases. Given any combination of cutoff scores on the predictor and criterion (X_c and Y_c in Figure 6.9, for example), the ratio of "hits" to "misses" will be greater when $r = .63$ than when $r = .41$.

Fourth, the utility of any "new" selection system (for replacing an "old," existing selection system) is influenced by the proportion of employees who have been selected using the "old" system who perform satisfactorily on their jobs. If Y_l in Figure 6.9 represented the dividing line between "successful" and "unsuccessful" job performance, it is obvious that almost all the individuals whose data make up this scattergram would be performing their jobs at levels that fall into the "satisfactory" range. In this case, the benefits to be gained by using a "new" selection system (that is, its utility) would be minimal or nonexistent. On the other hand, if Y_c or Y_h represented the difference between success and failure on the job, there would be enough "unsuccessful" employees to render a "new" selection system potentially useful. This parameter of a selection system is usually referred to as the *base rate of success.*

Fifth, the utility of a selection system is a function of the *selection ratio* and *hiring rate* that provide a context for that system. The selection ratio refers to the proportion of individuals in the population from which an organization draws its applicants whose scores on a predictor exceed a given cutoff score. Alexander, Barrett, and Doverspike (1983) distinguished between this selection ratio and a hiring rate, "which refers to the percentage of total applicants hired" (p. 342) and refers only to specific samples of applicants. These two indices are equivalent only when a sample of applicants represents a random sample of the larger population, a condition they claim tends to be the exception rather than the rule.

The important point here is that the utility of a selection system will increase as the cutoff score on the predictor is set increasingly higher (until, of course, it is set so high that *none* of the applicants' scores exceed it). Higher predictor cutoff scores mean that an organization is choosing the "cream of the crop." Predictor cutoff scores can only be set at such high levels when there is a large number of applicants relative to the number of jobs that must be filled (hiring rate), and when a sufficient proportion of the individuals in the applicant population have predictor scores that exceed that cutoff point (selection ratio).

You can see, then, that a statistically significant validity coefficient is only a step down the path to a useful personnel selection system. The ultimate goal is a system with demonstrable utility. As we said earlier, however, utility is not an altogether new and different idea.

Early Descriptions of Utility: The Taylor–Russell and Naylor–Shine Tables

Taylor and Russell (1939) generated a set of tables designed to show the percentages of newly hired employees who could be expected to achieve "successful" levels of job-performance, given specific predictor validities, specific selection ratios, and specific preselection base rates of job-performance success. Although these tables were very useful tools for personnel psychologists interested in the practical implications of a selection test or system, they suffered from some notable weaknesses. First, they required designation of a single criterion score that separated "success" from "failure" on the job; this is often an arbitrary exercise at best. A second, related problem was that they did not recognize different degrees of job success and failure; performance on a wide variety of jobs simply does not lend itself to neat, dichotomous categorization as "success" or "failure," with nothing in between.

Naylor and Shine (1965) responded to these weaknesses by publishing a second set of tables that treated job proficiency as a continuous variable. These tables identified the expected differences in average job performance scores for groups of employees selected under the "new" and "old" systems.

Contemporary Utility Formulas

Boudreau (1983b) described a typical formula for calculating the utility of a selection test or system:

$$\Delta U = (N)(T)(r_{xy})(SD_y)(\overline{Z}_x) - C, \text{ where}$$

ΔU = the increase in average dollar-value payoff that results from selecting N employees using a test or procedure (x) instead of selecting randomly
N = the number of employees selected
T = the expected average tenure of the selected group
r_{xy} = the correlation coefficient (for prescreened applicants) between predictor scores (x) and dollar-value payoff (y)
SD_y = the standard deviation of dollar-value payoff in the group of prescreened applicants
Z_x = the average **standard** predictor **score** of the selected group
C = the total selection cost for all applicants

Each of these parameters is relatively easy to estimate, with the notable exception of SD_y, the standard deviation of selected applicants' job-performance scores expressed in dollar-value terms.

Not surprisingly, a substantial portion of the recent literature pertaining to utility has addressed this problem of estimating SD_y. We can now point to several different estimation strategies. Schmidt, Hunter, McKenzie, and Muldrow (1979) made the basic assumption that job performance in dollar-value terms was distributed normally (see Chapter 2 for a description of the normal distribution), and then asked the supervisors of the workers in question to estimate the dollar value of employees whose job performance (according to the supervisors) placed them at either the 15th, the 50th, or the 85th **percentiles** of that normal distribution. The 15th and 85th percentiles represent those points in a normal distribution that lie approximately -1 and $+1$ standard deviation, respectively, away from the mean of the distribution, which coincides with the 50th percentile (see Figure 2.7). A final estimate of SD_y was obtained by averaging several supervisors' estimates of the dollar-value discrepancies between a 50th-percentile worker and either a 15th- or an 85th-percentile worker. Bobko, Karren, and Parkington (1983), who collected data in a large insurance company, provided empirical support for both the initial assumption of normality, and the use of the 15th, 50th, and 85th percentiles for estimating SD_y in utility equations.

A second approach to estimating SD_y equates this parameter with certain percentages of employees' salaries or the dollar value of their average work outputs. Schmidt and Hunter's (1983) accumulation of empirical data from the research literature offered support for these estimation procedures. A third approach, known as the CREPID (after "Cascio–Ramos estimate of performance in dollars") method (Cascio, 1982), "is based on the economic premise that the value of an individual's labor is equivalent to what an organization is willing to pay to obtain that labor" (Reilly & Smither, 1985, p. 652). Other methods for estimating this crucial parameter of the utility equation have been suggested by Burke and Frederick (1984) and Eaton, Wing, and Mitchell (1985). Although there has been a small number of simulated (Reilly & Smither, 1985) and empirical (Weekley, Frank, O'Connor, & Peters, 1985) comparisons of several of these approaches, it is still too soon to draw any conclusions about the relative superiority of any particular procedure(s).

The message that comes through "loud and clear" from most of the published utility studies is that the dollar value of using valid selection tests far surpasses most of our wildest expectations. For example, Schmidt, Mack, and Hunter (1984) examined the utility of using a valid test versus a structured interview for selecting park rangers for the U.S. Park Service. A portion of one of their tables, which shows the estimated increases in productivity (expressed in thousands of dollars) to be expected by using a general mental ability test instead of an interview for a period of one year, is presented in Table 6.1. You can see from this table, for instance, that:

> if 80 park rangers are hired in a given year (the 1978–81 average was 83 . . .) using a reliable test of general mental ability instead of the interview, the resulting increase in the dollar value of their output over their tenure will be approximately $1.16 million if they average 5 years on the job and approximately $2.3 million if they stay on the job an average of 10 years (p. 495).

Schmidt et al. (1979) predicted even more impressive monetary gains in productivity if computer programmers were selected on the basis of their scores on a programming aptitude test. Tables 6.2 and 6.3 show the estimated increases in productivity (expressed in millions of dollars) that would result if the Programmer Aptitude Test (Hughes & McNamara, 1959) were used for a period of one year to select computer programmers in the federal government and in the U.S. economy as a whole, respectively.

---

standard score: equal to the difference between a "raw" (untransformed) score and the mean of the distribution of scores, divided by the standard deviation of that distribution of scores

percentiles: values in a distribution of scores that separate specified percentages of those scores when they are arranged in rank order of magnitude; for example, the 85th percentile is that score that exceeds 85 percent of the scores in a distribution of scores

TABLE 6.1 Estimates of Productivity Increases Obtainable from One Year's Substitution of a General Mental Ability Test for an Interview in Selecting U.S. Park Rangers (in Thousands of Dollars)

	Number of years on the job	
Number selected	5	10
30	434	868
40	579	1158
50	724	1447
60	868	1737
70	1013	2026
80	1158	2316
90	1303	2606
100	1448	2895
110	1592	3184
120	1737	3474
130	1882	3764

SOURCE: Adapted from "Selection Utility in the Occupation of U.S. Park Ranger for Three Modes of Test Use," by F. L. Schmidt, M. J. Mack, and J. E. Hunter, *Journal of Applied Psychology*, 1984, 69, 490–497. Copyright 1984 by the American Psychological Association. Reprinted by permission.

Boudreau suggested that standard utility equations, such as the one presented above, are too simplistic because they ignore the fact that employees are continually moving in and out of the workforce (Boudreau, 1983b; Boudreau & Berger, 1985), and they ignore such key economic concepts as variable costs (bonuses and commissions), taxes, and "discounting," which refers to changes in monetary value over time (Boudreau, 1983a). The first of these omissions results in underestimates of utility, while the second group of oversights (economic concepts) results in overestimates. Nevertheless, the prospect of achieving monetary gains and/or savings anywhere near this magnitude should stimulate I/O psychologists to pursue their research in the area of utility, and should render the results of such research fascinating to managers and executives in a wide variety of organizations.

At this point, you should have a grasp of the science and some of the economics of personnel selection. All that remains is to describe the legal context that has influenced the selection process since the passage of the Civil Rights Act in 1964—the context that prompted Mr. Smith to send Dr. MacKeven the memo that appeared at the beginning of this chapter.

EEOC GUIDELINES

Formally entitled the *Uniform Guidelines on Employee Selection Procedures* (EEOC, 1978), this document was adopted by the Equal Employment Opportunity Commission (which is the federal agency charged with enforcing Title VII of the 1964 Civil Rights Act) to guide employers as they develop and modify their personnel procedures so that they comply with the law. The *Guidelines* have

TABLE 6.2 Estimates of Productivity Increases Obtainable from One Year's Use of the Programmer Aptitude Test to Select Computer Programmers in the Federal Government (in Millions of Dollars)

| Hiring rate* | True validity of previous procedure | | | | |
	.00	.20	.30	.40	.50
.05	97.2	71.7	58.9	46.1	33.3
.10	82.8	60.1	50.1	39.2	28.3
.20	66.0	48.6	40.0	31.3	22.6
.30	54.7	40.3	33.1	25.9	18.7
.40	45.6	34.6	27.6	21.6	15.6
.50	37.6	27.7	22.8	17.8	12.9
.60	30.4	22.4	18.4	14.4	10.4
.70	23.4	17.2	14.1	11.1	8.0
.80	16.5	12.2	10.0	7.8	5.6

*Number of jobs to be filled divided by the number of applicants for those jobs.

SOURCE: "Impact of Valid Selection Procedures on Workforce Productivity," by F. L. Schmidt, J. E. Hunter, R. C. McKenzie, and T. W. Muldrow, *Journal of Applied Psychology*, 1979, 64, 609–626. Copyright 1979 by the American Psychological Association. Reprinted by permission.

TABLE 6.3 Estimates of Productivity Increases Obtainable from One Year's Use of the Programmer Aptitude Test to Select Computer Programmers throughout the U.S. Economy

| Hiring rate* | True validity of previous procedure | | | | |
	.00	.20	.30	.40	.50
.05	1605	1184	973	761	550
.10	1367	1008	828	648	468
.20	1091	804	661	517	373
.30	903	666	547	428	309
.40	753	555	455	356	257
.50	622	459	376	295	213
.60	501	370	304	238	172
.70	387	285	234	183	132
.80	273	201	165	129	93

*Number of jobs to be filled divided by the number of applicants for those jobs.

SOURCE: "Impact of Valid Selection Procedures on Workforce Productivity," by F. L. Schmidt, J. E. Hunter, R. C. McKenzie, and T. W. Muldrow, *Journal of Applied Psychology*, 1979, 64, 609–626. Copyright 1979 by the American Psychological Association. Reprinted by permission.

also been adopted by federal and state judicial systems as a set of standards for determining whether or not organizations are, in fact, in compliance.

Because they are quite lengthy and complex, you can only achieve a complete understanding of the *Guidelines* by studying them yourself. Our goal here is to provide you with a general overview, and to acquaint you with several of the key concepts that make up the core of this document. These include the ideas of protected groups, adverse impact, and affirmative action. Finally, we shall describe some of the contributions to the I/O psychology literature that pertain to these *Guidelines*.

Protected Groups

The purpose of the *Guidelines* is to prohibit and prevent discrimination in employment on the bases of race, color, sex, religion, or national origin. In order to document compliance, an organization must maintain employment records (pertaining to recruiting, selecting, promoting, etc.) separately by sex and by the following racial and ethnic groups: (1) blacks; (2) American Indians, including natives of Alaska; (3) Asians, including Pacific Islanders; (4) Hispanics, including individuals of Mexican, Puerto Rican, Cuban, Central or South American, or other Spanish origin or culture, regardless of race; and (5) Caucasians, including whites other than Hispanics.

Each of these groups, except for Caucasians, is referred to as a "protected group," because it is discrimination against these specific groups of women and men that the *Guidelines* are expressly designed to prevent. If a personnel procedure does discriminate against one (or more) of these groups, that procedure is said to have an "adverse impact" on that group, and the organization is then obliged to defend its use of the discriminatory procedure. Such defense typically takes the form of demonstrating the validity of the personnel procedure in question, usually along the lines of one or more of the validity analyses described in the previous chapter.

Although space limitations preclude a detailed discussion, you should realize that such a demonstration is not always as straightforward as it sounds. Recall (from Chapter 2) that I/O psychologists typically report their research results in terms of the probability that their conclusions are justified by their data (statistical significance levels). If you have ever witnessed a judicial procedure (or even watched "Perry Mason" reruns on TV), you know that our judicial systems seek "yes" or "no" answers during testimony, answers that trained psychologists are often unable and therefore unwilling to give. We will have to bridge this communication gap if we are to enhance our contributions to judicial deliberations concerning employment legislation.

Adverse Impact

The *Guidelines* have adopted the "four-fifths rule" as a criterion for determining whether a personnel procedure has an adverse impact on any protected group. Stated as simply as possible, this standard stipulates that adverse impact exists whenever the hiring rate for a protected group is less than four-fifths of the hiring rate for whatever group is treated most favorably (usually white men) by the personnel procedure in question, except when the difference is based on small numbers of individuals and is not statistically significant. Thus, if five out of every ten white men who apply for a given job are hired on the basis of their scores on a particular selection test, adverse impact will exist when fewer than four out of every ten members of a protected group who apply are selected on the basis of their test scores.

As we stated earlier, once a **plaintiff** successfully demonstrates the adverse impact of a personnel procedure, the employing organization must then demonstrate that the procedure in question is a valid predictor of job performance. Even if the organization succeeds in so demonstrating, however, the *Guidelines* stipulate that it is the organization's responsibility to search for, identify, and use *other* valid selection procedures that do not have an adverse impact on any protected group.

The implicit assumption here is that there is no inherent relationship between a person's performance on a job, or on a valid selection test, and that person's status vis-à-vis any of the protected groups. Given the unfortunate history of racial, sex, and ethnic inequalities that have prevailed in the areas of education and socioeconomic status in our society, however, this assumption may not always be consistent with reality. It is the goal of affirmative action to eliminate the employment-related consequences of these past injustices.

Affirmative Action

Affirmative action refers to *voluntary* organizational policies and procedures that are designed to assure that jobs are accessible to qualified persons without regard to their sex, to their race, or to their ethnic-group membership. Such policies are intended to cover all stages of the employment process, from recruiting and selecting individuals to training and promoting them, and even to redesigning jobs.

In practice, this often amounts to hiring or promoting a member of a protected group when that person and a "majority group" member (usually a white man) are deemed *equally qualified.* Organizations are under *no* obligation to hire anyone, protected group member or not, who is *less qualified* to perform the work. Unfortunately, it is often very difficult to determine when two or more people are "equally qualified." Many organizations have therefore interpreted affirmative action to mean giving the protected group member the "benefit of the doubt" in equivocal situations. It is personnel actions based on this interpretation that have led to outraged cries from white men of "reverse discrimination."

Recent EEOC-Related Literature

A number of recent contributions to the professional literature have focused on adverse impact and affirmative action. Several of these have been specifically concerned with the appropriate procedures for diagnosing adverse impact. Wing (1981, 1982), for example, discussed how small sample sizes can undermine investigations of adverse impact, and pointed out that even so-called experts can be wrong in their choices of applicable statistical procedures. She suggested that findings of adverse impact should be based on *both* statistical significance *and* the four-fifths rule, rather than on just one or the other.

Drasgow and Kang (1984) compared differential validity analysis (which compares correlation coefficients) with differential prediction analysis (which compares regression coefficients), and concluded that the latter had more power in most situations to detect adverse impact. Ironson, Guion, and Ostrander (1982) proposed an alternative psychometric definition of adverse impact that is based on latent-trait theory (or IRT). We briefly described IRT in Chapter 5 as a particular type of measurement theory that specifies rules for converting test-item responses into estimates of the degree to which people possess

---

plaintiff: that party to a legal dispute that makes an accusation or brings charges against another party (the defendant)

underlying (latent) traits (Hulin, Drasgow, & Parsons, 1983). Raju and Edwards (1984) offered additional support for this approach.

To date, most of the EEOC's investigations into charges of adverse impact have concentrated on paper–and–pencil selection tests. As a result, many employers have grown wary of using these predictors (Olian & Wilcox, 1982). Although there is some evidence that biographical data and peer evaluations may be just as valid as standardized tests under various circumstances, there is no clear indication that these alternative procedures have less adverse impact (Reilly & Chao, 1982).

Kleiman and Faley (1985) reviewed 12 court cases since 1978 that have addressed the issue of adverse impact as it pertains to paper–and–pencil tests. They concluded that the courts are placing a heavy emphasis on proper test development procedures, which can sometimes be demonstrated through content validity analyses. They also described a general reluctance to accept recent research and theory that is inconsistent with the *Guidelines*; much of this reluctance centers on the topic of validity generalization.

Other authors have addressed procedures for implementing affirmative action, as well as some of the possible consequences of such programs. Ramos (1981) found that the use of Spanish test instructions resulted in small but significant gains in scores on a predominantly nonverbal test battery for Hispanic applicants whose language preference was Spanish. Heilman (1984) suggested that personnel decision makers are less likely to discriminate against female applicants or employees when those decision makers are provided with greater amounts of *relevant* information. Additional evidence indicates that employers may unknowingly discriminate against physically attractive women who apply for managerial jobs (Heilman & Saruwatari, 1979). These kinds of research findings may be extremely useful to organizations interested in strengthening their affirmative action programs.

Rosen and Mericle (1979) cautioned, however, that care must be taken to develop affirmative action policy statements and procedures that do not result in managerial "backlash" in selection and salary decisions. Others have suggested that an affirmative action policy that imposes a quota that is even slightly larger than a protected group's representation in the applicant population may necessitate extensive recruitment procedures, and result in substantial performance differences between selected subgroups (Kroeck, Barrett, & Alexander, 1983).

Considerable evidence exists that affirmative action "backlash" is not always limited to managers and decision-makers. Chacko (1982) reported that women who believed that they had been hired primarily because of their sex had lower levels of organizational commitment, lower levels of satisfaction (with their work, their supervisors, and their co-workers), and higher levels of role conflict and ambiguity. Similarly, Heilman and Herlihy's (1984) data suggested that increased proportions of women holding particular jobs tended to make those jobs appear more interesting to high school-aged women only when those teenagers believed that the women had been hired on the basis of their qualifications and not on the basis of affirmative action policies. Other researchers have given similar attention to the dynamics of age discrimination (Cleveland & Landy, 1983; Faley, Kleiman, & Lengnick-Hall, 1984; Pritchard, Maxwell, & Jordan, 1984).

There can be no question that Title VII of the 1964 Civil Rights Act has made personnel selection (and all human-resources decisions) more challenging than it has ever been before. When you consider the complexities of validity analysis and utility, and add the legal challenges of assessing adverse impact and the related issue of test fairness (Lawshe, 1983; Ledvinka, Markos, & Ladd, 1982; Norborg, 1984; Schmidt & Hunter, 1982), you can appreciate what Dr. MacKeven is up against as she tries to respond to both Mr. Schiftner's and Mr. Smith's concerns.

CHAPTER SUMMARY

Organizations can recruit new employees through radio, television and newspaper announcements, personal contacts, posted notices, and professional employment agencies. Because recruiting is part of the overall selection process, care must be taken to contact men and women of all races, ethnic groups, and religious preferences, and to encourage them to apply for vacant organizational positions. Realistic job previews that provide job applicants with relatively unbiased descriptions of the available job(s) may help to improve the efficiency and effectiveness of the recruiting process.

After one or more selection tests have been administered to job applicants, the information obtained can be organized and presented in several different ways in order to facilitate the decision-making process. Expectancy charts are easy to understand, but they convey only a global picture of a selection system's impact on workers' performance. Regression equations are more mathematically sophisticated and precise, and they can reveal the magnitude of the relationship between selection tests and job-performance criteria. They are compensatory, however, in that they allow an applicant's high score on one selection instrument to make up for a low score on another. Multiple cutoff and multiple hurdle decision strategies can be used in place of, or in combination with, regression strategies when a completely compensatory approach is inappropriate. Efforts to improve the effectiveness of these traditional personnel selection strategies have involved the use of moderator and suppressor variables, as well as investigations of synthetic validation and validity generalization techniques.

Beyond the validity of hiring decisions, personnel selection specialists have become concerned with the utility, or cost-effectiveness, of the systems used to make those decisions. The utility of a new selection system is determined by the reliability and validity of the selection test and job-performance measures, as well as the base rate of current employees' success on the job and the current selection ratio and hiring rate.

This all takes place in the legal and social context of the EEOC's *Guidelines*, which protect certain groups of applicants from selection tests with adverse impact, and encourage organizations to adopt affirmative action policies and procedures.

INTEROFFICE MEMO

TO: T. J. Smith, Legal Counsel

FROM: J. A. MacKeven, Human—Resources Coordinator

Thanks for the reminder. Jim Schiftner and I have already discussed, and agreed to solicit, your services and expertise as we go about assembling a selection system for staffing PPP's managerial ranks.

A quick review of our personnel records confirms that PPP is indeed an ''equal opportunity employer'' when it comes to women. We may have some problems, however, with respect to some of the other protected groups, especially blacks and Asians. Although I am unaware of the exact percentage representations of those groups in our applicant population, I suspect they are underrepresented among PPP's managers. I therefore plan to examine our recruiting strategies, and to conduct some specific ''subgroup analyses'' as part of our overall validity analyses of the selection measures we are currently considering (which you mentioned in your memo). I hope these efforts will shed some light on the seriousness and the dynamics of our underrepresen— tation problems with specific groups protected by the EEOC.

Jim or I will contact you soon to arrange an initial ''meeting of the minds,'' and then periodically thereafter, to keep you informed con— cerning our progress and problems. Thanks for your support.

REVIEW QUESTIONS AND EXERCISES

1. Describe recent research that suggests that Dr. MacKeven may be too complacent in her conviction that Peter's Pan Pizza has no "affirmative action problems" with women.

2. Although there are relatively few black or Asian managers on PPP's employment rolls, why might this not be a problem as far as the EEOC *Guidelines* are concerned?

3. What should Dr. MacKeven look for as she examines PPP's recruiting strategies in her search for the cause(s) of possible subgroups' underrepresentation as managers?

4. Describe the specific "subgroup analyses" that Dr. MacKeven referred to in her memo to Mr. Smith.

5. What kinds of information must Dr. MacKeven have at her disposal in order to determine the utility of whatever selection system she and Mr. Schiftner create?

6. Once that selection system is in place, should PPP use expectancy charts, regression equations, multiple cutoffs, or a combination of these decision-making strategies to select managers? Explain your answer.

7. When does "affirmative action" become "reverse discrimination"?

8. Describe the basic premise that underlies Title VII of the 1964 Civil Rights Act. Do you agree or disagree with it? Why?

CHAPTER 7

Personnel Training

Learning Points

After studying this chapter, you should

- be able to describe the three components of training-needs assessment, as well as the functional relationship between needs assessment and training evaluation

- be able to list examples of four different kinds of criteria for evaluating training effectiveness, and to cite the strengths and weaknesses associated with each kind

- know the three basic questions that must be answered during the course of training evaluation

- be able to describe several different "threats" to the internal and external validity of a training program

- know the differences that characterize pre- and quasi-experimental designs, as well as true experimental designs, and how those differences affect the capacity of a design to control the various threats to internal and external validity

- be aware of the legal context in which personnel training programs operate

- be able to describe, and to cite the advantages and disadvantages associated with, most of the training methods and procedures that are currently being used in industrial organizations

INTEROFFICE MEMO
TO: Dr. Jennilyn A. MacKeven, Human-Resources Coordinator
FROM: Robert Hammond, Director of Engineering

As you probably know, I have been with Peter's Pan Pizza for almost 25 years now. I was hired fresh out of college, with the ink on my bachelor of engineering degree barely dry. Due to a lot of hard work and, quite frankly, a bit of good luck, I have been promoted through the organizational ranks and, 8 months ago, became the director of my department. As these promotions accumulated, I quite naturally found myself doing less and less actual engineering, so that I could devote more time to my supervisory responsibilities. Although I believe that I have become a competent supervisor and manager, my only credential in that area is an imaginary diploma from the ''school of hard knocks.'' That is to say, I have never received any formal training in supervisory or managerial skills. I was made a first-level supervisor because I was the ''best'' engineer, I became a manager because I apparently excelled at first-level supervision, and so forth.

After 8 months as Director of Engineering, observing and evaluating my subordinate managers and especially my first-level supervisors, it has become clear to me that nothing has changed. People are still being promoted out of engineering specialties into supervisory positions not because they apparently know anything about supervising others, but because they are excellent engineers. Can we do anything to break this rather illogical chain of events? Is it possible, either at a departmental or an organizational level, to develop some sort of training program for professional engineers who are being asked to move into supervisory positions? Because of my own experience, and my recent observations, I am convinced that competent supervisors must possess more than a high level of motivation and a reasonable portion of common sense.

Do you agree? And, more importantly, can you help?

After receiving Bob Hammond's memo, Dr. MacKeven conducted an informal survey of Peter's Pan Pizza's vice presidents to determine the extent to which this problem was shared by other divisions of the organization. Much to her chagrin, she found that the facilities division had no monopoly in this area. Vice presidents Ryan in marketing, Clark in retail operations, Creighton in personnel, as well as the vice presidents of purchasing, distribution, and finance all decried the lack of programs for initiating technicians, specialists, and other lower-ranking personnel into the mysteries of supervision. It appears that supervisors throughout PPP, Inc., are expected to just "pick up" the necessary skills and abilities "along the way."

Mr. Hammond's memo highlights a very serious gap in Peter's Pan Pizza's personnel procedures. Dr. MacKeven may derive some small comfort from the knowledge that she is not alone. The assumption that "almost anyone" with adequate intelligence and motivation can become an effective supervisor is a common one. It is that very misconception that underlies the "Peter Principle," which stipulates that people in hierarchical organizations will be promoted, and rise in the ranks, until they reach their levels of *in*competence, at which point their promotions cease (Peter & Hull, 1969). Mr. Hammond, for a variety of reasons, including no small portion of good luck, has either managed to circumvent the Peter Principle, or has simply not yet reached *his* level of incompetence.

Fortunately for Peter's Pan Pizza, Dr. MacKeven is not one to rely on good luck. Mr. Hammond's memo will surely prompt her to investigate the need for a more-or-less formalized system of training procedures that can prepare men and women for the rigors of supervising other employees. Although she will probably concentrate initially on the engineering department, any training program that she may develop will probably also be useful in construction, maintenance, and custodial services, and throughout much of the organization, for the available job analyses and pertinent research (Dowell & Wexley, 1978) suggest that first-level supervision in all departments requires a common core of behaviors and tasks (such as observing, planning, communicating, and so forth).

This final chapter in the first section of your book examines the topic of personnel training in organizations. We will describe the preliminary work that must precede the development of any effective training program, and continue by examining the crucial, yet often overlooked, topic of how to evaluate the effectiveness of training programs. Finally, we will describe some of the diverse training techniques and methods that are currently available, paying particular attention to the extent to which they rely on widely recognized principles of learning. As always, we will try to facilitate your understanding of the material by frequently referring to the situation at Peter's Pan Pizza, Inc., and especially to Mr. Hammond's request for supervisory training in the engineering department.

Once again, we encourage you to consider how all of the topics discussed in this and in previous chapters are interrelated, in one way or another. Although we have divided the personnel (human resources) functions into separate chapters for the purposes of clarity and convenience, we are firmly convinced that an effective personnel system is one in which all these functions (job analysis, performance appraisal, personnel selection) fit together in an integrated fashion.

Title

Wexley and Latham (1981) defined training as "a planned effort by an organization to facilitate the learning of job-related behavior on the part of its employees" (p. 3), while Goldstein's (1986) definition focused on "the systematic acquisition of skills, rules, concepts, or attitudes that result in improved performance in another environment" (p. 3). Common to these two definitions is the idea that personnel training involves a systematic set of procedures and experiences that are planned and implemented by an organization for the purpose of bringing about some change in its employees that will result in improved job performance.

ASSESSING THE NEED FOR TRAINING

Regardless of which specific training technique or procedure is ultimately chosen for bringing about the desired changes, it's a safe bet that its implementation and subsequent evaluation will involve expenditures of time and money. It therefore makes a great deal of sense for an organization to determine whether such changes in employees' behavior are really necessary, and whether a systematic training program is the best way to bring those changes about. This process, known as needs assessment, also provides insight into the *kinds* of change that will contribute to improved organizational performance. As you will see, different kinds of change are best accomplished by different training techniques and procedures. Thus, for both financial and logical reasons, careful needs assessment should always precede the development of any training program.

A proper needs assessment consists of three phases that proceed in a logical order: (1) organizational analysis, (2) job or task analysis, and (3) person analysis (McGehee & Thayer, 1961). As we discuss each of these in turn, the logic of this sequence should become clear to you.

Organizational Analysis

Goldstein (1986) described organizational analysis as the study of "the system-wide components of an organization that may have impact on a training program . . . [including] an examination of the organizational goals, resources of the organization, climate for training, and internal and external constraints present in the environment" (p. 28). Simply stated, it is logically impossible to be dissatisfied with an organization's performance without a clear understanding of the purpose(s) for which that organization exists, and the goals that it has been created to achieve. The rationale for organizational analysis, then, is to identify those purposes and goals as unambiguously as possible.

This is not always as easy as it might seem. Except for charitable and nonprofit organizations, of course, companies in a capitalist society exist for the purpose of providing the owners with a financial return on their investments. This is, after all, the "bottom line," and Peter's Pan Pizza is no exception.

Specifying which objectives in particular will lead to this "bottom line," however, is often a tricky proposition.

Should Peter's Pan Pizza strive to maximize profits by offering customers a product made with only the highest-quality ingredients, or can more money be made by "skimping" whenever possible? Should PPPs be concerned with the morale and psychological welfare of its employees, or should the company concentrate on profit, and let the workers fend for themselves? Should the organization try to be a responsible community citizen (by sponsoring youth softball teams and senior citizens' discounts, by urging delivery people to be courteous drivers, and so on), or should it restrict resource expenditures to direct profit opportunities, to things that have an obvious and immediate impact on productivity and costs? These are just some of the questions that a careful organizational analysis must explicitly address. Failure to deal openly with such issues creates a breeding ground for idiosyncratic assumptions and innumerable misunderstandings and conflicts, some of which will surely affect the content and evaluation of any training program that might be developed (see Goodman, 1969; Lynton & Pareek, 1967; and Miller & Zeller, 1967, for examples of specific "horror stories").

As if this were not a sufficiently tall order, unambiguously identifying organizational goals is not enough. Organizational analysis must also determine the resources and the constraints and limitations, both inside and outside the organization, that will facilitate or frustrate goal attainment. Resources include people, money, physical facilities, reputation, and anything else at the company's disposal that will help it reach its goals. Constraints are the "flip side" of resources. They may include such internal factors as shortages of money, personnel, or equipment, or an organizational climate characterized by fear and suspicion. External constraints might include such things as local, state, or federal regulations that restrict certain activities (the EEOC *Guidelines,* for example), a severely limited pool of applicants from which new employees can be selected, or stiff competition from other pizza companies.

In short, organizational analysis refers to a careful specification of what the company wants to accomplish, as well as the conditions under which it must operate. Without such information, the second and third phases of needs analysis, job/task and person analysis, become meaningless. How can we know whether jobs are properly designed, or whether employees are performing those jobs properly, unless we know the overall organizational goal(s) to which those jobs are supposed to contribute? How can we train workers without knowing what they are supposed to be able to do?

Given the important role of organizational analysis in setting the stage for every other aspect of training, Wexley (1984) was "appalled" at the almost complete absence of any relevant empirical research. Although Goldstein's (1980) earlier review of the literature included a small number of (relatively hard-to-find) studies dealing with the negative impact of employees' resistance to organizational training programs (Anastasio & Morgan, 1972; Salinger, 1973), Wexley's more recent review uncovered "no additional empirical research studies" (p. 521).

Our own review was only marginally more productive. Glaser and Taylor (1973) reported that highly motivated research participants, who engaged in two-way communication with the researchers, were often associated with successful applied research projects. This finding has direct implications for research on training programs, which is, after all, extremely "applied" research. Baumgartel and Jeanpierre's (1972) data suggested that a favorable organizational climate is important to effective training; a more recent study by Russell, Terborg, and Powers (1985), however, was less enthusiastic about the role of organizational support.

Where does this leave Dr. MacKeven? Obviously, the absence of conclusive research findings doesn't negate the importance of careful organizational analysis. Effectively training Mr. Hammond's first-level supervisors presumes a knowledge of the engineering department's goals, which in turn depend on the goals of Vice President Nathanson's facilities division and, ultimately, on the goals of Peter's Pan Pizza, Inc. Of course, Dr. MacKeven must also identify the resources at her (and the organization's) disposal, and the constraints that may limit the way in which PPP achieves its goals. At this point, she can only hope that the next comprehensive review of the field will no longer be able to conclude that "training researchers have either intentionally or unintentionally chosen to ignore the influence of organizational variables on the training function" (Wexley, 1984, p. 521). That would certainly make her job easier. For now, her best bet may be to consult some of the work being done by organizational development (OD) specialists in the area of organizational diagnosis. Because we examine this work in our discussion of organizational development (in Chapter 13), we will not go into it here.

Task/Job Analysis

The second phase of needs assessment consists of identifying the tasks that must be performed if the organization is to reach its goals under existing conditions (resources, constraints, and so forth). Tasks that involve similar behaviors or that lead to similar outcomes are usually grouped together to form *jobs*. Task analysis, then, "results in a statement of the activities or work operations performed on the job and the conditions under which the job [or group of similar tasks] is performed" (Goldstein, 1986, pp. 36–37).

Our earlier discussion of job analysis (see Chapter 3) is relevant here. Recall that job-oriented job analysis identifies the outcomes or "end products" of jobs. The first step in task/job analysis is to ensure that existing jobs produce outcomes that are consistent with the overall organizational goals. In the event that significant "gaps" emerge, it may be necessary to redesign existing jobs, or to design new jobs, the outcomes of which fill those gaps.

Once these job outcomes have been specified, the second step involves what we called worker-oriented job analysis, which identifies the actual behaviors required of incumbents if they are to achieve the specified outcomes. Only now do we arrive at a point in the needs assessment process that has *direct* implications for personnel training activities. It makes no sense to speak of "training" organizational goals or job outcomes; we can only train employees to perform job-related behaviors that will lead to desirable job outcomes. Any of the job analysis techniques discussed in Chapter 3 (critical incidents, functional job analysis, and so on) may be used to accomplish this second phase of the needs assessment process.

As Goldstein (1980) acknowledged, proceeding from task analysis to the design of specific training programs is one of the most challenging aspects of personnel training. A widely used strategy for bridging this gap involves specifying the knowledge, skills, and abilities (KSAs) that individual employees must possess in order to successfully perform the necessary job-related behaviors identified through task analysis. KSAs are typically identified with the help of "job experts" (incumbents, supervisors, I/O psychologists, and so on). Training procedures can then be designed to facilitate the learning of these KSAs.

Person Analysis

The third phase of the needs assessment process focuses on the men and women who must perform the tasks that are necessary if the organization is to reach its goals. The first two phases, organizational and task analyses, result in a description of what employees must be able to do. This final phase yields a description of what employees are actually capable of doing at the present time.

There are two common sources of relevant information for conducting person analyses: (1) performance appraisal data for people who are already on the job, and (2) data obtained from selection procedures (interviews, selection tests, and so forth) concerning people who are about to be hired. These topics were discussed in Chapters 4 through 6.

Summary

Organizational, job/task, and person analyses permit Dr. MacKeven to answer the two questions that lie at the heart of needs assessment: (1) Is a training program necessary? and if so, (2) What should be the specific objectives of such a program? Comparing the results of organizational and task analyses, which tell her what is required of Peter's Pan Pizza's employees, with the results of person analyses, which describe employees' or applicants' capabilities (or deficiencies), puts Dr. MacKeven in a position to make intelligent decisions about training programs.

In the event that there is no apparent discrepancy between people's capabilities and what their jobs demand of them, there is no justification for training. Unfortunately, Mr. Hammond's memo suggests that this is not the case. It is just as important to recognize, however, that detecting such a discrepancy does not automatically indicate that a training program is the optimal solution. It may be that the discrepancy can be better eliminated by improved selection procedures or more attractive incentive conditions at the workplace (Thayer & McGehee, 1977). Training programs should be designed only after careful consideration and analysis of the relative costs and benefits associated with alternative solutions.

In the event that a training program does appear to be necessary, a needs assessment will suggest *specific* training objectives—things that must be accomplished if the discrepancies are to be eliminated. The importance of specific objectives cannot be overstated. At the departmental level, Dr. MacKeven and Mr. Hammond may stipulate that the percentage of first-level supervisors within the engineering department who are dismissed because of unsatisfactory performance should not exceed 5 percent among those who complete the training program. Given such a specific objective, it is relatively easy to evaluate the training program's effectiveness. Compare that with a less specific objective, such as "improving supervisors' appreciation of the complexity of supervisor-subordinate relations." How could Dr. MacKeven unambiguously determine whether this latter objective had been met?

At the individual level, good training objectives should unambiguously describe what employees should be able to do, or accomplish, following the training program, as well as the conditions under which they will be expected to perform. An example of a good behavioral objective is that first-level supervisors in the engineering department should be able to provide subordinates with timely and accurate performance feedback such that "spot checks" by upper-level managers *never* find employees who "just don't know where they stand" with their supervisor. Compare that with a less specific objective such as "developing better communication skills." Evaluation of the former is simple and unambiguous; evaluation of the latter is all but impossible.

You can see, then, that the benefits of needs assessment are two-fold. First, it provides information about whether a training program is necessary at all; if training is deemed advisable, it identifies the specific objectives that the training program must meet. Second, by identifying those specific objectives, needs assessment also points to the criteria that should be used to evaluate the effectiveness of the training program. A successful training program is one that meets its objectives. It is to that evaluation process that we now turn our attention.

EVALUATING TRAINING PROGRAMS

It may seem to you that we are "putting the cart before the horse" by discussing how to evaluate training programs before describing any specific training techniques or methodologies. Our rationale is quite simple. We have chosen to examine the evaluation phase of personnel training now, because this is what Dr. MacKeven would (or at least *should*) do. Just as training needs must be assessed prior to the initiation of training, the procedures that will be used to evaluate the effectiveness of that training should also be planned before training is actually begun. Such advanced planning makes it less likely that the training program will not be evaluated at all (a distressingly common state of affairs), and more likely that the training will be designed and conducted in a way that facilitates useful evaluation.

Our discussion of evaluation is divided into three parts. First, we will list the three basic questions that any training evaluation procedure must ultimately answer, and describe some of the factors and conditions that can produce misleading, or simply inaccurate, answers to those questions. Second, we will describe a variety of (research) designs, some experimental in nature and some not, that are used to evaluate training programs. Third, we shall briefly describe some alternative perspectives on training program evaluation. As always, we will (and you should) keep Mr. Hammond's opening memo in mind.

Questions and Question Marks

To evaluate a training program is to answer the following questions:

1. Did any change in employees occur? If the answer to this question is "no," the training program is, in almost every case, ineffective. If the answer is "yes," the second question becomes relevant.
2. If a change did occur, was the training program responsible for that change? If the answer is "no," the training program isn't effective. If the answer is "yes," then the third question becomes important.
3. If the training program was responsible for the change in a given sample of employees, will that program also be effective for a different sample of employees in the same, or perhaps in a different, organization?

An affirmative answer to the first two questions indicates that the training program has what is called "internal validity." This means that the program "worked" for a specific sample of trainees. If, in addition, the answer to the third question is also "yes," that training program is said to have "external validity," too. That is, it will probably also "work" for subsequent groups of trainees (Goldstein, 1986). Now let's examine the kinds of criterion measures available for assessing training effectiveness, as well as some of the factors and conditions that mislead I/O psychologists about the internal and external validity of training programs.

CRITERIA OF TRAINING EFFECTIVENESS

Kirkpatrick (1967) described four different kinds, or levels, of criteria that can be used to evaluate training program effectiveness. These are usually referred to as "reaction," "learning," "behavior," and "results" criteria. In the order in which we just listed them, they yield information that is increasingly useful for determining whether all the needs identified during needs assessment have been met.

Reaction criteria are nothing more than opinions concerning the perceived effectiveness of a training program. That is, they are the "reactions" of the trainees (and sometimes the trainers) to the question "What did you think of the training program (you) just completed?" The value of these measures is extremely limited. Although it is certainly interesting to know whether the individuals involved in a particular training program hated or enjoyed it, because a despised program may create more problems than it solves, employees' reactions to training tell us little or nothing about whether the organization's needs are being met.

Trainees may react favorably to a program for any number of irrelevant reasons, perhaps because it was fun or entertaining, perhaps because it got them away from their normally boring jobs, perhaps because they believe it will lead to faster promotions or greater pay increases, and so forth. Obviously, none of these responses constitute evidence that organizational needs are being met—unless, of course, the only (trivial?) purpose of the training program was to make employees happy. Further, reaction criteria do not logically require any "before versus after" comparisons. Without such comparisons, there is no way to answer the first important question about whether or not a *change* has occurred. The relative convenience of reaction criteria undoubtedly accounts for their popularity, in spite of the fact that they are all but useless for evaluation purposes. Eden's (1985) study of team development within the Israeli army confirmed that reactions can be very favorable, even when every other piece of evaluative information suggests that a training program produced *no* useful changes in employees or the organization.

Learning criteria are an improvement over reaction measures. These data are typically collected immediately following the completion of training, and are intended to reflect whatever trainees learned during the program. Final written or performance examinations at the completion of training are the most common forms of learning criteria. Rather than simply asking Mr. Hammond's first-level supervisors how they liked a training program, or how much they believed they benefited from it (reaction criteria), Dr. MacKeven might administer a paper-and-pencil examination immediately following training that tests the supervisors' knowledge of supervisory duties and responsibilities, company policies, or whatever else had been identified as a need that justified training.

You can see that such a criterion measure has the potential to answer the first of the three crucial evaluative questions we listed earlier. If Dr. MacKeven had administered some sort of pretest before beginning the training program, she could compare each trainee's final exam score with his or her pretest score and discover whether a change had occurred in supervisors' knowledge or skill, or whatever the pre- and posttests measured. Of course, in the absence of any pretraining data, no such comparisons are possible.

Unfortunately, systematic differences between trainees' pre- and posttest ("final exam") scores may emerge that have absolutely nothing to do with the training program. Conditions or factors capable of producing such changes will be examined in our discussion of "threats" to internal validity. Further, even the discovery of systematic changes that *are* produced by the training does not guarantee that those changes will be transferred back to the employees' work setting(s). In the absence of such transfer, the training program cannot meet identified needs.

Behavior criteria specifically address the issue of transfer of training to the job setting. The most common examples of behavior criteria of training effectiveness are (objective, personnel, or judgmental) measures of job performance that are collected *after* trainees have returned to their jobs. These might include the number of grievances filed by subordinates of each of Mr. Hammond's first-level supervisors (personnel data), or upper-level managers' ratings of those supervisors' job performance (judgmental data). You can readily see that behavior criteria can provide information that is much more useful for determining whether the organization's needs are being met.

Of course, in order to use behavior criteria to answer the questions listed at the beginning of this section, it is again necessary to have some pretraining data for comparison purposes. As you may have surmised, however, even the existence of such comparison data, and the emergence of systematic change in trainees' "before" and "after" scores, offer no assurance of the internal validity of the training program. Once again, any of the threats to internal validity discussed below may have been operating.

The fourth kind of criteria for assessing a training program's effectiveness are known as *results criteria*. Results criteria directly address the *organizational* needs identified during needs assessment. This level of criteria transcends mere measures of job performance, and speaks to the question of whether any emergent changes in work behavior are translated into the kinds of broad changes in the organization that prompted the training in the first place. Examples of results criteria that might pertain to Mr. Hammond's memo include favorable changes in organizational climate associated with more effective first-level supervision, or lower personnel costs attributable to less turnover among disgruntled engineers or frustrated supervisors.

Because results criteria reflect *change* at the level of the organization, you can see that they also imply a comparison of conditions before and after the training has taken place. Once again, however, all of the threats to internal validity described below may result in erroneous conclusions concerning the role of the training program in producing those changes.

We can summarize our discussion of training criteria as follows:

1. Results criteria are ultimately the most important to the organization, but behavior criteria are the most informative and useful to I/O psychologists, who (after all) are primarily concerned with individuals' behaviors. Learning and reaction criteria are much less useful, for they tell us nothing about trainees' subsequent job performance.

2. Unfortunately, results criteria are also the most difficult to assess, and behavior criteria can present a formidable challenge, too (see Chapter 4). Learning and reaction criteria are somewhat easier to assess.

3. Although the assessment of results, behavior, or learning criteria does not necessarily require a pretraining measure for comparison purposes, it is logically impossible to determine whether any relevant changes have occurred in the absence of some "baseline" measure. Reaction criteria, on the other hand, can be logically assessed in the absence of any pretraining information.

4. All four kinds of criteria are vulnerable to the threats to internal validity that we will discuss now, and none of them addresses the issue of external validity.

THREATS TO INTERNAL VALIDITY

These are factors or influences that can lead a training evaluator to *erroneously* conclude that a training program *was* responsible for changes in learning, behavior, or results criterion measures. Campbell and Stanley (1963) described a number of these factors, including "history," "maturation," testing, instrumentation changes, statistical regression toward the mean, differential selection of trainees, and experimental "mortality." We will briefly describe each of these potentially contaminating influences, and offer examples that pertain to Mr. Hammond's needs.

History refers to the passage of time or, more specifically, to particular events that occur while a training program is in progress. These events, rather than the training program itself, can be responsible for changes in training-criterion measures. Suppose, for example, that a newspaper article describing the brutal murder of an office supervisor by a subordinate is published during the time that Dr. MacKeven is training Mr. Hammond's first-level supervisors. She may find that the trainees treat their subordinates with a great deal more respect and consideration (and possibly fear) following the training program than they did prior to it (a behavior criterion). That altered behavior, however, may be due to supervisors' realization that poor interpersonal relations with their subordinates can have dire personal consequences. The training itself may have had no effect on the supervisors' behaviors at all. In this case, a training evaluator who is unaware of the newspaper article in question may erroneously conclude that the training program was responsible for the observed change.

Maturation is similar to history, in that it refers to changes that occur during the passage of time. It is different, however, in that maturation refers to biological and/or psychological changes that are not tied to any specific external, environmental event. People grow older, and more experienced with a given task, simply as a function of normal biological and psychological processes, respectively. Mr. Hammond's relatively inexperienced supervisors might show a greater awareness of how people react to authority on a paper-and-pencil test of such knowledge following a training program (a learning criterion), simply because they gained some experience in that area while the training was in progress—experience that was *not* a part of the training intervention.

Testing presents a threat to internal validity when trainees obtain higher scores on a test following a training program *because they were given a pretest* prior to training. Suppose Dr. MacKeven administers a test designed to measure supervisors' communication skills before she begins a training program that, among other things, is designed to improve such skills. (The purpose of such a pretest, you will remember, is to have something to which trainees' scores following training can be compared, so that any changes in knowledge or skill can be recognized.) It's entirely possible that Mr. Hammond's supervisors may actually learn something about communication skills from the very acts of reading and answering the questions on the pretest. If they obtain higher scores on a communications test following training (this posttest would be a learning criterion) because of what they learned on the pretest, and not because of the training program itself, Dr. MacKeven might mistakenly conclude that her training program was responsible for the observed change.

Instrumentation changes refer to alterations in the ways in which criteria are measured. Suppose that, prior to training, Mr. Hammond asked upper-level managers to use graphic rating scales to evaluate the first-level supervisors' abilities to organize others' work, and to delegate responsibility. Suppose further that, while Dr. MacKeven was training those supervisors to improve their organizing and delegating skills, Peter's Pan Pizza discarded those graphic rating scales and began to use a new performance appraisal technique that was (unexpectedly) *more* vulnerable to leniency errors than the old, graphic scales were. Trainees might therefore receive higher ratings on their abilities to organize and delegate after training simply because of the increased amount of leniency error in the managers' ratings, and not because they learned how to better perform these supervisory functions during Dr. MacKeven's training program.

Statistical regression toward the mean is a trickier concept to understand, because it depends on a grasp of classical psychometric theory (Campbell, 1976; Nunnally, 1978). Recall from our discussions in prior chapters that unreliable measurement is due to the influence of random error. Sometimes this random error artificially inflates peoples' scores, and sometimes it diminishes their scores (with respect to their "true" scores on whatever construct is being measured). Although we can never be certain, it is a "good bet" that people with *extremely* high or *extremely* low scores on a measure have probably had their true scores inflated or diminished by random error, respectively. Because this error is random and normally distributed, we should expect that individuals with extremely high scores on the first administration of a test might obtain somewhat lower scores (closer to the population mean score—thus the label "regression toward the mean") on the second administration of that test, or an equivalent form of that test, even though their true scores did not actually change. This is because the random error in their second test scores does not inflate those scores as much as it did the first set of scores, or possibly because the random error actually diminishes their scores the second time around. Conversely, people who obtained extremely low scores on the first administration (partly because random error diminished those scores) might be expected to obtain higher scores (again, closer to the population mean) on a second administration of the test, even though their true scores did not change. In this case, the random error on the second test does not diminish their true score as much as it did on the first test, or perhaps the error actually inflates their scores the second time around.

If those who are pretested, trained, and then posttested include people with a wide range of pretest scores (some very high, some moderate, some very low), statistical regression toward the mean should *not* threaten the internal validity of the training program. For everyone who obtains a higher score on the posttest because of regression, someone else should obtain a comparably lower score; this is the nature of random error variance. If, on the other hand, Dr. MacKeven decides to train only those first-level supervisors who obtained very low scores on a pretest of their supervisory skills (an ostensibly reasonable decision, especially if it is impossible or impractical to train all of Mr. Hammond's supervisors at the same time), then regression toward the mean *does* represent a threat. We would expect those initially low-scoring supervisors to obtain somewhat higher scores on a posttest simply because of error-score variation, and not because of any increase in their true scores on the test of supervisory skills. Their scores would improve because of this statistical artifact known as regression toward the mean.

You can see, then, that any effect of regression toward the mean depends on the way in which trainees are selected for a given training program. If they are chosen more-or-less randomly, threats to internal validity are minimized. Non-random selection, however, introduces such threats. Extreme pretest scores are not the only way in which trainees may be nonrandomly selected for a training program.

Mr. Hammond may ask for volunteers among his first-level supervisors to undergo Dr. MacKeven's experimental training program. Alternatively, he may select only more experienced supervisors for the "trial run" of the training program. If, in the first case, the subordinates of the volunteer trainees file fewer grievances during the six-month period following their supervisors' training (a results criterion) because of the volunteers' high levels of enthusiasm and commitment, and *not* because of anything that was learned during training, that is a clear threat to internal validity. Similarly, if the subordinates of the more experienced trainees file fewer grievances, that desirable outcome may be a function of the supervisors' experience, and *not* anything learned during training. You can probably imagine many other ways in which differential selection of trainees can threaten the internal validity of a training program.

Experimental mortality is not limited to those cases where trainees expire during training! It refers to any situation where trainees drop out of training, for any reason. As we saw with statistical regression toward the mean, if trainees drop out on a more-or-less random basis, there is little threat to internal validity. If there is a pattern to their departures, however, there may be a problem.

For example, if the "bottom" or poorest performing 20 percent of Mr. Hammond's first-level supervisors quit the training program (and, perhaps, their jobs) while it was in progress, Dr. MacKeven might conclude that her training intervention was effective when, in fact, it was not. The mean score on a posttest of (the "surviving") trainees' knowledge of supervisory responsibilities will undoubtedly be higher than the average of all the pretest scores, simply because the lowest one-fifth of the scores are not represented in the posttest mean.

As if all these threats to internal validity were not enough, Campbell and Stanley (1963), and later Cook and Campbell (1979), correctly acknowledged that two or more of them can interact to further undermine internal validity. Goldstein (1986) offered an example where maturation might interact with differential selection. In our context, if Mr. Hammond sent only his younger first-level supervisors to a rather lengthy training program, Dr. MacKeven might see improvement following training that would have been less apparent (or even nonexistent) if supervisors of all ages had gone through the program. Alternatively, differential selection of trainees could interact with testing, such that younger, less experienced (and perhaps more enthusiastic) supervisors may be more prone to being sensitized by, or to learn from, a pretest in a way that would "show up" on a subsequent posttraining test.

The value of the research designs, discussed in the next section, for evaluating the effectiveness of training programs depends on how well they reduce, control, or eliminate these threats to internal validity. To get just a bit ahead of ourselves, designs that use a "control group" as well as an "experimental group," and rely on random assignment of trainees to these groups, do a better job of controlling these threats than do other types of designs.

Interestingly, Dr. MacKeven must also contend with some threats to internal validity that cannot be controlled through rigorous experimental design—threats that arise mainly *because* the training program is being evaluated. Cook and Campbell (1979) described several of these.

First, since organization members who are assigned to a control group (randomly or otherwise) are very often acquainted with those employees in the group that receives the experimental training, these control-group members may benefit from the training "through the grapevine." Cook and Campbell (1979) called this "diffusion of treatments." To the extent that the control group does receive such "second-hand" training from their friends in the experimental group, any differences between the groups that might have resulted from training may be reduced.

Second, based on their (premature) faith in the value of the experimental training, managers and supervisors of employees assigned to the control group may go out of their way to provide these "deprived" employees with other benefits in order to "make up for" their being excluded from training. Such additional benefits and considerations, or what Cook and Campbell (1979) labeled "compensatory equalization of treatments," can also reduce any differences that might have emerged between the control and experimental groups as a result of training.

Third, members of the control group may behave in a systematically different fashion based on their perceptions of having been excluded from the experimental training program. They may band together in order to compete with the "favored" group going through training. This self-induced competition or "compensatory rivalry" (Cook & Campbell, 1979)—an effort to prove that they can perform as well as, or better than, the other group—might reduce or eliminate any differences on learning, behavior, or results criteria that may otherwise have emerged as a result of training. Alternatively, control-group members may become depressed and demoralized at having been "excluded" from the training group. Their resentment or despondency ("resentful demoralization" according to Cook & Campbell, 1979) may result in the control group obtaining lower scores on any of a variety of criteria, thereby artificially increasing any apparent difference between the control and training groups following training.

As Goldstein (1986) pointed out, careful experimental design will not eliminate any of these (latter) threats to internal validity. It will require other approaches, such as "working with the participants as part of the evaluation model so that they do not feel threatened by events such as being assigned to a control group" (pp. 152–153), to solve these last few problems.

THREATS TO EXTERNAL VALIDITY

Organizations that design and evaluate training programs are usually interested in using those programs over and over again. They are therefore concerned not only with whether the program was effective for the trainees who participated in the experimental evaluation of the program, but also with whether the same training program will be effective for subsequent groups of trainees. The third of the three questions we posed at the beginning of this section addresses this concern. At the very least, if Dr. MacKeven asks the control group to participate in designing the training-evaluation "experiment," as Goldstein (1986) suggested, she must be confident that any training program that proves effective for the experimental group will also be effective for the control group when their turn comes. Her confidence will depend on the external validity, as well as the internal validity, of that training program.

External validity is basically a question of the generalizability of research results (see Chapter 2). Threats to external validity tend to be factors or influences that render the "experimental" group of trainees used to evaluate the effectiveness of a training program somehow different in a systematic way from subsequent "run-of-the-mill" trainees, who will experience the training later on, as a regular part of their employment. Cook and Campbell (1979) also described several of these threats.

Just as taking a pretraining test can threaten internal validity, a pretest can also undermine external validity. If the pretest generates an unusual level of sensitivity to the material being taught, the training program may be less effective (or completely ineffective) for subsequent groups of trainees who do not take the pretest (because the training program itself is no longer "on trial"). Fortunately, Dr. MacKeven can solve this problem very easily by administering the pretest to *all* subsequent groups of trainees. That is, she can just include the pretest as a regular segment of the training program.

Other threats to external validity are not so easily resolved. One of the most persistent problems revolves around the manner in which experimental trainees are selected. Unless they are chosen randomly from the entire population of employees who will ultimately be trained, the danger exists that they are somehow systematically different from the rest of that population in a way that may render the training more, or less, effective for the larger group. Unfortunately, nonrandom selection in organizational field studies (such as training-evaluation studies) tends to be the rule rather than the exception; managers and supervisors often perceive random selection as too disruptive of ongoing organizational activities. For example, if Mr. Hammond selects one subsection of his engineering department to serve as "experimental" trainees, and the people in that subsection just happen to be more (or less) intelligent or experienced, older or younger, or systematically different in any way from the remainder of those in the department, there is a distinct danger that a training program that proves to be (in)effective for the select group of trainees may not produce a similar level of (in)effectiveness for the others.

A second process that we described in an earlier chapter can also represent a threat to external validity. Recall that the "Hawthorne effect" refers to an alteration in people's behavior that is attributable to their perceptions that they are being watched, that they are the focus of an unusual amount of special attention. Employees who participate in an experimental training program are especially vulnerable to this influence. If their subsequent criterion scores are affected by this attention, rather than by the actual content of the training program, that training will not be equally effective for subsequent trainees who participate in the program when it is no longer "bathed in the glare of the research spotlight."

The "Pygmalion effect" can also threaten external validity. Originally documented in the classroom (Rosenthal & Jacobson, 1968), this is where experimental trainees' performance on various criteria is inflated, not because of the content of the training program, but rather because of the trainer's strong expectations that the training program will be effective (Eden & Shani, 1982). These enthusiastic expectations, conveyed to trainees in a variety of ways that can influence their subsequent criterion scores (encouragement, increased personal attention, and so forth), may generate a self-fulfilling prophesy. If this enthusiasm is not maintained for later groups of "regular" trainees, their performance on the criterion measures may not equal that of their predecessors, who received a great deal more encouragement.

Once again, we must "add insult to injury" by acknowledging that two or more of these threats to external validity may combine or interact to further undermine our efforts to generate an accurate answer to the third question posed above. Trainees selected nonrandomly for the purpose of evaluating a training program, for example, may be differentially influenced by either the Hawthorne or the Pygmalion effect.

We should also point out that there can be two sides to the concept of external validity, depending on the goals of those who are evaluating a training program. They may be interested in generalizing their results only to other employees within a given organization. Or, they may be concerned with a training program's effectiveness in other organizations, or at least in other branches or offices of a large, parent organization. As you might suspect, generalization becomes riskier in these latter situations, where there is a greater likelihood of dissimilarities between "experimental" trainees and those who are the targets of generalization.

Now that you are aware of the many challenges that confront Dr. MacKeven as she sets out to develop an effective training program for Mr. Hammond's first-level supervisors, we will look at some of the research designs that can be used to evaluate a training program's effectiveness. We will pay particular attention to the capabilities of these designs to reduce or eliminate the many threats to internal and external validity that we have just examined.

Evaluation Designs

As we set out to evaluate the effectiveness of a training program, it is appropriate to think of that program as a social science experiment. There are many different ways to design such a training experiment. Each approach, however, can be classified as either a pre-experimental design, a true experimental design, or a quasi-experimental design (Campbell & Stanley, 1963). As we describe two examples from each of these three categories, we urge you to pay particular attention to their respective capabilities to control the various threats to internal and external validity.

Except where otherwise noted, we will use the following symbols throughout our discussion of research designs for evaluating training programs' effectiveness:

E = experimental training group
C = control group (receives no training)
T_1 = pretest (administered prior to training)
T_2 = posttest (administered following training)
X = the training program
R = random assignment of individuals to control and experimental (training) groups.

PRE-EXPERIMENTAL DESIGNS

The simplest of all designs, and really not a "design" at all, is the "one-group posttest only" design:

$$X \longrightarrow T_2$$

As you may already have surmised, this design controls for *none* of the threats to internal or external validity discussed earlier. Without a pretest, there is no way to know how to interpret individuals' posttest scores. Have they gone up, down, or remained unchanged? Even if (unknown to us) there has been some change in the criterion measure during the course of the training, this nondesign tells us nothing about whether that change is attributable to history, to maturation, or to any of the other threats to internal validity. Similarly, because this strategy does not even address the question of selecting those employees who are to receive the training, it provides no information about the generalizability (external validity) of the results.

About the only value associated with data collected in this manner is that they may be a rich source of descriptive information that may stimulate future hunches or hypotheses concerning training effectiveness. As a self-contained source of evaluative information, however, the "one-group posttest only" design is worthless.

A second pre-experimental design that is a slight improvement over the first is the "one-group pretest/posttest design:

$$T_1 \longrightarrow X \longrightarrow T_2$$

Because trainees' pretest scores are now available, it becomes possible to compare these to their posttest scores to determine whether any change has occurred. Also, by comparing the pretest scores of those who complete the training with the pretest scores of those who drop out, we can learn something about whether the change might be attributable to systematic experimental mortality. In the absence of a control group, however, we cannot determine whether any of the other threats to internal validity are responsible for that change. Nor can we say anything about external validity.

Citing Goldstein (1981) and Wexley and Latham (1981), Wexley (1984) lamented that "even in those cases when evaluation is attempted, it usually involves a pre-experimental design together with merely reaction and/or learning [criteria]" (pp. 538–539). The state of the art among training evaluators leaves much room for improvement.

EXPERIMENTAL DESIGNS

This category of designs is characterized by the use of at least one control group along with the experimental (training) group, as well as random assignment of employees to those groups. Campbell and Stanley (1963) described these as "the most strongly recommended designs" (p. 13), because of their ability to control for many of the threats to internal and external validity.

When experimental designs are used, the most popular is the "pretest/posttest control-group" design:

$$R_E \longrightarrow T_1 \longrightarrow X \longrightarrow T_2$$
$$R_C \longrightarrow T_1 \longrightarrow T_2$$

Because workers are randomly assigned to one of these two groups, there is no reason to suspect that there are any systematic differences between them, or between them and the larger population of workers from among whom they were chosen. Both groups take the pretest at the same time, and then, following training for the experimental group and a **control experience** for the control group, both groups take the posttest at the same time.

By comparing the two groups' changes in criterion scores from the pretest to the posttest, we can determine whether any changes are attributable to the training program, or whether they are attributable to such internal-validity threats as history, maturation, pretesting, instrumentation changes, or statistical regression toward the mean. If any of these threats are operating, they should affect the training and control groups to the same extent, because of the random-selection process. If the training program is effective, the difference between the training group's pre- and posttest scores should exceed the difference for the control group (which can only be attributed to history, maturation, and some of the other threats to internal validity, because the "control" employees did not experience the training). The crucial comparison, then, is *between the groups'* (pre- to posttest) *difference scores*, and not just between a single group's pre- and posttest scores.

Although this design does an excellent job of controlling for the internal-validity threats listed above, it does not control for any of the threats associated with intervention, such as diffusion of training "through the grapevine," supervisors' attempts to compensate the "deprived" control group, or the competitive or demoralized response of the control group. As we stated before, these can only be prevented by the experimenter/evaluator.

Random selection does minimize some of the threats to external validity (representativeness of the training-group sample, for instance), but not all of them. The effect of pretesting, as well as the Hawthorne and Pygmalion effects, can still threaten the external validity of the training evaluation. Nevertheless, when all factors are considered (financial and human resources requirements), we concur with Campbell and Stanley's (1963) strong endorsement of the "pretest/posttest control-group" design.

An even more powerful experimental design is the "Solomon four-group" design:

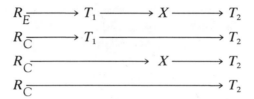

The four groups consist of one experimental group that is exposed to both the pretest and the training program, and three different control groups. One of the control groups takes the pretest, but is not exposed to the training; a second is exposed to the training without having taken the pretest; the third is exposed to neither the pretest nor the training program, and just takes the posttest at the same time as the other three groups.

This design controls for the same threats to internal validity as the previous experimental design. In addition, it permits us to determine the impact of the *interaction* between taking the pretest and experiencing the training program. In fact, an evaluator can determine the proportions of the overall change in the experimental group's criterion scores that are attributable purely to the training program, to the pretest, to the interaction between the pretest and the training, and to factors such as history, maturation, and other time-dependent threats to internal validity.[1]

[1]This requires systematic comparisons of the four groups' (pre- to posttest) difference scores. The average of the first two groups' pretest scores is used to estimate the mean pretest score for the third and fourth groups that did not take the pretest. Because subjects are assigned randomly to the four groups, there is no reason to assume any pretraining differences between or among the groups.

control experience: activities or stimuli to which the control group is exposed while the experimental group is undergoing training

Similar to the "pretest/posttest control-group" design, the "Solomon four-group" design does not control for any of the intervention threats to internal validity, nor any of the threats to external validity except for sample representativeness, because of random selection and assignment of subjects to the groups. It is also true that the four-group design makes demands on a company's human resources that are often excessive. Many organizations just do not have a sufficient number of potential trainees to create four separate groups of sufficient size to permit standard statistical analyses. When the required sample sizes are available, however, the "Solomon four-group" design represents the "cream of the crop."

QUASI-EXPERIMENTAL DESIGNS

This category of research designs represents a compromise between pre-experimental and experimental designs. As we indicated, pre-experimental designs are almost never justified. Experimental designs, on the other hand, are often impractical to implement in active, "real-life" organizations. Sometimes there are too few people to create a control group; sometimes it would be prohibitively disruptive to break up normal work groups for the purpose of randomly assigning workers to control and experimental (training) groups.

The "time-series" design is one such compromise:

$$T_1 \longrightarrow T_2 \longrightarrow T_3 \longrightarrow X \longrightarrow T_4 \longrightarrow T_5 \longrightarrow T_6$$

Rather than taking a single pretest and a single posttest, trainees take a series of pretests and a series of posttests; each sequential pair of tests is separated by a more–or–less constant time interval. In this way, a single group of trainees can serve as its own "control." Any changes in mean criterion score between pretests 1 and 2, between 2 and 3, or between posttests 4 and 5, or between 5 and 6, are most likely attributable to history, to maturation, or to some other time-related threat to internal validity. Any change in criterion scores between the last pretest (T_3 in the example shown above) and the first posttest (T_4), however, is a function of the training program, as well as these other factors. If this particular difference ($T_4 - T_3$) exceeds all of the others, the training program is probably responsible for at least part of that difference.

"Time-series" designs do not control for historical events that occur during the interval when training takes place. Nor do they control for any of the threats to external validity.

A second quasi-experimental design is the "nonequivalent control-group" design:

$$T_{1_E} \longrightarrow X \longrightarrow T_2$$
$$T_{1_C} \longrightarrow T_2$$

In this case, we have a control group that does not experience training, but workers are not assigned to the two groups on a random basis. (On the other hand, which of the two groups receives the training and which serves as the control *can* be determined randomly.) Instead, preexisting, intact organizational groups are used.

A primary advantage of this procedure is its practicality, in that the use of intact groups is usually less disruptive to ongoing organizational activities. The relative ease with which this design can be implemented *may* reduce some of the intervention-related threats to internal validity, as well as the negative impact of the Hawthorne effect on external validity.

The more alike the two intact groups, the more effectively this design controls for history, maturation, and instrumentation differences. Groups that are less similar undermine this design's capability to control for these threats to internal validity, and make the design especially vulnerable to any interactions between these influences and nonrandom selection of participants.

SUMMARY

Dr. MacKeven will certainly choose from among the true experimental or the quasi-experimental designs as she plans her strategy for evaluating a training program for Mr. Hammond's first-level supervisors. Even if the director of engineering permits *all* of his supervisors to participate in the training research, there will still be only 11 or 12 trainees. Unless she is able to enlist the cooperation and participation of other first-level supervisors from other departments or divisions, such a small number of trainees will probably preclude the use of any design that involves a separate control group. Under such circumstances, Dr. MacKeven may have to be satisfied with a "time-series" design, where a single group of trainees can serve as its own control.

If, on the other hand, she can include additional supervisors in the research design, Dr. MacKeven could use either the true experimental "pretest/posttest control-group" design, or the "nonequivalent control-group" design, depending on how much disruption in normal work groups is deemed tolerable. The human-resources demands associated with the "Solomon four-group" design would still, most likely, exceed the pool of available first-level supervisors (trainees).

Alternative Perspectives on Training Evaluation

Three additional considerations merit Dr. MacKeven's attention as she plans her evaluation strategy. The first is an alternative approach to training evaluation that does not rely on criterion-score changes. The second pertains to the legal context that has surrounded all personnel-related activities since the passage of the Civil Rights Act in 1964. The third, which we will mention only briefly because it is discussed in some detail in a later chapter, addresses three different ways that criterion-score changes can be interpreted or explained.

CONTENT EVALUATION

A number of researchers have approached training evaluation from a different direction (Bownas, Bosshardt, & Donnelly, 1985; Faley & Sundstrom, 1985; Ford & Wroten, 1984). Rather than examining change scores, these approaches share the common goal of empirically comparing the content of a training program with the content of the job(s) for which the training is designed. Training programs that emphasize knowledge, skills, abilities, and other personal characteristics (KSAOs) that are deemed important to successful job performance, and that employees are relatively unlikely to learn on the job, tend to be more useful and defensible than programs that ignore those job-relevant KSAOs, or programs that emphasize KSAOs that are not as crucial to effective job performance.

Researchers can choose from among several numerical indices capable of reflecting the "overlap" between the content of training and the content of jobs, including Lawshe's (1975) Content Validity Ratio. Nevertheless, these content-oriented approaches to training evaluation currently suffer from the same "second-class status" relative to empirical studies of criterion change scores that content validation strategies do relative to empirical, criterion-related validation strategies for personnel selection (EEOC, 1978).

LEGAL CONSIDERATIONS

A second perspective on training-program evaluation is a legal one. How does Title VII of the 1964 Civil Rights Act, and the ensuing EEOC *Guidelines*, affect the acceptability of organizational training programs? In his recent review of fair employment cases in the area of training, Russell (1984) provided three answers to this question.

First, whenever employees' performance in a training program is used as a criterion for assessing the validity of a selection test or system (interviews, paper-and-pencil tests, and so on), the organization must be prepared to demonstrate the validity of training performance as a *predictor* of subsequent on-the-job performance. Relevant U.S. Circuit Court rulings suggest that a wide variety of training criteria may be acceptable, including subjective ratings, if they are properly developed. Those rulings also suggest, however, that using selection tests to determine whether trainees possess the *minimum* skills necessary to successfully complete a training program is a legally risky procedure.

Second, training program content may either involve, or lead to, disparate treatment for different (protected) groups of employees. After describing the way in which charges of differential treatment are usually examined in court, as well as the results of relevant cases, Russell (1984) concluded that "the courts give employers considerable latitude in [implementing] training programs . . . [and that they] appear [especially] reluctant to critically examine the content of on-the-job training" (pp. 269–270).

Third, Russell (1984) found that the courts have been specific about the conditions under which pay differences between men and women may be justified on the basis of training programs. Such salary differences are less likely to be struck down when

- people are hired with the understanding that they will undergo training
- the training program is described in writing

- trainees are rotated through different departments or segments of the training program, and are subsequently placed in positions, on a *predetermined* schedule, and not simply on the basis of "organizational expediency"
- there is some "formal" aspect to the training (although this may include "self-study")
- and, most importantly, there has been no obvious history of excluding women from the training program

ALPHA, BETA, AND GAMMA CHANGES IN CRITERION SCORES

Our prior discussion of pretest-to-posttest changes in criterion scores directly addressed only what Golembiewski, Billingsley, and Yeager (1976) referred to as "alpha" changes: changes in criterion scores that reflect nothing more than numerical changes in the construct of interest. They suggested, however, that measured changes in criterion scores may reflect one or two quite different kinds of change. They called these "beta" and "gamma" changes.

Beta change refers to criterion score changes that are attributable to **calibration** changes in the measuring instrument, rather than to numerical changes in the construct that is being measured. Gamma change is even more fundamental. As a result of the training program, the criterion construct may be entirely reconceptualized. Because these changes were originally suggested in the context of organizational development (OD) research, we shall defer our discussion of them until Chapter 13. For now, you should simply realize that observed changes in criterion scores may be more complex than they might first appear to be.

Summary

At this point, it should be clear to you that evaluating the effectiveness of a training program is a very complex undertaking. It requires a knowledge of criterion-development procedures and experimental research designs, as well as an acute sensitivity to potentially contaminating variables (threats to internal and external validity). An awareness of alternative, content-based evaluation strategies, and an appreciation of the legal context in which training programs operate are also very important.

The complexity of the process is often enough to discourage trainers from evaluating the effectiveness of their programs. Others avoid the evaluation process because they are convinced of the inherent effectiveness of their procedures: "If I'm spending so much time and money doing this, then it *must* be effective!" Still others shun evaluation because they don't want to take a chance on "proving their own ineffectiveness," and thereby injuring their own pride or, perhaps, jeopardizing their jobs. Although she may occasionally

---

calibration: the process of attaching specific numbers to specific locations on a measuring instrument

experience such qualms, Dr. MacKeven knows that the difficulties and challenges that are necessarily a part of training evaluation can never justify a reluctance or refusal to evaluate. Whatever training methods she chooses for Mr. Hammond's first-level supervisors, their effectiveness will certainly be assessed.

Now let's turn to the final section of this chapter, where we discuss some of the many different techniques, methods, and procedures that are currently available for training employees.

TRAINING TECHNIQUES, METHODS, AND PROCEDURES

Having assessed training needs, and developed an evaluation plan, one of Dr. MacKeven's most crucial tasks is to select one or more training methods or procedures that can address those needs in a way that lends itself to careful evaluation. Her decision to include or exclude any particular procedure from her training program should be based on several factors: (1) the extent to which the technique relies on recognized principles and theories derived from many years of research on learning processes; (2) the suitability of the technique for helping trainees acquire the specific knowledge, skills, abilities, or other characteristics (KSAOs) identified during needs assessment; and (3) the practicality (time, money, and so on) of the technique.

Although the research and theory on animal and human learning is extremely vast (Hilgard & Bower, 1966; Schwartz, 1984), we can identify a limited number of principles that are known to facilitate learning, and are especially relevant to organizational training. These include motivation, feedback (or knowledge of results), and transfer of learning from the training environment to the actual work setting.

Motivation refers to the purposefulness or goal-directedness, and to the intensity and persistence of behavior (Steers & Porter, 1983). As you will learn in Chapter 8, "instrumentality" or "expectancy" theories are currently very popular for explaining human motivation. A common assumption that underlies these theories is that people's behavior in any given situation is largely governed by how they answer the old, familiar question: "What's in it for me?" Women and men are presumed to engage in, and repeat, behaviors that lead to favorable outcomes, while avoiding behaviors that result in unpleasant outcomes. Training methods that acknowledge and take advantage of these tendencies will, all else being equal, be more effective than those that do not.

Feedback, or knowledge of results, is fairly self-explanatory. As we indicated in Chapter 4, it is usually unrealistic to expect people to systematically change their behavior unless they are kept informed about how they are (or are not) progressing toward a given goal. Thus, training techniques that generate feedback for trainees will almost always be more effective than those that do not.

The importance of transfer of training to the actual job setting is equally obvious. Mr. Hammond would derive no consolation from the knowledge that his first-level supervisors performed magnificently in training, if they proved unable to transport their success back to the engineering department. Goldstein (1986) and others described two approaches to maximizing such transfer: identical elements, and transfer through principles.

Identical elements refers to the extent to which performance in training and performance on the job both depend on the same stimuli (visual displays, interpersonal situations, and so on), and require the same responses or behaviors. Transfer through principles occurs when trainees are able to use, on the job, general ideas or relationships among concepts that they learned during training; in this case, identical stimuli and responses are not necessary. Training programs that facilitate transfer through either or both of these approaches are typically more effective than those that ignore (or even inhibit!) such transfer.

There are a variety of ways to categorize the many different training methods and techniques that are currently available. Does the technique emphasize content (information), process (behaviors), or both? Does the training occur at the workplace, or must trainees be transported off-site? Does the training stress psychomotor skills, cognitive skills, social skills, or some combination of these?

Because we can see no particular advantage to any of these schemes, because many techniques seem to straddle the boundaries of any taxonomy, and because we make no pretense of providing you with a comprehensive list of every imaginable training procedure, we have refrained from using any of these classifications during the remainder of our discussion. Instead, our goal is to emphasize the importance of assessing each technique's appropriateness for meeting specific, identified needs, and to illustrate that process by discussing several different training techniques in the context of Mr. Hammond's need to transform competent engineers into competent first-level supervisors.

Lectures, Videotapes, and Films

Of all the different training techniques, you are probably most familiar with these (especially lectures!). We begin our look at the various techniques here precisely because of that familiarity. After following our analysis in an area that you know well, you should be better prepared to understand our assessments of techniques with which you have had little, or no, first-hand experience.

Videotapes, films, and lectures (in their purest form) are all characterized by a one-way flow of information from the trainer to the trainee(s). These techniques, therefore, do a singularly poor job of incorporating the important learning principles we mentioned earlier. Trainees' motivation is typically (and often mistakenly) taken for granted. Individual differences among trainees' needs and abilities are ignored, and these techniques offer little or no reward to trainees. In fact, they are sometimes quite aversive (boring, difficult to see or hear, and so forth). Feedback is usually nonexistent. Except for a lecture delivered by someone who is willing to respond to questions, these techniques require trainees to be passive, and offer them no opportunity to assess how well or how poorly they are learning the information that is being presented. Because very few employees' jobs entail listening to lectures or viewing films and tapes, transfer of training through identical elements is improbable. Transfer through general principles remains a possibility, however.

On the positive side, these procedures can be very efficient in their use of time and money. They are suitable for communicating vast amounts of information to large numbers of trainees in minimum amounts of time. In spite of the fact that some authors (Bass & Vaughan, 1966; Korman, 1971, 1977; McGehee & Thayer, 1961) and training directors (Carroll, Paine, & Ivancevich, 1972) have impugned the effectiveness of lectures, Goldstein (1986) concluded that "there appears to be little empirical reason for the bias against the procedure" (p. 188). As Zelko (1967) concluded more than two decades ago, the "lecture remains a most important method of training, and it probably always will be" (p. 151). Given the continuing advances in audiovisual and cinematic technologies and skills, we would extend Zelko's prophesy to videotapes and films as well.

Dr. MacKeven might choose the lecture method to orient Mr. Hammond's supervisors to the training program, and/or to present them with some basic information about the duties, responsibilities, and challenges inherent in first-level supervision. In addition, she may include films or videotapes as components of other training methodologies, such as computer-assisted training or behavioral role modeling (which we discuss below). It is highly unlikely, however, that she will rely solely on these one-way techniques in her effort to transform engineers into competent first-level supervisors.

Programmed and Computer-Assisted Instruction

Although it was designed as a "testing machine," Pressey (1950) is usually credited with developing the first teaching machine in the 1920s. The device "presented a series of questions to a student and informed him immediately whether his reply was right or wrong" (Lysaught & Williams, 1963).

The basic characteristics of programmed instruction (PI) are as follows (Bass & Vaughan, 1966; Goldstein, 1986):

1. Information is presented in small units ("frames"), each of which may vary in size from a single sentence to several paragraphs.
2. The trainee responds actively to each frame.
3. The trainee is informed immediately as to the correctness of his or her response. Since each frame contains only a limited amount of information, the trainee makes few errors.
4. The program is carefully designed to maximize learning. The programmer must consider the learning objectives, the nature of the material to be learned, and the prospective trainees' characteristics and abilities.
5. Each trainee works through the program independently, and at his or her own speed.

An example of a program that Goldstein adapted from a U.S. Civil Service document is reproduced in Table 7.1. This is a *linear* program, because the trainee

TABLE 7.1 Example of Linear Programmed Instruction (PI)

	1. You are now beginning a lesson on programmed instruction. The principle of *self-pacing* as used in programmed instruction allows all trainees to work as slowly or as fast as they choose. Since you can control the amount of time you spend on this lesson, this program is using the principle of self- _____ .
Pacing	2. People naturally learn at different rates. A program that allows all trainees to control their own rate of learning is using the principle of _____ .
Self-pacing	3. If a self-pacing program is to be successful, the information step size must be small. A program that is self-pacing would also apply the principle of small _____ .
Steps	4. The average trainee will usually make correct responses if the correct size step of information is given. This is utilizing the principle of small _____ .
Steps	5. A program that provides information in a step size that allows the trainee to be successful is applying the principle of _____ .
Small steps	6. A trainee knows the material being taught but has to wait for the remainder of the class. What programming principle is being violated? _____ .
Self-pacing	7. Two principles of programmed learning are: (1) _____ . (2) _____ .

1. **Self-pacing**
2. **Small steps**

Note: For practical reasons, the frames are arranged on one page rather than on succeeding pages. The answers should be covered until the preceding frame has been answered.

SOURCE: U.S. Civil Service Commission. (1970). *Programmed Instruction: A Brief Evaluation of Its Development and Current Status.* Washington, D.C.: U.S. Government Printing Office. [From Goldstein, I. L. (1986). *Training in Organizations: Needs Assessment, Development, and Evaluation* (2nd ed.). Pacific Grove, CA: Brooks/Cole.]

progresses through it in a rigid, step-by-step fashion. *Branching* programs are more complex; they can usher trainees directly through a program, or send them back to simpler material, or ahead to more difficult material, depending on the correctness of their responses and the nature of any mistakes they make.

Computer-assisted instruction (CAI) takes the basic characteristics of PI and adds the power and flexibility associated with our rapidly expanding computer technology. The tremendous growth in personal computers has rendered this technique even more accessible in homes and offices. Trainees can use the computer terminal as an infinitely patient tutor for "drill-and-practice" sessions on a given topic. Alternatively, they can better utilize the computer's immense potential by interacting with it in the form of a dialogue. A brief excerpt of a geography lesson in the form of such a dialogue appears in Table 7.2 (Collins & Adams, 1977).

PI and (especially) CAI make good use of two of the learning principles we discussed earlier. Trainees' motivation levels are often high, because they find the

TABLE 7.2 Annotated Excerpt from a Dialogue between a Student and a Computer-Assisted Instructional Device

Dialogue	Annotated comments
WHAT IS CHILE? ∗COUNTRY IN SOUTH AMERICA∗ VERY GOOD.	This is the most important property of Chile. (A tutor would suppress it on the assumption that the student knows the answer.) In evaluating the answer, it looks for "country," ignores the rest.
CORRECT OR INCORRECT? CHILE IS IN NORTHERN SOUTH AMERICA. ∗INCORRECT∗	Location is the next most important attribute under Chile.
YOU ARE CORRECT. CHILE IS IN SOUTHWESTERN SOUTH AMERICA.	The student answers correctly, so SCHOLAR will go deeper into Location.
THE EASTERN BORDERING COUNTRY OF CHILE IS— ∗I DON'T KNOW∗	This is the most important Bordering Country of Chile.
THE ANSWER IS: ARGENTINA. THE BOUNDARY OF THE EASTERN BORDERING COUNTRIES OF CHILE IS THE ANDES. THE NORTHERN BORDERING COUNTRY OF CHILE IS PERU. THE NORTHEASTERN BORDERING COUNTRY IS BOLIVIA.	Since the student has missed the question, SCHOLAR presents some related information about Bordering Countries.

Note: The student's responses are set off by asterisks.
SOURCE: Collins, A., & Adams, M. J. (1977). "Comparison of Two Teaching Strategies in Computer-Assisted Instruction," *Contemporary Educational Psychology, 2,* 133–148. Copyright 1977 by Academic Press, Inc. [From Goldstein, I. L. (1986). *Training in Organizations: Needs Assessment, Development, and Evaluation* (2nd ed.). Pacific Grove, CA: Brooks/Cole.]

procedures interesting, or even fun. They also receive immediate feedback (usually positive) concerning the accuracy of their responses, and they are allowed to progress through the material at their own pace. Transfer of training, however, is by no means assured, except in those cases where CAI is utilized to train people to use computer terminals, or when a computer is used to increase the realism of simulator training (which we will discuss soon).

Although research results have not always been consistent (Leib, Cusack, Hughes, Pilette, Werther, & Kintz, 1967), there is some consensus today that these autoinstructional techniques usually require less time of the trainees and the trainer (*during actual training*) than other techniques (such as the lecture) to teach a given amount of material, but that there are usually no meaningful differences in the achievement scores of trainees exposed to autoinstructional as opposed to more conventional training techniques (Goldstein, 1986; Wexley, 1984). Preparation of PI, and (again) especially CAI, packages can be very time consuming, and inordinately expensive, however.

Because of these drawbacks, and because other techniques are far more promising for training first-level supervisors, Dr. MacKeven will probably not rely on either of these autoinstructional methods, at least not right away. She may subsequently change her mind, if her training procedures for Mr. Hammond's engineers turn out to be very successful and she is inundated with requests from other managers throughout Peter's Pan Pizza to train their supervisors, too. In that case, considering Dowell and Wexley's (1978) conclusion that "there are few differences in the jobs of first-line supervisors regardless of technology or function" (p. 563), and Dossett and Hulvershorn's (1983) data suggesting that CAI training is just as effective when trainees work in pairs, she may save time in the long run by developing autoinstructional packages.

Conferences, Case Studies, and Sensitivity Training

These three training methodologies are similar, in that each relies heavily on verbal communication between and among trainees. A conference is a "carefully planned meeting with a specific purpose and goals" (McGehee & Thayer, 1961). It is particularly useful for helping trainees learn and understand conceptual information, and for helping them develop or modify certain attitudes. Conferences are, therefore, especially well suited for supervisory training (Busch, 1949).

Case studies typically present trainees with a written report describing an organizational problem. Each trainee usually analyzes the problem individually, and then prepares a set of solutions based on certain assumptions about available human and physical resources, as well as existing organizational, economic, and legal conditions. Trainees then meet as a group to present and discuss their solutions and, with the help of a "trainer," to identify the basic principles that underlie the case.

Sensitivity training (also known as laboratory training, T-group training, encounter-group training, and so forth) consists of face-to-face interactions among individuals where (1) the primary concern is with the "here and now"; (2) feelings and emotions are not only appropriate topics of conversation, they are paramount; (3) feedback and analysis involving self-disclosure is frequent; and (4) the choice of whether and how to respond to that feedback is left up to each individual trainee (Blumberg & Golembiewski, 1976; Goldstein, 1986). The goals are to promote self-awareness and sensitivity to others, to teach listening skills and an appreciation of group dynamics, and to provide a "psychologically safe" setting for people to experiment with different styles of social interaction (Campbell, Dunnette, Lawler, & Weick, 1970).

The role of the trainer or "leader" is crucial to the success of each of these techniques. Incompetence here can result in (1) poorly organized conferences; (2) case studies that convince trainees either that there is *no* solution to the organizational dilemma presented, or that the trainer's solution is the *only* acceptable solution to the problem; and (3) sensitivity groups that not only fail to promote constructive self-awareness, but that create or exacerbate emotional difficulties in trainees. The trainer's skills can also influence or determine trainees' motivation levels, and the degree to which feedback is made available to them.

Perhaps the most consistent criticism leveled against these techniques, however, focuses on the issue of transfer of training. Information gleaned in a conference, or from a sensitivity group, may prove to be irrelevant or even damaging, unless the trainee returns to an organizational environment that supports the use, or implementation, of that knowledge. Case studies may uncover principles that are extremely difficult to generalize to the trainees' "real-life" organizational situations. Once again, the trainer occupies a central role (Goldstein, 1986; Hinrichs, 1976; McGehee & Thayer, 1961).

Although Dr. MacKeven will probably opt not to use sensitivity groups, because of their ambiguous goals and inherent dangers, she may very well plan case studies and conferences that will help Mr. Hammond's engineers learn the basic principles of effective first-level supervision, and make them more comfortable in their new role. If her objectives are sufficiently specific, and she is skillful in her role as "leader" or discussion facilitator, these structured forms of face-to-face communication can make an important contribution to the training of inexperienced supervisors.

Simulations

Simulations are approximations of real-life situations and events. Training simulations can be divided into two types, those that emphasize the use of a machine, a piece of equipment, or a set of materials, and those that replicate a social or interpersonal situation. The purpose of simulation is to reproduce an actual work setting or situation in such a way that it is under the trainer's control. This control allows the trainer to influence trainees' motivation, and to provide them with timely and constructive feedback concerning their performance. The more realistic a simulator, physically and especially psychologically, the greater the expected transfer of training. In addition, simulation is usually far less expensive, both financially and emotionally, than training people in real-life situations.

Probably the best known machine simulator is a flight simulator for training pilots. A trainer can create all sorts of routine and hazardous situations, so that the trainee can learn the proper responses under controlled circumstances with no danger to life, limb, or extremely expensive equipment. Not all equipment simulators are that complex, however. Many factories expose new employees to "vestibule training," where they learn how to operate a piece of machinery away from the noise and confusion of the actual assembly line or factory floor.

Regardless of how complex or simple the machine simulation, the key issues are the trainer's control of the situation and the stimuli that confront the trainee, and the realism or fidelity of the approximation to real life. Although advances in computer technology have rendered many machine simulators far more realistic than they were in the past, we can never really be sure just how seriously trainees take these contrived reproductions of reality. Even in a multimillion-dollar flight simulator that is controlled by computers and augmented by audiovisual effects, the trainees still know that they are "playing make-believe," and that even if they "crash" into the side of a mountain, they'll still be able to go home to dinner that night.

Social or interpersonal simulations come in a variety of forms. Perhaps the most widely known is role-playing, where trainees act out various job-related situations. This technique can be very effective, when the trainees are willing and able to assume their assigned roles, and to behave as if they *really* were in their regular work setting (Campbell et al., 1970; Goldstein, 1986). Given an acceptable level of motivation, the trainer can provide timely and useful feedback to the actors. The accuracy of that feedback, and the fidelity of the role-play situation, will determine the extent to which training will be transferred back to the actual job setting. Interesting variants of standard role-playing include (1) reverse role-playing, where trainees whose jobs may place them in situations involving personal conflicts (with a supervisor or subordinate, or with the public, for example) assume the other person's role in order to appreciate another's perspective, and (2) multiple role-playing, where a large number of trainees are divided into teams, each of which acts out a situation, and then compares and discusses the results with the others.

Other forms of nonmachine simulation include business games and case studies (which we discussed earlier). Business games typically require trainees to make decisions in contrived situations that approximate normal business environments. Trainees receive feedback on the effect(s) of their decisions, and then go on to make subsequent decisions based on that feedback. Once again, advances in computer technology have made such games more realistic, and more fun. Far surpassing other social simulations in popularity among practitioners and researchers, however, is a set of procedures based on Bandura's (1969, 1977) social learning theory that are collectively known as behavioral role-modeling.

BEHAVIORAL ROLE-MODELING

Social learning theory suggests that observation, modeling, and **reinforcement** or reward (both direct and **vicarious**) can play important parts in modifying human behavior. Goldstein and Sorcher (1974) relied on these concepts when they designed a training procedure that was specifically intended to improve supervisors' interpersonal skills: behavioral role-modeling.

As summarized by Mann and Decker (1984), behavior-modeling training includes the following five components:

1. modeling, during which the trainee observes another person engaging in the desired behaviors, and receives vicarious reinforcement by watching the model receive rewards for his or her behavior
2. retention processes, whereby the trainee encodes those observations for later recall

---

reinforcement: a stimulus that increases the likelihood that a given behavior will be repeated when it (the stimulus) is presented contingent on that behavior

vicarious: experienced "secondhand," through imaginative participation in the experience of another person

3. rehearsal, when the trainee actually practices or rehearses the observed behaviors him- or herself
4. social reinforcement, where the trainer and the other trainees reward the individual for accurately imitating the previously observed model
5. transfer of training, when the trainee tries those newly learned behaviors in his or her actual job setting, and then reports successes and failures back to the training group

As you can see, the behavioral role-modeling approach attends to trainees' motivation, to feedback, and to transfer of training. It goes beyond traditional behavior modification techniques (Haynes, Pine, & Fitch, 1982; Luthans & Kreitner, 1985) by emphasizing the importance of observation and vicarious reinforcement to learning, in addition to actual practice and direct reinforcement.

Available research evidence suggests that Goldstein and Sorcher's (1974) behavioral role-modeling procedures have improved first-level supervisors' performance in a variety of different circumstances (Decker, 1979; Kraut, 1976; Latham & Saari, 1979; Porras & Anderson, 1981; Wexley, 1984). One of the more intriguing applications was that of Sorcher and Spence (1982), who successfully incorporated behavioral role-modeling in the InterFace Project (Nossel, 1982), which was an effort to improve interpersonal relations among black employees and their "mostly white" supervisors in a South African pharmaceutical company.

Because of the encouraging empirical evidence, and because behavioral role-modeling addresses the important issues pertaining to trainees' motivation, feedback, and transfer of training, this methodology will certainly play an important part in Dr. MacKeven's plans for responding to Mr. Hammond's and the engineering department's needs. Behavioral role-modeling may, in fact, be the cornerstone of Peter's Pan Pizza's training program for first-level supervisors (and perhaps higher-ranking managers and executives, too).

On-the-Job Techniques

A final category of training procedures that merit at least a cursory examination are those that occur right at the workplace, while the trainees are actually performing their jobs. These on-the-job training (OJT) techniques and procedures include orientation sessions, coaching, mentoring or apprenticeships, job rotation, and performance appraisal.

Orientations are common during the first few days of employment. Personnel representatives and supervisors, sometimes with the aid of audiovisual equipment, typically inform new employees about company policies, procedures, and benefits, as well as the role of their jobs in the overall organizational mission. As long as they are not inundated with too much information too rapidly, most new hires find such sessions to be useful. Coaching involves periodically providing employees with feedback and advice concerning their job performance. Immediate supervisors and co-workers are the most common sources of coaching.

Apprenticeships, which can "last anywhere from two to five years, . . . combine on-the-job instruction together with [many hours] of classroom and shop instruction" (Wexley & Latham, 1981). They are used to transform men and women in the skilled trades (bricklayers, carpenters, electricians, painters, plumbers, and so on) into competent "journeymen" through a lengthy and intensive relationship with more experienced workers, who can teach them the skills they will need to succeed in their chosen trade.

In management and professional circles, the senior men and women who take newcomers "under their wings" are known as "mentors." A substantial amount of evidence suggests that having a mentor can facilitate success and advancement through the ranks of an organization (Hennig & Jardim, 1977; Kanter, 1977; Stumpf & London, 1981). Hunt and Michael (1983) reviewed this literature, and even offered a model of the mentor–protégé relationship.

Job rotation consists of "giving trainees a series of job assignments in various parts of the organization for a specified period of time" (Wexley & Latham, 1981), or assigning trainees to different workstations or pieces of equipment on a rotating schedule. This technique serves not only to "cross-train" employees for a number of different jobs, but provides trainees with an overview of how their shop, department, or the organization as a whole operates. We'll have more to say about job rotation in Chapter 13.

Finally, as you learned in Chapter 4, one of the purposes of performance appraisal is to provide employees with both formal and informal feedback concerning their relative strengths and weaknesses on their jobs. From that perspective, the performance appraisal process can be construed as a somewhat more institutionalized form of coaching, and as such, a form of OJT.

Obviously, the major advantage of OJT techniques involves transfer of training. Except for the classroom component of apprenticeships, these techniques require no transfer at all; the training takes place right where it is intended to be used. Similarly, feedback is an important component of many OJT procedures, especially coaching/mentoring and performance appraisal.

Unfortunately, most OJT techniques pay little attention to the motivation levels of employees, either trainees or trainers. Trainees may, in the absence of any formal, off-site training program, conclude that the organization is unwilling to devote much in the way of time or resources to developing their job-related knowledge and skills, and consequently become demoralized. Trainers are often expected to provide new employees with OJT, without being offered any incentives or reinforcement for doing so effectively. In fact, coaching or other OJT techniques can often result in reduced levels of productivity, and perhaps fewer or smaller rewards, for those designated as "trainers." It seems clear that organizations that rely on OJT techniques should include the training function in the job descriptions of those who are asked to assist newcomers, and that they should be rewarded accordingly.

As you learned in Chapter 4, Peter's Pan Pizza is committed to improving its performance appraisal procedures, so some OJT is already in progress. Dr. MacKeven may also find that promoting mentor–protégé relationships, and even relatively superficial coaching sessions, will contribute to an overall training program with the potential to transform Mr. Hammond's selected engineers into first-rate first-level supervisors.

CHAPTER SUMMARY

Training involves a systematic set of procedures, designed and implemented by an organization, for bringing about changes in employees that will result in improved job performance. Comprehensive needs analysis is a necessary prerequisite to training. Only by explicitly acknowledging or determining the overall goals and constraints that characterize an organization (organizational analysis), and by defining the ways in which specific jobs and their associated tasks contribute to those overall goals (job/task analysis), and by assessing the capabilities of current employees and applicants to perform those tasks (person analysis), can we determine whether training is indicated and, if it is, what it must accomplish.

Competent needs assessment also suggests the kinds of criteria that will be appropriate for evaluating a training program's effectiveness. Although reaction and learning criteria are used most frequently, only behavior and results criteria can reveal the extent to which trainees apply their training in the work setting. Training evaluation involves answering three questions: (1) Did a change occur? (2) If so, was the training program responsible? (3) If so, will that change occur again with a new group of trainees?

Answers to the first two questions (which reflect a program's internal validity) can be contaminated by history, maturation, pretesting, instrumentation changes, trainee selection and mortality, and regression toward the mean. Answers to the third question (which reflects external validity) can be confounded by pretesting, trainee selection, and Hawthorne and Pygmalion effects. True experimental designs for evaluating training can minimize or eliminate many of these "threats" to validity. Quasi-experimental designs can also be informative, but pre-experimental designs reveal next to nothing about a training program's effectiveness.

A variety of techniques, methods, and procedures are currently available to organizational trainers. These include "one-way" techniques (lectures, films, videotapes), autoinstructional techniques (programmed and computer-assisted instruction), discussion-oriented techniques (case studies, conferences, sensitivity training), simulations, and on-the-job procedures (coaching, mentoring, performance appraisal). Whatever techniques are used, they should be chosen because they can address identified needs, and because of their capacity to motivate trainees, to provide them with feedback, and to facilitate transfer of training. Behavioral role-modeling does a good job of incorporating all three of these basic learning principles.

INTEROFFICE MEMO

TO: Robert Hammond, Director of Engineering

FROM: Jennilyn MacKeven, Human-Resources Coordinator

I couldn't agree more with your concerns about training supervisors.
I have therefore asked my assistant, Sandy Roberts, to prepare an
overall plan for determining your exact training needs, for designing
and implementing specific training methods and procedures that are
capable of addressing those needs, and for evaluating the effectiveness of whatever training "program" is eventually developed. I asked
Sandy to concentrate her initial efforts in Engineering but, because
your situation there is hardly unique, to consider the possibility of
including supervisors from other departments throughout PPP in her
plans.

Without presuming to forecast the exact outcome of Sandy's inquiries,
I strongly suspect that a set of procedures known as "behavioral
role-modeling" will occupy a central position in our eventual program
for training first-level supervisors. This approach will require a
great deal of cooperation not only from the "target" supervisors,
but also from their managers, and possibly from their subordinates as
well. It is therefore very important that we enlist the support of
Mr. Nathanson, Vice President for Facilities, at the very beginning
of our project.

You should be hearing from Sandy very soon, as she begins the "needs
assessment" phase of the project. Feel free to contact me any time.

REVIEW QUESTIONS AND EXERCISES

1. What information do you think Sandy Roberts will generate through her organizational, job/task, and person analyses in the engineering department? How are these three kinds of information logically interrelated?
2. Based on your response to (1), what kind(s) of criteria should be measured during training evaluation? Explain your answers.
3. Considering your responses to the first two questions, what design(s) should be used to evaluate training effectiveness in this situation? Why?
4. List the threats to internal and external validity that will be controlled or eliminated by the design(s) you recommended. Which threats will not be controlled? Explain how each threat is or is not controlled by your design.
5. What is the rationale that underlies "content" approaches to training evaluation?
6. Evaluate *each* of the specific training methods or procedures discussed in this chapter, paying particular attention to (*a*) how well or poorly a method addresses each of the "person" needs that you identified in response to the first question (above), and (*b*) how practical each method is in the context of Peter's Pan Pizza, Inc.

INTEROFFICE MEMO
TO: All Personnel
FROM: Michael N. Darling, President and Chairman

It is my distinct pleasure to announce that Peter's Pan Pizza, Inc., has finalized an agreement to purchase Flavio's Frozen Foods, Inc., located in Manhattan Harbor, Massachusetts. This acquisition will, in the opinion of the board of directors, strengthen the corporation by allowing rapid expansion into a profitable segment of the food industry.

I am aware that there have been numerous rumors about mergers, both friendly and unfriendly, in recent months, so I would like to tell you a little about Flavio's, and explain how our purchase can be expected to affect PPP employees.

Flavio's Frozen Foods is one of the top 25 businesses in the prepared—food industry, and has been experiencing an average 7 per—cent annual growth rate over the past five years. There are Flavio's plants in the Northeast and the Southwest U.S., with distribution centers in Phoenix, Arizona, and Manhattan Harbor. Flavio's major products are frozen pizza, frozen lasagna, and a variety of frozen dinners and appetizers.

Although both PPP and Flavio's are part of the food industry, it should be clear that they are in distinctly different segments of that industry. Consequently, this merger will have virtually no effect on the vast majority of PPP employees. We do plan to transfer some PPP managers into positions at Flavio's, but based on prelimi—nary discussions regarding expansion by Flavio's into additional seg—ments of the prepared—food market, we do not anticipate laying off any of Flavio's current managerial staff.

I hope that this information has addressed your major questions and concerns. Within the next few weeks, all PPP managers and supervisors will attend orientation meetings on the merger, and will then hold similar meetings with their own workers, at which time you will be able to ask questions about Flavio's. Until then, I hope that you will join me in welcoming Flavio's Frozen Foods into the PPP family.

CHAPTER 8

Work Motivation

Learning Points

After studying this chapter, you should

- know the three functions of motivation, and be able to evaluate motivation theories in terms of how they explain these functions
- be able to explain the factors that limit the usefulness of the motivation construct
- be able to define the concept of needs and explain how it has been used in various theories to explain work motivation
- be able to define the components of instrumentality theory and explain how, according to the theory, they combine to predict motivational force
- be able to describe the concept of equity, and explain how it might influence work behavior
- be able to list the factors that are necessary for effective goal setting
- understand how operant conditioning is used in work organizations
- be able to evaluate the research results for each of the motivation theories discussed in this chapter

INTEROFFICE MEMO
TO: J. A. MacKeven, Human—Resources Coordinator
FROM: Margaret Russell, Director of Consumer Research

For about eight years now Consumer Research, as well as several other units in the marketing division, has sponsored a number of interns each summer. These people are generally advanced undergraduates or graduate students in business or the social sciences from colleges and universities in the Rocky Mountain area. I usually have students with some training and experience in either research design or data analysis. The stated purpose of the program, according to Bill Ryan, the vice president of marketing, is to provide support to students interested in the marketing field, while providing Peter's Pan Pizza with qualified, short—term help in technical fields.

While the program sounds good on paper, I have consistently had prob—lems with the interns in our department. Occasionally we get a dedi—cated, hard—working student, but most of the people simply don't seem very interested in their jobs. We do all that we can to make sure that we select the best candidates, and in fact we had Personnel develop a biodata—based selection program for interns two years ago. I am convinced that these students are, for the most part, capable of performing the tasks we give them, but they just aren't putting in the effort. I would like to discuss this matter with you further, and see if there is anything that can be done to salvage this intern program.

Margaret Russell has presented Dr. MacKeven with what appears to be a problem in employee motivation. Ms. Russell believes that the interns in her department are capable of performing the work given to them, but most have not lived up to their potential. All organizations face this type of problem from time to time. In some cases, employees with good work records have unexplained lapses in performance; in other situations, previously cooperative workers develop "bad attitudes" and appear to become lazy. Of course, it also happens that "problem" employees begin to work harder, produce more, and cooperate with their co-workers. In order to explain why workers behave in the ways they do, and to help organizations improve their employees' performance, I/O psychologists have spent a great deal of time studying work motivation. In this chapter we will examine the topic of work motivation, the theories that have been developed to explain motivation, and some of the procedures that psychologists have suggested for improving motivation.

A DEFINITION OF MOTIVATION

Motivation has traditionally referred to the processes by which people are moved to engage in particular behaviors. In a work setting, such as Peter's Pan Pizza, motivation is often used as an explanation for workers' productivity, effort, and attendance (or the lack thereof). We often hear that some people are "highly motivated," while others "lack motivation." This common use of the term does not, however, suggest *why* some people seem to work harder or appear to be more conscientious about their attendance. In order to study work motivation scientifically and develop theories that will enable us to understand and improve work motivation, we need a more precise definition.

Although several definitions of work motivation have emerged over the years, most share three components that, together, represent the commonly accepted aspects of motivation: Motivation is that *which energizes, directs, and sustains behavior* (Steers & Porter, 1983). Let's examine each part of this definition to provide a clearer picture of the nature of motivation.

The *energizing* function of motivation is its most basic component. Motivation is a state that causes people to act, that drives them to engage in particular behaviors. People who are motivated are compelled to do something, while people who are not motivated (or who are less motivated) do not feel such a compulsion. According to motivation theories, few tasks would be initiated, much less completed, without this energization.

The *directing* function of motivation implies that motivated behavior has a purpose; it is directed toward achieving specific goals. People who are motivated know what they want to accomplish, and engage in behavior that they believe will help them achieve their goals. Less motivated people may be unsure of exactly what they want to accomplish, which certainly lowers their chances of getting anything done.

The *sustaining* function of motivation explains why we persist in our efforts to achieve our goals. It also explains why people sometimes appear to abandon a particular approach to a problem, or abandon the problem altogether if they don't succeed immediately. Motivation theories suggest that highly motivated people will sustain their goal-directed behavior longer than those who are less motivated. This does not mean, however, that highly motivated people will hesitate to drop a course of action that is not working. Rather, under conditions of high motivation, a person is likely to try a new, potentially more successful, approach to the problem, while under low motivation, the goal may be abandoned after initial failure.

A general model of the motivation process that is consistent with this definition was presented years ago by Dunette and Kirchner (1965; see Figure 8.1). The source of motivation is described as a "state of disequilibrium," or a sense of imbalance. This can be a need, desire, expectation, or some combination thereof, experienced by a person. For example, a person may feel a need for greater control over her work life or a desire to move to a better climate, or may expect that being late for work one more time will result in being fired. As you can see, the feeling of disequilibrium is an uncomfortable experience, and consequently provides the energizing component of motivation.

Accompanying these feelings is the anticipation that certain behaviors will satisfy the needs and desires, or fulfill the expectations. This anticipation provides the directive, or goal-oriented, function of motivation. Behavior is sustained, according to this model, by a *feedback* process. A worker engages in certain behaviors in order to achieve the goal of reducing the inner state of disequilibrium. By observing the results of the behavior (either directly or through information provided externally), the worker can judge whether or not the goal is closer to being achieved. Based on this judgment, the person can continue the current behavior or modify the behavior, or if the activation is weak or the goal unclear, give up.

Limitations to Motivation

While motivation is intended to be a general explanation for behavior, it is not sufficient to explain *all* behavior. There are a number of variables that do not

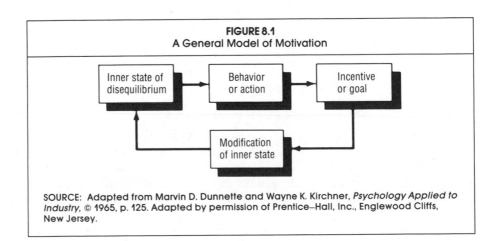

FIGURE 8.1
A General Model of Motivation

Inner state of disequilibrium → Behavior or action → Incentive or goal → Modification of inner state → (back to Inner state of disequilibrium)

SOURCE: Adapted from Marvin D. Dunnette and Wayne K. Kirchner, *Psychology Applied to Industry,* © 1965, p. 125. Adapted by permission of Prentice–Hall, Inc., Englewood Cliffs, New Jersey.

easily fit within the motivation framework. In certain cases, these factors can affect the relevance of motivation for understanding work behavior and performance.

MOTIVATION AND ABILITY

A common assumption of psychologists is that performance is a function of both motivation and ability. This means that in order to successfully perform a task, one must *both* be motivated to perform the task *and* have the skills, knowledge, experience, and so forth to perform. If either factor is lacking, successful performance is unlikely. Consider, for example, the situation described by Ms. Russell in Peter's Pan Pizza's consumer research department. Let's assume that the interns are all highly motivated to do their jobs well. Their poor performance, then, might be due to an inability to perform the required tasks. They might be expected, for example, to analyze data from marketing research, yet the college programs from which they are selected may not offer the necessary statistics courses. Ms. Russell mentioned that the students seem to be uninterested in their work, and are not putting much effort into their jobs. Although this may seem to be a clear-cut case of poor motivation, it is possible that once the interns discovered that they lacked the skills to perform the job, they saw further effort as being futile. The solution would, in this case, involve improving selection or training procedures, rather than trying to increase motivation.

INDIVIDUAL DIFFERENCES IN MOTIVES

One important way in which people differ from one another is in terms of the goals they pursue. If everyone was motivated to achieve the same goals, managers would have a much easier time getting workers to do what they wanted them to do. The fact that workers have different goals means that efforts to increase the motivation of one worker may have no effect, or even a negative effect, on another worker's motivation. Further, if management makes incorrect assumptions about the workers' goals, efforts to increase motivation may be useless. For example, in Peter's Pan Pizza's consumer research department, the students may view their internships as useful for reaching the goal of full-time employment after graduation. Some of the interns may believe that simply having an internship greatly increases the probability of receiving a job offer. Consequently, they may feel that what is learned *during* the internship is unimportant. Other students may have sought the internship in order to learn particular skills. Efforts by PPP to deal with either set of motives alone would have no beneficial effect on those interns motivated by the other set.

MOTIVATION AS AN INFERRED STATE

Many of the behaviors that I/O psychologists study are more-or-less objective; they can be measured in fairly (although not absolutely) unambiguous ways. Productivity, turnover, and absenteeism are some examples. Other variables, however, are not so clear-cut. Motivation is a psychological state of the individual worker. While it may have an effect on people's observable behavior, it is not the same as that behavior. Since we cannot observe motivation directly, we must *infer* it from our observations of the behavior that we *can* see. Unless everyone with the same level of motivation in a given situation behaves in the same way (and they do not), this presents a problem for studying and understanding motivation.

For example, the interns at Peter's Pan Pizza may all be equally motivated, yet their observable behaviors may differ greatly. Some interns may respond to motivation by engaging in bursts of activity, implementing the first plan of action that occurs to them. Others may respond to the same motives by stepping back to evaluate the situation and carefully planning their next course of action. Dr. MacKeven might observe the apparent energy level of the first group and conclude that they were more highly motivated, while another psychologist might note the careful thought of the second group and conclude that *they* were more highly motivated. Because psychologists and others must infer the state of workers' motivation, such disagreement and ambiguity is both common and problematic.

THE DYNAMIC NATURE OF MOTIVES

It would be nice for both organizations and I/O psychologists if people's motives did not change over time. Ms. Russell would like to know what motivates her workers, and she would like to be able to count on the same things motivating them tomorrow that motivate them today. Unfortunately, the factors that motivate workers *do* change, and when this happens managers can find themselves out of touch with their workers' needs, and unable to motivate them with the techniques that worked in the past.

Consider again the intern situation in Peter's Pan Pizza's consumer research department. The internship program may have been developed on the assumption that the interns would be highly motivated to learn all they can while at PPP, and that may have been true early in the life of the program when the students seemed to be "dedicated and hard-working." Today, however, it is possible that the interns are not motivated to learn or develop new skills, but rather by other factors, such as the opportunity to live in Suardell Springs during the ski season. Such a change might occur if the job market for these students had improved and they no longer needed to worry about polishing their skills during an internship in order to get a job.

STEREOTYPES

Understanding worker motivation is made more difficult by the fact that everyone holds stereotypical views about what motivates people. McCormick and Ilgen (1980) described two general stereotypes about motivation. The first of these they called the "trait" stereotype. This is a belief that motivation is a characteristic of individual workers, and that some people have more of it than others. People who hold this stereotype are likely to believe that the only way to improve work motivation is to replace the workers you have with more highly motivated people. Motivation thus becomes a selection problem. If Dr.

MacKeven held this view, she might conclude that the selection process for interns is not sensitive to differences in motivation, and suggest that the procedure be revised to include predictors of motivation.

The second stereotype is an "external-state" view of motivation. This approach stresses the working conditions and the nature of the supervision, pay, and other aspects of the job that are assumed to have an effect on worker motivation. If she held this viewpoint, Dr. MacKeven might suggest that the work environment of the interns be examined for possible reasons for low motivation. For example, the supervision supplied by management in the consumer research department may not be close enough, and consequently the students are not really sure what is expected of them.

THEORIES OF MOTIVATION

In the following sections we discuss several theories of work motivation. These theories are grouped into general categories, based on similarities in the underlying processes that they propose to explain motivation. Some of the approaches presented here are primarily of historical interest, having played an important role in the development and understanding of work motivation, although they are no longer considered to be adequate explanations for employees' behaviors. Other theories are currently very popular. Together, this collection of viewpoints should give you a good picture of how psychologists have addressed the issue of motivation.

Need Theories

Some of the earliest theories of motivation were based on the concept of **needs.** In general, these theories suggest that people have needs for certain outcomes or events. When these needs are not satisfied, people experience a **drive** to engage in behaviors that will lead to need satisfaction. The goal of motivated behavior, according to need theories, is to eliminate or satisfy the need, which serves to restore equilibrium. Some theories address basic **physiological needs** such as the needs we all have for food and water. In these cases the nature of the drives, hunger and thirst, are clear and familiar to everyone. Most need theories of work motivation, however, rely more heavily on **psychological needs.** The nature of these needs is not so clear, and attempting to define and measure them has been one of the biggest challenges for need theorists.

NEED HIERARCHY THEORY

Abraham Maslow (1943, 1970) proposed one of the earliest need theories of human motivation. He suggested that people are motivated to satisfy a number of specific needs. Like all need theorists, Maslow believed that an unsatisfied need produces behavior that is intended to satisfy it, after which that particular need is no longer motivating. What makes Maslow's theory different from other need theories is his belief that human needs are arranged in a **hierarchy.** That is, some needs are more basic, or "prepotent," than others, and therefore have greater potential for motivation. Further, when a basic need is unsatisfied or "deprived," it dominates a person's behavior, and she will seek to gratify that need. Once that need is gratified, the next most prepotent need is activated and becomes motivating, and so on up the hierarchy.

Maslow's hierarchy of needs is presented in Figure 8.2. The most basic needs in this model are *physiological needs*, such as needs for food, water, and sex. Since they are the most basic, when one or more of these needs are not satisfied, other potential motives are ignored until the physiological needs are fulfilled. Once this happens, *safety needs* begin to motivate the individual. These include needs to maintain a safe environment and a healthy existence that is free from threats. Once safety is reasonably assured, *belongingness needs*, or needs to be accepted and liked by others, become the primary motivators. Next are *esteem needs*, which include the need for a positive self-image, as well as needs for recognition from others for personal accomplishments.

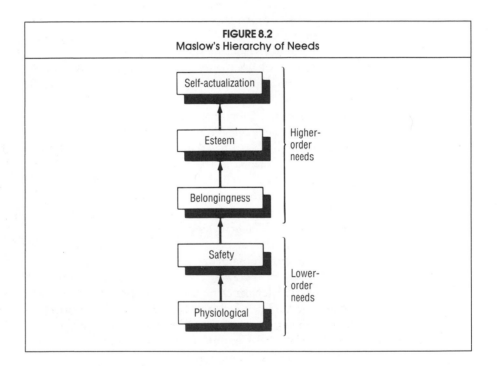

FIGURE 8.2
Maslow's Hierarchy of Needs

need: a condition in which there is a deficiency of something; a condition requiring relief

drive: an impulse or urge to act, resulting from the existence of a need

physiological needs: needs resulting from biological deficiencies

psychological needs: needs that have no direct cause in biological deficiencies; acquired or learned needs

hierarchy: a system in which objects are ordered in terms of status

Finally, once the first four levels of needs have been relatively well satisfied, *self-actualization needs* become the major motivating force in a person's life. Self-actualization refers to a process whereby an individual reaches her full potential, achieving all that she is capable of achieving. In some of his later work, Maslow suggested that the gratification of self-actualization needs, unlike that of other needs, results in a strengthening rather than a weakening of the need. This was apparently an effort to explain what would motivate people who were approaching self-actualization, since there are no higher needs to be activated (Maslow, 1965). The U.S. Army recently captured the spirit of self-actualization in its recruiting slogan "Be all you can be!"

The possible need hierarchy explanations for the problems in Peter's Pan Pizza's consumer research department are straightforward: Either all of the interns' needs are satisfied (which is unlikely), or performance of their jobs does not satisfy their currently active needs. The latter could happen if the job satisfies needs that are either too low or too high in the hierarchy. For example, the interns may have a great deal of responsibility, which would normally satisfy esteem needs. Since they still have the financial concerns of college students, however, the interns are likely to be motivated by lower-order needs, and not find the responsibility particularly attractive.

While Maslow's theory has been popular with managers and practitioners, there is little evidence to support the components of the theory. Wahba and Bridwell (1976) reviewed the research literature on need hierarchy theory, and did not find much support for the existence of the five categories of needs proposed by Maslow. They reviewed ten factor-analytic studies based on a variety of need measures. If Maslow's theory is valid, factor analyses should yield five independent factors, representing the levels in the hierarchy (see Chapter 5 for a more detailed discussion of factor analysis). In no case did the analyses reveal all of Maslow's needs, although there was some limited evidence that the higher-order needs and the lower-order needs formed separate clusters, as shown in Figure 8.2 (Lawler & Suttle, 1972). These reviewers also found that in studies where subjects were asked to rank the importance of Maslow's needs, the hierarchy proposed by the theory was never obtained.

Wahba and Bridwell (1976) also concluded that, contrary to the theory, there was little evidence for the notion that need deprivation leads to domination by that need. The needs rated as being the least satisfied were not always those rated as being most important. Research by Alderfer (1972), Lawler and Suttle (1972), Hall and Nougaim (1968), and Rauschenberger, Schmitt, and Hunter (1980) all reported similar results.

Finally, Wahba and Bridwell (1976) examined evidence bearing on the proposal that gratification of one need activates needs at the next highest level. One prediction consistent with this proposal is that the higher the level of a need, the less gratified, on the average, that need should be. Data from 23 studies, however, failed to support this prediction. Wahba and Bridwell found that either self-actualization or security (safety) needs were typically the least satisfied, while social (belongingness) needs were usually the most satisfied.

The limited research on need hierarchy theory offers little support for Maslow's ideas. One reason for this lack of support may be that most of this research has been "cross-sectional," comparing the needs of different people at one point in time, whereas the theory was intended to predict *changes* in individuals' needs. It is therefore possible that longitudinal designs, measuring the needs of people over time, would yield greater support for the need hierarchy. Of greater importance is the difficulty psychologists have had in defining constructs such as needs and self-actualization. While these notions are the cornerstones of Maslow's theory, he did not describe how they should be operationally defined for research purposes (Maslow, 1943).

ERG THEORY

In an effort to deal with some of the criticisms of Maslow's theory, Alderfer (1969, 1972) proposed a motivation theory based on the hierarchy-of-needs concept, but with substantial modifications in terms of both the number of needs and how the needs operate to motivate people. Rather than five needs, Alderfer suggested only three. The name of the theory, ERG, was derived from the names of these needs, which were defined by Alderfer (1969) as follows:

> *Existence* needs include all the various forms of material and physiological desires. Hunger and thirst represent deficiencies in existence needs. Pay, fringe benefits, and physical working conditions are other types of existence needs. . . .
>
> *Relatedness* needs include all the needs which involve relationships with significant other people. Family members are usually significant others, as are superiors, coworkers, subordinates, friends, and enemies. . . .
>
> *Growth* needs include all the needs which involve a person making creative or productive effects on himself and the environment. Satisfaction of growth needs comes from a person engaging problems which call him to utilize his capacities fully and may include requiring him to develop additional capacities . . . (pp. 145–147).

One similarity between Maslow's and Alderfer's theories is that the needs they specified are arranged in a hierarchy. Alderfer, however, claimed that it is a hierarchy of *concreteness* rather than prepotence, with existence needs being the most concrete and growth needs the least concrete. As with Maslow's theory, however, the gratification of needs at one level activates the motivating potential of needs at the next level. This *gratification/activation* principle, as it applies to ERG theory, is presented in Figure 8.3.

Unlike Maslow, however, Alderfer proposed that the hierarchy is not absolute, and that people can be simultaneously motivated by needs at different levels. Also unlike Maslow, ERG theory provides a means for people to go *down* the hierarchy. Alderfer referred to this process as *frustration/regression*. After repeated attempts to achieve gratification of needs at a given level, Alderfer said that people will essentially abandon those needs and become more concerned with satisfying needs at the next lowest level. Thus, rather than the relatively steady progression up the hierarchy described by Maslow's theory, ERG theory suggests that people may move up or down, depending on their success in gratifying needs at each level. The frustration/regression process is also illustrated in Figure 8.3.

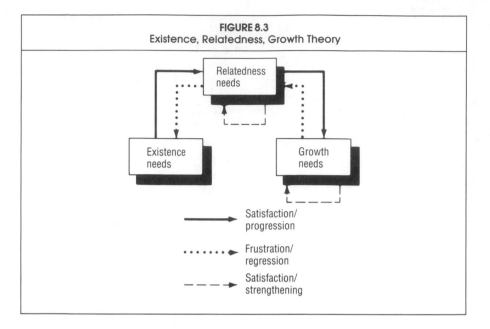

FIGURE 8.3
Existence, Relatedness, Growth Theory

Alderfer's theory suggests, too, that satisfaction of relatedness and growth needs results in the strengthening of those needs. This is represented by the arrows at the bottom of the relatedness and growth boxes in Figure 8.3. As in Maslow's theory, this process allows for continued motivation once a person reaches the higher need levels.

ERG is more sophisticated than Maslow's need hierarchy. By allowing for motivation by multiple needs as well as regression toward more basic needs, ERG appears to be more compatible with the experiences that most people have had while actually working in organizations. Peter's Pan Pizza's interns, for example, may have been motivated by unsatisfied existence needs when they started working. After the first few paychecks, however, they began to be concerned with relatedness needs, which they found more difficult to satisfy in a temporary job. According to ERG, continued frustration of relatedness needs would cause the interns to return to existence needs as the primary motivator. By this time, however, the interns probably learned that pay and performance are not directly related, which would explain why they are not putting forth the amount of effort they had originally exhibited.

Unfortunately, research testing ERG theory is sparse, and that which has been conducted has provided only mixed support for the theory. Some researchers have found positive evidence of the basic components of ERG (for example, Wanous & Zwany, 1977), while others have failed to find any support for the theory's principles (Rauschenberger, Schmitt, & Hunter, 1980). The lack of interest in ERG theory probably stems in part from the ambiguous nature of these research results, and in part from some of the problems that ERG shares with Maslow's need hierarchy. Both theories rely upon the concept of needs, which has never been operationally defined to the satisfaction of many researchers. This leads to problems in both testing and applying the theory. Each theory also suggests an ultimate goal of motivated behavior: self-actualization in Maslow's case, growth in Alderfer's, although exactly what is meant by these terms is not clear. Because of questions such as these, ERG, much like the need hierarchy, has proved to be of little use for understanding work motivation.

MANIFEST NEEDS THEORY

Another motivation theory based on human needs is manifest needs theory, the basic principles of which were developed by Murray (1938). According to Murray, human motivation is determined by a number of needs that provide for both the activation and direction of behavior. In this sense, manifest needs theory is similar to need hierarchy theory. Murray, however, differed from Maslow on a number of points that clearly distinguish this theory from other need theories.

The first, and most obvious, difference between manifest needs and need hierarchy theories is that rather than suggesting five basic needs, Murray identified as many as two dozen. Second, he believed that these needs are not instinctive, but rather are learned by people as they go about their day-to-day lives. This implies that not all people will experience the same needs, since each person's life, and what is learned during that life, is unique. Third, rather than being activated by either deprivation or the satisfaction of a lower-order need, Murray believed that needs are activated by events or cues in the person's environment. When the appropriate cues for a given need are present, then that need becomes active, or **manifest.** When the environmental cues are absent, the need is inactive, or **latent.** Of course, if a person does not possess a need in the first place, the cues will have no effect. Fourth, Murray did not believe that needs were arranged in any hierarchy of prepotence or concreteness. This means that any need can be activated at any time, regardless of the state of satisfaction of other needs. Finally, Murray did not limit motivation to the activation of a single need at any one time. Instead, manifest needs theory states that a person's motivation may be influenced by a variety of needs working together to determine the ultimate strength and direction of behavior.

Although Murray suggested that there were a relatively large number of human needs, research on the implications of his theory for work motivation has tended to focus on only a few (Steers, 1983). The need most often studied in organizational settings is *need for achievement,* or as it is commonly abbreviated, *n Ach.* People with high need for achievement are competitive, take responsibility for solving problems, have a strong desire for feedback, and are concerned with successfully accomplishing their tasks. High need achievers are likely to prefer tasks or problems with moderate levels of difficulty, rather than those that are extremely difficult or extremely easy. This is because accomplishing easy tasks does not represent adequate achievement, while difficult tasks present

---

manifest: evident; active; having an effect
latent: present, but hidden and inactive; invisible

a high probability of failure, which also does little to bolster feelings of accomplishment. Low need achievers are not likely to be strongly attracted to *any* task, with only a slight preference for moderately difficult challenges (Atkinson & Feather, 1966; McClelland & Winter, 1969).

Another dimension to achievement-oriented behavior is the tendency for some people to avoid tasks because of a fear of failing. This has been called the *need to avoid failure* or n AF (Atkinson & Feather, 1966). People who are high in n AF tend to avoid tasks with moderate difficulty. Instead, they are more attracted to either very easy tasks, where success is assured, or very difficult tasks, where failure can be blamed on the nature of the task rather than on the person's lack of ability.

A second need that has implications for work motivation is *need for power*, or n Pow. People high in n Pow are motivated to control their environment, including the other people in that environment. They attempt to influence others by offering opinions, making suggestions, and attempting to persuade. McClelland (1976) has identified two different forms of n Pow. *Personal power* involves the control and domination of other people as an end in itself. Individuals with needs for this type of power are not typically concerned with the goals or accomplishments of the organization. *Institutionalized power* also involves controlling other people, but with the goals of the organization rather than personal gain in mind. People with needs for institutionalized power are more likely to seek help with problems and are willing to forego their personal gain for the benefit of the organization.

Two other needs from manifest needs theory that have frequently been examined in organizational settings are *need for affiliation (n Aff)* and *need for autonomy (n Aut)*. People high in n Aff desire the approval of others, and often conform to the wishes of those around them, particularly if they value the friendship of those people. High n Aff individuals are also genuinely concerned with the feelings of others. People high in n Aut value freedom from the control of other people as well as from institutional rules. They prefer to work alone and control the pace of their own work (Steers, 1983).

Theory and research on the effects of manifest needs in organizations have focused primarily on how they relate to managerial motivation and performance. McClelland has stated that the most important need for managers to possess is the need for power, specifically the need for institutional power (McClelland, 1976). Recognizing that politics play an important role in business organizations, and that obtaining and using power is crucial to political behavior, the high n Pow manager is expected to have the best chances for success. High n Ach managers are too concerned with their own success to be sufficiently motivated by the needs of the organization; high n Aff managers may be unwilling to make the tough decisions necessary for effective management, for fear of offending a co-worker or subordinate; and managers high in n Aut tend to ignore pressures from the organization and are not committed to its goals (Zaleznik, 1970).

Indeed, research evidence supports the proposed advantages of n Pow among managers. McClelland and Boyatzis (1982) found that high n Pow, when combined with low n Aff, was predictive of success 8 and 16 years later among nontechnical managers of AT&T. This pattern of needs did not predict the success of managers in technical fields, such as engineering, where specific technical skills are apparently more important. High n Ach also predicted success, but only among managers at the lower levels of the organization. McClelland and Boyatzis explained the limited effects of n Ach by noting that individual contributions are more important at lower levels, while influencing others is more important at higher levels. There has been quite a bit of research on this "leadership motive pattern," and most of it is consistent with McClelland's findings. Because of its importance for managerial behavior and performance, we will discuss this aspect of motivation further in the chapter on leadership.

While recent research has suggested the advantages of n Pow among managers, there is also a substantial literature showing the positive effects of high n Ach. Particularly in settings where individual effort can have a substantial impact, such as in entrepreneurial situations or in developing countries, n Ach has been shown to be related to individual success (Brockhaus, 1980; McClelland, 1961, 1965, 1975, 1976).

EVALUATION OF NEED THEORIES

Need theories of motivation have been popular for quite some time. Much of this popularity probably stems from the fact that they make a great deal of sense. Few would argue with the basic logic that people who feel deprived of something that they need will try to satisfy that need. The problem with need theories has not been the logic underlying them, but rather the inability to develop adequate definitions of the needs that motivate people, as well as clear descriptions of how those needs should be measured. The hierarchical theories of Maslow and Alderfer in particular have been criticized on these grounds (Campbell & Pritchard, 1976; Mitchell, 1979; Staw, 1984).

Manifest needs theory, on the other hand, has proved to be somewhat more promising. Particularly in the area of managerial motivation and behavior, it appears that a number of the needs initially identified by Murray, and further studied by McClelland and Atkinson, are related to successful performance. It may be that manifest needs have had greater success because they represent relatively specific behavioral tendencies, whereas Maslow's and Alderfer's needs are too general to apply well to any one situation. Unfortunately, manifest needs theory seems to be more appropriate for predicting managerial performance, and may therefore not be a reasonable *general* model of motivation.

Expectancy Theory

Due in part to the problems of need theories, a number of cognitive theories of motivation have emerged over the years. Unlike need theories, which suggest that motivation results from largely irrational urges or drives to attain desired physiological or psychological states, cognitive theories emphasize the effects of peoples' thoughts, expectations, and judgments on the motivation process. The most popular cognitive motivation theory is expectancy theory.

VROOM'S EXPECTANCY MODELS

Modern expectancy theory has its origins in *path–goal theory*, which primarily concerned the role of motivation in worker productivity (Georgopoulos, Mahoney, & Jones, 1957). Vroom (1964) later developed the first formal description of expectancy theory. While the theory is complex, its basic premise is simple: The tendency for people to engage in a particular behavior is a function of (1) the strength of their expectation that the behavior will be followed by a given outcome, and (2) the anticipated value of that outcome.

Expectancy theory, as described by Vroom, consists of two related models. The first of these is the valence model, which is used to predict the *valences* that workers place on various *outcomes*.[1] In the terminology of expectancy theory, an outcome is any event that might follow a worker's behavior, such as praise, punishment, or increased productivity. The valence of an outcome is the satisfaction that the worker *anticipates* receiving, should he obtain the outcome.

According to the valence model, an outcome will have a positive valence if people believe that it has positive *instrumentality* for obtaining other valued outcomes. Vroom defined instrumentality as the extent to which the person believes that attaining one outcome is associated with attaining other outcomes, and said that instrumentalities could range from $+1.00$ to -1.00. In other words, an instrumentality is the perceived *correlation* between two outcomes, although many researchers have treated it as a perceived *probability*, which could limit the validity of their results (Mitchell, 1974).

Figure 8.4 illustrates how the valance model would predict the valence, for one of Peter's Pan Pizza's consumer research interns, of performing well on his internship. Four possible outcomes of performing well, and their valences, are listed on the left side of the figure. This particular intern, Keil Hardy, places positive values on earning higher pay in later jobs, developing new skills, and having greater flexibility in choosing jobs in the future, but places no value on making "business contacts" during the internship. In the center of the figure are instrumentalities of having a PPP internship for attaining each of the four outcomes. Mr. Hardy perceives a positive association between the internship and greater pay in future jobs, learning new skills, and making business contacts. The perceived instrumentality of the internship for flexibility in job choice, however, is negative.

Combining this information, the valence model would predict that the potential for higher pay and improved skills would increase the valence of the internship for Mr. Hardy, since he values these outcomes, and the internship is seen by him as a way to attain them. The opportunity to develop business contacts will have no effect on the valence in this case, because even though

---

[1]Formally, the valence model is expressed as

$$\mathbf{V}_j = f \sum_{k=1}^{n} (\mathbf{V}_k \mathbf{I}_{jk})$$

where $\mathbf{V}_j$ = the valence of outcome j; $\mathbf{I}_{jk}$ = the instrumentality of outcome j for attaining outcome k; $\mathbf{V}_k$ = the valence of outcome k; n = the number of outcomes.

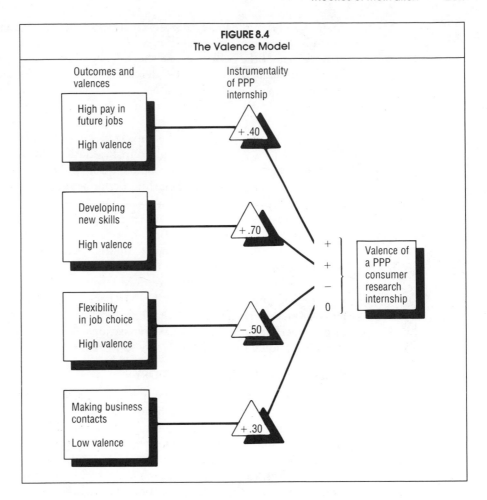

FIGURE 8.4
The Valence Model

Outcomes and valences

Instrumentality of PPP internship

High pay in future jobs

High valence

+ .40

Developing new skills

High valence

+ .70

Flexibility in job choice

High valence

− .50

Making business contacts

Low valence

+ .30

+
+
−
0

Valence of a PPP consumer research internship

Mr. Hardy believes that contacts can be made through the internship (positive instrumentality), he does not value this particular outcome. Finally, although Mr. Hardy would like to have flexibility in his job choices (positive valence), he believes that having a Peter's Pan Pizza internship will *decrease* the chances of this happening (negative instrumentality), which serves to lower the valence of the internship.

The second model in Vroom's version of expectancy theory predicts the motivational force acting on a person to perform a particular behavior.[2] This

---

[2]Formally, the force model is expressed as

$$F_i = \sum_{j=1}^{n} (E_{ij} V_j)$$

where F_i = the force on the individual to perform behavior i; E_{ij} = the strength of the expectancy that act i will be followed by outcome j; V_j = the valence of outcome j; n = the number of outcomes.

model states that the force, or strength of motivation, to engage in any behavior depends upon both the *expectancy* that various outcomes will follow the performance of the behavior, *and* the valence of those outcomes, as defined in the valence model. Vroom (1964) defined expectancy as the perceived *probability* that an outcome would follow a behavior, and thus it can range from zero to $+1.00$; nearly all research has treated expectancies in this way (Mitchell, 1974).

Figure 8.5 illustrates how the force model would predict the motivation for Keil Hardy to work hard on his internship duties. Positive expectancies are associated with three of the four outcomes in the figure. That is, Mr. Hardy believes that hard work will help him perform well, receive good evaluations from his supervisor, and limit his social life. He believes, however, that hard work will have no effect on his chances of receiving a job offer from Peter's Pan Pizza, due to a company policy not to hire their own interns for permanent jobs. Of the four outcomes, all except a limited social life have high valences. According to the force model, the limited social life and the possibility of a job offer from PPP will not contribute to Mr. Hardy's work effort, since *both* high valence and positive instrumentality are necessary for an outcome to increase motivational force. The belief that hard work *will* lead to the valued outcomes of good performance and positive evaluations, however, will in turn increase the motivational force for Mr. Hardy to work hard.

RESEARCH ON EXPECTANCY THEORY

Early research on expectancy theory focused on the ability of the valence and force models to predict various criteria. Mitchell (1974) classified research on the valence model into predictions of occupational preference, predictions of job satisfaction, and predictions of ratings of the valence of effective job performance itself. In each study reviewed, positive support for the model was obtained. Research on the force model, which typically tested predictions of work effort, also supported the theory, although not as strongly.

While the early tests of expectancy theory yielded fairly broad empirical support, Mitchell (1974) raised a number of methodological, empirical, and theoretical issues that subsequent research has addressed. One of Mitchell's points was that, at the time of his review, virtually all of the research on

THE WIZARD OF ID, by permission of Johnny Hart and News America Syndicate.

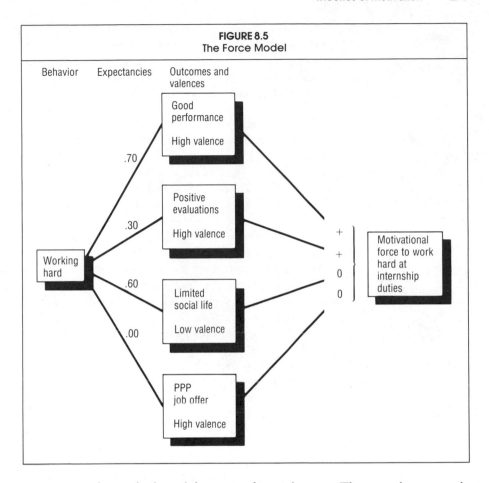

FIGURE 8.5
The Force Model

expectancy theory had used *between-subjects* designs. That is, the research typically presented groups of subjects with different combinations of the variables in the model, and compared the predicted choices or effort of the different groups. This practice is clearly contrary to Vroom's (1964) description of expectancy theory; he said that the theory was meant to predict individual choice—specifically which of a number of levels of effort a person would select. Consequently, the proper research design for testing expectancy theory is a *within-subjects* design. In this type of design, predicted levels of effort under different conditions for the *same* person can be computed, and the ability of the model to predict individual choices can be properly tested.

After Mitchell's review in 1974, researchers began to use within-subjects designs more frequently. Consistent with the original theory, Mitchell (1979) reported that a number of articles had found that within-subjects tests of the theory predicted performance better than between-subjects designs (Kopelman, 1976; Muchinsky, 1977a; Oldham; 1976). Wanous, Keon, and Latack (1983) drew similar conclusions in a review of 16 studies that used within-subjects designs to predict either organizational attractiveness or actual job choices.

Another issue that has received a great deal of attention is the manner in which instrumentalities, expectancies, and valences are combined to predict behavior. In order to test the theory as originally described by Vroom (1964), values of second-level outcomes and instrumentalities, as well as first-level valences and expectancies, should be multiplied together (see previous footnotes). In order to legitimately multiply the values of two variables, though, the measures of both variables must have ratio-scale properties (see Chapter 2). It is clear, however, that the rating scales commonly used to measure expectancy variables do not yield ratio-scale measurement. Consequently, the measures used in the research do not allow for tests of the multiplicative properties of the theory (Arnold & Evans, 1979; Hackman & Porter, 1968; Schmidt, 1973).

From a practical standpoint, the lack of ratio-scale measurement may not be a serious problem, since reasonably good predictions can be made from individual variables in the model. Schmitt and Son (1981) reviewed research suggesting that instrumentalities alone are as effective in predicting the valence of first-level outcomes as when they are multiplied by second-level valences. Their own research, predicting post-high school activities, verified this conclusion. Similar results were obtained by Pulakos and Schmitt (1983) for the prediction of job satisfaction.

Data showing that instrumentalities alone predict as well as instrumentalities weighted by valences seem to imply that valences are not important. However, you must remember that if the measures of valences and instrumentalities are not on ratio scales, the valence × instrumentality term may not be valid, and the conclusion that instrumentalities are more important than valences may be unwarranted. What is needed is a test of the multiplicative properties of the theory that avoids multiplying instrumentality and valence values together.

Such a test may have been provided by Wanous, Keon, and Latack (1983). Using a sample of applicants to graduate business programs, these researchers attempted to predict the attractiveness of the business schools. Organizational attractiveness is the valance of the first-level outcome (selecting a school) for these applicants. Each subject rated the valence and expectancy of being admitted to each of 4 graduate schools, the instrumentality of admission to the programs for each of 15 secondary outcomes, and the attractiveness of each school. Using a procedure they called *implicit weighting*, Wanous and his colleagues had subjects divide the 15 second-level outcomes into high, middle, and low thirds, based on valence. The researchers then summed the instrumentalities for each third and correlated those sums with the ratings of organizational attractiveness. They reasoned that if the multiplicative properties of the theory are valid, then instrumentalities for the outcomes with the highest valences should be the best predictor of attractiveness and instrumentalities for the outcomes with the lowest valences should be the least valid predictor.

Wanous, Keon, and Latack (1983) found support for their predictions. Correlations between instrumentalities and attractiveness were .63, .44, and .37 for the high-, medium-, and low-valence conditions, respectively. This suggests that people perceive stronger instrumentalities for more highly valued outcomes. Researchers and managers should therefore keep in mind that while instrumentalities may be good predictors of preferences or effort, valences may moderate that relationship, and should also be carefully considered.

Yet another topic of research on expectancy theory concerns the underlying cognitive processes implied by the theory. Expectancy theory assumes that people make decisions in a very careful, rational manner. For example, the theory specifies that even if a first-level outcome has a very positive valence, no effort to obtain that outcome will be made if there is not an expectancy that such effort will be effective. A less rational model would predict additional effort to obtain highly valued outcomes, even if the probability of doing so was virtually zero. It has, in fact, been suggested that expectancy theory is too complex to be an accurate model of how most people make decisions, and that the majority of decisions are made in a less rational, more haphazard manner (Slovic, Fischhoff, & Lichtenstein, 1977).

Stahl and Harrell (1981) conducted a series of four studies relevant to the issue of how people combine valences and expectancies. Their within-subjects design allowed the researchers to test whether each individual subject was using the rational decision-making process defined by expectancy theory, or a less rational process that ignored the interaction between valences and expectancies. The results of the studies showed that, overall, only 37 percent of the 157 subjects made decisions consistent with the predictions of expectancy theory. The remaining subjects were less rational than expectancy theory suggests, indicating, for example, that they would work hard to obtain a desired outcome even if the probability of obtaining it was very low, or that they would choose to pursue an outcome that has little or no value if it was sure to be obtained.

Stahl and Harrell (1981) suggested that expectancy theory might be modified to include two force models: one for those people who use careful, rational decision-making strategies, and one for people who are not as systematic. For such a distinction to be useful, however, we would have to be able to predict who is going to be rational, who is not going to be rational, and whether rational people are always rational or only occasionally rational. While these issues have not yet been settled, research such as Stahl and Harrell's provides important directions for future expectancy research.

EVALUATION OF EXPECTANCY THEORY

As we have indicated, expectancy theory has been very popular. Part of this popularity stems from the fact that the theory implies that people are logical, and it makes logical predictions of their behavior. Not only does the logical nature of the theory make it easy to understand, but it also makes it easy to use in organizations. If Margaret Russell finds that the interns in her department are not working hard because they do not value the outcomes associated with good work performance, she can try to provide outcomes that they *do* value, and thereby strengthen instrumentalities. If the lack of effort is due to a low expectancy that effort will improve performance, Ms. Russell can assign tasks with a relatively high probability of success in order to strengthen these expectancies. Because of the rational nature of the theory, such solutions to problems are easily defined.

Expectancy theory is also popular because, as you have seen, it is relatively valid for predicting certain types of behavior, specifically effort levels and decisions such as occupational choices and job preferences. As you have also seen, however, expectancy-based predictions are hardly perfect. Research on it continues, but expectancy theory remains the most highly developed cognitive motivation model, and it promises to be a useful tool for studying motivation in the foreseeable future.

Equity Theory

Another cognitive approach to motivation is embodied in *balance theories*. In general, balance theories state that a person's behavior is influenced by comparisons made between his current status and some standard. When the person's status is reasonably close to the standard, a state of *balance* results, and the person is not motivated to change his behavior. If, however, the person's status is substantially different from the standard, the lack of balance causes an uncomfortable sense of tension, and the person is motivated to restore balance.

The best known balance theory of work motivation is Adams' equity theory (Adams, 1965). Equity theory is based on workers' *inputs*, or what they believe they contribute to their job or organization, and their *outcomes*, or what they perceive that the organization provides them in return. Because of the notion of trading inputs for outcomes, equity theory is often referred to as an *exchange* theory.

Inputs can take a variety of forms, such as labor, time, skill, and the years of education or experience that provide workers with the ability to perform their jobs. Outcomes can also vary, ranging from pay and fringe benefits, to praise and recognition from a superior, to the opportunities for social interaction with co-workers. According to Adams (1965), each worker forms a *ratio* of her inputs to outcomes, which is compared to the perceived ratio of inputs to outcomes of an appropriate comparison person, or what Adams called a "significant other." The two ratios are equal when the worker and the comparison person are receiving the same level of outcomes for each unit of input. Under these conditions the worker will experience feelings of equity, and there will be no motivation to change behavior. If, on the other hand, the ratios are not equal, the worker will experience inequity, and tension will result.

In order to eliminate this unpleasant state, the worker will be motivated to engage in behaviors that will restore equity. The following list (summarized from Adams, 1965) suggests some of the ways that she can restore perceptions of equity; she can

1. Alter her own inputs to bring her O/I ratio into balance with the comparison person's ratio.

2. Alter her own outcomes to bring her O/I ratio into balance with the comparison person's ratio. (Adams believed that people will generally try to increase their outcomes, and avoid increasing inputs in their efforts to restore equity.)

3. Cognitively distort, or change perceptions of either her own or the comparison person's inputs and outcomes, to bring the two ratios into balance. (Adams said that people are likely to find it easier to distort perceptions of the inputs and outcomes of the other person than to distort their own.)

4. "Leave the field," or quit her job. (Adams said that this would usually happen only if the inequity was extreme.)

5. Engage in behaviors designed to change the inputs and/or outcomes of the comparison person.

6. Select a new comparison person for the purpose of judging equity. (Adams implied that this course of action is unlikely.)

The amount of tension and the strength of the motivation are proportional to the degree of the perceived inequity. Equitable and inequitable comparisons are illustrated in Figure 8.6. As indicated in this figure, feelings of inequity, and therefore motivation, result if the worker's ratio is *either* smaller or larger than the ratio for the comparison person.

To further illustrate equity theory, consider how it might explain the poor performance of the interns at Peter's Pan Pizza. The problem Margaret Russell described is that the interns are not putting forth enough effort, or in equity terms, they have reduced the level of their inputs. This happens, according to

---

FIGURE 8.6
Conditions of Equity and Inequity

Equity conditions   Examples

$$\frac{O_P}{I_P} = \frac{O_0}{I_0}$$

$O_P = O_0$ and $I_P = I_0$
$O_P = K(O_0)$ and $I_P = K(I_0)$,
    where K is any constant value

Inequity conditions   Examples

$$\frac{O_P}{I_P} < \frac{O_0}{I_0}$$

$O_P = O_0$ and $I_P > I_0$
$O_P < O_0$ and $I_P = I_0$
$O_P < O_0$ and $I_P > I_0$

- - - - - - - - - - - - - - - -

$$\frac{O_P}{I_P} > \frac{O_0}{I_0}$$

$O_P = O_0$ and $I_P < I_0$
$O_P > O_0$ and $I_P = I_0$
$O_P > O_0$ and $I_P < I_0$

P = person (worker)
0 = significant other (comparison person)

equity theory, if the interns believe that other workers are receiving greater outcomes for the same amount of input, or if others were receiving the same outcomes in return for lower inputs. Before Dr. MacKeven can suggest any solution, she would have to find out who the comparison persons are for the interns, and what inputs and outcomes the interns consider to be important. One possible explanation might be that the interns believe that they are contributing the same inputs as some higher-paid, permanent employees.

RESEARCH ON EQUITY THEORY

Most of the research on equity theory has examined the effects of inequity due to overpayment or underpayment, under either piece-rate or hourly-wage systems. The predictions made for these conditions are presented in Table 8.1. Notice that workers can alter their inputs by either changing the *quantity* of their work or by changing the *quality* of their work, and that the type of inequity and the type of pay system affect the nature of the predicted response.

Although equity research usually takes place in the laboratory, subjects are often led to believe that they are performing a temporary job, typically proofreading or interviewing. These tasks are quite simple, which makes it likely that any differences between groups are due to motivational differences rather than differences in skill or ability (Mowday, 1983). Feelings of equity are manipulated by convincing the subjects that they are either being overpaid or underpaid for their work, and the effects of these manipulations on the quantity and/or quality of the subjects' performance is determined.

Although there is fairly strong support for the predictions made for underpayment conditions, studies of overpayment yield results that are both less consistent and open to alternative explanations (Mowday, 1983). Overpayment is typically manipulated by telling subjects that they are not qualified for the "job," which is thought to result in beliefs that they deserve neither the job nor the accompanying compensation. While this type of manipulation *may* result in feelings of inequity, it may also threaten the subjects' self-esteem. Rather than working harder to increase inputs and reduce inequity, these subjects may be working harder to prove that they *are* qualified to perform the task (Andrews & Valenzi, 1970; Wiener, 1970). Studies using other manipulations of overpayment, such as giving higher-than-normal wages due to the unexpected availability of

TABLE 8.1 Predicted Responses to Pay Inequity Based upon Equity Theory

	Underpayment	*Overpayment*
Hourly wages	Production will decrease or be of lower quality.	Production will increase or be of higher quality.
Piece rate	Production will increase, but quality will be lower.	Production will decrease, but quality will be higher.

additional funds, have generally found less support for the predictions than those challenging subjects' qualifications (for example, Pritchard, Dunnette, & Jorgenson, 1972; Valenzi & Andrews, 1971). In fact, Locke (1976) has questioned the entire notion of overpayment in work organizations. He suggests that rather than feeling inequity, workers are more likely to adjust their perceptions of their inputs, based on the assumption that the organization would not pay them more than they are actually worth.

Because of the mixed results of equity research, psychologists have begun to examine variables that might improve the predictive power of the theory. One issue that has received some attention is the way in which workers select comparison persons. For example, Goodman (1974) pointed out that workers could compare their outcome/input ratios to a number of different standards:

- the ratios of other people in the same or in other organizations
- any of the ratios that the workers themselves have experienced in the past, either in the same organization or in other organizations
- formal or informal understandings or agreements with the organization concerning outcomes and inputs, such as collective-bargaining agreements

Goodman found, among a sample of managers, that satisfaction with pay was related to all three of these equity standards.

Greenberg and Ornstein (1983) examined another aspect of equity theory: the possibility that one outcome might compensate for the lack of another outcome. These researchers paid subjects to proofread written material for three 12-minute work periods spread over a one-hour session. After the first work period, the subjects were told privately that the experimenter would like them to proofread for an additional hour without pay. Some subjects were told that they would be "senior proofreaders," and that they had been selected for this duty based upon their excellent performance during the first period. This condition was labeled the "earned title" group. Subjects in a second condition, called the "unearned title" group, were given the title of senior proofreader, but were not told why. A third "no title" group was simply asked to work the second hour, and a control group was neither asked to do the additional work, nor given the title.

Greenberg and Ornstein (1983) found, consistent with equity theory, that in the "no title" condition, the number of lines proofread dropped considerably in the final two periods. This was apparently an effort to reduce current inputs in anticipation of additional inputs during the second hour. In the "earned title" condition, performance did not change after the title was bestowed. These subjects apparently saw the title as an additional, valuable, outcome. Consequently, the title compensated for the anticipated lack of pay in the second hour, and equity was maintained.

Compared to the other experimental conditions, subjects in the "unearned title" group behaved unexpectedly. Greenberg and Ornstein (1983) had predicted that since there was no reason given for the title, these subjects would not view it as an additional outcome; they would focus instead on the extra inputs required, and lower their performance to compensate. Instead, during the work period following the title bestowal, the number of lines proofread *increased* to a level far above that of the "earned title" condition. Then, during the final work period, performance dropped to a level *below* that of the "earned title" group.

Greenberg and Ornstein (1983) replicated their study with another sample of subjects and reported the same results. Analysis of a questionnaire used in the second study revealed that in the "unearned title" condition, the title was seen as an additional outcome immediately after it was bestowed. Since the title was not earned on the basis of merit, the subjects apparently increased their inputs to restore equity. By the second post-title period, however, the subjects began to focus on the additional work expected of them, and they lowered inputs to make up for the additional effort to be expended later.

These studies demonstrated that one outcome (a title) may substitute for another (pay). They also showed that a set of events, such as title bestowal and assignment of additional responsibilities, may be seen as an outcome at one point in time, and as an input a short time later. Thus, while the situation used in this research was highly artificial (organizations seldom bestow new titles on employees without a reason), it does illustrate the potentially dynamic nature of equity evaluations.

A third issue in equity theory is the possibility that individual differences, or personality variables, may moderate the relationship between perceived equity and behavior. An interesting example is a study by Vecchio (1981), who examined the role of moral maturity in predicting reactions to piece-rate overpayment. He reasoned that people whose views of morality were governed by concern for rights or responsibilities (high in moral maturity) would be more sensitive to the unfairness of being overpaid than those whose ideas of right and wrong are based on need fulfillment or adherence to rules and authority (lower in moral maturity; see Kohlberg, 1968, for more information on the notion of moral maturity). Subjects high in moral maturity would therefore behave in a manner consistent with equity theory. Subjects low in moral maturity were expected to behave in a more "hedonistic" manner, doing more work of lower quality in order to *maximize* (not equalize) the input-to-outcome ratio. Such behavior would be predicted on the basis of expectancy theory.

Vecchio (1981) found that students performing an interviewing task who were classified as high in moral maturity responded to overpayment in the manner predicted by equity theory: they produced less, although their work was of a higher quality, than equitably paid subjects. Subjects low in moral maturity performed in the opposite pattern, as predicted by expectancy theory (see Figure 8.7). Vecchio's study is interesting and important not only because it helps clarify the nature of responses to overpayment, but also because it represents an effort to reconcile conflicting predictions from two theories, thereby improving the usefulness of *both* theories.

EVALUATION OF EQUITY THEORY

Equity theory seems to have made a useful contribution to the motivation literature. Although it is true that its best predictions are made for underpayment conditions, where the predictions may seem obvious or even trivial, recent

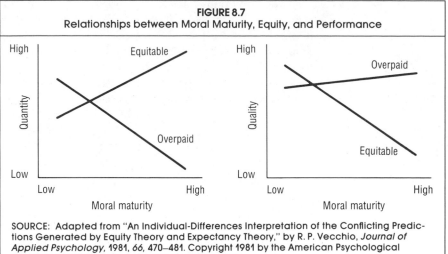

FIGURE 8.7
Relationships between Moral Maturity, Equity, and Performance

SOURCE: Adapted from "An Individual-Differences Interpretation of the Conflicting Predictions Generated by Equity Theory and Expectancy Theory," by R. P. Vecchio, *Journal of Applied Psychology*, 1981, *66*, 470–481. Copyright 1981 by the American Psychological Association. Reprinted by permission of the author.

research on such topics as personality and compensating outcomes promises to help clarify the rather inconsistent literature on overpayment. There is, of course, no theoretical reason to limit equity theory to conditions of overpayment and underpayment. Perhaps as additional outcomes are considered in conjunction with pay, the ability to predict the level of worker inputs will be enhanced.

Goal Setting

A third cognitive approach to motivation is goal setting. While goal setting involves a simpler, more straightforward process than either expectancy theory or equity theory, the theoretical basis for goal setting is also less highly developed. Some authors have classified goal setting not as a theory, but rather as a general approach to motivation, consistent with a variety of theoretical viewpoints (McCormick & Ilgen, 1985). Indeed, goals, such as the outcomes in expectancy theory, are explicit or implied components of many motivation models (Locke, 1978). It is also true, however, that goal setting has attracted as much attention as most formal motivation theories. We will therefore examine goal setting in some detail.

The basic ideas behind goal setting were developed by Locke. The central theme is that the behavior of people is guided most directly by their **intentions,** and that in organizations intentions are reflected in **performance goals** (Locke, 1968; Locke, Shaw, Saari, & Latham, 1981). According to Locke, goals serve

intentions: commitments based on a determination to do a specified thing in a specified manner

performance goals: specific behaviors or results that an individual strives to perform or achieve

a number of functions relevant to worker motivation. The first of these is the *direction* provided by goals. That is, goals clarify what needs to be accomplished, and set standards for judging progress toward that accomplishment. The more specific the goals are, the more effective they will be in directing behavior toward particular aspects of performance.

Goals also provide for the energization or *mobilization* of behavior, allowing workers to judge the effort requirements of tasks. All else being equal, the more difficult the goal, the greater workers' effort. Further, when combined with performance feedback, goals also provide for the *sustaining* of task behavior. That is, workers adjust their levels of effort, based on feedback, in order to assure goal attainment. Also important for effective goal setting, according to Locke, is *goal acceptance*. Goal acceptance means that workers have agreed to commit themselves to achieving certain goals. Without such acceptance, goals will be irrelevant to worker performance.

The predictions derived from goal setting have direct implications for increasing worker performance: Provided that workers accept the goals, have the necessary skills to perform at goal levels, and have adequate performance feedback, then specific, difficult goals will result in better performance than less specific or easier goals. An important task of management, therefore, is to assure the establishment of specific, difficult goals that are both within the range of workers' abilities and acceptable to the workers.

RESEARCH ON GOAL SETTING

Locke and his associates conducted a series of laboratory studies testing goal-setting predictions, and found strong and consistent evidence of a positive relationship between goal difficulty and productivity (Locke, 1968). Similar results have been obtained by other researchers in laboratory studies, although the support in correlational field studies is not as strong (see Locke et al., 1981, for a review of this research).

The finding that goal-difficulty effects are stronger in lab research than in field settings should not be surprising. First, lab studies typically use easy tasks, such as addition, naming objects belonging to specific categories, and naming uses for objects (Locke, 1968). Difficult goals are introduced by setting high quantity standards, not by changing the difficulty of the tasks. In field studies the tasks are both more complex and more difficult. It may be more difficult to increase productivity in such situations, which would restrict goal effects. Second, much of the lab research includes instructions to subjects in easy-goal conditions to stop once the goal is reached (for example, Locke, 1982c; Locke, Cartledge, & Knerr, 1970). In at least one case, data from easy-goal-condition subjects who went beyond their goals were removed from the analysis because they did not "accept" the goal. This suggests that the goal-difficulty effect may be, in part, due to the *suppression* of productivity in easy-goal conditions, rather than, or in addition to, the positive effect of difficult goals (Locke, 1982).

In addition to goal difficulty, there have also been a large number of studies comparing the effects of specific, hard goals to the effects of instructions to "do your best." Again, as predicted by the model, specific hard goals almost always result in better performance than either "do your best" instructions or no goals at all (for example, Latham, Mitchell, & Dossett, 1978; Latham & Steele, 1983; Locke, 1968; Umstot, Bell, & Mitchell, 1976). This effect favoring specific goals is probably due to the ambiguity of the instruction to "do your best," which provides little guidance for defining what is expected from the worker. No matter how subjects interpret "do your best," the results are obviously *not* their best, in light of the higher performance of those with specific goals. The clear advantage of specific, clear performance goals over pleas for best efforts is the most important lesson to emerge from goal setting.

A number of other issues have been studied by goal-setting researchers. One relatively clear finding is that feedback is an important component of successful goal setting, as proposed by Locke. Although by itself feedback has little effect on performance, without feedback goal-setting effects are drastically reduced (Locke et al., 1981). Recent research by Ivancevich and McMahon (1982), based on a sample of engineers, found not only that feedback conditions were superior to nonfeedback conditions, but also that self-feedback conditions, where the engineers kept their own performance records, were better than those in which feedback was received from external sources. Self-feedback may have important implications for the use of goal setting, since it can be both more timely and less expensive to administer than external feedback.

Research has also been conducted on the relative merits of goals assigned by management and goal setting in which the workers participate. Based on their review, Locke and his associates concluded that although there are theoretical reasons to expect better performance when workers participate in goal setting, there is little consistent evidence of such an effect (Locke et al., 1981). For example, Latham and Marshall (1982) had government employees brainstorm to produce lists of critical incidents for a job analysis. Goals for the number of incidents were set in one of three ways: self-set, participatively set, and assigned. They found relatively strong correlations (*r*s from .62 to .74) between goal difficulty and performance in all three conditions, and concluded that *how* goals are set is less important than *whether* they are set.

UNDERSTANDING GOAL SETTING

While it is clear that goal setting can have positive effects on performance, it is not at all clear *why* goal setting works. In an effort to explain the effects of goals, a considerable amount of research has attempted to reconcile the predictions of goal setting with the apparently contradictory predictions of other theories (see Table 8.2). Most of this research has examined the possible role of expectancy theory in goal setting. Matsui has suggested that difficult goals present a dilemma for the worker, since the lower expectancy of success should decrease the probability of goal acceptance, while the difficulty presents an attractive (high-valence) challenge. The positive correlations typically found between goal difficulty and performance would therefore suggest that valences

TABLE 8.2 Comparison of Predicted Effects of Task Difficulty

EXPECTANCY THEORY	Task difficulty	Performance
Difficult tasks lower expectancies for success, thereby lowering motivation. Easy tasks raise both expectancies and motivation.	Easy	High
	Moderate	Moderate
	Hard	Low

NEED THEORY	Task difficulty	Performance
Workers high in *n* Ach are not motivated by easy tasks (no challenge), nor by very difficult tasks (low probability of success).	Easy	Moderate
	Moderate	High
	Hard	Low

GOAL SETTING	Task difficulty	Performance
Difficult goals set performance standards that result in higher performance than do easy goals.	Easy	Low
	Moderate	Moderate
	Hard	High

are more important for predicting goal acceptance than are expectancies (Matsui, Okada, & Mizuguchi, 1981).

Garland (1984) noted that when goals are held constant, positive correlations between expectancy and performance are obtained, as predicted by expectancy theory. When comparisons are made *across* goal levels, however, the positive relationships between goal difficulty and performance predicted by goal-setting theory are obtained. Garland concluded that the two theories are not necessarily in conflict, and that goal difficulty and expectancies make independent contributions to the prediction of performance.

Concerning the role of needs in goal setting, Matsui, Okada, and Kakuyama (1982) found a positive relationship between need for achievement and productivity in a perceptual-speed task. However, when goal difficulty was held constant, *n* Ach and performance were unrelated, suggesting that achievement motivation affects performance through its effects on goals.

EVALUATION OF GOAL SETTING

The positive effects of specific, difficult goals on productivity are well documented. It is clear that goal setting is a technique that may be useful in a wide variety of settings where productivity is low, or where workers are directing their efforts inappropriately. A goal-setting analysis of the situation in Peter's Pan Pizza's consumer research department might find that the interns are not sure which tasks are most important and which are peripheral to successful performance. If Margaret Russell were to set specific performance goals for each intern, their efforts should, according to Locke, be channeled into the desired activities. Alternatively, the interns may be mistaken about the overall quantity of work that is expected. Again, goal setting should alleviate this problem. Finally, it may be that while the interns have realistic expectations about what is important and how much work is expected, the performance feedback that they receive is inadequate for evaluating their goal progress. Perhaps Ms. Russell could arrange the interns' work so that self-feedback is possible.

In sum, goal setting seems to be a useful technique for increasing worker productivity, although the research on expectancies, achievement motives, and other variables suggests that the relationship between goals and performance is not as simple as was once thought. We can expect additional research on the processes by which goals affect behavior to both clarify the relationship further and to raise new issues concerning the use of performance goals.

Reinforcement

One of the most prominent schools of thought in psychology is **behaviorism,** which focuses on the learning of behaviors through conditioning processes. Of particular interest in I/O psychology is the approach known as **operant conditioning,** which was popularized by B. F. Skinner (1959). Skinner believes that behavior is controlled by its consequences. When a person (or other organism) engages in a behavior, that behavior is followed by an event, or *consequence.* The consequence might be obvious, such as being "chewed out" by the boss, or it might be subtle, such as a nod of approval from a co-worker. The nature of these consequences can affect the probability that the person will repeat the behavior. This viewpoint has a simple yet powerful implication for behavior in organizations: control the consequences of workers' behavior and you will have a great deal of influence over that behavior.

Skinner described two types of consequences that have implications for learning. The first of these is *reinforcement.* Reinforcement is any consequence that has the effect of increasing the probability that the preceding behavior will be repeated. In organizations we usually have such things as pay, praise, recognition, promotions, and other rewards in mind when we think of reinforcement. The second type of consequence discussed by Skinner is *punishment.* Punishment occurs when the consequence of a behavior has the effect of making it *less* likely that the behavior will be repeated. Examples of punishment in organizations might include docking a worker's pay, denying a manager a promotion, or simply scolding a worker. Note that no reference is made to needs, expectancies, equity, or any other emotional state or cognitive process. Instead, the emphasis is strictly on the effects of reinforcing and

---

behaviorism: the doctrine that observable behavior is the only legitimate data in psychology; rejects cognitive concepts

operant conditioning: a learning technique based on the belief that behavior is controlled by consequences or events that follow the behavior; the use of rewards and punishments

punishing events on the overt, observable behavior of workers (Luthans & Kreitner, 1985).

Skinner and other behaviorists have strongly emphasized the superiority of reinforcement over punishment as a means for controlling behavior (Luthans & Kreitner, 1985; Skinner, 1969; Wiard, 1972). Perhaps the most compelling reason for this is that while punishment may keep undesirable behaviors in check, it does not provide any means for workers to learn what they *should* be doing. Reinforcement, on the other hand, not only teaches workers what they should be doing, but by making certain that no rewards follow undesired behaviors, those behaviors will eventually be **extinguished.**

In order to use reinforcement effectively, any rewards given by an organization must be **contingent** upon the behaviors management desires. If rewards are distributed in a manner that does not emphasize the connection between the rewards and the desired behavior, the rewards will be ineffective. For example, consider again the situation in the consumer research department of Peter's Pan Pizza. If Dr. MacKeven were to start monthly pay bonuses for interns whose work met certain standards, it would not be a proper use of reinforcement because such a bonus is a **noncongintent reward.** Skinner has said that workers do not work on Monday for pay they will receive on Friday, and the reason is that there is no clear relationship between any specific behavior and the paycheck. People work between Monday and Thursday, according to Skinner, because they will be fired if they don't, which is hardly reinforcing (Jordan, 1972). A more promising approach to reinforcement would start by identifying specific behaviors that are related to high performance among PPP's interns, such as completing reports within a specified period of time. Supervisors could then be trained to provide immediate reinforcement, such as praise or recognition, when these behaviors are observed.

This example raises some interesting points about the ways in which most people are paid for their work. Hourly wages and salaries are both noncontingent forms of pay. That is, as long as workers show up for work they will be paid, and the manner in which they behave and how well they perform make little difference. Consequently, these types of pay should not be useful as reinforcers. Some psychologists have suggested that piece-rate pay systems are better examples of contingent reinforcement, because the amount of money a worker gets under piece rates depends directly upon productivity (Landy, 1985). There are problems associated with using piece-rate pay as a reinforcer, however. First, there is the issue of the timing of the reinforcement. Piece-rate workers are paid once every week or two, just the same as other workers, and Skinner's statements about the timing of pay should apply to piece rates as well as other forms of pay. Second, rewards are effective when they are used to reinforce specific behaviors. Piece-rate systems reward productivity, which is not a behavior, but the result of behavior and a number of other factors, such as skill, health, the behavior of co-workers, the weather, and so on. Unless the workers' jobs are very simple, so that it is clear to the workers how to improve performance, there is no assurance that piece-rate pay reinforces the behaviors that will lead to higher productivity.

In laboratory research with animals, behaviorists have extensively studied the effects of different *reinforcement schedules* on behavior. A reinforcement schedule refers to the timing and frequency of reinforcement. For example, a continuous schedule involves reinforcing the desired behavior each time it is performed. Other schedules are referred to as intermittent schedules, since they involve reinforcement on a less-than-continuous basis; a summary of intermittent-reinforcement schedules is provided below:

1. *Fixed-ratio schedule:* A specific number of responses, or occurrences of the behavior, must take place before reinforcement is given. For example, Peter's Pan Pizza's interns could be given praise after turning in every third report.
2. *Variable-ratio schedule:* Reinforcement occurs after the behavior is performed a certain number of times *on the average*, although the actual number varies from one reinforcement to another. For example, PPP's interns could be praised after turning in two reports, then after turning in five, then after three, and so on, with the average equaling reinforcement every three reports.
3. *Fixed-interval schedule:* Reinforcement occurs only after a specific interval of time has elapsed since the last reinforcement. Using this schedule, PPP's interns could be reinforced weekly, with praise following the first report filed, for example, after the start of work each Thursday.
4. *Variable-interval schedule:* Reinforcement occurs after a specific interval of time has elapsed since the last reinforcement *on the average*, although the actual amount of time varies from one reinforcement to the next. Here, PPP's interns might be reinforced after five days, then after eight, then after three, and so on, with the average interval equaling one week.

Differences in reinforcement schedules have been shown to have substantial and predictable effects on the rate of learning and the persistence of behavior, with intermittent schedules, particularly variable schedules, maximizing persistence, and continuous schedules minimizing learning time (Skinner, 1959).

Research on reinforcement schedules in organizations, however, has been less consistent. For example, Saari and Latham (1982) compared the effectiveness of a continuous-reinforcement schedule to that of a variable-ratio schedule and found that workers on the variable-ratio schedule had higher performance than those reinforced continuously. However, in other field studies, continuous and variable schedules showed no differences in effectiveness (Yukl & Latham, 1975; Yukl, Latham, & Pursell, 1976). Pritchard and his associates found that while comparisons between different contingent-reinforcement schedules revealed no

---

extinguish: to eliminate a behavior by withholding reinforcement
contingent: depending upon a certain event or set of circumstances
noncontingent reward: a reinforcing event that does not clearly follow nor depend upon the behavior to be rewarded

differences in effectiveness, *all* contingent schedules resulted in better performance than noncontingent reinforcement (Pritchard, Hollenback, & DeLeo, 1980; Pritchard, Leonard, VonBergen, & Kirk, 1976).

One problem in the use of reinforcement is the amount of time and effort that it entails. Careful records of employee behavior must be maintained, in order for rewards to be administered. While in some cases proof that the behavior was performed is easy to obtain, in other cases employees must actually be observed. Further, there is evidence that once a contingent-reinforcement policy is established, it must be maintained in order to continue its effectiveness. Haynes, Pine, and Fitch (1982) found that an incentive program based on operant principles was effective in reducing the accident rates of bus drivers during the time of the program, but that the improved performance did not carry over into the following months. Greene and Podsakoff (1981) found that when a reward program was discontinued, employee perceptions of management's use of punishment increased, while perceptions of the use of rewards, legitimate influence, and interpersonal power decreased.

EVALUATION OF REINFORCEMENT

The weight of the evidence strongly indicates that contingent reinforcement is a reliable means for improving performance, if it is designed and administered properly. As with goal setting, however, it is not clear *why* it works. Of course, radical behaviorists such as Skinner would argue that the issue of why reinforcement works is unimportant. In fact, the entire issue of *motivation* is irrelevant to these psychologists. All that is needed to understand behavior from their perspective is knowledge of workers' behaviors and the events in the environment that reinforce or punish those behaviors; motivation, reasoning, needs, and other such constructs are unnecessary baggage. Cognitive psychologists, however, are not satisfied with simply knowing that reinforcement works. Rather, they are interested in discovering the underlying processes that make certain events reinforcing. Let's examine a well-known case of reinforcement, and show how two cognitive theories, expectancy theory and goal setting, might explain the results.

Emery Air Freight is a large air-freight forwarder. An important key to success in such a business is the use of air-freight containers. These are large shipping crates that hold many smaller packages. By putting packages into the freight containers, Emery saves handling time and expense, and can earn greater profits for the same costs. The company had spent a lot of money instructing employees on how to use the freight containers, and so management was surprised to find that they were being used only 45 percent of the times possible (Where Skinner's theories work, 1972). To remedy this problem, Emery executives implemented a program of positive reinforcement and self-feedback. Workers recorded their performance on a checklist, which kept them informed of how closely they were meeting management's goals for container usage. In addition, supervisors were trained to provide positive reinforcement, or praise, to workers who were meeting their goals or showing improvement (At Emery Air Freight, 1973). The results of this program were dramatic. Performance approached the goal on the first day, and during the first three years, Emery attributed savings of $2 million to the program.

Behaviorists often cite the Emery case as an example of the power of reinforcement (Jordan, 1972; Luthans & Kreitner, 1985). However, Locke (1980) suggested that this type of program might work because of the performance goals that are established, and that attributing the effects simply to reinforcement and self-feedback is misleading. Similarly, expectancy theorists could argue that the praise of supervisors serves to establish strong instrumentalities between performance and second-level outcomes, or that the setting of goals might increase the valence of achieving those goals, either of which could increase motivation. Of course, the question of *why* reinforcement works is unimportant to most people in organizations. Psychologists, however, cannot be satisfied with predicting and controlling behavior; they also want to understand and explain behavior, and in this regard reinforcement has fallen short. We agree with Landy (1985) that reinforcement is more of a technology than a theory, and that while it is a useful tool, it has not promoted our understanding of work behavior.

Other Motivation Issues

In addition to general theories of motivation such as those just presented, psychologists have also examined a number of more specific motivation issues. Most of these concern the application or use of motivational techniques. We shall briefly present two such issues. The first concerns the combination of different motives, while the second deals with the motivational effects of worker participation in decision making.

INTRINSIC MOTIVATION

While present in earlier theories (Herzberg, 1966), the notion of intrinsic motivation received renewed attention following the work of Deci (1975, 1976). According to Deci, work behavior can be motivated by both *intrinsic* and *extrinsic* factors. Intrinsic motivation occurs when people achieve feelings of competence and control from their work. Extrinsic motivation occurs when people are given rewards from external sources, such as pay from their employer. Deci claims that extrinsic rewards for intrinsically motivating work will reduce feelings of control, which will in turn lower the overall level of motivation. One conclusion to be drawn from Deci's theory is that it is best to rely upon either extrinsic or intrinsic rewards alone, rather than combining them in some fashion.

Deci and others have found support for his predictions (for example, Deci, 1972, 1975; Lepper & Greene, 1975). Many researchers, however, have been unable to replicate Deci's results (these include Arnold, 1976, and Scott &

Erskine, 1980). Several studies have found that the effects of extrinsic and intrinsic rewards depend upon the nature of the job. Specifically, it seems that on uninteresting or boring tasks, extrinsic rewards *increase* intrinsic motivation (Calder & Staw, 1975; Mossholder, 1980). Conversely, on interesting tasks, extrinsic rewards have been shown to *decrease* intrinsic motivation (Daniel & Esser, 1980; Mossholder, 1980). It therefore seems that while Deci's (1972, 1975) original notions of the effects of intrinsic motivation may have been overstated, the process he described may indeed operate under certain conditions.

PARTICIPATIVE DECISION MAKING

One of the most widely advocated motivational techniques is participative decision making, or PDM. PDM is based on the premise that worker motivation, as well as satisfaction, morale, creativity, and other favorable characteristics, can be enhanced by allowing workers to participate in making decisions that are relevant to their jobs.

A huge number of research programs have studied the issue of participation, and some have found impressive support for the effectiveness of the technique. A number of reviews of the participation research show, however, that support for PDM is mixed at best (Dachler & Wilpert, 1978; Locke & Schweiger, 1979).

While Locke and Schweiger (1979) seem to take an unusual amount of pleasure in criticizing PDM, we think that their conclusions about the effectiveness of participation are fair. They said that the research provided only equivocal support for the effects of PDM, although the effects on satisfaction seemed to be stronger than those on productivity. They also concluded that the effects of PDM depend upon a number of situational factors. Indeed, the once-wide acceptance of PDM seems to be giving way to consideration of the types of situations in which participation is most appropriate and in which it will be most effective (Vroom & Yetton, 1973).

Combining Motivation Theories

We have presented three theories of motivation based on needs, three cognitive approaches to motivation, and the behaviorist viewpoint on work behavior. Most of these theories have been supported, to some extent, by research. None of these theories, however, has proved to be more than moderately successful in predicting worker performance or any other criterion. One way to improve our understanding of motivation is to combine the processes specified in several theories into a more comprehensive model, thereby playing the strengths of each approach against the weaknesses of the others.

There have been a number of general theories of organizational behavior that combine aspects of different motivation theories, such as the ambitious model developed by Naylor, Pritchard, and Ilgen (1980). Perhaps the best known of these models is that of Porter and Lawler (1968). The Porter–Lawler model provides a good illustration of how components of several motivation theories can be combined to provide a broader perspective than any single theory can (see Figure 8.8).

The Porter–Lawler model was developed as an expanded version of expectancy theory, as you can see by examining the first three cells in the diagram. Here valences (Cell 1) and expectancies (Cell 2) combine to produce effort (Cell 3). Consistent with Vroom's (1964) description of expectancy processes, effort does not determine performance directly, but rather combines with ability and other worker characteristics (Cell 4) and the worker's perceptions of what is expected on the job (Cell 5) to produce performance (Cell 6). As Deci (1975) later emphasized, performance can result in intrinsic and/or extrinsic rewards (Cells 7a and 7b), the levels of which may have implications for future expectancies. Consistent with equity theory, the rewards received are compared to a standard representing what the worker believes is fair (Cell 8). This comparison can have positive or negative effects on job satisfaction (Cell 9), which in turn has implications for the valence of rewards available in the future.

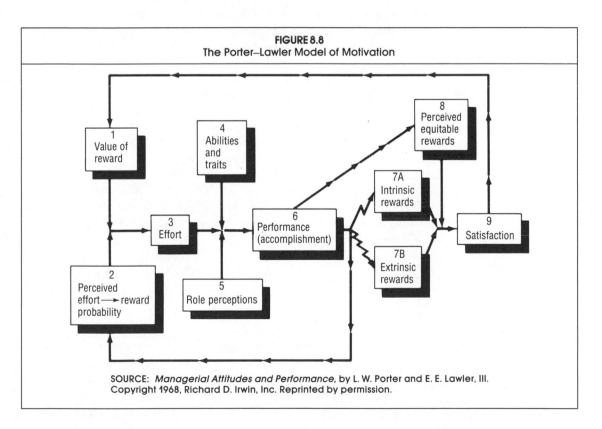

FIGURE 8.8
The Porter–Lawler Model of Motivation

SOURCE: *Managerial Attitudes and Performance,* by L. W. Porter and E. E. Lawler, III. Copyright 1968, Richard D. Irwin, Inc. Reprinted by permission.

The Porter–Lawler model is not the final word on motivation, but it is a good example of the direction that we believe will be most productive in future motivation research and theory. Rather than relying on any one process, it combines the basics of several viable models in a framework that allows for dynamic changes in workers' motives, as represented by the feedback arrows between rewards and expectancies and between satisfaction and valence. Given the flexibility and change that permeate our society and our workplaces, it is unlikely that the "final word" on motivation will ever be uttered. Dynamic, multifaceted theories such as Porter and Lawler's are therefore probably the best chance we have for understanding the activation, direction, and persistence of work behavior.

CONCLUSION

In this chapter we presented a number of theories designed to explain work motivation. These theories reflect a wide range of perspectives on human behavior. With the exception of the earliest need approaches, all of these theories have received at least modest support from research: We clearly know more about what motivates workers than did previous generations.

Even though psychologists have been able to identify many factors related to work motivation, problems such as the one involving Peter's Pan Pizza's interns have not become less frequent or less important. This is true in part because managers often fail to take advantage of what we have learned from motivation research when dealing with their employees. There are many reasons for this, including a lack of awareness of the theories, the difficulties associated with applying motivation theories in dynamic, complex organizations, and, in some cases, managers' fears that following the psychologist's advice will limit their freedom to supervise subordinates as they see fit. These considerations illustrate some of the problems facing Dr. MacKeven as she develops a plan to deal with the situation in the consumer research department. As you evaluate her recommendation to Ms. Russell, keep these considerations, as well as what you have learned about the theories themselves, in mind.

CHAPTER SUMMARY

Work motivation is concerned with people's goal-directed behavior in the workplace. Specifically, motivation theories attempt to explain the energizing, directing, and sustaining of behavior that leads to the achievement of individual or organizational objectives. Although motivation is a potentially powerful concept, its effects can be limited by such factors as individual ability level, changes in motives, and the operation of stereotypes about workers.

Theories developed to explain work motivation specify a variety of processes by which behavior may be directed. Some of the better-known theories based on need satisfaction, such as Maslow's need hierarchy and Alderfer's ERG, have not received much empirical support, although models based on the manifest-needs system of Murray show more promise. The most widely researched cognitive theory of motivation is Vroom's expectancy model, which states that motivation is a function of workers' expectations that behavior will result in the attainment of desired outcomes. Other motivation theories propose that behavior is controlled by perceptions of equity, the setting of performance goals, and the use of reinforcement and punishment. Each of these approaches has received some research support, but none has proved to be a good general explanation for worker motivation.

In addition to general theories of work motivation, I/O psychologists have studied such issues as the effects of extrinsic rewards on intrinsic motivation, and the value of participative decision making. Research on these more specific issues has been useful for defining the limits of motivation, and in efforts to integrate motivation theories, such as the Porter–Lawler model.

INTEROFFICE MEMO

TO: M. Russell, Director of Consumer Research

FROM: J. A. MacKeven, Human—Resources Coordinator

I have just completed a meeting with my staff, at which we discussed the situation involving the summer interns in your division. Let me briefly summarize what we have done regarding this situation, and out-line our recommendations.

After receiving your memo describing the motivation problems that you have been experiencing, we interviewed a number of the interns in the program—both good and poor performers, as identified by your staff. Our major goal in doing this was to determine what the interns per-ceived to be the major responsibilities of their jobs, as well as what they believed were management's expectations of them. I person-ally interviewed the immediate supervisors of these interns, to determine <u>their</u> perceptions of these same issues. Upon comparing notes from the intern and supervisor interviews, it was clear that there were two totally different perspectives on what the intern pro-gram is all about.

A detailed report on our research will be forthcoming in the next two weeks, in which we will explain the differences between interns' and supervisors' views. Also in that report will be detailed recommenda-tions for policy changes to help avoid this sort of misunderstanding in the future. Briefly, these recommendations will propose that detailed performance standards be established for each intern, and that each intern be required to submit weekly reports describing his or her status relative to those standards. After you have had time to study the report, we should meet to work out specific details of the program.

REVIEW QUESTIONS AND EXERCISES

1. Dr. MacKeven's recommendation could be justified by several theories presented in this chapter. Which theories are these, and how would each of them explain the potential success of the proposed program?

2. Dr. MacKeven's suggestion, as we have described it, is somewhat incomplete. What *additional* recommendations would you make to help assure the program's success?

3. Although Dr. MacKeven's recommendation is consistent with several theories, a number of alternative programs could have been proposed. Given what you have learned about motivation, describe one such alternative, and contrast its strengths and weaknesses with those of Dr. MacKeven's proposal.

4. Early in the chapter we presented a list of factors that limit the practical usefulness of the motivation concept. Discuss how each of these factors might cause the proposed program to fail (or appear to fail).

CHAPTER 9

Job Satisfaction and Attitudes

Learning Points

After studying this chapter, you should

- be able to define "attitude," and explain how job satisfaction is an attitude
- be able to describe the basic ideas of scientific management, and explain how the Hawthorne and Hoppock studies changed the way I/O psychologists thought about work behavior
- be able to describe two-factor theory, differentiating between the role of motivators and the role of satisfiers
- understand the basic principles of comparison theories of job satisfaction, and be able to explain how these principles were used by Maslow, Murray, Locke, and Lawler
- be able to explain the roles of social learning and attributions in the development of job attitudes
- be able to define withdrawal, and describe the relationship between withdrawal and job satisfaction
- be able to describe the relationship between job performance and job satisfaction, and explain why this relationship is not what many people believe it should be
- be able to define work and nonwork, and describe how they seem to be related
- be able to discuss various measures of job satisfaction, and recommend different measures for different uses

INTEROFFICE MEMO

TO: J. A. MacKeven, Human-Resources Coordinator

FROM: Joanna Richmond, Director of Inspections

I am writing to see if you might be able to help me with a puzzling, and in fact embarrassing, problem that I recently became aware of. Last month I called a meeting of my staff to discuss the latest federal regulations that apply to our store operations, and how they might have implications for the enforcement of certain common state regulations. Quite unexpectedly, Ed Clark, Vice President of Retail Operations, attended the meeting. Normally this would not be threatening to me, and it wasn't in this case until Mr. Clark mentioned that he didn't seem to recognize many of the people at the meeting, and asked me to introduce everyone. It was clear to me that he was making a point when he mentioned the ''importance of keeping good people'' after the meeting. While I was aware that there had been a number of people leaving from my division in recent months, I was surprised to find, upon checking, that the annual turnover rate has been running at approximately 50 percent. I did some more checking with the directors of the policy and quality standards divisions, and found that both turnover and absenteeism are problems throughout retail operations. While I cannot judge the extent of the problem elsewhere in the company, it is a very real problem here, especially given the large number of inspectors and the high costs of training. I would like to arrange a meeting with you to discuss this situation in detail.

INTRODUCTION

In this chapter we will discuss job satisfaction and other attitudes that workers may have regarding their jobs. It is clear, by examining our own experiences in schools, families, businesses, or other organizations, that people have attitudes toward many aspects of the groups to which they belong. I/O psychologists have studied both *how* such attitudes develop and the *effects* of these attitudes on work behavior. The turnover and absenteeism problems described by Joanna Richmond are typical of those that psychologists have found to be related to job satisfaction. If such attitudes have an effect on work behavior, then an understanding of how work attitudes develop would be invaluable. Before examining the research on these issues, we will first consider the nature of attitudes in general, and then take a closer look at job satisfaction, the most widely studied job attitude.

The Nature of Attitudes

Psychologists, particularly social psychologists, have been studying attitudes for many years. Attitudes can be defined as *relatively stable affective, or evaluative, dispositions toward a specific person, situation, or other entity*. The thing about which we have an attitude, such as a job, is commonly referred to as an "attitude object." Attitudes are typically described as consisting of three basic components. The first is a **belief** about the attitude object, sometimes referred to as the cognitive component of attitudes. For example, the store inspectors at Peter's Pan Pizza may believe that their work is dull and boring. That belief, however, does not necessarily mean that they have a negative attitude toward their jobs—it may be that they *enjoy* dull and boring work!

The second component of an attitude is an **evaluative** or emotional component. If you have an attitude toward something, you either like it or dislike it to some degree. It is the evaluative component that distinguishes attitudes from simple beliefs. For example, a store inspector from Peter's Pan Pizza might be overheard to say, "I am paid $5.10 an hour." In this case the inspector has simply reported what she believes to be true. A second inspector might be overheard to say, "I am paid $5.10 per hour, and I'm worth a lot more." In this case, the inspector has expressed a degree of dislike or dissatisfaction with her pay, thereby revealing a negative attitude. Finally, another inspector, paid the same $5.10 per hour, might be overheard to say, "I can't believe they pay me so much money to do this work!" This also indicates an attitude, but positive in nature rather than negative. It is important to note that there are no "neutral" attitudes. If you find yourself in a situation that evokes no evaluative response, positive or negative, then although you may have *beliefs* about that situation, you do not have an attitude toward it.

The third component of attitudes is a tendency or disposition to act in a certain way toward the attitude object. Returning to our store inspectors, the person who feels she is underpaid is likely to display a tendency to look for a new job, whereas the person who feels she is overpaid is less likely to engage in job hunting. Thus, work attitudes should have implications for work motivation.

Job Satisfaction: A Constellation of Work Attitudes

As we stated, job satisfaction refers to a worker's emotional, affective, or evaluative response toward his job. It should be clear, however, that jobs are complex and have many characteristics or facets. Consequently, it is possible for a single worker to have very different attitudes toward the different aspects of a job. For example, Dr. MacKeven suspects that the employees in Peter's Pan Pizza's retail operations division are experiencing low job satisfaction, and that this dissatisfaction is resulting in the high rates of turnover and absenteeism in this unit. She may therefore administer an attitude survey, and find that the workers are indeed unhappy with their jobs. What Dr. MacKeven would then want to know is precisely what it is about their jobs that the workers dislike. It is possible that the inspectors about whom Joanna Richmond wrote are all reasonably happy with their pay, benefits, and the work that they do, but are very unhappy about the amount of travel that their jobs require and the amount of time that they must spend away from their families.

Psychologists describe the complex nature of job satisfaction by saying that it is multidimensional, meaning that it has a number of distinct, relatively independent components. This multidimensionality has at least two important implications. The first is that it may be misleading to speak of job satisfaction without specifying the precise aspect of the job to which the satisfaction refers. In some cases, such as when Dr. MacKeven tries to find out if workers are generally happy or not, she is interested in general or global job satisfaction. This would reflect some combination of a worker's satisfaction with all aspects of his job. In other cases, such as when Dr. MacKeven must recommend what should be done to improve workers' satisfaction, it might be more useful to know exactly what it is about the job that is causing the problem.

The second implication of the multidimensionality of job satisfaction concerns the measurement of satisfaction. Clearly, if you are interested in workers' global satisfaction, you need to use a very different measure of satisfaction than if you are only interested in satisfaction with a single facet of the job, such as pay or the quality of supervision. Consequently, psychologists have developed a variety of measures of satisfaction, ranging from very general measures of overall feelings toward a job, to very specific readings of attitudes toward individual job components. We will discuss some of the issues involved in the measurement of satisfaction later in this chapter. For now, just keep the complex, multidimensional nature of job satisfaction in mind as we examine some of the theories of satisfaction that have been developed over the years.

---

belief: an opinion or conviction that something is true
evaluative: assessing the value or desirability of something

THE ORIGINS OF JOB SATISFACTION RESEARCH

While preparing to write this book, we reviewed all of the articles published in numerous journals over a number of years. We found that more articles addressed some aspect of job satisfaction than any other single topic. I/O psychologists have certainly shown a great interest in worker attitudes. This was not always the case, however, as evidenced by the perspective taken in one of the earliest systematic approaches to dealing with worker behavior—Frederick Taylor's "scientific management."

Scientific Management

Frederick W. Taylor was an engineer who, in the early part of the 20th century, became interested in increasing workers' efficiency. As might be expected, given his engineering background, Taylor's efforts focused on ways to change or redesign jobs in order to allow workers to be more efficient. In his book *Principles of Scientific Management* (1911), Taylor described what he saw as the necessary steps toward increased efficiency. Although critics do not always realize this, he advocated the development of cooperation and shared responsibility between management and labor. The major aspects of scientific management, however, concerned the systematic study and design of jobs in order to eliminate inefficient behaviors and techniques. To this end, Taylor introduced time-and-motion studies, which analyzed the individual movements made by workers, and identified the most efficient set of behaviors to perform the tasks required by a job. One result of performing time-and-motion studies was that the jobs were greatly simplified; workers performed only a few, very simple tasks.

Taylor's view of the role of workers was based on a simple, and much disputed, assumption about motivation. He believed that *all* workers desired *only* economic rewards, and that they would increase their levels of effort in order to obtain these rewards. Consequently, it was assumed that once pay was linked with productivity, workers would accept whatever job changes were introduced in order to get higher pay. The result of this perspective was that workers were seen as interchangeable components of jobs. Since motivation was assured by the link between productivity and economic rewards, and since time-and-motion studies could be used to simplify jobs so that ability made little difference, research on worker behavior focused on working conditions that might improve productivity, such as temperature and illumination levels, and the identification of even more efficient worker behaviors that all workers could be trained to perform. Workers' attitudes toward their jobs were simply not considered to be important.

The Hawthorne and Hoppock Studies

In 1924 a series of long-term research projects was begun at the Hawthorne plant of the Western Electric Company (Landsberger, 1958; Roethlisberger & Dickson, 1939; see Chapter 1 for additional details). Consistent with the then-prevalent view of worker behavior and the emphasis on efficiency, the original purpose of the Hawthorne studies was to determine the level of illumination at which workers' productivity and efficiency were highest. One early study showed that the performance of *both* experimental and control groups, rather than that of the experimental group alone, increased during the course of the research. Other studies showed that productivity increased even when the level of illumination was dramatically lowered, or when the researchers tricked the workers into *believing* that the lights had been changed when *in fact* the illumination levels were the same as before.

These results left the Hawthorne researchers "in the dark," and prompted the researchers to conduct a number of additional studies, in the hope of identifying factors that could explain the workers' bizarre behavior. In some studies the workers kept diaries, and their comments clearly indicated that the experimental manipulations were accompanied by changes in the workers' attitudes toward their co-workers and company management. Further, these attitudes provided a better explanation for the changes in workers' productivity than did the manipulations themselves.

The Hawthorne studies have been criticized for poor experimental design, inaccurate reporting of results, and a variety of other shortcomings (see Chapter 1). They remain, however, one of the most important research projects in the history of I/O psychology. This is due to the impact of two general conclusions that were drawn from the studies. The first of these is that workers' attitudes toward their jobs, and their perceptions of job characteristics, determine (at least in part) the effects of such things as pay, hours of work, working conditions, and the physical work environment. Managers no longer assume that all workers respond in the same way to similar jobs, nor that their reactions are easily predictable. The second conclusion was that workers respond not only to the rules, goals, and expectations of the formal organization, but also to the pressures and norms established by informal work groups, over which management has little or no control.

These conclusions led researchers to ask new questions about the effects of workers' attitudes, emotions, and perceptions, and the differences between workers or groups of workers on these types of variables. Some of the earliest influential studies of job satisfaction to follow the Hawthorne studies were conducted by Robert Hoppock (1935). In the best known of these, he surveyed all adult residents of New Hope, Pennsylvania, in 1933. New Hope was described by Hoppock as a "typical" American town of about 1100 residents, of whom 351 were employed adults. One notable aspect of Hoppock's results is their similarity to those of more recent surveys discussed later in the chapter (Weaver, 1980). For example, he found that, overall, New Hope residents were quite satisfied with their jobs, with 77 percent reporting that they "liked," were "enthusiastic about," or "loved" their jobs. Also, virtually no differences were found between the mean satisfaction levels of men and women. There were, however, more substantial differences between the mean satisfaction levels for different occupational/ socioeconomic groups, with professional, managerial, and executive workers having the highest satisfaction levels, and unskilled manual workers having the lowest satisfaction levels.

Whereas the Hawthorne studies focused attention on the importance of workers' needs and perceptions, Hoppock's (1935) work addressed many of the practical issues involved in conducting job satisfaction research. Together, these pioneering efforts shaped much of the theory and research on job attitudes that was to follow.

THEORIES OF JOB SATISFACTION

Over the years there have been a number of theoretical approaches to explaining the causes and effects of job satisfaction. Many of these theories are more than simply theories of satisfaction: They are also concerned with worker motivation, work group interaction, and leader–follower relationships. Consequently, as we examine these theories you will recognize many of the concepts from previous chapters, and you will also be getting a preview of some of the things to come in later chapters.

Frederick Herzberg's Two-Factor Theory

In 1957, Herzberg, Mausner, Peterson, and Capwell published a review of the early satisfaction research literature. Contrary to other reviews that had found no relationships between job satisfaction and work performance (for example, Brayfield & Crockett, 1955), Herzberg concluded that there *were* systematic relationships between workers' attitudes and their behavior, but that these relationships had gone unnoticed because researchers had confused job satisfaction and job *dissatisfaction.* According to Herzberg, job satisfaction depends upon a certain set of conditions, whereas job dissatisfaction is the result of an entirely different set of conditions. Thus, although it is possible to think of satisfaction and dissatisfaction as the two extremes on a single continuum, they are determined by different factors. Failure to recognize this, said Herzberg, had resulted in the mistaken conclusion that work attitudes were unrelated to work behaviors.

MOTIVATORS AND HYGIENE FACTORS

Herzberg, Mausner, and Snyderman (1959) conducted new research to test the relationship between satisfaction and performance, and formalized a theory based on their results. According to the theory, people have two major types of needs. The first of these Herzberg called **hygiene needs,** which are influenced by the physical and psychological conditions in which people work. Herzberg called the second set of needs **motivator needs,** and described them as being very similar to the higher-order needs in Maslow's (1943) need hierarchy theory (see Chapter 8).

Herzberg et al. (1959) claimed that these two types of needs were satisfied by different types of outcomes or rewards. Hygiene needs were said to be satisfied by the level of certain conditions called hygiene factors, or dissatisfiers. The factors that Herzberg found to be related to hygiene needs are listed here.

- Supervision
- Interpersonal relations
- Physical working conditions
- Salary
- Company policies and administrative practices
- Benefits
- Job security

These factors are all concerned with the *context* or *environment* in which the job exists. When these factors are unfavorable, then job dissatisfaction is the result. This might be the case in the retail operations division at Peter's Pan Pizza if the workers believe they are being paid too little, or if the travel involved in their jobs is a hardship. When hygiene factors are positive, such as when workers perceive that their pay is fair and that their working conditions are good, then barriers to job satisfaction are removed. The fulfillment of hygiene needs, however, cannot by itself result in job satisfaction, but only in the *reduction* or elimination of *dis*satisfaction. Herzberg compared hygiene factors to modern water- and air-pollution controls: Whereas such controls do not cure any diseases, they serve to *prevent* the outbreak of disease. In the same way, he believed that hygiene factors did not cause satisfaction, but that they could prevent dissatisfaction.

Unlike hygiene needs, motivator needs are fulfilled by what Herzberg et al. (1959) called motivator factors or satisfiers. They identified the following motivator factors.

- Achievement
- Recognition
- Work itself
- Responsibility
- Advancement

Whereas hygiene factors are related to the context of work, motivator factors are concerned with the nature of the work itself and the consequences of work. According to the theory, the factors that lead to job satisfaction are those that satisfy an individual's need for self-actualization in one's work, and it is "only from the performance of a task that the individual can get the rewards that will reinforce his [or her] aspirations" (Herzberg et al., 1959, p. 114).

Compared to hygiene factors, which result in a "neutral state" when present, positive motivator factors result in job satisfaction. When recognition, responsibility, and other motivators are absent from a job, however, the result

---

hygiene needs: human needs relevant to the health, safety, and security of individuals

motivator needs: human needs relevant to the self-esteem and personal achievement of individuals

will not be dissatisfaction, as with the absence of hygiene factors, but rather the same neutral state associated with the *presence* of hygiene factors. Figure 9.1 illustrates the nature of the relationships between hygiene factors, motivator factors, job satisfaction, and job dissatisfaction.

EVALUATION OF TWO-FACTOR THEORY

It is easy to imagine how two-factor theory might work in a particular situation. For instance, Dr. MacKeven might suspect that the turnover problem in retail operations stems from employee dissatisfaction. If she were to base her recommendations on two-factor theory, she might try to eliminate dissatisfaction by suggesting that a higher mileage rate be provided to inspectors who must travel, or perhaps by adjusting pay and fringe benefits. By improving these deficient hygiene factors, Dr. MacKeven would be removing the source of worker dissatisfaction. If she wished to make the workers *satisfied,* however, she would have to bolster their feelings of esteem or self-actualization. This would require changes in jobs that would enable workers to receive recognition for their achievements, and to have responsibility for what they do and how it is done. These changes should also affect the actual work they perform, such that it has personal meaning and significance.

Unfortunately, two-factor theory just doesn't work out in practice. One problem with the theory is that it is based on face-to-face interviews of workers conducted by Herzberg and his colleagues. This is a problem because unhappy workers are likely to claim that their dissatisfaction is due to circumstances beyond their control, such as the boss, the working conditions, or company policy. When something happens that satisfies a worker, such as receiving recognition or a promotion, it is more likely to be attributed to the worker's own skills or effort. Thus, the theory may reflect the way in which the data were gathered, more than the actual causes of satisfaction and dissatisfaction. Indeed, efforts to replicate Herzberg's results using noninterview techniques have generally not been successful (for example, Ewen, Smith, Hulin, & Locke, 1966; Hulin & Smith, 1965). Another factor that has probably contributed to the lack of support for two-factor theory is that Herzberg et al. (1959) based the theory solely on samples of accountants and engineers. It is hardly surprising that efforts to replicate their results with more representative samples of workers have failed—the same could be expected with any theory based on a restricted sample of workers from highly technical occupations.

King (1970) pointed out another, more theoretical problem. Specifically, he noted that Herzberg did not remain consistent in his description of two-

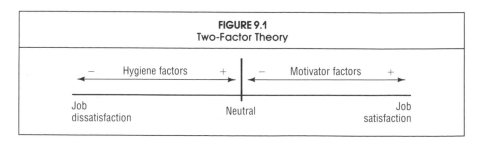

FIGURE 9.1
Two-Factor Theory

— Hygiene factors + | — Motivator factors +

Job dissatisfaction   Neutral   Job satisfaction

factor theory, or in the roles played by motivation and hygiene factors. King identified at least five different versions of two-factor theory in Herzberg's writings (for instance, Herzberg, 1964, 1966), ranging from the statement that, collectively, motivators have a stronger effect on satisfaction than on dissatisfaction whereas hygiene factors have a stronger effect on dissatisfaction than on satisfaction, to the relatively strict statement that *only* motivators influence satisfaction and *only* hygiene factors influence dissatisfaction. This inconsistency, however, seems to make little practical difference, since King found little support for *any* version of two-factor theory.

The problems associated with two-factor theory, particularly the difficulty researchers have had replicating Herzberg's results, served to virtually halt research on this approach during the late 1970s and early 1980s. An interesting exception is a study by Machungwa and Schmitt (1983), who used a critical incidents technique to examine motivation in the developing country of Zambia. Three hundred and forty-one Zambian employees provided detailed critical incidents describing a time when they worked exceptionally hard, and a time when they put very little effort into their work. A content analysis of the incidents resulted in 27 demotivating and 23 motivating themes. These themes were further clustered into six general themes that seemed to be consistent with the basic premises of two-factor theory. Two of the themes, growth/advancement opportunity and work nature, were predominantly related to high motivation and favorable attitudes. The remaining themes, material and physical provisions, relations with others, fairness in organizational practices, and personal problems, were predominantly associated with a lack of motivation and negative work attitudes.

It is not possible to say, on the basis on this one study, whether two-factor theory might have some particular relevance for developing countries, where workers undergo rapid changes in economic and social status. Machungwa and Schmitt's (1983) study does, however, support Landy's (1985) contention that two-factor theory is valuable, if not for *predicting* worker attitudes and motivation, then at least for *describing* what people find satisfying or dissatisfying, on the average and after the fact.

Comparison Theories of Job Satisfaction

Two-factor theory states that certain aspects of work are related to job satisfaction, whereas other aspects are related to dissatisfaction. Workers who have, on balance, more satisfiers in their jobs will tend to be more satisfied, whereas those with more dissatisfiers will be more dissatisfied. If you change the level or amount of either factor, the theory would predict a change in satisfaction. Further, since two-factor theory focuses on work and job characteristics as the causes of satisfaction (and dissatisfaction), the same changes would be predicted for *all* workers. Most satisfaction theories, however, specify more complex processes that involve a comparison between a worker's current status and some standard or expectation. These comparison theories differ as to what this standard of comparison is, but they have in common the notion that meeting the standard leads to satisfaction, whereas failure to meet the standard leads to dissatisfaction.

NEED THEORIES

Perhaps the earliest application of the comparison approach to job satisfaction involved the concept of needs. Need theories were developed primarily to explain motivation, and were discussed in detail in Chapter 8. Briefly, need theories state that we have certain physiological and psychological requirements or needs that may be fulfilled through the work that we do. We continually compare the current status of our needs to the level of need fulfillment that we desire from our jobs. When our needs are unfulfilled, an unpleasant state of tension results and we are not likely to experience job satisfaction. Fulfillment of our needs removes the tension, thereby allowing us to feel satisfied.

The best-known need theories are those of Abraham Maslow and Henry A. Murray. Recall that Maslow's (1943, 1970) need hierarchy theory positions human needs in a hierarchy of importance or prepotence, with lower-level needs, such as physiological needs and safety needs, dominating behavior until they are fulfilled, at which time higher-level needs, such as needs for esteem and belongingness, are activated. This gratification/activation principle has an interesting implication for job satisfaction: Because the fulfillment of any one level of needs activates the next level, a worker will always have an active need, making long-term job satisfaction seem unlikely.

Murray's manifest needs theory, and the related theories of Atkinson and McClelland, differ significantly from Maslow's theory. In need hierarchy theory, different people may be motivated by, or satisfied with, different conditions, depending upon their current level in the hierarchy. However, *all* of the needs are potentially of equal importance to *all* people under the appropriate circumstances. Manifest needs theory, on the other hand, allows for relatively permanent differences between people in the overall importance of different needs (Atkinson & Feather, 1966; McClelland, 1961; Murray, 1938). Consequently, those workers who are high in need for achievement are likely to be most satisfied when they are solving problems and successfully accomplishing their job tasks. In contrast, those workers who are high in need for affiliation will probably be most satisfied by maintaining social relationships with their co-workers.

Need theories have received a lot of research attention, and this research has identified a number of problems with this approach to studying behavior. The most troublesome of these problems is the inability of psychologists to adequately define the concept of needs, or to identify a set of needs that is adequate to explain behavior over a variety of situations (see Chapter 8). Based on the research evidence so far, it appears that although the manifest needs approach may have some value in explaining and predicting managerial behavior, including satisfaction, more general satisfaction theories will have to rely on other processes.

LOCKE'S VALUE THEORY

A second comparison theory of job satisfaction is the value theory developed by Locke (1976). Rather than focusing on needs, Locke suggested that job satisfaction may be more closely related to whether or not our work provides us with what we *want*, *desire*, or *value*. We examine what our jobs provide us in terms of, for example, pay, working conditions, and promotion opportunities. We then compare those perceptions to what we value or find important in a job. To the extent that the two match, job satisfaction results.

To illustrate Locke's theory, consider the absenteeism and turnover problems in Peter's Pan Pizza's retail operations division. Assuming that these problems are indeed related to poor job satisfaction, value theory would lead Dr. MacKeven to determine what outcomes the workers value from their jobs and, if possible, adjust the level of those outcomes to match their values. It should be noted that because different workers have different values, this would not be an easy task.

There is a subtle difference between Locke's (1976) viewpoint and that of need theories such as Maslow's (1943) that can be illustrated by considering the effects of a potential pay raise for the workers at Peter's Pan Pizza. Let's assume that PPP pays its employees very well compared to other companies in the food industry. Despite this, however, few of us would be surprised to learn that PPP workers *want* a pay raise. It would be unlikely that money could be identified as a *need* for these workers, in the way that either Maslow or Murray (1938) define needs. It is easy, however, to believe that most workers would *value* more money than they are currently receiving.

An interesting implication of Locke's (1976) theory is that while knowing the importance or value that a worker attaches to a particular outcome does not by itself predict how satisfied the worker will be, importance should predict the *range* of potential worker attitudes. Consider, for example, the possible effects of pay on the satisfaction of workers at Peter's Pan Pizza. Some workers attach a high value to the level of their pay; to them money is one of, if not *the*, major outcome associated with working. Consequently, variations in pay will be strongly related to their satisfaction, as illustrated in Figure 9.2. (We only show positive effects for pay on satisfaction, although some equity approaches suggest a negative effect for overpayment, as described in Chapter 8.) Other workers, once they are making enough money to satisfy their basic needs, are not as concerned with how much they make. Variations in the pay of these workers will not have much effect, either positive or negative, on satisfaction, again as shown in Figure 9.2. Thus, value theory suggests that the more important a job-related factor is to a worker, the greater its potential effect on his satisfaction.

Whereas there is some evidence consistent with Locke's value theory (for example, Locke, 1969; Mobley & Locke, 1970), there has been little empirical research on this approach. Nevertheless, the concept of values is an important addition to the satisfaction literature, and may remedy some of the problems associated with need theories of satisfaction. Need theories imply that the satisfaction of all workers depends on the fulfillment of a small number of basic needs. This in turn implies that satisfaction can be achieved through a limited number of strategies designed to address whichever of these needs are unfulfilled for a particular worker. Worker values, however, introduce another dimension to this situation. Even though outcomes such as pay, fringe benefits, and working conditions are the same for two workers, and even though these outcomes may provide equivalent levels of need fulfillment, the workers' satisfaction will differ to the extent that their values differ. This approach seems to be more consistent

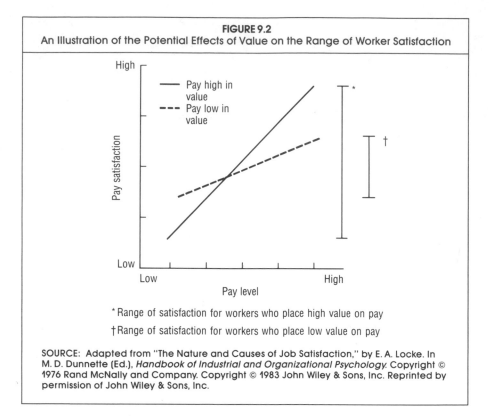

FIGURE 9.2
An Illustration of the Potential Effects of Value on the Range of Worker Satisfaction

* Range of satisfaction for workers who place high value on pay

† Range of satisfaction for workers who place low value on pay

SOURCE: Adapted from "The Nature and Causes of Job Satisfaction," by E. A. Locke. In M. D. Dunnette (Ed.), *Handbook of Industrial and Organizational Psychology.* Copyright © 1976 Rand McNally and Company. Copyright © 1983 John Wiley & Sons, Inc. Reprinted by permission of John Wiley & Sons, Inc.

with the ways in which people actually react to their jobs. Further, as Landy (1985) pointed out, value theory is theoretically consistent with more general models of emotion, which state that emotional responses, such as attitudes, are triggered by a general state of physiological and psychological arousal (for example, Schachter & Singer, 1962). Landy notes that valued outcomes are more likely to lead to arousal, and thereby have implications for satisfaction, than are nonvalued outcomes (Landy, 1978).

LAWLER'S FACET SATISFACTION MODEL

A third comparison theory of satisfaction is Lawler's Facet Satisfaction Model (Lawler, 1973). This theory is an elaboration on portions of the Porter–Lawler motivation model discussed in Chapter 8 (see Figure 8.8, p. 289). We described the Porter–Lawler model as a combination of some of the basic ideas from several prominent motivation theories. The facet satisfaction model is an expansion of that part of the Porter–Lawler model related to equity theory (Adams, 1965). The facet model, illustrated in Figure 9.3, derives its name from the fact that it is intended to describe the processes by which satisfaction with any individual job component, or **facet,** is determined.

The comparison specified in Lawler's theory is between perceptions of what a worker believes he *should* receive, in terms of job outcomes such as pay, recognition, and promotions, and perceptions of the outcomes that are *actually*

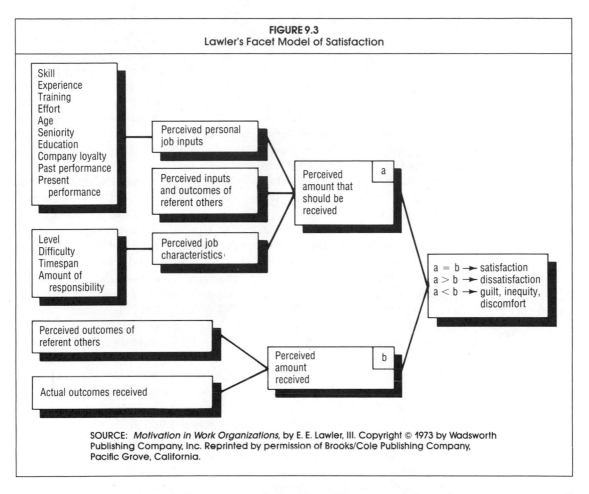

FIGURE 9.3
Lawler's Facet Model of Satisfaction

Skill
Experience
Training
Effort
Age
Seniority
Education
Company loyalty
Past performance
Present
    performance

Level
Difficulty
Timespan
Amount of
    responsibility

Perceived outcomes of
referent others

Actual outcomes received

Perceived personal
job inputs

Perceived inputs
and outcomes of
referent others

Perceived job
characteristics

Perceived
amount that
should be
received   a

Perceived
amount
received   b

a = b → satisfaction
a > b → dissatisfaction
a < b → guilt, inequity,
            discomfort

SOURCE: *Motivation in Work Organizations*, by E. E. Lawler, III. Copyright © 1973 by Wadsworth
Publishing Company, Inc. Reprinted by permission of Brooks/Cole Publishing Company,
Pacific Grove, California.

received. Perceptions of what *should* be received depend upon perceptions of
the inputs the worker brings to the job, such as skill, education, and experience,
as well as perceptions of job characteristics, such as responsibility and difficulty,
and perceptions of the inputs and outcomes of others. Perceptions of *actual*
outcomes depend, of course, on the outcomes themselves, as well as perceptions
of the outcomes of referent others, or people holding similar jobs with whom
workers compare themselves. It should be obvious, with all of this talk about
perceptions, that the facet model is highly cognitive in nature, and reflects the
view that people respond to their *perceptions* of reality more directly than to
reality itself.

As is the case with Adams' (1965) equity theory, the facet model states
that the only desirable or satisfying condition is one in which the comparison
process indicates equality, when perceptions of what should be received balance
perceptions of what is actually received. If the worker feels that she is receiving

facet: an individual aspect or component of a larger entity

less than is warranted, dissatisfaction with the job results. If the worker perceives that she is receiving *more* than is deserved, uncomfortable feelings of inequity, and possibly guilt, ensue. The notion of feeling overpaid or overcompensated is the most controversial aspect of the equity theory of motivation, and it remains a problem in Lawler's (1973) satisfaction theory. As we saw in our discussion of equity theory in Chapter 8, there are a number of things we can do to avoid feeling overpaid. For example, we can compare our own inputs and outcomes to those of a different reference person. We can also enhance our perceptions of our own inputs, thereby justifying the higher outcomes, or we can devalue the outcomes ("A dollar isn't what it used to be!").

Research on Lawler's model has been limited and inconclusive. A telling example involves a study by Wanous and Lawler (1972), who examined satisfaction with 23 different job facets using several measures of satisfaction. One of the measures, as specified by the facet satisfaction model, was the difference between the current level of the facet and the level that the worker believed should be associated with her job. Wanous and Lawler found that overall job satisfaction ratings could be predicted from this difference score, as suggested by the theory. The same data, however, were later reanalyzed by Wall and Payne (1973), who found that perceptions of the level of outcomes *received* predicted overall satisfaction best, with those workers who perceived greater outcomes being more satisfied. Further, what the workers thought they *should* receive did not improve the prediction of satisfaction. Indeed, Wall and Payne argued that the type of difference score suggested by Lawler's model is inherently flawed. Whereas this does not necessarily invalidate Lawler's theory, it raises questions about how to validly measure perceptions of equity.

Another problem is that the facet model assumes that people use very rational cognitive processes, carefully weighing their own, as well as others', inputs and outcomes, and basing their attitudes on the logical conclusions derived from those comparisons. There are good reasons to suggest that many people are *not* this rational (Slovic, Fischhoff, & Lichtenstein, 1977). Further, it is not at all clear, even if people do compare inputs and outcomes, that this comparison is as simple as Lawler's (1973) model suggests. Weiner (1980) showed that job satisfaction can be predicted more accurately if the difference between what you actually receive and what you think you should receive is computed as a percentage of what you actually receive (satisfaction = [actual − desired]/actual), rather than as a simple difference (satisfaction = actual − desired).

The following computations show the effects of these two approaches to equity for two of Peter's Pan Pizza's employees, Ed Clark, Vice President of Retail Operations, and Dennis Foss, one of the store inspectors. Assuming that Mr. Clark has a salary of $63,000 and that Mr. Foss has a salary of $21,000, we can see the effects on satisfaction when each believes that he should be paid $1,000 more than he is currently being paid, based on comparisons of their own inputs and salaries to those of their co-workers.

Ed Clark, Vice President, Retail Operations
   Actual salary: $63,000
   Desired salary: 64,000

   Difference prediction of satisfaction:
      $63 - 64 = -1$
   Averaging prediction of satisfaction:
      $(63 - 64)/63 = -.016$

Dennis Foss, Store Inspector
   Actual salary: $21,000
   Desired salary: 22,000

   Difference prediction of satisfaction:
      $21 - 22 = -1$
   Averaging prediction of satisfaction:
      $(21 - 22)/21 = -.048$

Using the simple difference between what is desired and what is actually received, the same level of satisfaction is predicted for both men. Dividing this difference by their current salaries as Weiner (1980) suggested, however, we see that Mr. Foss should be less satisfied than Mr. Clark (negative values indicate perceived underpayment and dissatisfaction), since $1,000 represents a larger percentage of Mr. Foss' current salary, and therefore greater perceived underpayment. In fact, according to Weiner's averaging process, for Mr. Clark to feel the same dissatisfaction with pay that Mr. Foss is experiencing, he would have to desire a $67,000 salary.

Equity is a compelling idea, and in the social environment of organizations it would seem to be an important factor in determining satisfaction. The research on theories that rely on equity principles, however, makes it quite clear that psychologists do not yet understand the cognitive processes that determine perceptions of equity and inequity. Until these processes are more fully specified, equity theories will probably not provide acceptable answers to questions of job satisfaction.

Social and Cognitive Construction Theories of Job Satisfaction

Some recent approaches to studying job satisfaction are based upon social and cognitive construction processes. These theories attempt to explain satisfaction by describing the cognitive processes that workers use when evaluating or otherwise making decisions about their jobs. Specifically, these theories state that workers build or "construct" beliefs and attitudes based on events that they observe, such as the behavior and attitudes of co-workers. Workers are seen as active gatherers of information, which they use to build and define their personal "realities." It is these subjective, socially constructed realities, not objective events, that determine satisfaction.

SOCIAL LEARNING

Social learning approaches to job satisfaction and attitudes are similar to Lawler's (1973) facet model, in that attitudes are determined in part by an examination of the behavior of other workers. Instead of comparing inputs and outcomes, however, social learning theory says that we use other people as sources of information for selecting appropriate attitudes and behaviors. Our own attitudes, at least in part, are copied or modeled from the attitudes of our co-workers. Specifically, by observing our co-workers, we infer their attitudes toward the organization, the job as a whole, and specific job facets. We perceive certain co-workers, usually those with similar jobs and interests, or those who we believe are successful or powerful, as being appropriate *models*, and base our own attitudes on what we believe theirs to be (Salancik & Pfeffer, 1977a).

A number of studies conducted by Weiss examined the social learning of work attitudes. Weiss and Shaw (1979) studied the effects of models' evaluative comments on the task satisfaction of subjects. They had subjects watch an instructional videotape, on which could be seen the hands of a "trainee" who was assembling a simple electric circuit, while the voice of the "trainer" explained the steps involved in the task. The subjects could also hear, in the background, the voices of the trainee and another person. In some conditions the trainee made positive comments about the task, while in others he made negative comments. Weiss and Shaw found that subjects who overheard the positive comments had more favorable attitudes after performing the task than did those who overheard the negative comments.

Weiss (1978) also found that situational and personal factors play a role in the social learning of work attitudes. He found that the modeling of work values was influenced by supervisors' behavior; there was greater similarity between the values of workers and supervisors when the supervisors demonstrated consideration toward their subordinates. He also discovered that workers who were low in self-esteem, or who had relatively negative perceptions of their own abilities and worthiness, modeled the values of successful and competent supervisors more strongly than did high self-esteem subordinates. Weiss suggested that high self-esteem people may have greater confidence in their own judgments of the job, and therefore feel less of a need to rely on cues provided by others.

Social learning appears to be an important means by which people develop attitudes, not only in work settings, but also in other social situations (Bandura, 1971). Research shows, however, that not everyone is equally likely to model the behavior of others, nor is everyone equally likely to serve as a model. Consequently, social learning is apt to be a better explanation for job satisfaction and other attitudes in certain situations and for certain people than for others.

SATISFACTION AS AN ATTRIBUTION

Landy (1985) recently suggested an approach to job satisfaction that is based on a general theory of emotions developed by Schachter and Singer (1962). According to Schachter and Singer, certain events or environmental conditions cause a state of general physiological arousal. The qualitative, physiological nature of this arousal is the same for any such event; differences from one situation to the next involve only the intensity or level of arousal. So, for example, when a well-paid Peter's Pan Pizza store inspector receives a paycheck, he experiences arousal. The same physiological state of arousal occurs when the inspector must be in Mary Esther, Florida, rather than in Suardell Springs on his daughter's birthday. As you might imagine, however, the *emotions* experienced by the inspector are quite different in these two cases. To understand the differences in emotions, we need to understand how the individual interprets the feelings of arousal.

According to Schachter and Singer (1962), specific emotions depend on our attributions, or perceived causes, for physiological arousal. In other words, once we experience arousal, we examine the situation or context in which it has occurred, and infer our emotions from the cues that are present. The inspector who has just received a large paycheck is therefore likely to attribute his arousal to the money, and is likely to be satisfied with the job (or at least with the pay). When the inspector is forced to miss his child's birthday party, arousal is more likely to be attributed to the "unreasonable" travel demands of the job, and dissatisfaction is the likely result.

Not only can the same physical arousal result in different emotions, but arousal caused by the *same event* can have different emotional consequences, depending on the attributions we make. Store inspectors are likely to experience arousal upon being told that they will be responsible for inspecting an additional ten stores each month. Those inspectors who attribute this to the trust placed in them by their superiors are likely to feel satisfied as a result, whereas those who attribute it to an effort by management to get more work out of them are likely to feel dissatisfied.

This approach to job satisfaction is a dramatic change from most theories, which assume that environmental, psychological, or physiological conditions have some sort of direct effect on satisfaction. It suggests instead that the effects of such conditions depend, to a great extent, on individuals' perceptions of the causes of those conditions, which in turn may be determined by a number of factors that are unlikely to be the same for everyone. Whereas this possibility complicates the research on satisfaction, it may be more realistic than other approaches.

An emerging topic of research consistent with the social/cognitive construction view of job satisfaction deals with the *effects* of emotions on other types of behavior. Staw (1984) noted that it is unusual and unfortunate that I/O psychologists have largely ignored the role of mood or emotion as an independent variable. The research of O'Reilly and Caldwell demonstrates that work attitudes can indeed be related to other perceptions about jobs, such as the variety of tasks that make up a job, and the skills required to perform the job (Caldwell & O'Reilly, 1982b; O'Reilly & Caldwell, 1979). This research is consistent with the notion that emotional responses may help determine employees' reactions to their jobs, and with Landy's (1985) suggestions that general theories of emotion may be useful for understanding job attitudes.

Evaluation of Satisfaction Theories

We have examined a number of job satisfaction theories, ranging from such classics as two-factor theory to relatively new attribution approaches. During most of the past three decades, the predominant theories of job satisfaction have been based on comparison processes. As was the case with two-factor theory, however, comparison theories have enjoyed only limited empirical support. In some cases, such as Maslow's (1943) need hierarchy, it appears that the basic premises underlying the theories are flawed. In other cases, such as Locke's (1976) and Lawler's (1973) theories, there is little empirical research upon which to base an evaluation. The research that does exist, however, suggests that these theories may be unable to account for differences in the type and complexity of cognitive comparisons made by workers. Emerging perspectives, such as social learning theory and an emphasis on emotions, represent the newest phase of satisfaction theory. We expect, however, that the development of work attitudes is influenced by such a variety of personal and situational factors that no single theory is likely to provide a complete explanation. Rather, some combination of perspectives will ultimately provide the best understanding of job satisfaction.

CORRELATES OF JOB SATISFACTION

Whereas many theories of job satisfaction have been proposed to explain the development of workers' attitudes, much of the satisfaction research has addressed a more practical question: What behaviors, personal characteristics, and working conditions are related to job satisfaction? Knowing what variables are related to satisfaction can serve at least two important purposes. First, it can allow us to make predictions about what types of people will be more or less satisfied under a given set of circumstances, often suggesting ways to improve satisfaction. Second, it can allow us to establish the *practical* importance of job satisfaction. That is, knowing what variables are typically associated with satisfaction lets us estimate the extent to which improving satisfaction might in turn help solve various organizational problems, such as low performance or high turnover.

Job Satisfaction and Work Behaviors

To most managers and many psychologists, job satisfaction is interesting because we expect it to have positive effects on work behaviors. In fact, for many years following the Hawthorne studies the beneficial effects of high job satisfaction were taken for granted. As empirical research on satisfaction accumulated, however, it became clear that the effects of satisfaction on employee behavior were much weaker than had once been believed. This is seen clearly in the research on the relationships between satisfaction and withdrawal, and between satisfaction and performance.

WITHDRAWAL

Withdrawal is the general term used to refer to behaviors by which workers remove themselves, either temporarily or permanently, from their jobs or workplaces. Two forms of withdrawal that have been studied extensively are absenteeism and turnover.

Absenteeism is a major problem in work organizations. In 1978, Steers and Rhodes estimated that nonmanagerial absenteeism in the United States cost industry between $8.5 and $26.4 billion annually. Considering the additional costs of managerial absenteeism, as well as the effects of inflation since 1978, these figures certainly underestimate the current costs of absenteeism.

As recently as 1977, Muchinsky concluded that there was a "highly consistent" negative relationship between job satisfaction and absenteeism, although he did not estimate the strength of that relationship (Muchinsky, 1977b). Most subsequent reviews and research, however, have been less positive, typically reporting small and inconsistent satisfaction–absenteeism correlations. Further, this research has shown that other variables often have stronger relationships to absenteeism than does satisfaction (Breaugh, 1981; Cheloha & Farr, 1980; Keller, 1983; Locke, 1976; Nicholson, Brown, & Chadwick-Jones, 1976; Watson, 1981).

One of the earliest efforts to elaborate on the job satisfaction–absenteeism relationship was the Process Model of Attendance developed by Steers and Rhodes (1978), which is illustrated in Figure 9.4. The model states that work attendance is a function of both motivation to attend and ability to attend. Thus, we might not come to work because we don't *want* to come to work (motivation), and/or because we are *prevented* from coming to work (ability). Job satisfaction, rather than being the direct cause of attendance, is seen as only one of the factors that determine attendance motivation. Thus, whereas satisfaction is an important component in the Steers and Rhodes model, it is easy to see how any of a variety of other factors could moderate the effects of satisfaction.

Subsequent research suggests that even this indirect role of the effects of job satisfaction on absenteeism may be exaggerated. For example, Watson (1981) found that personal characteristics such as age and marital status, and job characteristics such as tenure and shift work, predicted job satisfaction. The correlations between satisfaction as measured by the Job Descriptive Index (see page 324) and absence were very low, however, ranging from $-.09$ to $.08$ (Watson, 1981). Keller (1983) also found that nonattitudinal variables predicted attendance better than did satisfaction. In general, the research evidence provides little reason to expect any consistent relationship between workers' satisfaction and absenteeism.

Before leaving the topic of absenteeism, and in light of job satisfaction's failure to live up to psychologists' expectations in this regard, we should mention that some variables *do* predict who will come to work. Among the best of these, not surprisingly, is a worker's previous history of absenteeism (for example, Breaugh, 1981). Also predictive of attendance is work-group cohesiveness

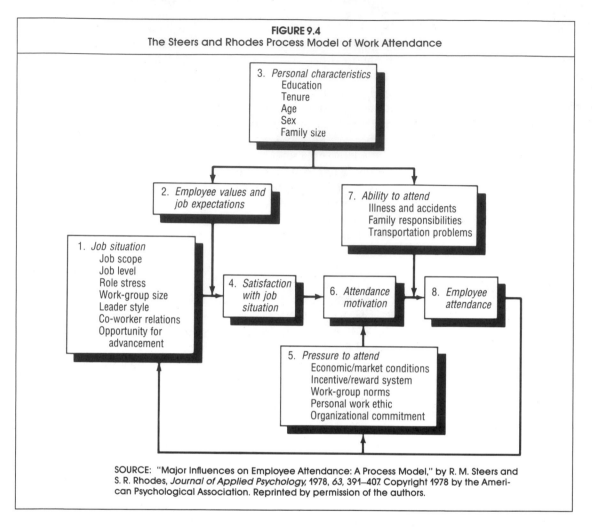

FIGURE 9.4
The Steers and Rhodes Process Model of Work Attendance

SOURCE: "Major Influences on Employee Attendance: A Process Model," by R. M. Steers and S. R. Rhodes, *Journal of Applied Psychology,* 1978, *63,* 391–407. Copyright 1978 by the American Psychological Association. Reprinted by permission of the authors.

(Keller, 1983). Steers and Rhodes (1978) suggested that members of smaller work groups have fewer absences because small groups develop greater cohesiveness or closeness than do larger groups. This seems to be true, whether work-group size is varied across groups or across time. Markham, Dansereau, and Alutto (1982) studied 66 work groups that changed in size during the period of the research. In 74 percent of these groups, the researchers found a significant negative relationship between group size and absenteeism.

Chadwick-Jones, Nicholson, and Brown (1982) have taken a new approach to understanding absenteeism. Their theory is not based on the common assumption, explicit in the Steers and Rhodes model, that absenteeism is based on an *individual's* motivation, satisfaction, and ability to attend. Rather, they offer a **social-exchange** explanation for absenteeism. In this view, employers will tolerate a certain level of absence in return for such behaviors as loyalty to the company, hard work, or innovative ideas. They also suggest that group norms and co-worker expectations concerning attendance play an important role. The research of Dalton and Perry (1981) supports this line of thought. Comparing absenteeism rates in a number of organizations, Dalton and Perry found that those organizations paying higher wages had higher rates of absenteeism. This suggests that workers will be absent more if they can *afford* to be absent. Dalton and Perry also found greater absenteeism in companies where sick leave accumulates fast and where unused sick leave is not remunerated. Such policies pressure workers to "use or lose" their sick-leave benefits, and it should not be surprising that absenteeism is the result.

The exchange model of absenteeism should be carefully considered by the management at Peter's Pan Pizza. Company policy on such matters as sick leave, vacation, and maternity leave may account for much of their absenteeism problem. In a similar fashion, it is possible that the workers may have developed norms or expectations about what they can "get away with," and that these norms have only recently developed to the point that management is aware of their effects. In any case, it would be unwise to ignore these possibilities, particularly given the low probability that the problem will be solved by efforts to improve satisfaction.

The second form of withdrawal, turnover, is also a potentially costly problem for organizations. When a productive employee quits her job, the employer is faced with the costs and inconvenience of recruiting, selecting, and training a replacement. Turnover also has the potential for disrupting social relationships within work groups, which may have implications for the performance of workers remaining on the job. We should be careful, however, not to view *all* turnover as avoidable, dysfunctional, or problematic. Dalton, Krackhardt, and Porter (1981) found that among the tellers in 190 bank branches, 52 percent of all turnover was *unavoidable*. That is, the tellers quit for reasons related to their families, educational opportunities, or other personal concerns. They also found that 71 percent of all turnover was functional, in that the employee who left was later rated by supervisors as having performed unsatisfactorily. Whereas we suspect that some of these low performance ratings may have been given *because* the employee quit (what manager wants to admit that a good employee got away?), it is clear that *some* voluntary turnover represents a useful process by which unsatisfactory or marginal employees remove themselves from the organization. It's likely that many of these people, had they stayed on the job, would have become victims of *involuntary turnover;* they would have been fired.

Although some turnover may be functional, all organizations occasionally lose valuable employees, making turnover an important practical concern. The most popular model of the turnover process was developed by Mobley (Mobley, 1977; Mobley, Griffeth, Hand, & Meglino, 1979; Mobley, Horner, & Hollingsworth, 1978). The Mobley model of turnover is presented in Figure 9.5. In this model, job satisfaction is viewed as having no *direct* effect on turnover. Rather, the model specifies that dissatisfaction causes the employee to *think* about quitting. This in turn leads to the decision to search for a different job, provided that acceptable alternatives to the current job are available. Depending on the

---

social exchange: a form of interpersonal interaction in which one party performs certain acts in return for considerations from another party

FIGURE 9.5
The Mobley Model of Turnover

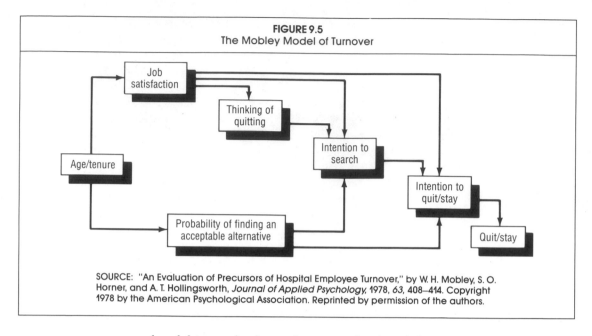

SOURCE: "An Evaluation of Precursors of Hospital Employee Turnover," by W. H. Mobley, S. O. Horner, and A. T. Hollingsworth, *Journal of Applied Psychology,* 1978, *63,* 408–414. Copyright 1978 by the American Psychological Association. Reprinted by permission of the authors.

results of this search, the employee next develops definite intentions about either staying or quitting. This intention to quit is, according to the model, the immediate precursor of quitting. As a theory of the turnover process, the Mobley model has yielded some evidence of validity. Although the specific relationships among the variables in the model vary across studies, Mobley and a number of other researchers have found general support for the model, particularly for the idea that intention to quit is the best single predictor of actual turnover (Michaels & Spector, 1982; Miller, Katerberg, & Hulin, 1979; Mobley, Horner, & Hollingsworth, 1978; Mowday, Koberg, & McArthur, 1984; Youngblood, Mobley, & Meglino, 1983).

An important aspect of Mobley's model is the role of labor-market conditions in the turnover decision. Even if they are dissatisfied, even if they have thought about quitting, and even if they have gone as far as to look for another job, workers will not intend to quit if there are no acceptable alternative jobs available. Indeed, Dreher and Dougherty (1980) found that the greater the competition in the labor market, the fewer the workers who resigned from their jobs. Concerns for future employment do not always influence intentions to quit, however. Michaels and Spector (1982), for example, did not find any effect for availability of alternative employment. They suggested that availability has no effect on intentions to quit, but rather that intentions to quit will only be *acted upon* if alternative jobs are available.

In general, research on turnover has shown that there is a link between job dissatisfaction and quitting. This link, however, is neither simple nor direct. Job dissatisfaction seems to trigger or contribute to a chain of decisions on the part of the worker, and the exact nature of those decisions will vary across individuals, jobs, and economic conditions. Consequently, many psychologists have suggested that in order to understand turnover, investigators should study variables more closely related to behavioral intentions. The most promising of these variables is organizational commitment. We will briefly examine the issue of commitment, for it provides insight into why job satisfaction is not more closely related to turnover.

Organizational commitment is defined as the relative strength of an individual's identification with, and involvement in, a particular organization. It is characterized by (1) a strong belief in and acceptance of the organization's goals and values; (2) a willingness to exert considerable effort on behalf of the organization; and (3) a strong desire to maintain membership in the organization (Mowday, Steers, & Porter, 1979). Mowday, Porter, and Steers (1982) carefully examined the role of organizational commitment in the turnover process, and concluded that it is far superior to satisfaction as a predictor of turnover. This may be because commitment is a general emotional reaction to a worker's employing *organization*, rather than to a specific job or set of tasks. Also, unlike satisfaction, commitment is thought to develop slowly, and is therefore not likely to change with day-to-day events in the workplace, whereas satisfaction is believed to be more sensitive to such events. Jackson, Stafford, Banks, and Warr (1983) illustrated the potential psychological importance of commitment in an examination of its effects on people who had lost their jobs. Although psychological distress was higher among unemployed persons than among those who were working, it was particularly high for those unemployed who had been highly committed to their organizations. As more research is conducted on the origins of commitment, we can expect to learn more about turnover, and perhaps better understand the role of job satisfaction in this complex process.

PERFORMANCE

Over the years, one of the most strongly held beliefs among managers, supervisors, and I/O psychologists has been that there is a relationship between a worker's job satisfaction and his performance. Unfortunately, this belief has not proved to be valid. For over 30 years psychologists have been looking for the link between satisfaction and performance, and for over 30 years they have found little or nothing of substance (Brayfield & Crockett, 1955; Vroom, 1964). Iaffaldano and Muchinsky (1985) speculated that one reason for the continuing research on satisfaction and performance, in the face of growing evidence that the two are largely independent, is a belief that the two variables *should* be related, and that more research might reveal the nature of that relationship. Using modern meta-analysis techniques, Iaffaldano and Muchinsky examined 217 correlations, found in the published research literature, between measures of satisfaction and performance. The mean correlation was .146, which is not only very small, but also virtually identical to the result obtained by Vroom 21 years earlier (Vroom, 1964).

The failure to find any clear association between satisfaction and performance has led many researchers to suggest that this relationship may be moderated by other variables. That is, perhaps the expected positive relationship between satisfaction and performance holds for certain people, but not for others, or in certain types of organizations, but not in others. To test this possibility, Iaffaldano and Muchinsky (1985) included information about factors such as white-collar vs. blue-collar samples, longitudinal vs. cross-sectional research designs, and quality vs. quantity performance measures in their meta-analysis. They concluded that these types of variables were "of little consequence" in understanding the satisfaction–performance relationship.

One condition not examined by Iaffaldano and Muchinsky (1985) that *may* make a difference is the manner in which rewards are administered in an organization. It appears that when rewards are based on performance, so that good performers receive greater rewards than poor performers, the satisfaction–performance correlation is positive, whereas inappropriate rewards result in negative correlations (Cherrington, Reitz, & Scott, 1971; Jacobs & Solomon, 1977; Podsakoff, Todor, & Skov, 1982).

Despite the lack of evidence that satisfaction is related to performance, psychologists continue to conduct research as if they were in fact related. For example, there has been a substantial amount of research examining the issue of whether the level of worker satisfaction causes, or has an effect on, the level of worker performance, or whether workers who perform better are more satisfied because they are able to demonstrate or use their skills. This research has tended to support the notion that people will become satisfied after performing well, rather than vice versa (for example, Wanous, 1974a). Indeed, Locke's (1968) research on goal setting suggests that people derive satisfaction from accomplishing difficult goals (see Chapter 8). There are instances, however, in which satisfaction *seems* to be causing performance (as an example, see Organ, 1977). Given the inconsistent and weak relationship between satisfaction and performance overall, these conflicting findings are hardly surprising. How can the question of whether satisfaction causes performance or performance causes satisfaction be answered when the two variables are, for the most part, independent? In general, it appears to us that psychologists interested in performance would better spend their time studying variables other than satisfaction.

Satisfaction and Personal Characteristics

Another line of satisfaction research has attempted to identify certain types of people who tend to be more satisfied than others. Research on these personal or demographic characteristics typically involves comparing job satisfaction ratings for different subsamples, such as men and women, blacks and whites, the young and the old, and so forth. Table 9.1 contains data from a longitudinal survey conducted during the 1970s (Weaver, 1980). The most striking aspect of these data is that, overall, different types of people seem to have about the same level of job satisfaction. There are some differences between groups in this table that are consistent with other research findings, though. For instance, whites tend to report higher levels of satisfaction than blacks, although the size of the differences is, on the average, quite low (Moch, 1980; Weaver, 1977). Both blacks and whites, however, seem to derive satisfaction from the same aspects of their jobs (Weaver, 1978a). In a similar fashion, older workers and those with more education report greater satisfaction than those who are younger or less educated. Also, not surprisingly, workers with professional and managerial jobs, and those who are paid more, have greater satisfaction than lower-level, lower-paid workers. Again, however, these differences tend to be very small, accounting for approximately 2 to 5 percent of the variance in satisfaction ratings (Weaver, 1977).

As indicated in Table 9.1, overall differences in the job satisfaction of men and women are small and inconsistent. Any sex differences in job attitudes, however, are likely to be related to differences in education, pay, and tenure. Thus, if you compare men and women who are equal on these variables, you should find no sex differences in satisfaction (Hulin & Smith, 1964; Sauser & York, 1978). Recent research has supported this conclusion. Smith and Plant (1982) compared 51 male and 51 female university professors who had been

TABLE 9.1 Mean Job Satisfaction among Full-Time Workers in the United States, 1972–1978, by Selected Demographic Variables

| | Year of survey | | | | | | | |
Variable	1972	1973	1974	1975	1976	1977	1978	M
Race								
White	2.36	2.34	2.38	2.43	2.44	2.37	2.43	2.39
Black	2.09	2.32	2.17	2.34	2.13	2.36	2.01	2.19
Sex								
Male	2.32	2.31	2.35	2.44	2.41	2.33	2.38	2.36
Female	2.28	2.40	2.36	2.40	2.42	2.42	2.39	2.38
Education								
Grade school	2.32	2.22	2.28	2.32	2.32	2.33	2.35	2.31
High school	2.25	2.28	2.38	2.46	2.39	2.38	2.37	2.36
Some college	2.26	2.45	2.35	2.52	2.38	2.36	2.31	2.37
College degree or more	2.44	2.52	2.41	2.37	2.54	2.46	2.49	2.46
Age								
Less than 20	1.43	1.95	2.25	2.08	1.73	2.17	2.14	1.95
20–29	2.06	2.18	2.18	2.24	2.25	2.19	2.67	2.20
30–39	2.37	2.39	2.26	2.48	2.53	2.33	2.35	2.38
40–49	2.36	2.34	2.41	2.48	2.45	2.39	2.43	2.41
50 or more	2.51	2.46	2.55	2.55	2.53	2.55	2.55	2.53
Personal income*								
Less than $5,000	—	—	2.23	2.23	2.21	2.21	2.21	2.22
$5000–$6999	—	—	2.21	2.47	2.44	2.46	2.14	2.35
$7000–$9999	—	—	2.26	2.38	2.37	2.32	2.31	2.33
$10,000–$14,999	—	—	2.42	2.44	2.47	2.35	2.43	2.42
$15,000 or more	—	—	2.58	2.60	2.55	2.48	2.50	2.53
Occupation								
Professional–technical	2.48	2.45	2.48	2.50	2.61	2.46	2.55	2.50
Managerial–administrative	2.51	2.65	2.59	2.64	2.56	2.52	2.55	2.57
Sales	2.24	2.35	2.33	2.71	2.41	1.96	2.48	2.33
Clerical	2.27	2.32	2.25	2.47	2.37	2.33	2.28	2.33
Craftsmen–foremen	2.34	2.19	2.44	2.33	2.56	2.42	2.50	2.39
Operatives	2.13	1.99	2.12	2.15	2.14	2.26	2.18	2.14
Laborers	1.89	2.21	2.29	2.50	2.16	2.36	1.89	2.16
Service	2.20	2.42	2.24	2.42	2.30	2.41	2.31	2.33

*Not available for 1972 and 1973.

Note: 3 = very satisfied, 0 = very dissatisfied.

SOURCE: "Job Satisfaction in the United States in the 1970s," by C. N. Weaver. In *Journal of Applied Psychology*, 1980, 65, 364–367. Copyright 1980 by the American Psychological Association. Reprinted by permission of the author.

matched on years of service, education, organizational level (rank), and academic department. They found extremely small, yet significant, differences in the men's and women's satisfaction with supervision and satisfaction with co-workers, and no other attitude differences. Similarly, Fry and Greenfeld (1980) compared the work attitudes of male and female police officers. This study is particularly interesting because no sex differences were found despite the traditional masculine stereotype associated with this job. Finally, it seems that not only do men and women with comparable jobs have comparable levels of satisfaction, but as was the case with black and white workers, both men and women derive satisfaction from the same aspects of their jobs (Weaver, 1978*b*).

One danger in interpreting the literature on race and sex differences in job satisfaction is concluding that blacks and whites, and men and women, are equally satisfied. It should be kept in mind that in any single organization, such as Peter's Pan Pizza, very real differences may exist between the satisfaction levels of such groups. Further, simply because a difference in satisfaction can be explained by differences in pay, education, tenure, and the like, this does not make the low-paid, less-educated, short-tenured worker any happier. As long as segments of the population differ on variables such as these, differences in satisfaction are likely to exist.

Work and Nonwork Satisfaction

The relationship between work behavior and behavior off the job has been of interest to psychologists for many years. A particularly large body of literature has been generated by researchers studying the relationship between job satisfaction and other types of satisfaction. Psychologists have been especially interested in *nonwork satisfaction,* or the satisfaction a person experiences when engaging in activities away from the job, and *general life satisfaction,* or one's level of satisfaction considering all aspects of life, including both work and nonwork. If a person's feelings about work are related to feelings about other aspects of life, work may have important implications beyond the walls of the factory or office, and outside of the regular 40-hour workweek. At the same time, characteristics of a person's nonwork life may have implications for work behavior.

GARFIELD, © 1985 United Feature Syndicate, Inc.

Early research on the relationship between work and nonwork variables was conducted by Dubin (1956), who developed the notion of a central life interest. Central life interest refers to a person's preference for behaving or acting in specific locales or settings. Dubin classified people as having one of three basic central-life-interest patterns. The first he called *job-oriented* central life interest, which describes people who perceive their jobs as the focal points of their lives. The second pattern is *nonjob-oriented* central life interest, held by people for whom the job is not the primary activity in life, but who instead place more emphasis on such things as family, church, or other interests. The third type Dubin called *flexible-focus* central life interest. These people demonstrate no preference for either work or nonwork activities.

Whereas Dubin's (1956) categories help us classify the dominant interests in a worker's life, they do not explain the relationships between work and nonwork activities, and people's satisfaction with those activities. More recently, Kabanoff (1980) reviewed theoretical and philosophical writings on the nature of work, and identified three possible relationships between work and nonwork. The first of these is a *compensatory* hypothesis, which says that nonwork activities compensate for deficiencies in a person's work life, and vice versa. According to this hypothesis, there should be a negative relationship between work and nonwork satisfaction: Those with low job satisfaction will engage in satisfying nonwork activities, whereas people dissatisfied with their nonwork lives will seek satisfaction at the workplace. The second relationship is a *generalization* or *spillover* hypothesis, which specifies a positive relationship between work and nonwork satisfactions. Basically, this hypothesis says that satisfying aspects of one's job will make nonwork life more pleasant, whereas dissatisfying work elements will also spill over into other domains. The final hypothesis specifies a *segmented* relationship between work and nonwork satisfactions. This means that work and nonwork are independent in their effects on a person's attitudes and life.

Perhaps before worrying about the nature of the relationship between work and nonwork satisfaction, we should first be concerned with whether the two are related at all. As it turns out, there is both positive and negative evidence of such a relationship. Gechman and Wiener (1975) found that teachers with higher job satisfaction had better mental health, and concluded that job satisfaction leads to benefits in nonwork areas. Other researchers, however, found little evidence that satisfaction with one's job predicts satisfaction with life in general (London, Crandall, & Seals, 1977). Kabanoff (1980) found support in the literature for each of the compensatory, spillover, and segmentation hypotheses. He also found, however, that the relationships between work and nonwork attitudes were generally weak.

Kabanoff (1980) concluded, too, that the research on work and nonwork suffers from methodological problems that make interpretation difficult. One of the most basic of these problems is defining what is "work" and what is "nonwork." For example, if we define nonwork as everything that occurs outside the workplace, how do we classify the time spent traveling to work, mowing the lawn, or painting the house? By the same token, if the work–nonwork distinction is primarily psychological, based on differences in pleasure, freedom, or relaxation, how do we classify the on-the-job activities of people who enjoy their jobs and experience freedom and relaxation in the workplace? Based on his own data, Kabanoff supported a "conservative segmentalist" hypothesis, stating that work and nonwork are not consistently related, and that when they *are* related, the relationship tends to be weak (Kabanoff & O'Brien, 1980).

Despite the lack of evidence of any consistent relationship between work and nonwork satisfaction, another line of research has attempted to determine whether differences in job satisfaction *cause* differences in life satisfaction, or vice versa. Orpen (1978), using **causal correlational analyses,** found that the causal effects of work satisfaction were stronger than those of nonwork satisfaction among his sample of first-line managers. Schmitt and Mellon (1980), however, drew the opposite conclusion in a study of civil service employees. More recent research suggests that the causal effects may go in *both* directions. Schmitt and Bedeian (1982) examined the satisfaction ratings of 875 civil service workers, and concluded that high job satisfaction had a positive effect on life satisfaction, whereas life satisfaction also had a positive effect on job satisfaction. Near, Smith, Rice, and Hunt (1984) found a similar "cross-domain spillover effect" in a survey of 1515 working people. They found that living conditions had a reliable, although small, effect on job satisfaction, *and* that working conditions had a similar effect on life satisfaction. Chacko (1983) also found evidence for spillover effects in both directions, although he concluded that the effects from job to life satisfaction were more prevalent.

In general, whereas there may be relationships between work and nonwork satisfaction, the nature of the relationships remains ambiguous. Perhaps we should heed Kabanoff and O'Brien's (1980) advice, and abandon attempts to identify *the* relationship between work and nonwork, and focus instead on why people develop *different* work/nonwork patterns.

Summary of Job Satisfaction Correlates

The relationships between job satisfaction and other variables are fewer and weaker than psychologists once believed. There is no consistent relationship between satisfaction and absenteeism, and only an indirect association between satisfaction and turnover. Similarly, research has shown no meaningful relationship between job satisfaction and work performance. Only small differences in satisfaction across occupational and demographic groups have been discovered, and even these may be better explained by differences in pay, education, and job tenure. Finally, the relationships between job satisfaction and nonwork or general satisfaction are weak at best.

About now you may be wondering if job satisfaction is worth bothering with. We will address that specific question later in the chapter. One possible explanation for the negative results in satisfaction research, however, is that the measures of job satisfaction used by psychologists are somehow flawed. If these instruments do not really measure workers' attitudes toward their jobs, then we are unlikely to find meaningful results. In the following sections we examine several of these measures and present some of the more important issues in job-attitude measurement.

MEASUREMENT OF JOB SATISFACTION

In this chapter we have presented the results of a wide variety of research studies on the origins, correlates, and possible effects of job satisfaction. Without measures of worker satisfaction, this research, and the theories it has spawned, would not be possible. We will now turn briefly to some of the issues involved in measuring job satisfaction. At first glance, measuring satisfaction may seem to be a straightforward process. Closer examination, however, reveals that it is anything *but* straightforward.

Facet vs. Global Satisfaction

At the beginning of this chapter, we defined job satisfaction as a multifaceted construct. Job satisfaction measures clearly reflect this multidimensionality. Over the years, as researchers studied different job facets and investigated the multitude of variables that might be related to satisfaction, hundreds of different satisfaction measures were developed. Whereas these instruments have in common the purpose of gauging worker attitudes, they differ in many significant ways; most importantly, they differ in the specific facets of satisfaction that they are designed to measure.

The large number of job satisfaction measures in use has slowed the development of job satisfaction theory. Specifically, the use of different measures, no two of which yield completely comparable scores, has made it extremely difficult to accumulate information about satisfaction, or to compare the results of different studies. It has also contributed to the inconsistency in research results that we have encountered in this chapter. Addressing these issues, Schneider (1985) concluded that I/O psychologists should develop a single measure of *global*, or overall, job satisfaction. The widespread use of such a measure would avoid the problem of noncomparable data being gathered in different studies. Further, Schneider suggested that with a global satisfaction measure that could be used as both a dependent variable in studies of the causes of satisfaction, *and* as an independent variable in studies of the effects of satisfaction, sound theories of work attitudes might emerge.

Popular Job Satisfaction Measures

Psychologists have not agreed on a single measure of global job satisfaction, nor even that such a measure would be desirable. There *has*, however, been a trend in recent years for researchers to use one of a small number of standardized job satisfaction measures. In the following sections we will present two of these scales, as well as an interesting single-item scale that uses a unique approach to attitude measurement.

---

causal correlational analyses: statistical procedures designed to test for evidence supporting (but not proving) causal relationships among two or more variables; used primarily when experimental research designs are not feasible

THE JOB DESCRIPTIVE INDEX

The Job Descriptive Index (JDI) is far and away the most frequently used measure of job satisfaction. Developed by Smith, Kendall, and Hulin (1969), the JDI measures satisfaction with five facets of a worker's job: the work itself, supervision, pay, promotions, and co-workers. It is also possible to combine the facet measures to obtain a global-satisfaction measure (Hulin, Drasgow, & Komocar, 1982; Parsons & Hulin, 1982). A "job in general" scale was added in 1985.

Examples of the types of items used in the JDI follow. For each descriptive phrase or word, the worker indicates "Yes" if that phrase describes the relevant aspect of his job (that is, the work itself, pay, and so on), "No" if it does not describe that aspect of the job, and "?" if he is uncertain.

Work itself:	_____	Routine
	_____	Satisfying
	_____	Good
Pay:	_____	Bad
	_____	Well paid
	_____	Less than I deserve
Promotions:	_____	Dead-end job
	_____	Infrequent promotions
	_____	Good chance for promotion
Co-workers:	_____	Helpful
	_____	Lazy
	_____	Loyal
Supervision:	_____	Hard to please
	_____	Asks my advice
	_____	Around when needed
Job in general	_____	Better than most
	_____	Rotten
	_____	Acceptable

SOURCE: Adapted from *The Measurement of Satisfaction in Work and Retirement,* by P. C. Smith, L. M. Kendall, and C. L. Hulin. Copyright 1969 by Rand McNally and Company Job Descriptive Index copyright 1975; revised 1985 by the Department of Psychology, Bowling Green State University, Bowling Green, Ohio 43403. Reprinted by permission for this book. Rights to duplicate must be purchased from Bowling Green State University.

In general, although there is some evidence that the JDI may actually measure satisfaction with more than five job facets (Yeager, 1981), the reliability and validity of the scales appear to be good. For example, Johnson, Smith, and Tucker (1982) found three-week test–retest reliabilities from .68 to .88, and internal consistency reliabilities from .75 to .93.

The primary problem with the JDI is that there are many aspects or facets of jobs that are not included in the measure. Consider again the turnover problem in Peter's Pan Pizza's retail operations division. As we have seen, it is possible that job dissatisfaction is playing a role in this situation. Let's assume that the aspect of the job with which the store inspectors are most dissatisfied is the amount of time they must be away from home. The JDI would be inadequate for measuring these specific feelings.

THE MINNESOTA SATISFACTION QUESTIONNAIRE

Another popular job satisfaction measure is the Minnesota Satisfaction Questionnaire (MSQ; Weiss, Dawis, England, & Lofquist, 1967). The MSQ contains 100 items that measure satisfaction with 20 job facets:

1. Ability utilization
2. Achievement
3. Activity
4. Advancement
5. Authority
6. Company policies and practices
7. Compensation
8. Co-workers
9. Creativity
10. Independence
11. Moral values
12. Recognition
13. Responsibility
14. Security
15. Social service
16. Social status
17. Supervision–human relations
18. Supervision–technical
19. Variety
20. Working conditions

Even with 20 facets, however, there is no guarantee that the specific attitude of importance, such as satisfaction with travel policy, is being measured.

THE FACES SCALE

A unique approach to measuring global job satisfaction is represented by the Faces Scale (Kunin, 1955). A version of this single-item scale is shown in Figure 9.6. As a measure of global satisfaction, the Faces Scale appears to be quite good (Cook, Hepworth, Wall, & Warr, 1981). It also has the advantage of not relying on complex, often ambiguous verbal anchors, but using instead universally recognized facial expressions. The principle underlying the Faces Scale is flexible, and could probably be applied to the measurement of other attitudes.

FIGURE 9.6
The Faces Scale

Put a check under the face that expresses how you feel about your
<u>job in general</u>, including the work, the pay, the supervision, the
opportunities for promotion, and the people you work with.

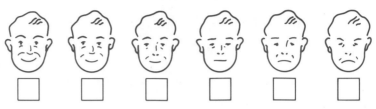

SOURCE: *The Measurement of Satisfaction in Work and Retirement,* by P. C. Smith, L. M.
Kendall, and C. L. Hulin. Copyright 1969 by Rand McNally & Company. Adapted from "The
Construction of a New Type of Attitude Measure," by T. Kunin. In *Personnel Psychology,* 1955,
8, 65–77. Copyright 1955 by Personnel Psychology, Inc. Reprinted by permission.

Custom Job Satisfaction Measures

The JDI and the MSQ measure only a limited range of all possible work attitudes.
Organizations such as Peter's Pan Pizza are often interested in more specific
worker attitudes for which standardized measures do not exist, such as satisfaction
with company policies. The common response to such a problem has been to
design a custom job satisfaction measure. Although it seems reasonable, this
task should not be undertaken lightly. It may be that the desired scale already
exists. Cook, Hepworth, Wall, and Warr (1981) identified about 250 work
attitude measures, providing a useful source of information about available
satisfaction scales. Also, developing a *good* satisfaction measure takes a lot of
time, work, and expertise. The JDI, the MSQ, and the Faces Scale are each a
product of long hours of work. It is doubtful that anyone with limited resources
could do as good a job.

Be that as it may, it is common for a researcher or organization to need a
specific measure of satisfaction for which there is no existing scale. The only
option in such circumstances is to develop a custom-made measure. A variety
of item formats can be used in attitude measures, three of which follow.

A. LIKERT FORMAT

Instructions: Indicate your agreement with the following statements, using the
following scale:

SA: Strongly agree
 A: Agree
 N: Neither agree nor disagree
 D: Disagree
SD: Strongly disagree

1. My work is boring.   SA   A   N   D   SD
2. My work is challenging.   SA   A   N   D   SD
3. My work is meaningful.   SA   A   N   D   SD
4. My work is unpleasant.   SA   A   N   D   SD

B. SEMANTIC DIFFERENTIAL FORMAT

Instructions: Mark (X) the point between each pair of words that best describes your job. Example: If you find your job extremely exciting, you would mark as shown below.

Boring ____ ____ ____ ____ __X__ Exciting

1.   Boring   ____ ____ ____ ____ ____ Exciting
2. Challenging   ____ ____ ____ ____ ____ Easy
3. Meaningful   ____ ____ ____ ____ ____ Useless
4.   Pleasant   ____ ____ ____ ____ ____ Unpleasant

C. CHECKLIST FORMAT

Instructions: Mark (X) the words in the following list that describe your job.

1. Boring   ____   5. Meaningful   ____
2. Exciting   ____   6. Useless   ____
3. Challenging ____   7. Pleasant   ____
4. Easy   ____   8. Unpleasant   ____

More important than the format of the questions, however, are the reliability and validity of the measure. An unreliable scale, or a scale that is not valid for the purpose for which it is used, will create more problems than it solves.

CONCLUSIONS

Schneider (1985) stated that whereas an aim of all management and motivation theories is to have a satisfied work force, we lack the comprehensive theories of the causes of satisfaction necessary to control worker attitudes. Since job satisfaction is one of, if not *the* most widely studied topic in I/O psychology, this is discouraging. Schneider suggested three hypotheses to explain the importance that researchers have apparently placed on job satisfaction. The first of these is that it is *easy* to study the relationship between job satisfaction and other variables. With the variety of satisfaction measures available, correlational studies of satisfaction and sex, age, status, and so on have proliferated, although as we have seen, the results concerning the causes of satisfaction are often less than conclusive.

The second hypothesis is that satisfaction is *expected* to be a useful predictor of important work behaviors. This predictive relationship seems to prevail for some behaviors, such as turnover, but research on the relationship of satisfaction with other behaviors, such as performance, seems to have progressed *in spite of* the accumulated empirical evidence. One general conclusion that can be drawn from this research is that job satisfaction is not as strongly related to work behaviors as the Hawthorne studies and the human relations movement once led us to believe.

Each of these first two hypotheses undoubtedly accounts for much of the satisfaction research activity. However, given the volume of data that has been generated, we know relatively little about *either* the causes of satisfaction *or* the effects of satisfaction. It is Schneider's (1985) final hypothesis, we believe, that captures the flavor of the most interesting satisfaction studies, and which seems to offer the best rationale for future research. This hypothesis states that satisfaction is simply an important human *outcome* of organizational life, and researchers study satisfaction because it is as much a part of work organizations as productivity, motivation, or anything else. All workers are more or less satisfied with the various aspects of their jobs. Those attitudes are important, if for no other reason than that they are experienced by workers. Until we study and understand job satisfaction in its own right, we are not likely to learn about its relationships with other behaviors.

CHAPTER SUMMARY

Job satisfaction is an attitude or "evaluative disposition" that people have toward their jobs. Because jobs are multidimensional, this attitude is most accurately perceived as a collection or network of specific attitudes toward specific job dimensions. The importance of these job attitudes was first brought to the attention of I/O psychologists through the pioneering research of the Hawthorne and Hoppock studies.

One of the earliest influential theories of job satisfaction was Herzberg's two-factor theory, which stated that job satisfaction and dissatisfaction stemmed from different aspects of the job. Research, however, has failed to support Herzberg's ideas. Most other satisfaction theories, including need theories, Locke's value theory, and Lawler's facet theory, propose that a worker's level of satisfaction results from a comparison between his or her current status (for example, level of need satisfaction) with some standard or ideal. Although this comparison notion is popular, research support for these theories has been mixed, at best.

Relatively recent approaches to understanding job attitudes suggest that satisfaction is based on social modeling of the attitudes and behaviors of other workers, or on attribution processes influenced by the work context. Both of these approaches emphasize the importance of social factors in work-attitude development.

Research has also examined the relationship between job attitudes and workers' behaviors. These efforts have found weak, inconsistent associations between satisfaction and absenteeism, and only somewhat stronger, indirect relationships between satisfaction and turnover. Similarly, only very small correlations between satisfaction and job performance, or between work attitudes and nonwork attitudes and behaviors, have been obtained.

A substantial amount of research has been dedicated to developing sound measures of job satisfaction. Notable among these measures are the Job Descriptive Index and the Minnesota Satisfaction Questionnaire, each of which measures satisfaction with a number of job dimensions or facets, and the Faces Scale, which uses a simple, single-response item to measure global job satisfaction.

INTEROFFICE MEMO
TO: Joanna Richmond, Director of Inspections
FROM: J. A. MacKeven, Human-Resources Coordinator

This memo is to follow up on our discussion of last Tuesday, and to provide you with a little more detail on what my staff and I have done with regard to the turnover problem in store inspections and Retail Operations in general.

The first thing we did was to examine the personnel records of the store inspectors who have left the company. We found that about 20 percent of the turnover was for personal reasons and classified as unavoidable. Another 20 percent was what we call "functional" turn-over—either the employees were fired or they probably would have been fired if they had not quit. The remaining 60 percent were employees in good standing who voluntarily left for other jobs. The majority of these have remained in the retail food business, but virtually none have taken inspection jobs.

Next, we conducted a job satisfaction survey of all retail operations employees. In addition to using a well-respected measure of job sat-isfaction known as the Job Descriptive Index, my staff interviewed a sample of the store inspectors. Based on those interviews, we devel-oped questions specifically addressing the issue of travel require-ments, as well as questions concerning intention to leave PPP. The results of the survey showed that the store inspectors are generally satisfied with the work they perform, their pay, and their supervi-sion, while being somewhat dissatisfied with the opportunities for promotion. The questions regarding travel clearly show that the inspectors are very dissatisfied with this aspect of their jobs. Also, over 50 percent of the inspectors said they were thinking about changing jobs.

Based on this information, I make the following suggestions:

1. The travel schedules of all store inspectors should be exam-ined, and if possible adjusted so as to minimize the time spent on the road.
2. When hiring new inspectors, be certain that the travel requirements are clearly understood by all prospective employees.
3. Consider changing the store inspection system so as to allow inspectors to live in the general area of the stores for which they are responsible, rather than working out of Suardell Springs.

REVIEW QUESTIONS AND EXERCISES

1. Dr. MacKeven seems to have focused on the issue of travel in making her recommendations. What other factors are implied by the data she gathered, and how do you think they should be dealt with?

2. Given what you know about the nature of the store inspectors' jobs, what variables *not* measured in Dr. MacKeven's survey might be expected to be related to their satisfaction levels and/or rate of turnover?

3. What steps, other than reducing travel requirements and improving other factors that could be causing employees to leave, might be taken to lower the overall turnover rate?

4. Evaluate each of Dr. MacKeven's recommendations. Upon which assumptions do they seem to be based? What are the "hidden costs" or possible disadvantages of each?

CHAPTER 10

Leadership and Management

Learning Points

After studying this chapter, you should

- be able to describe the different ways leadership has been defined over the years, and distinguish between leadership and management
- be able to describe French and Raven's bases of social power and how they relate to both formal and emergent forms of leadership
- understand the relationship between different personal traits and leadership, and be able to describe recent research findings on leader traits
- be able to describe the Ohio State leadership measures, and explain the importance of implicit theories for such measures of leader behavior
- be able to explain the basic principle of contingency theories of leadership, and evaluate Least-Preferred Co-worker and path–goal theories
- understand the purpose of the Vroom–Yetton normative theory of leadership, and describe how it is used
- be able to define vertical dyad linkage and average leadership style, and explain how they operate according to Vertical Dyad Linkage theory
- understand the potential importance of attribution processes and charisma in organizational leadership
- be prepared to speculate on the importance of leadership in organizations

INTEROFFICE MEMO
TO: J. A. MacKeven, Human—Resources Coordinator
FROM: Richard Roe, Senior Vice President, Frozen Foods

Following the acquisition by Peter's Pan Pizza of Flavio's Frozen
Italian Foods, and our subsequent entry into the frozen food market,
there were a number of changes in the way that Flavio's factories and
distribution network operate. I am writing to let you know about one
such change in the management of Flavio's, and to ask you for your
advice on a problem it seems to have created.

When Peter's Pan Pizza and Flavio's merged, top management felt that
it would be helpful to move managers who were familiar with PPP's
overall operation into positions at Flavio's. The expansion of
Flavio's operations at the time of the merger allowed us to move
these managers in without displacing any of the people at Flavio's.
Currently, about one—third of the lower— and middle—level managers in
frozen food production and distribution are former PPP managers.

In the six months following this move, I have noticed some problems,
primarily in four of the units supervised by former PPP managers.
First, production in these units is low, compared to similar units
supervised by people who had been with Flavio's before. Second, there
has been an increase in the number of grievances against management
from these units. Third, in talking to the managers themselves, I
have been told that their workers are unresponsive to efforts to deal
with these problems.

I realize that there could be many explanations for these events,
such as a lack of familiarity with the frozen food industry. However,
the managers involved are not novices, and were placed in jobs that
were similar in terms of management responsibility to those they held
at PPP. I would like you to look into this and suggest what should be
done to remedy the situation.

The memo from Richard Roe suggested a leadership problem to Dr. MacKeven. Because the actual operation of Flavio's Frozen Foods had changed little since the merger with Peter's Pan Pizza, it did not seem likely to Dr. MacKeven that changes in procedure were responsible for the problems Mr. Roe had reported. Further, the lower production and increased number of grievances were found only in some of Flavio's production and distribution units, and in each case these units were among those whose managers had recently transferred from PPP's retail division. Because the new managers were the only substantial changes in these units, it seemed likely to Dr. MacKeven that the events described by Mr. Roe were related to the new managers, and to the employees' reactions to the managers.

In this chapter we will explore the topic of organizational leadership and supervisory influence. As you will see, Dr. MacKeven is faced with a great deal of conflicting research and theory concerning what makes a person a good leader. In the following pages we will look at several approaches to leadership, and discuss how they might apply to the problem in Flavio's Frozen Foods. First, however, we will need to define exactly what we mean when we use the term "leadership," and just as important, what we *don't* mean when we call someone a leader.

THE NATURE OF ORGANIZATIONAL LEADERSHIP

Leadership is one of the most widely researched topics in I/O psychology. Stogdill (1974) reviewed and summarized the published research on leadership, and his work was later updated and expanded by Bass (1981). Whereas Stogdill's book summarized over 3000 published works, Bass cited more than 5000 studies only seven years later. Leadership has clearly been an important topic in psychology and, based on the continued growth of leadership research, it is safe to predict that it will continue to be a major area of discussion and debate in the future.

Definitions of Leadership

With so much research on leadership, you might assume, or at least hope, that psychologists are in fairly good agreement about what leadership is. Unfortunately, this is not the case. Bass (1981) described the situation well when he said "There are almost as many different definitions of leadership as there are persons who have attempted to define the concept" (p. 7). He went on, though, to group the definitions into several categories. We'll look at some of these general approaches to leadership, and then present a definition that takes most of them into account. It is important to develop such a definition because without it we would be unable to either adequately describe what we expect from leaders, or to study their behavior and identify ways to improve their effectiveness. Keep in mind that some of the following definitions of leadership are considered by most psychologists to be far too simplistic by today's standards.

Many of the basic ideas contained in these definitions, however, have been incorporated into the modern theories that we will discuss.

LEADERSHIP AS PERSONALITY

This approach claims that leadership is determined by certain personality traits or characteristics (for example, Bernard, 1926; Jenkins, 1947). People with these traits have the potential to influence others and become leaders, whereas people without these traits are destined to be followers. This definition would imply that the managers who had transferred from Peter's Pan Pizza into Flavio's Frozen Foods simply have the wrong personalities. Personality is the basis for the trait theories of leadership that we will discuss later.

LEADERSHIP AS INFLUENCE

When we define leadership as influence, we are saying that leader behavior has some desired effect on follower behavior. This approach does not really suggest reasons for leadership problems, such as in Flavio's Frozen Foods, but it does stress the fact that leadership involves people getting others to do what they want. The notion of influence is implied by most modern definitions of leadership (House & Baetz, 1979).

LEADERSHIP AS BEHAVIOR

This is a deceptively simple definition of leadership. Assuming that you know who the leaders in an organization or group are, leadership is defined as those behaviors in which the leaders engage (Fiedler, 1967; Hemphill, 1949). In practice, this approach has virtually always equated leadership with *managerial* or *supervisory* behavior. Ineffective leadership, such as in Flavio's Frozen Foods, results when supervisors engage in the wrong (that is, ineffective) behaviors. You should notice an important difference between this approach and the influence definition of leadership. If you define leadership as influence, then you must examine the behavior of the followers to see whether or not leadership has taken place. If you view leadership as simply the behavior of people in supervisory positions, then the reactions of the followers are less important.

LEADERSHIP AS POWER

According to Raven and French (1958a, b), power is the extent to which one person (the leader) can exert more force on other group members than they, in turn, can exert to resist the leader's intentions. It should be clear that power depends upon the reactions of followers as well as the behavior of leaders. In fact, unlike most leadership definitions, the power approach does not automatically assume that supervisors and managers are the only leaders in an organization. Depending upon their ability to influence others, *all* members of an organization can, at times, be leaders. For example, perhaps some of the new managers in Flavio's Frozen Foods lack the necessary power to overcome workers' resistance to their plans or policies. Of course, it could also be that some of the workers have enough power to have become strong leaders themselves. Because power is such a prominent characteristic of formal organizations, we will discuss it in more detail later.

LEADERSHIP AS GOAL ACHIEVEMENT

This view of leadership stresses the outcome of behavior, in terms of whether or not it helps the group or organization achieve its goals (Bellows, 1959; Cowley, 1928). Whether the leader was effective because of power, personality, coercion, or for other reasons is not particularly important, as long as the organization's goals are met. As was the case with influence definitions, goal achievement illustrates an important aspect of leadership, but it does not suggest why problems might exist.

LEADERSHIP AS AN ATTRIBUTION

This view of leadership, which is currently gaining popularity, emphasizes that leadership does not, by itself, affect important outcomes in organizations. Rather, it is an attribution, or an explanation used by people to account for events in the workplace (Calder, 1977; House & Baetz, 1979; Pfeffer, 1977, 1981). This definition suggests that the problems in Flavio's Frozen Foods may not be due to leadership issues, but that people, including Mr. Roe and Dr. MacKeven, naturally **attribute** what happens in organizations to leaders.

LEADERSHIP AS A DYADIC RELATIONSHIP

This is another approach that has emerged in recent years (Dansereau, Graen, & Haga, 1975; Graen, Novak, & Sommerkamp, 1982; Liden & Graen, 1980). The basic idea is that leadership depends not only on the behavior, personality, power, and so forth of the leader, but also on the reactions of the followers, which in turn have implications for the leader's subsequent behavior. This approach says that a **dyadic,** or one-on-one, relationship develops between leaders and each of their followers. Consequently, leaders interact with their subordinates in different ways, depending on the nature of the individual dyadic relationships. Whereas other definitions imply that dyadic relationships between leader and follower are important, this approach views the dyadic relationship as the *essence* of leadership. Returning again to Flavio's Frozen Foods, this definition suggests that the new managers have not yet established dyadic relationships with their workers, or perhaps that they have attempted to establish relationships with which the employees are not comfortable (for example, giving the workers too much or too little responsibility).

Given the diversity of opinion about the nature of leadership, you might wonder if it is even possible to come up with a single meaningful definition. For our purposes, a good definition of leadership is one that is general enough to accommodate various theories and research studies, while being specific enough to distinguish leadership from other organizational phenomena such as motivation or job satisfaction. We believe that the following definition meets these standards: Leadership is social influence in an organizational setting, the effects of which are relevant to, or have an impact upon, the achievement of organizational goals. Let's examine the implications of this definition.

First, leadership is social influence. This means that leadership takes place when one person determines, at least in part, the behavior of other people. We are *not* dealing with leadership when behavior is determined by situational factors generally beyond individual control, such as the level of noise or the temperature of the work environment, or by characteristics of the worker, such as skill level or temperament. Rather, leadership occurs when the behavior of one person results in behavior on the part of others that would not have otherwise occurred.

Some people, notably Pfeffer (1977), have argued that leadership, defined as social influence, cannot be distinguished from other forms of social influence. Consequently, Pfeffer argues that leadership is redundant with the concept of influence itself, and is therefore unnecessary for understanding behavior in organizations. We disagree with Pfeffer. Along with House and Baetz (1979), we believe that leadership has unique characteristics that do distinguish it from other forms of social influence. The first of these is the organizational setting in which leadership takes place. Organizations have certain formal and informal structures, rules, and processes that both limit some opportunities for influence while creating others. These structures and rules also define, to a large extent, the means by which influence can be attempted. The second characteristic is the general purpose of leadership, namely to help the organization achieve its goals. Influence concerning issues other than goal achievement, whether it occurs within the organization or outside of the organization, is *not* leadership, whereas influence that helps determine organizational performance *is* leadership. Together these two aspects of leadership distinguish it from other types of influence.

To show how this definition can accommodate various approaches to leadership, consider that social influence can be based on many factors, including the personality of the leader (Mills & Bohannon, 1980; Sanders & Malkis, 1982; Spector, 1982), the behavior of the leader (Butterfield & Powell, 1981; Tziner & Vardi, 1982; Weed & Mitchell, 1980), or the power held by the leader (Cobb, 1980; Price & Garland, 1981). It is important, however, that attempts to influence be accepted, for unless followers perceive such attempts as legitimate, leadership may be rejected (House & Baetz, 1979). One factor that could affect the acceptance of leadership is the type of attributions that followers make for the leader's behavior. Greater acceptance would be expected, for example, if followers attribute leaders' actions to expertise in the field, or concern for the welfare of the workers and the organization, rather than blind allegiance to company policy (Calder, 1977; Eagly, Wood, & Chaiken, 1978; Harvey & Weary, 1984).

The Scope of Leadership

Having defined what we mean by leadership, we should consider the ways in which leadership operates in organizations. Who are the leaders, and who are

---

attribute: to think of as belonging to, produced by, or resulting from something
dyadic: consisting of two units

the followers? This is not a simple question to answer, but, as we have explained, it is a question that should be carefully considered.

LEADERSHIP VS. MANAGEMENT

Leadership takes place in organizations, and in organizations some people have more **authority** than others. In this context, it is tempting to say that leaders are the people with the most authority, that is, the managers and supervisors. People who study leadership have generally taken this view. Nearly all theories of leadership are concerned with managerial influence and, in fact, the terms leadership and management are often used interchangeably. The temptation to equate leadership and mangement is apparently a very strong one. Wilpert (1982) commented on three presentations from a symposium on leadership. This symposium was intended, among other things, to address the differences between leadership and management and the relevance of leadership research for the practice of management (Bussom, Larson, & Vicars, 1982; Lombardo & McCall, 1982; Stewart, 1982). You would expect these papers to have made a clear distinction between leadership and management. Wilpert noted, however, that whereas each paper implied a difference between the two constructs, none of them described this difference, and all used the terms synonymously. Even Wilpert fell into this trap, making the assumption that "managers always perform some leadership function due to their organizational position" (p. 69).

How reasonable is this assumption? Do all managers perform leadership functions, as we have defined leadership? To answer these questions, we need to examine what is meant by "management" more closely. Mintzberg (1980) offered one popular view of management. After observing senior managers, he concluded that the manager's job could be described in terms of ten roles. These roles are grouped into interpersonal roles, informational roles, and decisional roles. As you can see from the following list, "leader" is only one of the ten managerial roles; most of the functions performed by managers are not directly related to leadership or even social (interpersonal) in nature. Thus, if all managers are leaders, they are many other things as well (Hunt, Sekaran, & Schriesheim, 1982).

INTERPERSONAL ROLES
1. *Figurehead:* Involves the performance of symbolic duties stemming from the manager's position as the head of the unit or organization.
2. *Leader:* Involves motivating employees to work toward achieving the goals of the organization, and establishing a beneficial work atmosphere.
3. *Liaison:* Involves establishing and maintaining contacts outside of the unit or organization for the purpose of obtaining necessary information or other resources.

INFORMATIONAL ROLES
4. *Monitor:* Involves collecting information necessary for proper unit or organizational functioning.
5. *Disseminator:* Involves the transmission of information coming from outside the organization or unit to its members.

6. *Spokesperson:* Involves the transmission of information generated by the unit or organization to the outside.

DECISIONAL ROLES

7. *Entrepreneur:* Involves changing the unit or organization to adapt to changes in the outside environment.
8. *Disturbance handler:* Involves handling disturbances or other unforeseen events.
9. *Resource allocator:* Involves making policy decisions about the use of resources.
10. *Negotiator:* Involves negotiating or bargaining with other organizations or with individuals.

SOURCE: Adapted from *The Nature of Managerial Work,* by H. Mintzberg. Copyright 1973 by Henry Mintzberg. Adapted by permission.

But do *all* managers act as leaders as a regular, day-to-day, part of their jobs? We think not. Mintzberg (1980) said that different managers emphasize different roles, depending on the functions of the units they manage. For example, when managers were asked to rate the importance of Mintzberg's roles, sales managers rated "leader" and the other interpersonal roles as being more important than did other managers (Alexander, 1979; Paolillo, 1981; Pavett & Lau, 1983). Pavett and Lau also found that lower-level managers rated the leader role as more important than did middle-level or upper-level managers. Thus it appears that not all managers are leaders, at least not to the same extent.

A second question about the scope of leadership concerns whether all leaders are managers. That is, do people have to be in positions of formal authority in order to exercise goal-relevant social influence? We strongly believe that they do not. There is no reason why anyone, given the right circumstances, can't exercise leadership in an organization. This is not to say that managers aren't more *likely* to be leaders, because they are more apt to have resources that are unavailable to other members of organizations. Managers are also more likely to exercise *broader* leadership, or to have influence over a wider variety of issues than nonmanagers. The ability to influence others, however, does not stem solely from formal authority.

BASES OF SOCIAL POWER

The potential for nonmanagerial leadership is illustrated by the various ways people come to have power in organizations. The best-known approach to studying social power was developed many years ago by French and Raven (1959). According to these authors, there are five distinct sources, or bases, of social power, and people's ability to influence others depends on the degree to which they possess one or more of these types of power.

Legitimate power stems from the acknowledgment that certain people in organizations have the *right* to lead others. This type of power usually takes the

---

authority: the power or right to give commands, enforce obedience, or take final action

form of accepting the authority of management to make decisions and enforce rules. Research has shown that power can be legitimized by election to a position (Goldman & Fraas, 1965; Hollander, Fallon, & Edwards, 1977; Hollander & Julian, 1970; Read, 1974) as well as appointment by an authority (Julian, Hollander, & Regula, 1969; Knight & Saal, 1984; Knight & Weiss, 1980). For example, Watson (1982) had student subjects select a leader for a management exercise. She found that the group members complied with the requests of the person whose authority had been legitimized in this fashion, whereas the influence attempts of other members were resisted.

Reward power concerns the ability of people to administer valued rewards, or to help others obtain desired outcomes. According to operant conditioning principles (Luthans & Kreitner, 1985; Scott, 1977), the effective use of reward power requires that the leader know which rewards are valued by each subordinate. It does little good to offer overtime as a reward if workers do not like their jobs or need the extra money and would prefer to spend more time at home. When monetary rewards are available, the use of reward power is usually simplified, because most people value money; indeed managers seem to prefer to use money as a reward when it is available (Hinton & Barrow, 1975; Kipnis, 1972).

Because people value things other than money, reward power is not limited to management. A person's co-workers or subordinates can administer rewards through the use of praise, attention, or ingratiation. This contrasts with legitimate power, which is necessarily limited to those people authorized by the organization.

Coercive power stems from the ability to impose penalties for failure to comply with influence attempts. Such penalties may involve either punishment or the withholding of rewards (Bass, 1981). As with reward power, coercive power is not limited to managers. Any person with the means to punish another, such as by filing grievances against a supervisor or refusing to cover for a co-worker who misses work, has the potential to exercise coercive power.

Several research studies have found that coercive power is used primarily in reaction to poor performance, whereas rewards are used in response to good performance (Greene, 1976; Sims, 1977, 1980; Sims & Szilagyi, 1975). This is true even though rewards are generally more effective than punishments for improving performance (Arvey & Ivancevich, 1980; Sims, 1980). The relative ineffectiveness of coercive power was demonstrated long ago by French and Raven (1959), who found that its use led to *conformity* on the part of followers. This means that whereas workers may publicly accept the leadership of coercive managers, they will privately reject it, and go along with influence attempts only while they are being watched. Coercion is therefore unlikely to result in long-term influence.

Expert power is based on perceptions of another person's competence or possession of knowledge necessary for the organization to achieve its goals. People who are believed to have expertise relevant to the organization's goals will be powerful. This should be especially true if the person is the sole source of that expertise. A substantial amount of research in the 1950s showed that people are indeed more easily influenced by the opinions of experts than by the opinions of nonexperts (for example, Mausner, 1953, 1954), and that expert information can improve performance (Levi, 1954; Torrance, 1953).

More recently, research on expert power has examined how it might interact with other variables. For example, Price and Garland (1981) found that followers were more willing to comply with the wishes of an expert leader when they thought that their own level of competence was low, rather than high. Knight and Saal (1983) examined ratings of leader expertise as a function of both leader sex and the sex-type of the group's task. When the group's task dealt with a topic that had been rated as "feminine" (early childhood education), we found that female leaders had higher expertise ratings than male leaders, although the female leaders were *not* more influential. Wiley and Eskilson (1982) examined perceptions of male and female managers as a function of the type of power the manager used. They found that the use of expert power resulted in more favorable ratings when the manager was male rather than female, whereas women received higher ratings when they used reward power.

Research on expert power has shown that perceptions of expertise can develop from either observing a person succeed (Mausner, 1954; Price & Garland, 1981) or simply being told that a person is an expert (Mausner, 1953). Knight (Knight & Saal, 1983; Knight & Weiss, 1980) has shown that perceptions of leader expertise can also be based on the expertise of the person who selects the leader. Knight and Weiss found that a group leader chosen by the experimenter was rated as having more expertise when the experimenter himself claimed to be an expert on the subjects' task than when he claimed to have no task expertise. Knight and Weiss also found that the leader selected by an expert was more influential than the leader chosen by a nonexpert.

Keep in mind that expert power depends on how much knowledge or expertise people *think* a person has. Newcomers are therefore likely to have to prove their ability on the job. This would be particularly true in a situation such as we have in Flavio's, where employees who have worked for the company for some time and who know the operation well are supervised by people without any experience in the organization.

The final base of power described by French and Raven (1959) is *referent power*. Referent power is based on attraction to the leader, and on subordinates' desires to be like the leader. This form of power is quite different from the other four, because it depends on the interpersonal relationships between workers, and is less dependent on job-related factors such as authority, rewards, or task knowledge. An example of a situation in which referent power is likely to be important is *charismatic* leadership, which we will discuss later in this chapter.

Whereas French and Raven's (1959) bases of power model is the best-known system for classifying sources of social influence, it has been criticized for several shortcomings (Bass, 1981). One problem concerns power that does not clearly fit into one of the five categories. For example, Allen and Panian (1982) found that the personal relationships between corporate managers and families controlling large amounts of stock in the corporation predicted the amount of power and control the managers had over their own careers. It is not clear whether this was due to a desire to identify with the stockholders (referent power), or if the relationship with the stockholders legitimized the managers' authority (legitimate power), or if some other process was operating.

There has been a great deal of research on French and Raven's (1959) approach to social influence, allowing us to evaluate the effectiveness of different types of power. Yukl (1981) reviewed 11 field studies that compared the effectiveness of French and Raven's power categories, and concluded that referent and expert power were more commonly associated with positive results. He also presented a list of recommended strategies for the effective use of other power bases as well; a brief summary is included below:

EXPERT POWER

1. *Promote an image of expertise.* Make sure that people are aware of your skills and special training. Avoid projects with a low probability of success, especially when starting out.
2. *Maintain credibility.* Avoid careless statements. Do not lie to subordinates.
3. *Act confident and decisive in a crisis.* Never express doubts or appear confused.
4. *Keep informed.* Technical knowledge is the basis for expert power.
5. *Recognize subordinate concerns.* Expertise that is irrelevant to the needs of the workers will not be effective.
6. *Avoid threatening the self-esteem of subordinates.* Do not use expertise to make subordinates feel ignorant.

LEGITIMATE POWER

1. *Make polite requests.* Do not emphasize status differences by being rude.
2. *Make requests in a confident tone.* Enthusiasm implies that the request is important.
3. *Make clear requests and check for comprehension.* If subordinates don't understand what is requested, all the legitimate power in the world won't help.
4. *Make sure that requests appear legitimate.* The supervisor's authority to make a request should be clear.
5. *Explain the reason for the request.* Do not assume that the logic for a decision is obvious.
6. *Follow proper channels.* Do not rely upon subordinates to implement your orders.
7. *Exercise authority regularly.* Frequent requests enhance legitimacy.
8. *Insist on compliance and check to verify it.* Noncompliance will undermine authority.
9. *Be responsive to subordinate concerns.* Understand the reasons for noncompliance.

REWARD POWER

1. *Be sure compliance can be verified.* Rewards cannot be administered if compliance cannot be checked.
2. *Be sure the request is feasible.* Subordinates will not comply if the request seems impossible.

3. *Be sure the incentive is attractive.* A reward is not a reward unless the subordinate desires it.

4. *Be sure that the leader is a credible source of the reward.* Subordinates must believe that the leader can deliver the reward.

5. *Be sure that the request is proper and ethical.* Rewards should not be perceived as bribes.

COERCIVE POWER

1. *Inform subordinates about rules and penalties for violations.* It is unfair to punish workers who are unaware of the rules.

2. *Administer discipline consistently and promptly.* Failure to act can encourage further disobedience.

3. *Provide sufficient warning before resorting to punishment.* Indicate what is expected and give subordinates a chance to learn from their mistakes.

4. *Get the facts before using reprimands or punishment.* Wrongful punishment will undermine respect for the manager's authority.

5. *Stay calm and avoid appearing hostile.* Managers who lose their tempers risk making the problem worse.

6. *Maintain credibility.* Follow through with punishments, but do not threaten to use punishments beyond your authority.

7. *Use appropriate punishments.* Actions should be consistent with policy and rules, as well as with the severity of the infraction.

8. *Administer warnings and punishments in private.* Embarassing a subordinate in public could lead to resentment and retaliation.

SOURCE: Adapted from G. A. Yukl, *Leadership in Organizations,* © 1981, pp. 47–58. Adapted by permission of Prentice–Hall, Inc., Englewood Cliffs, New Jersey.

These guidelines are useful in any situation involving leadership. Basically, Yukl advocates self-assurance, consideration for the people you are trying to influence, and careful planning, whatever type of power you attempt to use.

You should also recognize that the use of one basis of power might affect perceptions of the others. Greene and Podsakoff (1981) compared ratings of managers' use of the five bases of power in two paper mills. One of the plants had recently abandoned a performance-contingent incentive plan, whereas the other continued to use an incentive plan, as it had for the previous six years. Incentive plans of this type are good examples of the use of reward power. Greene and Podsakoff found that in the mill where the incentive plan had been abandoned, employees perceived an increased use of coercive power and a decreased use of reward, referent, and legitimate power. It is clear that although the change in policy concerned only the reward behavior of the managers, it had implications for the other sources of power as well.

EMERGENT LEADERSHIP

The concept of power illustrates that people other than managers and supervisors can be influential in organizations. To actually become a leader without the benefit of formal authority, however, may depend upon more than power. The development of leadership in previously leaderless situations is known as emergent leadership. Research on emergent leadership, much of it conducted by social psychologists in laboratory settings, typically involves a "leaderless group." This is a group of people, brought together for the purpose of the research, that is given a task to perform without a leader being appointed. Depending on the issue being studied, the researcher manipulates such independent variables as the number of group members, the nature of the group's task, or the sex composition of the group. The behavior of the group members is then observed in order to determine the effects of the independent variables on the emergence of leadership behaviors within the group.

Because the members of leaderless groups used in this type of research have no previous history of interaction, and because the groups lack the formal structures and rules found in all organizations, the generalizability of much of this research may be limited. It should be kept in mind, however, that people in organizations frequently work in **ad hoc** groups, such as committees and task forces, in which there is no formal leadership (Galbraith, 1977). Consequently, emergent leadership research may indeed have implications for certain organizational settings.

Bass (1981) listed several factors that have been found to be related to the emergence of leadership. For example, as you might expect, group members who attempt to lead or to control group interaction are more likely to emerge as leaders than are those who do not make such attempts (Gray, Richardson, & Mayhew, 1968). Emergence as a leader has also been found to be related to the amount of time group members spend talking (Lord, 1977; Stein & Heller, 1979), and to the quality of their talk and skill in communication (Alpander, 1974; Klauss & Bass, 1981). That is, the more people talk, the more likely they are to become leaders; the better they are at communicating information to other members, the more likely they are to assume leadership positions. Gintner and Lindskold (1975) examined the joint effects of talkativeness and expertise on emergence, and found that when the group members thought that a person was an expert, that person was likely to emerge as the leader no matter how much he talked. If the person was not thought to be an expert, then talkativeness increased chances for leadership. Other variables that have been found to be related to emergence are assertiveness (Megargee, Bogart, & Anderson, 1966), competence (Penner, Malone, Coughlin, & Herz, 1973; Winter, 1978), and the acceptance of other group members (Bass, 1967).

One factor that might be expected to affect leader emergence is the sex of the group members. Whereas women now account for more than half of the paid work force (U.S. Bureau of the Census, 1984), they are present in much smaller numbers in managerial positions. Kanter (1977) suggested that one reason there are relatively few women in management positions is that promotion to such jobs depends first on being perceived as having leadership ability (that is, emerging as an informal leader). There is a substantial amount of evidence that women are generally seen as having neither the ability to be leaders, nor the personal characteristics that are typically attributed to managers (Bass, Kruskell, & Alexander, 1971; Schein, 1973, 1975). These perceptions make the emergence of female leaders unlikely. There is evidence, too, that women have been reluctant to accept authority (Eskilson & Wiley, 1976; Megargee, 1969), which would also make them unlikely to engage in many of the behaviors associated with emergent leadership. Despite these apparent barriers to emergence, however, there is only limited evidence of sex differences in emergent leadership. Schneier and Bartol (1980), for example, found no difference in the proportion of men and women who emerged as leaders in a study of 52 leaderless groups from a personnel administration class. They also found that there were no differences in the behaviors of male and female leaders during the semester, and that the performance of groups led by women was the same as that of groups led by men.

One reason why sex differences in leader emergence have not been found is suggested by Eagly's (1983) review of the literature on sex differences in influence. She pointed out that there are many status differences favoring men, and many social pressures for women to accept the influence of men and for men to reject the influence of women in organizations. These factors are not present in the laboratory or the classroom. Eagly also stated that women in organizations tend to have low-status models, whereas men have high-status models, thereby perpetuating the tendency for men to be more influential and women to be more easily influenced. Eagly suggested that the relatively small sex differences found in leadership research are due to the absence of these types of social processes and pressures in laboratory settings, and that the tendency for men to emerge as leaders is probably stronger in organizations.

It is important to keep in mind that emergent leadership is not something that you can acquire singlehandedly. Rather, it is granted by the other people with whom you work. Consequently, the characteristics of the entire work group are important in understanding emergence. Lord, Phillips, and Rush (1980) examined the effects of sex and personality characteristics on emergent leadership in groups working on a variety of tasks. They found that both the sex and the personality of the subjects were related to leadership ratings, ratings of influence, and ratings of French and Raven's (1959) bases of social power. The most consistent finding was that women provided higher ratings on all measures than did men. Thus, although it may be difficult for female leaders to emerge, leaders, whether male or female, may emerge more readily if there are women in the group.

THEORIES OF LEADERSHIP

We have spent quite a bit of time discussing the issues of power and leader emergence. These are important topics because they illustrate that leadership is not limited to managers. However, as we stated earlier, most of the leadership theories that have been developed over the years are concerned with the influence exercised by managers and other supervisors. In the following sections we will describe and discuss several of these theories. You will notice that in the course of time new theories have emerged in response to the limitations of older theories. In this sense, leadership has been a truly "evolutionary" topic.

---

ad hoc: for a specific purpose only; without general authority

Trait Theories

Trait theories of leadership assume that leadership ability stems from certain characteristics shared by leaders that are lacking among nonleaders. In other words, leaders are different from nonleaders, and those differences account for the ability of leaders to be influential. The trait approach to leadership has its roots in what has come to be known as the "great man" theory. If this name sounds sexist, that's because it is; it reflects an attitude that has prevailed over the years that one necessary characteristic of a leader is that he be male. The great man theory is based on the assumption that the course of history and the nature of society have been shaped by individual acts. Examples include the decision of Queen Isabella of Spain to fund the expedition of Columbus (which certainly raises questions about the masculine nature of great leadership); Jefferson's decision to purchase the Louisiana Territory from France, thereby expanding both the borders and the natural wealth of the United States; and Eisenhower's decision to proceed with the D-Day invasion of Normandy during a storm, thereby catching the German defenders off guard.

In the 19th century, Sir Francis Galton, a British scientist who was strongly influenced by Charles Darwin's theory of evolution, examined the hereditary background of eminent men. He found that such men tended to have had eminent fathers, and tended themselves to have eminent sons (Galton, 1869). This resulted in a movement known as "social Darwinism," which stated that socioeconomic standing was the result of traits inherited by the higher classes in society. Because most of the leaders of that time came from these higher classes, this implied to the adherents of social Darwinism that leadership ability was also inherited.

TRAIT RESEARCH

The emphasis on great leaders naturally led to attempts to identify those characteristics that distinguish leaders from nonleaders. Until the late 1940s, most leadership research was designed to identify these traits.

Stogdill (1948) reviewed the early literature on leader traits, and found consistent evidence that leaders were higher than other members of their work groups on such characteristics as intelligence, scholarship, dependability, activity, participation, and socioeconomic status. Stogdill also found that leaders tended to score higher on measures of sociability, initiative, persistence, self-confidence, insight, popularity, adaptability, cooperativeness, verbal skills, and task knowledge. More important than having summarized the traits relating to leadership, however, Stogdill concluded that people do not become leaders simply because they possess a certain combination of traits, but rather that these traits must be appropriate for the situations in which leaders find themselves. In other words, leadership depends on an interaction between the characteristics of the leader and those of the environment, including followers, organizational goals, competition from outside the group, and so on. Stogdill based this conclusion on the fact that whereas some traits were frequently found among leaders, no single trait was *necessary* for leadership. Further, the traits associated with successful leadership varied from situation to situation.

Stogdill's (1948) paper had the effect of nearly halting research on leadership traits, as researchers sought to identify situational and behavioral variables related to leadership. As Stogdill (1974; Bass, 1981) later pointed out, his 1948 review was widely misunderstood. He did not intend to imply that personal characteristics were unimportant, but rather that their importance could be determined only in the context of specific organizational situations. Thus, research that examines situational characteristics but ignores characteristics of the leader is not better than early trait research that ignored the situation. Stogdill's (1974) review of the trait research from 1947 to 1970 uncovered sufficient evidence to conclude that such traits as responsibility, self-confidence, influence, and persistence distinguished leaders from nonleaders, and in some cases effective leaders from ineffective leaders. Similarly, a recent meta-analysis of the early leadership-trait literature by Lord, De Vader, and Alliger (1986) showed that the relationships between perceptions of leadership and intelligence, masculinity, and dominance were substantially stronger than those suggested by the reviews of Stogdill and others (Mann, 1959). These authors also pointed out that this literature addresses the relationship between leader traits and *perceptions* of leadership, not between traits and leader *effectiveness*. Nevertheless, Stogdill's review essentially halted leadership research involving these types of traditional personality traits.

MOTIVATION TO MANAGE

One trait that has received a lot of attention in recent years is managerial motivation. Miner (1965, 1978b) developed a model of motivation appropriate for managers in large, bureaucratic organizations. Based on previous research describing effective managers in large organizations, Miner concluded that an effective pattern of motivation involves having positive attitudes toward performing a number of behaviors:

1. Managers must be able to obtain support from those at higher levels, and thus should have a positive attitude toward their superiors.
2. Because resources, both within and outside of organizations, are limited, managers must be favorably disposed toward engaging in competition for those resources.
3. Managers are expected to take charge of situations and take disciplinary actions as needed. This behavior requires an active and assertive nature, and those preferring more passive roles are not likely to be successful.
4. Managers must direct and control the behavior of subordinates, and therefore should feel comfortable using both rewards and punishments.
5. Because of their status relative to other members of the organization, managers must assume a position of high visibility and perform behaviors that invite attention and perhaps criticism. People who are uncomfortable

with this type of behavior will not be likely to engage in effective managerial behavior.

6. Management involves more than supervising the work behavior of others. There are also a wide variety of administrative duties that involve repetitive, detailed work. Managers must be willing to perform, and preferably enjoy, such work. Those not willing to attend to such details are destined to failure.

SOURCE: Adapted from "Twenty Years of Research on Role-Motivation Theory of Managerial Effectiveness," by J. B. Miner. In *Personnel Psychology*, 1978, *31*, 739–760. Copyright 1978 by Personnel Psychology, Inc. Adapted by permission.

Miner (1978*a*) also developed a projective test of managerial motivation called the Miner Sentence Completion Scale. As the name implies, this test involves completing partial sentences, and is based on the theory that people will "project" their personalities into their responses. (This is the same principle that operates in the famous Rorschach "inkblot" test, where personality characteristics are supposedly revealed in people's descriptions of inkblots.) Miner's test is scored to give measures of a person's willingness to engage in the six types of behavior described in the preceding list.

Research has shown that high motivation to manage, as measured by Miner's scale, is related to both promotion within organizations and to managerial performance (Miner, 1965, 1967, 1977*b*, 1978*b*). Miner has also found that university students with high motivation to manage are more likely to include managerial activities in their career plans (Miner, 1968*a*, 1968*b*; Miner & Crane, 1981; Miner & Smith, 1969). Significant differences between the motivation-to-manage scores of male and female managers have generally not been found (Miner, 1974*a*, 1977*a*), but both Miner (1974*b*) and Bartol, Anderson, and Schneier (1981) reported that female business students scored lower on some scales of Miner's test, indicating lower motivation to manage. Bartol et al. also found that black students scored lower than white students on some of the scales.

Bartol et al. (1981) suggested that the reason for these differences between managers' and students' results is that people who are in managerial positions obtained their status through high motivation to manage, whereas student samples include those lower in motivation who will probably not succeed as managers. This suggestion is troubling, given that women and minorities are among the students who score lower on the test. It is also interesting to note that when managers in smaller, nonhierarchical organizations have been examined, motivation to manage has not been correlated with success or performance (Miner, 1967, 1977*a*). It is possible that behaviors not measured by Miner's test are important in smaller organizations (Yukl, 1981).

Let's assume that Dr. MacKeven believes that the problems in Flavio's production and distribution units might be due to a lack of motivation to manage on the part of the new supervisors. Let's also assume that she gives these supervisors the Miner Sentence Completion Scale, and finds, as she suspected, that the managers in the poorly performing units have lower motivation to manage than the other managers. The most direct solution to this problem would be to replace these managers with others who are higher in motivation to manage.

Given that characteristics such as motivation to manage are based on a number of personality traits that develop throughout life, it should be difficult to change these motives in a reasonably short period of time. However, Miner (1975) has developed a training course designed to increase managerial motivation by teaching managers and potential managers to behave in a manner consistent with his six managerial roles. He has found that this course significantly increases scores on the Miner Sentence Completion Scale (Miner, 1978b), although it is not clear whether the training has actually changed managerial motivation, or only trained the managers how to get higher scores on the test.

SEX

Sex is an important trait to consider in leadership for at least two reasons. First, everyone is either male or female, and to the extent that there are sex differences in leadership, those differences will have implications for all organization members. Second, the practical importance of sex in organizations has recently become more obvious due to the increase in the number of women in the work force. According to U.S. Census Bureau figures, in 1982 women accounted for 51 percent of the paid work force aged 15 or older, and 37 percent of the year-round, full-time workers (U.S. Bureau of the Census, 1984). These figures reflect a steady growth in women's representation in the work force over the years. The same census report also showed that in 1982 there were 2.6 million women classified as full-time executives, managers, and administrators. This accounted for 29 percent of these jobs, and 11 percent of full-time working women. These figures represent a substantial increase over those reported by Baron (1977), which showed that only 18 percent of managers were women, and only 5 percent of women workers were managers. One fact that has not changed concerns the salaries of women managers. The 1984 Census Bureau report showed that the median income of male managers was $28,820, whereas the median income of female managers was $17,326. This was partially due to women having less seniority and holding lower-level managerial positions than men, but illegal wage discrimination undoubtedly contributed in some cases.

A number of explanations for the history of sex inequality in management have been suggested. Recall that Eagly (1983) suggested that because of status differences between traditional male and female occupations, and status differences of male and female role models, women tend to be both less influential and more easily influenced than men. This difference should make it less likely that women would emerge as informal leaders, which in turn would make it less likely that they would be appointed or promoted to formal management positions. Another barrier to the emergence or appointment of female leaders is the popular stereotype that women are less suited to be leaders or managers than are men (Bass, Kruskell, & Alexander, 1971; Rosen & Jerdee, 1973; Schein, 1973, 1975). To the extent that people believe that women, as a group, do not possess the skills necessary for management, women are not likely to obtain managerial jobs. Further, it has been shown that when women are successful, this success is likely to be attributed to factors beyond their control, such as luck, whereas men's success is attributed to their skill (Deaux & Emswiller, 1974). These attribution differences should also have negative implications for women managers.

White, Crino, and DeSanctis (1981) identified two general barriers to women's success and effectiveness as managers. The first of these is a lack of encouragement and appropriate training that results in low interest in management on the part of many women. The second is prejudice and discrimination on the part of people in organizations, who either believe that women are not capable of being good managers, or who simply do not want women in positions of authority. The lack of encouragement and management training results in relatively few women seeking leadership positions, while prejudice often prevents those women who are interested in management from succeeding.

White et al. (1981) noted that whereas there have been a number of programs designed to help women develop managerial skills, the validity and utility of these programs have not been clearly demonstrated. In addition, Gordon and Strober (1975) suggested that although little has been done to recruit women managers, much of the recruiting that *has* taken place has been in response to EEOC pressure, and represents efforts to avoid lawsuits more than change in attitudes toward women.

Another area of research concerns the effectiveness of female managers. Whereas Bass (1981) concluded that men and women do differ on a number of traits related to leader emergence, once a woman is in a managerial position her behavior is not likely to be different from that of her male counterparts. The weight of the evidence shows that there are more similarities between male and female managers than there are differences on such factors as the characteristics associated with success (Gaudreau, 1975; Kanter, 1977), work-group performance (Bartol, 1978), and employee satisfaction (Bartol, 1974, 1975; Bartol & Wortman, 1975; Osborn & Vicars, 1976). For example, Rice, Instone, and Adams (1984) examined the effects of leaders' sex among cadets at West Point. They looked for sex differences in leader success, sex differences in the nature of leader–follower relationships, sex differences in leader behaviors, and interactions between leader and follower sex on success and relationships. This study is particularly interesting, because even though the subjects in the study were military cadets with very traditional attitudes toward women, there were no significant leader-sex effects. It seems clear that whereas women have been discouraged from accepting managerial responsibility, and although many people continue to resist women as leaders, sex may not be all that important when it comes down to employee performance and attitudes.

Leader Behavior: The Ohio State Studies

Following Stogdill's (1948) critique of leadership-trait research, psychologists turned away from personality explanations for leadership. Many began to examine the possibility that leader effectiveness was determined by the specific behaviors in which leaders engage. Instead of saying that people become leaders because they possess a particular profile of traits, these behavior theories viewed leadership as the consequence of a person's behavior.

This change in perspective had important implications for leadership and management in organizations. If trait theories are valid, then having strong leaders depends on either effective recruiting or being simply lucky enough to have "natural" leaders come along. If, however, behavior theories are valid, then it's possible that effective leadership methods can be *taught* to employees. This simplifies the leadership problems of organizations since, theoretically, all that is needed are reasonably intelligent, trainable employees, and a list of the appropriate behaviors to teach them. The first task of behavior researchers, therefore, was to identify those behaviors that distinguished leaders from followers and effective leaders from ineffective leaders. Whereas many researchers addressed the issue of effective leader behavior, the best-known and most influential behavior theory emerged from Ohio State University.

In order to identify important leader behaviors, researchers at Ohio State wrote approximately 1800 brief descriptions of managerial behaviors. Members of the research team then sorted these items into nine different groups, each emphasizing a different aspect of managerial leadership. Of the original items, 150 were used to develop the first version of the Leader Behavior Description Questionnaire, or LBDQ (Hemphill & Coons, 1957). Whereas the LBDQ was intended to measure nine different leader behaviors, it was later determined that the questionnaire actually measured only two primary types of behavior (Halpin & Winer, 1957), which were named consideration and initiation of structure.

Consideration is defined as the degree to which managers display concern for the well-being of their subordinates. Considerate managers display trust, warmth, and respect for their workers, whereas inconsiderate managers are unconcerned with subordinates' feelings or needs. Initiation of structure is defined as the degree to which managers organize, define, or otherwise structure the job activity of their workers. Managers high in initiation of structure define specific roles for both themselves and others, determine the schedule of work activities, and keep track of their groups' progress toward achieving organizational goals.

Over the years a number of different questionnaires have been developed to measure consideration and initiation of structure. The original LBDQ has 40 items, which are used by subordinates to describe their supervisor's behavior. A similar measure intended for industrial settings, the Supervisory Behavior Description Questionnaire (SBDQ; Fleishman, 1953), and a version to be completed by managers to describe ideal leadership behavior, the Leader Opinion Questionnaire (LOQ; Fleishman, 1957b), were also developed. The most recent and most widely used measure of consideration and initiation of structure is the LBDQ-XII (Stogdill, 1963).

Whereas the different measures of consideration and initiation of structure contain similar items, they are not identical, which makes comparisons between them difficult. One important difference concerns the measurement of initiation of structure. Both the original LBDQ and the SBDQ initiation-of-structure scales contain items describing punitive or punishing behavior. Although this type of behavior can be used to control employees, it is not the same as structuring. The LBDQ-XII initiation-of-structure scale is relatively free of these coercive, dominating behaviors (Schriesheim & Kerr, 1974; Schriesheim & Stogdill, 1975), which is one reason for its popularity as a measure of leader behavior.

Another problem with the original LBDQ is its emphasis on only two dimensions of leader behavior, which is an obvious oversimplification. Stogdill (1959, 1963) suggested 10 additional behaviors that were included in the LBDQ-XII, listed below.

1. *Consideration:* Regards the comfort, well-being, status, and contributions of followers.
2. *Initiation of structure:* Clearly defines own role, and lets followers know what is expected.
3. *Representation:* Speaks and acts as representative of the group.
4. *Demand reconciliation:* Reconciles conflicting organizational demands and reduces disorder in the system.
5. *Tolerance of uncertainty:* Is able to tolerate uncertainty and postponement without anxiety or upset.
6. *Persuasiveness:* Uses persuasion and argument effectively; exhibits strong convictions.
7. *Tolerance of freedom:* Allows followers scope for initiative, decision, and action.
8. *Role retention:* Actively exercises leadership role rather than surrendering leadership to others.
9. *Predictive accuracy:* Exhibits foresight and ability to predict outcomes accurately.
10. *Production emphasis:* Applies pressure for productive output.
11. *Integration:* Maintains a closely knit organization; resolves intermember conflicts.
12. *Influence with superiors:* Maintains cordial relations with superiors; has influence with them; is striving for higher status.

SOURCE: Adapted with permission of The Free Press, a Division of Macmillan, Inc. from *Handbook of Leadership: A Survey of Theory and Research,* by Ralph M. Stogdill. Copyright © 1974 by The Free Press.

Although some of these scales have not provided consistent research results, and although they are relatively minor compared to consideration and initiation of structure, they do provide a more complete picture of management activities than the original two dimensions alone.

There have been many studies examining the relationships between consideration and initiation of structure and other organizational variables. For example, significant positive correlations have been found between initiation of structure and group performance (Fleishman, 1957a) and employee satisfaction (House & Filley, 1971), whereas negative correlations have been reported between initiation of structure and employees' feelings that their needs are being met (Hammer & Dachler, 1973). Consideration has been found to be positively correlated with such variables as productivity (Lawshe & Nagle, 1953), attendance (Fleishman,

Harris, & Burtt, 1955), satisfaction and low turnover (Michaels & Spector, 1952; Petty & Bruning, 1980), and performance (Butterfield & Powell, 1981).

It soon became evident that the relationships between leaders' behaviors and criteria are not simple, but that they depend on situational or environmental conditions. For example, J. Schriesheim (1980) found that initiation of structure was positively related to measures of satisfaction and productivity, but only in groups where the members did not feel personally close to one another (that is, groups with low interpersonal cohesiveness). In groups with high cohesiveness, consideration was positively related to satisfaction and performance. In a classic study by Fleishman and Harris (1962), it was even found that the effects of consideration depended upon the level of a manager's initiation of structure. In addition to measuring leader behavior, Fleishman and Harris examined the number of grievances that were filed against each manager in the study. Their results are presented in Figure 10.1. Managers who were low in consideration received quite a few grievances, no matter how much structure they imposed on their workers. On the other hand, managers who were high in consideration received relatively few grievances across the board. The grievance rate for those managers who were rated as medium in consideration, however, depended on their initiation of structure: the more they structured the work of their subordinates, the more grievances they received.

Because the effects of leader behaviors are frequently moderated by other factors, it would be difficult for Dr. MacKeven to make any recommendations about Flavio's problem based solely on LBDQ measures of behavior. For instance, if she found that the new production managers had lower-than-average initiation-

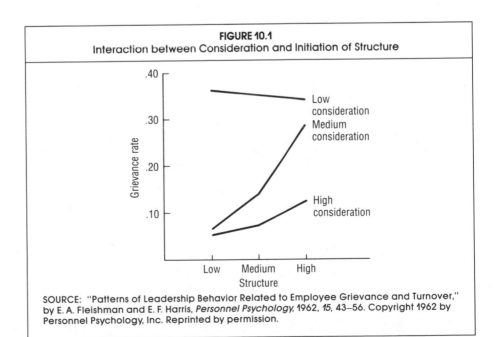

FIGURE 10.1
Interaction between Consideration and Initiation of Structure

SOURCE: "Patterns of Leadership Behavior Related to Employee Grievance and Turnover," by E. A. Fleishman and E. F. Harris, *Personnel Psychology,* 1962, *15,* 43–56. Copyright 1962 by Personnel Psychology, Inc. Reprinted by permission.

of-structure scores, it could mean that the production tasks are ambiguous, and the poor performance is due to the fact that the workers need more guidance than the supervisors are providing. It could also mean that the previous supervisors were high in structuring, and the workers have come to expect a great deal of guidance. In this case, the lower production might be due to a lack of self-confidence based on a history of relying on the boss. In any case, Dr. MacKeven needs information about the leaders' situations in order to make reasonable suggestions to Mr. Roe.

IMPLICIT LEADERSHIP THEORIES

Although the LBDQ is the most widely used leadership scale, it does not measure actual leader behavior. Instead, it asks workers to indicate how their boss might be *expected* to behave along the dimensions of consideration and initiation of structure. It is quite possible that in many cases supervisors' actual behaviors are not reflected in these ratings. It has been suggested that when workers use questionnaires such as the LBDQ, they do not rely on memories of their supervisor's actual behavior, but rather upon their implicit theories of leadership (Eden & Leviathan, 1975; Schneider, 1973). An implicit theory of leadership is a set of expectations or stereotypes about how leaders are likely to act, and according to some critics of leader behavior questionnaires, it is these stereotypes that people describe when they respond to the LBDQ, and not actual behavior.

To demonstrate this, Rush, Thomas, and Lord (1977) asked subjects to describe a manager using the LBDQ-XII. These subjects had read only a brief description of the manager that did not include any information about consideration or structuring behavior. The researchers found that factor analyses of the scores from these ratings resulted in factors that were very similar to those based on descriptions of real leaders (Schriesheim & Stogdill, 1975). Because Rush, Thomas, and Lord's ratings could not have been based on the leader's behavior (since there was no behavior!), they concluded that the consideration and initiation-of-structure factors that emerged must reflect their subjects' stereotypes, or implicit theories of leadership. Further, because these ratings of a bogus manager resulted in the same factors as ratings of real managers, Rush et al. suggested that *all* leader behavior ratings may reflect nothing more than respondents' implicit theories.

Schriesheim and DeNisi (cited in Bass, 1981) showed that reliance on implicit theories is strongest in situations where there is little or no information about the leader's actual behavior. When people have had an opportunity to observe the behavior of the manager they are rating, however, they will not need to rely on stereotypes. Schriesheim and DeNisi asked workers to describe both their own supervisor and "supervisors in general" on the LBDQ-XII. When the two sets of ratings were factor analyzed separately, both analyses yielded the familiar consideration and initiation-of-structure factors. However, when the two sets of ratings were combined in the same factor analysis, separate factors emerged for the two sets of ratings. This demonstrated that the workers were not relying on their implicit theories when they rated their real supervisors. If they had, those ratings would have been essentially the same as the ratings of the supervisor in general, and only one set of factors would have emerged. Further, the ratings of the real manager had strong correlations with worker satisfaction, whereas the ratings of supervisors in general had much lower correlations.

Although Schriesheim and DeNisi's study showed that raters do not rely solely upon implicit theories when describing leader behavior, it by no means indicates that implicit theories do not have important effects on leader ratings. Lord, Foti, and Phillips (1982) developed a "cognitive categorization" model of leader behavior perception. This theory is based on the idea that leader behavior is too complex for workers to observe accurately, much less recall and describe. In order to rate the behavior of their supervisors, workers therefore rely on a prototype of leadership. A prototype is an abstract description of the typical member of a category, such as leader or supervisor, and it is based on a person's history of experience with members of that category. Workers who have had friendly supervisors are likely to have supervisor prototypes that include the trait "friendly," whereas those who have had unfriendly supervisors are likely to have quite different prototypes. According to this theory, when workers *observe* their boss' behavior, they rely on their prototype for "supervisor," and tend to classify the behavior as being similar to the prototype. When they are asked to *rate* their boss' behavior, they do not have to actually remember the behavior, but only that the boss belongs to the "supervisor" category. They can then describe the behavior as they would describe the prototype's behavior.

Recent research has revealed that people do indeed rely on prototypes when they describe leader behavior (Foti, Fraser, & Lord, 1982; Lord, Foti, & Phillips, 1982; Phillips & Lord, 1982). For example, Phillips (1984) asked subjects to rate identical videotapes of a leader working with a group. He described the leader as an "effective leader" to some of the subjects, and as an "ineffective leader" to others. Phillips found that these prototype labels had an effect on ratings of behaviors typical of effective and ineffective leaders, but no immediate effects on behaviors not typical of leaders.

Although the research results have not been entirely conclusive, the potential for implicit theories and stereotypes to influence leader-behavior ratings has certainly been demonstrated. Dr. MacKeven should keep this in mind as she examines the leadership situation in Flavio's, and she should probably avoid relying on such ratings alone to measure leader behavior.

Contingency Theories

As we have noted, both trait theories and behavior theories were found to be inadequate explanations for leadership and managerial influence. One major reason for their failure was that the effects of any particular trait, or of any particular leader behavior, often varied across situations. Thus, whereas Stogdill (1974) was able to conclude that intelligence was one characteristic typical of leaders, he could not say that all leaders were more intelligent than their followers.

One result of this inconsistency was the development of contingency theories of leadership. Whereas all behavior theories assume that leadership is related to leader behavior, and all trait theories assume a relationship between leadership and personal traits, contingency theories are more diverse. The only common characteristic of contingency theories is an assumption that the effects of one variable on leadership depend, or are *contingent,* on one or more other variables. One theory may contain entirely different variables, and be concerned with different aspects of leadership than a second theory, but both will be classified as contingency theories if they propose that two variables interact to determine leader effectiveness.

Rather than trying to identify a limited number of traits or behaviors, the notion of contingencies raised the possibility that leadership was different in each situation, and that what was important in one location could be irrelevant in another. As you will see in the following examples of contingency theories, psychologists have considered a variety of different leader contingencies. At present, it is difficult to tell whether any one of these theories is more or less valid or useful than the others, but it is safe to say that contingency theories reflect a more realistic view of the complexity of leadership than did the earlier trait and behavior approaches.

TRAIT–SITUATION CONTINGENCIES

The first theory to popularize the contingency approach to leadership was developed by Fiedler (1964, 1967). It is known as the "LPC" theory, or sometimes simply as the "Contingency Theory." In order to avoid confusion with other contingency theories, we will refer to it as the LPC theory. According to Fiedler, leader effectiveness depends on the interaction of two factors: (1) the degree to which the leader's situation is favorable for the exercise of influence, and (2) leadership style. We will describe each of these components of Fiedler's theory and how they interact, and then discuss the relevant research.

According to Fiedler (1967), leader effectiveness depends on how easy it is for a leader to influence followers, a factor that he calls situational favorability. Situational favorability is determined by three characteristics of the leader's situation. The first and most important of these is leader–member relations, or how well the leader and the subordinates get along. The second characteristic is task structure. This is defined as the extent to which the workers' tasks are clearly defined and their performance easily monitored, thereby making supervision easier. The third situational characteristic is position power, or the extent to which leaders can obtain compliance with their wishes based upon the power of their position in the organization. (This is similar to French and Raven's [1959] "legitimate" power.) Finally, the eight different combinations of high and low leader–member relations, structure, and power can be combined to form eight cells or "octants," ranging from the highest situational favorability in octant 1 to the lowest in octant 8 (see Figure 10.2).

The second component of Fiedler's (1967) theory is leader style, which is measured by the Least Preferred Co-worker scale, or LPC. The LPC consists of a list of bipolar adjective pairs (for example, Tense—Relaxed, Gloomy—Cheerful),

FIGURE 10.2
Components of Situational Favorability

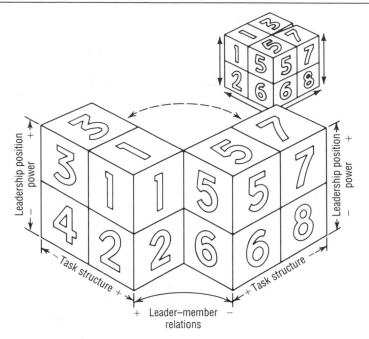

on which supervisors are asked to rate the one person with whom they "can work least well." High LPC scores mean that the leader described this person in relatively positive terms. According to Fiedler, describing the least-preferred co-worker in positive terms indicates a strong concern with interpersonal relationships. Low scores mean that the least-preferred co-worker was described in negative terms, which Fiedler claims reflects a lack of concern with relationships, and a stronger concern with accomplishing job tasks.

Although Fiedler (1967) claims that LPC scores reflect a task vs. relationship orientation, it is not at all clear what psychological processes the LPC actually measures. At various times it has been described as a measure of **social distance,** motivation, or **cognitive complexity** (Rice, 1978). The most recent interpretation offered by Fiedler (1972) is that the LPC measures a "motivational hierarchy."

social distance: the degree to which a person is aloof, or psychologically removed, from others in a group

cognitive complexity: the degree to which a person is able to consider or evaluate multiple dimensions or aspects of a situation or circumstance; the ability to mentally process multiple elements of information

According to this view, low-LPC leaders are primarily motivated to achieve task success; maintaining good social relationships with their subordinates is only a secondary goal. For high-LPC leaders the opposite pattern holds, with social relationships being the primary concern, and task success being secondary. According to the theory, these motives are important because they determine whether a supervisor's behavior is appropriate for a given situation.

Fiedler (1967) found that situational favorability and leader style combined to determine leader effectiveness in the manner illustrated in Figure 10.3, and he predicted that similar relationships would be found with other samples. In

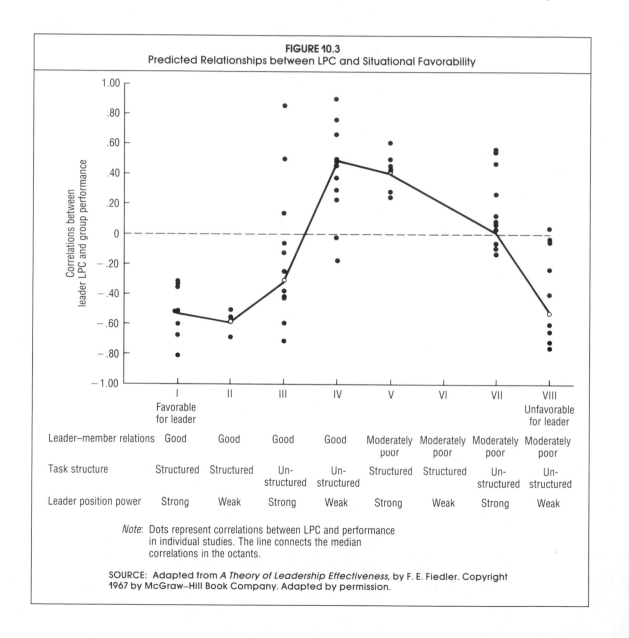

FIGURE 10.3
Predicted Relationships between LPC and Situational Favorability

Note: Dots represent correlations between LPC and performance in individual studies. The line connects the median correlations in the octants.

SOURCE: Adapted from *A Theory of Leadership Effectiveness,* by F. E. Fiedler. Copyright 1967 by McGraw–Hill Book Company. Adapted by permission.

situations with high favorability, the correlations between supervisor LPC scores and group performance were negative. This means that groups led by low-LPC supervisors performed better than those led by high-LPC supervisors in these situations. In low-favorability situations, Fiedler found that low-LPC-supervisors' groups again performed better than groups with high-LPC supervisors, as indicated by the negative correlations. Positive correlations between LPC and performance were found only in medium-favorability situations, meaning that high-LPC supervisors did better.

The reasoning behind Fiedler's (1967) predictions is based on the motivational hierarchy supposedly measured by the LPC. In favorable situations, managers stress their *secondary* motives, because their primary motives are already satisfied. This means that low-LPC supervisors will stress social relationships, which Fiedler claims is effective managerial behavior in favorable situations. High LPCs will stress task performance, which Fiedler says will be ineffective because successful task performance is virtually assured in favorable situations, and the supervisor's task emphasis is likely to be resented by workers. Thus the low-LPC supervisors are more effective in these situations.

In unfavorable situations, Fiedler says that managers will stress their *primary* motives, because they see this as the key to solving the difficult problems that they face. For high-LPC supervisors this means stressing social relationships, which is not likely to be effective in such negative circumstances. A better strategy would be to stress task performance, which is what the theory predicts low-LPC managers will do, making them more effective in this setting as well. In moderately favorable situations it is difficult to say which motives will govern supervisory behavior. The superior performance predicted for high-LPC supervisors may be due to an ability to sort out the variety of favorable and unfavorable factors in these octants, and select the appropriate behavior. Low LPCs apparently lack this ability, and continue to stress task performance in these situations (Rice, 1978).

Athough many studies on LPC theory have been published, it has received only mixed support. Some reviews of the theory have concluded that the theory is valid (Rice, 1978; Strube & Garcia, 1981, 1983), whereas others have found what they believe to be serious problems with the model (Kabanoff, 1981; Singh, 1983; Vecchio, 1977, 1983). Critics of the theory point out that Fiedler's data analyses are unorthodox and difficult to evaluate. They also believe that there are serious problems in defining situational favorability, and that the validity of the LPC scale has not been adequately demonstrated. One author (Vecchio, 1977, 1983) noted that whereas Fiedler and his students seem to be able to find support for the theory, other researchers have generally failed to do so. Vecchio also pointed out that much of the supporting evidence for the theory is based on samples of military officers, which raises questions about the generalizabililty of the model. Yet another commonly mentioned problem is that the theory fails to consider managers with moderate LPC scores, although there has recently been some effort to examine their leadership effectiveness (Kennedy, 1982).

At present there are too many unresolved questions about Fiedler's theory to accept it as a reasonable explanation for leader effectiveness. It is, however, a very important theory from the standpoint of having made contingency approaches to leadership popular. Also, because Fiedler has frequently modified the theory in response to criticisms and new findings, continued research on LPC and situational favorability may someday provide acceptable answers to his critics.

If Dr. MacKeven were to apply LPC theory to the situation in Flavio's, she would find a number of possible courses of action. Because LPC scores reflect a personality trait, they are not likely to change, at least not very quickly. Consequently, the remedy must focus on changing the situation. One way to do this is to measure the situational favorability of each job and the LPC of each supervisor, and then assign the supervisors to units where they are likely to be most effective. High-LPC leaders would be assigned to medium-favorability situations, and those with low LPC scores to the others. Although this procedure is consistent with the theory, it raises the possibility of frequent disruptive transfers as situational favorability changes. Another possibility is to train managers to measure the favorability of their situations and their own LPC, and then teach them to alter their situation to maximize their effectiveness. Fiedler, Chemers, and Mahar (1976) developed a program called Leader Match that teaches managers to do exactly that. Although Leader Match has met with some success (for example, Fiedler & Mahar, 1979), the many unanswered questions about LPC (Schriesheim & Hosking, 1978) are likely to cause Dr. MacKeven to look elsewhere for a solution.

Fiedler and some of his associates have also studied the relationship between the leader's intelligence and group performance, in a framework they call the Multiple Screen Model (Fiedler & Leister, 1977; Potter & Fiedler, 1981). Fiedler and Leister noted that most research has found relatively low correlations between leader intelligence and group performance. They suggested that there are several factors that form a "screen" between the potential of a leader's intelligence and its effects on task performance (see Figure 10.4).

Potter and Fiedler's (1981) data, based on U.S. Army infantry squad leaders, supported most of the relationships illustrated in the figure, with stronger relationships between leaders' intelligence and performance when the leaders were

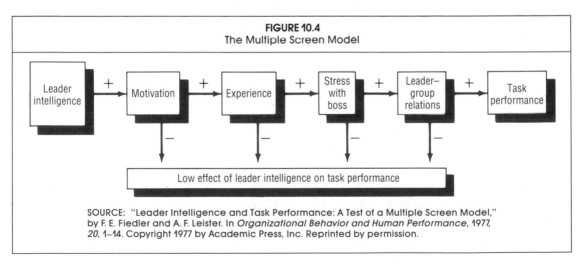

FIGURE 10.4
The Multiple Screen Model

Leader intelligence → + → Motivation → + → Experience → + → Stress with boss → + → Leader–group relations → + → Task performance

Motivation − ; Experience − ; Stress with boss − ; Leader–group relations −

Low effect of leader intelligence on task performance

SOURCE: "Leader Intelligence and Task Performance: A Test of a Multiple Screen Model," by F. E. Fiedler and A. F. Leister. In *Organizational Behavior and Human Performance*, 1977, *20*, 1–14. Copyright 1977 by Academic Press, Inc. Reprinted by permission.

experienced, motivated, lacked stress, and when they viewed their relationships with subordinates as good. In a later study of U.S. Coast Guard personnel, Potter and Fiedler (1981) found that when stress with the boss was low, intelligence was uncorrelated with performance evaluations; when stress with the boss was high, however, intelligence was negatively correlated with performance. This negative relationship between stress and the effects of intelligence was also found by Fiedler, Potter, Zais, and Knowlton (1979). It is interesting that Fiedler has found that the effects of intelligence, a characteristic that might be expected to have a uniformly positive association with performance, depend on a variety of situational factors.

BEHAVIOR–SITUATION CONTINGENCIES

LPC theory states that leader effectiveness is a result of contingencies between leader personality and situational variables. Other theories have been developed that stress contingencies between leader *behavior* and situations. One such theory that has received a lot of attention is path–goal theory (House, 1971; House & Mitchell, 1974). Based on the principles of expectancy theory of motivation (see Chapter 8), this theory states that the primary function of a leader is to help workers develop behaviors ("paths") that will lead them to the outcomes they desire ("goals"), thereby increasing work motivation. According to path–goal theory, good leaders are people whose behavior (1) helps followers identify the paths to their goal; (2) rewards followers for goal achievement; and (3) removes barriers that prevent followers from attaining their goals (House, 1971). The theory attempts to specify which of a number of different leader styles will be more effective in accomplishing these goals in different situations (see Figure 10.5).

The types of behavior that will result in improved worker motivation depend on a number of situational factors. Some of these concern the nature of the task. For example, House (1971) said that if a task is intrinsically satisfying, then supervisor consideration will not improve worker satisfaction or motivation, because the satisfying effects of consideration would be redundant with the satisfying effects of the task itself. If, however, the task is not satisfying, then supervisor consideration will result in greater satisfaction, because the leader's behavior would provide a means for attaining satisfaction on an otherwise unsatisfying job. Other contingencies involve the characteristics of the followers. House found that the correlation between initiation of structure and performance was lower for workers who were high in autonomy, apparently because they did not believe that the structure was necessary for achieving their goals.

As you can see, path–goal theory is more than just a theory of leadership. It is an effort to bring together several areas of organizational research and theory, including leadership, motivation, and job satisfaction. We agree with Muchinsky (1983) that for this reason alone, path–goal theory represents an important advance in I/O psychology.

As a theory of leadership, however, path–goal theory has met with only mixed success. Some research has supported the theory (Dessler, 1972; Fulk & Wendler, 1982; House & Dessler, 1974; Schriesheim & DeNisi, 1979, 1981),

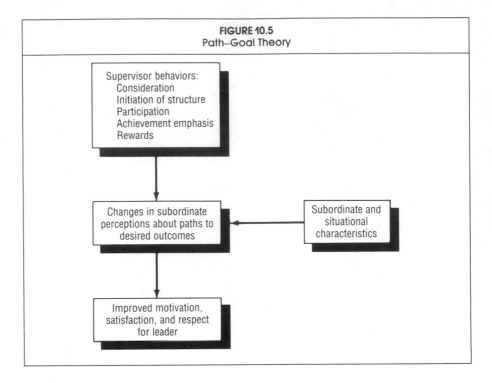

FIGURE 10.5
Path–Goal Theory

whereas other studies have not found support (Downey, Sheridan, & Slocum, 1975; Szilagyi & Sims, 1974). When negative results are found, the failure to support the theory is usually attributed to problems with the research, rather than to problems with the underlying logic of the theory. One problem facing path–goal researchers is measuring constructs such as "paths" and "goals." Because they are likely to be different for different people and situations, it is hard to develop reliable measures of these variables. Another problem centers on the large number of variables that might moderate the relationship between leader behavior and follower motivation. Unless all such variables are identified, results may be unexpected and unexplainable (Schriesheim & Schriesheim, 1980). If these types of problems can be resolved, path–goal theory may prove to be valuable in clarifying the relationships between leadership and other organizational variables.

Dr. MacKeven might use path–goal theory to examine the supervision in Flavio's Frozen Foods. The problem could be that the new supervisors are making wrong assumptions about the goals of the workers. For example, some of the supervisors may believe that the workers, who are paid on a piece-rate basis, would like to be able to improve their productivity, and thereby their pay. To do this, changes in the work schedule might be made. However, these changes may restructure some of the work groups, and the workers, many of whom have established strong relationships within their work groups, may react negatively, which might result in turn in lowered production and satisfaction. If the managers had known that the goal of maintaining social relationships was more important than making more money, this situation could have been avoided. Thus, Dr. MacKeven might be wise to survey the workers and supervisors in Flavio's to see if there are misunderstandings about goals that might explain the problems.

Another behavior–situation contingency theory of leadership that has received a lot of attention is rational decision-making theory, or as it is more commonly known, the Vroom–Yetton theory (Vroom, 1976; Vroom & Yetton, 1973). Unlike the other leadership theories that we have discussed, the Vroom–Yetton theory is a *normative* theory. This means that its purpose is to describe what leaders *should do* in specific situations. It is also very limited in scope compared to most other leadership theories. Rather than attempting to account for all aspects of leadership, the Vroom–Yetton theory is only concerned with how much subordinate participation supervisors should allow in the decision-making process.

The best-known of Vroom and Yetton's (1973) models concerns group decisions, for which they described five decision processes, ranging from autocratic to fully participative:

AI: You solve the problem or make the decision yourself using the information available to you at the time.

AII: You obtain necessary information from subordinates, then decide on the solution to the problem yourself. You may or may not tell subordinates what the problem is in getting the information from them. The role played by your subordinates in making the decision is clearly one of providing the necessary information to you, rather than generating or evaluating alternative solutions.

CI: You share the problem with relevant subordinates individually, getting their ideas and suggestions without bringing them together as a group. Then *you* make the decision, which may or may not reflect your subordinates' influence.

CII: You share the problem with your subordinates as a group, collectively obtaining their ideas and suggestions. Then you make the decision, which may or may not reflect your subordinates' influence.

GII: You share the problem with your subordinates as a group. Together you generate and evaluate alternatives and attempt to reach agreement (consensus) on a solution. Your role is much like that of a chairman. You do not try to influence the group to adopt "your" solution and you are willing to accept and implement any solution which has the support of the entire group.

SOURCE: Reprinted from *Leadership and Decision Making* by Victor H. Vroom and Philip W. Yetton by permission of the University of Pittsburgh Press. © 1973 by University of Pittsburgh Press.

They then specified a series of seven questions that managers should ask themselves about each decision they must make. These questions form a "decision tree"; based on the answers to the questions, the tree indicates which of the five decision processes are appropriate for the particular problem facing the manager (see Figure 10.6).

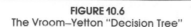

FIGURE 10.6
The Vroom–Yetton "Decision Tree"

A. Does the problem possess a quality requirement?
B. Do I have sufficient information to make a high-quality decision?
C. Is the problem structured?
D. Is acceptance of the decision by subordinates important for effective implementation?
E. If I were to make the decision by myself, am I reasonably certain that it would be accepted by my subordinates?
F. Do subordinates share the organizational goals to be attained in solving this problem?
G. Is conflict among subordinates likely in preferred solutions?

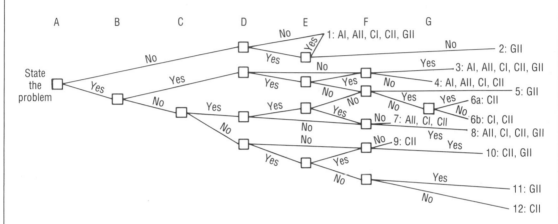

SOURCE: Reprinted from *Leadership and Decision Making* by Victor H. Vroom and Phillip W. Yetton by permission of the University of Pittsburgh Press. © 1973 by University of Pittsburgh Press.

For each problem, then, there is a "feasible set" of decision processes that should result in acceptable solutions. According to Vroom and Yetton (1973), any of the processes in the feasible set should result in decisions of adequate quality; if acceptance of the decision by subordinates is important, that too will be assured. In addition, Vroom and Yetton suggested that managers should select the *least*-participative decision process in the feasible set, because it is always the least time-consuming.

Support for the Vroom–Yetton theory is fairly strong. Vroom and Yetton (1973) had managers specify the decision processes they would use in a series of problems, and found that these decisions fit the appropriate feasible sets about two-thirds of the time. Vroom and Jago (1978) had managers describe actual problems they had faced and the decisions they had made in solving them. Not only did they find that 65 percent of the decision processes used were in the feasible set, but also that 68 percent of decisions consistent with the feasible set were rated by the managers as having been effective. Only 22 percent of the decision processes that were outside the feasible set were rated as effective. Field (1982) also found support for the model, but suggested that only some of the questions were useful in identifying effective decision rules. Jago and Vroom (1982) compared the decision processes used by men and women, and found that women were more participative, and their decisions fit the model better than did those of men.

Field (1979) noted that every feasible set in the Vroom–Yetton decision tree contains either decision process CII or decision process GII, or both. He therefore recommended a simpler decision rule to select between these two processes: "If acceptance of the decision by subordinates is critical to effective implementation and it is not reasonably certain that subordinates would accept an autocratic decision, but they share organizational goals (or decision quality is not important), use GII; otherwise use CII" (p. 256). Jago and Vroom (1980) compared the Vroom–Yetton model to the process proposed by Field, and found that the Vroom–Yetton model was the better predictor of managers' decisions. However, because the Vroom–Yetton theory is supposed to be normative, we think that Jago and Vroom's study does not change the implications of Field's comments. Field's decision rule will always yield a decision process in the Vroom–Yetton feasible set, and consequently, it should result in decisions equal in quality to those prescribed by the Vroom–Yetton model.

Jago and Vroom (1980) pointed out that Field's (1979) decision rule will always select one of the two most participative decision processes. These are also the two most time-consuming processes, and although they should work, quicker strategies may be overlooked. Jago and Vroom also suggested that managers are not likely to engage in this much participation. Consistent with this, Heilman, Hornstein, Cage, and Herschlag (1984) found that people who role-played managers were more favorable toward autocratic leadership than those who role-played followers. Vardi, Shirom, and Jacobson (1980) noted that although managers typically express favorable attitudes toward participation, they also tend to doubt the leadership abilities of others, making participation less likely. It appears, then, that although the Field decision rule is simpler, the presence of more autocratic processes may make the Vroom–Yetton procedure more attractive to managers.

Using the Vroom–Yetton model to investigate the situation at Flavio's might involve first training the supervisors to assess the decision-making requirements of the problems they face. Second, Dr. MacKeven would need to encourage the supervisors to use decision processes from the feasible set appropriate for the problem, pointing out particularly the advantages of using participative processes when they are needed. The result of this program should be a greater assurance of quality decisions, and greater acceptance of those decisions by subordinates.

Vertical Dyad Linkage Theory

As we noted earlier, leadership theories have paid more and more attention to followers. Whereas early trait and behavior theories did not consider followers at all, more recent theories include descriptions of how followers might affect leadership. For example, Vroom and Yetton's (1973) normative model suggests that followers' acceptance of leaders' decisions may be critical. In some theories, however, followers play a role equal to, or surpassing, that of the leader.

Graen and his colleagues (Dansereau, Graen, & Haga, 1975; Graen, 1976; Graen & Schiemann, 1978) developed the most widely known of these theories. The vertical dyad linkage theory (VDL) is an attempt to explain how the nature of the relationship between leader and follower can affect the leadership process. According to the theory, a manager's subordinates can be divided into two groups: the *in-group* and the *out-group*. The in-group consists of those workers believed by the supervisor to be competent, trustworthy, and motivated to work hard and accept responsibility. The out-group includes those who the leader believes do not possess these traits. The nature of the relationship between the leader and in-group members is thought to be different from the relationship between the leader and out-group members. In-group members are given responsibility for important tasks, thereby making the supervisor's job easier. In return, the leader provides in-group members with support, understanding, and a more personal relationship. Out-group members are given tasks requiring less ability and responsibility, and do not benefit from a personal relationship with the supervisor. Interaction with the out-group members is based on the supervisor's formal authority rather than on respect or friendship.

Research on VDL has generally supported the theory. For example, Liden and Graen (1980) found that in-group foremen accepted greater responsibility and were rewarded with more support, feedback, and personal attention than out-group foremen. Howat and London (1980) examined the relationship between conflict and dyadic relationships, and found that the closer the relationship approached an in-group style, the fewer the interpersonal conflicts between supervisor and subordinate.

One implication of VDL theory is that leadership can be better understood by examining individual leader–member dyads rather than the supervisor's "averge leadership style" (ALS), which assumes that all subordinates are treated the same. A number of studies have tested this prediction. Graen, Liden, and Hoel (1982) compared predictions of turnover based on leader–member interactions with those based on managers' overall styles. Consistent with the theory, the dyadic approach resulted in better prediction. Katerberg and Hom (1981) examined the relationship between national guardsmen's ratings of their superiors' consideration and initiation of structure, and measures of satisfaction and role perceptions. They found that within-unit differences, corresponding to differences in dyadic relationships, predicted the criteria better than between-unit differences, which represent average leadership styles. However, *both* measures were significantly related to the criteria, indicating that they are both important considerations. Vecchio (1982) found similar results in a study of Air Force personnel, but only for predicting attitudes such as job satisfaction. The VDL approach did not predict performance any better than the leader's average style. Vecchio's study illustrates the need for further research on factors that both influence and are influenced by the nature of the relationship between leader and follower.

VDL theory suggests that the problems at Flavio's are due to inappropriate or ineffective dyadic relationships. For example, Dr. MacKeven might find it useful to interview the workers to see what informal duties they had performed in the past. Although it should not be expected that two managers would develop the same in-groups, it may be useful to know who had been trusted with additional responsibility in the past. Dissatisfaction on the part of employees who made up the previous manager's in-group may result if they are denied that responsibility by the new manager.

Other Leadership Theories

The previous sections describe the dominant themes in leadership theory and research. Not all leadership theories, however, fit neatly into one or more of these general approaches. In this section we will briefly present two leadership theories that expand the traditional scope of organizational leadership. The first attempts to explain supervisors' perceptions of their subordinates' performance. The second is concerned with a type of influence that is usually thought of only in terms of political or religious leadership.

GREEN AND MITCHELL'S ATTRIBUTION THEORY

A problem typical of those that all supervisors face is what to do about employees whose performance does not meet standards or expectations. Why do some managers seem to ignore the mistakes of their subordinates, while others get very upset over seemingly trivial incidents? These issues, the causes of leader behavior and how leaders respond to their subordinates, have been addressed by Green and Mitchell's (1979) attribution model. Unlike most leadership theories, which attempt to explain the *consequences* of what a leader does, this theory focuses on the antecedents or *causes* of leader behavior.

The basis for this attribution approach to leadership is the notion that leaders operate in an uncertain environment. They therefore examine the environment for cues about what is happening and how they should react; a major focus of their attention is the behavior of their subordinates. When supervisors must make decisions about how to interact with workers, the subordinates' behaviors become particularly important.

According to Green and Mitchell's (1979) theory, leaders use their subordinates' behaviors, and other information in the environment, to draw conclusions, or make attributions, about why the subordinates behave or perform their jobs the way they do. The nature of these attributions in turn determines leaders' behavior toward their subordinates. A number of research studies have supported these ideas. For example, Mitchell and Wood (1980) had nursing supervisors read cases describing nurses who had made mistakes on the job, such as giving patients the wrong medication. In some of the cases the mistakes were described as being unusual for the nurse (implying a good work history), and in other cases as being common (implying a poor work history); the results of the mistakes were described as either serious to the patient involved or as not so serious. Mitchell and Wood found that nurses with poor work histories and those whose mistakes were serious were seen by the supervisors as being more responsible for their actions, and that punitive actions were seen as more appropriate for these nurses. Knowledge of the nurses' previous work histories helped determine whether the supervisors would attribute the error to the nurse or to circumstances beyond the nurse's control, as well as whether or not punitive action should be taken.

One topic that has been addressed in this attribution framework is the nature of the interaction between supervisors and subordinates of the opposite sex. Dobbins, Pence, Orban, and Sgro (1983) found that the sex of both supervisor and subordinate was important in determining leader attributions and leader actions. Their data showed that leaders who were the same sex as their subordinate were less likely to hold the subordinate responsible for missing a deadline when the cause of the missed deadline was beyond the subordinate's control. Supervisors who were the opposite sex of the subordinate, however, were more likely to hold the worker responsible. This has grave implications for female workers, because most supervisors and managers are men, and women are therefore more likely than men to be the subordinate in a mixed-sex dyad.

HOUSE'S THEORY OF CHARISMATIC LEADERSHIP

House (1977) developed a unique theory to explain charismatic leadership. Charismatic leaders are defined as people who have extraordinary effects on their followers, not due to any formal authority, but due rather to the force of their personalities and their interpersonal skills. The followers, according to House, are relatively unconcerned with careers, promotions, or money, but they follow instead out of love, passionate devotion, and enthusiasm for the leader.

In order to become a charismatic leader, House (1977) stated that a person must articulate a "transcendent goal" for her followers. That is, charismatic leaders define the moral mission of the group and the means whereby the members can accomplish that mission. These leaders instill confidence in their followers, serve as role models, and express special beliefs, values, and shared ideologies.

Charismatic leaders certainly don't sound much like typical industrial supervisors, and we believe that typical industrial organizations are unlikely places for charismatic leaders to emerge. Concerns about profit, personnel, research and development, and so on, are not conducive to moral missions, shared ideology, or passionate devotion and enthusiasm for leaders. It is, therefore, not surprising that little research on charismatic leaders has been published (cf. Bass, 1985). We believe, however, that House's (1977) theory is of great potential value for understanding leadership in *voluntary* organizations, such as charitable groups, service organizations, and religious groups. Organizational psychology has, for the most part, ignored these types of organizations, yet nearly everyone belongs to one or more of these groups, and many people devote a great deal of time to them. We hope that psychology begins to pay attention to voluntary organizations, and that more theories with special implications for these groups are developed.

THE IMPORTANCE OF LEADERSHIP

We began this chapter by noting the vast number of articles that have been published on the issue of leadership. We also noted that there was not general agreement about what leadership is, and that the evidence concerning the effects of leadership is at best mixed. Pfeffer (1977) stated that these are symptoms of some fatal problems with leadership research, and with the construct of leadership itself. He listed three problems with leadership as it is studied by I/O psychologists: (1) The concept of leadership is ambiguous. It is conceptually indistinguishable from other types of social influence, and psychologists have not even been able to agree on a definition of leadership. (2) There is little evidence for the effects of leaders. Selection processes used by organizations result in most leaders being alike, which means that it makes no difference who leaders are. Also, the social systems in organizations limit the decisions that can be made by leaders, and many of the factors that determine organizational success (cost of supplies, for example) are beyond leaders' control. (3) Merit and ability do not account for much in leader selection. Becoming a leader is more a matter of who you know than what you can do.

Pfeffer (1977) went on to state that leaders are little more than symbols used by people to explain what happens in organizations. Further, what happens in organizations is attributed to leaders simply because some people have been identified as leaders, and we have been led to believe that leaders are responsible for what happens. Calder (1977) offered similar arguments in his discussion of the status of the construct of leadership.

We find this blanket rejection of the relevance and importance of leadership to be unconvincing. In fact, Pfeffer (1977) was not talking about leadership as we have defined it; rather he was talking about the importance of *management*. Consider a study that Pfeffer used to support his arguments (Salancik & Pfeffer, 1977b), showing that changes in mayors had little or no effect on the functioning of city governments. We believe that this says more about municipal bureaucracy than about leadership. Salancik and Pfeffer offered no evidence that the new mayors in their study did anything differently than their predecessors, so there was no reason to expect them to make a difference. In fact, we believe that leadership usually operates at the lower levels of organizations, where there is more contact with a greater number of workers, and that studies of changes in the upper levels of management are not likely to be useful for understanding leader influence.

It is not likely, however, that leadership is equally important in all situations. Kerr and Jermier (1978) noted that most theories suggest that leadership, in some form, will be important in any situation, an assumption that they questioned. They proposed that there are characteristics of workers, of job tasks, and of organizations that make it unnecessary, difficult, or even impossible for managers to have an effect on their subordinates. They referred to these factors as potential substitutes for leadership, and predicted that certain substitutes would have implications for certain types of leader behavior (see Table 10.1).

Research has demonstrated that there are indeed personal and situational variables that seem to make leadership less important. Sheridan, Vrendenburgh, and Abelson (1984) examined the effects of both head nurses' behavior and potential leadership substitutes on the job performance of hospital nurses. They found that only one head-nurse behavior, assertiveness, had a significant effect

TABLE 10.1 Substitutes for Leadership

	Will tend to neutralize	
Characteristic:	Relationship-oriented, supportive, people-centered leadership: consideration, support, and interaction facilitation	Task-oriented, instrumental, job-centered leadership: initiating structure, goal emphasis, and work facilitation
Of the subordinate		
1. ability, experience, training, knowledge		X
2. need for independence	X	X
3. "professional" orientation	X	X
4. indifference toward organizational rewards	X	X
Of the task		
5. unambiguous and routine		X
6. methodologically invariant		X
7. provides its own feedback concerning accomplishment		X
8. intrinsically satisfying	X	
Of the organization		
9. formalization (explicit plans, goals, and areas of responsibility)		X
10. inflexibility (rigid, unbending rules and procedures)		X
11. highly specified and active advisory and staff functions		X
12. closely knit, cohesive work groups	X	X
13. organizational rewards not within the leader's control	X	X
14. spatial distance between superior and subordinates	X	X

SOURCE: "Substitutes for Leadership: Their Meaning and Measurement," by S. Kerr and J. M. Jermier. In *Organizational Behavior and Human Performance*, 1978, *22*, 375–403. Copyright 1978 by Academic Press, Inc. Reprinted by permission.

on performance, whereas a number of the substitutes, including the staff nurses' education, work-group cohesion or closeness, and work technology also had direct effects on performance. Howell and Dorfman (1981), however, found that although a number of variables were related to the job satisfaction and job commitment of hospital employees, only one of these **(organizational formalization)** had a strong enough relationship to make leadership unnecessary.

It seems clear that in some situations job tasks are so structured, rules are so rigid, or workers are so skilled and dedicated that certain leadership functions are not necessary. However, a comparison of the Sheridan, Vrendenburgh, and Abelson (1984) and the Howell and Dorfman (1981) studies, which were conducted in very similar hospital settings, shows that the effects of such substitutes depend on a variety of subtle factors. Indeed, although leadership theory and research have come a long way from the days of the "great man" theory, there is still a lot to learn about what makes people influential in organizations.

CHAPTER SUMMARY

Leadership has been characterized in many ways over the years. We have defined leadership as social influence in organizations that has implications for achieving organizational goals. It is important to distinguish this type of influence from the more general functions of management, which include a variety of administrative duties that lie beyond the scope of leadership. It is also important to realize that *anyone* in an organization may exercise leadership. This potential is illustrated by French and Raven's five bases of power, only one of which is limited to people with formal authority.

Theories of leadership have undergone an evolutionary process, beginning with the belief that personal traits distinguish leaders from followers. The failure to identify such traits led to attempts to specify behaviors that characterize effective leaders (although recent work on managerial motivation shows that the trait approach is not dead). The most prominent of these behavior theories is based on the Ohio State leader-behavior dimensions of consideration and initiation of structure.

As did earlier trait approaches, behavior theories proved inadequate for explaining leadership, and I/O psychologists turned to contingency theories. These theories specify that leader effectiveness depends on certain *combinations* of conditions, traits, or behaviors. The best known of these is Fiedler's LPC theory, which states that leader effectiveness depends on the level of situational favorability and a leader trait measured by the LPC scale. Other well-known contingency theories include path–goal theory and Vroom and Yetton's rational decision-making model.

Another influential approach to leadership considers the nature of individual leader–follower dyads. Graen's Vertical Dyad Linkage theory explores the quality of supervisor–subordinate relationships, and their effects on individual and group performance.

Finally, leadership theory has come under attack by those who believe that it is indistinguishable from other constructs, or that it is simply a convenient explanation for events in organizations. We believe that most of these critics have confused leadership with management, and that their comments are misdirected. It should be acknowledged, however, that under certain circumstances leadership may be rendered unnecessary by situational factors.

---

organizational formalization: the degree to which plans, goals, and areas of responsibility are explicitly defined within an organization

INTEROFFICE MEMO
TO: Richard Roe, Senior Vice President, Frozen Foods
FROM: J. A. MacKeven, Human-Resources Coordinator

As you know, over the past month I have been looking into the productivity problem that you reported in some of your production and distribution units. Specifically, I have been examining the four
"problem" units that you identified, to see if any of the changes
that have occurred as a function of the merger might be responsible
for the productivity decline.

The first thing that we did was to add some questions about changes in
workers' jobs since the merger to the regular quarterly employee survey. We also interviewed the four supervisors in question, as well as
the supervisors of four units that have not experienced a production
decline since the merger. In addition to these interviews, we talked
to a small sample of "opinion leaders" (as identified by the supervisors) from each of the problem units.

We found quite a "hodgepodge" of opinions and ideas about what is
good and what is bad in Flavio's since the merger. Regarding your
specific problem, however, two recurring themes seem to have the most
relevance: First, employees in the problem units seem to believe that
their supervisors are "in over their heads." That is, the supervisors are trying to tackle problems that they don't have the expertise
or experience to handle, and they are not seeking help from their
experienced subordinates. Second, some employees in these units feel
that they have been "set adrift" by their new supervisors. It seems
that in the past these workers had a degree of responsibility for
certain tasks, but now they have lost that responsibility and see
their work as having less impact on the organization.

The first of these complaints suggests that the supervisors of these
units are failing to take advantage of the experience and expertise
of their workers. General supervisory experience cannot prepare them
for making quality decisions about specific technical problems. We
need to train them to be more sensitive to their own limitations, and
how best to use the human resources available to them.

The second complaint clearly illustrates a lack of awareness of the
roles that different workers played prior to the merger. As in most
work groups, some of the workers had established their own "turfs,"
or areas of responsibility, which were sources of pride and satisfaction for them. Unaware of these traditions, the new supervisors dele-
gated these responsibilities to other workers. This will not be an
easy situation to resolve. Perhaps the best first step would be to
meet with the supervisors, share these findings with them, and see
what happens. We may be able to link this with the issue of untapped
human resources—pointing out that the workers who had responsibility
in the past probably had knowledge and skills to back it up. Clearly,
things will improve when the skills and experience of the workers in
these units are more fully utilized.

REVIEW QUESTIONS AND EXERCISES

1. What theory or theories of leadership does Dr. MacKeven seem to be relying on to make her recommendations? Describe the specific processes by which these theories would explain the problems presented in the memos.
2. Consider the distinction between leadership and management. What alternative explanations for the productivity decline in Flavio's does this distinction suggest? What solutions are suggested by these explanations?
3. We have stressed the role of social power in the exercise of organizational leadership. Use French and Raven's (1959) categories of power to both diagnose, and recommend solutions for, the problems that the new managers in Flavio's seem to be having.
4. Explain how implicit leadership theories might have led Dr. MacKeven to incorrectly conclude that Flavio's productivity decline was due to leadership/management problems. If the decline is *not* due to leadership factors, what might be its cause?

CHAPTER 11

Labor Unions

Learning Points

After studying this chapter, you should

- understand what labor unions are, and why they have become prominent in North American workplaces
- be able to describe the steps in union organization, and discuss the factors that are related to pro-union behavior
- understand the typical viewpoint of management on labor unions
- be able to describe the purpose of collective bargaining, and explain how impasses can be resolved
- be able to explain why grievances occur, and discuss factors that are related to the filing of grievances
- be able to explain why I/O psychologists have conducted relatively little research on unions
- be able to discuss the factors that contribute to union commitment and union satisfaction

INTEROFFICE MEMO

TO: J. A. MacKeven, Human-Resources Coordinator

FROM: T. J. Smith, Legal Counsel

I would like to have your input on a matter that is of some concern to the senior management team. As you know, prior to our merging with Flavio's Frozen Foods, we had no unionized employees. While it would be nice to attribute this to our enlightened management practices, it is probably more likely due to the nature of the pizza business: Most of our employees in the pizza end of the business are either in man- agement or staff positions at headquarters here in Suardell Springs, or in management positions at the individual restaurants owned by the company. Workers at franchise restaurants are the employees of the franchise owner, not of PPP. Consequently, PPP was not an attractive target for unionization. With the acquisition of Flavio's, however, this picture has changed dramatically. Both the manufacturing and distribution divisions of Flavio's are labor intensive, and in fact 30 percent of the Flavio's work force were members of unions at the time of the merger. Most of the union shops are in the Midwest and Northwest, but there has been increasing union activity in the South- west. In fact, authorization cards are being circulated at the Flavio's plant in Phoenix this month. We can probably expect increased efforts to unionize our employees during the next year or two.

I would like you to serve on an ad hoc committee on union activity. This committee's job will be to analyze Peter's Pan Pizza regarding the potential for additional unionization, and plan how the company should deal with such activity. The committee will also be concerned with how the company should approach dealing with the currently unionized shops. I particularly hope that you will be able to provide some information on the psychological variables that lead workers to unions, and suggest how we can prevent this type of activity.

The memo Dr. MacKeven received from the legal counsel's office expresses concern and uncertainty that is shared by the mangement of many organizations that are dealing with labor unions for the first time. In this chapter we will discuss the role of labor unions in work organizations, and the reasons why workers might join unions (as well as the reasons why they might not). We will also examine the unique relationship between employer and union, as well as the dual roles of union members.

A DEFINITION OF LABOR UNIONS

Labor unions are found in most countries, and their activities vary as a function of the political, social, and economic conditions around the world. The politically active, independent unions of western Europe are therefore dramatically different from the carefully controlled unions found in the communist bloc. In the United States and Canada, a labor union can be defined as *an association of workers, the purpose of which is to represent the interests of its members on issues of wages, policy, and working conditions.* The primary technique by which unions represent these interests is collective bargaining, in which representatives of the union negotiate, or bargain, with representatives of company management over various issues. The techniques of collective bargaining, and other union activities, are described in more detail later in this chapter. Collective bargaining illustrates, however, the basic philosophy of unions, which is that workers can better achieve their common goals by dealing with management as a group, rather than as individuals.

LABOR UNIONS IN NORTH AMERICA

The modern labor movement in North America began shortly before the turn of the century. To a large extent, it was a response to changes in the workplace that resulted from the Industrial Revolution. As the economy shifted from its agricultural base and became more heavily industrialized, workers migrated from farms and rural communities to the cities in search of more dependable and more financially rewarding livelihoods. The resulting abundance of labor, however, kept wages low, and few working-class people amassed the wealth they had expected. Further, although growth in terms of production and jobs was rapid during this time, working conditions in the factories were often noisy, abusive, unsanitary, and even unsafe. In summary, whereas the Industrial Revolution provided many workers with a new way of life, it had negative consequences as well. Early labor-organizing efforts, often anchored in **socialist** philosophy, were aimed at gaining a share of the newly created wealth for workers, while improving their general working conditions.

There have been trade unions and local labor organizations of various types in North America since at least the end of the eighteenth century. The first widely influential labor organization, however, was the American Federation of

Labor, or AFL, founded in 1881 under the leadership of Samuel Gompers. The AFL was actually a collection of relatively independent unions that supported one another in their efforts to organize various industries. Other unions, dedicated to socialist principles of class struggle and revolutionary change, emerged during this time, but were uniformly unsuccessful in attracting members. The more moderate AFL, which was committed to improving the lives of workers through collective bargaining, and using political "persuasion" rather than violence to bring about desirable changes in society, quickly became the dominant labor organization: Through the early 1930s, 70 percent to 80 percent of all organized workers were members of the AFL.

In 1933 the National Industrial Recovery Act became law, and guaranteed the right of workers to organize and engage in collective bargaining. Although this law was later declared unconstitutional, the 1935 National Labor Relations Act that followed also guaranteed the right to organize. These laws led to the rapid growth of unions, as industries previously resistant to unionization were organized (see Table 11.1). Another period of rapid union growth began in 1938, when several AFL unions with members in the skilled crafts broke away to form the Congress of Industrial Organizations (CIO), which competed with the AFL for members. The last dramatic period of growth in union membership occurred during World War II. Unlike previous eras of union expansion, this growth was not due to an increase in the number of unions, but rather to the very rapid expansion of those industries involved in war production, most of which were already unionized. After the war, the growth of union membership proceeded more slowly. This period was marked by the reunification in 1955 of the AFL and CIO into a single organization, the AFL-CIO, which remains the largest labor organization in North America.

The number of workers in unions continued to grow throughout the 1960s, although the percentage of the work force that belonged to unions remained fairly constant. During the 1970s, and more dramatically in the 1980s, union membership reversed its long history of growth. Both the number of workers belonging to unions and the percentage of the work force that they made up began to fall, as illustrated in Table 11.1. This shrinkage is due to a number of factors, but it can be accounted for primarily by the change in the types of industries experiencing growth. Through the 1960s, traditional industrial organizations, especially manufacturing companies, experienced steady growth. This growth slowed, and then reversed, in the 1970s and 1980s, as the number and proportion of workers in service industries (for example, financial institutions, custodial services, food services, "high-tech" industries) and government jobs increased. These new growth industries are not as heavily unionized as those of previous decades. One effect of this shift in employment, therefore, was a decrease in the membership and influence of labor unions. However, even today approximately one in five workers belongs to a union, and for these millions of employees and their employers, unions are an important fact of life.

---

socialist: advocating the control and ownership of the means of production and distribution by society, rather than by private individuals

TABLE 11.1 Labor Union Membership: 1900–1985

Year	Number of union members (in thousands)	Percentage of total work force belonging to unions
1900	791	4.9
1910	2,116	9.1
1920	5,034	17.5
1930	3,632	6.8
1940	8,944	15.5
1950	15,000*	22.3*
1960	18,117	23.6
1970	20,752	22.6
1980	20,095	23.0
1985	16,996	18.0

*Approximate

SOURCES: 1900–1970: U.S. Bureau of the Census, 1975, pp. 176–177; 1980: Adams, 1985, p. 26; 1985: U.S. Department of Labor, 1986, p. 213.

Peter's Pan Pizza illustrates the trend in union membership mentioned above: The PPP franchise business, a decentralized service organization, is not unionized. This is primarily because most of the employees in the retail franchises work for the individuals who own the restaurants. These owners pay a franchise fee to PPP for the right to use the company name, recipes, advertising, and so forth. The franchise owners also buy supplies and equipment from PPP. Because each franchise is actually a small, independent business, often with a largely part-time student work force, PPP restaurants have not been attractive targets for union organization. Many of the employees who actually worked at PPP's corporate headquarters prior to the merger with Flavio's were either in managerial positions, and therefore not subject to unionization, or aspired to managerial positions, and therefore not sympathetic to the union movement. Flavio's Frozen Foods, on the other hand, is a more labor-intensive organization, with traditional manufacturing and distribution functions. It is this type of company that is an attractive target for unionization efforts. As we have seen, the proportion of the work force in such jobs has been falling, although in PPP's case, the acquisition of Flavio's led to a net *growth* in employee unionization.

UNION ORGANIZATION

Millions of workers belong to labor unions, but many millions more do not. What factors contribute to an employee's decision to join a union? To what extent are employees free to make this choice? To answer these questions, we will examine basic processes involved in union organization, and outline several of the individual and situational characteristics that seem to be related to union status. Although we cannot specify why any one individual might want to join a union, or why another worker is opposed to union membership, we can identify factors related to attitudes toward unions, as well as conditions beyond the control of workers that often dictate the presence or absence of a union.

Certification Elections

In order for a union to represent the employees of an organization, those employees must first vote to accept, or certify, the union as their legal bargaining representative. U.S. law requires that prior to an election, a substantial number of employees must indicate an interest in voting on whether or not the union should be certified. Specifically, 30 percent or more of the employees must sign cards authorizing an election. In order to obtain the necessary number of signatures, representatives of the union will campaign in support of the election. Management, however, will campaign to *prevent* the authorization of the election, for reasons that we will discuss later in the chapter. There is obviously the potential for abuse on both sides of these campaigns, and so laws have been enacted that regulate the behavior of both the union and management representatives. For example, management cannot discipline workers for signing cards or openly supporting the union, whereas union organizers cannot interfere with the performance of the workers' jobs. These laws, as well as regulations governing all other aspects of the unionization process, are enforced by the National Labor Relations Board (NLRB), an agency of the federal government.

It should be noted that not all of a company's employees will necessarily be asked to sign authorization cards, nor be eligible to vote in the election if one is authorized. In some cases, different employees of a single company may belong to different unions, depending on the type of work they perform. For example, the International Brotherhood of Teamsters might attempt to organize the truck drivers in Flavio's distribution unit, but would not be likely to represent other types of workers. The Food and Beverage Trades Department of the AFL-CIO might try to organize the workers who prepare the food, whereas the Office and Professional Employees' International Union might distribute authorization cards among Flavio's office staff. It is up to the NLRB to determine who is eligible to vote in each election, although in general, only managerial employees are prohibited from voting.

If fewer than 30 percent of the eligible workers sign cards, the union must either give up or start its organization campaign over again. If 30 percent or more of the eligible employees do sign authorization cards, however, the NLRB schedules an election by secret ballot. Campaigning by both parties is supervised closely by the NLRB, which also conducts all aspects of the actual election. If more than half of the voters approve the union, it becomes the legal bargaining agent for all of the eligible employees. If a majority does not approve the union, the union's supporters can, if they wish, try again.

Workers' Reasons for Joining Unions

Although there is no single explanation for why workers vote to join unions, there has been some research on the factors that predict pro-union behavior. Perhaps the most consistent result has been that the best predictor of pro-union behavior (that is, voting for the union, intention to vote for the union, signing authorization cards, and so on) is dissatisfaction with extrinsic aspects of the job, such as pay, promotions, and working conditions (for example, Bigoness,

1978; Hamner & Smith, 1978; Schriesheim, 1978). This is consistent with the stated purpose of most unions, which is to protect the economic interests and improve the work environment of their members.

Recently, a more sophisticated approach to understanding the voting behavior of workers has emerged. DeCotiis and LeLouarn (1981) presented a model of the union-vote decision process, based on a review of the previous research. This model, presented in Figure 11.1, relies on the concept of instrumentality as the primary factor in determining whether a worker will vote in favor of the union. Instrumentality, in this model, refers to a worker's perception that the union will help her attain personal outcomes that she values (see Chapter 8 for a more complete discussion of instrumentality). More specifically, the model states that workers who believe that the union will help them get what they want will have positive attitudes toward the union. Workers with positive attitudes toward the union will, in turn, express an intent to vote for the union when given the opportunity. Finally, workers who have made up their minds to vote for the union are very likely to actually do so.

The instrumentality of a union, according to the model, is a function of the work context and a worker's individual characteristics. DeCotiis and LeLouarn (1981) defined work context as a combination of (1) the employee's reaction to work, including satisfaction with extrinsic factors (such as pay), job stress, and role conflict and ambiguity; (2) organizational climate, which serves to define acceptable behaviors; (3) workers' perceptions of the organization's structure; and (4) closeness of supervision and the nature of worker–supervisor communication. Personal characteristics identified from previous research as being related to pro-union behavior were age, education, race, hours worked, and prior union-voting behavior.

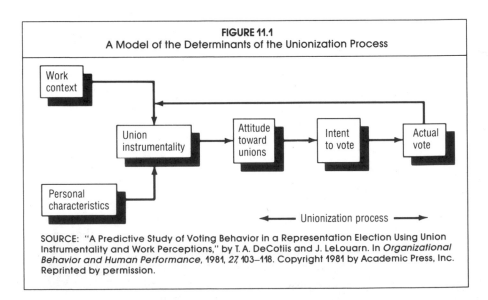

FIGURE 11.1
A Model of the Determinants of the Unionization Process

SOURCE: "A Predictive Study of Voting Behavior in a Representation Election Using Union Instrumentality and Work Perceptions," by T. A. DeCotiis and J. LeLouarn. In *Organizational Behavior and Human Performance*, 1981, *27*, 103–118. Copyright 1981 by Academic Press, Inc. Reprinted by permission.

DeCotiis and LeLouarn tested their model, using a sample of registered nurses who had recently voted in a union-representation election. As specified by the model, the results showed that the best predictor of intent to vote, as well as of the actual vote cast, was union instrumentality. Consistent with the previous research in this field, extrinsic dissatisfaction was also strongly correlated with intent to vote, but it was *more* strongly correlated with union instrumentality. This suggested to these researchers that lack of satisfaction causes an employee to consider alternative ways to reach his goals on the job, but does not *necessarily* result in a pro-union attitude. Overall, four variables were found to be significant predictors of union instrumentality: extrinsic job satisfaction, stress, fairness (a dimension of organizational climate), and worker–supervisor communications.

This model of union-voting behavior is consistent with a number of other studies that have examined factors contributing to union voting. For example, Allen and Keaveny (1981) found, among other effects, that a perceived *lack* of instrumentality between job performance and pay raises was associated with a strong belief in the need for a union. Apparently, these workers believed that a union would be instrumental in developing a stronger link between pay and performance.

Hammer and Berman (1981) found that whereas satisfaction with pay predicted voting behavior, distrust of management was even more strongly related to pro-union voting. They interpreted this result in the context of a power theory of unionization, suggesting that when workers distrust management, they are more likely to vote for a union in an effort to gain more power. The unstated assumption in their theory seems to be that dissatisfied workers see the union as instrumental in acquiring the power that they need in order to gain control from their distrusted supervisors.

Gordon, Philpot, Burt, Thompson, and Spiller (1980) found that those workers with the strongest pro-union attitudes were most likely to perceive that the union membership was instrumental in attaining personal gain. Finally, Bigoness and Tosi (1984) found that college faculty who perceived their union as instrumental for improving employment conditions were *less* likely to vote to decertify the union. (Decertification is the process by which workers remove a union as their legal representative.)

Although the notion that perceived instrumentality is a strong determinant of one's attitudes toward unions and union-voting behavior appears to have a good deal of support, it cannot explain why *all* union members vote for, or join, unions. As discussed in Chapter 8, instrumentality theories of behavior imply that people make carefully considered, rational decisions. There is abundant evidence, however, that people are not always rational, and that they will in fact often behave in ways that are irrelevant, or even contrary, to their own best interests.

For example, workers may vote for, or against, a union because their co-workers are voting that way, rather than because of any rational analysis of the instrumentality of union membership. Workers may also accept or reject unions because of their general political beliefs. "Liberals" may be more likely to vote in favor of unions than are "conservatives," whether or not the union would prove to be beneficial in their particular circumstances. Consequently, whereas the research on union attitudes and voting behavior suggests some general conclusions about what makes a union attractive, it cannot adequately explain the behavior of *individual* workers.

A study by Zalesny (1985) illustrates the role of emotional and social factors in determining union behavior. Zalesny studied the attitudes and behaviors of university faculty involved in a union election. She found that although instrumentality of the union predicted pro-union behavior, affect toward unionization, or simply whether a person evaluates unionization positively or negatively, improves the prediction of union-voting behavior beyond that made from instrumentality alone. Also identified as a contributing factor to union voting in Zalesny's study were social pressures based on such things as roles and norms related to the faculty members' jobs.

Finally, you must remember that not all of the men and women who belong to a union voted in favor of accepting that union, and that some members would prefer not to be members. Often, those workers who vote against the union in elections *must* join the union if the union wins. In this arrangement, called a union shop, all workers must join and pay dues to the union regardless of their personal attitudes or desires regarding union membership. In other situations, workers are not required to join the union per se, but are required to pay a fee to the union to help cover the union's expenses as the legal bargaining agent for the employee. Many states, however, have passed right-to-work laws, which guarantee workers that union membership cannot be a condition for employment in any organization.

Workers' Reasons for Not Joining Unions

As we have seen, the number and proportion of workers who belong to unions have been dropping in recent years. Even during the heyday of unions, from the 1940s through the 1960s, only a minority of workers belonged to labor unions. In our examination of workers' reasons for joining unions, we have alluded to their reasons for rejecting unions as well. In many companies, and in some industries, there has simply been no effort to organize employees. This may be because union officials feel that the workers in a particular company would never accept a union, so that they don't bother to spend their time and resources trying to get authorization for an election.

Many nonmanagerial employees, such as engineers, accountants, and research scientists, work closely with management in planning their companies' policies. Such workers may come to identify with the management goals they have helped to define and achieve, and reject unions on the same philosophical and practical grounds as do managers. In a similar fashion, some companies, such as Peter's Pan Pizza prior to its merger with Flavio's, have few jobs involving traditional blue-collar work, but numerous opportunities for promotion to management. If a large proportion of the employees of a company aspire to managerial positions, it is less likely that a union's organizing effort would be successful.

It is clear from the research discussed in the previous section that the *best* explanation for the rejection of unions, and one that encompasses the considerations listed above, is that workers reject unions when they perceive that unions are not instrumental for achieving their personal goals, or when they perceive that there are *other* options in the workplace (for example, aligning themselves with management's goals) that have *greater* instrumentality than union membership. That is, if a worker believes that belonging to a union will increase her chances for promotion, pay raises, and a safer working environment, *and* if she values these outcomes, then a pro-union attitude is likely to result. A pro-union attitude will be less likely to develop, however, if any of the following conditions exist: (1) The worker believes that unions will lead to these outcomes, but does not value them (not all workers desire to be promoted, for example); (2) the worker values the available outcomes, but does not believe that unions will help get them (perhaps because no promotions are available); or (3) the worker believes that by *not* joining a union the chances for attaining these outcomes will be enhanced.

Management Reactions to Unionization Efforts

Unions represent a threat to the management of a company. In a nonunionized organization, management is relatively free to set policy regarding hours, wages, and conditions of work. Once a union is authorized to represent the employees in a company, however, many of these issues will become subject to collective bargaining, and thereafter will be governed by a contract, rather than the desires of management. Some examples of management concerns with issues commonly covered by union contracts are listed below:

1. *Promotions:* Many union contracts include clauses regarding promotion. Although there is variation in the content of these clauses, management is most concerned with clauses that specify seniority as a, if not *the*, criterion for promotion.

2. *Discipline:* Contracts often indicate a specific series of steps to be taken in the disciplining of an employee. These clauses are intended to protect employees from unfair and arbitrary discipline, and often limit the types of behaviors that can be disciplined, the period of time over which evidence of misdeeds can be accumulated, and the form that discipline can take.

3. *Layoffs and firings:* Union contracts usually specify that layoffs be made on the basis of seniority. In most cases, management would prefer to make layoffs strictly on the basis of employee ability and productivity. Under most contracts, an employer must demonstrate "due cause" for firing an employee. If the employee or the union wishes to challenge the firing, an arbitrator may be called in to make the final decision about the employee's status.

4. *Transfers:* Transfers, or job changes to equal-status or lower-status jobs, are usually governed by the principle of seniority, rather than ability or performance. The same is true for selection of work shifts or choices among several open jobs. A trial period to learn the new job is often specified by the contract.

5. *Work schedules:* Union contracts, especially in manufacturing companies, frequently specify work schedules and the rate of production. Increases in the rate of production due to technological improvements are made difficult by many contracts, as the union tries to avoid changes that would increase profits for the company without corresponding increases in wages.

6. *Overtime:* Most union contracts specify that overtime must be distributed equally within a work unit. As with other personnel actions, management would prefer to offer overtime on the basis of worker performance.

In sum, management loses some of its authority to operate the organization as it sees fit when its relationships with workers are governed by a contract. From management's standpoint, therefore, the ideal situation is to never even be faced with a unionization campaign. To this end, it behooves management to be aware of the factors that contribute to pro-union attitudes, and to be willing to take action to satisfy those needs and desires that might otherwise result in union activity.

There is a great deal of advice available on how to prevent unions from succeeding in their certification efforts. Occasionally, this advice involves practices prohibited by U.S. law, such as taking disciplinary action against pro-union employees, or promising employees benefits if a union is kept out. More reputable advice is offered by those who emphasize a positive employee-relations atmosphere as the key to avoiding unionization. For example, lawyers who specialize in helping companies fight unionization suggest that supervisors express appreciation of employees' work, be sensitive to personal problems, be fair and consistent in dealings with employees, and maintain integrity (DeMaria, 1974).

Although the employee-relations approach to discouraging unions involves behaviors that are certainly desirable and likely to be appreciated by employees, it doesn't address most of the fundamental factors that lead workers to perceive a need for a union. As we have seen, workers are likely to develop pro-union attitudes, and therefore vote in favor of unions, when union membership is seen as useful for attaining certain valued goals. Of particular importance is the perceived instrumentality of unions for attaining goals related to extrinsic satisfaction, such as pay, promotion, and working conditions. If management at Peter's Pan Pizza sincerely wishes to avoid unionization, their best bet is to be aware of the extrinsic needs of their employees, and to provide alternative "nonunion" paths to those goals. This can be expensive, as it may involve changes in pay structure, benefits, hours, and other work conditions. These costs, however, are not likely to be greater than the costs a company will incur if a union is successful, and these types of voluntary benefits do not involve any loss of management's right to run the company as it sees fit, or to make organizational changes as economic conditions change.

THE ROLE OF LABOR UNIONS

We have discussed the process by which a company becomes unionized. Once a union is "in," what is its role in the workplace? Clearly, the most important role of unions is to represent the workers in contract negotiations with management. Although there are other union functions, such as representing employees during grievance procedures, these other activities are governed by the terms of the labor contract. Consequently, the strength of a union depends on its ability to obtain favorable contract terms during negotiations. We will therefore examine the collective-bargaining process in some detail in the following sections, and then discuss the grievance procedure, which is one of the most important union activities between contract negotiations.

Collective Bargaining

The labor contract is the legal document governing employment conditions during the time that the contract is in effect, and it is the result of a process known as collective bargaining. In collective bargaining, management and union representatives meet and try to come to an agreement about such issues as employee compensation, working conditions, workers' security, and management's rights. These negotiations are typically drawn-out, combative affairs, and their success or failure can depend on many factors, including the expectations of each party, the state of the economy, and the ground rules that have been set up prior to formal bargaining.

BARGAINING POSITIONS AND NEGOTIATION

It is obvious that union representatives will want to maximize the benefits received by their members; this is the primary reason why the union was elected to represent the workers. Because of the costs of providing these benefits, management will naturally wish to maintain a limit on what the workers receive. Labor knows that management will not agree to everything that the workers desire; and management, in turn, knows that labor will not accept what the company would like to offer. Each side also knows that some give-and-take is expected in negotiations. Negotiators, therefore, present initial bargaining positions that are usually extreme and far apart from one another.

The union representatives in Flavio's negotiations, for example, are going to demand wages that are higher than they realistically expect to obtain, and ask for benefits that they know are probably too costly for Flavio's to provide. They are also likely to demand contract clauses, unacceptable to management, that either mandate or encourage union membership in order for a person to obtain a job at Flavio's (although in states with right-to-work laws, such clauses are illegal), that specify seniority as the primary criterion for promotion, layoffs, transfers, and recalls, and that give the rank-and-file workers more say in setting company policy. These union demands are likely to be influenced by the nature of contracts in similar organizations, and the desire of Flavio's workers to meet or exceed these standards. They might also be affected by such things as economic conditions and the local labor situation. Greater demands are typically made when the economy is good and the labor supply tight; demands are lower when the company is not doing as well or when there are many people looking for jobs.

For their part, Flavio's management will anticipate the costly demands of the union, so that their initial bargaining position will include offers that are far below what they know the union will be willing to accept. These offers will typically reflect lower wages and benefits than those sought by the union. They will also contain clauses allowing nonunion workers to be employed, specifying merit or performance as the basis for promotions, layoffs, transfers, and recalls, and denying the rank-and-file workers any role in setting certain company policies.

Because the initial bargaining positions of both union and management are extreme, everyone involved knows that each side must compromise if a contract agreement is to be reached. On each issue, there is a certain amount that each side will be willing to sacrifice in order to reach an agreement. The limit of what each side will give up is called the tolerance limit (Stagner & Rosen, 1965; see Figure 11.2). As was true for the initial bargaining positions, tolerance limits are likely to be determined by specific conditions in the industry. For example, if Flavio's is facing stiff competition from a newcomer in the frozen-lasagna market, the union may tolerate lower wages than they otherwise would. If, however, the company has paid large dividends to stockholders for several years, the union is likely to reject anything other than a large hike in wages.

When the union's tolerance limit overlaps with management's tolerance limit, as in Figure 11.2a, a "bargaining zone" is created that includes solutions acceptable to both parties. When this bargaining zone exists, it *should* be possible for negotiations, at least on that issue, to be successful. Occasionally there is no overlap between the tolerance limits, and therefore no bargaining zone, as in Figure 11.2b. In this case, the minimum that the union will accept is still more than the maximum that management is willing to give. It is therefore unlikely that the give-and-take of negotiations will resolve the issue, and an impasse has been reached.

IMPASSE RESOLUTION

When the union and management bargainers are so far apart either on a single issue or on the contract as a whole that agreement is virtually impossible, that is known as an impasse. Without some technique for breaking impasses, many contract negotiations would grind to a halt, ultimately resulting in a strike or lockout, which are costly to both sides. Because an impasse is always a possibility in collective bargaining, it is common for both parties to agree to take certain measures in the event an impasse is reached. This agreement may be part of the previous labor contract, or it may be less formal, and agreed upon only when it becomes evident that an impasse has occurred.

There are three common techniques for resolving impasses. Each involves the services of an independent third party, but they vary in terms of the power

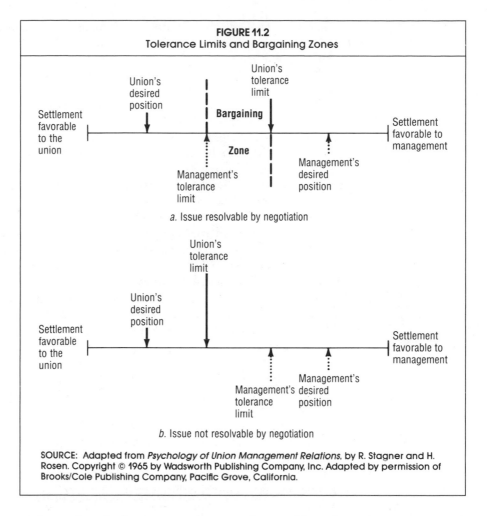

FIGURE 11.2
Tolerance Limits and Bargaining Zones

a. Issue resolvable by negotiation

b. Issue not resolvable by negotiation

SOURCE: Adapted from *Psychology of Union Management Relations,* by R. Stagner and H. Rosen. Copyright © 1965 by Wadsworth Publishing Company, Inc. Adapted by permission of Brooks/Cole Publishing Company, Pacific Grove, California.

given to that third party to impose a solution. They share the same general purpose, however: to ensure the completion of the contract negotiations and hasten the resumption of "business as usual."

The least-structured, least-formal method for dealing with an impasse is mediation. In mediation an impartial third party, the mediator, is called in to help negotiators overcome their differences. It is important to note that mediation is a voluntary process, and that the mediator has *no authority* to unilaterally impose a solution to the impasse. One of the most important functions of mediation is reopening the lines of communication between union and management. Once an impasse is reached, there are often hard feelings on each side. Even if a "bargaining zone" existed prior to the negotiations, neither union nor management representatives are likely to display a desire to compromise any further. By privately discussing each side's position with its representatives, away from the eyes and ears of "the enemy," the mediator may identify avenues that will bring the parties closer together.

Although mediators have no power to enforce a settlement, they are still important people with delicate jobs to perform. In case of an impasse during contract negotiations at Flavio's Frozen Foods, a mediator will need to find out such things as how far each side is actually willing to go in order to come to an agreement, which issues are most important to them, and where they are willing to compromise in order to gain concessions from the other side. Because this sort of information could easily be used to bias the negotiations one way or the other, the mediator must be trusted completely by both sides. He must therefore be fair, impartial, and discreet. In some cases there is a third party, familiar to both sides, that can play this role. If this is not the case, the negotiators can turn to the Federal Mediation and Conciliation Service, which maintains a staff of experienced, qualified mediators.

A second, and less common, method of impasse resolution is fact finding, where an impartial third party gathers all the relevant information about the disputed issues, reviews it, and makes a public recommendation about how the impasse should be settled. At Flavio's, a fact finder brought in to settle a dispute over wages might consider such things as the profits or losses experienced by Flavio's in recent years, the prevailing wages in the food industry, local economic and labor conditions, and the final offers and demands of the bargainers.

Fact finders also have *no power* to enforce their recommendations. The theory behind fact finding is that making the recommendation public will pressure the parties to accept the fact finder's solution. Unfortunately, most people do not seem to care about contract negotiations unless they are personally inconvenienced by a strike, and so public pressure from fact finding tends to be minimal (Kochan, 1980). Clearly, it isn't very likely that the threat of a strike at Flavio's, and the resulting possibility of a frozen-pizza shortage, will inspire the public to demand that a fact finder's advice be adopted! On the other hand, the threat of being without a daily newspaper or public transit might result in such pressure.

The third form of impasse resolution is arbitration. As is the case with mediation and fact finding, arbitration involves the services of a third party, known in this case as an arbitrator. Unlike the other methods of resolving impasses, however, the decision of an arbitrator is *legally binding* on both parties. That is, whatever the arbitrator decides *must* go into the contract. For this reason, arbitration, if used, is always the last step in negotiations. Also, because of the binding nature of an arbitrator's decisions, the procedures involved in this technique are spelled out in more formal, specific terms than are those of the other methods, in order to protect the rights of both parties.

There are several ways to classify the various types of arbitration. Conventional arbitration is when the arbitrator is free to make any settlement she wishes. This often results in the arbitrator "splitting the difference" between the two offers, although she *could* select a settlement that is closer to either the union or the management offer. Final-offer arbitration gives the arbitrator less freedom in settling the impasse. In this system, the arbitrator *must* select either the union or the management offer; no compromise settlement is allowed. Final-offer arbitration was developed because in conventional arbitration, negotiators found that the settlement often falls halfway between the two offers. This results in a "chilling effect," in which the parties tend to begin the negotiations far apart and resist moving closer together. Figure 11.3 shows what might happen under conventional arbitration if management made concessions without similar concessions from the union: Management would lose out in arbitration, assuming that the arbitrator settled about halfway between the two *final* offers. The rationale for final-offer arbitration is that extreme offers are not likely to be selected by the arbitrator, and so the bargainers will take more moderate bargaining positions, and perhaps settle more issues without an impasse.

Research on the effectiveness of conventional vs. final-offer arbitration supports the usefulness of the final-offer technique. Starke and Notz (1981) reviewed the brief literature comparing the two types of arbitration, and found that most studies report that bargainers anticipating final-offer arbitration were closer to settlement at the end of negotiations than were bargainers anticipating conventional arbitration. In their own laboratory study of bargaining behavior, Starke and Notz found that final-offer arbitration resulted in lower prenegotiation expectations, closer agreement at the conclusion of bargaining, and greater commitment to the settlement, whether negotiated or arbitrated.

Final-offer arbitration can be further broken down into final offer by issue or final offer by package. In final offer by issue, the bargainers identify the individual issues on which they cannot negotiate a settlement, and make a final offer on each one. The arbitrator must select one of these offers for each issue. The result of arbitration by issue is that the union position may be selected on some issues, and the management position selected on others. For example, at Flavio's the union and management bargainers may be unable to agree on the issues of wages and health benefits. The union may be demanding $8.50 per hour as a starting wage and full health-insurance coverage for all members of an employee's family. Management may be offering $7.00 per hour as a base wage and paid insurance only for the employee, with insurance premiums for family coverage coming out of the workers' wages. It is conceivable that under arbitration by issue, an

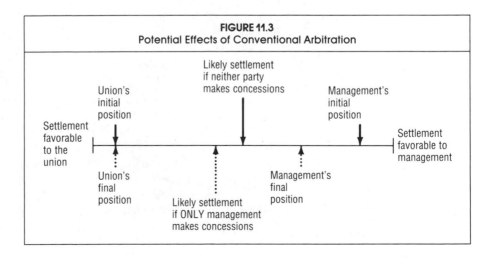

FIGURE 11.3
Potential Effects of Conventional Arbitration

arbitrator would award the $8.50 starting wage, but accept management's offer of the limited health benefits.

In final offer by package, the negotiators make offers on each of the unsettled issues, but the arbitrator must either select the union's offers on *all* of the issues, or management's offers on *all* of the issues. In our example above, the arbitrator must select between awarding both the higher wages and the more costly health benefits, or awarding the lower wages and the limited benefits.

In a study comparing these two types of final-offer arbitration and conventional arbitration, Grigsby and Bigoness (1982) found that there were significantly fewer issues left unsettled before arbitration when subjects anticipated final-offer arbitration by package than when they anticipated either final-offer arbitration by issue or conventional arbitration. The largest number of unsettled issues occurred in the conventional-arbitration situation. It is interesting to note that there were no differences between the final-offer arbitration conditions when the subjects believed that mediation would be used prior to arbitration. The anticipation of mediation led the groups expecting final-offer arbitration by issue to resolve more issues than when no mediation was anticipated. These results suggest that combining impasse-resolution techniques, such as mediation and arbitration, might be effective.

One final way to categorize arbitration is to consider whether it is voluntary arbitration or compulsory arbitration. In voluntary arbitration, both parties agree to abide by the decision of an arbitrator, once they have realized that a negotiated settlement is unlikely. There is no legal requirement, either by statute or by a previous contract, to engage in arbitration, so that voluntary arbitration is unlikely unless both sides anticipate that the settlement will be in their own best interest. In compulsory arbitration, the parties are *required* to submit offers to an arbitrator if they are unable to come to an agreement, usually by a specified deadline. This requirement may be enforced by law, or by the terms of the existing contract.

You can see that there are many different impasse-resolution methods. Which of these methods are used in a particular situation depends on a number of factors, including the common practices in the industry, preferences of top management and union leaders, and external pressures on the two parties. For example, in the case of labor disputes involving public employees, it is common for arbitration to be used as the means for settling disputes. The reason for this practice is that strikes by such groups as fire fighters, police, and sanitation workers can pose threats to the welfare of the public, and are therefore illegal in many places. In most cases, the binding nature of arbitration guarantees that public strikes will be avoided. Mediation, on the other hand, is more likely to be used to settle impasses in the private sector. This may be because mediation does not require negotiators to give final control of the bargaining process to a third party, or perhaps because union and management leaders often want to demonstrate that they can settle their differences effectively. The risk that is run when mediation is used, however, is that the mediator will not be able to bring the two sides together. When that happens, a strike may result.

STRIKES, LOCKOUTS, AND OTHER TACTICS

When arbitration is not used, and when mediation and fact finding prove to be ineffective, both management and the union can turn to more drastic actions. The best-known of these tactics, designed to bring pressure to bear on management, is a strike. In a strike, the workers simply stop working, thereby forcing management (they hope) to suspend operations and causing financial hardship for the company. Of course, workers do not get paid when they are on strike, nor are they eligible for unemployment benefits, and so they usually experience financial hardship themselves. Because a strike is costly to both employer and employee, the decision to strike is not usually taken lightly. A majority of the union members must vote to authorize a strike. The decision to strike can be made easier if union members have contributed all along to a strike fund, which is used to make payments to strikers while they are not working. These payments, however, are usually only a fraction of the workers' normal wages; even if there is a strike fund, workers may be reluctant to walk off the job.

A union will often use the *threat* of a strike to pressure management. Typically, workers will vote to authorize a strike if a negotiated settlement is not reached by a certain "target date," usually midnight on the day that the current contract expires. Knowing that a strike has already been authorized often prompts management's negotiators to be more receptive to the union's demands, especially if a strike will be particularly costly. Unions therefore try to negotiate contracts that expire at times that correspond to critical periods in the business cycle. Truck drivers, for example, like contracts that end when there is a lot of perishable food to be shipped to markets; employees of toy manufacturers like to be negotiating new contracts during the late summer and early fall, when toys are being stockpiled for Christmas. In some cases, a union will ask its members to work without a contract until such a critical period arrives. Not very long ago, professional baseball players worked under the terms of an expired contract in order to threaten a strike just before the all-star game, and umpires timed a strike so that it occurred immediately prior to the onset of the major league championship series.

Without question, a strike is unpleasant for everyone involved. Because of this, there are less severe forms of pressure that a union can bring to bear. Chief among these is a work slowdown. During a slowdown, workers remain on the job and collect their wages. They limit their productivity, however, thereby bringing financial pressure to bear on the company. A slowdown may be instigated if economic conditions are such that workers would find it difficult to obtain temporary jobs during a strike, if there is no strike fund, or if strikes are illegal, as is often the case in public-sector jobs.

Although we are accustomed to hearing about strikes and slowdowns, management also has pressure tactics at its disposal during contract negotiations. Specifically, management can institute a lockout. A lockout basically means that the company is closed down. The workers therefore have no jobs and no wages.

In terms of its economic impact on both the company and the workers, a lockout is similar to a strike. The difference is that a strike is usually called when management is in a vulnerable position; a lockout is more likely to occur when management knows that the workers would not be able to go very long without their wages, and that alternative employment is difficult to find. Under these conditions, a lockout is likely to initiate pressure *within* the union to accept management's offers, as workers increasingly feel the effects of forced unemployment.

Management can also take actions in response to strikes by the union. For example, if there are a large number of unemployed workers in the local economy, the company can hire nonunion workers to replace the strikers. Whereas this may seem to be a logical solution to a strike, it entails certain risks on the part of management. First, in most situations the new employees will have neither the training nor the experience to perform the jobs, and a costly training program will have to be instituted. Second, the striking employees will naturally resent the presence of these new workers (referred to by union members as "scabs"), and violence directed toward both the company and the replacement workers is not unheard of. It is also possible in a small proportion of cases, particularly in highly automated industries, for management to fill in for striking workers, although union resentment and its effects are again a possibility. Farsighted managers who anticipate a strike may try to increase production prior to contract negotiations, so that an ample supply of products will be available if and when a strike is actually called. Of course, farsighted union leaders will perceive this tactic and try to prevent the production increase, possibly through a slowdown.

It should be clear to you by now that failure to resolve an impasse through mediation or arbitration can result in unpleasant and costly actions by *both* union and management. Strikes, lockouts, slowdowns, and other pressure tactics cost the participants a great deal, and in some cases serve simply to strengthen the resolve of the opposition. It is in the best interest of both parties to settle their differences through negotiation, and indeed most negotiations are successfully completed. Whether a contract settlement comes through negotiation, the efforts of an arbitrator, mediator, or fact finder, or as the result of a strike, the interaction of union and management does not end when the contract is signed. Indeed, depending on the terms of the labor contract, the union often plays an important role in the day-to-day activities of the organization, particularly the relationship between labor and management.

Union Activity between Negotiations

Union and management negotiators hope that the labor contract will address all the important issues that might arise, and that the contract is clear regarding what should be done in every circumstance involving labor and management disagreement. Bear in mind, however, that in order to reach a contract settlement, both sides had to make concessions and compromises. There will therefore be terms in the contract that one side or the other may be able to "live with," but about which they are not really happy. We can expect, then, that management and the union may interpret some contract clauses in slightly (or not so slightly) different ways.

Different interpretations of the contract usually lead to disagreement and friction between employer and employee. Virtually all labor contracts give the union authority to represent workers when such conflicts occur, through a formal process known as a grievance procedure. Although the specific nature of grievance procedures varies from place to place, a grievance is usually filed when an employee believes that management has violated her rights, as defined by the labor contract. The grievance itself is a formal protest, and sets into a motion a series of events that are designed to determine whether or not the employee's complaint is valid, and if so, what steps should be taken to remedy the injustice.

An example of a management action that might result in a grievance would be if Flavio's management were to promote a worker with eight years of experience rather than one with 15 years of experience, and the labor contract specified that seniority was to be used as the basis for promotions whenever possible. To the union, this seniority clause seems straightforward: More senior employees will be promoted whenever such employees are available and want the promotion. Management, however, is likely to see things as being more complex. Specifically, management may interpret the "whenever possible" portion of the seniority clause as giving them license to select the most senior employee *with experience in jobs similar to the one to which the promotion is to be made.* That is, management may feel that it is "not possible" to promote an employee who has not demonstrated the skills necessary to perform the new job. The union, on the other hand, may expect management to promote the most senior person who wants the job, and if that person needs special training, then management must provide that training.

As we said, grievance procedures are defined by the labor contract, and so there is a great deal of variability in the specific steps that a grieving employee might follow. In many cases, once the grievance has been filed, the employee and her supervisor meet to try to settle the dispute. If the employee is still not satisfied, the shop steward may get involved in the process. The shop steward is the formal representative of the union in the workplace, more or less the union equivalent of a foreman. Stewards will often represent the grieving employee because they have a more detailed knowledge of the contract, and are likely to have had special instruction or training from the union in how to handle grievances.

If the steward is not able to resolve the grievance by working with the supervisor, the next step might be to present the grievance to a representative from the personnel department, and if that is not successful, to a higher member of management, and so on. Eventually, the grievance procedure may be exhausted. That is, the chain of appeal specified by the contract may be followed to its end without the employee being satisfied with the result. At this point, if allowed by the contract, the issue may be settled by arbitration. Here, the job of the arbitrator is to study the facts of the case, and decide if the action taken by management is warranted under the terms of the contract. As in the case of arbitration during contract negotiations, the decision of the grievance arbitrator is binding on both sides.

There is only a limited amount of psychological research on the grievance process. Perhaps the most interesting are the studies conducted by Dalton and Todor (1979, 1982). These authors noted that the shop steward is often very influential in determining whether or not a grievance is filed. They therefore suggested that the personalities of stewards, as reflected in the strengths of their various needs, may predict the pattern of grievances in the stewards' units. They found that the higher a steward's need for dominance, the more grievances that steward filed. They also found, however, that stewards with higher needs for dominance were more likely to discuss potential grievances with management, and therefore settle the issue before actually filing charges (Dalton & Todor, 1979). In the same study, Dalton and Todor found that stewards with high needs for affiliation were also likely to avoid grievances by first discussing the incidents with management, which may reflect a preference for interpersonal techniques of conflict resolution over formal procedures.

In another study of union stewards, Dalton and Todor (1982) found that the attitudes of stewards predicted the pattern of grievances filed in their units. Specifically, stewards who were more committed to the employing company, and those who had higher job satisfaction, were less likely to file grievances than those with less commitment or job satisfaction. The committed or satisfied stewards were also less likely to encourage workers to file grievances when the workers showed no desire to file, and they filed fewer grievances over the objections of workers. The more committed stewards were to the *union*, however, the less likely they were to discourage a grievant from filing, and the less likely they were to resolve the grievance by discussing the issue with management before filing charges.

Dalton and Todor's (1979, 1982) research not only identifies characteristics of stewards that predict whether or not grievances will be filed, but also illustrates the degree of control that stewards have over the grievance process. Dalton and Todor (1982) developed a model of the grievance process, which is shown in Figure 11.4. The bottom line of the model indicates that stewards may file grievances without consulting the workers who may have been harmed. In this situation, the steward controls the grievance activity completely, and the types of personal characteristics identified in Dalton and Todor's research are probably quite important in determining grievances.

The steward can also encourage workers to file when they are reluctant to do so, or the steward can discourage workers from filing when they are anxious to do so. The amount of influence exercised by the steward in these cases depends on his persuasive skills and the worker's resolve. Finally, the steward can try to avoid filing a grievance by dealing with management on a more informal basis. An aspect of this model that should not be overlooked is the potential power of management to avoid grievances. As envisioned by Dalton and Todor (1982), management can avoid grievances by trying to prevent grievable situations, by dealing with the aggrieved employee after an incident, or by negotiating with the

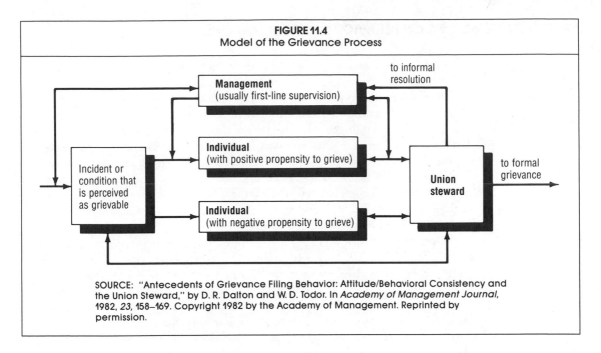

FIGURE 11.4
Model of the Grievance Process

SOURCE: "Antecedents of Grievance Filing Behavior: Attitude/Behavioral Consistency and the Union Steward," by D. R. Dalton and W. D. Todor. In *Academy of Management Journal,* 1982, *23,* 158–169. Copyright 1982 by the Academy of Management. Reprinted by permission.

shop steward. Clearly, if incentives are available for both union and management, there are ample opportunities to avoid filing grievances.

Concession Bargaining

Before we leave the discussion of union–management relations, we should mention a relatively new phenomenon called concession bargaining, where the union concedes, or "gives back," some of the benefits that its members had previously won through collective bargaining. Concession bargaining received a great deal of attention in the early 1980s when the Chrysler Corporation, on the verge of bankruptcy, won concessions from the United Auto Workers that resulted in Chrysler employees making less money than workers at other auto companies. Those concessions allowed Chrysler to cut costs, however, and so helped to ensure that the federal government would give them the loan that eventually kept the company in business.

There is little research on either the effects of, or the factors that contribute to, concession bargaining. Plovnick and Chaison (1985) found that economic hardship alone does not increase the probability of unions agreeing to concessions. Their data did, however, suggest that concessions by management (such as Chrysler chairman Lee Iacocca giving up his salary) may lead to better union–management relations, which in turn may improve the chances for union concessions.

THE EFFECTS OF UNIONS ON BEHAVIOR IN ORGANIZATIONS

Research on the effects of unions on workers' behavior has been scarce. Gordon and Nurick (1981) noted that union leaders tend to distrust I/O psychologists, and view the profession as a tool of management to be used against labor. This distrust stems from the fact that union members often associate psychology with unpopular efforts to increase worker productivity, such as the work of Frederick Taylor (see Chapters 1 and 9). Also, psychologists who conduct research in organizations have traditionally been employed by management, and have often worked to achieve management goals opposed by unions. Consequently, union leaders have often rejected psychologists' attempts to study the work behavior of their members. Dr. MacKeven should keep this history of distrust in mind as she works with the unionized employees at Flavio's.

Gordon and Nurick (1981) also pointed out that psychologists have not exactly fought to gain access to unions for research purposes. These authors believe that this lack of effort is due largely to two basic beliefs held by most I/O psychologists. First is the notion, developed during the human relations movement of the late 1950s and early 1960s, that workers and their managers share common interests and concerns. This in turn led to the conclusion that unionization was a symptom of poor management, and focused psychologists' efforts on developing ways to increase management–labor harmony. The tendency to view unionization in this way, as a symptom of a problem rather than as a legitimate effort on the part of workers to protect their interests, discouraged research on unions *as organizations*.

A second factor that has limited research on unions is a belief among I/O psychologists that they do not need to be concerned with the *uses* to which their research is put, but rather only with developing the *means* by which the goals of management can be reached, regardless of the nature of those goals. Hugo Münsterberg expressed this view in 1913, and it can be argued that I/O psychologists have followed it ever since. Gordon and Nurick (1981) believe that this practice has led psychologists to be unaware of, or perhaps to ignore, the natural conflict between management and unions, and so unions have not been the focus of their research efforts. Again, to the extent that Dr. MacKeven may have acquired either of these attitudes toward unions, she should strive to be especially objective when dealing with the unionization issues raised in Mr. Smith's memo. In any case, unions have only recently become the focus of psychologists' research. What follows is a sample of the types of issues psychologists have begun to examine when considering the role of unions in the workplace.

Unions and Job Satisfaction

You have seen that low job satisfaction, particularly with extrinsic factors such as pay, is related to pro-union attitudes and behavior. A related but separate issue is whether belonging to a union is related to workers' levels of job satisfaction; the research evidence suggests that it is. Odewahn and Petty (1980), for example, compared 100 union members to 100 workers who did not belong to unions, and found that the union members had lower overall job satisfaction.

When research focuses on satisfaction with more specific aspects of work, however, the results are more complex. Kochan and Helfman (1981) found that unionized hourly workers were more satisfied with their pay than were non-unionized workers, but that the union members had *lower* satisfaction with nonpay facets of their jobs. A similar pattern of pay and nonpay satisfaction was found by Berger, Olson, and Boudreau (1983). These researchers polled a nationwide sample of 386 union members and 769 nonmembers, and their findings led them to conclude that whereas unionization has an effect on satisfaction with various facets of work, this effect is indirect, and operates through the direct effects of unionization on work-related values and perceived rewards. Specifically, Berger and his colleagues concluded that union members were more satisfied with pay *because* of the positive effects of unions on pay, whereas unions had negative effects on satisfaction with the actual work performed *because* union members perceived that their jobs had fewer responsibilities. Satisfaction with supervision was also lower for union members *because* of less favorable perceptions of relations with supervisors, and satisfaction with promotions was lower *because* of a lower value placed on promotions by union members.

A slightly different picture emerged from the research of Gomez-Mejia and Balkin (1984). In a study comparing unionized and nonunionized college faculty, they found, as have other researchers, that the union members were more satisfied with their pay. What is different about this study is that Gomez-Mejia and Balkin controlled for differences in pay between the two groups, and the union members were *still* more satisfied with their pay. This is contrary to Berger, Olson, and Boudreau's (1983) conclusion that unionization has an effect on pay satisfaction only because it results in higher pay. These conflicting results illustrate that the effects of unionization on job satisfaction are probably dependent on a number of situational factors, such as the type of industry within which the unions operate, as well as personal factors, such as the type of person attracted to certain jobs.

Attitudes toward Unions

I/O psychologists have long been interested in studying attitudes toward work and employers (see Chapter 9). With increased recognition of the role of unions in determining worker behavior, there has been greater interest in studying attitudes toward the union itself. We now discuss research on two such attitudes: union commitment and satisfaction with the union.

UNION COMMITMENT

Gordon, Philpot, Burt, Thompson, and Spiller (1980) spearheaded the research on commitment to unions by developing a measure of union commitment. They constructed a questionnaire that included measures of such factors as loyalty to the union, satisfaction with the union, participation in union activities, socialization experiences occurring early in a worker's union membership, and various demographic variables (for example, age and sex). This questionnaire was administered to 1377 nonprofessional, white-collar union members. A factor analysis of these data identified four dimensions of union commitment. The first and most important dimension was *union loyalty*, which reflects, to a great extent, the degree to which the union is seen by members as providing desired benefits (that is, union instrumentality), as well as one's intentions to remain in the union. The second dimension, *responsibility to the union*, taps members' willingness to fulfill day-to-day union obligations. The third, *willingness to work for the union*, concerns members' desire to perform services for the union that go beyond normal obligations. Finally, the fourth dimension reflects an attraction to unions based on ideology, and was labeled *belief in unionism.*

Gordon and his colleagues correlated scores on their union-commitment scales with a variety of other measures, and found that the best predictors of union loyalty and belief in unionism were union socialization experiences, such as the nature of workers' interactions with other members during their first year in the union. On the other hand, the best predictors of responsibility to the union and willingness to work for the union were previous union activities; those who worked for the union before were most likely to work for the union again.

Ladd, Gordon, Beauvais, and Morgan (1982) administered the same questionnaire to both professional and nonprofessional union members. Their analyses showed the same four dimensions that were identified in the earlier study, thereby demonstrating that these dimensions generalize to a variety of union populations. A later study by Fukami and Larson (1984) found that personal characteristics (age, years with the company, and education), work-role characteristics (job scope and stress), and work experiences (pay equity, supervisory relations, and social involvement) *all* predicted commitment to the *employing organization;* only work experiences, however, predicted commitment to the *union*. This is consistent with Gordon et al.'s (1980) finding that union loyalty, the strongest component of their model, is related to on-the-job socialization experiences. What remains to be seen is the extent to which psychologists will continue to show an interest in union commitment, given the lack of cooperation that has historically existed between psychologists and union leaders. Perhaps the existence and continued development of union-oriented measures (such as Gordon et al.'s) will help to stimulate more cooperation.

SATISFACTION WITH UNIONS

In an interesting and unique study, Stagner and Eflal (1982) examined the effects of the most dramatic form of union activity—a labor strike—on the attitudes and perceptions of union members. Stagner and Eflal's study was made possible by the unusual bargaining practices in the U.S. automotive industry. Typically, when contracts with the automakers are about to expire, the United

Auto Workers (UAW) international leadership selects one of the "big three" automakers, General Motors, Ford, or Chrysler, as a strike target. The union bargains with that one company, and if an agreement is not reached by the deadline, the UAW locals associated with the target company go out on strike, while the other two companies maintain operations. Whether a strike is called or not, the companies that were not targeted usually agree to contracts identical to the one that the UAW eventually negotiates with the target company. It is therefore possible to evaluate the effects of a strike by measuring the attitudes of union members in all three companies before the strike target is named, during the strike, and after the contracts have been signed.

Stagner and Eflal (1982) did exactly that, comparing the union attitudes of Ford workers, who struck in 1976, with the attitudes of General Motors and Chrysler workers, who did not strike but ended up with the same contract terms as the Ford workers. The researchers found that during the strike the Ford workers had more favorable attitudes toward the UAW international leadership, less favorable perceptions of their current economic (for example, wages) and "leisure" (for example, vacation) benefits, more militancy or hostility toward their employer, and greater willingness to help the union than General Motors and Chrysler workers. Seven months after the strike, however, these differences had essentially disappeared. Clearly, members' attitudes toward both the union and the employer are a function not only of union membership, but also the activity of the union.

Unions and Organizational Effectiveness

A final example of research on the impact of unionization concerns the question of whether or not unions influence the effectiveness of the employing organization. Certainly, most managers would argue that unions have a detrimental effect on the ability of organizations to function, but there is very little empirical research to support this belief. Cameron (1982) addressed this issue when he compared the effectiveness of colleges with unionized faculty to that of colleges without unions. Effectiveness of the colleges was measured along three general dimensions: ability to acquire resources, morale, and academic quality. On all three dimensions, nonunionized institutions were more effective than their unionized counterparts.

Cameron (1982) suggested that the inability to acquire resources may be a *cause* of unionization, rather than an effect of unions, and that unions may be seen by faculty at colleges with few resources as a tool for acquiring more resources. He further suggested that the lower morale among the unionized institutions may be a function of the nature of the difficult unionization process itself, because morale was higher the longer a college had been unionized (although morale never reached the levels of nonunionized schools). Finally, and perhaps most importantly for institutions of higher education, Cameron raised the possibility that the lower academic quality of unionized schools may be due to a number of factors, such as the additional time required of faculty for administrative duties, a lower rate of research activity, an emphasis on economic issues at the expense of academic quality, or a lower level of collegiality among the faculty of unionized colleges.

Cameron's (1982) research shows that there is at least the potential for negative effects of unions on organizational performance. It should be kept in mind, however, that his research only examined the relationship between unionization and effectiveness in colleges in the Northeastern United States. As we have seen in other types of research, unions may have different effects among college faculty than among traditional industrial workers. Also, much of Cameron's data were gathered from administrators, who are the management of colleges. The negative effects of unions may have resulted from an anti-union bias on the part of these respondents. Further, because Cameron's research was strictly correlational, it is not legitimate to conclude that unionization *caused* the lower effectiveness that he identified. It may well be, as he suggested for the acquisition of resources, that unionization is a response to poor conditions. Given the potential effects found here, however, we can expect further research on these types of issues.

CONCLUSION

It is somewhat ironic that the general level of interest in unions among I/O psychologists is increasing at a time when union membership is experiencing a somewhat dramatic decline. As we have said before, even with this decline the number of workers belonging to unions is vast, and we do not believe that unions will stop being an important factor in the workplace in the foreseeable future. However, the recent changes they have experienced illustrate the fact that like the organizations for which their members work, unions must react to changes in the economy. We hope that I/O psychologists continue to develop their interests in unions, and as they do, explore the issues that emerge in this field, such as concession bargaining and the unionization of new industries. We believe that the failure to do so would create a major gap in our knowledge of work behavior. Of course, the ability of I/O psychologists to fill that gap depends to a great extent on overcoming the adversary relationship that they have historically had with unions. Only time will tell whether or not this will happen, but the recent increase in research on unions leads us to be optimistic.

CHAPTER SUMMARY

Labor unions are associations of workers that represent the interests of their members in dealings with company management. The labor movement in North America began in the late nineteenth century, and unions grew steadily in terms of both membership and power through the 1960s. A crucial factor in this growth was the National Labor Relations Act of 1935, which guaranteed workers the right to organize. The recent decline in union membership is largely due to basic changes in the economy, most notably a shift from manufacturing to service industries.

Unions are authorized to represent workers through a democratic process called certification. This process, like other aspects of union–management relations, is overseen by the National Labor Relations Board. Research on worker support for unions has found that dissatisfaction with such factors as pay and benefits, as well as the perceived ability of unions to improve these conditions, are the best predictors of pro-union attitudes and behaviors.

Once workers are organized, the union's most important function is to represent them in collective bargaining, which is the process by which the labor contract specifying employment conditions is arrived at. If a contract cannot be agreed upon by the bargainers (that is, if an impasse is reached), a number of techniques relying on the services of an independent third party are available for breaking the deadlock. These techniques include mediation, fact finding, and several forms of arbitration. In some cases, when these impasse-resolution techniques fail or are not used at all, a strike or a lockout may be called, which essentially shuts down the company and prevents the employees from working. Between contract negotiations, the most visible union function is representing workers in the grievance procedure.

I/O psychologists have conducted relatively little research on labor unions. This is probably due to a history of distrust of psychologists on the part of unions, as well as psychologists' lack of concern over the issues that unions believe are important. Recently, however, there has been an increase in research on such topics as negotiating strategies, attitudes toward unions, and the relationship between union membership and both job satisfaction and performance.

INTEROFFICE MEMO

TO: T. J. Smith, Legal Counsel

From: J. A. MacKeven, Human-Resources Coordinator

I have been preparing my preliminary report for the ad hoc committee on unions, and I am writing this memo to share my major recommendations with you before the committee meets.

Concerning the probability of additional unionization, I am not too concerned about the situation at PPP. As you pointed out in your memo to me, we simply do not have the type of work force that is likely to be a target for such efforts. Besides, PPP has traditionally had good employee relations, so I don't think we have much to worry about here.

It might be a different story, however, in the Flavio's divisions. The substantial presence of unions in these units shows that there have been serious problems in the past. I believe that an immediate effort should be made to examine the attitudes of all Flavio's employees, particularly toward pay and other benefits. To the extent that there is any substantial dissatisfaction with these aspects of employment, we may expect additional union activity. I suggest that we pay particular attention to plants in locations where unionization is common, because that is where the contrast between union and non-union benefits is likely to be most salient to the workers. Eventually, top management will have to make a decision about whether to spend money to address any dissatisfaction with benefits or risk additional unionization.

As far as ''dealing'' with currently unionized shops, I don't have much advice to offer. As you know, federal law governs the nature of our relationships with existing unions, so the best we can do is comply with the law and hope for changes in union commitment among Flavio's workers, and eventually some decertifications.

REVIEW QUESTIONS AND EXERCISES

1. Do you think that Dr. MacKeven's assessment of the chances of unionization among Peter's Pan Pizza employees is realistic? Describe conditions under which unionization of the staff in Suardell Springs would be more likely than she indicates.

2. Dr. MacKeven has suggested that PPP's management keep close tabs on the satisfaction of Flavio's employees. Outline in more detail what this would entail. If dissatisfaction with pay or benefits were discovered in a Flavio's unit, what should be done? How might this action influence other PPP and Flavio's employees?

3. Dr. MacKeven suggests that there have been "serious problems" in Flavio's in the past, as indicated by the presence of unions. Is this a reasonable analysis on her part? What types of problems might she be talking about? What other explanations are there for Flavio's unionization?

4. Dr. MacKeven states that a decrease in commitment to the union might eventually result in decertification. What do you think would have to happen in order for this change in commitment to take place?

CHAPTER 12

Organizations and Behavior

Learning Points

After studying this chapter, you should

- be able to explain the basic principles of bureaucratic theory, and discuss its strengths and weaknesses
- understand the basic viewpoint of the human relations movement, and explain how that viewpoint is expressed in the theories of McGregor and Argyris
- be able to define an open system, and explain the similarities in, and differences between, the open systems theories of (1) Lawrence and Lorsch and (2) Katz and Kahn
- be able to describe the organizational communication process, as well as factors that influence the effectiveness of communication
- be able to define both organizational climate and organizational culture, and explain why they are important for I/O psychologists to consider
- be able to describe how effective organizations can be identified, and the factors that appear to contribute to effectiveness
- be able to define stress, and discuss how stress might best be controlled in the workplace

INTEROFFICE MEMO

TO: J. A. MacKeven, Human-Resources Coordinator

From: Ed Clark, Vice President, Retail Operations

Please take a look at the attached memo, which was forwarded to me by Joanna Richmond, director of the store inspection unit. I think that we have a serious problem with information flow in my division, and I intend to do something about it. Please let me know if you have any advice, or if there are any programs that we can institute to remedy this problem.

INTEROFFICE MEMO

TO: Joanna Richmond, Director of Store Inspections

From: Greg Bombyk, Quality Standards

I have just become aware that you have developed a new set of inspection guidelines for your people. I am writing because I also understand that these guidelines specify a series of quality points that are not consistent with the standards that my people have developed for the stores. Our most recent quality standards are dated over one year ago. You probably should have taken them into consideration when revising your inspection guidelines. For example, the inspectors should not only examine the physical condition of lavatory facilities, but also the procedures followed by store employees to guarantee sanitary conditions following use of the facilities. Please examine the attached copy of our standards, and we'll meet to go over them at your convenience.

The memos that open this chapter describe an interesting problem that is not well defined, and has no single, obvious cause. In fact, there are a variety of theories and perspectives in I/O psychology that offer potential explanations for the situation described in Mr. Bombyk's memo. Ed Clark, the vice president of retail operations, suggests that the problem is one of "information flow," which is an aspect of what we will refer to as organizational communication. It is also possible, however, that this situation reflects a long-standing conflict between the store inspection and quality standards units, with both groups claiming (or denying) responsibility for the same duties. Perhaps the general climate or culture of the organization encourages competition and friction between work groups. Maybe the company was organized on the basis of certain principles that are not valid under current economic and business conditions, and the lack of understanding or cooperation between these two groups is a symptom of this more general problem.

In this chapter we will present a variety of topics that may seem to be essentially unrelated at first. What they have in common is a focus on the role of the individual worker in the larger context of the organization as a whole. This is often referred to as a macro-level or system-wide perspective, as opposed to the more micro-level or individual approach that we have taken so far. We will also look at some meso-level issues, which are concerned with the interactions between subsystems or units within larger organizations. We will not, of course, abandon our primary interest in the individual and his behavior, as this is the appropriate emphasis for any psychology text. We will, however, try to illustrate the effects that macro-level and meso-level variables have on individual behavior, as well as the importance of individuals in determining overall subsystem or organizational performance.

ORGANIZATIONAL THEORIES

Throughout the history of I/O psychology, organizational theories have been developed to guide the organization of workers and their tasks into effective systems. The average person doesn't worry much about how to organize a company, but it must be explicitly addressed before any organization can begin to work toward meeting its goals. For example, who reports to whom? Should **research and development** managers and production managers have some formal way to communicate with one another, or is this unnecessary? Should there be many managers, or only a few, and what should be the limits of their official authority? In general, organizational theories are concerned with describing how all of the various parts of a company relate to each other (and, in some cases, to the external environment), in such a way as to maximize efficiency, productivity, and ultimately the attainment of the company's primary goals.

In practice, organizational theories have been used in two basic ways. The first is *prescriptive*, which means that an organizational theory can suggest how a company *should be put together*, or how it *should be changed*, in order to improve the way it functions. Second, organizational theories can be *heuristic*, meaning they can be used by psychologists to suggest how organizations *should be studied.* That is, these theories can suggest which conditions, characteristics, innovations, or procedures are important in an organization, as well as ways to implement and evaluate those suggestions. In the opening sections of this chapter, we will present some examples of both old and new organizational theories, and show how thinking on the nature of ideal organizations and on how organizations should be studied has changed over the years.

"Classic" Organizational Theory: Bureaucracy

The earliest organizational theories were, to a great extent, responses to the changes in business organizations that resulted from the Industrial Revolution. Prior to this time, businesses operated in what now seems to be a very haphazard fashion. There were no generally accepted guidelines for organizing a company, and so each business functioned in a slightly, or not so slightly, different way. Business was often conducted and employees managed in the same manner practiced by the owner's parents and grandparents. Relying on family tradition didn't present much of a problem for companies when they were small, and their business dealings were limited to specific geographic areas. As companies grew larger and more complex, however, and as manufacturing processes and procedures became more sophisticated, lack of organization became a serious handicap. It was simply not possible to manage a large business effectively on the basis of the same principles that small family businesses had used in the past.

The best-known and most influential of the early, or "classic," organizational theories that were developed to address the issue of chaos in industrial organizations was bureaucracy. The idea and principles of bureaucracy were developed by German sociologist Max Weber in the early part of this century (Weber, 1947). Today, the term "bureaucracy" carries negative connotations of large, impersonal, and wasteful organizations. In developing his theory, however, Weber was motivated by what might be considered a humanitarian concern for workers. He saw the typical organization of his day as being a chaotic place to work. There were usually no rules concerning such things as job assignments, promotions, and discipline. Power and authority were used in an arbitrary fashion, leaving the individual worker in the bind of not really knowing what was expected, or what the consequences of his behavior might be. This disarray led to inefficient, wasteful practices that had a direct and significant effect on organizational productivity.

Weber viewed organizations as collections of offices or positions. People with the necessary skills were hired to *occupy* those offices, but their jobs, and their conduct in those jobs, were determined by the formal organizational rules. The

---

research and development: a process by which new products are developed; the combination of basic research and technical design that results in an idea or product

word bureaucracy stems from this concept: Weber likened a business to a *bureau*, or chest of drawers, with each drawer representing an office. The content of the drawers (employees in the organization) may change over time, but the bureau itself, the relationships between the drawers, and the function and purpose of the entire system are unaffected by such changes.

Weber believed that the solution to the problems of businesses in his day was a formal, structured organizational system that was governed by legal–rational authority. That is, rather than basing power and authority on either tradition or the personal charisma of managers and supervisors, power and authority should be based on *rules*. A consequence of legal–rational authority, according to Weber, is that workers' loyalty and obedience are owed not to a particular person or group of people, but rather to *offices* that are defined by the rules and principles of the organization. Weber believed that placing authority in offices, governed by rules, would make work more predictable and fair for individual workers.

Based on studies of large, stable industrial organizations that he considered to be successful, Weber developed a set of characteristics that could be used to describe bureaucratic organizations. It is an indication of the impact that Weber has had on both business and the study of organizations that these concepts are still widely used to describe and categorize organizations.

Perhaps the best-known characteristic of bureaucracy is division of labor, or job specialization. In a bureaucracy each job is specialized, with the jobholder having responsibility for only a limited range of tasks or activities. The primary advantage of division of labor, in Weber's view, is that it allows extremely complex tasks to be performed efficiently as a series of simpler tasks. It also allows management to know who is responsible for each of the activities of the organization. The Peter's Pan Pizza organizational chart, reproduced in Figure 12.1, illustrates the concept of division of labor. There are nine divisions in PPP, each responsible for a certain range of activities. Further, within each of the divisions there is a finer division of labor among several units; although not shown in the chart, there is an even finer division of labor within each of the units, with work groups and individuals being responsible for *specific* tasks.

Although division of labor allows for the execution of complex tasks and accountability for different activities, it also presents managers in bureaucracies with the monumental task of coordinating workers' efforts. Of course, Weber believed that this coordination should be governed by formal authority. He also believed that authority was most efficient, and coordination most effective, when power was arranged in a hierarchy, which is the second of Weber's characteristics of bureaucracy.

In a hierarchy, such as Peter's Pan Pizza (Figure 12.1), ultimate authority resides in the office at the top of the organization, in this case the board of directors and the president. Offices at each level in the organization have authority over the levels below. This authority is expressed as each office coordinates the activities of the next lower level. For example, the senior vice president for operations at PPP has authority over all of the positions in the purchasing, marketing, distribution, and retail operations divisions. In practice, and according to the principles of the bureaucratic system, this authority is exercised through

FIGURE 12.1
Peter's Pan Pizza

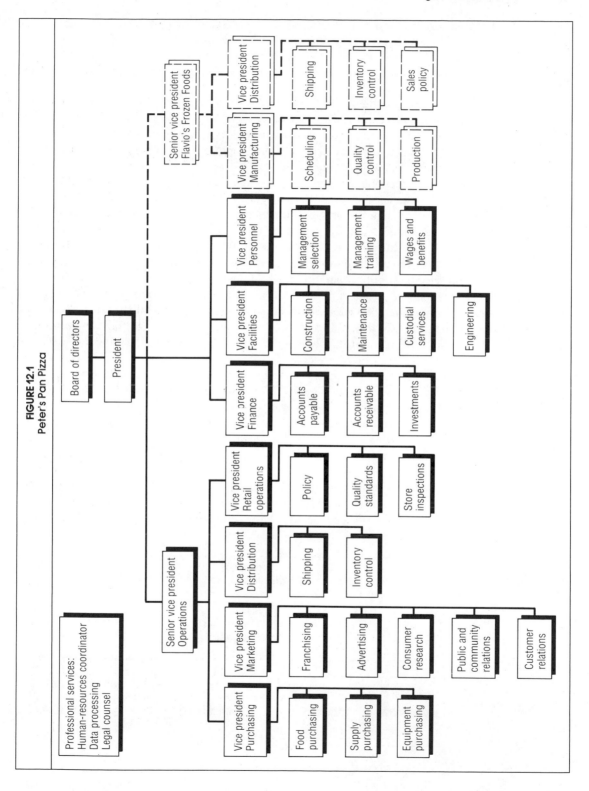

the senior vice president's coordination and supervision of the four vice presidents of these divisions. The vice presidents, in turn, have authority within their respective divisions, and this authority is exercised through their coordination and supervision of the activities of the unit directors, and so on throughout the organization.

Thus, in a hierarchy there is a clear chain of authority from the top of the organization on down, with each office being responsible to the office immediately above it in the hierarchy. Weber believed that hierarchical authority prevented the arbitrary use of power, and therefore improved both organizational functioning and individual well-being.

Two other characteristics of bureaucratic organizations introduced by Weber concern the *shape* of organizations. The first of these is span of control, which refers to the number of subordinates that are supervised by the occupant of a particular office. You can appreciate the concept of span of control by comparing Figure 12.2 with Figure 12.3. Figure 12.2 shows the marketing division of Peter's Pan Pizza; Figure 12.3 shows the distribution division. Five departments report to the vice president of marketing, who therefore has a larger span of control than does the vice president of distribution, to whom only two departments report.

The final characteristic of bureaucracies that we will discuss is known as structure. Typically, this term has been used to distinguish "tall" organizations from "flat" organizations. Figures 12.4 and 12.5 illustrate the difference between these two types of bureaucracies. In Figure 12.4 we show Peter's Pan Pizza's facilities division as it exists in the organizational chart that we have been using throughout the book. In Figure 12.5 we show the same division with an additional level of management between the vice president and the directors of the subunits. The first figure illustrates a flat bureaucratic structure, with relatively few levels in the hierarchy and a wide span of control. The second figure demonstrates a taller bureaucratic structure, with a greater number of hierarchical levels and a narrower span of control.

Weber believed that for each of these four characteristics (division of labor, hierarchy of authority, span of control, and structure) there is a single "best level," and therefore a single ideal bureaucratic form for organizations. Identifica-

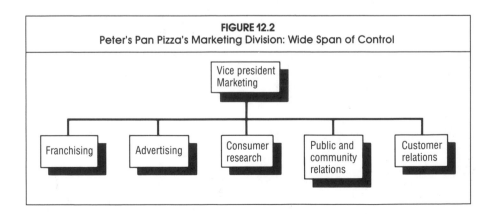

FIGURE 12.2
Peter's Pan Pizza's Marketing Division: Wide Span of Control

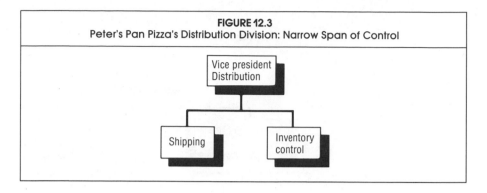

FIGURE 12.3
Peter's Pan Pizza's Distribution Division: Narrow Span of Control

tion of this ideal form has eluded researchers and practitioners, and this notion is not generally accepted today.

The belief that the ideal organization can be described using only the characteristics developed by Weber points out one of the most important weaknesses of his theory. Specifically, Weber's description of bureaucracy focused exclusively on the nature of the formal organization. It excluded consideration of activities or interactions that do not show up on the organizational chart, although such behaviors obviously *do* occur, even in the strictest of bureaucracies. Also, bureaucracy represents a **closed system,** in that it does not consider the powerful effects of events and conditions outside the formal boundaries of the organization. Later theories, some of which are discussed below, included informal processes and environmental effects, and more closely reflect the reality of how organizations function. It should be noted, however, that even though the bureaucratic model is widely viewed as being deficient, it remains very influential. Most modern organizations still conform to the characteristics that Weber described, most notably division of labor, hierarchy of authority, and systems of formal rules. It

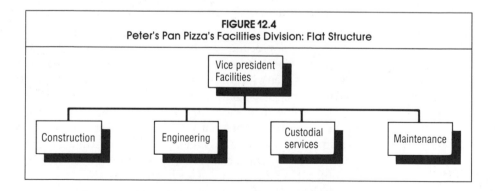

FIGURE 12.4
Peter's Pan Pizza's Facilities Division: Flat Structure

closed system: a collection of parts or components that work together, but are unaffected by, and have no effect on, the environment within which they operate

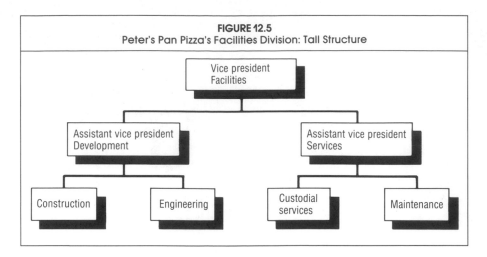

FIGURE 12.5
Peter's Pan Pizza's Facilities Division: Tall Structure

was the failure of bureaucratic theory to consider factors beyond these that limited its usefulness.

Even though newer approaches have removed bureaucracy from its position as the dominant organizational theory, some of its basic concepts have remained the focus of research. For example, Ivancevich and Donnelly (1975) studied the relationship between organizational structure (flat vs. tall) and the job attitudes, perceptions, and performance of sales personnel. They found that the sales forces in flat organizations tended to be more satisfied, experienced less stress, and had higher performance than those in taller organizations. Snizek and Bullard (1983) gathered longitudinal data examining the relationship between perceptions of bureaucratic characteristics and job satisfaction among a sample of professional park rangers. They found that over the five-year period of their study, *changes* in perceptions of these characteristics predicted satisfaction better than did current perceptions. Specifically, Snizek and Bullard's data showed that those rangers who perceived an increase in either division of labor or hierarchy of authority had lower satisfaction, whereas those who perceived an increase in the standardization of work procedures had higher satisfaction.

In yet another study of the reactions of sales personnel to bureaucratic structure, Chonko (1982) found that greater span of control on the part of managers was associated with perceptions of higher role ambiguity and role conflict among their subordinates. (We will discuss conflict and ambiguity later in this chapter.) Apparently, when a worker's boss has a large number of subordinates and must therefore divide his time among more people, the subordinates experience uncertainty about what is expected of them, and pressure to conform to more than one set of role demands.

It seems, then, that the organizational characteristics that Weber described have implications for the functioning of organizations, and in particular for the perceptions and reactions of workers. Indeed, Blackburn and Cummings (1982) found that affective (emotional) reactions to organizations were closely related to bureaucratic variables such as hierarchy of authority in workers' descriptions of their organizations' structure. This factor was only one of five that emerged from their data, however. Therefore, although bureaucracy illustrates and seems to influence some important aspects of organizations, it is safe to conclude that it only "scratches the surface." More recent theories, described in the following sections, attempt to deal with some of the facets of organizations that Weber did not consider.

Human Relations Theories

As we have seen, classic theories such as bureaucracy stressed formal structure and rules as the keys to understanding how organizations operate. Those theories failed to consider the importance of several other factors, however, not the least of which is the role played by *individuals* in organizations. Although the bureaucratic model may describe important dimensions of formal structure, its treatment of individual employees as interchangeable components does not allow us to consider the potentially important effects of individual behavior, motives, skills, and other characteristics. The human relations movement in psychology produced several organizational theories that explicitly addressed the role of individual workers in the functioning of organizations. We therefore examine the human relations perspective, and some representative theories, in more detail.

The human relations view of behavior in organizations is based on the premise that the needs and motives of individual workers, interacting with formal structure, goals, and processes, determine the ways in which an organization functions, and ultimately its success or failure. This idea is often thought to have originated with the Hawthorne studies, in which the identification of informal social influence and the apparent effects on performance and attitudes of close personal attention led to new ways of thinking about organizations (see Chapters 1 and 9 for more detailed discussions of the Hawthorne research). Whether the data from these studies actually demonstrated the effects that the Hawthorne researchers claimed is now in doubt (for example, Franke & Kaul, 1978), but even if the original interpretation was erroneous, this research laid the groundwork for subsequent studies and theory that ultimately culminated in the human relations approach to organizations.

Perhaps the essence of the human relations viewpoint can be illustrated by comparing the formal, bureaucratic structure of Peter's Pan Pizza (Figure 12.1) with the diagram in Figure 12.6. This figure shows some of the *informal* lines of communication and influence that might operate at PPP, but are not to be found in the formal organizational chart. These links develop partially because the demands of the business make them more practical than using the channels dictated by the formal structure. They also emerge, in part, because of the personalities, interests, and skills of the people in the company. Human relations theories of organizations were designed to incorporate these considerations into the way we think about, and operate, organizations.

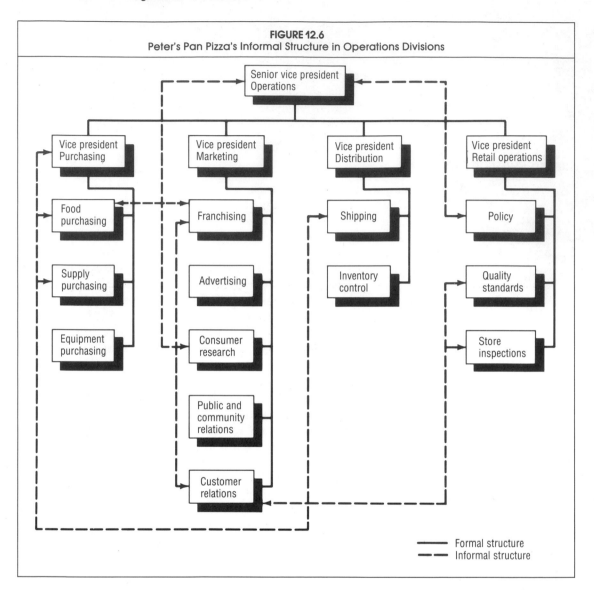

FIGURE 12.6
Peter's Pan Pizza's Informal Structure in Operations Divisions

—— Formal structure
–– Informal structure

McGREGOR'S THEORY X AND THEORY Y

Perhaps the best-known human relations theory was developed by McGregor (1960). His work focused on managers in organizations and the subjective "theories" or beliefs that they have concerning how to motivate workers. McGregor felt that every managerial action was based on a theory, or set of assumptions, about human nature and behavior. He believed that these assumptions influence managerial strategy and organizational policy in important ways. It is therefore critical, according to McGregor, to examine and understand the nature of managers' belief systems and their effects on organizations and the people in them.

To illustrate his ideas, McGregor described two belief systems or theories that he claimed operated in organizations. The basic assumptions of these theories are presented in the following lists:

THEORY X
1. The average human being has an inherent dislike of work and will avoid it if he [or she] can.
2. Because of this human characteristic of dislike of work, most people must be coerced, controlled, directed, [or] threatened with punishment to get them to put forth adequate effort toward the achievement of organizational objectives.
3. The average human being prefers to be directed, wishes to avoid responsibility, has relatively little ambition, [and] wants security above all.

THEORY Y
1. The expenditure of physical and mental effort in work is as natural as play or rest. The average human being does not inherently dislike work. Depending upon controllable conditions, work may be a source of satisfaction (and will be voluntarily performed) or a source of punishment (and will be avoided if possible).
2. External control and the threat of punishment are not the only means for bringing about effort toward organizational objectives. Man [and woman] will exercise self-direction and self-control in the service of objectives to which he [or she] is committed.
3. Commitment to objectives is a function of the rewards associated with their achievement. The most significant of such rewards, e.g., the satisfaction of ego and self-actualization needs, can be direct products of effort directed toward organizational objectives.
4. The average human being learns, under proper conditions, not only to accept, but to seek responsibility. Avoidance of responsibility, lack of ambition, and emphasis on security are generally consequences of experience, not inherent human characteristics.
5. The capacity to exercise a relatively high degree of imagination, ingenuity, and creativity in the solution of organizational problems is widely, not narrowly, distributed in the population.
6. Under the conditions of modern industrial life, the intellectual potentialities of the average human being are only partially utilized.

SOURCE: *The Human Side of Enterprise,* by D. McGregor. Copyright 1960 by McGraw–Hill Book Company. Reprinted by permission.

The first theory, called Theory X, embodies the belief that because of an inherent dislike of work on the part of employees, and a subsequent lack of concern for organizational objectives, the attainment of organizational goals depends on strictly controlling workers. Control, in turn, depends on the use of formal, hierarchical authority, and externally administered rewards and punishments—a sort of "carrot-and-stick" philosophy of motivation. McGregor claimed that most of classic organizational theory seems to have been based on Theory X assumptions. It is difficult to disagree with him.

The second belief system described by McGregor is Theory Y. As you can see in the list, the assumptions about workers made by Theory Y managers are quite different from those made by Theory X managers. McGregor claimed that the most important assumption of Theory Y is that the limitations of people in organizations are not due to shortcomings in human nature, but rather to a lack of ingenuity on the part of managers, who are often unable to discover and utilize their workers' potential.

McGregor claimed that the central principle of organization to be derived from Theory Y assumptions was what he called *integration*. That is, it is the duty of management to create conditions in which the goals of workers and the goals of the organization are integrated, so that workers can *best* achieve their personal goals by working toward organizational goals. (In many ways, this is similar to the concept of instrumentality from Vroom's expectancy theory, in which behavior is thought to be motivated by the perception that it will result in valued outcomes; see Chapter 8.) The utilization of worker potential is achieved, according to McGregor, when management is aware of the needs and desires of workers, and then creates an environment in which the performance of normal job duties will result in the satisfaction of those individual needs. One way to develop such an environment, he believed, was to manage on the basis of Theory Y assumptions; one way to preclude such an environment was to operate on the basis of traditional Theory X assumptions.

Theory X and Theory Y were based on managerial behavior that McGregor had observed, and in that sense, these inferred belief systems are real, not hypothetical. It is important to realize, however, that these two sets of assumptions were only meant to be *examples* of the many possible belief systems that managers may hold. That is, although McGregor's comparisons between Theory X and Theory Y were specific, his underlying purpose was to illustrate the *general* importance of belief systems for determining managerial strategies and the effectiveness of organizations. He later suggested that there may be a great many distinct "theories" of this type, each with different implications for organizations (McGregor, 1967). The fact that McGregor never described theories other than X or Y has led many to believe that he saw these two types of managers as the *only* types, but this misses the larger implications of his work.

ARGYRIS' THEORY OF ORGANIZATIONS: INTEGRATION OF NEEDS

Another influential human relations theory of organizations was developed by Argyris (1957). This theory is based on the assumption that people are naturally predisposed toward psychological growth as they progress from childhood to adulthood. Specifically, Argyris claimed that people develop along the following lines:

- from being passive to being active
- from being dependent on others to being independent
- from being able to behave in only a few ways to being capable of behaving in many different ways

- from having casual, shallow interests to having deeper interests
- from having a short time perspective to having a long time perspective
- from being subordinate to the control of others to being equal to or superordinate to others
- from having a lack of self-awareness to having self-awareness and self-control

As you can see, these assumptions are similar to the assumptions that McGregor ascribed to Theory Y managers. Argyris stated that problems can develop in organizations when the demands of workers' jobs are such that they either inhibit this natural development, or even worse, demand childlike or infantile modes of behavior. For example, imagine that Peter's Pan Pizza decided to install a pizza assembly line at the Flavio's frozen pizza factories. Like most assembly lines, this one would require each worker to perform a single task, such as spreading sauce or sprinkling cheese, at a rate dictated by the pace of the line. Such a job, according to Argyris' perspective, demands childlike behaviors: It limits workers' activities and forces passivity. Workers become dependent on, and are subordinate to, the technology of the assembly line. Their tasks are brief and repetitive, which fosters impatience, and only a very small range of worker abilities are utilized.

In short, many jobs in traditional, bureaucratic organizations inhibit or arrest workers' normal psychological development. As shown in Figure 12.7, this can result in defensive behaviors, which in turn lead to a variety of problems including poor performance, absenteeism, turnover, and sabotage. In response to these problems, managers with traditional (Theory X) perspectives are likely to see the problem as one of workers' laziness or carelessness. These managers then increase the amount of control and direction that the job imposes, which, unknown to them, caused the problem in the first place. Thus, a vicious cycle like the one at the bottom of Figure 12.7 is started, in which conditions get progressively worse for both management and workers.

Argyris mentioned two possible solutions to this problem. First, and with tongue in cheek, he said that the frustration that stems from working in traditional organizations can be avoided by hiring only workers who do not aspire to be healthy mature adults. Second, he suggested that formal organizational structure, directive leadership, and management controls be changed so that employees can continue their psychological development. Chief among the ways to make such changes is the integration of individual needs and organizational goals. In this sense, Argyris' and McGregor's theories are similar in their prescriptions for healthy organizational functioning.

OUCHI'S THEORY Z

A currently popular organizational theory that is in many ways consistent with older human relations approaches is Ouchi's (1981) Theory Z. This theory is an attempt to combine what Ouchi believes are the useful aspects of both the traditional American style of management and the Japanese style of management. The American style that he described is a mixture of bureaucratic principles (for example, formal control, specialization) and human relations principles

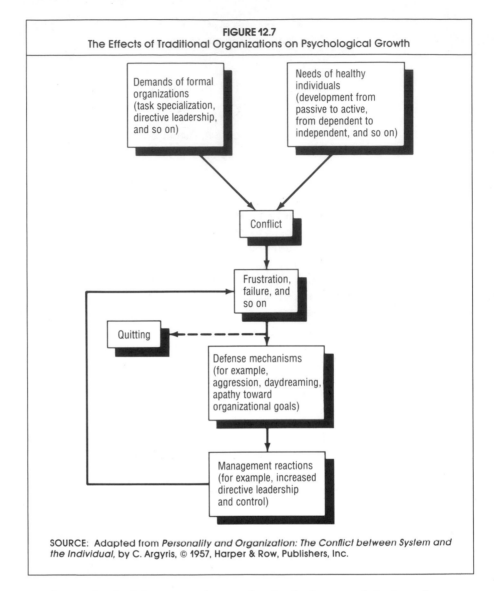

FIGURE 12.7
The Effects of Traditional Organizations on Psychological Growth

SOURCE: Adapted from *Personality and Organization: The Conflict between System and the Individual,* by C. Argyris, © 1957, Harper & Row, Publishers, Inc.

(such as individual decision making and individual responsibility), with expectations of short-term employment on the part of workers. The Japanese style stresses collective responsibility, informal control, a lack of specialization, and an expectation of lifetime employment with the same company. The Type Z organization retains the traditional American emphasis on individual responsibility and career specialization, but advocates group decision making, less formal control, long-term employment, and a concern for all aspects of workers' lives, both on and off the job.

Ouchi (1981) claims that Theory Z organizations should be superior to traditional organizations in terms of workers' attitudes and productivity, and he cites several examples of successful organizations that have Theory Z characteristics. This does not mean, however, that the Theory Z characteristics of these organizations caused them to be successful, nor that there are no unsuccessful Theory Z organizations. Further, Schein (1981) pointed out that Theory Z is basically an application of Maslow's (1943) need hierarchy, which has often been criticized on theoretical grounds and has received little empirical support. Thus, although the future of Theory Z awaits more rigorous research, we strongly suspect that the results of that research (if it is ever conducted) will lead to general disillusionment with this particular approach.

Open Systems Theories of Organizations

Both the classic approach of bureaucracy and the human relations approaches of McGregor and Argyris treat organizations as relatively static, unchanging entities. That is, in bureaucratic theory the ideal organizational structure is sought and then if possible is maintained without any substantial alterations. In a similar fashion, although human relations theories addressed many of the potentially destructive effects of rigid adherence to formal authority and structure, they also failed to consider the inevitable changes that all organizations constantly experience. A more dynamic approach to studying organizations is needed in order to account for an organization's ability to survive both internal and external changes. An open systems approach offers this type of flexibility.

An open systems theory emphasizes the interrelationships and dependence (1) between different components within an organization, and (2) between the system components and the environment within which the organization operates. For example, whereas bureaucratic theory emphasizes division of labor and specialization, open systems theories emphasize the importance of the coordination of the activities of various organizational units, and how this coordinated activity yields a final outcome that is not possible by any single unit operating alone. Also, although human relations theories consider the importance of workers' characteristics (needs, for example), and how these characteristics interact with formal structures and rules to determine organizational effectiveness, open systems theories stress that the effects of worker characteristics, formal structure, and all other components of an organization are dependent on the environment. Environmental conditions (such as the economic and legal contexts in which an organization operates) and changes in that environment therefore have implications for organizations that earlier theories ignored.

It may be easier to get a "feel" for open systems theory by considering an analogy to a smaller, more clearly defined system, such as an automobile. Like an organization, an automobile is a collection of smaller units or subsystems, each with a specific function. For example, the fuel system delivers gasoline to the engine, whereas the electrical system charges the battery, fires the sparkplugs, and supplies power to lights and accessories. Combined, these subsystems form the larger system, and can achieve the overall goal of providing transportation. Separately, these subsystems have little usefulness: A fuel system without an engine is little more than a fire hazard, and an electrical system without a car is only a high school science project. The same conclusions apply to organizational systems. At Peter's Pan Pizza, for instance, the finance division would have no accounts to receive or pay if it were not for the retail operations divisions and the business they generate.

Another system characteristic illustrated by our automobile example is the interdependence of the subsystems, on one another as well as on conditions in the environment. When a single subsystem, such as the electrical system, malfunctions in an automobile, the entire car is either rendered useless or at least becomes less efficient. Further, the automobile and all of its component subsystems depend on the environment in order to operate efficiently. Without oil, gas, or water, each of which can only come from the environment, the car will not operate. Also, environmental catastrophes, such as a truck running into the car in a parking lot, can influence the usefulness of each component as well as the overall system. Analogous examples from Peter's Pan Pizza might include the following: A failure to collect accounts on the part of the finance division could force the facilities division to postpone plans to build new stores. Alternatively, a strike at the meat-packing company from which PPP buys its pepperoni could temporarily force a halt to the production of pepperoni products, or perhaps force PPP to buy high-priced, imported pepperoni.

Although we can apply the general idea of open systems to many examples, such as an automobile, there are components of open systems that have particularly important implications for organizations. We will therefore examine two influential organizational theories based on the open systems model.

LAWRENCE AND LORSCH'S DIFFERENTIATION, INTEGRATION, AND RESPONSE TO CHANGE

An early example of open systems theory applied to organizations was that of Lawrence and Lorsch (1967), who were concerned with two basic issues. The first of these dealt with the effects of division of labor or specialization within organizations. Lawrence and Lorsch believed that when organizations are segmented, managers in each segment become specialists, and develop unique working styles and ways of thinking. Specifically, these authors identified three dimensions along which managers in different units might differ:

1. *Orientation toward particular goals:* To what extent are managers in different units concerned with different goals or objectives?
2. *Time orientation:* To what extent do managers in different units differ in their emphasis on immediate vs. long-range goals?
3. *Interpersonal orientation:* To what extent do managers in different units differ in the ways they typically deal with their colleagues?

Differences in these orientations, along with differences in the formal structures of work units, combine to define what Lawrence and Lorsch called differentiation, or differences in cognitive and emotional orientation among managers in various functional departments of an organization. When there are large differences in these characteristics across departments, differentiation is high; when there are only small differences, differentiation is low.

Differentiation is a matter of concern because high levels can make it difficult for managers to reach agreement about both specific and general policies that are necessary for an organization to function effectively. In order to deal with differentiation, Lawrence and Lorsch claimed that organizations must achieve an appropriate level of integration, which they defined as the quality or degree of collaboration existing among departments that are required to work together because of the demands of the environment.

Lawrence and Lorsch rejected the notion, basic to classic theories such as bureaucracy, that the needed level of collaboration can be achieved automatically by using a rational, hierarchical system of authority. They stated that there are other means of settling conflict and achieving integration, such as "integrating committees" that work to coordinate the efforts of different units. They further pointed out that classic theories, with their emphasis on rationality, fail to consider the role of emotions and interpersonal skills in developing collaboration between units.

At the same time, Lawrence and Lorsch rejected the idea, common in human relations theories, that all disagreement and conflict within an organization is to be avoided. Instead, they argued that whereas extreme differentiation can be dysfunctional, some level of differentiation and conflict is *necessary* in order for a large organization to perform its many functions. They emphasized, therefore, that achieving integration, without sacrificing necessary differentiation, should be a top priority.

The second basic issue that Lawrence and Lorsch's theory addressed is the effect on organizations of differences and changes in the environment. They proposed that technical and economic conditions dictate the structure and pattern of interactions within an organization, but more importantly that these conditions dictate the extent to which an organization is differentiated, and the means by which integration can be achieved. For example, consider what might happen if an increase in the public's concern about health and fitness caused a dramatic decline in the sales of Flavio's (mostly fattening) products, thereby threatening the future of the entire company. We would predict that a common "cognitive and emotional orientation," one geared toward company survival, would develop among Flavio's (and Peter's Pan Pizza's) managers. In other words, differentiation would decrease. Further, managers are likely to be open to new types of collaboration with their peers in other departments, as they coordinate their efforts to adapt to the changes in the public's tastes. That is, integration would increase. Therefore, rather than trying to define the *one* best way to organize, or the *one* best way to coordinate the needs of individuals and the organization, Lawrence and Lorsch believe that managers must be prepared to make changes as environmental conditions change.

KATZ AND KAHN'S OPEN SYSTEMS THEORY

Another influential open systems theory was developed by Katz and Kahn (1978). Although this theory has much in common with that of Lawrence and Lorsch, it has a very different emphasis. Specifically, Lawrence and Lorsch's theory has a relatively narrow focus: It is concerned primarily with the effects of specialization or division of labor at the department or subunit level. Katz and Kahn's work, however, applies the concept of open systems to *all* levels of organizations, and discusses the implications of the theory for a variety of topics, including motivation, performance, communication, leadership, and organizational change. Although we will not go into these specific implications, we will describe the theory and some of the *general* implications of viewing organizations from a total systems perspective.

Katz and Kahn listed ten characteristics of open systems. Although these characteristics apply to all open systems, our interest is, of course, in their implications for organizations. The characteristics of open systems are the following:

1. *Importation of energy:* No open system can sustain itself without taking in resources or "energy" from the environment. In organizations, these inputs take the form of labor, raw materials, ideas, and anything else that is required to maintain functioning.

2. *Throughput:* This refers to the transformation of the energy inputs discussed in (1). Organizations manufacture products, train employees, and in general perform work toward achieving specific goals.

3. *Output:* Once inputs have been transformed, some of the resulting products are returned to the environment. Organizations distribute their manufactured goods or their services, as well as deliver unwanted output, such as industrial pollution.

4. *Cycles of events:* The input–throughput–output functions form a cycle in which energy is transformed and exchanged. That is, the products that are output into the environment, such as manufactured goods, provide the means (money) for an organization to obtain additional inputs of raw materials.

5. *Negative entropy:* Entropy refers to the tendency for systems to "run down" and eventually die. In order for an organization to be successful, it must reverse this tendency and achieve *negative* entropy. That is, organizations must take in more than they use, maximizing the ratio of inputs to expended energy. The excess energy and resources are stored, and during crises the organization can use these stored resources to maintain itself while making any necessary adjustments.

6. *Information input, negative feedback, and the coding process:* The inputs discussed in (1) above are primarily raw materials necessary for the organization to produce its products or provide its services. Organizations also need inputs in the form of information that will let management know how well the organization is functioning. The most basic performance information is *negative feedback,* which can be anything that tells the organization when it has deviated from its intended course. For example, if Peter's Pan Pizza's management learned that its share of the take-out pizza business had dropped by 10 percent, that would be negative feedback indicating that a change is necessary. With all of the information available in the environment, systems must be selective about the performance information they accept. This selection is carried out by the *coding process,* in which irrelevant or less relevant information is filtered out, and a few critical sources of information are emphasized.

7. *The steady state and dynamic homeostasis:* In a healthy system, the input of energy and resources is balanced with the output of products. This constancy of energy exchange is known as a *steady state.* In order to react to changes in the environment, however, an organization will probably have to make changes in its outputs, which may require corresponding changes in inputs. An organization might also need to change its structure, or change in terms of the number of employees or divisions that it has. Therefore, the steadiness of an organization refers to an equilibrium in its *basic character,* rather than in its structure or size. Katz and Kahn refer to this property of constant change in order to maintain organizational character as *dynamic homeostasis.*

8. *Differentiation:* Systems, including organizations, develop specialized structures to perform specialized tasks. This is an evolutionary process, with new structures, or subsystems, developing as new needs arise. This use of the term differentiation, therefore, refers more to division of labor than to the differences in orientation discussed by Lawrence and Lorsch.

9. *Integration and coordination:* As we have already seen, if a system is to be effective, its components must be integrated and coordinated to work together to achieve the overall purpose of the system.

10. *Equifinality:* Because of their open and flexible nature, systems can achieve the same final outcome in many different ways. Katz and Kahn referred to this property as *equifinality.* Equifinality is a particularly important characteristic for organizational systems, because it allows them to adjust to changing environmental demands while working toward established goals.

As the above characteristics illustrate, Katz and Kahn's theory describes a dynamic, ever-changing system. Organizations must interact with, and react to, their environments. They must also maintain themselves through hard times, coordinate the tasks of many individuals and groups, and manage the critical input, throughout, and output processes.

Another important aspect of Katz and Kahn's theory is their use of the concept of roles. Roles are defined as sets of behaviors that are required of a person by virtue of her position in an organization. These behaviors interact with the role behaviors of others to produce predictable outcomes in the organization. In this sense, Katz and Kahn defined organizations as *systems of roles:* The throughput processes by which work gets done are defined by the interdependent role behaviors of workers.

Roles are similar to the concept of "offices" in bureaucratic theory, because they define tasks and the ways in which different employees must work together to achieve organizational objectives. There are, however, at least two important ways in which Katz and Kahn's use of roles differs from the bureaucratic concept of offices. The first of these concerns the way in which roles are developed. In a bureaucracy, the role and the office are one and the same. That is, the behaviors expected of an officeholder are defined by the office, and are independent of any personal characteristics of the officeholder. In open systems theory, roles are acquired through social interaction with other people, in a process called the role episode (see Figure 12.8). Basically, people with whom a worker interacts, the

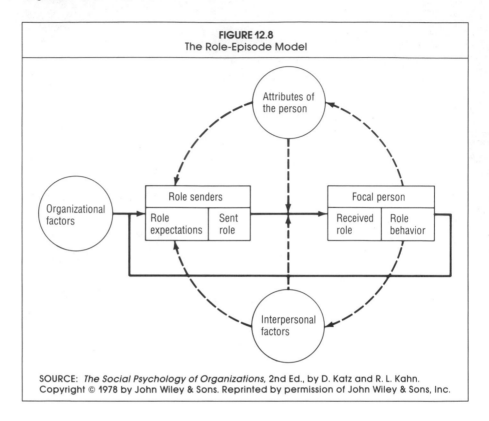

FIGURE 12.8
The Role-Episode Model

SOURCE: *The Social Psychology of Organizations*, 2nd Ed., by D. Katz and R. L. Kahn.
Copyright © 1978 by John Wiley & Sons. Reprinted by permission of John Wiley & Sons, Inc.

role senders, have certain expectations about that worker's role in the organization, and through direct and indirect communication they send those expectations to the worker. The worker, in turn, receives these role expectations, which determine, to a greater or lesser extent, his role behaviors.

Note that because of personal, interpersonal, and organizational factors, the role expectations of the role senders and the messages that they send to the worker may or may not be the same. For example, in our opening memos for this chapter, we saw that there was some confusion about who was responsible for setting store inspection standards. Ed Clark, the vice president for retail operations, probably has specific expectations about who should fulfill this role, but these expectations may not have been clearly communicated. It may be, for instance, that Mr. Clark has a very nondirective interpersonal style, and his expections were interpreted as suggestions rather than as directions.

In a similar way, the received role, or what the worker perceives to be the expectations of the role senders, may not correspond to the expectations that were actually sent. Also, the actual role behavior may not reflect the received role for any of a variety of reasons. Consequently, there is a good chance that the role expectations that exist within a company will not correspond to the role behavior of the worker. Because of this, as well as changes in the organizational and interpersonal factors that influence role expectations, the role episode is a constant, ongoing process.

The second distinctive aspect of Katz and Kahn's treatment of roles is the concept of partial inclusion. This refers to the fact that, psychologically, only a portion of each worker is "in" the organization. That is, every worker performs numerous nonorganizational roles. Organizations, however, often expect employees to abandon some of these roles; this can be dehumanizing to the employee, and in some cases counterproductive to the organization.

Partial inclusion has particularly important implications for those organization members who are in boundary positions. These are employees whose roles require them to interact with people, groups, or other organizations *outside* of their own group or organization. In effect, boundary positions link an organization with its environment. People in boundary positions therefore have partial inclusion not only in their employing organization, but also in that part of the environment to which they represent the organization. This situation can lead to conflicting role behaviors that threaten the well-being of the organization.

For example, a sizable proportion of Flavio's frozen pizza sales are to taverns and bars, where they are cooked in microwave ovens and sold along with beer and wine. Many pizza companies are trying to move into this market. In the struggle for a competitive advantage, there is pressure for salespersons to conform to the role demands of their customers. One of Flavio's sales representatives, whose name we will not mention, apparently decided to become friends with as many bar owners as he possibly could. He spent many hours in bars, drinking and discussing the "ins and outs" of life on the road. The bar owners liked him, but he failed to conform to the role behaviors of a pizza sales representative. Consequently, he didn't sell many pizzas, and was eventually fired.

Of course, most workers in boundary positions do not succumb to these types of pressures. In general, however, the notion of partial inclusion is a valuable component of Katz and Kahn's theory, as it draws attention to the multiple roles of workers, both within and outside of the organization, and forces us to consider the effects of these roles.

In summary, open systems theory is perhaps the most comprehensive organizational theory to date. As does any organizational theory, it provides a certain perspective from which to consider the operation and structure of organizations. Like the classic and human relations theories that preceded it, open systems theory is perhaps most valuable as a device for suggesting new ways of doing things in organizations. Although not all of these suggestions have worked out, open systems theories have increased our understanding of many important dimensions of organizations.

We have spent a fair amount of time discussing theories of what organizations are and how they function. Although organizational theories certainly have implications for more specific issues, we need to examine some of these issues in more detail. One such issue, which is important for the macro-level functioning of the organization, the meso-level integration and coordination of units within the organization, and the micro-level behavior of workers, is organizational communication.

ORGANIZATIONAL COMMUNICATION

Communication is one of the most central processes in organizations. Information exchange between divisions, units, work groups, and individuals is necessary to perform both simple and complex tasks. Understanding communication processes is therefore important to understanding the functioning of organizations. In fact, it is possible to view organizations not as bureaucratic structures or role systems, but as communication networks.

Regardless of whether you view organizations as formal structures, informal role systems, or communication networks, the importance of communication in day-to-day organizational activity is obvious. For example, training programs depend on effective communication of information about desired behaviors and performance standards (see Chapter 7). Performance appraisal hinges on the ability of supervisors or other evaluators to communicate information about employees' performance (Chapter 4). Leadership involves, among other things, the effective communication of directives, goals, and reinforcements such as praise and personal attention (Chapter 10). A failure to communicate effectively may result in dissatisfaction (Chapter 9) and perhaps, if that dissatisfaction is severe enough, a unionization effort on the part of the employees involved (Chapter 11). We could give many more such examples, but our point is simple: Communication is critical to every topic in the field of I/O psychology.

The Communication Process

The means by which communication takes place are complex and variable, so that any description of the communication process must necessarily be a simplification. All communication events, however, have certain common components that allow us to describe the *general* communication process, and illustrate some of the many ways in which communication can fail.

An early, but still useful, model of communication was presented by Shannon and Weaver (1948). A diagram of the components of their model is presented in Figure 12.9. The communication cycle begins with the source, or the person sending the message. The source has certain ideas, facts, opinions, or other information that she wishes to convey to one or more other people, either within or outside of the organization. Because humans are not by nature telepathic, the source cannot simply transmit her thoughts directly; the information must be put into a form that can be conveyed to, and understood by, the intended receiver, or target. This process of converting the intended message into what we hope is understandable language is called encoding. Communication depends on the ability of individuals to transform thoughts into words, and this ability depends in turn on verbal skills, emotional states, experience, and many other factors.

Once the information has been encoded it is called a message. The message must, in turn, be transmitted to the target via a particular medium. A variety of media are used to facilitate communication in organizations. Some of the more common of these are listed here:

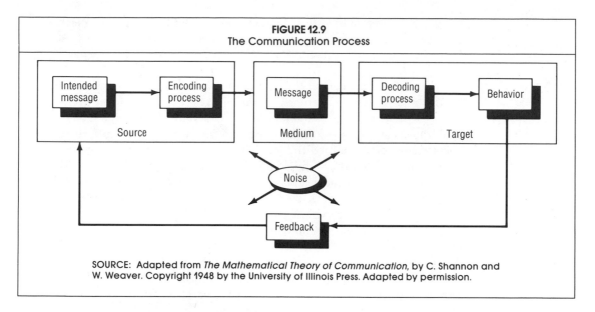

FIGURE 12.9
The Communication Process

SOURCE: Adapted from *The Mathematical Theory of Communication*, by C. Shannon and W. Weaver. Copyright 1948 by the University of Illinois Press. Adapted by permission.

WRITTEN COMMUNICATION
- Memoranda and letters
- Instruction manuals
- Policy manuals
- Employee handbooks
- Company newsletters
- Annual reports to stockholders
- Grievance and suggestion systems

ORAL COMMUNICATION
- Face-to-face communication
- Telephone
- Employee meetings
- Training sessions

As you can see, the nature of the message will often influence the selection of the medium. For example, it would not be appropriate to print a disciplinary message in the company newsletter, nor would it be worthwhile or effective to publish a change in the safety procedures in the annual report to the stockholders.

When (or if) the encoded message is received, the first thing the target must do is decode or interpret it, to try to determine the source's intent. As is the case with encoding, effective decoding depends on the verbal skills, frame of reference, emotional state, and experience of the target. Based on his interpretation of the message, the target will respond in some way. Perhaps work behavior will change on the basis of a recommendation, or perhaps the target will become angry and quit. In any case, the target's reaction forms the basis for feedback to the source. Feedback can take many forms, but it serves the general function of letting the source know whether or not the message was effective. For example, a desirable change in behavior on the part of the target following a disciplinary message would constitute feedback that the message had its intended effect.

The final component of this communication model is noise, which includes anything that alters, interrupts, or inhibits the communication cycle at any point. It is possible, for example, that a typographical error in a memorandum could drastically change the meaning of a message. For example, if the legal counsel's secretary omitted the word "not" from a memo advising Peter's Pan Pizza managers that they "should *not* discuss the lawsuit filed against PPP with subordinates," the memo would have an effect *opposite* of what was intended. In a similar fashion, the target could incorrectly interpret the intent of a message that was worded ambiguously. Consider, for example, the opening memos for this chapter. Mr. Bombyk may have intended to make a friendly offer to discuss inspection policies with Ms. Richmond. Ms. Richmond, however, may have interpreted the memo as a challenge to her authority.

We have referred to the communication process as a "cycle"; this choice of term was not accidental. The diagram in Figure 12.9 is really only a "snapshot" or a segment of the continual cycle of communication that takes place among individuals and groups in organizations. Messages often prompt the target to assume the role of communication source, encoding and sending a response through an appropriate medium to the former source, who becomes the target. Any given message is likely to elicit a series of additional messages that form such a cycle. This is important to keep in mind, because it illustrates the importance of longitudinal analyses of any potential communication problems.

Functions of Communication

Scott and Mitchell (1976) examined the uses of communication in organizations, and identified four very general functions that different types of communication serve: information, motivation, control, and emotion. Most organizational communication serves all of these functions to some degree, as we can see below by considering the memos that opened this chapter.

INFORMATION

The information function of communication is the most obvious. All communication involves the transmission of some type of information, of course, but often this information is simply a means to achieve another purpose. However, in some cases the purpose of communication is strictly informative, as when a worker provides her supervisor with information needed to make a decision. An example of the information function of the opening memos is Ed Clark sending a copy of Bombyk's memo to Dr. MacKeven. The purpose of Clark's communication was to provide MacKeven with information, so that she could decide whether or not she would be able to help with the problem.

MOTIVATION

Much of the communication in an organization is designed to influence the behavior or attitudes of workers. Both managers and nonmanagers spend a lot of their time trying to get others to commit themselves to doing certain things, or to change how others feel about certain aspects of the job. The most straightforward examples of communication designed to motivate are praise and criticism, although more subtle forms of communication can also achieve the motivating function. In our memos, we can see the attempt to motivate on the part of Greg Bombyk when he requests that Ms. Richmond change her guidelines to conform to those developed in his own unit. We don't know whether or not she actually changed the guidelines, but Bombyk's memo certainly motivated her to take the issue to Mr. Clark.

CONTROL

Given the complexity of modern organizations, responsibility for specific tasks and authority over particular workers is not always clear. A significant proportion of communication is therefore directed toward clarifying duties and establishing authority, which in turn allow management to control the functioning of the organization. Clearly, one of the primary purposes of Bombyk's memo was to establish the responsibility and authority for setting inspection standards in his unit.

EMOTION

We are all familiar with communication that is designed, in whole or in part, to express feelings or emotions. Suggestion boxes, in addition to providing a medium for informative communication, allow employees to air their feelings on virtually any aspect of work. Annual award ceremonies are designed not only to reward and motivate, but also to express management's appreciation for a job well done. Again, Bombyk's memo certainly has an emotional quality to it, as it clearly conveyed his disappointment with the inspection guidelines established by Ms. Richmond.

Communication Effectiveness

These functions of communication are obviously important to organizations and the people in them. Unfortunately, communication does not always work as well as we would like. We have referred to the general concept of "noise" in the communication cycle, but that is too general to describe the actual conditions that render communication ineffective. In the following sections we discuss some of the more specific factors that influence the communication process.

ACCURACY, FIDELITY, AND DISTORTION

Accuracy refers to the perceived validity or truth of the message sent by the source to the target. It should therefore not be confused with questions of fidelity, or whether or not the message is being altered by the communication process itself. An example of a problem involving fidelity would be a malfunction in a computer printer that caused characters to be switched, making it impossible to read memos printed on that printer. A problem involving accuracy would be a perfectly legible memo that no one believed.

Certainly, if the target of the communication has doubts about the fidelity of the communication process, she will also be likely to have doubts about the accuracy of any messages sent via that process. High fidelity, however, does not guarantee perceived accuracy. For example, research suggests that perceptions of message accuracy are influenced by the expertise of the communication source, as well as the trust that the target places in the source (Hanser & Muchinsky, 1980; O'Reilly & Roberts, 1976). If a source isn't trusted, or seen as knowing what he is talking about, message fidelity will not improve overall communication.

In contrast to accuracy, which refers to the target's perception of a message, communication distortion usually refers to changes in the *content* of a message on the part of the source, whether intentional or not. This can happen, for example, when a target passes on a received message, therefore becoming a source. Distortion is apparently most common in *upward* communication, or communication from subordinates to their superiors. Specifically, subordinates sometimes omit information that is unfavorable to themselves, while emphasizing information that puts them in a more favorable light, particularly when there is a lack of trust between the parties (O'Reilly, 1978).

Accuracy and distortion are important aspects of communication to consider for a number of reasons. Most obviously, communication that is free from distortion and perceived as being accurate will facilitate the exchange of information. Further, there is evidence that these types of communication problems can have negative psychological effects as well. Hatfield and Huseman (1982), for example, found that when subordinates agreed with their supervisors concerning the nature of their previous communication, they were also more satisfied with both the nature of their supervision and with their work in general. It is not likely that communication plagued with distortion and inaccuracy would result in this type of agreement between supervisor and subordinate.

COMMUNICATION OVERLOAD

Communication overload describes a situation in which more information is sent than the target can receive, interpret, and act upon. The result of overload seems to be that some or most of the information is inadequately processed or improperly interpreted, and the effectiveness of both the employee and the organization are reduced. For example, O'Reilly (1980) examined the effects of communication overload among samples of U.S. Navy personnel working on decision-making tasks. His results are intriguing, because although subjects who experienced overload had *lower performance* than those provided with less information, the overloaded subjects were *more satisfied* with the task. These results suggest that employees may seek more information than they can use.

Of course, there are individual differences in people's abilities to receive and process information, so that one worker's overload may be the optimal amount of communication for another worker. These individual differences are even more important because, up to some optimal point, more communication does indeed improve performance. O'Reilly (1980) found this pattern in his data; it was only when communication went beyond a certain level that there was a negative effect on subjects' behavior. Because this point is likely to be different for different employees, supervisors and managers must be sensitive to the levels of communication skills among their employees.

ATTITUDES

The efficiency of the communication cycle is likely to be influenced by the participants' attitudes toward each other, as well as toward the subject of their communication. This potential was illustrated in a study by Tjosvold (1982), who asked executives attending a business school course to participate in a laboratory exercise on conflict resolution. The executives played the role of managers whose job was to settle a conflict with workers over job rotation. Some of the executives were led to adopt a cooperative strategy, some a competitive strategy, and some a strategy in which they were instructed to avoid controversy. The results showed that the cooperative strategy apparently improved communication, as subjects in this condition demonstrated a greater understanding of the workers' position than did subjects in the other two conditions.

STRUCTURAL VARIABLES

There are two types of structure in organizations that have implications for communication. The first of these includes the types of structural variables normally associated with bureaucracy, such as size, hierarchy, and division of labor. It is obvious that as an organization grows, either in number of employees or number of functional units, there is a greater need for communication in order to control and coordinate the activities of workers. As the amount of communication increases, there is a tendency for formal channels of communication to be established in order to make communication more efficient. A major means by which efficiency is achieved is to *limit* the amount of communication by formally specifying the timing of messages and the appropriate content for various communication channels.

Communication is also restricted by gatekeeping. Gatekeeping refers to a less-formal process, engaged in by many employees, that involves making decisions about what information will be communicated and what will not. Gatekeepers decide whether other people need to know certain facts, thus filtering out irrelevant or sensitive material that might result in inefficiency or other problems if passed along. The need for gatekeeping, and the organization's reliance on gatekeepers to control the flow of information, increases with organizational size and communication volume.

The second type of structure relevant to communication is the structure of the communication network. Just as we can draw a chart showing which workers are responsible to which supervisors and managers, we can also draw a chart showing who communicates with whom in an organization. These communica-

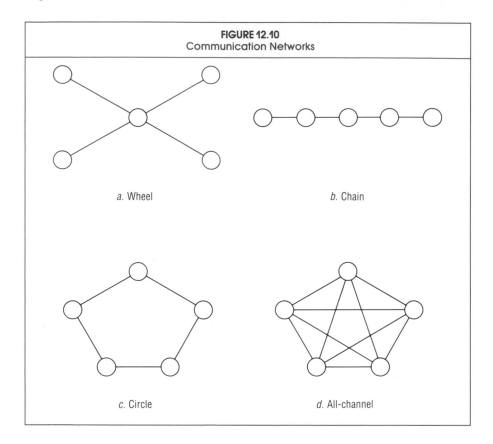

FIGURE 12.10
Communication Networks

a. Wheel

b. Chain

c. Circle

d. All-channel

tion patterns, or networks, have typically been studied in laboratories, where experimenters can carefully control the flow of information.

Simple networks involving small numbers of people, such as those in Figure 12.10, have often been compared. Shaw (1964) reported that with simple tasks, networks in which communication is channeled through a single person (12.10*a*) or otherwise limited (12.10*b*) were most effective, whereas networks allowing communication between more parties (12.10*c*, 12.10*d*) led to better performance on more complex tasks. It would therefore seem that a contingency model of communication networks may be warranted, with the freedom to communicate with others dependent on task characteristics.

Research on communication patterns in actual organizations has recently begun to appear. For example, Keller and Holland (1983) examined characteristics of research-and-development department employees who were both high in volume of communication and innovative in their ideas. Among other personal characteristics such as having high self-esteem and a low need for clarity, these communicators/innovators held central positions in communication networks. That is, they controlled the flow of communication between others in their departments. Similarly, Boje and Whetten (1981) found that administrators who were centrally located in communication networks were seen by their peers as being more influential than other administrators. These studies illustrate that the ability to control communication can lead to definite benefits. In Keller and Holland's study, it is not unreasonable to suspect that the increased innovativeness of workers in central communication positions stemmed, at least in part, from their access to the ideas of their co-workers, which they could combine and assimilate in unique, innovative ways.

A particularly important role in communication is played by boundary spanners. Tushman and Scanlan (1981) stated that boundaries develop in organizations because each unit within an organization develops its own unique language and ways of looking at problems. It is the primary duty of boundary spanners to recode communication that crosses boundaries, from the "semantic space" of one unit into that of the second, without any change in meaning. In order to perform this function, boundary spanners must be linked to the internal communication network of their own unit, as well as to sources and targets of communication outside of the unit. Thus, Tushman and Scanlan argued that people in boundary positions, such as sales representatives, are not actually boundary *spanners* unless they are (1) aware of events within the organization, (2) aware of events and conditions in the environment, and (3) capable of facilitating the communication of these types of information between the organization and the environment. Consistent with the implication that boundary spanners must be able to function well both within and outside of their units, Caldwell and O'Reilly (1982a) found that high-performing boundary spanners were able to adjust their self-presentation styles, thereby altering their communication roles to fit different situations.

As textbook authors we have found ourselves serving as boundary spanners between the field of I/O psychology and you, the reader of this book. Our responsibilities in this role include communicating the issues, concerns, and desires of a diverse body of researchers and theoreticians in the field, and doing so in such a way that the educational goals of the course you are taking can be achieved. We can safely say that this boundary-spanning experience has been a challenge. We hope that it has also been successful.

Conclusion

You should now recognize the importance of organizational communication for all aspects of organizational life. It is easy to forget just how important communication is, however, because most people tend to take it for granted, and are largely unaware of its complexities. We hope that you will *not* take it for granted, and that you keep these complexities in mind as you consider the role of communication in the following sections of this chapter (and as you review earlier chapters).

OTHER ORGANIZATIONAL TOPICS

Organizational theories provide a framework from which to study, or design, organizations. They also suggest appropriate management styles, or means of coordinating employees' activities. Communication, as one of the critical processes in all organizations, is of great importance in determining whether or not organizations operate according to plan. These are, however, only two of the many macro-level and meso-level issues that have been studied by I/O psychologists and other organizational researchers. Unfortunately, the practical limitations on the length of a textbook make it impossible to discuss all of these issues. In the remaining sections of this chapter, we must be content with brief presentations of several of the more interesting topics. Even these brief discussions, though, should give you a better feel for the complex issues psychologists face when trying to understand behavior in organizations.

Organizational Climate and Culture

Organizational climate refers to an organizational characteristic that has proved to be both difficult to define and difficult to measure. Typical definitions of climate state that it represents employees' *shared perceptions* of their organization. Thus, if Peter's Pan Pizza's employees believe, as a group, that their company is generous in its rewards for hard work, then PPP can be said to have a climate of generosity, or perhaps of fairness. This would be the climate *regardless* of the objective reward practices of the company. Schneider (1985) pointed out that climate definitions have at various times included the dominant interpersonal practices of an organization, such as supervisory style and how workers relate to each other, as well as formal and informal policies that encourage certain types of behavior, such as safety (Zohar, 1980) and innovation (Abbey & Dickson, 1983).

Research on climate has focused on the analysis of activities and policies that distinguish organizations from one another, as well as those that distinguish units within organizations. In this sense, climate may be thought of as an organization's personality. Although climate research can be traced back to Lewin, Lippett, and White's (1939) classic study of the effects of **authoritarian, democratic,** and **laissez-faire** social climates, modern research on organizational climate stems largely from the work of Litwin and Stringer (1968), who identified the following eight dimensions of climate:

1. Structure
2. Individual responsibility
3. Rewards
4. Risk and risk taking
5. Warmth and support
6. Tolerance for conflict
7. Organizational identity and group loyalty
8. Performance standards and expectations

Campbell, Dunnette, Lawler, and Weick (1970) reviewed the early climate literature, and identified these four factors:

1. Degree of structure present
2. Individual autonomy
3. Reward orientation
4. Support and consideration

Muchinsky (1976) and others have found similar, although not identical, factors. Despite criticism of the construct (for example, Guion, 1973), there has been a considerable amount of research on climate over the years. Schneider (1985) noted, however, that research on climate has recently declined, and suggested that this may be due to the widespread acceptance of the construct, and the ability that we now have to measure multiple dimensions of policies and other organizational characteristics.

In the place of climate, the concept of organizational culture has emerged. Whereas climate focuses on employees' perceptions of organizational characteristics, culture research attempts to understand the *meaning* that employees attach to events in the organization. The predominant approach to studying culture is to examine stories and **myths** that are told in organizations. Culture theorists believe that stories and myths shared by employees are important channels for the communication of the meaning of events (Koprowski, 1983; Mitroff, 1983). For example, there is a story at Peter's Pan Pizza about the company president seeing a senior vice president drive into the parking lot of a competitor's pizza parlor. According to the story, the president drove in behind the vice president and fired him on the spot. This story may or may not be true, but in either case it serves to convey a certain message about the loyalty that is expected when a person works at PPP.

Perhaps one of the most significant aspects of the research on climate and culture, at least for psychologists, is that it illustrates the importance of considering the organization as a single unit while we examine the behavior of individual workers. Inconsistent research results and differences between apparently similar organizations *may* be explained by differences in variables such as climate and culture. We hope that the research in these areas becomes more sophisticated, and that the role of these factors can be more fully documented.

---

authoritarian: describing a social system in which individual members are under strict domination by the formal authority of a specific person or small group of persons

democratic: describing a social system in which authority is vested in the members, and exercised by them or their elected representatives

laissez-faire: describing a social system in which formal authority is limited, so that individual freedom and discretion are interfered with as little as possible

myths: traditional or legendary stories that attempt to state basic truths

Organizational Effectiveness

Organizational effectiveness is the term used to refer to various aspects of an organization's overall performance. As you might imagine, there are many ways in which an organization can be effective or ineffective. Cameron (1980) described four major approaches to evaluating effectiveness. First, an organization can be described as effective if it is successful in accomplishing its goals, usually with respect to outputs or production. Second, an organization can be considered effective if it is successful in acquiring the resources it needs from the environment. In particular, this approach emphasizes successful competition for scarce resources. Third, effective organizations can be defined as those where internal functioning is smooth and free of major problems. Such characteristics as trust and benevolence toward individual workers, smooth information flow, and freedom from conflict between work units would typify such an organization. Fourth, effective organizations may be seen as those that are able to keep their "strategic constituencies" satisfied. Strategic constituencies are groups of people who have a stake in the organization, such as customers, workers, and stockholders. Keeley (1984) identified a special case of this last definition in theories that view effectiveness as satisfying the interests of different groups of workers, or "participating individuals."

There have been a lot of recent studies on organizational effectiveness, as researchers have attempted to identify the factors that determine global organizational performance. One critical variable that has emerged is the passage of time. That is, the nature of effectiveness is likely to change as organizations and their environments change. For example, Cameron and Whetten (1981) found that in the life cycle of an organization, individual effectiveness and effectiveness at acquiring inputs became less important over time, whereas overall organizational effectiveness and effectiveness at producing outputs became more important. These considerations should remind you of our discussion of proximal, distal, and dynamic criteria, way back in Chapter 3.

Another important conclusion, demonstrated in empirical research (for example, Cameron, 1981), and implicit in the different approaches to measuring effectiveness mentioned above, is that effectiveness is a multidimensional rather than a unitary construct. That is, we cannot measure a single aspect of an organization's performance and hope to have captured the essence of its effectiveness. We must either limit our interest in an organization's effectiveness to a restricted range of criteria, or we must consider multiple measures and perspectives. Once again, our earlier discussion of single, multiple, and composite criteria should "come back" to you here.

In general, researchers are just beginning to deal with the complexity of organizational effectiveness. The consensus among these researchers seems to be that the measure of effectiveness that is used in a given situation should be contingent upon a variety of factors (Connolly, Conlon, & Deutsch, 1980). Cameron (1980) suggested six critical questions that should be asked when evaluating organizational effectiveness (see Table 12.1). The answers to these questions should help a manager or researcher identify the most important

TABLE 12.1 Six Critical Questions in Evaluating Organizational Effectiveness

Critical question	Examples
1. What domain of activity is being focused on?	Internal activities vs. external activities
2. Whose perspective, or which constituency's point of view, is being considered?	Internal constituencies vs. external constituencies; satisfying all constituencies minimally vs. satisfying one constituency maximally
3. What level of analysis is being used?	Individual effectiveness, subunit effectiveness, or organizational effectiveness
4. What time frame is being employed?	Short time perspective vs. long time perspective
5. What type of data are to be used?	Perceptual (from individuals) vs. objective (from organizational records)
6. What referent is being employed?	Comparative—relative to a competitor; normative—relative to a theoretical ideal; goal-centered—relative to a stated goal; improvement—relative to past performance; trait—relative to effective traits

SOURCE: Reprinted, by permission of the publisher, from "Critical Questions in Assessing Organizational Effectiveness," *Organizational Dynamics*, Autumn 1980, p. 75, © 1980 American Management Associations, New York. All rights reserved.

dimensions of effectiveness for a particular organization at a particular time. We believe that such an approach is bound to be more successful than attempts to assess more general types of effectiveness.

Stress in Organizations

As was the case with organizational effectiveness, research on stress in organizations has increased dramatically in recent years, and stress has also proved to be a difficult concept to pin down. Many definitions of stress in general, and job stress in particular, have been offered (stress as a stimulus, stress as a response, and so on). Although each of these definitions has its own advocates, we have adopted Beehr and Newman's (1978) definition of job stress as a condition arising from the interaction of people and their jobs, characterized by changes in people that force them to deviate from their normal functioning.

There are a variety of situations that may result in stress on the job. Brief, Schuler, and Van Sell (1981) compiled a list of potential job-related **stressors,** organized into three basic categories: (1) organizational characteristics and processes, (2) job demands and role characteristics, and (3) individual characteristics and expectations. Each variable in the following list has been found to result in stress and therefore to affect job behavior. The nature of the relationship between stress and behavior, however, is not at all clear.

stressor: anything that causes a person to experience stress; something that interrupts normal functioning or causes a disturbance of equilibrium

Organizational characteristics and processes
Organizational policies
Inequitable or inadequate performance evaluations
Pay inequities
Ambiguous or arbitrary policies
Rotating work shifts
Frequent relocation
Idealistic job descriptions before hiring
Organizational structure
Centralization; low participation in decision making
Low opportunity for advancement or growth
Increased size
Excessive formalization
Excessive specialization and division of labor
Interdependence of organizational units
Organizational processes
Poor communication
Poor or inadequate feedback on performance
Ambiguous or conflicting goals
Ineffective delegation
Training programs
Job demands and role characteristics
Working conditions
Crowding
Lack of privacy; poor spatial arrangements
Noise
Excessive heat or cold
Lights: inadequate, glaring, or flickering
Presence of toxic chemicals
Safety hazards
Air pollution, including radiation
Interpersonal relationships
Inconsiderate or inequitable supervisors
Lack of recognition or acceptance
Lack of trust
Competition
Difficulty in delegating responsibilities
Conflict within and between groups
Job demands
Repetitive work
Time pressures and deadlines
Low skill requirements
Responsibility for people
Underemployment; overemployment
Role characteristics
Role conflict

>   Role ambiguity
>   Role underload/overload
>   Role–status incongruency
> **Individual characteristics and expectations**
> *Career concerns*
>> Under/overpromotion
>> Midcareer crises
>> Obsolescence
>> Unmet expectations and goals
>> Job insecurity
> *Individual characteristics*
>> Type A behavior pattern
>> Anxiety
>> Intolerance of ambiguity
>> Flexibility/rigidity
>> Introversion/extroversion

SOURCE: A. P. Brief, R. S. Schuler, and M. Van Sell, *Managing Job Stress*, pp. 66–67. Copyright © 1981 by Arthur P. Brief, Randall S. Schuler, and Mary Van Sell. Reprinted by permission of Little, Brown and Company.

In a review of recent research on stress, Staw (1984) concluded that there was clear evidence of a positive relationship between stress and physical factors such as noise, extreme temperatures, and pollution, and that this stress was in turn related to reduced performance. When the stressors being studied are more psychological in nature, however, Staw reported inconsistent and contradictory results. For example, both jobs with little influence and responsibility (French & Caplan, 1972) and jobs with substantial responsibility (Cooper & Payne, 1978) have been found to be stressful.

On the basis of his own research and a literature review, Jamal (1984) drew three tentative conclusions about the effects of stress on workers' behaviors. First, when stress is measured in terms of workers' perceptions of stressors such as role conflict (incompatible expectations on the parts of others), role overload (expectations beyond the worker's capability), or inadequacy of resources, the relationship between stress and job performance is negative and linear. That is, people who perceive these types of stressors have lower performance than those who do not. However, when stress is measured directly (for example, physiological measures such as muscle tension or heart rate), the relationship between stress and performance is unclear.

Second, the relationship between job stress and absenteeism, intention to quit, and actual turnover is positive. The greater the stress experienced by a worker, the more likely he is to withdraw from the workplace. Jamal (1984) argued quite logically that stress creates an adverse environment for workers, and that escape from such an environment is a natural response.

Third, Jamal (1984) concluded that both organizational and professional commitment, or the extent to which workers identify with and become "attached to" their organizations or professions, moderate the relationship between stress and behavior. Highly committed workers seem to be better able to cope with stress, and are less likely to suffer such negative consequences as reduced performance or increased withdrawal.

There is, as we have said, extensive research on job stress, and we have presented only a brief sample. Staw (1984) drew two relevant conclusions about the effects of stress. First, conditions that are stressful, and individuals' reactions to stress, are likely to be determined in part by situational variables, such as support from co-workers (for example, Seers, McGee, Serey, & Graen, 1983). Second, there are significant differences between people in their reactions to stress, and how they cope with stressors.

It is also fairly safe to conclude that job stress has contributed to the dramatic increase in drug and alcohol use on the job. One estimate of the combined costs of drug and alcohol use to the U.S. economy in 1983 is $177 billion (Castro, 1986). Of this, approximately $70 billion was due to reduced productivity alone (Quayle, 1983). A frequently cited factor in employee drug and alcohol use is stress, whether resulting from work overload and time pressures, or extremely boring, repetitive, unenriching work (Castro, 1986). Of course, not all on-the-job drug and alcohol use is an effort to cope with stress, but any success in understanding and reducing stress will certainly help alleviate this costly problem.

Fortunately, drug use is not the only way employees can cope with stress, and there has been an extensive effort aimed at developing stress-reduction and stress-management programs (for example, Brief, Schuler, & Van Sell, 1981). Although there has been relatively little systematic research on the effectiveness of stress-reduction and stress-management techniques, that which exists does show some promise. For example, Ganster, Mayes, Sime, and Tharp (1982) found that a program that taught workers to recognize conditions that cause them stress and to respond in adaptive rather than self-defeating ways, when combined with instruction in muscle-relaxation techniques, resulted in lower employee "strain." Rose and Veiga (1984) described a similar program of relaxation and cognitive modification that reduced anxiety.

Although these results are promising, Ganster and his colleagues did *not* advocate the widespread use of these types of programs. They argued that their program, which involved 16 hours of training over an eight-week period, is about the minimum amount of training necessary for reliable stress reduction, and that it resulted in relatively small effects. Virtually all commercially available programs, however, are *much* shorter, often lasting only a few hours over one or two days. Further, these authors argued that programs designed to alter reactions to stress do not address the basic problem. They would rather see more effort aimed at making work organizations inherently less stressful. They therefore suggested that stress-management programs be used as supplements to organizational change programs, given that a great deal of organizational stress is due to conditions that are not under management control, such as the time pressures experienced by the tax accountants every spring no matter what their organizations might do. We agree with this general advice, and believe that Ganster and his associates have articulated one of the most important, and most imposing, tasks facing I/O psychology in the near future.

CONCLUSIONS

In this chapter we presented a number of issues that focus on the individual's role in work settings; that is, on how she contributes to the operation of the organization and how it influences her. These issues are both fascinating and frustrating. On one hand they include the most basic questions concerning the nature of organizations (organizational theories) and how they function (communication). On the other hand they include concepts that I/O psychologists and others who study work organizations have not even been able to agree *exist*, much less define (organizational climate and culture). The common lesson of these topics for I/O psychologists and students of I/O psychology is that behavior in organizations is both *collective* and embedded within a *context*. To the extent that we forget that lesson, our science and our discipline lose their relevance.

CHAPTER SUMMARY

Organizational theories are statements about how organizations should be designed or structured, and about how organizations should be conceptualized and studied. The earliest influential organizational theory was bureaucracy, the principles of which are still evident in the structure of most organizations. Limitations to bureaucratic theory, and the rise of the human relations movement, led to organizational theories such as McGregor's Theory Y and Argyris' need-integration theory that focused on the needs and motives of individual workers. More recently yet, open systems theories have attempted to describe organizations in terms of the interrelationships between units within organizations, as well as interactions between the organization and its environment.

A great deal of effort has been directed toward understanding the communication process in organizations. Understanding this process is critical because communication is an essential component of virtually every organizational function. A number of distinct communication functions have been identified, as have factors that influence communication effectiveness.

Two other popular research topics are organizational climate and organizational culture. These concepts involve employees' shared perceptions of their organization and the psychological meaning they attach to organizational events, respectively. Not all I/O psychologists agree on the importance of climate and culture, however, and there have been problems developing definitions of, and clarifying the differences between, these concepts.

Topics that have recently become frequent targets of research are organizational effectiveness and stress in organizations. Effectiveness has been found to be a very complex phenomenon to study, and sophisticated models of effectiveness are just beginning to emerge. Results of research on stress clearly demonstrate its negative effects on health and performance, although there is no general agreement on how stress should best be managed.

INTEROFFICE MEMO
TO: Ed Clark, Vice President, Retail Operations
From: J. A. MacKeven, Human-Resources Coordinator

I have been considering the memo that you sent concerning the flap between Bombyk and Richmond. You seem to imply that there is a communication problem in your division, and that is certainly a possibility There is, however, a more basic factor that seems to be involved, and we should consider it before taking any action.

First, in terms of the communication issue, it would appear that Quality Standards and Store Inspections are unaware of each other's activities, which has led to some duplication of effort. In terms of formal lines of communication, your office is the link between these departments. I think we need to examine the procedures by which your staff controls interdepartmental communication. Perhaps we need to set up some direct liaisons between departments, bypassing your office.

The more basic issue here concerns the fundamental structure of your division. That is, which department should have the responsibility for defining these standards (as well as for other specific activities)? We simply shouldn't have two groups that are able to logically claim responsibility for the same functions. I think we need to understand what each department head sees as the major tasks of his or her unit, and how they came to hold those opinions. I would not be surprised to find that some type of reorganization within Retail Operations would be helpful. For example, do we need these two departments, or would it be more effective (including in terms of communication!) to combine them? With your permission, I will start looking into both the specific communication issues and the more general issue of duplication of responsibility, and we'll see if my suspicions are warranted.

REVIEW QUESTIONS AND EXERCISES

1. The problem in the retail operations division seems to involve communication at some level. Given what you know about the general communication process (Shannon & Weaver, 1948) and communication networks, what might be the specific cause(s) of this problem? What remedies might be effective?

2. Dr. MacKeven has suggested that there may be problems in the basic functioning of the retail operations division. In terms of (*a*) bureaucratic theory and (*b*) Lawrence and Lorsch's theory of organizations, what might the nature of these problems be?

3. Aside from any breakdown in communication, there may be differences of opinion on the parts of Mr. Bombyk and Ms. Richmond concerning the functions for which their respective departments have responsibility. Use the role-episode model of Katz and Kahn to describe a series of events that might have led to this misunderstanding.

4. Examine the dimensions of organizational climate identified by Litwin and Stringer (1968) and by Campbell et al. (1970) that were listed earlier in the chapter. Given your knowledge of Peter's Pan Pizza, describe its climate in terms of these dimensions.

CHAPTER 13

Organizational Change

Learning Points

After studying this chapter, you should

- be able to describe the dimensions along which organizational change varies
- be able to describe scientific management, and explain why it is no longer a popular approach to job design
- be able to define job scope, and both describe and evaluate three techniques for increasing job scope
- be able to explain what the job characteristics model is, describe the components of the model and how they interact, and evaluate both the model and the Job Diagnostic Survey; you should also be able to suggest how the job characteristics model might be improved
- understand what organizational development is, and describe the processes involved in each stage of planned change according to Lewin's model
- be familiar with examples of individual-, group-, and organization-level organization development techniques
- be able to explain the arguments for and against the effectiveness of OD

INTEROFFICE MEMO

TO: All vice presidents and senior vice presidents

From: J. A. MacKeven, Human—Resources Coordinator

I recently attended a meeting, along with some of you, at which plans to expand operations into several new fields were discussed. Two plans in particular were met with enthusiastic support, and are being pursued in greater detail. These plans are (1) development and marketing of products for vending machine sales, and (2) marketing of current products in institutional markets, such as schools, airlines, and children's camps.

I have been asked by the president to study the ramifications of these plans for our human resources. These ramifications fall into two basic categories. First, there are the obvious issues of selecting, placing, and training the new employees who will have to be hired to implement these plans. Second, there are the equally important issues of job design, and it is these issues that I am writing to you about today. Specifically, if these plans are implemented, there will be a substantial number of new jobs created, and there will have to be substantial changes to a number of existing jobs. Recognizing that there are a variety of ways to accomplish any given set of tasks, we would like to design these jobs such that there is maximum benefit for both the employees and the company.

In the next few weeks, directors and supervisors in your divisions will be contacted by members of the human resources staff to get their input on a number of issues, such as the effectiveness of the design of current jobs, how new jobs necessitated by the proposed changes might be integrated into the relevant units, and what changes in the total organization might be necessary in order to facilitate the plans. Information on likely changes, in terms of new/changed jobs, in each department will be forwarded to the appropriate managers in the immediate future. Please encourage your management staffs to examine these changes carefully, and to think about the ways in which they might be implemented.

In this chapter, we will be discussing change in organizations. Although some of the issues that we will address in the first part of this chapter, such as job and task design, have broader implications, they are often critically important components of organizational change. In the later sections of the chapter we will discuss techniques specifically designed to facilitate change in organizations. Before we begin describing the theory and research on organizational change, however, we would like to make a few points about the nature of change in organizations, focusing on issues raised in the opening memo.

The memo that opens this chapter was selected because it discusses *anticipated* changes at Peter's Pan Pizza: If PPP's management decides to proceed with one or both of the plans mentioned in the memo, there will be dramatic, large-scale changes in many aspects of the company's operations. The memo was also selected because the types of change that the proposed programs would require are the types that can, to some extent, be *planned*. The importance and advantages of planning for change in organizations will, we hope, become evident as you read this chapter.

One way to classify organizational change is in terms of its **scope.** In previous chapters we have seen widespread change at Peter's Pan Pizza. The most obvious example was their acquisition of Flavio's Frozen Foods, which not only made the company larger, but also brought them into new markets with new products. The acquisition of Flavio's, and the types of changes discussed in the current chapter memo, are at one end of a continuum of organizational change. They represent large-scale, organization-wide events that may require major alterations in the basic structure and philosophy of the company. These types of changes have historically been relatively infrequent, although they are more common in growing, entrepreneurial companies than in older, established organizations. They have also become more common in recent years as the number of corporate mergers has dramatically increased. At the other end of the continuum we find smaller-scale changes that have more limited effects on the organization. For example, the purchase of a new machine to shred cheese will probably not trigger a series of events that will be felt throughout PPP and the rest of the pizza industry, but it will make an important difference to those workers who use the machine.

When all degrees of change, from global to specific, are considered, a somewhat contradictory conclusion must be drawn: *Organizational change is constant.* That is, organizations are always undergoing change in one form or another. This fact is acknowledged in open systems theories of organizations, discussed in Chapter 12 (for example, Katz & Kahn, 1978). Open systems theories stress the interdependence of various parts of an organization, and how a change in one part will normally require changes in other parts if the organization is to function effectively. For example, Peter's Pan Pizza's plan to begin institutional service will make it necessary, among other things, to change policies and procedures regarding shipping and inventory control. Even if gearing up for institutional service required no other *direct* changes (which would certainly not be the case), the changes in shipping and inventory would result in other changes, such as how the finance division handles accounts payable and accounts receivable, which would in turn affect the cash flow throughout the company and therefore have indirect effects on numerous other units. When the organization is viewed as a system, the importance of anticipating and planning for change, even when relatively limited in scope, should not be underestimated.

Another important lesson to be learned from open systems theories that will help us understand organizational change is the interdependence of the organization and its environment. Katz and Kahn (1978) described organizations in terms of a continuous cycle in which inputs are taken from the environment, transformed in some way, and returned to the environment in the form of products or services. In the simplest sense, environmental change (changes in available inputs, or changes in the demand for outputs) will have direct effects on the functioning of organizations that are using those inputs and producing outputs. Environmental change therefore makes change in the organizational system necessary, or at least desirable. At Peter's Pan Pizza, the decision to expand into vending and institutional markets should be based on an unmet demand for those products and services in the environment. Further, in order for the expansion to be successful, PPP will need to have ready access to the inputs necessary to meet those needs. Changes in either consumer demand or required resources could influence the effectiveness of PPP's changes.

We said earlier that organizational change can be defined in terms of the size or scope of the change. Another dimension along which change can be defined, which is also highlighted by the open systems view of organizations, concerns the response of the organization to environmental change. At one end of this continuum is a **reactive** response. By this we mean that in some cases organizations respond only after dramatic environmental change has taken place, occasionally after having experienced serious problems because a response was not made sooner. An example of this can be seen in the American auto industry, which did not respond to growing consumer demand for smaller, more efficient vehicles until "foreign" automakers had already stepped in and claimed most of that market.

At the other end of the continuum is a **proactive** response to change. Here, management attempts to anticipate environmental change before it can adversely affect the company, and institutes plans that will allow the company to use the change to its advantage. The obvious examples of this type of response are the "foreign" carmakers, who responded more quickly to changing consumer demand than did their U.S. counterparts. As far as Peter's Pan Pizza is concerned, it remains to be seen whether they are responding to market changes that have already put the company at a competitive disadvantage, or anticipating a demand for fine Italian-style specialties in previously untapped markets.

---

scope: the range or extent of an activity
reactive: caused by, or in response to, something
proactive: anticipating, or taking place in expectation of, something

A final note in our overview of organizational change: We have made a point of emphasizing the importance of planning for change and anticipating the need for change. It should be kept in mind, however, that a great deal of the change that occurs in organizations is haphazard, and therefore difficult if not impossible to anticipate. For example, an unexpected blight that wipes out the anchovy harvest could have devastating effects at Peter's Pan Pizza, if the company had invested a great deal of time and money in developing a new frozen anchovy-filled pastry. There may not be acceptable anchovy substitutes, and the company may have to "write off" its investment in the project. Although this sort of unexpected change can always happen, we believe that much of the change in organizations, particularly changes that are made necessary by environmental conditions, *can* be anticipated. Doing so, however, requires careful monitoring of these conditions, and conscious efforts to manage and control the change process.

JOB AND TASK DESIGN

Except in Chapter 3 (where job analysis was considered), our discussion of I/O psychology has generally centered on characteristics of workers; the characteristics of jobs and job tasks have been taken as "givens." We have discussed methods for selecting and training workers so that they would be able to perform specific jobs in the organization. Later, we discussed how individual characteristics, such as needs or leadership style, can be important in determining workers' behavior. In short, this approach emphasized selecting or changing individuals in order to achieve certain goals. Although the traditional psychological emphasis on individual characteristics is evident in most I/O theories, there is another general approach to dealing with these issues: *Jobs* rather than people can be changed. For example, rather than training workers how to perform a complicated and dangerous task, it might be better to change the task so that workers can perform it without as much training and without being endangered.

In a way, job and task design represents an individual-level application of the philosophy underlying the organizational theories presented in Chapter 12. That is, organizational theories are concerned with how best to design and coordinate total organizations, and job- and task-design theories are concerned with how best to design individual jobs. In both cases, individual characteristics are usually only considered as moderating variables, while the major emphasis is on structural, procedural, and relational aspects of the job or organization.

Origins of Job Design

The earliest influential approaches to job design resulted from more general theories of organizations and management. One such approach was based on the scientific management theory of Frederick Taylor (1911), which we discussed in Chapter 9. Taylor was primarily concerned with organizational and individual efficiency, and emphasized job designs that would maximize efficiency. He believed that job tasks could be broken down into elemental motions, and that by replacing slow, inefficient motions with those that are faster and more efficient, overall organizational and individual productivity could be increased.

The best-known tool for achieving this goal was the time-and-motion study (Gilbreth, 1919). In this technique, workers' motions were timed, and when faster ways of accomplishing the job tasks were identified, they were incorporated into the job. As a result of using time-and-motion studies, jobs were greatly simplified to involve only a few elementary movements that were repeated continually. This simplification of jobs also resulted in worker specialization and job standardization. Each person was trained to perform only a handful of simple operations, and each of the simplified jobs had to be performed in only one way, if it was to "fit" with the rest of the jobs in the company.

Similar job-design implications evolved from Weber's (1947) bureaucratic model (see Chapter 12). One of the basic principles of bureaucracy is strict division of labor, with each worker performing a limited number and type of tasks. As with scientific management, the consequences of bureaucracy include simplification, standardization, and specialization of jobs and job tasks.

There is little question that jobs designed on the basis of scientific management and bureaucratic principles *are* more efficient in terms of time spent to perform specific tasks, and that these approaches resulted in economic savings for the companies that used them. However, these savings were typically short-lived, because simplification and standardization have negative long-term side effects (such as monotony and boredom) that can in turn have a negative impact on workers' attitudes (Dunham, 1979). As we saw in Chapter 9, negative attitudes toward work and low job satisfaction are related to withdrawal behaviors such as absenteeism and turnover, which are usually costly for companies. Also, extreme standardization and specialization are likely to result in inflexibility and resistance to change, which, as we have seen, limit an organization's ability to adapt to changing internal and external conditions.

The negative consequences of scientific management and bureaucracy for job design are only examples of the many limitations of these approaches. Both of these theories were popular during the early part of the twentieth century, but managers came to question some of the basic assumptions underlying them when the economic consequences of worker alienation became evident. At about this time, however, the human relations movement, spurred on by the Hawthorne studies, began to take shape. The new emphasis on worker attitudes and perceptions led to the next major advance in job and task design, the job-scope approaches.

Job Scope

As we stated during our discussion of job attitudes and satisfaction, during the 1930s and 1940s managers and organizational researchers began to attend to the needs and desires of workers in addition to the efficiency of individuals and organizations. One of the key principles of this human relations movement was the idea that workers desire a sense of achievement or accomplishment from what they do. That is, rather than being motivated only by economic factors such as pay and benefits, human relations theories assumed that rank-and-file workers identified with their jobs, and were motivated by meaningful tasks and opportunities to utilize their skills. Jobs designed along the lines of scientific management or bureaucratic principles, because of their emphasis on specialization and the underlying assumption that workers are primarily motivated by economic issues, were unlikely to provide this sense of achievement.

These changing attitudes about workers' responses to their jobs led to job-design principles that were diametrically opposed to those derived from Taylor's and Weber's theories. Rather than making jobs simpler and more efficient, the emphasis shifted to designing jobs that involved a broader range of tasks and utilized a wider variety of workers' skills and abilities. Because of the emphasis on the span of activities and skills involved in job performance, this approach to job design is often referred to as the job-scope approach. The basic rationale for this type of change was that only by making jobs more challenging (by including more tasks), or more meaningful (by using more worker skills), would workers feel the sense of accomplishment that they desired, and be motivated to work hard and to perform well as a result.

Two major job-change techniques emerged during the early years of the human relations era. One of these was job enlargement. Job enlargement involves giving workers a greater *number* of tasks to perform. Enlargement is contrary to Weber's (1947) bureaucratic notion of division of labor, and it is essentially the opposite of the job-simplification techniques introduced by Taylor. In this sense, it represents job expansion in a *horizontal* direction (see Figure 13.1).

An example of job enlargement would be if Peter's Pan Pizza decided to start marketing vending machine products, and asked the same sales representatives who have been selling Flavio's frozen products to supermarkets to also sell the new products to vending companies. Each sales representative would have *more* to do, although their new responsibilities would be essentially similar to their old responsibilities. It is important to notice that job enlargement can come about because of management's belief that increasing the number of tasks will satisfy employee needs, or because there is simply more work to be done in the organization and the new tasks are "naturally" assigned to those who are already performing similar tasks.

The second job-scope technique is job enrichment, where workers are given greater control over how their jobs are performed. Typically, job enrichment involves giving workers authority and responsibility, either solely or shared with a supervisor, to do such things as planning work activities, setting goals, and making decisions about how to deal with problems that arise. This is dramatically different from how decisions are made and authority is exercised in traditional organizations. Specifically, it is at least partially inconsistent with the widely practiced bureaucratic principle of hierarchy of control. That is, in most organizations there is a clearly defined authority structure, in which each worker is responsible to his immediate supervisor, who in turn is responsible to the manager at the next level, and so on. In a similar fashion, each supervisor is

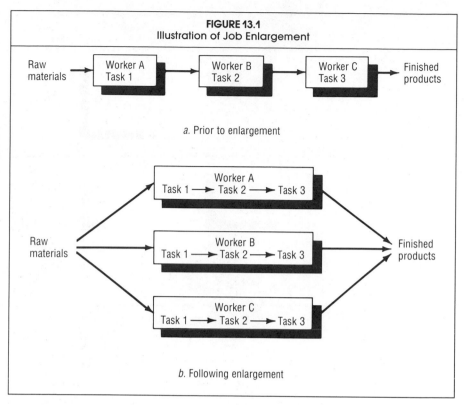

FIGURE 13.1
Illustration of Job Enlargement

responsible for defining subordinates' jobs, and specifying how those jobs should be performed. Under job enrichment, however, a worker may be responsible to her supervisor only for the *results* of her work, and have the freedom to organize and perform the job in whatever way best suits her. Job-enrichment programs, therefore, have an impact on the level at which decisions are made in an organization, with supervisors and managers giving their subordinates some authority to define the nature of work. Compared to job enlargement, enrichment represents job expansion in a *vertical* direction (see Figure 13.2).

Job enrichment among Peter's Pan Pizza's sales force might entail giving the sales representatives the freedom to decide which products should be "pitched" to which clients, to set their own schedules for visiting their clients, to plan special promotions for their territories, and to exercise similar functions normally carried out by their supervisors.

A third, less common technique that can be used to expand the scope of a job is job rotation. Here, rather than changing the number of tasks that make up any one job or set of jobs, workers switch from one job to another on a regular basis. From a job-design standpoint, this is similar to job enlargement, in that each rotation will usually result in different skill requirements for the workers, so that over time a greater range of worker skills are called into play. It can be argued quite effectively, however, that the tasks that a worker is performing at any given time will still be relatively limited in scope. For this

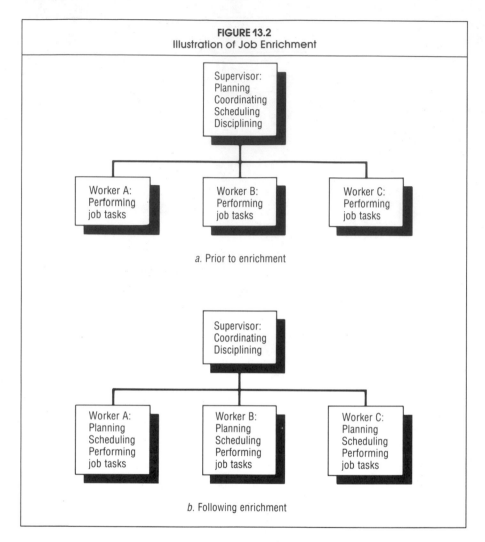

FIGURE 13.2
Illustration of Job Enrichment

Supervisor:
Planning
Coordinating
Scheduling
Disciplining

Worker A:
Performing
job tasks

Worker B:
Performing
job tasks

Worker C:
Performing
job tasks

a. Prior to enrichment

Supervisor:
Coordinating
Disciplining

Worker A:
Planning
Scheduling
Performing
job tasks

Worker B:
Planning
Scheduling
Performing
job tasks

Worker C:
Planning
Scheduling
Performing
job tasks

b. Following enrichment

reason, and because employees who rotate between jobs have to spend a great deal of their time training for each new position, job rotation has never received as much attention as the other methods as a way to increase job scope.

Job enlargement and job enrichment were very popular for many years, and there were numerous reports of success using these techniques. Often, however, the changes in job scope were confounded with other changes, and experimental control was often inadequate, making it impossible to attribute changes in workers' behavior or attitudes to the changes in the jobs. Further, when changes due to job scope were observed, they were frequently shorted-lived (for example, Maher & Overbagh, 1971). Theorists began to claim that most workers, especially blue-collar workers, did not desire enriched jobs (for example, Shrank, 1974), and research supported this view, showing that increasing job scope did not have positive effects for all workers (see Brief & Aldag, 1975; Robey, 1974, Wanous, 1974*b*).

A number of possible moderators of the enrichment–satisfaction relationship were suggested, including urban vs. rural upbringing and Protestant work ethic. Investigations of these variables, however, failed to reveal any consistent effect on the relationship between job scope and satisfaction (White, 1978). Indeed, it has been suggested that increasing job scope might lead to increased role ambiguity, which itself has been associated with such outcomes as increased stress and anxiety (Korman, Greenhaus, & Badin, 1977).

The implementation of job enrichment and job enlargement was also hampered by the somewhat limited, overgeneralized theory on which they were based—the human relations view that workers obtain satisfaction from accomplishments and use of their skills. Although this provides an optimistic view of workers, it provides little practical guidance in terms of *how* to design jobs, what sorts of changes workers will find enriching, or what types of additional tasks will utilize workers' skills most efficiently. Consequently, it is not surprising that the evidence for the effectiveness of job-scope approaches to job design was mixed. Clearly, the *potential* for task design to influence behavior and attitudes had been demonstrated. What was needed was some sort of guiding theory that would suggest which types of job changes, in which types of situations, would produce the desired results.

Job Characteristics Model

The seeds of a comprehensive model of the effects of job and task design on worker behavior and attitudes were sown in the work of Turner and Lawrence (1965). Taking the position that certain attributes or characteristics of jobs were likely to be associated with desirable worker responses, such as high performance, good attendance, and high satisfaction, they constructed a list of six attributes that they believed would show favorable results: (1) variety of tasks performed, (2) worker autonomy, (3) worker knowledge and skill required by the job, (4) worker responsibility, (5) interaction with others required by the job, and (6) optional interaction with others. Turner and Lawrence did not provide any experimental tests of their hypothesis that these characteristics resulted in desirable behaviors; however, they did provide correlational evidence that these attributes were associated with attendance and satisfaction, although only among workers from rural communities.

A number of authors presented elaborations and extensions of Turner and Lawrence's (1965) basic idea that task variety, autonomy, and other task characteristics affect worker behavior and attitudes. However, Hackman and Oldham's (1976) model quickly became, and still remains, the best-known and most widely researched theory of task attributes. This theory, the job characteristics model, is described and evaluated in the following sections.

THEORETICAL BASIS OF THE JOB CHARACTERISTICS MODEL

As you will soon see, the job characteristics model is complex, and includes a number of direct and indirect relationships between several types of variables. The basic theory underlying the model, however, is straightforward. Hackman and Oldham (1976) believed that properly designed tasks could satisfy the psychological needs of certain workers. Specifically, they focused on Maslow's (1943) need theory (see Chapter 8), and proposed that jobs with characteristics such as those described by Turner and Lawrence (1965) would satisfy Maslow's higher-order needs or growth needs. Thus, workers who had progressed through Maslow's need hierarchy to the point where they were motivated to satisfy esteem or self-actualization needs would find these sorts of jobs satisfying and motivating. Of course, these jobs would not be as appropriate for workers motivated to satisfy lower-order needs.

As we pointed out in Chapter 8, Maslow's need hierarchy theory of motivation has had very little empirical support. Relying on Maslow's theory to explain the effects of job design has therefore been a problem for the job characteristics model from the start (for example, Korman, Greenhaus, & Badin, 1977). This has not completely deterred psychologists from conducting research on the model, but it may help explain some of the inconsistencies that characterize the research results.

CORE JOB CHARACTERISTIC DIMENSIONS

The key to Hackman and Oldham's (1976) model is a set of five core job dimensions that can be used to describe jobs in terms of design characteristics that have implications for workers' behavior. These core dimensions are similar to the characteristics listed by Turner and Lawrence (1965), and include

• *Skill variety:* This refers to the extent to which a worker's job requires the worker to use numerous skills or talents in order to perform the job successfully. An example of a job high in skill variety is that of the Peter's Pan Pizza's sales representatives mentioned before. Among other things, they must make judgments about how the products they have to offer meet different market demands, prepare and deliver sales presentations, and keep accurate records of customers' orders. An example of a job low in skill variety is that of the people who sprinkle cheese on Flavio's frozen pizzas, who only need a reasonable amount of eye–hand coordination to perform their job tasks.

• *Task identity:* Jobs high in task identity are those in which the worker is able to perform a complete, identifiable piece of work, starting with raw materials or information and ending with a product that is ready to be used, either by a customer or by another person or group of people in the company. A low-task-identity job at Peter's Pan Pizza might involve performing only one step in the assembly of a pizza, such as being the person who spreads the sauce onto the crust. A high-task-identity job would be one in which a single person performed all of the steps in pizza assembly, starting out with some crust, sauce, cheese, and assorted toppings, and finishing with a ready-to-bake pizza.

• *Task significance:* Task significance refers to the impact that a person's work has on other people. A person's job has high task significance if what she does is critical to the successful performance of other jobs in the company. Clearly, the Peter's Pan Pizza's sales representatives have jobs that are significant in this way. A job would also be significant if it had an impact on the lives of people who are not members of the organization. Although pizza may not seem to be a very important product, the ways in which PPP's employees perform their jobs *do* have an effect on the livelihoods of people who supply the company with raw materials, as well as on those of the people who work for the supermarkets and stores that sell PPP's products. These jobs therefore have significance beyond the workplace. Although no job has a total lack of task significance, an example of one *lower* on this dimension might be that of the janitor who cleans managers' offices in the Suardell Springs headquarters. We at least *hope* that these managers can perform their jobs with dusty shelves as well as they can with clean shelves!

• *Autonomy:* A job is high in autonomy if the worker has the freedom to decide, independently of his supervisor, the procedures used to perform the job and the scheduling of the job. Clearly, some jobs more readily lend themselves to autonomy than do others. Returning again to our pizza salesforce, it would seem that they would have a fair amount of autonomy, because they are not under the direct, day-to-day supervision of their bosses, and must therefore make most decisions about how to perform their jobs themselves. Other jobs, such as those involved in the preparation of the food, would have less autonomy, because much of the scheduling of that work and the procedures used to perform the work are dependent on technology and relationships to other jobs in the organization.

• *Task feedback:* Task feedback refers to whether or not a worker can tell, simply from performing her job in the normal fashion, whether the job is being done effectively. For example, a truck driver who delivers supplies to Peter's Pan Pizza's pizzerias has a job with high task feedback: either the supplies are delivered on time and undamaged, or they are not. On the other hand, marketing employees whose job is to develop new products do not have as high a level of task feedback. Do you remember the idea they had for a frozen anchovy-filled pastry? They won't really know if this idea is going to work until the product is marketed and consumer reaction is studied.

Hackman and Oldham (1976) stated that each of the core dimensions will be positively related to favorable worker attitudes and behaviors. The motivating properties of a job, however, are not conceptualized as a simple combination of the five dimensions. Instead, Hackman and Oldham specified the following formula for combining these characteristics into what they called the motivating potential score, or MPS:

$$\text{MPS} = \frac{\text{Skill variety} + \text{Task identity} + \text{Task significance}}{3} \times \text{Autonomy} \times \text{Feedback}$$

This formula has important implications for job design. First, notice that skill variety, task identity, and task significance are averaged together in the formula. This means that jobs with low levels of one or even two of these dimensions can still have motivating potential if there are high levels of the remaining dimension(s) in this group. Note, too, that this average is multiplied together with both autonomy and feedback. This implies that if the average of the first three dimensions is zero (that is, the job has *no* variety, *no* identity, and *no* significance), *or* if autonomy is zero, *or* if feedback is zero, then the motivating potential of the job will be zero. In other words, for a job to have motivating potential, it *must* have both autonomy and feedback, in addition to one or more of the remaining three dimensions.

In order to increase the MPS for a job, we need to know what can be done to improve the core job dimensions. Hackman, Oldham, Janson, and Purdy (1975) suggested the following implementation concepts as possible ways to do this:

• *Combining tasks:* This involves reversing the processes of specialization and division of labor made popular in the scientific management and bureaucratic theories, by combining a number of specific tasks into more complex, multidimensional jobs. In essence, this is the same as job enlargement. According to Hackman and Oldham (1976), combining tasks will increase both task variety and task identity.

• *Forming natural work units:* Often, a worker is unable to see how his or her job "fits in" with the jobs of others, or with the overall company goals and plans. By giving workers responsibility for complete, identifiable units of work, this strategy attempts to increase both task identity and task significance.

• *Establishing client relationships:* Although they seldom consider their jobs in these terms, each worker has a number of "clients," both within the organization and outside of the organization. For example, each of the stores to which Peter's Pan Pizza's truck drivers deliver supplies is a client whom they serve. By having employees develop personal relationships with each of their clients, the model predicts that task variety, autonomy, and feedback will be increased.

• *Vertical loading:* Vertical loading is very similar to the concept of job enrichment. A vertically loaded job provides workers with more freedom and independence in making decisions about how, and in some cases when, their work will be done. This strategy is expected to have a positive effect on task variety, task identity, task significance, and autonomy.

• *Opening feedback channels:* This implementation concept is intended to have a direct effect on the core job dimension of feedback. Feedback channels include the job itself, as we have mentioned before, as well as information provided by supervisors and co-workers.

SOURCE: Adapted from "A New Strategy for Job Enrichment," by J. R. Hackman, G. Oldham, R. Janson, and K. Purdy, *California Management Review*, 1975, 17(4), 51–71. © 1975 by the Regents of the University of California. Reprinted by permission from the *California Management Review*, vol. 17, no. 4. By permission of the Regents.

These are only examples of what can be done to affect job dimensions—many other actions could be taken as well—but they should give you a good idea of the types of changes that the job characteristics model advocates.

CRITICAL PSYCHOLOGICAL STATES

According to the Hackman and Oldham (1976) model, the core job dimensions influence individual behavior and attitudes through critical psychological states. These states are basically perceptions on the part of workers about the nature of their jobs. As you might expect, changes in different core job dimensions have effects on different perceptions. Specifically, skill variety, task identity, and task significance combine to determine a worker's experience of the *meaningfulness* of his work. That is, according to the model, workers will perceive jobs that are high on these dimensions as being meaningful, both to the workers themselves and to other people. The degree of autonomy in a job determines the second critical psychological state, the experienced *responsibility for outcomes of work*. The more a worker is free to structure, schedule, and define her job, the greater will be the responsibility felt for the results or outcomes of that job. Third, the amount of feedback present in a job determines the final critical psychological state, *knowledge of the actual results of work activities*. Without adequate feedback, workers are unable to judge the effects of their behavior; but with adequate feedback, a fairly accurate picture of how they are doing, and how they contribute to the performance of the entire organization, is possible.

PERSONAL AND WORK OUTCOMES

So far we have explained that the job characteristics model specifies that certain changes in jobs (implementation concepts) can affect important task characteristics of those jobs (core job dimensions), which in turn play an important role in determining workers' perceptions of their jobs (critical psychological states). The next step in the model is to describe the expected effects of these perceptions on workers' behaviors and attitudes. Hackman and Oldham (1976) described four general results that can be expected when workers experience meaningfulness, responsibility, and knowledge of results. The first two of these, *high internal work motivation* and *high-quality work performance*, can be thought of as motivational outcomes. That is, workers who experience high levels of the critical psychological states will be motivated to perform well, not because of external incentives such as pay, but because of internal motives stemming from the nature of their jobs. The other outcomes, *high satisfaction with work* and *low absenteeism and turnover*, can be thought of as attitudinal outcomes. Jobs that result in favorable psychological states should be enjoyable and satisfying, resulting in positive attitudes toward the job and the organization. As we saw in Chapter 9, these types of attitudes are not good predictors of work performance, but they *do* predict withdrawal behaviors such as absenteeism and turnover.

GROWTH NEED STRENGTH

The final component in the job characteristics model is growth-need strength. As we said when we introduced the model, Hackman and Oldham (1976) based their work on the idea that properly designed jobs will satisfy workers' growth needs. However, consistent with Maslow's need hierarchy, Hackman and Oldham believed that jobs designed to satisfy growth needs will not be appropriate for, and therefore will not motivate, workers who are currently motivated by lower-order needs. Thus, the degree to which workers are motivated by growth needs, or growth need strength (GNS), was proposed as a moderator variable in the model. That is, improving the core job dimensions was predicted to have favorable results only for those workers who were *high* in GNS. Only for high-GNS workers would the core job dimensions affect the critical psychological states, and only for these same workers would those critical states result in favorable personal and work outcomes. For workers low in GNS, the effects of changing jobs according to this model could be expected to be negative, because the emphasis would be placed on needs that are, for them, irrelevant.

The complete job characteristics model is illustrated in Figure 13.3. As we said earlier, this is a fairly complex model, but the logic behind it is relatively straightforward. In order to test the model, however, a special measure had to be developed. It is to this measure, and the research that has used it, that we now turn our attention.

THE JOB DIAGNOSTIC SURVEY

In order to implement or test the job characteristics model, a measure of core job dimensions and motivating potential was needed. Hackman and Oldham (1975) developed such a measure, called the Job Diagnostic Survey or JDS. The key features of the JDS are scales designed to measure each of the five core job dimensions from the model. Also included in the instrument, however, are scales measuring two supplementary dimensions (*feedback from agents* and *dealing with others*), as well as scales measuring the critical psychological states, internal motivation, satisfaction, and growth need strength. Most dimensions and states are measured in two different sections of the survey, using more than one item format.

Hackman and Oldham (1975) presented evidence of the reliability and validity of the JDS, including its ability to measure the core job dimensions. A number of other researchers, however, have failed to confirm that the JDS measures what it was intended to measure. For example, rather than obtaining the five core dimensions specified by the model, Dunham (1976) performed a factor analysis on the JDS and found only *one* dimension, which he called "job variety." Dunham, Aldag, and Brief (1977) found that the number of dimensions depended upon the type of job, and varied from two to five. Other researchers have had similar problems replicating or reproducing the proposed structure of the JDS (for example, Lee & Klein, 1982; Pokorney, Gilmore, & Beehr, 1980).

A recent study by Harvey, Billings, and Nilan (1985) used a technique called confirmatory factor analysis to examine the structure of the JDS. This technique is designed to test hypotheses concerning the number and type of dimensions measured by a scale, and therefore allowed the researchers to compare a number of specific models, including Hackman and Oldham's (1976) model and Dunham's (1976) single-factor model. Harvey and his colleagues found that if certain methodological problems, such as the use of more than one response format and

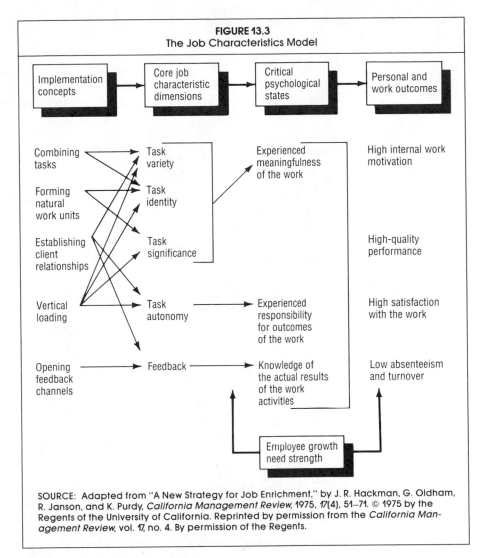

FIGURE 13.3
The Job Characteristics Model

| Implementation concepts | Core job characteristic dimensions | Critical psychological states | Personal and work outcomes |

Combining tasks

Forming natural work units

Establishing client relationships

Vertical loading

Opening feedback channels

Task variety

Task identity

Task significance

Task autonomy

Feedback

Experienced meaningfulness of the work

Experienced responsibility for outcomes of the work

Knowledge of the actual results of the work activities

High internal work motivation

High-quality performance

High satisfaction with the work

Low absenteeism and turnover

Employee growth need strength

SOURCE: Adapted from "A New Strategy for Job Enrichment," by J. R. Hackman, G. Oldham, R. Janson, and K. Purdy, *California Management Review*, 1975, *17*(4), 51–71. © 1975 by the Regents of the University of California. Reprinted by permission from the *California Management Review*, vol. *17*, no. 4. By permission of the Regents.

a mixture of positively and negatively worded items, are controlled, the Hackman and Oldham model, with separate core dimensions, provided the best description of their data, whereas the Dunham model provided the most parsimonious (simple, yet adequate) description. We think this study is important, because the other factor-analytic studies of the JDS, many of which failed to support the model, used a type of factor analysis that is not appropriate for model testing. Thus, although Harvey's data are not by themselves conclusive, and in fact he and his colleagues offer several suggestions for improving the JDS, it is interesting that the only study that used the appropriate factor analysis supported the original model.

Another issue in using the JDS concerns the manner in which the scores on the individual core dimensions should be combined to predict behavior and attitudes. Ferris and Gilmore (1985) reviewed research on the JDS, and found three basic techniques for computing what they called "job-complexity indices." The first of these is to compute the motivating potential score (MPS) as suggested by Hackman and Oldham (1976). As we have seen, because this technique multiplies three values together, low scores on any of the three will yield a low MPS score. The second method is a "weighted-average" technique suggested by Stone (1974):

$$\text{Complexity} = (2 \times \text{Variety}) + (2 \times \text{Autonomy}) \\ + \text{Task identity} + \text{Feedback}$$

The third method is an unweighted additive index, obtained simply by summing the five core-dimension scores. Ferris and Gilmore's results showed that the weighted-average method predicted job satisfaction better than the other methods, but that growth need strength had the predicted effect on the relationship between complexity and satisfaction only when the original MPS formula was used.

There are undeniable problems in using the JDS as a measure of core job dimensions. Research has provided inconsistent results regarding its validity; the individual job-dimension scales have questionable reliability, because they consist of relatively few items; there are methodological concerns regarding the use of multiple item formats and negatively worded items; and research results based on the JDS do not seem to be stable from sample to sample. It is important to note these shortcomings, because the JDS is essential to testing the job characteristics model. If this scale is faulty, then it is difficult to draw any conclusions about the model.

Harvey, Billings, and Nilan (1985) argued, however, that there is evidence that the JDS and the MPS, although flawed, have some validity and might be improved by rewording and adding items. The larger question is whether it would be worth the effort. That is, does the available research support the validity of the job characteristics model as an explanation of the effects of job design? If not, then improving the JDS may be a waste of time.

RESEARCH ON THE JOB CHARACTERISTICS MODEL

From the mid-1970s to the early 1980s there was a tremendous amount of research on all aspects of the job characteristics model. Most reviews of this research literature have not supported the theory. For example, the model has been criticized because it relies on poor measures such as the JDS, because the job characteristics lack conceptual independence, because it uses perceptual measures rather than objective measures of job characteristics (although cognitive theories suggest that workers respond to their perceptions rather than to "objective reality," and so perceptual measures are the *only* appropriate measures), and because most of the research that supports the model has used **cross-sectional designs** that do not allow tests of the effects of actual changes in jobs on workers' attitudes and behavior (Aldag, Barr, & Brief, 1981; Roberts & Glick, 1981).

A recent meta-analysis of JDS research (Loher, Noe, Moeller, & Fitzgerald, 1985) found that the best estimate of the correlation between core job characteristics and job satisfaction is .39. For people high in growth need strength, the correlation was .68; for those low in GNS it was .38. Although both of these correlations were significantly different from zero ($p < .05$), the difference between them is consistent with the original model. Thus, although we can have some confidence that perceptions of job characteristics are related to job satisfaction, and that this relationship may be moderated by GNS, we cannot conclude from this research that changes in job design are *responsible* for those perceptions. Unfortunately, field experiments that can test the effects of job-design changes are few in number, and offer little support for the model (Staw, 1984).

The widespread use of cross-sectional, correlational research designs on the job characteristics model leaves us in something of a quandary. Although the theory states that job satisfaction is the result of certain job and task characteristics, it may (also) be that perceptions of those characteristics are actually the *result* of workers' levels of job satisfaction. That is, the theory states that Peter's Pan Pizza's workers will be satisfied if their jobs are high in motivating potential, as determined by the core job characteristics. It could be, however, that satisfied PPP workers *perceive* their jobs as being high in motivating potential as a result of being satisfied, regardless of the actual characteristics of their jobs.

Adler, Skov, and Salvemini (1985) found evidence to support this possibility when they gave subjects phony feedback from a job satisfaction measure, and then asked them to complete the JDS. They found that subjects who had been told they were highly satisfied with their tasks rated the core job dimensions higher than did those who had been told they were dissatisfied. (It should be noted that Adler et al. claim that none of their subjects expressed doubts about this phony satisfaction feedback.) James and Tetrick (1986) also found that job satisfaction influenced job perceptions and vice versa. What is noteworthy about James and Tetrick's study, however, is that this reciprocal relationship between satisfaction and perceptions was found to be *preceded* by a direct effect of job attributes on perceptions (see Figure 13.4). This means that although satisfaction can influence job perceptions and vice versa, these effects depend on the effect that objective job characteristics have on perceptions, which is again consistent with the job characteristics model.

Another controversy surrounding the job characteristics model concerns whether or not job characteristics really *are* important in determining workers' perceptions of, and reactions to, their jobs. A number of theorists (for example, Salancik & Pfeffer, 1978; Weiss, 1977, 1978) have suggested that individuals' perceptions of their jobs may be determined by social cues in the work

---

cross-sectional designs: research designs in which data are gathered from all groups at one point in time (rather than being gathered at more than one point in time), which makes it impossible to properly evaluate changes that occur over time

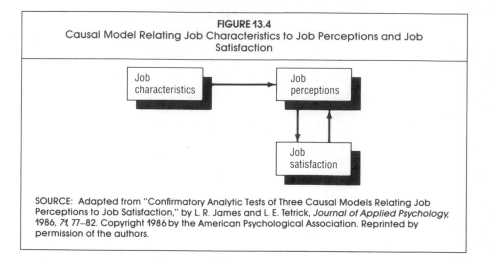

FIGURE 13.4
Causal Model Relating Job Characteristics to Job Perceptions and Job Satisfaction

SOURCE: Adapted from "Confirmatory Analytic Tests of Three Causal Models Relating Job Perceptions to Job Satisfaction," by L. R. James and L. E. Tetrick, *Journal of Applied Psychology,* 1986, *71,* 77–82. Copyright 1986 by the American Psychological Association. Reprinted by permission of the authors.

environment. That is, perceptions of jobs, and job satisfaction, may be more a function of the behavior of other workers than of objective job characteristics.

In partial support of this view, Griffin (1983) conducted a field experiment involving two manufacturing plants, in which he found that *both* objective task characteristics and information provided by supervisors influenced workers' perceptions of core job dimensions, interpersonal task attributes (such as friendship opportunities), and satisfaction. *Only* objective task characteristics, however, had an effect on worker productivity. Staw (1984) pointed out that advocates of both task-characteristic and social-information approaches to job design have utilized research that favors their respective positions, and that neither side is likely to emerge as a clear "winner." He argued that research examining the joint effects of social cues and objective task changes may be more useful than studying either by itself. We agree.

ALTERNATIVES TO THE JOB CHARACTERISTICS MODEL

By now it should be clear that the evidence supporting or refuting the job characteristics model is *anything* but clear. The body of research on the model shows inconsistencies regarding the number and nature of significant core job dimensions, the relationship between job dimensions and workers' perceptions, the importance of growth need strength, and the suitability of the JDS as a measure of job characteristics.

In response to these problems, a number of alternative job-design models have been proposed. These models have tended to rely on theoretical bases other than need theory, such as expectancy theory (Schwab & Cummings, 1976) and goal setting (Umstot, Mitchell, & Bell, 1978), in this way addressing what may well be one of the basic problems with the job characteristics model. Unfortunately, these alternatives have not yet attracted the amount of research attention that has been lavished on the Hackman and Oldham model, and we therefore cannot evaluate their usefulness for confronting the problems that plague job characteristics research.

We are reluctant to suggest, as some authors have, that the job characteristics model be abandoned, or that its only usefulness has been to stimulate research on task design (for example, Landy, 1985; O'Brien, 1982; Schwab & Cummings, 1976). Particularly in light of the recent research that finds support using techniques such as meta-analysis and confirmatory factor analysis, we think that the model may yet prove to be of some value. We do not, however, believe that the support for the model is either strong or conclusive, and we certainly do not view it as a comprehensive explanation for the effects of job design. More realistically, the job characteristics model probably offers a *partial* understanding of the relationships between job and task design and workers' behaviors and attitudes.

Recognizing the importance of valid measures of job characteristics for testing job-design theories, Stone and Gueutal (1985) used a sophisticated scaling technique to determine the dimensions along which people perceive job characteristics. Their rationale for conducting this study was that all of the commonly used measures of job characteristics, such as the JDS, contain essentially the same dimensions, and that these dimensions were derived from the list of characteristics presented by Turner and Lawrence (1965). Unfortunately, Turner and Lawrence did not base their characteristics on empirical research, but rather on their own experiences and reviews of theories. Stone and Gueutal pointed out that although these dimensions may reflect the way Turner and Lawrence perceived jobs, they may not have much in common with the way most workers perceive jobs. Their analyses showed that one dimension along which jobs are perceived, called "job complexity," contained virtually all of the traditional JDS characteristics. In addition to complexity, however, two other dimensions not measured by the JDS nor by any other commonly used scales were also found. Stone and Gueutal named these dimensions *serves the public,* which includes such behaviors as interacting with and providing services to people outside of the organization, and *physical demand,* which involves such characteristics as required strength, health hazards, and physical activity.

Campion and Thayer (1985) also addressed the measurement of job-design characteristics, but from a different perspective. Instead of focusing on worker perceptions, as most psychologists have, they first examined the ways in which job design is studied in a *number* of disciplines. They came up with four basic perspectives on job design, only one of which resembles what is measured by the JDS. Based on these four approaches to job design, Campion and Thayer developed a measure called the Multimethod Job Design Questionnaire, or MJDQ, which taps each of the four perspectives:

- *Motivational:* This approach is based on research and theory in traditional I/O psychology. It includes work on job enrichment, job enlargement, and the job characteristics approach to job design, as well as a number of theories of motivation. Of the four dimensions in the MJDQ, it is the most similar to what is measured by the JDS.
- *Mechanistic:* This perspective is based on "classic" industrial engineering, and emphasizes many of the same concepts as Frederick Taylor's scientific management, such as task simplification and economy of motion.

- *Biological:* The biological approach to job design emphasizes biomechanics and physiology. Included in this view are such things as strength, endurance, vibration, and posture.
- *Perceptual/motor:* This perspective is most similar to human engineering, human factors, or "ergonomics" (see Chapter 14). Here we are concerned with such things as lighting, the design of displays and machine controls, and the safety of the workplace. Also included in this approach are cognitive requirements of jobs, such as information processing and memory.

SOURCE: Adapted from "Development and Field Evaluation of an Interdisciplinary Measure of Job Design," by M. A. Campion and P. W. Thayer, *Journal of Applied Psychology*, 1985, *70*, 29–43. Copyright 1985 by the American Psychological Association. Reprinted by permission of the authors.

Although the results of Campion and Thayer's research using the MJDQ are too complex to present in detail here, it is important to note that the four scales had very different correlations with various criteria. For example, scores on the motivational scale were positively correlated with measures of work motivation and job satisfaction, which is similar to what has been found with the JDS. The biological scale, however, was negatively correlated with measures of effort, pain, and need for medical care. High scores on the mechanistic scale were associated with high skill utilization and low training requirements, and high perceptual/ motor scores were associated with low levels of accidents, errors, stress, work overload, and mental demands.

Both the Stone and Gueutal (1985) and the Campion and Thayer (1985) studies have important implications for the future of job-design research. First, they share the conclusion that JDS-type measures of job characteristics are incomplete, from the perspective of worker perceptions as well as from the standpoint of total job design. If this is true, and we have every reason to expect that it is, it might explain some of the inconsistencies in the psychological job-design research. That is, variation in dimensions that were not measured by the JDS could have affected the research results in unpredictable ways. Second, both of these studies suggest that the types of dimensions measured by the JDS, although not a complete picture of job design, *are* nonetheless important and should be preserved in any comprehensive theory of job design. Thus, whether or not the JDS and the job characteristics model continue to be used, the research based on them has revealed important aspects of the effects of job design. Perhaps in the context of other design parameters, the effects of job characteristics will be identified with more precision.

SUMMARY

The job characteristics model has proved to be a useful, if incomplete, description of the effects of job and task design. Its most notable shortcoming is its failure to consider the effects of nonmotivational factors in job design, although this is not surprising for a *psychological* theory. Its most notable contribution has been as the stimulus for the vast number of research studies on the psychological effects of task characteristics, and the resulting knowledge about the importance and limitations of job characteristics and growth need strength in determining job attitudes.

ORGANIZATIONAL DEVELOPMENT AND CHANGE

As we have seen, much of the research on change in organizations has dealt with changes in either jobs or the tasks that jobs comprise. These types of changes tend to be concentrated at the "narrow" end of the scope-of-change continuum introduced at the beginning of this chapter. That is, although changes in one job may also have important implications for other jobs, their primary impact will be on the specific job being changed. I/O psychologists and other organizational researchers have, however, also focused on methods of systematic change that affect either entire organizations or large portions of organizations. The most widely studied and widely known of these techniques have come to be known collectively as organizational development or OD procedures. In the remaining sections of this chapter we will examine the topic of OD, and see how it has been used to improve the functioning of organizations.

Definition and Description of Organizational Development

Organizational development has been a popular topic in organizational research and practice for nearly three decades. During that time, the number and nature of activities that are considered part of OD have increased dramatically. Today, "OD" is used to refer to so many different theoretical notions and applied practices that telling you that Peter's Pan Pizza is "using OD" really reveals little about what PPP is actually doing. Fortunately, there are enough common elements among most OD techniques that a general definition *can* be developed. Different techniques will stress different aspects of OD, as you will see when we describe some of the more common methods, but the following definition captures the essential philosophy behind virtually all of OD: *Organizational development is the planned use of interventions based on behavioral science knowledge, aimed at encouraging organizational self-examination and acceptance of changes that will improve organizational effectiveness and health.*

Let's examine this definition more closely to see what we are really talking about. First, OD is planned, which means that it is based on a careful analysis of the current status of the organization and on the development of specific courses of action to deal with any problems that have been detected. Ideally, OD does not involve "seat-of-the-pants" organizational changes, nor changes based on management's hunches about what might improve the organization, but rather changes that are suggested by a careful diagnosis of the organization's problems. This diagnostic process is similar to the organizational analysis that should precede the development of a training program (Chapter 7).

Second, OD involves techniques, or interventions, that are based on the body of knowledge about organizations that has developed within the "behavioral sciences." (I/O psychology has, of course, been a major contributor to this body of knowledge.) There are many things that could be done to improve organizations, but many of these either have little to do with individual or collective behavior, or have no basis in scientific research and theory. Again, ideally, OD interventions rely on techniques that have some empirical evidence of effectiveness.

Third, OD techniques have historically been designed to encourage organization members to examine the interpersonal processes that take place in the organization as it performs its many tasks. This "consciousness-raising" function is designed to make managers and workers aware of how things are being done at the present, as well as helping them to see the need for changes that will improve the organization. This emphasis on interpersonal processes originated in the human relations movement, from which many early OD approaches took their inspiration. OD is sometimes criticized for this association with human relations (for example, Alderfer, 1977), although today, as we indicated above, OD has come to encompass such a broad range of activities that this criticism is overstated.

Finally, the definition points out that the primary purpose of OD is to improve the effectiveness and health of organizations. Effectiveness can be defined in terms of the organization's ability to achieve its goals, and a healthy organization can be defined as one in which individuals and groups work toward those goals in an efficient manner.

There are two additional conditions that are usually associated with OD. The first of these is that in order to be successful, OD procedures require the active support of top management. This "top-down" philosophy of OD is intended not only to obtain the support of upper managers, but also to communicate the importance of the OD intervention to all other employees in the organization. Second, OD is often described as an "organization-wide" activity. As you will see later in this chapter, there are many OD procedures that focus on either individual or group processes, rather than organizations as a whole. It should be kept in mind, however, that in most cases these individual and group interventions are intended to solve problems that have been identified through organization-wide analyses.

A final note before outlining the basic processes of OD concerns what is known as Quality of Work Life (QWL). QWL programs are designed to improve workers' experiences on the job in such a way as to increase motivation, satisfaction, commitment, and other employee attitudes, thereby increasing organizational effectiveness and performance. QWL is currently a very popular topic among organizational researchers, but the differences between it and OD are elusive. Some authors have gone to great lengths to distinguish between these two concepts, without much success (Faucheux, Amado, & Laurent, 1982). You will probably run across references to QWL if you do additional reading in organizational research journals or other books, and so we wanted to make it clear that QWL procedures are similar or identical to those common in OD programs.

Basic Processes in Organizational Development

Because it encompasses such a broad spectrum of activities, it is difficult to describe OD processes in general terms. Certainly, a number of theoretical models of OD have been proposed over the years, each attempting to describe the essential elements of OD interventions. Perhaps the simplest model of organizational change was developed by Kurt Lewin (1958). By being simple,

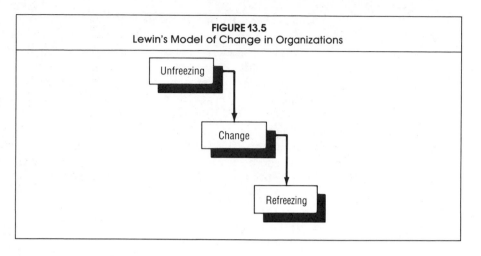

FIGURE 13.5
Lewin's Model of Change in Organizations

Unfreezing

Change

Refreezing

this model has the virtue of being able to incorporate the variety of OD techniques that have been used. We will therefore use this three-stage model, which is illustrated in Figure 13.5, to describe the major processes that are involved in most OD efforts. Keep in mind that specific OD techniques may have more or fewer steps than we outline here, and that other models are usually more complex. Our purpose, however, is not to teach you how to perform OD, but rather to help you understand the basic theory underlying its use.

STAGE ONE: UNFREEZING

According to Lewin (1958), there are forces in organizations that attempt to maintain the status quo, and there are forces that push for change. In order for change to occur, those forces that are resisting change (or maintaining the status quo) must be reduced or modified, so that the forces for change may prevail. Lewin referred to this stage of the model as *unfreezing,* during which the organization prepares for change. It is in this early phase of OD that the OD consultant or change agent begins her interaction with the organization. The change agent is the individual who is responsible for coordinating the changes that will come about as a result of the OD intervention.

Typically (but not always), the change agent is a person from outside of the organization. There are two major reasons why this is so: First, many organizations do not have employees with the basic knowledge and skills in diagnosis, problem solving, and theories of organizational behavior that are considered to be necessary for successful OD. For example, although Dr. MacKeven had a brief experience with OD in her internship during graduate school, she is probably not familiar enough with the variety of available OD techniques to adequately evaluate each of them. Consequently, these organizations hire consultants who have this expertise. Second, and more basic to the process of OD, the role of the change agent is to help identify and implement the changes that will be the most beneficial to the organization. In order to do this, the agent must be trusted by all of the employees with whom she works, and must be seen as unbiased and independent. It is widely believed that an outside consultant is more likely to be perceived as having this independence than is an "in-house" agent, who *may* be suspected of having hidden motives that favor certain groups or individuals in the organization. It is possible, for example, that if Dr. MacKeven has worked frequently or closely with one group of managers, she will be perceived as favoring their interests over those of other managers.

Several important activities must occur during the unfreezing stage in order for OD to be successful. First, as we have already mentioned, it is important to secure the *active participation of top management* early in the OD process. Representatives of top management should therefore meet with the change agent during this time, both to demonstrate their endorsement of the project and to achieve a clear understanding with the change agent about what is expected from the OD process. Often, this understanding will take the form of a contract in which the expectations of each party are explicitly stated. Such a contract is useful because of the broad scope of OD, and the very real possibility that the original purpose of the intervention may be overlooked or downplayed over the course of the months, and even years, that many OD techniques require.

A second important activity during the unfreezing stage is the *diagnosis of the organization's current status,* and the identification of ways in which OD might be able to improve organizational and individual effectiveness. Our definition of OD includes the goal of organizational self-examination, which is necessary if management is to become aware of the organization's shortcomings and the need for change. The change agent plays a critical role in this self-examination, because it is often difficult for managers to take an objective view of the organization that they have helped to build or sustain. Also, experienced change agents should have skills and techniques that will facilitate the diagnostic process. The end result of this process is typically a set of goals specifying the changes that the OD intervention is expected to produce.

A third function that occurs during the unfreezing stage of OD is *planning the actual intervention.* Here again, the change agent's expertise comes into play, as he selects methods that are best suited for meeting the goals identified earlier. Two special points must be raised here. First, you should be aware by now that given the complex nature of organizational systems, there can be no *one* procedure that will be useful in *all* situations. A technique that solves a problem for Peter's Pan Pizza may not be of much use in another organization, nor for other problems within PPP itself. Consequently, organizations should be wary of consultants and change agents who advocate *one* best way to solve all types of problems. An effective OD change agent should be familiar with a variety of techniques, and must be able to recognize when the skills that he can offer will not help the organization, and in such cases withdraw his services.

The second point concerns the two basic forces identified by Lewin: forces to maintain the status quo and forces for change. Ideally, the involvement of management and other employees during the early phases of OD will help reduce the pressure to maintain the status quo. However, as specific plans for change are laid, resistance to those plans is likely to grow. Organizational members may be concerned that OD will cost more than its benefits are worth, or they may believe that the planned changes will alter their jobs in unpleasant ways, or they simply may not like change. For example, the changes mentioned in the opening memo for this chapter would seem to benefit the Flavio's divisions, which are responsible for frozen and prepared foods, more than the Peter's Pan Pizza divisions, which are responsible for pizza restaurants and franchising. It is important that this resistance be anticipated, and that plans be made for dealing with it.

STAGE TWO: CHANGE

This stage of the OD process involves the implementation of the plans developed by the change agent, in conjunction with management. Again, resistance is likely to be a problem, particularly if the employees affected by the change (which *could* be all of them) are not prepared. *Involving workers* in the actual change process may reduce this resistance by giving them a sense of "ownership" of the changes. That is, by participating in the implementation of the plans, workers may see the changes as being *their* changes, rather than changes imposed by external agents.

Another issue in the implementation phase of OD is *transfer of effects*. As we said before, most traditional OD techniques emphasize interpersonal relationships and skills; they may also involve training that occurs away from the workplace. When training takes place outside of the work context, there is always concern about whether changes that occur during training will recur when the employee is back on the job. We will not discuss transfer of training in any detail here (see Chapter 7), but you should be aware that in the implementation of organizational change, the transfer of behavioral changes to the workplace is an important issue. Of particular concern in OD is the presence of a supportive environment following the intervention. If co-workers are critical of, or unresponsive to, the changed behavior of employees who have undergone OD training, these changes are unlikely to be maintained.

STAGE THREE: REFREEZING

The third stage of Lewin's model of organizational change is refreezing. Although the goal of OD is to change the status quo, once the desired changes have occurred it is necessary to make those changes permanent. That is, a new status quo, incorporating the changes introduced in the change stage, replaces the old. Actually, a number of distinct processes can be identified in the refreezing stage.

The first of these processes involves *evaluation* of the OD intervention and *rediagnosis* of the organization's status. Clearly, if the intervention did not have the intended effects, or if it had undesirable effects, then it would be foolish to make any changes that did occur permanent. The effectiveness of OD in general is a topic that has generated a great deal of debate among organizational researchers, and we will examine that debate in a later section of this chapter.

For now, keep in mind that without proper evaluation of change programs, there will always be questions about their effectiveness.

Assuming that an OD program has been shown to be effective, the company will want to make that program, and the changes associated with it, a permanent part of the organization. This is known as *institutionalization* of change, and represents formal approval of the change. Institutionalization may take a variety of forms, such as alterations to organizational structure, new training programs, changes in supervisor–subordinate relations, or virtually any other change dictated by the nature of the OD program. Of course, management can easily institutionalize some changes, such as changes in formal organizational policy, but it is not as easy to institutionalize others, such as those involving the nature of interpersonal relations between employees and supervisors. Resistance to institutionalizing changes may occur if there is no clear evidence for the effectiveness of the changes, or if the changes are complex and require a large number of individuals or groups (possibly with incompatible goals) to work together. Again, we see the importance of anticipating resistance to OD, and the benefits of involving those who will be affected by OD in the planning and implementation stages.

Part of the refreezing process may also involve attempts to *export* successful OD interventions to other parts of the organization. That is, change is often planned and introduced on a limited scale, and if effective it is spread to other units and divisions that were not involved in the original program. This appears to be a logical way of doing things. When the intervention is a failure, a great deal of time and money may be saved by limiting the scope of the unsuccessful change. However, just because a program worked in one unit of an organization is no guarantee that it will have similar effects in other units. In fact, such factors as a lack of top management support, differences in technology, union resistance, and the incompatibility of the changes with existing policies and structures have been found to inhibit the spread of organizational change, making such diffusion rare (Walton, 1975). We might expect this sort of problem if OD changes first developed in the Flavio's divisions were exported to the Peter's Pan Pizza divisions.

Finally, we should recognize that the refreezing stage of organizational change is a relative phenomenon. As we have said before, given the dynamic nature of organizations and the environments within which they operate, the need for change is constant. Organizational change is therefore a *cycle* of events, with successful change followed by a rediagnosis of the organization's health, followed by additional change efforts, and so on. What we said at the beginning of the chapter about organizational change being constant also applies to planning for organizational change.

Examples of Popular OD Interventions

It's possible that the diagnosis phase of OD will detect situations that call for interventions at individual, group, or organizational levels. Consequently, although the emphasis of OD is on problems affecting the entire organization, intervention techniques are often aimed at the group or individual levels. Examples of popular OD interventions that focus on each of these levels are given below.

INDIVIDUAL CHANGE: LABORATORY TRAINING

Perhaps the best-known OD technique is *laboratory training,* also known as *sensitivity training.* Laboratory training was discussed in Chapter 7 (personnel training), so we will not describe it in detail here. As an OD technique, however, laboratory training is designed to improve the interpersonal skills of employees, primarily of managers. As we said in Chapter 7, there are questions about how well the effects of laboratory training transfer to the workplace, as well as concerns that some participants experience unacceptable levels of distress as a result of the training procedures.

GROUP CHANGE: TEAM BUILDING AND SURVEY FEEDBACK

Whereas laboratory training is intended to provide individual workers with interpersonal skills that will benefit the organization, the next two techniques are designed to change entire groups of workers. Team building is in many ways the group-level counterpart of laboratory training. Its purpose is to help people with related or interdependent jobs examine the ways in which their "team" works together, identify strengths and weaknesses, and develop plans to improve team functioning. Although team building does emphasize interpersonal inter-action, as does laboratory training, it is more task-oriented. That is, there is greater emphasis on changes that will improve specific aspects of team perfor-mance. Team building begins with a diagnostic meeting. During this session the members of the team, along with the change agent, discuss the current level of team functioning in an open, unstructured format. Each member of the group is allowed time to present his or her views on what the strengths and weaknesses of the team are, and what changes are needed to improve team effectiveness. These viewpoints then serve as stimuli for discussion, which, if all goes well, culminates in an agreed-upon list of desirable changes for the team. Later sessions are then dedicated to developing plans to implement these changes.

Survey feedback is another OD technique that can be used to improve group functioning, but unlike team building, it can also be helpful in examining either the effectiveness of the total organization, or the relationships between work units. Survey feedback entails systematically collecting data from and about the group or groups in question, summarizing the data, and then feeding the results back to all of the group members. Depending on the total size of the group, one or more workshop sessions are held to discuss the feedback, to identify problems revealed in the data, and to plan action to solve those problems. Survey feedback is therefore used primarily for diagnostic purposes, because the interventions endorsed by the group members will depend on the nature of the group and the problems that have been identified. In order to be successful, survey feedback requires reliable and valid measures of group and organizational characteristics, the results must be presented in an easy-to-understand manner, and change agents must be able to conduct group workshops or discussions characterized by free and open expression of ideas.

ORGANIZATION-WIDE CHANGE: MANAGERIAL GRID® AND MANAGEMENT BY OBJECTIVES

Finally, there are OD techniques that are applied to entire organizational systems. These procedures are appropriate when the problems facing the organization are widespread, or when there is a desire to ensure that the changes have an organization-wide impact. The *Managerial Grid* intervention, which is among the most popular OD techniques, was originally developed by Blake and Mouton in 1964, and recently updated (Blake & Mouton, 1985) as a way to improve the functioning of total organizations. The basic premise of the Managerial Grid is that managerial style can be defined in terms of two dimensions. The first dimension is *concern for people,* which reflects a manager's interest in subordinates' well-being, and his or her relationships with subordinates. The second dimension is *concern for production,* which includes a manager's interest in accomplishing the production tasks of his or her unit. Each of these dimensions is represented by a 1-to-9 scale, which together form the Managerial Grid (see Figure 13.6). Each cell within the Grid represents a different managerial style. Included in Figure 13.6 are descriptions of five illustrative styles. As you can see, the 1,1 style of management involves little concern for either production or people, and is essentially a "do nothing" approach to management. The 1,9-oriented manager, often called the "country club" manager, emphasizes the well-being of subordinates at the expense of production, whereas the 9,1-oriented manager, or "taskmaster," does the opposite, ignoring interpersonal relationships and stressing production. The "middle-of-the-road" or 5,5-oriented manager has a balanced emphasis on people and production, but neither concern is strong. Finally, the 9,9-oriented manager has a strong concern for *both* production and people. This "team-management" style is clearly seen by Blake and Mouton as the ideal for all organizations (contrary to a great deal of research supporting contingency theories of leadership and management; see Chapter 10), and the Managerial Grid intervention is designed to promote 9,9 leadership throughout all levels of an organization.

The implementation of Grid management involves a six-phase program, beginning with what is called a "Grid seminar." Members of top management typically attend a seminar first, and then conduct the seminars for the other managers in the company. The role of the consultant or change agent is thereby downplayed. The seminar itself is the key to the Grid technique, and involves a very structured approach to teaching managers the theory and philosophy of the Grid, as well as analyzing their own positions on the Grid. The remaining phases are designed to facilitate the implementation of the 9,9 managerial style, and involve team building, fostering of intergroup relationships, and the development, implementation, and evaluation of an ideal model for achieving individual, group, and organizational goals.

As we said, the Managerial Grid is a very popular OD approach. Thousands of organizations throughout the world have used the Grid, hundreds of thousands

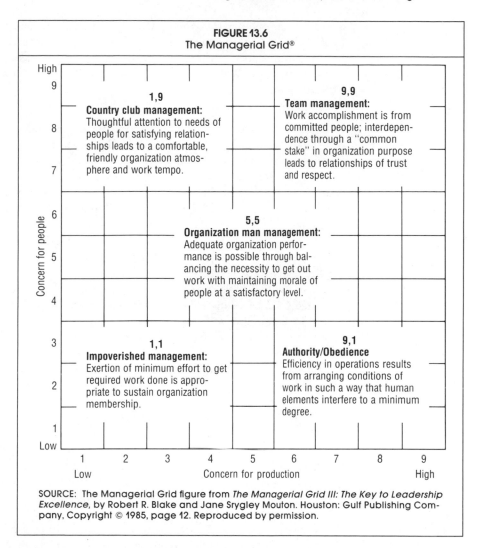

FIGURE 13.6
The Managerial Grid®

SOURCE: The Managerial Grid figure from *The Managerial Grid III: The Key to Leadership Excellence,* by Robert R. Blake and Jane Srygley Mouton. Houston: Gulf Publishing Company, Copyright © 1985, page 12. Reproduced by permission.

of managers have participated in these programs, and the approach is widely accepted (Using the Managerial Grid, 1974). Unfortunately, there is little empirical support for the Managerial Grid, a problem shared with many OD interventions. Equally damaging is the fact that Blake and Mouton claim that a *single* management style is the solution to a wide variety of organizational problems. Although we have made this point before, it bears repeating: The complexity of organizations and their environments makes it extremely unlikely that any one procedure will be effective in all, or even in a large proportion, of organizations. We also believe that the emphasis on two dimensions of leadership style is overly simplistic. Concern for production and concern for people are conceptually similar to the Ohio State leadership factors of initiating structure and consideration; as we saw in Chapter 10, these factors are, at best, an incomplete explanation for the effects of managerial behavior.

Another organization-wide OD technique is management by objectives, or MBO. Unlike Grid management, which is highly structured and fairly similar from organization to organization, MBO has taken a variety of forms over the years. Szilagyi and Wallace (1983, p. 578) identified eight steps common to most MBO programs:

Step 1—Diagnosis: This first step concerns the preliminary activities that are directed toward an understanding of the important employee needs, jobs, technology, and issues in the organization.

Step 2—Planning: Involved in this MBO step are issues related to the overall goals and strategies of the organization, receiving management commitment to the MBO process, and training and development in learning how to use the technique.

Step 3—Defining the employee's job: Possibly one of the most difficult steps, the employee is required to describe his or her particular job, its content, duties, requirements, and responsibilities. The important aspect of this step is that before individual goals can be set, one must know what work is being done.

Step 4—Goal setting: The employee initiates the superior–subordinate interaction by developing a set of goals for the upcoming period, usually one year. Concern is shown for the type of goal, setting priorities, target dates, and methods of measurement.

Step 5—Superior review: The employee's superior reviews the initial goals, offers suggestions for improvement, and so on.

Step 6—Joint agreement: Steps 4 and 5 are repeated until both the employee and the manager agree on the established set of goals for the period.

Step 7—Interim review: During the period of evaluation, the employee and manager get together to review the progress toward goal accomplishment. These meetings can be scheduled for once, twice, or more during the year. The focus of these interim reviews is not only to see what progress has been made, but to adjust the goals should new information or changing environmental events become important.

Step 8—Final review: At the end of the goal-setting period, the employee and manager formally get together to review the results. Emphasis is placed on analysis, discussion, feedback, and input to the next MBO cycle. At the end of this step, the cycle is repeated for the next period.

SOURCE: *Organizational Behavior and Performance,* 3rd ed. by A. D. Szilagyi, Jr., and M. J. Wallace, Jr. Copyright © 1983 by Scott, Foresman and Company. Reprinted by permission.

The key elements are identifying organizational goals, setting specific goals for employees that will help achieve the organization's goals, and evaluating employees' progress toward meeting those individual goals.

In Chapter 8 we saw that setting specific, difficult goals was an effective way to improve employees' performance. It is therefore not surprising that MBO has attracted a great deal of attention, and has become one of the most popular OD techniques. Another reason for the popularity of MBO is undoubtedly its flexibility, which allows it to be applied to a wide variety of issues. For example, motivation and productivity problems can be addressed via the goal-setting procedures, sensitivity to changing environmental conditions is ensured by the planning and diagnosis steps, and up-to-date information on individual, group, and organizational performance is made available throughout the MBO cycle by regularly scheduled reviews.

Evaluation of Organizational Development

So far we have not said very much about the effectiveness of organizational development. One reason for this is that despite the widespread use and acceptance of OD, there has been little systematic evaluation of its effects. This is true for even the most popular techniques. Much of the support for OD techniques is based on testimonials from managers who have used them and are satisfied with the results. As students of psychology, however, we should all be wary of this sort of "evidence" (reaction criteria) concerning OD. There is, in fact, research suggesting that when managers have invested a great deal of time and money in a program, as would be the case with any OD intervention, they will tend to maintain their support for the program, even when it has clearly failed (Staw, 1981). Thus, it is *possible* that the popular support for OD programs does not reflect actual intervention effectiveness.

The concern over OD effectiveness has generated considerable debate. One of the more intriguing contributions to this debate was the work of Terpstra (1981), who examined the relationship between the results of OD evaluation research and the methodological rigor of the research. OD evaluation research is designed to determine whether or not a particular intervention had its desired effects. Methodological rigor refers to how well the research was designed; the less rigorous the research, the less faith you can place in the results. Terpstra found that more rigorous evaluation research was less likely to find evidence of OD effectiveness. That is, research that used control groups, random assignment of subjects, and sophisticated statistical analyses was less likely to report that the OD intervention had positive effects on organizations. To explain this finding, Terpstra suggested that because the results of less rigorous research are often ambiguous, there is an unconscious bias on the part of OD researchers to interpret the results of these studies as supporting OD. He also thought that the high expectations of, and pressure from, top management might contribute to this bias.

Similarly negative conclusions about the evidence of OD effectiveness have been presented by others (for example, Alderfer, 1977; Porras & Berg, 1978; Woodman & Sherwood, 1980). Bass (1983), however, offered a number of alternative explanations for Terpstra's (1981) findings. Bass suggested that rather than a bias favoring OD on the part of those using less rigorous research, there may be a bias *against* OD on the part of those using *more* rigorous research. He also suggested the possibility that OD interventions may be more relevant to "socioemotional" issues such as employee commitment and the integration of individual and organizational interests than to productivity and profit. Because these socioemotional variables are difficult to measure reliably, finding positive OD effects is less likely.

Other explanations offered by Bass (1983) include (1) the possibility that a given OD intervention may move the organization toward one goal, while unintentionally moving it away from another, thereby canceling any overall effect, or (2) that more rigorous research examines short-term effects when, in fact, OD effects tend to be long-term. Thus, whereas there *may* be biases for or against reporting beneficial OD effects among different groups of OD researchers, it is difficult to prove either way. Bass argued, however, that the huge number of claims for OD success, although seldom documented with empirical data, cannot *all* be the result of bias, and that the sheer weight of these numbers suggests that OD has some positive effect. He also pointed out that given the complexity of most OD interventions and the difficulties involved in conducting rigorous research in organizations, well-controlled OD evaluation research is unlikely.

Another explanation for the failure to find support for OD interventions is based on the three types of change in training criteria mentioned in Chapter 7. Recall that Golembiewski, Billingsley, and Yeager (1976) labeled real changes in the criteria in which a researcher is interested alpha change. In terms of OD research, an example of alpha change would be a team-building effort that resulted in increased worker satisfaction. The failure to find such changes, according to Golembiewski et al., could be because the OD resulted in one of the other types of change, beta change or gamma change.

Beta change is when the intervention results in a *change in the scale* with which the criterion is measured. In this case, the team building may have raised workers' expectations about how high their satisfaction might someday be. If so, although they found the OD experience to be positive, using their new expectations as a benchmark they might report experiencing *lower* satisfaction *after* OD than they had reported before OD. Gamma change is when OD results in a *redefinition of the construct* that the criterion is attempting to measure. An example would be team building that caused workers to redefine what job satisfaction meant to them, perhaps downplaying the importance of economic factors such as pay, and increasing their emphasis on interpersonal relationships. The effects of this type of change would be unpredictable, and would depend on pre- and post-OD perceptions of both economic and interpersonal factors. In any case, to the extent that virtually all OD evaluation research has focused exclusively on alpha changes, the possible existence of beta and gamma changes makes it difficult to draw any meaningful conclusions about the effects of OD.

What, then, can we say about organizational development? OD has many supporters and many critics. It is clearly important to determine whether or not OD techniques are effective, for if they are not, then many millions of dollars are being wasted each year. Unfortunately, the most honest conclusion that we can draw is that the evidence is inconclusive. This is partially due to the low quality of OD evaluation research, but we believe that a more important contributor is the nature of OD itself. By trying to deal with problems in dynamic, complex systems, and by focusing on some of the more abstract, perceptual processes within those systems, OD has staked out a territory in which effectiveness may be impossible to demonstrate. Although the identification of alpha, beta, and gamma changes offers hope that measurement of different types of OD effects may clarify things, the problems of achieving rigorous control in OD research will continue to plague these efforts. In the end, the decision to use or not to use OD will remain subjective, based on the experience and best judgment of management, and the best advice of change agents who are familiar with the relative merits of a variety of OD interventions.

CHAPTER SUMMARY

Change is a constant phenomenon in organizations and, ideally, it should be anticipated and controlled. Some types of change, however, are beyond the ability of organizational personnel to foresee, and can only be dealt with after the fact. Two types of change that *can* be controlled are job/task design and organizational development.

Job design is concerned with how to design or change jobs to maximize worker effectiveness. Early job-design efforts, such as those based on scientific management, stressed job simplification and worker specialization. These programs, however, proved to be ineffective in the long run because of their negative impact on workers' attitudes. Following the advent of the human relations movement, job-design theories focused on helping workers achieve a sense of accomplishment by expanding the scope of their jobs. The results of these efforts were inconsistent.

The most widely known job design theory is the Hackman and Oldham job characteristics model, which is based on the notion that properly designed tasks can satisfy psychological needs, such as those in Maslow's need hierarchy. Hackman and Oldham described five critical job characteristics that they believed determine certain critical psychological states, which in turn influenced important work-related criteria. Research on this model has not been supportive, however, and although there is evidence that the job characteristics in the model are important, they are not a sufficient basis for a comprehensive theory of job design.

Organizational development (OD) is the planned use of interventions designed to encourage organizational self-examination, and to improve organizational effectiveness and health. Different OD techniques focus on individuals, groups, or organizations, but nearly all can be analyzed in terms of Lewin's unfreezing–change–refreezing model of change. Despite its widespread acceptance and use, there is little solid evidence of OD's effectiveness. This may be due to problems with the actual OD techniques, the inadequacies of OD evaluation research, or the use of inappropriate types of change in OD models. In any case, OD interventions should be used with a certain degree of caution.

INTEROFFICE MEMO
TO: All vice presidents and senior vice presidents
From: J A. MacKeven, Human—Resources Coordinator

The Human Resources staff has recently completed its evaluation of
the potential impact of entry into vending and institutional sales. I
would like to thank each of you for the cooperation my staff received
from the people in your divisions. Your managers and supervisors
helped make our job much easier.

As most of you probably know, feasibility studies have shown that the
best locations for any expansion along these lines are at our current
Flavio's plants. This is due to (1) the similarities between the pro—
posed new products and Flavio's current products, (2) a desire on the
part of top management to avoid duplication of management functions,
and (3) tax incentives from several of the municipalities in which
Flavio's plants are currently located, which make it financially
attractive to expand rather than build totally new facilities. I men—
tion these points because they have had a significant impact on the
recommendations that we at Human Resources have developed.

It is certain that if the expansion is made, we will have a dramatic
increase in the number of workers in the Flavio's facilities, and a
relatively smaller increase in the number of supervisors and man—
agers. In order not to overburden our supervisory staff, we recommend
that the jobs in these plants be expanded in terms of the decision—
making responsibility held by the typical rank—and—file worker. Fur—
ther, we believe that effective use of this additional responsibility
will be promoted if the jobs are also expanded in terms of the vari—
ety of tasks that workers perform. That is, effective decisions are
more likely to be made by workers if they have greater familiarity
with the entire production process. In addition to addressing the
problem of relatively few managers, these changes in the jobs should
have some positive motivational effects on the workers.

Of course, the degree to which these types of changes can be made
depends on the nature of individual jobs and work groups. To that
end, we are also proposing that the following two activities be com—
pleted prior to further planning: First, we need to carefully assess
the task requirements of the new jobs and the skill and ability
requirements of those tasks. Second, because of the concern expressed
by some managers and supervisors that there could be resistance to
these changes, team—building exercises should be conducted. All mem—
bers of a given work group will participate in a series of these
exercises, which will involve identifying current weaknesses and
strengths of the group, examining how the proposed changes will
affect the group, and developing <u>group</u> proposals to deal with any
anticipated problems. These proposals will be incorporated into any
job or work—group changes whenever feasible.

A more detailed description of our proposals, and the rationale for
them, will be sent to you next week. Please feel free to comment on
these proposals as you see fit.

REVIEW QUESTIONS AND EXERCISES

1. Dr. MacKeven stated that the fact that the new operations will, if approved, be located in existing Flavio's plants had a significant impact on her recommendations. What do you think was the nature of that impact? How might her recommendations have been different if new factories were being planned?

2. Explain the theoretical basis for Dr. MacKeven's recommedation that the jobs of Flavio's workers be expanded. Is that basis sound? Why or why not?

3. Dr. MacKeven recommended that the "task requirements" and the "skill and ability requirements" of the expanded jobs be assessed. What procedure is she advocating? Given what you have learned in earlier chapters, describe a series of steps that she might take in making these two assessments.

4. Describe how the team-building exercises mentioned by Dr. MacKeven would help overcome resistance to change. What other positive effects might they have? What negative effects? What should Dr. MacKeven and her staff do to ensure the success of these exercises?

CHAPTER 14

Work Conditions and the Work Environment

Learning Points

After studying this chapter, you should

- be able to explain what shift work is, and describe the effects of working different shifts on workers' attitudes and behaviors
- be able to discuss the merits and drawbacks of compressed workweeks, including practical problems encountered when trying to establish compressed schedules
- be able to describe a typical flextime schedule, and explain the theoretical and practical advantages and disadvantages of this system
- understand the nature of light, noise, and the factors that contribute to the sensation of heat. You should also be able to describe the effects of illumination, noise levels, and thermal conditions on workers
- be able to explain what an accident is, evaluate the concept of accident "proneness," and describe an effective accident-prevention program
- understand what human factors are, and be able to describe the concept of the "worker–machine system"

INTEROFFICE MEMO
TO: J. A. MacKeven, Human-Resources Coordinator
FROM: Andrew LeGette, Director of Wages and Benefits

I have been appointed to the management negotiating team for the upcoming contract negotiations with unions representing the organized shops within Flavio's. Although I am on the team primarily for dealing with wage and benefit demands, I have also been asked to look into the feasibility of offering some incentives outside of the benefits package in return for union movement on whatever benefit demands are made. We can estimate the costs of most of these programs fairly easily, but we do not want to offer anything that might save money now if it will cost us more down the road. Of particular concern to top management are the effects that these programs might have on productivity, although they are also interested in the probable effects on employee attitudes and commitment. I would like to have you or one of your staff prepare a report on the likely effects of instituting the following types of programs. We know that some of these things would be welcomed by the workers, but we don't want to bring them up at the negotiations unless we have good reason to believe that they will be beneficial. We need the report early next month. Please let me know ASAP if this will be possible.

- Four-day work week
- Flextime
- Employee safety programs

P.S. Feel free to suggest other nonpay incentives that would be desirable to workers and beneficial to the company.

In previous chapters we stressed the importance of the environment within which an organization operates. This is most clearly illustrated by open systems theory (Chapter 12), which takes the view that organizations are embedded in a complex environmental network from which they draw their resources, and into which they distribute the fruits of their labors. The importance of the external environment was also seen in our discussion of employee selection (Chapter 6). That is, the skills that exist in the available labor pool will to a great extent determine an organization's recruiting efforts, and the utility of whatever selection system the organization implements. Those skills will also have an impact on the training programs needed to help new employees acquire necessary skills (Chapter 7). We have also considered the psychological environment, or climate, within the organization, and the ways in which shared values and perceptions might influence individual and organizational performance (Chapter 12).

In this final chapter of the text, we will continue to examine the environment of the organization, but from a very different perspective. Specifically, the environment that we are referring to now is the environment within which employees must work on a day-to-day basis. That is, it is the environment that is defined by work schedules, physical conditions, and the equipment that workers use to perform their jobs. We will refer to these conditions collectively as the *work environment*. We will also examine the issue of job-related accidents, and the role of the work environment in their cause and prevention. In the opening memo to this chapter, Mr. LeGette suggested that programs to improve the work environment will not only be valued by workers, but will also prove to be valuable to Peter's Pan Pizza's "bottom line." Dr. MacKeven's task, as well as ours, is to see if this is indeed likely to be the case.

WORK CONDITIONS

An important component of the work environment is what we will call work conditions. These refer to aspects of employment or the workplace that do not *directly* determine worker behaviors, but rather have implications for the effectiveness of those behaviors, as well as employee reactions to their work. For example, the physical environment of the workplace represents one set of work conditions that we will discuss. How hot or cold the workplace is has little to do with the way in which workers who pack frozen anchovy treats do their jobs—the tasks involved do not change as a function of temperature. How the workers feel about their jobs, however, and perhaps how well they perform those jobs, *are* likely to be affected by this type of physical characteristic. To the extent that work conditions can be manipulated to maximize employees' productivity and satisfaction, the individual workers and the entire organization stand to benefit.

Scheduling of Work

In recent decades, the traditional weekly work schedule has consisted of five eight-hour workdays, Monday through Friday, each beginning about 8:00 a.m.

and ending around 5:00 p.m. There have, of course, always been notable exceptions to this "normal" work schedule, such as firefighters who might be on duty for several consecutive days followed by several days off, or night security guards in office buildings who begin work when the rest of the work force goes home. Also, manufacturing industries, such as the automotive industry, have long used **shift-work** schedules, in which one-third of the employees work the traditional "day shift" from, for example, 7:00 a.m. to 3:00 p.m., one-third work "afternoons" or the "swing shift" from 3:00 p.m. to 11:00 p.m., and the rest work "nights" or the "graveyard shift" from 11:00 p.m. until the day shift comes on again at 7:00 a.m. In her examination of the attitudes of Flavio's workers toward their working conditions, Dr. MacKeven will be likely to find that the perishability of the foods used in many of the frozen products requires that they be processed as rapidly as possible, and that shift work is therefore necessary. (As you might suspect, nothing is worse than an anchovy that has been sitting around since 3:00 the previous afternoon.) As the number of workers in manufacturing industries declines, and the number in service industries increases, it becomes less necessary for companies to operate around-the-clock, or even to operate at full capacity during normal business hours. The implications of traditional work schedules, and the possible benefits of alternative schedules, have therefore come under psychologists' scrutiny.

SHIFT WORK

Approximately one in four workers in the United States and Canada is on shift work (Tasto & Colligan, 1977). For those who work the day shift, shift work is no different from the schedules of the majority of workers. The work schedules of those who work the later shifts, however, can disrupt other aspects of their lives. For example, many shift workers are either asleep or at work during the evenings when their young children are home from school. Similarly, they are unavailable during the hours when most social activities take place, and they may find it difficult to make and keep necessary business and personal appointments. Although these may seem more like inconveniences than serious problems, research on the effects of shift work shows that a variety of negative consequences can result from nonstandard work hours.

Dunham (1977) reviewed the research on the effects of shift work, and found that there were a number of negative consequences that are typically associated with working nontraditional shifts. In addition to effects on social activity, such as less contact with friends, lower rates of participation in social organizations, and a higher rate of solitary leisure activities, shift workers experienced a higher incidence of family-related problems, such as sexual difficulties, divorce, and restricted parent–child contact. Equally or more disturbing is the evidence that shift work has a variety of negative effects on physical health. For example, shift workers not only obtained fewer hours of sleep than their traditional-schedule counterparts, but their sleep tended to be

shift work: a work-schedule arrangement in which different groups of workers have different, usually nonoverlapping, workdays

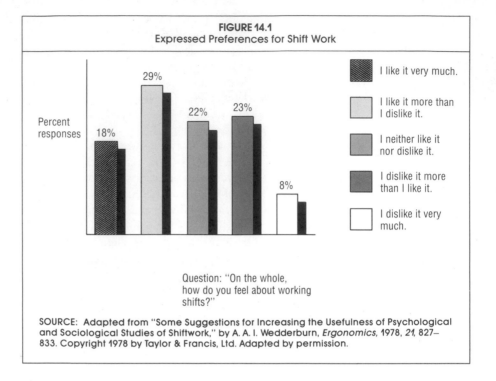

FIGURE 14.1
Expressed Preferences for Shift Work

Percent responses

18% 29% 22% 23% 8%

I like it very much.

I like it more than I dislike it.

I neither like it nor dislike it.

I dislike it more than I like it.

I dislike it very much.

Question: "On the whole, how do you feel about working shifts?"

SOURCE: Adapted from "Some Suggestions for Increasing the Usefulness of Psychological and Sociological Studies of Shiftwork," by A. A. I. Wedderburn, *Ergonomics*, 1978, *21*, 827–833. Copyright 1978 by Taylor & Francis, Ltd. Adapted by permission.

interrupted more frequently. Problems associated with appetite, digestion, elimination (bowel movements), and upper gastrointestinal disorders such as ulcers were also found to be associated more strongly with shift work than with traditional schedules. Oddly, Dunham found no evidence that shift workers had poorer general health (for example, total number of health complaints) than day workers.

Evidence that shift work affects satisfaction or productivity is mixed; there are people who prefer each of the shifts, and who are more productive on those shifts than they are on the others. On the other hand, there are people who do *not* like shift work, and who do not perform well when they deviate from a traditional day schedule. Regarding satisfaction, Figure 14.1 shows the percentage of workers in one study who expressed various degrees of preference for shift work. The important things to notice are that, contrary to what many people might expect, there is no universal dislike of shift work, and some people have definite preferences in favor of working specific shifts (Wedderburn, 1978).

Although there seems to be no effect of shift work on general satisfaction, some fairly large differences were found when more specific reactions to shift work were solicited. For example, both afternoon- and night-shift workers were likely to claim that working their shift restricted their social lives and "wasted their day," whereas day workers were more likely to say that their shift gave them more spare time and was good for their family life. Not all responses were quite so predictable, however. Afternoon-shift workers said that their jobs were less tiring, less likely to disturb their sleep, and more peaceful than did either day- or night-shift workers (Wedderburn, 1978).

Regarding productivity, Dunham (1977) cited several articles that either demonstrated or suggested that production is lower on night shifts than on day shifts. Two studies by Malaviya and Ganesh K. (1976, 1977), however, showed that the effects of shift work on performance are not so clear. Although these researchers found that day-shift workers in an Indian textile plant performed better than the same workers on an afternoon shift, they also found that there were workers who were consistently more productive during the afternoon shift than they were on the day shift. Further, in the latter of the two studies they were able to evaluate the consistency of this shift difference in productivity for 18 workers who were in both studies. They found that for 16 of these workers, their relative day and afternoon productivity remained unchanged over the course of the intervening year, demonstrating that the effects of shifts on individual productivity can be consistent over time. We cannot be certain that these results would generalize to U.S. or Canadian workers, but we know of no specific reason to suspect cross-cultural differences in reactions to shift work.

It seems that shift work does have some negative effects on some workers, particularly regarding their physical health, social interactions, and family relationships. The effects of shift work on actual work behaviors and attitudes, however, are less consistent. Dunham (1977) concluded, on the basis of his review, that many of the negative effects of shift work stem from the fact that it interferes with the rhythms or cycles that govern normal human life. In particular, there is not only evidence of a 24-hour cycle of bodily functions (known as a *circadian rhythm*), but also a 24-hour cycle of social and personal functions on which people come to depend. Shift work upsets the biological rhythms, as evidenced by the numerous health problems listed above, and interferes with workers' efforts to coordinate their activities with the social rhythms of their communities. This can be a particularly severe hardship for dual-career couples with children, who must work nontraditional hours and maintain adequate child care.

Although workers can eventually adjust to changes in the biological cycle, it may not be so easy to adjust the social cycle. For example, consider the case of the Flavio's factory in Jeddo, Michigan. This plant operates three shifts each day, and is the only industrial facility in town. It employs only a small percentage of Jeddo's population, however, because most of the residents are dairy farmers. Consequently, when the afternoon-shift workers leave work at 11:00 p.m., there is literally nothing for them to do, unless they want to drag their neighbors out of bed for a few hands of pinochle. The night shift workers have a slightly different problem: Everyone else in town is awake when they get off work, but at 7:00 in the morning there are few people with the time or inclination to socialize. Dunham suggested that there will be fewer problems associated with shift work in communities that adapt to accommodate the shift worker, because these communities will have a more flexible schedule of social activities. He also suggested that these are likely to be communities, unlike Jeddo, in which there is a relatively large proportion of shift workers.

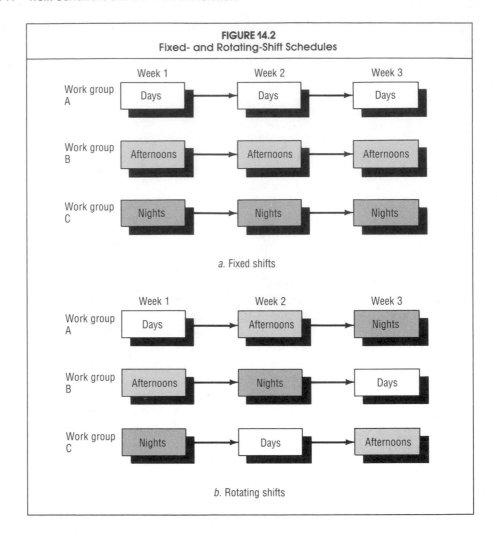

FIGURE 14.2
Fixed- and Rotating-Shift Schedules

Whether or not a particular worker is more or less satisfied or productive on one shift than another, afternoon and night shifts are typically perceived as being less desirable than are day shifts. Either as an incentive to get workers to volunteer for these shifts, or as additional compensation for those who are assigned to these shifts, most companies pay an hourly bonus to afternoon workers, and an even larger bonus to night workers. Although these bonuses may encourage workers to accept alternate-shift work, they cannot be expected to alleviate its negative physical, psychological, and social consequences.

In an apparent effort to be fair to all workers, some companies institute rotating shifts. In this type of schedule, workers "rotate" through the shifts, with one group working days for a period of time, then moving to afternoons, and finally to nights. The group that was originally working afternoons rotates to nights, and then to days, and so on (see Figure 14.2b). Rotating shifts in this way supposedly minimizes the negative effects of shift work, as no one worker remains on the afternoon or evening shifts for too long a period. Also, all workers have the opportunity to receive the shift bonuses.

Rotating shifts is a fairly common practice, and in fact much of the research on shift work has not compared people working one shift with those on another, but has rather followed the same group of people through two or more shifts and examined changes in their attitudes or behavior. Malaviya and Ganesh K. (1976, 1977), for example, used this technique to compare the performance of day and afternoon workers in the research cited earlier. Because the rotation of shifts is designed to remedy some of the problems that accompany shift work, however, it is necessary to compare the behavior of workers on "fixed-shift" schedules with those on rotating-shift schedules. If the negative effects of shift work can be explained solely by the fact that shift workers work late hours and are alienated from normal social cycles, then rotating shifts could be beneficial. That is, by guaranteeing that each worker has at least one-third day shift hours in a given period, the problems associated with working the later shifts should be reduced.

Several recent studies have specifically addressed the effectiveness of rotating-shift schedules. Jamal (1981) compared the work attitudes and absenteeism/tardiness behaviors of Canadian hospital nurses and manufacturing employees who worked either fixed or rotating shifts. He reasoned that the negative effects of shift work would be amplified when shifts were rotated, because workers would be unable to develop routines that would allow them to cope with the demands of their work schedules. Workers on fixed shifts, however, *would* be able to develop such routines regardless of the shift on which they worked. The establishment of these routines should, according to Jamal, result in improved work attitudes and behaviors.

Consistent with his expectations, Jamal's (1981) results showed that fixed-shift workers were better off than their rotating-shift counterparts in terms of mental health, job satisfaction, organizational commitment, and social participation. Further, fixed-shift workers were absent and tardy less often, and had lower expectations of leaving their jobs. Part of the difference between Jamal's fixed- and rotating-shift subjects could have been due to the fact that most of his fixed-shift group worked days. His results, however, are consistent with other studies that demonstrate that fixed-shift workers, even those working nights, have fewer physical and psychological problems than rotating-shift workers (for example, Colligan, Frockt, & Tasto, 1979; Mott, Mann, McLoughlin, & Warwick, 1965; Taylor, 1967).

In another study involving rotating-shift schedules, Zedeck, Jackson, and Summers (1983) suggested that Dunham's (1977) identification of an inherently dissatisfying element of shift work was oversimplified. They argued that individual differences in adaptation to shift schedules may be important in determining shift work's eventual effects. Zedeck and his colleagues analyzed questionnaire responses from over 700 public utility employees who worked a 28-day rotating-shift schedule, during which they worked six day shifts, seven afternoon shifts, and seven night shifts, with eight days off. Consistent with their expectations, the researchers found that there were indeed individual differences in responses to shift work. Workers who were most satisfied with the rotating-shift schedule had fewer physical complaints such as digestion problems or muscle pain, had higher job satisfaction, were more satisfied with the time available to them for social and family activities, had more positive attitudes toward the organization, and were less tense and less tired. In a similar fashion, workers who expressed a desire for changes in the shift schedule reported a greater number of physical and psychological problems, as did workers who expressed a desire to leave the organization.

Zedeck, Jackson, and Summers (1983) suggested that an important factor in reactions to shift work is the ability to adjust to shift demands. That is, to the extent that workers adjust their nonwork lives to accommodate their work schedules, they will avoid many of the possible negative consequences of rotating shifts. Further, older subjects in this study had poorer health, but were nonetheless more satisfied with the shift-work schedule than were younger workers. Zedeck and his colleagues suggested that the poorer health of these older workers was due to the normal aging process, rather than the effects of shift work, and that the longer a worker is exposed to shift work, the more fully she adapts, and the more willing she is to accept the schedule. Of course, it could also mean that the older workers who did not adapt to shift work had left the job before the study was conducted.

In summary, there is fairly solid evidence of negative physical, social, and psychological effects of shift work, and that these effects are magnified by the practice of rotating shifts. This suggests that part of the shift-work problem is adjusting to changes in routines and cycles of activity, although the inability of fixed-shift workers to coordinate their activities with the schedules of their family and friends also contributes to these problems. Perhaps the most important lesson from the research on shift work is that there are workers who prefer the afternoon and evening shifts, and that these workers tend to be more productive on those shifts. Consequently, in industries that must have continuous production (such as Flavio's anchovy pastry factory), and must therefore use around-the-clock shift work, it would be beneficial to consider workers' preferences when assigning shifts. Of course, day shifts are likely to remain the most popular time to work, so that it will not be possible to assign all workers to the shifts they want. There seems to be little reason, however, to force workers who prefer afternoon or night shifts to work days.

NONTRADITIONAL WORKWEEKS

Most U.S. and Canadian workers, whether they work the traditional hours of 8 to 5 or some other shift, go to work five days a week at a fixed hour and work for eight hours each day. Deviations from this five-day, 40-hour schedule (also known as 5/40) have become more and more common in the past few decades, however. These changes typically involve variations in the number of days worked per week (and therefore the number of hours worked per day), or changes in workers' arrival and departure times. Examples of both types of alterations to work schedules are examined below.

One common way to adjust the "normal" workweek is to maintain a 40-hour schedule for each worker, but to have people complete that schedule in four days rather than five. This four-day, 40-hour schedule, or 4/40, is the most common example of a **compressed workweek.** Logic suggests that a 4/40 schedule will be popular with workers, as it gives them a three-day weekend without losing a day's wages. Indeed, a review of research on compressed workweeks by Ronen and Primps (1981) found that most workers report being more satisfied with 4/40 schedules than with 5/40 schedules. Of course, the attractiveness of 4/40 may stem not only from the longer weekend it provides. That is, to the extent that workers are dissatisfied with their jobs, they will probably prefer 4/40 simply because it requires one *less* day each week at work, rather than one *additional* day of leisure (Dunham & Hawk, 1977). Of course, like shift work, 10-hour days can interfere with child-care arrangements and social activities of dual-career or single-parent families.

There is little evidence that 4/40 has any consistent effect on the quantity or the quality of workers' output. Ronen and Primps' (1981) review found only a few studies that had examined the relationship between compressed workweeks and productivity. Two studies measured actual changes in production, and found that compressed schedules had no effect. Four out of five studies that examined employees' responses found that the workers *believed* that they had increased their productivity under compressed schedules. These results should be interpreted with caution, however, because they may be due to the generally positive attitudes that workers have toward compressed workweeks, rather than to actual increases in productivity. Supervisor ratings of productivity showed improvement with compressed workweeks in three studies, but decreases in two others. As you can see, if compressed work schedules *do* affect productivity, it is only in a very unpredictable fashion.

Ronen and Primps (1981) also summarized research on two productivity-related behaviors, fatigue and absenteeism. All five of the studies of fatigue found that it was more severe under compressed schedules than under traditional schedules. Three out of five studies reported that absenteeism decreased under compressed schedules.

Even if compressed schedules do not improve productivity over traditional 5/40 schedules, there may be sound economic reasons for an organization to consider a change to something similar to 4/40. For example, if Flavio's could produce enough frozen pizza to meet demand by operating its factories 40 hours each week, they could save on heating, cooling, janitorial services, and other overhead expenses by operating four days per week rather than five.

Other types of businesses, however, would not be likely to benefit from 4/40. One type of organization for which 4/40 may be inappropriate is one that operates 24 hours a day. When an organization must operate 24 hours a day, whether because of high demand for a product (such as Flavio's frozen anchovy

---

compressed workweek: a work-schedule arrangement in which workers complete the standard 40-hour workweek in fewer than five days

treats), the nature of the service being offered (such as those provided by hospitals), or production technology that cannot be easily stopped and restarted (such as that used in nuclear power facilities), it is virtually impossible to institute a 4/40 schedule. This is because in order to staff the organization for 24 hours, the length of shifts must be even divisors of 24. For example, two ten-hour (4/40) shifts per day would only cover 20 hours, and there would be four hours left that would have to be covered by overtime or some other costly arrangement. The common way to cover a 24-hour schedule is to use three eight-hour shifts, but this is at the cost of any benefits that a compressed workweek might provide. Breaugh (1983) suggested the only logical means by which a compressed workweek could be adapted to a 24-hour schedule, and that is to use two 12-hour shifts. For example, half of the workers could work a 3/36 schedule one week, and a 4/48 schedule the next, while the other half worked the opposite pattern. Because laws require that workers be paid overtime for any hours worked beyond 40 in any week, there may be additional costs to using this type of schedule. However, it may be that eliminating one shift saves enough money in administrative costs relative to 5/40 that it would still be cost-effective for some companies to adopt 12-hour shifts.

Little research has been conducted on 12-hour shifts. Although their research did not examine *exactly* 12-hour shifts, Foster, Latack, and Reindl (1979) found that a 3/38 workweek resulted in higher productivity than did a 5/40 workweek. They also found that workers who had actually worked the 3/38 schedule had more positive reactions to it than did workers who had not worked 3/38 but had been asked to evaluate it nonetheless. Breaugh (1983) also found that experience with a 12-hour shift was accompanied by more positive evaluations of that schedule. It is not surprising, given the negative disruptions of social and biological cycles that result from shift work, that Breaugh also found that workers on the noon-to-midnight shift saw the 12-hour workday as more desirable than did workers on the midnight-to-noon shift.

We are uncertain about the future of compressed workweeks. There is little research on the effects of these schedules, particularly when you go beyond 4/40 into even longer workdays. For those organizations that can fit them into their systems, however, compressed work schedules may be a viable method for improving worker attitudes while reducing overhead costs.

FLEXTIME

Another popular variation on the traditional work schedule is flextime, where workers' arrival and departure times are variable, within certain limits, allowing them to tailor their workdays to meet their own unique needs. Specifically, most flextime programs include the following five components (Golembiewski & Proehl, 1978):

1. a "band width," or total number of hours to be worked each day
2. a "core time," or period in the workday during which all full-time employees are required to be at work

3. flexible bands of hours before and after the core time, during which workers may arrive at work and depart for home, respectively
4. "banking," or carrying a balance of excess or deficient hours from one work period to the next; typically there is a limit to the number of hours that can be "banked"
5. variable schedules, which give workers the authority to change their working hours from one period to the next without supervisory approval

An example of a flextime system at Peter's Pan Pizza would be if workers in the finance departments could come to work at any time between 7:00 a.m. and 10:00 a.m., and leave work at any time between 3:00 p.m. and 6:00 p.m., but *must* be at work between 10:00 a.m. and 3:00 p.m.

The logic behind flextime is fairly straightforward: Flexibility in arrival and departure times is expected to reduce tardiness and absenteeism because it provides discretionary time for workers to perform tasks that would cause them to be late under more rigid schedules (Nollen, 1979). This is a particularly important benefit for two-career or single-parent families, in which a worker must frequently be absent in order to take children to school or to visit doctors, banks, and other businesses with fixed hours, and still have time for normal family and social activities. Further, it has been hypothesized that flextime will allow workers to select working hours during which they are most productive, thereby increasing organization effectiveness.

Organizations may benefit in other ways from a flextime system under certain circumstances. For example, because flextime virtually ensures that a company will be at least partially staffed more than the traditional eight hours each day, it may be easier for customers and suppliers to do business with a company using flextime. Also, with companies such as Peter's Pan Pizza, which has facilities across the continent, communication between organizational units in different time zones should be more convenient with flextime.

Of course, there are situations that do not lend themselves to flextime, such as production facilities that require a certain number of tasks to be performed simultaneously. At Flavio's, for example, the cheese is the last ingredient to go onto a pizza before it is frozen, and it would not work to have the cheese sprinkler come to (or leave) work four hours before the people who put on the sauce and pepperoni. Flextime would also be difficult to implement if there was more than one shift, because flexible arrival and departure times would make it likely that the organization would be overstaffed at some times and understaffed at others.

Flextime may present particularly troublesome problems for supervisory personnel. It could, for example, be very difficult to coordinate the activities of workers who are coming and going at different times of the day. Of course, some jobs require less supervision and coordination than others, so that this may not be a problem in all organizations, or even in all sections of a single organization. To the extent that workers must work together or supervisors must observe workers' performance, however, flextime may be a burden, requiring additional time and effort to coordinate workers' activities and provide for adequate supervision.

Ronen (1981) studied the effects of flextime on time of arrival and time of departure for 162 Israeli workers, and found that the average arrival and departure times before and during flextime were very similar (see Table 14.1). Further, 83 percent of the workers developed and maintained a consistent individual arrival pattern. That is, they tended to arrive at work at about the same time each day. Also, 68 percent maintained a consistent departure pattern. For these consistent workers, the arrival and departure times centered around the pre-flextime average for arrivals and departures. Ronen also found that tardiness was lower under flextime. Prior to the institution of flextime, the average worker in the study was late for work six times per month. Under the flextime program, this rate dropped to 0.67 times per month. Ronen's general conclusion was that contrary to the fears of some managers, workers on flextime schedules come and go in predictable patterns, and that it is possible to plan and coordinate workers' activities with reasonable assurance that the workers will be there when you need them.

Flextime seems to offer a number of potential benefits for certain types of organizations. One fairly consistent effect of flextime is a reduction in worker absenteeism, although the exact nature of this effect varies from study to study (Harvey & Luthans, 1979; Narayanan & Nath, 1982). For example, Golembiewski, Hilles, and Kagno (1974) found that flextime reduced long-term, but not short-term (one day or less), paid absences; Kim and Campagna (1981), however, found a different pattern of results, with only short-term (two hours or less in a given day), unpaid absences being reduced by the program.

TABLE 14.1 Distributions of Arrivals and Departures: Cumulative Percentage

	Present on the job at	Pre-flextime	Under flextime
Arrivals	06:30	0%	2%
	07:00	0%	11%
	07:30	65%	46%
	08:00	85%	69%
	08:30	95%	85%
	09:00	100%	92%
	10:00	100%	99%
	10:30	100%	100%
	Average	07:36 a.m.	07:44 a.m.
Departures	14:00	100%	100%
	14:30	98%	90%
	15:00	81%	73%
	15:30	40%	57%
	16:00	9%	39%
	16:30	4%	23%
	17:00	3%	16%
	18:00	0%	10%
	Average	03:17 p.m.	03:39 p.m.

Note: Results represent percentage of arrivals and departures, not percentage of employees.

SOURCE: "Arrival and Departure Patterns of Public Sector Employees before and after Implementation of Flexitime," by S. Ronen, *Personnel Psychology*, 1981, *34*, 817–822. Copyright 1981 by Personnel Psychology, Inc. Reprinted by permission.

Less consistent is the effect of flextime on job satisfaction. Although workers express overwhelming support for flextime (Golembiewski & Proehl, 1978), and in some cases say that they are more satisfied under flextime schedules than under traditional schedules (Evans, 1973; Orpen, 1981; Partridge, 1973), there are also studies showing that flextime has no positive effect on job satisfaction (Hicks & Klimoski, 1981; Narayanan & Nath, 1982). Hicks and Klimoski noted that in most of the flextime research, workers were aware that they were being asked about their attitudes in order to evaluate the flextime program. Consequently, if the workers in these studies desired to keep the program, they may have biased their job satisfaction responses in a favorable direction. Certainly, there seem to be adequate reasons for workers to want to maintain flextime. Hicks and Klimoski, for example, found that under flextime workers had fewer travel problems, less role conflict, greater feelings of control, and more opportunities for leisure activities. Similarly, Narayanan and Nath found that flextime workers were more flexible in attending to personal and work-related matters, and that they believed that they had improved work-group and superior–subordinate relations. Apparently, however, because neither study found higher job satisfaction under flextime, these benefits do not necessarily translate into greater satisfaction with the job itself.

The evidence for effects of flextime on productivity is even weaker than for job satisfaction. Schein, Maurer, and Novak (1977) examined the effects of a four-month flextime experiment on the productivity of five groups of clerical workers. They found that two of the groups significantly increased their productivity over pre-experimental levels, but in one of these groups the introduction of flextime was confounded with other structural and technological changes that could have accounted for the increase in performance. In the remaining three groups, there was no evidence of any change in productivity as a function of flextime. In the study by Kim and Campagna (1981) mentioned earlier, only one of four groups of workers showed a significant increase in productivity during the flextime period; the remaining three groups performed at essentially pre-flextime levels throughout the experiment. Orpen's (1981) study of the effects of flextime on South African clerical personnel found that neither supervisory ratings of performance nor objective measures of productivity were affected by the change in schedules.

To summarize the research on flextime, it seems to have a positive effect on attendance, although there is some conflict in the literature as to whether it reduces long-term absences or short-term absences. The evidence for flextime effects on employees' job satisfaction is mixed, and there may be methodological problems with some of the supportive studies in which subjects knew that the flextime programs were being evaluated. There is no persuasive evidence that flextime improves employee productivity, although as both Schein, Maurer, and Novak (1977) and Kim and Campagna (1981) concluded, there is no evidence that flextime has any *negative* effect on productivity either. The decision to use flextime should therefore probably be based on a need to reduce absenteeism, provided that the organization's operation is flexible enough to accommodate partial staffing early and late in the workday.

Physical Conditions of the Workplace

So far we have discussed the effects of *when* people work. Once a worker is on the job, however, he is confronted by a variety of other work conditions that may have effects on both attitudes and performance. The most obvious of these are the physical conditions of the workplace. Each of us is familiar with situations in which physical variables in the environment make the performance of even simple tasks very difficult and frustrating. For example, as a student you may have found it very hard, at times, to concentrate on reading your assignments because of disturbing noises from a neighbor's room or apartment. In an industrial setting, noise may be combined with uncomfortable temperatures, smoke or other pollution, and poor lighting, just to name a few examples. In the following sections we examine some of these physical variables, and evaluate their possible effects on workers' behavior.

ILLUMINATION

The study of illumination, or lighting, has a long history in psychology, as well as in various related fields. You may recall that the Hawthorne studies were designed to examine the effects of illumination on workers' performance (Chapters 1 and 9), among other issues. Since that time, research on illumination has become much more sophisticated. Much of this research has been conducted by people known as illuminating engineers, who concern themselves with complex physical concepts with which we need not be concerned here. The fact that lighting can have important effects on performance, however, is not in doubt, and so we'll present a few general findings.

In order to understand the research on illumination, you must understand what illumination is and something about how it is typically measured. First, light sources have a certain intensity that is measured in units called *candelas*. Second, light is thought of as flowing from its source, much the same as water flows through a pipe. The flow of water is expressed in terms of gallons per minute; the flow of light from its source is expressed in terms of units called *lumens*. The flow from a 1-candela light source is 12.57 lumens. Third, the amount of light that strikes the surface of an object is known as illumination. Illumination is measured in terms of lumens per unit of area, with two standard measures in common use: One lumen per square foot is known as a *footcandle*, which is used primarily in the United States, and one lumen per square meter is known as a *lux*, which is an international, metric-based measure. Because light typically moves in all directions from its source, the surface area used to define illumination must be a section of a sphere in order for the definition to be technically correct. The relationships between candelas, lumens, and measures of illumination are shown in Figure 14.3. As you can see in the figure, a 1-candela light source casts 1 footcandle at a distance of 1 foot, and 1 lux at a distance of 1 meter.

In designing a workplace, engineers are of course concerned with illumination, although illumination by itself does not determine the adequacy of

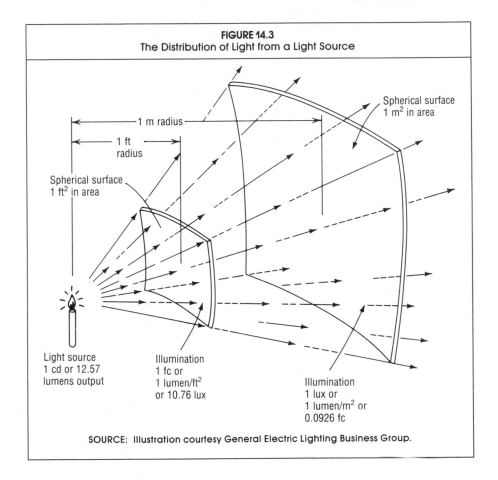

FIGURE 14.3
The Distribution of Light from a Light Source

Spherical surface
1 m² in area

1 m radius

1 ft
radius

Spherical surface
1 ft² in area

Light source
1 cd or 12.57
lumens output

Illumination
1 fc or
1 lumen/ft²
or 10.76 lux

Illumination
1 lux or
1 lumen/m² or
0.0926 fc

SOURCE: Illustration courtesy General Electric Lighting Business Group.

lighting. An important distinction is that between illumination, which (as we have said) is the amount of light striking a surface, and luminance, which refers to the amount of light that is *reflected* from an object's surface, and which therefore determines how well we see that object. Illumination and luminance are not always directly related, because different objects reflect different percentages of the light that strikes them. Thus, you may be able to see a highly reflective object under low illumination better than you can see a less reflective object under higher illumination. All of these factors—illumination, luminance, reflectance—as well as many others are considered in designing lighting systems for the workplace. Guidelines have been developed by the Illuminating Engineering Society, and are outlined in its *IES Lighting Fundamentals Course* (1976) and *IES Lighting Handbook* (1981a, 1981b). Interested readers are referred to these sources for more detailed information.

As students of I/O psychology, we are primarily concerned with how lighting affects workers' performance. There is a vast amount of research on this topic, and so we will only summarize the general results. One fairly consistent finding

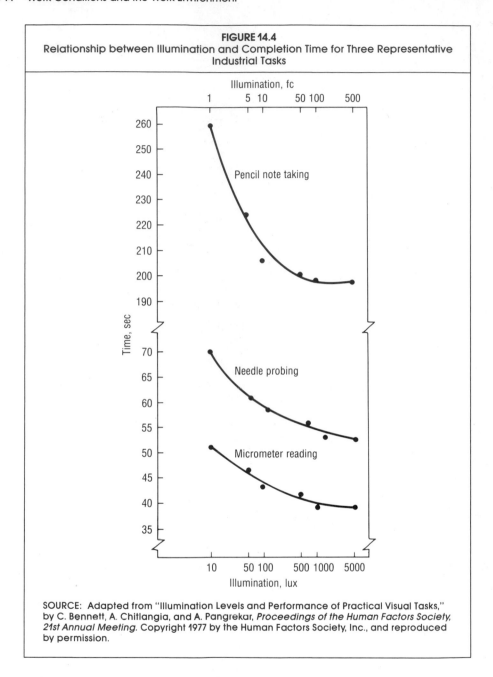

FIGURE 14.4
Relationship between Illumination and Completion Time for Three Representative Industrial Tasks

SOURCE: Adapted from "Illumination Levels and Performance of Practical Visual Tasks," by C. Bennett, A. Chitlangia, and A. Pangrekar, *Proceedings of the Human Factors Society, 21st Annual Meeting.* Copyright 1977 by the Human Factors Society, Inc., and reproduced by permission.

is that increasing illumination, up to a point, leads to improvements in performance; but past that point, further increases are not beneficial. For example, Figure 14.4 shows the results of a study of the effects of illumination on the amount of time it takes to perform various tasks typical of those found in industrial settings. As the figure shows, performance speed improves as illumination increases, but the rate of improvement slows at the higher illumination levels.

You should keep in mind that although the results illustrated in Figure 14.4 are typical, the ideal lighting for any task will depend strongly on task characteristics. The details of a surface may be more difficult to see under direct, bright light than under low-intensity, low-angle "surface-grazing" illumination.

The level of illumination also has implications for the amount of **glare** that is present. There are two basic types of glare: *Direct* glare is the result of a light source that is in the field of view; *reflected* glare is the result of light being reflected from polished surfaces. Glare is determined by a variety of factors, including the reflectance of surfaces, the position of light sources, and the luminance of backgrounds. All else being equal, however, the higher the illumination, the greater the possibility for discomforting or disabling glare. It may be possible to design a workplace using brighter lighting without the problems of glare if other factors, such as background luminance, can be controlled (Bennett, 1977). If these variables cannot be controlled, however, it may be that a lower level of illumination would be more effective.

NOISE

Complete silence is something that very few people have ever experienced. We are constantly surrounded by sounds, in the workplace as well as elsewhere, but in most cases we are able to ignore this "ambient noise" as we perform our jobs. As the amount of noise increases, however, the probability that it will become disturbing and interfere with job performance also increases. Of course, the effects of noise depend on the tasks that are being performed. For example, people talking very quietly can be quite disturbing if you are studying in a library, but athletes are able to work in extremely noisy stadiums, usually without any negative effects on their performance. In the design of a workplace, it is therefore important to consider the level of noise that will be present, as well as the type of job to be performed.

Just as an understanding of the nature of light was useful in understanding illumination, it is helpful to understand something about the nature of sound when trying to understand the effects of noise on workers' behavior. Sound is a form of physical energy that is created by the vibration of objects. As an object vibrates, such as a bell after it has been struck by a hammer, its movement causes alternating "waves" of high and low pressure to radiate from its surface. These "soundwaves" are the physical stimuli to which our ears are sensitive. The larger the vibrations of the object, the greater the *amplitude* of, or the amount of energy contained in, the soundwaves. All else being equal, the greater the amplitude of a sound, the louder it is perceived to be. The speed of vibration is also important in determining the nature of sound. The faster the vibration, the greater the sound's *frequency*. Frequency is typically expressed in units called *hertz*, or *Hz* (1 Hz = 1 cycle or wave per second). Higher-frequency

---

glare: a dazzling, harsh light

sounds are perceived as being higher in pitch than lower-frequency sounds. Humans can hear tones from approximately 20 Hz to 20,000 Hz, depending on age and other factors that might impair hearing. "Pure" tones, such as those from a tuning fork, contain only one frequency. Most sounds, however, are complex mixtures of various frequencies, most notably multiples of the main frequency known as *harmonics*. It is differences in harmonics that cause instruments, such as a piano and a saxophone, to sound very different, even though they are playing the same note.

One frequently used measure of sound is a measure of sound pressure or amplitude known as the *decibel* or *dB* scale. Actually, there are several dB scales, each developed for different purposes. The dB scale that you are probably familiar with is the dBA, or A scale. Figure 14.5 illustrates the dBA levels for a number of common sounds. It should be noted that 0 dBA corresponds to the threshold of human hearing—the softest sound that can be heard by a person with normal hearing in a very quiet environment. Also note that the dBA scale is a *logarithmic* scale, which means that an increase of 10 dB represents an increase in sound pressure to 10 times the original level, and an increase of 20 dB represents an increase in pressure to 100 times the original level.

In spite of, or perhaps *because* of, its widespread use as a measure of sound intensity, many people believe that the dBA scale measures how loud a sound is perceived to be. Unfortunately, even though there is a positive relationship between sound pressure and perceived loudness, the relationship is less than perfect. For example, humans are less sensitive to low-frequency sounds than they are to higher-frequency sounds, so that a 60 dBA, 100 Hz tone will not be perceived as being as loud as a 60 dBA, 2000 Hz tone. For this reason, scales to measure *perceived* loudness have been developed. The most commonly used of these is the *sone* scale, for which we have also provided illustrative examples in Figure 14.5. A 1-sone sound has been arbitrarily defined as equal to a standard 1000 Hz, 40 dBA tone; a 2-sone sound is one that is perceived as being twice as loud as that standard, a 3-sone sound is perceived as being three times as loud, and so on. Although the sone scale is a better reflection of our perceptions than the dB scale, most intensity measures still utilize dB scales because they are based on objective, physical properties, rather than subjective, psychological judgments.

Research on the effects of noise on work performance provides a somewhat confusing and contradictory picture. Some studies show that high levels of noise cause performance to worsen, others show that noise enhances performance, and still others show that the level of noise has no effect at all (for example, Broadbent, 1979). As we suggested earlier, some of this inconsistency results from differences in task characteristics. For example, for most tasks, the noise level must be quite high (greater than 95 dBA) before it has any effect on performance. For short-term memory tasks, however, substantially lower sound levels, beginning around 70 dBA, can impair performance (Hockey, 1978). On the other hand, high sound levels seem to *improve* performance on very simple tasks, perhaps because they require the person to attend more carefully to the task (Broadbent, 1976). It should be kept in mind that nearly all of the research

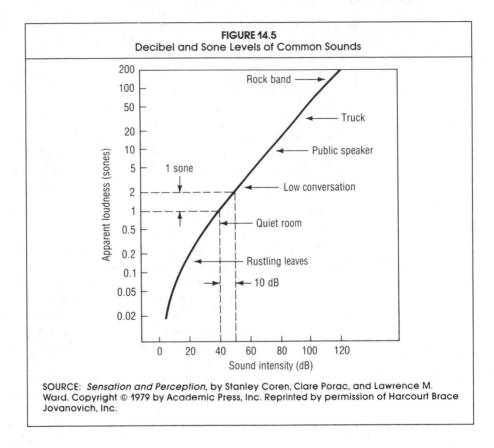

FIGURE 14.5
Decibel and Sone Levels of Common Sounds

SOURCE: *Sensation and Perception*, by Stanley Coren, Clare Porac, and Lawrence M. Ward. Copyright © 1979 by Academic Press, Inc. Reprinted by permission of Harcourt Brace Jovanovich, Inc.

on noise and performance has been conducted in the laboratory; the effects of noise in typical work settings have not been widely studied. It seems reasonable to expect, however, that the complexity and inconsistency of the laboratory results would be magnified by the complexity and inconsistency of most work environments.

Evidence of the effects of noise on hearing is more consistent than that for performance. Continuous exposure to loud noise typically results in temporary hearing loss. This loss takes the form of a shift in the threshold for detecting a sound. That is, after continuous exposure to a loud noise, the minimum intensity at which a sound can be detected, or threshold, is temporarily raised. Exposure to sounds below 75 dBA results in little or no hearing loss, whereas sounds of greater and greater intensity result in larger and larger threshold shifts. Most of this shift occurs in the first few minutes of exposure to the noise, followed by less rapid changes (McCormick & Sanders, 1982). Long-term exposure to continuous noise can result in permanent threshold shifts. These shifts first affect perceptions of tones around 4000 Hz, but gradually spread over a wider band of frequencies if the exposure is maintained.

A number of steps can be taken to reduce noise levels in the workplace, and thus to reduce the potential for hearing loss. Sound-absorbing materials can be used on walls, ceilings, and floors. Loud machines can sometimes be enclosed in acoustical chambers that muffle their noise. When nothing can be done to reduce the actual sound levels in the environment, workers can still protect themselves from the effects of excessive noise. The most common examples of such protection are devices such as headphones or earplugs that prevent soundwaves from entering the ear. Unfortunately, this is only a partial solution to the problem, as sound can reach the middle and inner ear by traveling through the bones of the head as well as through the outer ear. Indeed, a study by Machle (1945) showed that repeated exposure to the noise of gunfire resulted in substantial hearing loss among gunnery instructors, even though the subjects wore protective headphones.

HEAT AND COLD

Another environmental factor that may affect work behavior is the thermal condition of the workplace. We use the term "thermal condition" rather than "temperature" because the effects of heat or cold depend on factors other than temperature, the most important of which are the humidity level and the amount of airflow. This is because the body produces heat during normal metabolic processes, and this heat must be dissipated in order to maintain a normal internal body temperature. Some of this heat is lost via convection (through the air) and radiation (through other objects), but the higher the temperature in the environment, the less the heat that can be exchanged in these ways. Heat is also lost through evaporation, primarily of perspiration on the skin. When humidity is high, or there is little air circulation, this form of heat exchange also becomes less efficient. Of course, when temperatures are low, the problem is one of *preventing* the loss of body heat by limiting these heat-exchange processes.

Because normal temperature scales do not reflect the effects of humidity and airflow, alternative measures that do adjust for these variables have been developed. Two commonly used examples are **wet bulb globe temperature (WBGT)** and **effective temperature (ET).** Both of these scales are expressed in terms of degrees Celsius or degrees Fahrenheit, but they do not correspond directly to traditional temperature measures, because they reflect the effects of other atmospheric conditions.

Extreme levels of either heat or cold can have detrimental effects on the performance of job tasks. The negative effects of heat on the performance of physically demanding tasks have been known for many years (Leithead & Lind, 1964). Basically, tolerance for heat (the length of time heat can be endured) decreases as both temperature and the amount of physical effort or energy expended by workers increase. Excessive heat also has damaging effects on the performance of mental tasks, as illustrated in Figure 14.6 (Wing, 1965). As you can see, as effective temperature increases, the amount of time during which a person can be exposed to the temperature without impaired mental performance decreases. An indication of the quantitative effects of exposure to heat on intellectual performance can be seen in research by Fine and Korbrick (1978),

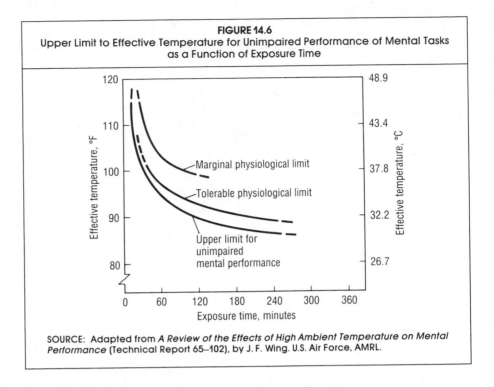

FIGURE 14.6
Upper Limit to Effective Temperature for Unimpaired Performance of Mental Tasks as a Function of Exposure Time

SOURCE: Adapted from *A Review of the Effects of High Ambient Temperature on Mental Performance* (Technical Report 65–102), by J. F. Wing. U.S. Air Force, AMRL.

who had subjects perform complex mental tasks under high heat and humidity conditions (95°F, 88 percent humidity) or under more moderate conditions (75°F, 25 percent humidity). Their results, shown in Figure 14.7, illustrate the dramatic negative effects of heat and humidity on error rates.

The effects of cold on task performance are usually linked with the lowering of the skin temperature. As the body adjusts to cold temperatures, blood vessels in the skin contract to prevent heat loss, which causes the skin to cool. As the temperature of the skin lowers, discomfort and, if the skin becomes cool enough, pain are experienced. This is particularly true in the hands and feet, which cool before other parts of the body. This discomfort is typically accompanied by a reduction in the performance of manual tasks when skin temperature falls below about 55°F (13°C).

There are relatively few jobs in which extreme temperatures present a problem for employees. Most modern buildings have adequate heating, dehumidification, air conditioning, or ventilation to avoid the negative effects that

---

wet bulb globe temperature (WBGT): an index consolidating the effects of dry bulb (normal) temperature, relative humidity, radiant temperature, and air velocity

effective temperature (ET): an index that consolidates the effects of temperature and humidity

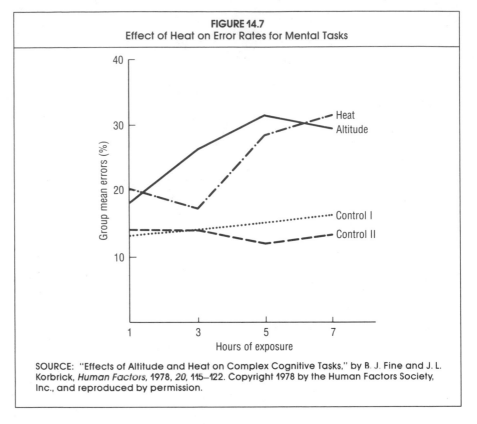

FIGURE 14.7
Effect of Heat on Error Rates for Mental Tasks

SOURCE: "Effects of Altitude and Heat on Complex Cognitive Tasks," by B. J. Fine and J. L. Korbrick, *Human Factors*, 1978, *20*, 115–122. Copyright 1978 by the Human Factors Society, Inc., and reproduced by permission.

we have described. The major exceptions are outdoor jobs, such as construction or road maintenance. In these types of jobs, special steps should be taken to prevent temperature and humidity from affecting workers. Proper clothing is an important consideration for outdoor workers, particularly when cold temperatures begin to chill hands and feet. In extreme heat, lightweight clothing promotes heat exchange and body cooling. Safety considerations, however, might dictate that heavier clothes be worn, even on the hottest days. In these cases, regular rest breaks, preferably out of the extreme heat, should be scheduled so that workers can recover from heat stress (Krajewski, Kamon, & Avellini, 1979).

OTHER PHYSICAL CONDITIONS

Psychologists and others have conducted a considerable amount of research on the effects of illumination, noise, and temperature. There are other physical variables in the workplace that have not received as much attention, but most certainly have implications for workers' attitudes and performance. For example, many industrial processes use hazardous chemicals or create pollution. If allowed to come into contact with workers, these substances can cause both immediate and long-term health problems. A well-known example of this type of hazard is "black lung" disease, which is common among coal miners, whose jobs virtually force them to breathe coal dust. A similar affliction, called "brown lung" disease, occurs in the textile industry, and is caused by inhaling tiny cloth fibers.

What makes the two above examples particularly noteworthy is that they do not involve smoke, noxious fumes, or other substances that we normally think of as pollution. When a physical threat is unexpected in this way, its effects can be overlooked for long periods of time. Such was the case with asbestos, which was used extensively as a building and insulation material, but only recently has been revealed as a powerful carcinogen, or cancer-causing substance. Another well-known example of an unexpected physical threat is that which was posed by "Agent Orange," a defoliant used by U.S. military forces in Vietnam. In addition to killing plants, exposure to Agent Orange has been found to have caused long-term health problems for many Vietnam veterans. A work environment free of these hazards is desirable for a number of reasons. Most obviously, workers' health and well-being are promoted by the elimination of pollution and unclean conditions. Given that personnel costs are frequently the largest expense of a company, a healthy workplace is usually cost-effective to the company as well. By removing the causes of illness that are present in the workplace, health-related absences are reduced, company-paid insurance costs may be lowered, and training costs may be reduced due to increased employee longevity.

In the past 30 years, another potential environmental hazard, radiation, has become prevalent in the workplace. The most obvious types of jobs in which radiation may be a problem are those in nuclear facilities of some type, such as power plants, nuclear powered naval vessels, or nuclear-fuel-refining operations. Radiation is also present in a variety of other, less obvious, settings. Medical and dental offices, for example, frequently contain X-ray machines, the use of which poses little threat to patients, but can be dangerous to employees if they are repeatedly exposed to the radiation on a regular basis. Further, natural forms of radiation can also present an unexpected threat to workers. It is now recognized that excessive or prolonged exposure to sunlight is a major cause of skin cancer. Workers whose jobs require them to be outside for substantial proportions of the workday face an increased risk of contracting skin cancer, unless appropriate precautions (such as the use of protective clothing and "sunscreen" lotions) are taken.

THE CUMULATIVE EFFECTS OF PHYSICAL VARIABLES

We have discussed the effects of several specific physical factors in the workplace, from illumination to pollution and radiation. Because research has tended to examine these variables one at a time, it has generally failed to demonstrate their *cumulative* effects, although it is reasonable to expect that such effects exist. That is, given that improper lighting, excessive noise, extreme temperatures, pollution, and radiation can have negative effects on employees, two or more of these operating together will probably have even greater effects. Unfortunately, many workers are exposed to several of these undesirable conditions in their jobs. It is therefore important that as organizations such as Peter's Pan Pizza make changes in the workplace, *all* aspects of the physical environment, and the interactions among them, be carefully considered. Attention to only selected environmental variables is likely to result in inadequate work conditions.

SAFETY AND ACCIDENTS

As described earlier, there are physical conditions in many work settings that pose threats to employees' health. A similar threat to workers' well-being is the potential for on-the-job accidents. By accidents, we are referring to unexpected events that have a negative effect on productivity or other aspects of performance. These negative effects could be due to worker injury, loss of time, damage to equipment, or loss of material. Whatever their form, accidents are costly to organizations, with annual estimated losses in the tens of billions of dollars.

Causes of Accidents

We often use the word "accident" to imply that an unfortunate event was unintended, unforeseeable, and unpreventable. This use of the word implies that little can be done to avoid accidents, and that no one should be held responsible for their occurrence. Most psychologists agree that accidents are unintended, but would argue that they have definite causes, and that understanding those causes should lead to the ability to prevent accidents from happening. Recognizing that there may be as many specific reasons for an accident as there are accidents, the potential causes for accidents can be grouped into two general categories, job-related factors and worker-related factors.

JOB-RELATED CAUSES OF ACCIDENTS

Although accidents always involve workers' behavior, it is clear that some jobs present a greater risk of accidents than others, regardless of the behavior of the individual workers on those jobs. For example, it is unlikely that Dr. MacKeven will ever have an accident that will either injure someone or cause extensive

GARFIELD, © 1984 United Feature Syndicate, Inc.

damage to expensive equipment. Peter's Pan Pizza's production workers, however, are more likely to have accidents simply due to the nature of their jobs. The difference in accident rates for various occupations was documented by Pimble and O'Toole (1982). They found, for example, that only 1.9 percent of the painters in their sample of British workers were "at risk," or likely to have an accident each year. Seventeen percent of the scaffolders, however, were likely to have an accident within the same period. Although it could be argued that scaffolding simply attracts more careless workers than does painting, it is unlikely that this could account for a nearly tenfold difference in accident rates.

What sort of characteristics are likely to make one job more dangerous than another? Perhaps the most important factors are job requirements that place workers in *potentially* unsafe conditions. For example, in order to erect a scaffold, a worker *must* climb very high, on precarious footing, while manipulating heavy pieces of iron or steel. Painters, on the other hand, seldom need to carry anything heavier than a bucket of paint, and when they climb, it is rarely more than one or two stories, on a ladder that has been designed for safe climbing (if used properly).

Another potential cause for accidents is the *presence* of unsafe conditions that do not necessarily "come with the job," such as missing handrails on stairways, or the use of dangerous or poorly maintained equipment. Even an otherwise safe machine can be a hazard if it does not function properly, thereby tempting unqualified workers to "fix" it themselves. For example, one of the machines used to chop anchovies for Peter's Pan Pizza's famous anchovy pastries has a tendency to "throw" a belt, causing the machine to stop. The operator, after a few such incidents, may try to replace the belt, and in the process catch her hand in a pulley. This is an illustration of how an unsafe worker behavior can stem from unsafe conditions: If the machine had been properly maintained, with belts properly adjusted and replaced, this accident would never happen.

WORKER-RELATED CAUSES OF ACCIDENTS

As we have indicated, although accidents may be facilitated by unsafe conditions, workers' behaviors are always involved. Further, accidents occur even when conditions are as safe as possible, which indicates that many mishaps can only be explained as the result of unsafe behaviors. Theoretically, at least, it is possible to improve equipment and work conditions to make them optimally safe. A major motive for research on worker-related causes of accidents has been to do the same for the work force, by identifying and eliminating workers' characteristics that seem to be related to accidents.

One popular explanation for accidents is the concept of accident proneness. Essentially, this concept is based on the notion that certain people have characteristics, or habitually engage in behaviors, that lead to repeated accidents. If such characteristics and behaviors exist, then it should be possible to identify accident-prone people, and avoid hiring them for risky jobs (such as working on scaffolding). Consistent with the idea of accident proneness, surveys show that a relatively small proportion of workers have a relatively large proportion of accidents. For example, DeReamer (1980) reported data showing that in a

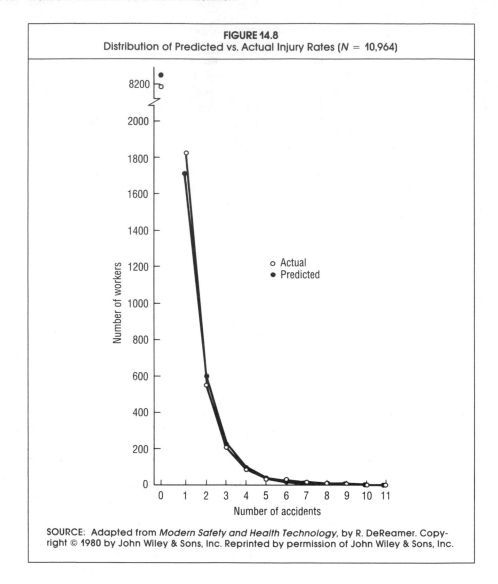

FIGURE 14.8
Distribution of Predicted vs. Actual Injury Rates ($N = 10,964$)

SOURCE: Adapted from *Modern Safety and Health Technology*, by R. DeReamer. Copyright © 1980 by John Wiley & Sons, Inc. Reprinted by permission of John Wiley & Sons, Inc.

sample of 10,964 workers, just 90 workers (0.8 percent of the total sample) suffered 531 injuries (11.9 percent of the total number of injuries).

Are these workers with high accident rates accident prone, engaging in behaviors or possessing characteristics that cause them to have more than their share of mishaps, or are they simply the unlucky victims of circumstances? The frequency diagram in Figure 14.8 summarizes DeReamer's (1980) data by plotting the number of workers having different numbers of injuries. Also plotted are the numbers of workers who can be *expected* to have different numbers of injuries, simply as a matter of chance, assuming that there is no accident-proneness construct operating. As you can see, the distribution of actual injuries is extremely similar to the predicted distribution of random injuries. This suggests quite strongly that the apparent accident proneness of some workers is simply the result of chance, and that the widely accepted concept of accident proneness has little merit.

Although there do not seem to be people who are *generally* accident prone, this doesn't mean that there aren't *any* individual characteristics or behaviors that are associated with accident rates. In the following sections on accident prevention, we will see that visual skills and perceptual style may be related to the number of accidents a person has in certain situations. For example, we might predict that "scaffolders" with poor depth perception will have more accidents than those with good depth perception. Poor depth perception, however, is not likely to lead to accidents on jobs that do not require climbing or judging distances. Consequently, the worker who appears to be accident prone on one job could have an excellent safety record on a different job. It is therefore better to focus on characteristics that predict accidents *in particular job settings* than to search for evidence of general accident proneness.

Accident Prevention

Given the potential costs of accidents to both individual workers and organizations, there has been a great deal of effort to develop ways to prevent accidents. Just as there are two general causes of accidents (job-related and worker-related), there have been two general approaches to accident prevention, changing workers (through selection or training) and changing jobs. While reading about accident-prevention techniques, you should keep in mind that there is no *single* cause for on-the-job mishaps, and that it is therefore unreasonable to expect any *single* accident prevention program to be 100-percent effective. Research suggests, however, that with the use of a comprehensive safety program, it should be possible to significantly reduce the number of accidents in most organizations.

SELECTION AND PLACEMENT

The first method for reducing accidents focuses on workers' characteristics. It is reasonable to expect that one way to prevent accidents in a given job is to select workers with a low probability of having accidents on that job. The process of **actuarial prediction** is used to determine who is likely to have an accident. That is, measures of various personal characteristics are correlated with accident rates for a large number of workers with the same or similar jobs. If a significant relationship is found between a characteristic and accident rate (and properly cross-validated), that characteristic can be used to predict who is likely to suffer an accident.

---

actuarial prediction: the prediction of behavior or outcomes based on biographical data (biodata)

For example, the premium that you pay on a life insurance policy depends to a great extent on your age. It is a sad fact of life that as we get older, the chances of our dying in the near future increase. Thus, age predicts the death rate, and in order to be able to pay insurance benefits when we die and still make a profit, the insurance company must charge older people higher premiums. In a similar fashion, if we can identify characteristics that predict accidents in a given situation, and accident rates are an important part of our ultimate performance criterion, we can use those characteristics as part of the selection procedure.

Relatively few individual characteristics have been found to predict the rate of work-related accidents. Among the most consistent predictors are perceptual variables, such as visual skills. It has long been known that workers with better vision have, on the average, fewer accidents than do workers with poorer vision (for example, Kephart & Tiffin, 1950). Also related to accident rates is a measure of perceptual style called field dependence. Field-*dependent* people are those who are socially dependent, conforming, and sensitive to their social environment. Field-*independent* people are self-reliant, inner-directed, and independent. Operationally, field-dependent people have a difficult time detecting shapes embedded in a complex background, whereas field-independent people find it much easier to perform these tasks. A number of studies have suggested that field-dependent individuals are more likely than field-independent individuals to have accidents, apparently because they have more difficulty detecting subtle cues that might warn them of hazardous conditions (for example, Barrett & Thornton, 1968; Mihal & Barrett, 1976).

Although there are studies linking accident rates with a wide variety of nonperceptual variables, few if any systematic relationships with accidents have been found. For example, some surveys show that younger workers have a greater number of accidents than older workers (Gordon, Akman, & Brooks, 1971), whereas others show that accident rates increase from middle age to old age (Cooke & Blumenstock, 1979). This does not necessarily mean, however, that in a given situation, with a particular applicant population and specific job characteristics, predictors of accident rates cannot be found. It *does* mean, unfortunately, that psychologists have not identified any traits that serve as predictors of accidents, in general, for all types of jobs.

TRAINING

As with selection, training programs focus on the worker as the key to reducing accident rates. Training is discussed in detail in Chapter 7, and so we will not repeat what we have said there, except to remind you that the motives of the workers and the supportiveness of management are important in determining the success of accident-prevention training.

The importance of management commitment to accident-reduction efforts was illustrated by Zohar (1980), who compared employee ratings of "safety climate" with evaluations made by safety inspectors. Zohar found that stronger perceptions of a safety climate were associated with greater management commitment to safety, as shown by the inspectors' estimates of the authority held by company safety officers, and the involvement of upper management in safety issues. Butler and Jones (1979) also found that management behavior was related to accident reduction, particularly in settings where hazards were not obvious. It seems clear that when training programs are developed to deal with accident prevention, management support for those programs is essential.

In terms of the effectiveness of safety training, research by Komaki and her colleagues has consistently shown that the most important factor in reducing accident rates and improving safety records is not explaining, describing, or discussing safe and unsafe behaviors, but rather providing workers with *feedback* on how they are doing relative to safety goals (for example, Komaki, Barwick, & Scott, 1978; Komaki, Heinzmann, & Lawson, 1980). In one study, Komaki, Collins, and Penn (1982) compared a traditional safety training program with a program centered around safety performance feedback. The traditional training program involved explaining safety rules with the aid of slide presentations, displaying safety rules in work areas, emphasizing a new rule three times each week, and holding weekly safety meetings. In the feedback program, a safety graph that showed the percentage of desired behaviors performed safely was explained to workers, posted in the work areas, updated three times each week, and discussed at weekly meetings. The results showed that the traditional training program led to a 6-percent improvement over the previous safety record, but that the feedback program resulted in an 18-percent improvement, and an 11-percent improvement over the results of the training program alone. Of course, the feedback would not have been effective without some training to let the workers know which behaviors needed to be changed. However, mere presentation of that information, which represents the bulk of most safety programs, is clearly not the most effective way to improve safety. Komaki's research also demonstrates the importance of maintaining safety feedback: Once feedback is halted, worker behaviors return to their pre-feedback levels (Komaki, Barwick, & Scott, 1978).

HUMAN FACTORS

A third general technique for increasing safety and reducing accidents focuses on changing jobs rather than on changing the behavior of workers. This is the human factors approach to accident prevention, and it is based on the premise that safety can be enhanced not only by encouraging safer behavior, but also by designing safer workplaces. Human factors as a discipline will be described in more detail in the last section of this chapter, as the safety of the workplace is only one of the many concerns addressed by human factors.

An example of a safety problem with which a human factors specialist could deal would be in the design of control devices for Peter's Pan Pizza's anchovy chopping equipment. One control on this machine might regulate the amount of material (anchovies) that is fed into a storage hopper, whereas another control would regulate the flow of material from the hopper into the actual chopping compartment. If these two controls were placed too close together, or if they were difficult to distinguish, it might be easy for a worker to accidently waste anchovies by overflowing an already-full hopper when he intended to empty the hopper into the chopper. On the other hand, if the controls were placed too far apart, attempts to operate them simultaneously might result in worker injury. Proper design of the equipment, as determined by human factors research, could avoid both types of accidents.

Safety Legislation

Worker safety and accident prevention are obviously desirable goals, both in terms of benefits for workers, and the potential for increased efficiency and profit for employers. Safety programs, however, can be costly and time-consuming to implement, leading some managers to resist their implementation in spite of the potential benefits. Since 1971, though, a federal law has mandated that employers must provide their workers with safe and healthful working conditions. This law, the Occupational Safety and Health Act, established the Occupational Safety and Health Administration, or OSHA. It is the responsibility of OSHA to establish and enforce safety and health standards for industry, to aid in the development of safety education and training, and to promote research on safety. OSHA has been most active in the area of safety and health *standards*, with literally thousands of regulations and guidelines currently in effect. These range from requirements for protective clothing, to pollution standards, to detailed specifications for safety devices on buildings and equipment.

Establishing standards, however, turned out to be the relatively easy part of OSHA's job. The more difficult aspect has been enforcing these standards. OSHA is empowered to inspect workplaces for violations of its standards, and to issue warnings and penalties to employers who are not in compliance. This enforcement activity has been hindered by two factors. First, even the best safety program will be ineffective if workers are not motivated to accept it, and there are many reasons why they might find it easier to behave unsafely rather than safely. Common needs that conflict with safety considerations are described in the following list.

1. *Safety vs. saving time:* If the safe way takes more time than an unsafe way, some people will choose the unsafe way to save time.
2. *Safety vs. saving effort:* If the safe way requires more work than the unsafe way, some people will choose the unsafe way to save the effort.
3. *Safety vs. comfort:* If the safe way is less comfortable than an unsafe way, some people will choose the unsafe way to avoid discomfort.
4. *Safety vs. getting attention:* If an unsafe way attracts more attention than the safe way, some people will choose the unsafe way.
5. *Safety vs. independence:* If an unsafe way gives greater freedom from authority than the safe way, some people will choose the unsafe way simply to assert their independence.
6. *Safety vs. group acceptance:* If an unsafe way has greater group approval than the safe way, many people will choose the unsafe way to get or maintain group acceptance.

SOURCE: *Management Guide to Loss Control*, by F. E. Bird. Copyright 1974 by Institute Press, Santa Monica, California.

Second, OSHA's budget has never allowed it to have a truly adequate inspection and enforcement staff, and many employers realize that there is little chance that infractions of the law will come to OSHA's attention. Of course, most companies voluntarily comply with safety laws, and we are confident that the overall safety of U.S. workplaces has improved since safety legislation has been enacted.

WORKER–MACHINE SYSTEMS: HUMAN FACTORS

There are probably an unlimited number of ways in which a tool, a machine, or even an entire factory could be designed to fulfill a given purpose. Clearly, some of these designs will be more efficient, easier to use, and will accomplish their goals better than others. Human factors is the scientific and technical discipline that is dedicated to promoting the design of workplaces, as well as other human environments, that can most effectively meet the needs of their users. That is, as it applies to work behavior, human factors is concerned with the relationships between workers and the physical objects with which they perform their jobs. Because the design of equipment, facilities, products, and other aspects of the environment have implications for behavior, human factors is also concerned with developing proper procedures for effectively performing a variety of tasks.

Human factors is a multidisciplinary field, with aspects of engineering, physiology, architecture, and various other areas of expertise, in addition to psychology. We will therefore not attempt to provide an exhaustive overview of human factors; interested readers can refer to any of a number of textbooks in this field (for example, Kantowitz & Sorkin, 1983; McCormick & Sanders, 1982). Instead, we will describe one of the major, guiding concepts of human factors, the worker–machine system, and show how human factors provides answers to problems that are often quite different from those suggested by the purely psychological theories.

The Worker–Machine System

It is common to view human factors as a discipline that is dedicated to improving worker–machine systems. A worker–machine system can be defined as an arrangement of people and machines, tools, and other devices, interacting within the work environment in order to achieve a set of system goals (Kantowitz & Sorkin, 1983). The role of the human factors specialist is to design the interface, or link, between the human and machine components of the system, so that the system can achieve its goals most efficiently. The way in which this is typically accomplished illustrates an important difference between the perspective of the I/O psychologist and the human factors specialist. Whereas psychologists emphasize selection, training, reinforcement, and other actions aimed at changing the *worker*, the human factors approach is likely to alter the *machine* components of the system. This does not reflect the opinion that human behavior is not important, but rather a belief that it may be easier to change a machine to make it compatible with people than it is to change people to make them compatible with machines. Certainly, to the extent that a machine is

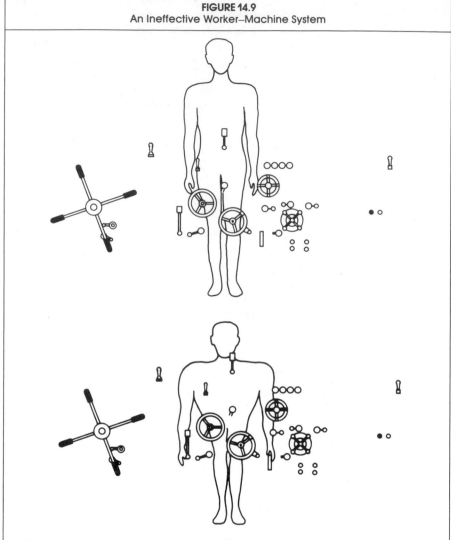

FIGURE 14.9
An Ineffective Worker–Machine System

The controls of a lathe in current use are not within easy reach of the average person. They are placed so that the ideal operator should be 1372 mm (4¼ feet) tall, 640 mm (2 feet) across the shoulders, and have a 2348 mm (8 feet) arm span.

SOURCE: "Industrial Use of Ergonomics," *Applied Ergonomics,* 1969, *1,* 26–32. Copyright 1969 by Butterworth Scientific Ltd. Reprinted by permission.

poorly designed, it may not be possible to train any worker to use it effectively (Figure 14.9).

The basic components of a worker–machine system are illustrated in Figure 14.10. In this system, there are certain components that are important to human factors specialists, and certain components that are of little interest to them.

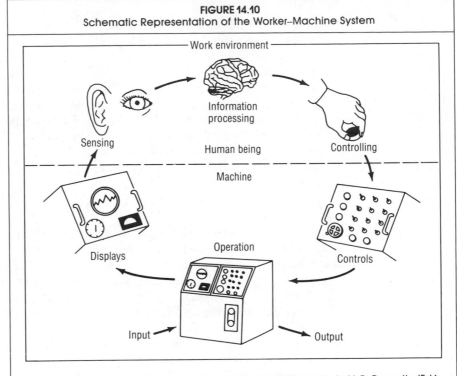

FIGURE 14.10
Schematic Representation of the Worker–Machine System

SOURCE: Adapted from "Engineering Psychology," by A. Chapanis. In M. D. Dunnette (Ed.), *Handbook of Industrial and Organizational Psychology.* Copyright © 1976 by Rand Mc-Nally and Company. Copyright © 1983 by John Wiley & Sons, Inc. Reprinted by permission of John Wiley & Sons, Inc.

On the machine side of the system, displays and controls are the most relevant components. On the human side sensory and motor functions are emphasized. The emphasis on these four components reflects the fact that they define the interface between the worker and the machine: The machine displays provide the worker's senses with information necessary to monitor and evaluate the machine's performance, whereas the worker's motor behavior allows him to adjust machine controls that will cause corrections or other changes in the machine's operation.

Of course, both the worker and the machine do much more than send information to each other. The machine's major function is to perform the operations that it was designed to perform, while the worker's most important tasks within the system are cognitive, processing and making judgments about the information provided by the machine, and deciding what changes in the controls are needed. These machine operations and information-processing functions, however, are largely irrelevant to the human factors specialist, who is primarily concerned with the compatibility of worker and machine at their interface.

INPUTS

Data about the machine's operation form the inputs for the human side of the worker–machine system. (These data, of course, also form the *outputs* for the machine side of the system, but to avoid repetition and confusion, and to remain consistent with our psychological perspective, we will discuss the system from the worker's perspective.) Research on these inputs has focused on two general topics. The first of these is the sensory capabilities of humans. In order for a worker to accurately perceive information displayed by a machine, that information must be compatible with the human senses. Consequently, in order for human factors experts to design effective displays, they must first understand human sensation. Failure to take the worker's sensory capabilities into account could lead to disastrous results.

For example, one type of display on Peter's Pan Pizza's anchovy chopping machine shows the pressure within the hydraulic system that powers the chopping blades. When the pressure is within normal limits a green light is displayed on a control panel; if the pressure rises above those limits, however, the green light is extinguished and a red light comes on, signaling the operator to perform certain safety actions. For most people, a quick glance at the panel would tell them which light is on, but for workers with red-green color blindness, who have difficulty distinguishing between red and green, this color-coded information will be much less effective, and may result in costly accidents. Although only a small minority of people have this sort of color vision disorder, it would be a simple matter to have the red warning light *flash* on and off, so that in the rare case of a color-blind operator, the risk of a pressure buildup will be reduced.

The other component of the information input process is the machine display itself. Not all displays can be as quickly or as accurately interpreted as others, even when all are within the range of normal human sensation. Figure 14.11 illustrates a case in point. This figure summarizes data from a study of the effectiveness of four different airplane altimeter designs (Simon & Roscoe, 1956). Each design indicates (1) the present altitude of the plane, (2) the predicted altitude of the plane in one minute, and (3) the "command altitude," or the altitude at which the plane is supposed to be flying. The subjects, 24 pilots, were presented problems consisting of different combinations of these three altitudes, from which they were to decide what needed to be done to reach the command altitude. The data at the bottom of the figure show the pilots' average time to solve the problems, and the number and percentage of errors for each altimeter design. On all of the performance measures, the integrated vertical design showed clear advantages, probably because it presents the information, which concerned the relative *vertical* position of three altitudes, in a *vertical* format. The other designs require the pilot to cognitively transfer a *digital* or *circular* representation into information about relative vertical positions.

This example, of course, illustrates only one of a variety of display-format issues that human factors specialists have addressed. In each case, however, the goal is to design a display that provides specific information in a readily interpretable manner. The nature of that display will depend both on the type of

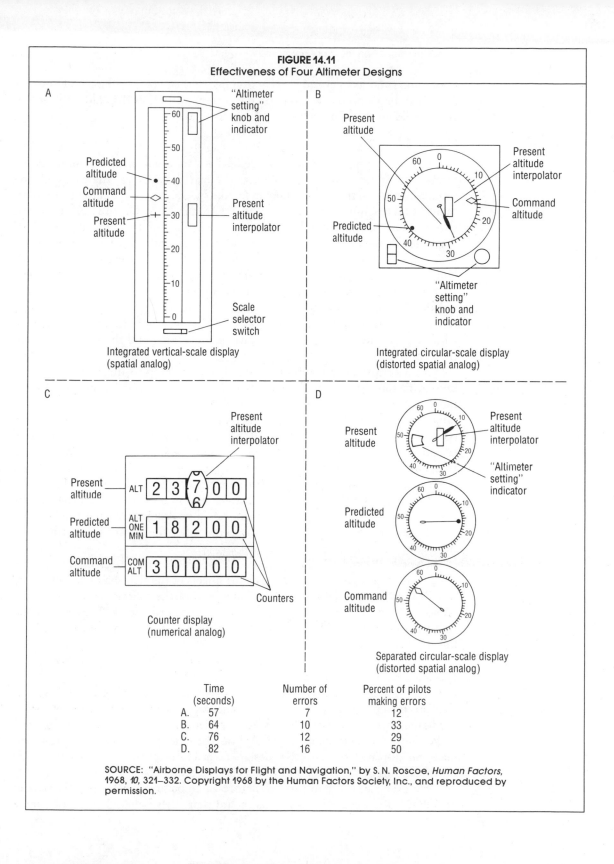

FIGURE 14.11
Effectiveness of Four Altimeter Designs

A

"Altimeter setting" knob and indicator

Predicted altitude

Command altitude

Present altitude

Present altitude interpolator

Scale selector switch

Integrated vertical-scale display (spatial analog)

B

Present altitude

Present altitude interpolator

Command altitude

Predicted altitude

"Altimeter setting" knob and indicator

Integrated circular-scale display (distorted spatial analog)

C

Present altitude interpolator

Present altitude

Predicted altitude

Command altitude

Counters

Counter display (numerical analog)

D

Present altitude

Present altitude interpolator

"Altimeter setting" indicator

Predicted altitude

Command altitude

Separated circular-scale display (distorted spatial analog)

	Time (seconds)	Number of errors	Percent of pilots making errors
A.	57	7	12
B.	64	10	33
C.	76	12	29
D.	82	16	50

SOURCE: "Airborne Displays for Flight and Navigation," by S. N. Roscoe, *Human Factors,* 1968, *10,* 321–332. Copyright 1968 by the Human Factors Society, Inc., and reproduced by permission.

information and its intended use. For example, if the pilots in Simon and Roscoe's study had simply been asked to judge the current altitude of the plane, the digital counter design would probably have been most effective.

OUTPUTS

The output portion of the human side of the worker–machine system takes the form of instructions from the worker to the machine. As was the case with the input functions of the system, human factors specialists are concerned with both human and machine components of this output process. On the human side, it is important to understand the motor capabilities of the typical worker. If machines demand input that is beyond the physical abilities of workers to provide, the system will not be able to function at its maximum potential. Human factors researchers have therefore studied such variables as workers' energy expenditure, strength, endurance, speed, accuracy of movements, and workload (McCormick & Sanders, 1982). Knowledge gained through this research has helped us to design workplaces that maximize human performance while minimizing such outcomes as fatigue and stress, and the errors to which they contribute.

An example of research on motor skills may help to illustrate its role in human factors. In recent decades there has been a dramatic increase in the number of workers whose jobs involve what is known as "data entry." These range from long-familiar jobs, such as typists, to those that are relatively new, such as the variety of computer-operator positions that now exist in many modern organizations. All of these jobs involve the use of some sort of keyboard, and therefore require a controlled, but rapid, tapping movement of the fingers. In order to design a keyboard for maximum efficiency, it would be useful to know whether or not, for the average person, some fingers are better suited than others for this type of task. If so, the keyboard should be designed so that the "better" fingers perform most of the work, while the other fingers are used only when necessary.

Dvorak, Marrick, Dealey, and Ford (1936) conducted research on this specific issue many years ago. They found that the fingers of the right hand can tap more rapidly than those of the left hand, probably because the majority of their subjects, like a majority of the general population, were right-handed. They also found that the index and middle fingers of both hands were faster than the ring or little fingers of the same hand. Consequently, in the design of equipment to be used in tasks requiring rapid finger movement, such as data entry, it is probably best to maximize the use of index and middle fingers.

The machine component of the output process consists of control devices that are manipulated by the worker. These devices can take a variety of forms, including knobs to be turned, levers to be pulled, switches to be flicked, and keys to be pressed, just to name a few. As was the case with human sensation and machine displays, the effective design of machine controls relies on a good understanding of the motor abilities of the operator.

For example, based in part on their research on finger movement, Dvorak et al. (1936) developed a typewriter keyboard that, they believed, would be more

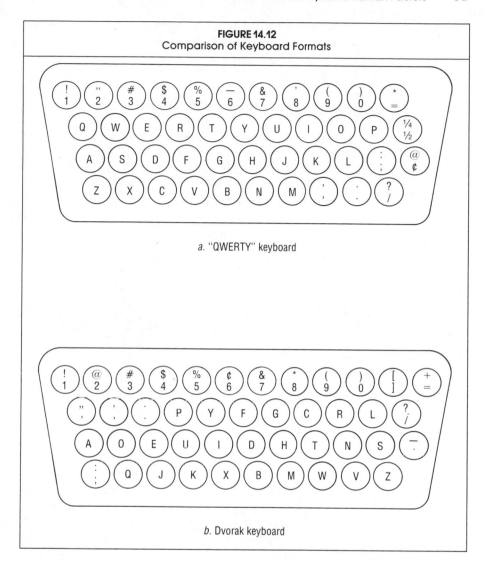

FIGURE 14.12
Comparison of Keyboard Formats

a. "QWERTY" keyboard

b. Dvorak keyboard

effective than the standard "QWERTY" keyboard (named for the sequence of keys on the second row). The QWERTY keyboard and the Dvorak keyboard are illustrated in Figure 14.12. Dvorak believed that his keyboard would lead to improved typing speed and accuracy. The QWERTY arrangement requires the left hand to do most of the work, and forces the typist to perform difficult finger movements to type common sequences of characters. The Dvorak keyboard equalizes the work of the two hands, and eliminates many difficult movements by placing the most commonly used letters on the middle row of keys, where the fingers typically rest while typing.

Dvorak's efforts to design a better typewriter keyboard are a good example of designing machine controls based on knowledge of human motor abilities.

Unfortunately, it is not clear whether this particular effort at improving the worker–machine interface has been effective. There are many claims of tremendous improvements in typing speed and accuracy as a result of using the Dvorak keyboard, but most of these claims are undocumented.

For example, McCauley and Parkinson (1971) reported that some typists increased their typing speed from 50 words per minute on the QWERTY to 150 words per minute on the Dvorak, and that 6-to 12-year-old children have learned to type over 40 words per minute in only a few weeks with the Dvorak keyboard. They cited no hard evidence to support these dramatic accomplishments, however. More scientific examinations of the Dvorak keyboard failed to support the claims of its followers. For example, Kinkead (1975) compared typing speeds obtained on the QWERTY, the Dvorak, and a third keyboard designed specifically to optimize typing speed. His results showed that the Dvorak keyboard resulted in only a 2.6-percent time savings over the QWERTY, and that the "optimal" keyboard was only 7.6 percent faster than the QWERTY.

It could be argued that a 7.6-percent time savings, or even a 2.6-percent time savings, would result in substantial savings over a long enough period of time, and that an improved keyboard design should therefore be attractive to organizations with large numbers of data-entry positions. All else being equal, this may be true; but all else is seldom equal, and in this case the adoption of the Dvorak keyboard would require the expensive and time-consuming retraining of large numbers of workers who have become used to the standard QWERTY keyboard. This would probably not be an easy retraining task either, because these experienced keyboard operators would probably experience "negative transfer" of training, as their old habits and skills interfere with learning new skills. Further, very few keyboards are produced with the Dvorak layout, and so any retraining would be a waste of time unless the Dvorak keyboard became widely available. Of course, until there are substantial numbers of Dvorak typists to create a demand for the Dvorak design, manufacturers of data entry equipment will not be likely to market alternative keyboards. This is not to say that an alternative keyboard design is not a good idea, but rather that even the best of ideas will not be acceptable if people do not want them, and refuse to use them.

CHAPTER SUMMARY

In this chapter we have divided the issue of work environment into three general topics. The first of these, *work conditions*, refers to aspects of employment or the workplace that influence employees' effectiveness and their reactions to work, rather than directly influencing their behaviors. Included in this category are work schedules, shift work, compressed workweeks, and flextime. Working nonstandard or irregular shifts has been found to have negative effects on workers' health, social interactions, and family relationships. The ability of workers to adjust to the demands of shift work is an important key to coping with these problems. Compressed workweeks are popular with workers, although longer workdays can increase workers' levels of fatigue. Flextime, in which workers' arrival and departure times are allowed to vary, lets workers adjust their schedules to meet their needs, but may present problems for supervisors and managers. Neither compressed workweeks nor flextime seem to have effects on employee satisfaction or performance, although flextime has been shown to reduce tardiness.

Another set of work conditions are the physical aspects of the workplace. These include illumination, noise level, thermal conditions, and pollution. Of course, any toxic pollution is undesirable, but the ideal levels of illumination, noise, and temperature depend in part on the nature of the job. Extreme levels of any of these factors, however, are detrimental to both workers' health and their performance.

The second general topic is *safety and accidents*. Causes of work-related accidents have been categorized as either job-related or worker-related. The former refers to unsafe conditions in the workplace, whereas the latter refers to unsafe worker behaviors. Although there appears to be no evidence of any "accident-prone" personality trait, some personal characteristics do predict accidents. Accident-prevention efforts have utilized employee selection, safety training, and human factors techniques.

The third general topic is *human factors,* which is the discipline dedicated to designing workplaces for maximum human performance. Human factors is often viewed as dealing with "worker–machine systems," trying to optimize the link between workers and the machines and tools with which they perform their job tasks. The design of machine displays and controls is the most obvious aspect of this effort.

INTEROFFICE MEMO
TO: Andrew LeGette, Director of Wages and Benefits
FROM: J. A. MacKeven, Human-Resources Coordinator

My staff has finished its research into the programs that you mentioned as possible nonpay incentives to offer during the contract negotiations. I will discuss each of the programs in turn:

<u>Four-day workweek:</u> There are potential advantages of a four-day workweek to Peter's Pan Pizza. The most important of these is that by cutting one day from the normal workweek, up to 20-percent savings in certain overhead costs (heat, custodial, etc.) may be realized. One major limitation is that you can't fit more than two 10-hour shifts in a day, so if a plant is currently on a 24-hour/day schedule it will be difficult to shorten the workweek. (Further, it would be difficult to get the union to accept four-day workweeks in only some of the plants.) Another drawback is that if you need to operate a plant more than four days/week, some people will have to work weekends and take days off in the middle of the week, which will probably be unpopular with the union. From a productivity standpoint, there is little evidence that a four-day workweek will have much effect on performance.

<u>Flextime:</u> Flextime may be acceptable for nonproduction workers, but we believe that it would be impossible to operate Flavio's production operations normally under this system, due to the high likelihood of understaffing both early and late in the day.

<u>Safety programs:</u> The human resources office has not been involved in developing company safety policy, so I'm not sure what is currently being done. I <u>hope</u> that we are conforming to all OSHA regulations, and that the workers are basically safe. You might want to offer some periodic safety education courses or workshops on company time, although they will probably only be attractive to the union if there is a general perception that the workplace is <u>unsafe.</u>

I think that you should know that, in general, there is little reason to believe that the union will ''trade'' these sorts of programs for wage and benefit increases. Union negotiators know that economic issues are what the rank-and-file want the union to concentrate on, and they tend to focus on those issues.

REVIEW QUESTIONS AND EXERCISES

1. Dr. MacKeven has pointed out some of the practical problems that arise when instituting nonstandard workweek or flextime programs. How might some of these problems be solved? Are the potential benefits of these programs worth the effort it would take to implement them? Defend your answer.

2. Assume that worker safety *was* a major concern of the union negotiators representing Flavio's workers. Describe the most effective safety program, in terms of both improving safety and cost, that Peter's Pan Pizza could offer to implement. Evaluate Dr. MacKeven's suggestion in comparison to your own.

3. Throughout this chapter we have mentioned Flavio's anchovy products. One task in the preparation of these products is chopping the anchovies. Describe the general human factors issues involved in designing an anchovy chopping machine.

4. Now that you have "designed" the anchovy chopper, you need a factory in which to put it. Describe the physical aspects of this workplace that could affect workers' behaviors and performance, and explain what some of the potential hazards might be in such a workplace.

REFERENCES

ABBEY, A., & DICKSON, J. W. (1983). R & D work climate and innovation in semiconductors. *Academy of Management Journal, 26,* 362–368.

ADAMS, J. S. (1965). Inequity in social exchange. In L. Berkowitz (ed.), *Advances in experimental social psychology* (vol. 2). New York: Academic Press.

ADAMS, L. T. (1985). Changing employment patterns of organized workers. *Monthly Labor Review, 108*(2), 25–31.

ADLER, S., SKOV, R. B., & SALVEMINI, N. J. (1985). Job characteristics and job satisfaction: When cause becomes consequence. *Organizational Behavior and Human Decision Processes, 35,* 266–278.

AIKEN, L. R. (1979). *Psychological testing and assessment* (3rd ed.). Boston: Allyn & Bacon.

ALDAG, R. J., BARR, S. H., & BRIEF, A. P. (1981). Measurement of perceived task characteristics. *Psychological Bulletin, 90,* 415–431.

ALDERFER, C. P. (1969). A new theory of human needs. *Organizational Behavior and Human Performance, 4,* 142–175.

ALDERFER, C. P. (1972). *Existence, relatedness, and growth.* New York: Free Press.

ALDERFER, C. P. (1977). Organization development. *Annual Review of Psychology, 28,* 197–223.

ALEXANDER, L. D. (1979). The effect level in the hierarchy and functional area have on the extent Mintzberg's roles are required by managerial jobs. *Proceedings of the Annual Meeting of the Academy of Management,* 186–189.

ALEXANDER, R. A., BARRETT, G. V., & DOVERSPIKE, D. (1983). An explication of the selection ratio and its relationship to hiring rate. *Journal of Applied Psychology, 68,* 342–344.

ALLEN, M. J., & YEN, W. M. (1979). *Introduction to measurement theory.* Pacific Grove, CA: Brooks/Cole.

ALLEN, M. P., & PANIAN, S. K. (1982). Power, performance, and succession in the large corporation. *Administrative Science Quarterly, 27,* 538–547.

ALLEN, R. E., & KEAVENY, T. J. (1981). Correlates of university faculty interest in unionization: A replication and extension. *Journal of Applied Psychology, 66,* 582–588.

ALLUISI, E. A., & MORGAN, B. B., JR. (1976). Engineering psychology and human performance. *Annual Review of Psychology, 27,* 305–330.

ALPANDER, G. G. (1974). Planning management training programs for organizational development. *Personnel Journal, 53,* 15–21.

AMERICAN EDUCATIONAL RESEARCH ASSOCIATION, AMERICAN PSYCHOLOGICAL ASSOCIATION, & NATIONAL COUNCIL ON MEASUREMENT IN EDUCATION. (1985). *Standards for educational and psychological testing.* Washington, DC: American Psychological Association.

ANASTASIO, E. J., & MORGAN, J. S. (1972). Factors inhibiting the use of computers in instruction. *Educational Testing Service* NSF GJ 27427. Princeton, NJ: Educational Testing Service.

ANDERSON, C. D., WARNER, J. L., & SPENCER, C. C. (1984). Inflation bias in self-assessment examinations: Implications for valid employee selection. *Journal of Applied Psychology, 69,* 574–580.

ANDREWS, I. R., & VALENZI, E. (1970). Overpay inequity or self-image as a worker: A critical evaluation of an experimental induction procedure. *Organizational Behavior and Human Performance, 5,* 22–27.

ARGYRIS, C. (1957). *Personality and organization: The conflict between system and the individual.* New York: Harper & Row.

ARNOLD, H. J. (1976). Effects of performance feedback and extrinsic reward upon high intrinsic motivation. *Organizational Behavior and Human Performance, 17*, 275–288.

ARNOLD, H. J. (1982). Moderator variables: A clarification of conceptual, analytic, and psychometric issues. *Organizational Behavior and Human Performance, 29*, 143–174.

ARNOLD, H. J. (1984). Testing moderator variable hypotheses: A reply to Stone and Hollenbeck. *Organizational Behavior and Human Performance, 34*, 214–224.

ARNOLD, H. J., & EVANS, M. G. (1979). Testing multiplicative models does *not* require ratio scales. *Organizational Behavior and Human Performance, 24*, 41–59.

ARNOLD, J. D., RAUSCHENBERGER, J. M., SOUBEL, W. G., & GUION, R. M. (1982). Validation and utility of a strength test for selecting steelworkers. *Journal of Applied Psychology, 67*, 588–604.

ARVEY, R. D. (1979). Unfair discrimination in the employment interview: Legal and psychological aspects. *Psychological Bulletin, 86*, 736–765.

ARVEY, R. D., & CAMPION, J. E. (1982). The employment interview: A summary and review of recent research. *Personnel Psychology, 35*, 281–322.

ARVEY, R. D., DAVIS, G. A., McGOWEN, S. L., & DIPBOYE, R. L. (1982). Potential sources of bias in job analytic processes. *Academy of Management Journal, 25*, 618–629.

ARVEY, R. D., & HOYLE, J. C. (1974). A Guttman approach to the development of behaviorally based rating scales for systems analysts and programmer/analysts. *Journal of Applied Psychology, 59*, 61–68.

ARVEY, R. D., & IVANCEVICH, J. M. (1980). Punishment in organizations: A review, propositions, and research suggestions. *Academy of Management Review, 5*, 123–132.

ASH, R. A., & EDGELL, S. L. (1975). A note on the readability of the Position Analysis Questionnaire (PAQ). *Journal of Applied Psychology, 60*, 765–766.

ASH, R. A., & LEVINE, E. L. (1985). Job applicant training and work experience evaluation: An empirical comparison of four methods. *Journal of Applied Psychology, 70*, 572–576.

ASHFORD, S. J., & CUMMINGS, L. L. (1983). Feedback as an individual resource: Personal strategies of creating information. *Organizational Behavior and Human Performance, 32*, 370–398.

At Emery Air Freight: Positive reinforcement boosts performance. (Winter, 1973). *Organizational Dynamics*, 41–50.

ATKINSON, J. W. (ed.). (1958). *Motives in fantasy, action, and society*. Princeton, NJ: Van Nostrand.

ATKINSON, J. W., & FEATHER, N. T. (1966). *A theory of achievement motivation*. New York: Wiley.

BALMA, M. J. (1959). The concept of synthetic validity. *Personnel Psychology, 12*, 395–396.

BANDURA, A. (1969). *Principles of behavior modification*. New York: Holt, Rinehart & Winston.

BANDURA, A. (1971). *Social learning theory*. Morristown, NJ: General Learning Press.

BANDURA, A. (1977). *Social learning theory*. Englewood Cliffs, NJ: Prentice-Hall.

BANKS, C. G., & MURPHY, K. R. (1985). Toward narrowing the research–practice gap in performance appraisal. *Personnel Psychology, 38*, 335–345.

BANKS, C. G., & ROBERSON, L. (1985). Performance appraisers as test developers. *Academy of Management Review, 10*, 128–142.

BANKS, M. H., JACKSON, P. R., STAFFORD, E. M., & WARR, P. B. (1983). The Job Components Inventory and the analysis of jobs requiring limited skill. *Personnel Psychology, 36*, 57–66.

BARNES, J. L., & LANDY, F. J. (1979). Scaling behavioral anchors. *Applied Psychological Measurement, 3*, 193–200.

BARNES-FARRELL, J. L., & WEISS, H. M. (1984). Effects of standard extremity on mixed standard scale performance ratings. *Personnel Psychology, 37*, 301–316.

BARNES, V., POTTER, E. H., III, & FIEDLER, F. E. (1983). Effect of interpersonal stress on the prediction of academic performance. *Journal of Applied Psychology, 68*, 686–697.

BARON, A. S. (1977). Selection, development and socialization of women into management. *Business Quarterly, 28*, 61–67.

BARON, R. A. (1983). "Sweet smell of success"? The impact of pleasant artificial scents on evaluations of job applicants. *Journal of Applied Psychology, 68*, 709–713.

BARRETT, G. V., CALDWELL, M. S., & ALEXANDER, R. A. (1985). The concept of dynamic criteria: A critical reanalysis. *Personnel Psychology, 38*, 41–56.

BARRETT, G. V., PHILLIPS, J. S., & ALEXANDER, R. A. (1981). Concurrent and predictive validity designs: A critical reanalysis. *Journal of Applied Psychology, 66*, 1–6.

BARRETT, G. V., & THORNTON, C. L. (1968). The relationship between perceptual style and driver reaction to an emergency situation. *Journal of Applied Psychology, 52*, 169–176.

BARRETT, R. S., TAYLOR, E. K., PARKER, J. W., & MARTENS, L. (1958). Rating scale content: I. Scale information and supervisory ratings. *Personnel Psychology, 11,* 333–346.

BARTLETT, C. J., & O'LEARY, B. S. (1969). A differential prediction model to moderate the effects of heterogeneous groups in personnel selection and classification. *Personnel-Psychology, 22,* 1–17.

BARTOL, K. M. (1974). Male vs. female leaders: The effect of leader need for dominance on follower satisfaction. *Academy of Management Journal, 17,* 225–233.

BARTOL, K. M. (1975). The effect of male versus female leaders on follower satisfaction and performance. *Journal of Business Research, 3,* 33–42.

BARTOL, K. M. (1978). The sex structuring of organizations: A search for possible causes. *Academy of Management Review, 3,* 805–815.

BARTOL, K. M., ANDERSON, C. R., & SCHNEIER, C. E. (1981). Sex and ethnic effects on motivation to manage among college business students. *Journal of Applied Psychology, 66,* 40–44.

BARTOL, K. M., & WORTMAN, M. S., JR. (1975). Male versus female leaders: Effects on perceived leader behavior and satisfaction in a hospital. *Personnel Psychology, 28,* 533–547.

BASS, A. R., & FIRESTONE, I. J. (1980). Implications of representativeness for generalizability of field and laboratory research findings. *American Psychologist, 35,* 463–464.

BASS, B. M. (1954). The leaderless group discussion. *Psychological Bulletin, 51,* 465–492.

BASS, B. M. (1962). Further evidence on the dynamic character of criteria. *Personnel Psychology, 15,* 93–97.

BASS, B. M. (1967). Social behavior and the orientation interview: A review. *Psychological Bulletin, 68,* 260–292.

BASS, B. M. (1981). *Stogdill's handbook of leadership.* New York: Free Press.

BASS, B. M. (1983). Issues involved in relations between methodological rigor and reported outcomes in evaluations of organizational development. *Journal of Applied Psychology, 68,* 197–199.

BASS, B. M. (1985). *Leadership and performance beyond expectations.* New York: Free Press.

BASS, B. M., & BARRETT, G. V. (1981). *People, work, and organizations: An introduction to industrial and organizational psychology* (2nd ed.). Boston: Allyn & Bacon.

BASS, B. M., KRUSKELL, J., & ALEXANDER, R. A. (1971). Male managers' attitudes toward working women. *American Behavioral Scientist, 15,* 221–236.

BASS, B. M., & VAUGHAN, J. A. (1966). *Training in industry: The management of learning.* Pacific Grove, CA: Brooks/Cole.

BASSETT, G. A., & MEYER, H. H. (1968). Performance appraisal based on self-review. *Personnel Psychology, 21,* 421–430.

BAUMGARTEL, H., & JEANPIERRE, F. (1972). Applying new knowledge in the back-home setting: A study of Indian managers' adaptive efforts. *Journal of Applied Behavioral Science, 8,* 674–694.

BAXTER, J. C., BROCK, B., HILL, P. C., & ROZELLE, R. M. (1981). Letters of recommendation: A question of value. *Journal of Applied Psychology, 66,* 296–301.

BEEHR, T. A., & NEWMAN, J. E. (1978). Job stress, employee health, and organizational effectiveness: A facet analysis, model, and literature review. *Personnel Psychology, 31,* 665–699.

BELLOWS, R. M. (1959). *Creative leadership.* Englewood Cliffs, NJ: Prentice-Hall.

BENDIG, A. W. (1952a). A statistical report on a revision of the Miami instructor rating sheet. *Journal of Educational Psychology, 43,* 423–429.

BENDIG, A. W. (1952b). The use of student rating scales in the evaluation of instructors in introductory psychology. *Journal of Educational Psychology, 43,* 167–175.

BENDIG, A. W. (1953). The reliability of self-ratings as a function of the amount of verbal anchoring and the number of categories on the scale. *Journal of Applied Psychology, 37,* 38–41.

BENDIG, A. W. (1954a). Reliability and number of rating scale categories. *Journal of Applied Psychology, 38,* 38–40.

BENDIG, A. W. (1954b). Reliability of short rating scales and the heterogeneity of the rated stimuli. *Journal of Applied Psychology, 38,* 167–170.

BENGE, E. J., BURK, S. L. H., & HAY, E. N. (1941). *Manual of job evaluation.* New York: Harper and Brothers.

BENNETT, C. (1977, January). The demographic variables of discomfort glare. *Lighting Design and Application,* 22–24.

BENNETT, C., CHITLANGIA, A., & PANGREKAR, A. (1977). Illumination levels and performance of practical visual tasks. *Proceedings of the Human Factors Society 21st Annual Meeting.* Santa Monica, CA: Human Factors Society.

BERGER, C. J., OLSON, C. A., & BOUDREAU, J. W. (1983). Effects of unions on job satisfaction: The role of work-related values and perceived rewards. *Organizational Behavior and Human Performance, 32,* 289–324.

BERKOWITZ, L., & DONNERSTEIN, E. (1982). External validity is more than skin deep: Some answers to criticisms of laboratory experiments. *American Psychologist, 37,* 245–257.

BERKSHIRE, J. R., & HIGHLAND, R. W. (1953). Forced-choice performance rating—A methodological study. *Personnel Psychology, 6,* 355–378.

BERMAN, F. E., & MINER, J. B. (1985). Motivation to manage at the top executive level: A test of the hierarchic role-motivation theory. *Personnel Psychology, 38,* 377–391.

BERNARD, L. L. (1926). *An introduction to social psychology.* New York: Holt.

BERNARDIN, H. J. (1978). Effects of rater training on leniency and halo errors in student ratings of instructors. *Journal of Applied Psychology, 63,* 301–308.

BERNARDIN, H. J., & BEATTY, R. W. (1984). *Performance appraisal: Assessing human behavior at work.* Boston: Kent.

BERNARDIN, H. J., & PENCE, E. C. (1980). Effects of rater training: Creating new response sets and decreasing accuracy. *Journal of Applied Psychology, 65,* 60–66.

BERNARDIN, H. J., & WALTER, C. S. (1977). Effects of rater training and diary-keeping on psychometric error in ratings. *Journal of Applied Psychology, 62,* 64–69.

BHAGAT, R. S., MCQUAID, S. J., LINDHOLM, H., & SEGOVIS, J. (1985). Total life stress: A multimethod validation of the construct and its effects on organizationally valued outcomes and withdrawal behaviors. *Journal of Applied Psychology, 70,* 202–214.

BIGONESS, W. J. (1978). Correlates of faculty attitudes toward collective bargaining. *Journal of Applied Psychology, 63,* 228–233.

BIGONESS, W. J., & TOSI, H. L. (1984). Correlates of voting behavior in a union decertification election. *Academy of Management Journal, 27,* 654–659.

BIRD, F. E. (1974). *Management guide to loss control.* Santa Monica, CA: Institute Press.

BLACKBURN, R., & CUMMINGS, L. L. (1982). Cognitions of work unit structure. *Academy of Management Journal, 25,* 836–854.

BLAKE, R. R., & MOUTON, J. S. (1985). *The managerial grid III.* Houston: Gulf.

BLANZ, F., & GHISELLI, E. E. (1972). The mixed standard scale: A new rating system. *Personnel Psychology, 25,* 185–199.

BLOOD, M. R. (1974). Spin-offs from behavioral expectation scale procedures. *Journal of Applied Psychology, 59,* 513–515.

BLOOD, M. R., & MULLET, G. M. (1977). *Where have all the moderators gone: The perils of Type II error.* Altanta, GA: College of Industrial Management, Georgia Institute of Technology.

BLUM, M. L., & NAYLOR, J. C. (1968). *Industrial psychology: Its theoretical and social foundations* (rev. ed.). New York: Harper & Row.

BLUMBERG, A., & GOLEMBIEWSKI, R. (1976). *Learning and change in groups.* Clinton, MA: Colonial Press.

BOBKO, P., KARREN, R., & PARKINGTON, J. J. (1983). Estimation of standard deviations in utility analyses: An empirical test. *Journal of Applied Psychology, 68,* 170–176.

BOEHM, V. R. (1980). Research in the "real world"—A conceptual model. *Personnel Psychology, 33,* 495–503.

BOEHM, V. R. (1982). Are we validating more but publishing less? (The impact of governmental regulation on published validation research—An exploratory investigation). *Personnel Psychology, 35,* 175–187.

BOJE, D. M., & WHETTEN, D. A. (1981). Effects of organizational strategies and contextual constraints on centrality and attributions of influence in interorganizational networks. *Administrative Science Quarterly, 26,* 378–395.

BOOKER, G. S., & MILLER, R. W. (1966). A closer look at peer ratings. *Personnel, 43,* 42–47.

BORMAN, W. C. (1974). The rating of individuals in organizations: An alternate approach. *Organizational Behavior and Human Performance, 12,* 105–124.

BORMAN, W. C. (1975). Effects of instructions to avoid halo error on reliability and validity of performance evaluation ratings. *Journal of Applied Psychology, 60,* 556–560.

BORMAN, W. C. (1979). Format and training effects on rating accuracy and rater errors. *Journal of Applied Psychology, 64,* 410–421.

BORMAN, W. C. (1982). Validity of behavioral assessment for predicting military recruiter performance. *Journal of Applied Psychology, 67,* 3–9.

BORMAN, W. C., EATON, N. K., BRYAN, J. D., & ROSSE, R. L. (1983). Validity of army recruiter behavioral assessment: Does the assessor make a difference? *Journal of Applied Psychology, 68,* 415–419.

BOUDREAU, J. W. (1983a). Economic considerations in estimating the utility of human resource productivity improvement programs. *Personnel Psychology, 36,* 551–576.

BOUDREAU, J. W. (1983b). Effects of employee flows on utility analysis of human resource productivity improvement programs. *Journal of Applied Psychology, 68,* 396–406.

BOUDREAU, J. W., & BERGER, C. J. (1985). Decision-theoretic utility analysis applied to employee separations and acquisitions [Monograph]. *Journal of Applied Psychology, 70,* 581–612.

BOUDREAU, J. W., & RYNES, S. L. (1985). Role of recruitment in staffing utility analysis. *Journal of Applied Psychology, 70,* 354–366.

BOWNAS, D. A., BOSSHARDT, M. J., & DONNELLY, L. F. (1985). A quantitative approach to evaluating training curriculum content sampling adequacy. *Personnel Psychology, 38,* 117–131.

BRAMEL, D., & FRIEND, R. (1981). Hawthorne, the myth of the docile worker, and class bias in psychology. *American Psychologist, 36,* 867–878.

BRAMEL, D., & FRIEND, R. (1982). Is industrial psychology none of Marxism's business? *American Psychologist, 37,* 860–862.

BRAYFIELD, A. H., & CROCKETT, W. H. (1955). Employee attitudes and employee performance. *Psychological Bulletin, 52,* 396–424.

BREAUGH, J. A. (1981). Predicting absenteeism from prior absenteeism and work attitudes. *Journal of Applied Psychology, 66,* 555–560.

BREAUGH, J. A. (1983). The 12-hour work day: Differing employee reactions. *Personnel Psychology, 36,* 277–288.

BRIEF, A. P. (1980). Peer assessment revisited: A brief comment on Kane and Lawler. *Psychological Bulletin, 88,* 78–79.

BRIEF, A. P., & ALDAG, R. J. (1975). Employee reactions to job characteristics: A constructive replication. *Journal of Applied Psychology, 60,* 182–186.

BRIEF, A. P., SCHULER, R. S., & VAN SELL, M. (1981). *Managing job stress.* Boston: Little, Brown.

BROADBENT, D. (1976). Noise and the details of experiments: A reply to Poulton. *Applied Ergonomics, 7,* 231–235.

BROADBENT, D. (1979). Human performance and noise. In C. Harris (ed.), *Handbook of noise control.* New York: McGraw-Hill.

BROCKHAUS, R. H., SR. (1980). Risk taking propensity of entrepreneurs. *Academy of Management Journal, 23,* 509–520.

BROGDEN, H. E. (1949). When testing pays off. *Personnel Psychology, 2,* 171–185.

BROGDEN, H. E., & TAYLOR, E. K. (1950). The dollar criterion—Applying the cost accounting concept to criterion construction. *Personnel Psychology, 3,* 133–154.

BROWN, E. M. (1968). Influence of training, method, and relationship on the halo effect. *Journal of Applied Psychology, 52,* 195–199.

BROWN, S. H. (1981). Validity generalization and situational moderation in the life insurance industry. *Journal of Applied Psychology, 66,* 664–670.

BRUMBACK, G. (1972). A reply to Kavanagh. *Personnel Psychology, 25,* 567–572.

BRYAN, W. L. (1904). Theory and practice. *Psychological Review, 11,* 71–82.

BRYAN, W. L., & HARTER, N. (1897). Studies in the physiology and psychology of the telegraphic language. *Psychological Review, 4,* 27–53.

BULLOCK, R. J., & SVYANTEK, D. J. (1985). Analyzing meta-analysis: Potential problems, an unsuccessful replication, and evaluation criteria. *Journal of Applied Psychology, 70,* 108–115.

BURKE, M. J. (1984). Validity generalization: A review and critique of the correlational model. *Personnel Psychology, 37,* 93–115.

BURKE, M. J., & FREDERICK, J. T. (1984). Two modified procedures for estimating standard deviations in utility analyses. *Journal of Applied Psychology, 69,* 482–489.

BUROS, O. K. (1974). *Tests in print II.* Highland Park, NJ: Gryphon Press.

BUROS, O. K. (ed.). (1978). *The eighth mental measurements yearbook.* Highland Park, NJ: Gryphon Press.

BUSCH, H. M. (1949). *Conference methods in industry.* New York: Harper and Brothers.

BUSSOM, R. S., LARSON, L. L., & VICARS, W. M. (1982). Unstructured, nonparticipant observation and the study of leaders' interpersonal contacts. In J. G. Hunt, U. Sekaran, & C. A. Schriesheim (eds.), *Leadership: Beyond establishment views.* Carbondale, IL: Southern Illinois University Press.

BUTLER, M. C., & JONES, A. P. (1979). Perceived leader behavior, individual characteristics, and injury occurrence in hazardous work environments. *Journal of Applied Psychology, 64,* 299–304.

BUTTERFIELD, D. A., & POWELL, G. N. (1981). Effect of group performance, leader sex, and rater sex on ratings of leader behavior. *Organizational Behavior and Human Performance, 28,* 129–141.

CAIN, P. S., & GREEN, B. S. (1983). Reliabilities of selected ratings available from the *Dictionary of occupational titles. Journal of Applied Psychology. 68,* 155–165.

CALDER, B. J. (1977). An attribution theory of leadership. In B. M. Staw & G. R. Salancik (eds.), *New directions in organizational behavior.* Chicago: St. Clair.

CALDER, B. J., & STAW, B. M. (1975). Self-perception of intrinsic and extrinsic motivation. *Journal of Personality and Social Psychology, 31,* 599–605.

CALDWELL, D. F., & O'REILLY, C. A., III. (1982a). Boundary spanning and individual performance: The impact of self-monitoring. *Journal of Applied Psychology, 67,* 124–127.

CALDWELL, D. F., & O'REILLY, C. A., III. (1982b). Task perceptions and job satisfaction: A question of causality. *Journal of Applied Psychology, 67,* 361–369.

CALDWELL, D. F., & SPIVEY, W. A. (1983). The relationship between recruiting source and employee success: An analysis by race. *Personnel Psychology, 36,* 67–72.

CALLENDER, J. C., & OSBURN, H. G. (1981). Testing the constancy of validity with computer-generated sampling distributions of the multiplicative model variance estimate: Results for petroleum industry validation research. *Journal of Applied Psychology, 66,* 274–281.

CALLENDER, J. C., & OSBURN, H. G. (1982). Another view of progress in validity generalization: Reply to Schmidt, Hunter, and Pearlman. *Journal of Applied Psychology, 67,* 846–852.

CALLENDER, J. C., OSBURN, H. G., GREENER, J. M., & ASHWORTH, S. (1982). Multiplicative validity generalization model: Accuracy of estimates as a function of sample size and mean, variance, and shape of the distribution of true validities. *Journal of Applied Psychology, 67,* 859–867.

CAMERON, K. (1980). Critical questions in assessing organizational effectiveness. *Organizational Dynamics, 9,* 66–80.

CAMERON, K. S. (1981). Domains of organizational effectiveness in colleges and universities. *Academy of Management Journal, 24,* 25–47.

CAMERON, K. (1982). The relationship between faculty unionism and organizational effectiveness. *Academy of Management Journal, 25,* 6–24.

CAMERON, K. S., & WHETTEN, D. A. (1981). Perceptions of organizational effectiveness over organizational life cycles. *Administrative Science Quarterly, 26,* 525–544.

CAMPBELL, D. T., & FISKE, D. W. (1959). Convergent and discriminant validation by the multitrait–multimethod matrix. *Psychological Bulletin, 56,* 81–105.

CAMPBELL, D. T., & STANLEY, J. C. (1963). *Experimental and quasi-experimental designs for research.* Chicago: Rand McNally.

CAMPBELL, J. P. (1976). Psychometric theory. In M. D. Dunnette (ed.), *Handbook of industrial and organizational psychology.* Chicago: Rand McNally.

CAMPBELL, J. P. (1982). Editorial: Some remarks from the outgoing editor. *Journal of Applied Psychology, 67,* 691–700.

CAMPBELL, J. P., DUNNETTE, M. D., ARVEY, R. D., & HELLERVIK, L. V. (1973). The development and evaluation of behaviorally based rating scales. *Journal of Applied Psychology, 57,* 15–22.

CAMPBELL, J. P., DUNNETTE, M. D., LAWLER, E. E., III, & WEICK, K. E., JR. (1970). *Managerial behavior, performance, and effectiveness.* New York: McGraw-Hill.

CAMPBELL, J. P., & PRITCHARD, R. D. (1976). Motivation theory in industrial and organizational psychology. In M. D. Dunnette (ed.), *Handbook of industrial and organizational psychology.* Chicago: Rand McNally.

CAMPION, J. E. (1972). Work sampling for personnel selection. *Journal of Applied Psychology, 56,* 40–44.

CAMPION, M. A. (1983). Personnel selection for physically demanding jobs: Review and recommendations. *Personnel Psychology, 36,* 527–550.

CAMPION, M. A., & THAYER, P. W. (1985). Development and field evaluation of an interdisciplinary measure of job design. *Journal of Applied Psychology, 70,* 29–43.

CARDY, R. L., & KEHOE, J. F. (1984). Rater selective attention ability and appraisal effectiveness: The effect of a cognitive style on the accuracy of differentiation among ratees. *Journal of Applied Psychology, 69,* 589–594.

Careers in psychology (4th ed.). (1980). Washington, DC: American Psychological Associaton.

CARROLL, S. J., JR., PAINE, F. T., & IVANCEVICH, J. M. (1972). The relative effectiveness of training methods—Expert opinion and research. *Personnel Psychology, 25,* 495–510.

CARROLL, S. J., & SCHNEIER, C. E. (1982). *Performance appraisal and review systems: The identification, measurement, and development of performance in organizations.* Glenview, IL: Scott, Foresman.

CASCIO, W. F. (1982). *Costing human resources: The financial impact of behavior in organizations.* Boston: Kent.

CASS, E. L., & ZIMMER, F. G. (eds.). (1975). *Man*

and work in society. New York: Van Nostrand Reinhold.

CASTRO, J. (1986, March 17). Battling the enemy within. *Time,* pp. 52–61.

CHACKO, T. I. (1982). Women and equal employment opportunity: Some unintended effects. *Journal of Applied Psychology, 67,* 119–123.

CHACKO, T. I. (1983). Job and life satisfactions: A causal analysis of their relationships. *Academy of Management Journal, 26,* 163–169.

CHADWICK-JONES, J. K., NICHOLSON, N., & BROWN, C. (1982). *The social psychology of absenteeism.* New York: Praeger.

CHAPANIS, A. (1976). Engineering psychology. In M. D. Dunnette (ed.), *Handbook of industrial and organizational psychology.* Chicago: Rand McNally.

CHELOHA, R. S., & FARR, J. L. (1980). Absenteeism, job involvement, and job satisfaction in an organizational setting. *Journal of Applied Psychology, 65,* 467–473.

CHERRINGTON, D. J., REITZ, H. J., & SCOTT, W. E. (1971). Effects of contingent and non-contingent reward on the relationship between satisfaction and task performance. *Journal of Applied Psychology, 55,* 532–536.

CHHOKAR, J. S., & WALLIN, J. A. (1984). A field study of the effect of feedback frequency on performance. *Journal of Applied Psychology, 69,* 524–530.

CHONKO, L. B. (1982). The relationship of span of control to sales representatives' experienced role conflict and role ambiguity. *Academy of Management Journal, 25,* 452–456.

CHRISTAL, R. E. (1974, January). *The United States Air Force occupational research project* (AFHRL-TR-73-75). Brooks Air Force Base, TX: Air Force Systems Command.

CLEVELAND, J. N., & LANDY, F. J. (1983). The effects of person and job stereotypes on two personnel decisions. *Journal of Applied Psychology, 68,* 609–619.

COBB, A. T. (1980). Informal influence in the formal organization: Perceived sources of power among work unit peers. *Academy of Management Journal, 23,* 155–161.

COHEN, B., MOSES, J. L., & BYHAM, W. C. (1974). *The validity of assessment centers: A literature review.* Pittsburgh, PA: Development Dimensions Press.

COLARELLI, S. M. (1984). Methods of communication and mediating processes in realistic job previews. *Journal of Applied Psychology, 69,* 633–642.

COLLIGAN, M. J., FROCKT, I. J., & TASTO, D. L. (1979). Frequency of sickness absence and work-site clinic visits among nurses as a function of shift. *Applied Ergonomics, 10,* 79–85.

COLLINS, A., & ADAMS, M. J. (1977). Comparison of two teaching strategies in computer-assisted instruction. *Contemporary Educational Psychology, 2,* 133–148.

CONNOLLY, T., CONLON, E. J., & DEUTSCH, S. J. (1980). Organizational effectiveness: A multiple-constituency approach. *Academy of Management Review, 5,* 211–217.

COOK, J. D., HEPWORTH, S. J., WALL, T. D., & WARR, P. B. (1981). *The experience of work.* New York: Academic Press.

COOK, T. D., & CAMPBELL, D. T. (1979). *Quasi-experimentation: Design and analysis issues for field settings.* Chicago: Rand McNally.

COOKE, W. N., & BLUMENSTOCK, M. W. (1979). The determinants of occupational injury severity: The case of Maine sawmills. *Journal of Safety Research, 11*(3), 59–67.

COOPER, C. L., & PAYNE, R. (eds.) (1978). *Stress at work.* New York: Wiley.

COREN, S., PORAC, C., & WARD, L. M. (1979). *Sensation and perception.* New York: Academic Press.

CORNELIUS, E. T., III, DeNISI, A. S., & BLENCOE, A. G. (1984). Expert and naive raters using the PAQ: Does it matter? *Personnel Psychology, 37,* 453–464.

CORNELIUS, E. T., III, & LANE, F. B. (1984). The power motive and managerial success in a professionally oriented service industry organization. *Journal of Applied Psychology, 69,* 32–39.

CORNELIUS, E. T., III, & LYNESS, K. S. (1980). A comparison of holistic and decomposed judgment strategies in job analyses by job incumbents. *Journal of Applied Psychology, 65,* 155–163.

CORNELIUS, E. T., III, SCHMIDT, F. L., & CARRON, T. J. (1984). Job classification approaches and the implementation of validity generalization results. *Personnel Psychology, 37,* 247–260.

COWLEY, W. H. (1928). Three distinctions in the study of leaders. *Journal of Abnormal and Social Psychology, 23,* 144–157.

CRONBACH, L. (1951). Coefficient alpha and the internal structure of tests. *Psychometrika, 16,* 297–334.

CRONBACH, L. J. (1957). The two disciplines of scientific psychology. *American Psychologist, 12,* 671–684.

CRONBACH, L. J. (1975). Beyond the two disciplines of scientific psychology. *American Psychologist, 30,* 116–127.

CRONBACH, L. J., & GLESER, G. C. (1965). *Psycho-*

logical tests and personnel decisions. Urbana, IL: University of Illinois.

CRONSHAW, S. F., & ALEXANDER, R. A. (1985). One answer to the demand for accountability: Selection utility as an investment decision. *Organizational Behavior and Human Decision Processes, 35,* 102–118.

CUNNINGHAM, J. W., BOESE, R. R., NEEB, R. W., & PASS, J. J. (1983). Systematically derived work dimensions: Factor analyses of the Occupation Analysis Inventory. *Journal of Applied Psychology, 68,* 232–252.

DACHLER, H. P. (1983). I/O psychology in Switzerland: New developments. *The Industrial-Organizational Psychologist, 20*(2), 50–56.

DACHLER, H. P., & WILPERT, B. (1978). Conceptual dimensions and boundaries of participation: A critical evaluation. *Administrative Science Quarterly, 23,* 1–39.

DALTON, D. R., KRACKHARDT, D. M., & PORTER, L. W. (1981). Functional turnover: An empirical assessment. *Journal of Applied Psychology, 66,* 716–721.

DALTON, D. R., & PERRY, J. L. (1981). Absenteeism and the collective bargaining agreement: An empirical test. *Academy of Management Journal, 24,* 425–431.

DALTON, D. R., & TODOR, W. D. (1979). Manifest needs of stewards: Propensity to file a grievance. *Journal of Applied Psychology, 64,* 654–659.

DALTON, D. R., & TODOR, W. D. (1982). Antecedents of grievance filing behavior: Attitude/behavioral consistency and the union steward. *Academy of Management Journal, 25,* 158–169.

DANIEL, T. L., & ESSER, J. K. (1980). Intrinsic motivation as influenced by rewards, task interest, and task structure. *Journal of Applied Psychology, 65,* 566–573.

DANISH, S. J., & SMYER, M. A. (1981). Unintended consequences of requiring a license to help. *American Psychologist, 36,* 13–21.

DANSEREAU, F., GRAEN, G., & HAGA, W. J. (1975). A vertical dyad linkage approach to leadership in formal organizations. *Organizational Behavior and Human Performance, 13,* 46–78. ___

DAVIS, K. R., JR. (1984). A longitudinal analysis of biographical subgroups using Owens' Developmental-Integrative Model. *Personnel Psychology, 37,* 1–14.

DEAN, R. A., & WANOUS, J. P. (1984). Effects of realistic job previews on hiring bank tellers. *Journal of Applied Psychology, 69,* 61–68.

DEAUX, K., & EMSWILLER, T. (1974). Explanation of successful performance: What's skill for the male is luck for the female. *Journal of Personality and Social Psychology, 29,* 80–85.

DECI, E. L. (1972). The effects of contingent and noncontingent rewards and controls on intrinsic motivation. *Organizational Behavior and Human Performance, 8,* 217–229.

DECI, E. L. (1975). *Intrinsic motivation.* New York: Plenum.

DECI, E. L. (1976). Notes on the theory and metatheory of intrinsic motivation. *Organizational Behavior and Human Performance, 15,* 130–145.

DECKER, P. J. (1979). Modesty and caution in reviewing behavior modeling: A reply to McGehee and Tullar. *Personnel Psychology, 32,* 399–400.

DECOTIIS, T. A., & LELOUARN, J. (1981). A predictive study of voting behavior in a representation election using union instrumentality and work perceptions. *Organizational Behavior and Human Performance, 27,* 103–118.

DEMARIA, A. T. (1974). *The supervisor's handbook on maintaining non-union status.* New York: Executive Enterprises Publications.

DENISI, A. S., CAFFERTY, T. P., & MEGLINO, B. M. (1984). A cognitive view of the performance appraisal process: A model and research propositions. *Organizational Behavior and Human Performance, 33,* 360–396.

DENMARK, F. L. (1980). Psyche: From rocking the cradle to rocking the boat. *American Psychologist, 35,* 1057–1065.

DEREAMER, R. (1980). *Modern safety and health technology.* New York: Wiley.

DESSLER, G. (1972). A test of the path-goal theory of leadership. *Proceedings of the annual meeting of the Academy of Management,* 178–181.

DICKINSON, T. L., & ZELLINGER, P. M. (1980). A comparison of the behaviorally anchored rating and mixed standard scale formats. *Journal of Applied Psychology, 65,* 147–154.

DIPBOYE, R. L., & FLANAGAN, M. F. (1979). Research settings in industrial and organizational psychology: Are findings in the field more generalizable than in the laboratory? *American Psychologist, 34,* 141–150.

DISTEFANO, M. K., JR., PRYER, M. W., & ERFFMEYER, R. C. (1983). Application of content validity methods to the development of a job-related performance rating criterion. *Personnel Psychology, 36,* 621–631.

DOBBINS, G. H., PENCE, E. C., ORBAN, J. A., & SGRO, J. A. (1983). The effects of sex of the leader and sex of the subordinate on the use of organizational control policy. *Organizational Behavior and Human Performance, 32,* 325–343.

DORFMAN, P. W., & HOWELL, J. P. (1984). Production sharing in the Mexican Maquiladora industry: A challenge for I/O psychology. *The Industrial-Organizational Psychologist, 22*(1), 20–26.

DOSSETT, D. L., & HULVERSHORN, P. (1983). Increasing technical training efficiency: Peer training via computer-assisted instruction. *Journal of Applied Psychology, 68*, 552–558.

DOVERSPIKE, D., & BARRETT, G. V. (1984). An internal bias analysis of a job evaluation instrument. *Journal of Applied Psychology, 69*, 648–662.

DOVERSPIKE, D., CARLISI, A. M., BARRETT, G. V., & ALEXANDER, R. A. (1983). Generalizability analysis of a point-method job evaluation instrument. *Journal of Applied Psychology, 68*, 476–483.

DOWELL, B. E., & WEXLEY, K. N. (1978). Development of a work behavior taxonomy for first-line supervisors. *Journal of Applied Psychology, 63*, 563–572.

DOWNEY, H. K., SHERIDAN, J. E., & SLOCUM, J. W., JR. (1975). Analysis of relationships among leader behavior, subordinate job performance and satisfaction: A path goal approach. *Academy of Management Journal, 18*, 253–262.

DRASGOW, F., & KANG, T. (1984). Statistical power of differential validity and differential prediction analyses for detecting measurement nonequivalence. *Journal of Applied Psychology, 69*, 498–508.

DREHER, G. F., & DOUGHERTY, T. W. (1980). Turnover and competition for expected job openings: An exploratory analysis. *Academy of Management Journal, 23*, 766–772.

DRORY, A. (1982). Individual differences in boredom proneness and task effectiveness at work. *Personnel Psychology, 35*, 141–151.

DUBIN, R. (1956). Industrial workers' worlds: A study of "Central Life Interests" of industrial workers. *Social Problems, 3*, 131–142.

DUBOIS, P. H. (1970). *A history of psychological testing.* Boston: Allyn & Bacon.

DUNHAM, R. B. (1976). The measurement and dimensionality of job characteristics. *Journal of Applied Psychology, 61*, 404–409.

DUNHAM, R. B. (1977). Shift work: A review and theoretical analysis. *Academy of Management Review, 2*, 626–634.

DUNHAM, R. B. (1979). Job design and redesign. In S. Kerr (ed.), *Organizational behavior.* Columbus, OH: Grid.

DUNHAM, R. B., ALDAG, R. J., & BRIEF, A. P. (1977). Dimensionality of task design as measured by the Job Diagnostic Survey. *Academy of Management Journal, 20*, 209–221.

DUNHAM, R. B., & HAWK, D. L. (1977). The four-day/forty-hour week: Who wants it? *Academy of Management Journal, 20*, 644–655.

DUNNETTE, M. D. (1963). A note on *the* criterion. *Journal of Applied Psychology, 47*, 251–254.

DUNNETTE, M. D. (1972). *Validity study results for jobs relevant to the petroleum refining industry.* Washington, DC: American Petroleum Institute.

DUNNETTE, M. D. (ed.). (1973). *Work and nonwork in the year 2001.* Monterey, CA: Brooks/Cole.

DUNNETTE, M. D. (ed.). (1976). *Handbook of industrial and organizational psychology.* Chicago: Rand McNally.

DUNNETTE, M. D., & BORMAN, W. C. (1979). Personnel selection and classification systems. *Annual Review of Psychology, 30*, 477–525.

DUNNETTE, M. D., & KIRCHNER, W. K. (1965). *Psychology applied to industry.* Englewood Cliffs, NJ: Prentice-Hall.

DVORAK, A., MARRICK, N., DEALEY, W., & FORD, G. (1936). *Typewriting behavior: Psychology applied to teaching and learning typewriter.* New York: American Book Co.

EAGLY, A. H. (1983). Gender and social influence: A social psychological analysis. *American Psychologist, 38*, 971–981.

EAGLY, A. H., WOOD, W., & CHAIKEN, S. (1978). Causal inferences about communicators and their effect on opinion change. *Journal of Personality and Social Psychology, 36*, 424–435.

EATON, N. K., WING, H., & MITCHELL, K. J. (1985). Alternate methods of estimating the dollar value of performance. *Personnel Psychology, 38*, 27–40.

EBERHARDT, B. J., & MUCHINSKY, P. M. (1984). Structural validation of Holland's hexagonal model: Vocational classification through the use of biodata. *Journal of Applied Psychology, 69*, 174–181.

EDEN, D. (1985). Team development: A true field experiment at three levels of rigor. *Journal of Applied Psychology, 70*, 94–100.

EDEN, D., & LEVIATAN, U. (1975). Implicit leadership theory as a determinant of the factor structure underlying supervisory behavior scales. *Journal of Applied Psychology, 60*, 736–741.

EDEN, D., & SHANI, A. B. (1982). Pygmalion goes to boot camp: Expectancy, leadership, and trainee performance. *Journal of Applied Psychology, 67*, 194–199.

ELLSON, D. G., & ELLSON, E. C. (1953). Historical note on the rating scale. *Psychological Bulletin, 50*, 383–384.

EMBRETSON (WHITELY), S. (1983). Construct validity: Construct representation versus nomothetic span. *Psychological Bulletin, 93*, 179–197.

EQUAL EMPLOYMENT OPPORTUNITY COMMISSION (EEOC). (1978). Uniform guidelines on employee selection procedures. *Federal Register, 43,* 38290–38309.

ESKILSON, A., & WILEY, M. G. (1976). Sex composition and leadership in small groups. *Sociometry, 39,* 183–194.

Ethical principles of psychologists. (1981). *American Psychologist, 36,* 633–638.

EVANS, M. G. (1973). Notes on the impact of flextime in a large insurance company: I. Reactions of nonsupervisory employees. *Occupational Psychology, 47,* 237–240.

EWEN, R. B., SMITH, P. C., HULIN, C. L., & LOCKE, E. A. (1966). An empirical test of the Herzberg two-factor theory. *Journal of Applied Psychology, 50,* 544–550.

FALEY, R. H., KLEIMAN, L. S., & LENGNICK-HALL, M. L. (1984). Age discrimination and personnel psychology: A review and synthesis of the legal literature with implications for future research. *Personnel Psychology, 37,* 327–350.

FALEY, R. H., & SUNDSTROM, E. (1985). Content respresentativeness: An empirical method of evaluation. *Journal of Applied Psychology, 70,* 567–571.

FAUCHEUX, C., AMADO, G., & LAURENT, A. (1982). Organizational development and change. *Annual Review of Psychology, 33,* 343–370.

FELDMAN, J. (1982). Ideology without data. *American Psychologist, 37,* 857–858.

FERRIS, G. R., & GILMORE, D. C. (1985). A methodological note on job complexity indexes. *Journal of Applied Psychology, 70,* 225–227.

FIEDLER, F. E. (1964). A contingency model of leader effectiveness. In L. Berkowitz (ed.), *Advances in experimental social psychology* (vol. 1). New York: Academic Press.

FIEDLER, F. E. (1965). Engineer the job to fit the manager. *Harvard Business Review, 43,* 115–122.

FIEDLER, F. E. (1967). *A theory of leadership effectiveness.* New York: McGraw-Hill.

FIEDLER, F. (1972). Personality, motivational systems and the behavior of high and low LPC persons. *Human Relations, 25,* 391–412.

FIEDLER, F. E., CHEMERS, M. M., & MAHAR, L. (1976). *Improving leadership effectiveness: The LEADER MATCH concept.* New York: Wiley.

FIEDLER, F. E., & LEISTER, A. F. (1977). Leader intelligence and task performance: A test of a multiple screen model. *Organizational Behavior and Human Performance, 20,* 1–14.

FIEDLER, F. E., & MAHAR, L. (1979). The effectiveness of contingency model training: A review of the validation of LEADER MATCH. *Personnel Psychology, 32,* 45–62.

FIEDLER, F. E., POTTER, E. H., III, ZAIS, M. M., &

KNOWLTON, W. A., JR. (1979). Organizational stress and the use and misuse of managerial intelligence and experience. *Journal of Applied Psychology, 64,* 635–647.

FIELD, R. H. G. (1979). A critique of the Vroom–Yetton contingency model of leadership behavior. *Academy of Management Review, 4,* 249–257.

FIELD, R. H. G. (1982). A test of the Vroom–Yetton normative model of leadership. *Journal of Applied Psychology, 67,* 523–532.

FINE, B. J., & KORBRICK, J. L. (1978). Effects of altitude and heat on complex cognitive tasks. *Human Factors, 20,* 115–122.

FINKLE, R. B. (1976). Managerial assessment centers. In M. D. Dunnette (ed.), *Handbook of industrial and organizational psychology.* Chicago: Rand McNally.

FINN, R. H. (1972). Effects of some variations in rating scale characteristics on the means and reliabilities of ratings. *Educational and Psychological Measurement, 32,* 255–265.

FLANAGAN, J. C. (1954). The critical incident technique. *Psychological Bulletin, 51,* 327–358.

FLANAGAN, M. F., & DIPBOYE, R. L. (1981). Research settings in industrial and organizational psychology: Facts, fallacies, and the future. *Personnel Psychology, 34,* 37–47.

FLEISHMAN, E. A. (1953). The measurement of leadership attitudes in industry. *Journal of Applied Psychology, 37,* 153–158.

FLEISHMAN, E. A. (1957a). A leader behavior description for industry. In R. A. Stogdill & A. E. Coons (eds.), *Leader behavior: Its description and measurement.* Columbus, OH: Bureau of Business Research, Ohio State University.

FLEISHMAN, E. A. (1957b). The leadership opinion questionnaire. In R. A. Stogdill & A. E. Coons (eds.), *Leader behavior: Its description and measurement.* Columbus, OH: Bureau of Business Research, Ohio State University.

FLEISHMAN, E. A. (1975). Toward a taxonomy of human performance. *American Psychologist, 30,* 1127–1149.

FLEISHMAN, E. A., & FRUCHTER, B. (1960). Factor structure and predictability of successive stages of learning Morse code. *Journal of Applied Psychology, 44,* 97–101.

FLEISHMAN, E. A., & HARRIS, E. F. (1962). Patterns of leadership behavior related to employee grievances and turnover. *Personnel Psychology, 15,* 43–56.

FLEISHMAN, E. A., HARRIS, E. F., & BURTT, H. E. (1955). *Leadership and supervision in industry.* Columbus, OH: Bureau of Educational Research, Ohio State University.

FORD, J. K., & WROTEN, S. P. (1984). Introducing new methods for conducting training evaluation and for linking training evaluation to program redesign. *Personnel Psychology, 37,* 651–665.

FORSYTHE, S., DRAKE, M. F., & COX, C. E. (1985). Influence of applicant's dress on interviewer's selection decisions. *Journal of Applied Psychology, 70,* 374–378.

FOSTER, L. W., LATACK, J. C., & REINDL, L. J. (1979). *Effects and promises of the shortened workweek.* Paper presented at the 39th Annual Meeting of the Academy of Management, Atlanta, GA.

FOTI, R. J., FRASER, S. L., & LORD, R. G. (1982). Effects of leadership labels and prototypes on perceptions of political leaders. *Journal of Applied Psychology, 67,* 326–333.

FRANKE, R. H., & KAUL, J. D. (1978). The Hawthorne experiments: First statistical interpretation. *American Sociological Review, 43,* 623–643.

FREDERIKSEN, N. (1968). *Organization climates and administrative performance.* Princeton, NJ: Educational Testing Service.

FREEBERG, N. E. (1969). Relevance of rater–ratee acquaintance in the validity and reliability of ratings. *Journal of Applied Psychology, 53,* 518–524.

FRENCH, J. R. P., & CAPLAN, R. D. (1972). Organizational stress and individual strain. In A. J. Morrow (ed.), *The failure of success.* New York: AMACOM.

FRENCH, J. R. P., & RAVEN, B. (1959). The bases of social power. In D. Cartwright (ed.), *Studies in social power.* Ann Arbor, MI: Institute for Social Research, University of Michigan.

FRIEDMAN, H. S. (1983). On shutting one's eyes to face validity. *Psychological Bulletin, 94,* 185–187.

FRIEND, R., & BRAMEL, D. (1982). More Harvard humbug. *American Psychologist, 37,* 1399–1401.

FROMM, E. (1941). *Escape from freedom.* New York: Farrar & Rinehart.

FRY, L. W., & GREENFELD, S. (1980). An examination of attitudinal differences between policewomen and policemen. *Journal of Applied Psychology, 65,* 123–126.

FUKAMI, C. V., & LARSON, E. W. (1984). Commitment to company and union: Parallel models. *Journal of Applied Psychology, 69,* 367–371.

FULK, J., & WENDLER, E. R. (1982). Dimensionality of leader–subordinate interactions: A path-goal investigation. *Organizational Behavior and Human Performance, 30,* 241–264.

FUSILIER, M. R., & HOYER, W. D. (1980). Variables affecting perceptions of invasion of privacy in a personnel selection situation. *Journal of Applied Psychology, 65,* 623–626.

GAITO, J. (1980). Measurement scales and statistics: Resurgence of an old misconception. *Psychological Bulletin, 87,* 564–567.

GALBRAITH, J. R. (1977). *Organization design.* Reading, MA: Addison-Wesley.

GALTON, F. (1869). *Hereditary genius: An inquiry into its laws and consequences.* London: Macmillan.

GANSTER, D. C., MAYES, B. T., SIME, W. E., & THARP, G. D. (1982). Managing organizational stress: A field experiment. *Journal of Applied Psychology, 67,* 533–542.

GARLAND, H. (1984). Relation of effort–performance expectancy to performance in goal-setting experiments. *Journal of Applied Psychology, 69,* 79–84.

GARRETT, H. E., & SCHNECK, M. R. (1933). *Psychological tests, methods, and results.* New York: Harper and Brothers.

GAUDET, F. J. (1963). *Solving the problems of employee absence.* New York: American Management Associations.

GAUDREAU, P. A. (1975). Investigation of sex differences across job levels. *Dissertation Abstracts International, 36,* 1957B.

GECHMAN, A. S., & WIENER, Y. (1975). Job involvement and satisfaction as related to mental health and personal time devoted to work. *Journal of Applied Psychology, 60,* 521–523.

GEORGOPOULOS, B. S., MAHONEY, G. M., & JONES, N. W. (1957). A path-goal approach to productivity. *Journal of Applied Psychology, 41,* 345–353.

GHISELLI, E. E. (1956). Differentiation of individuals in terms of their predictability. *Journal of Applied Psychology, 40,* 374–377.

GHISELLI, E. E. (1964). *Theory of psychological measurement.* New York: McGraw-Hill.

GHISELLI, E. E. (1966). *The validity of occupational aptitude tests.* New York: Wiley.

GHISELLI, E. E. (1973). The validity of aptitude tests in personnel selection. *Personnel Psychology, 23,* 461–478.

GHISELLI, E. E., & BROWN, C. W. (1955). *Personnel and industrial psychology* (2nd ed.). New York: McGraw-Hill.

GHISELLI, E. E., & HAIRE, M. (1960). The validation of selection tests in the light of the dynamic character of criteria. *Personnel Psychology, 13,* 225–231.

GIFFORD, R., NG, C. F., & WILKINSON, M. (1985). Nonverbal cues in the employment interview: Links between applicant qualities and interviewer judgments. *Journal of Applied Psychology, 70,* 729–736.

GILBRETH, F. B. (1919). *Applied motion study.* New York: Macmillan.

GILMER, B. v. H. (1966). *Industrial psychology* (2nd ed.). New York: McGraw-Hill.

GINTNER, G., & LINDSKOLD, S. (1975). Rate of participation and expertise as factors influencing leader choice. *Journal of Personality and Social Psychology, 32,* 1085–1089.

GLASER, E. M., & TAYLOR, S. H. (1973). Factors influencing the success of applied research. *American Psychologist, 28,* 140–146.

GLASS, G. V. (1976). Primary, secondary, and meta-analysis of research. *Educational Research, 5,* 3–8.

GOLDMAN, M., & FRAAS, L. A. (1965). The effects of leader selection on group performance. *Sociometry, 28,* 82–88.

GOLDSTEIN, A. P. (1981). *Psychological skill training: The structured learning technique.* New York: Pergamon Press.

GOLDSTEIN, A. P., & SORCHER, M. (1974). *Changing supervisor behavior.* New York: Pergamon Press.

GOLDSTEIN, I. L. (1980). Training in work organizations. *Annual Review of Psychology, 31,* 229–272.

GOLDSTEIN, I. L. (1986). *Training in organizations: Needs assessment, development, and evaluation* (2nd ed.). Pacific Grove, CA: Brooks/Cole.

GOLEMBIEWSKI, R. T., BILLINGSLEY, K. R., & YEAGER, S. (1976). Measuring change and persistence in human affairs: Types of change generated by OD designs. *Journal of Applied Behavioral Science, 12,* 133–157.

GOLEMBIEWSKI, R. T., HILLES, R., & KAGNO, M. S. (1974). A longitudinal study of flexitime effects: Some consequences of an OD structural intervention. *Journal of Applied Behavioral Science, 10,* 503–531.

GOLEMBIEWSKI, R. T., & PROEHL, C. W. (1978). A survey of the empirical literature on flexible workhours: Character and consequences of a major intervention. *Academy of Management Review, 3,* 837–853.

GOMEZ-MEJIA, L. R., & BALKIN, D. B. (1984). Faculty satisfaction with pay and other job dimensions under union and nonunion conditions. *Academy of Management Journal, 27,* 591–602.

GOMEZ-MEJIA, L. R., PAGE, R. C., & TORNOW, W. W. (1982). A comparison of the practical utility of traditional, statistical, and hybrid job evaluation approaches. *Academy of Management Journal, 25,* 790–809.

GOODMAN, P. S. (1969). Hiring and training the hardcore unemployed: A problem in system definition. *Human Organization, 28,* 259–269.

GOODMAN, P. S. (1974). An examination of referents used in the evaluation of pay. *Organizational Behavior and Human Performance, 12,* 170–195.

GORDON, F., & STROBER, M. (1975). *Bringing women into management.* New York: McGraw-Hill.

GORDON, J. B., AKMAN, A., & BROOKS, M. L. (1971). *Industrial accident statistics: A re-examination.* New York: Praeger.

GORDON, L. V., & MEDLUND, F. F. (1965). The cross-group stability of peer rating of leadership potential. *Personnel Psychology, 18,* 173–177.

GORDON, M. E., KLEIMAN, L. S., & HANIE, C. A. (1978). Industrial-organizational psychology: Open thy ears O house of Israel. *American Psychologist, 33,* 893–905.

GORDON, M. E., & MILLER, S. J. (1984). Grievances: A review of research and practice. *Personnel Psychology, 37,* 117–146.

GORDON, M. E., & NURICK, A. J. (1981). Psychological approaches to the study of unions and union–management relations. *Psychological Bulletin, 90,* 293–306.

GORDON, M. E., PHILPOT, J. W., BURT, R. E., THOMPSON, C. A., & SPILLER, W. E. (1980). Commitment to the union: Development of a measure and an examination of its correlates [Monograph]. *Journal of Applied Psychology, 65,* 479–499.

GOUGH, H. G. (1984). A Managerial Potential scale for the California Psychological Inventory. *Journal of Applied Psychology, 69,* 233–240.

GOUGH, H. G. (1985). A Work Orientation scale for the California Psychological Inventory. *Journal of Applied Psychology, 70,* 505–513.

GRAEN, G. (1976). Role-making processes within complex organizations. In M. D. Dunnette (ed.), *Handbook of industrial and organizational psychology.* Chicago: Rand McNally.

GRAEN, G. B., LIDEN, R. C., & HOEL, W. (1982). Role of leadership in the employee withdrawal process. *Journal of Applied Psychology, 67,* 868–872.

GRAEN, G., NOVAK, M. A., & SOMMERKAMP, P. (1982). The effects of leader–member exchange and job design on productivity and satisfaction: Testing a dual attachment model. *Organizational Behavior and Human Performance, 30,* 109–131.

GRAEN, G., & SCHIEMANN, W. (1978). Leader–member agreement: A vertical dyad linkage approach. *Journal of Applied Psychology, 63,* 206–212.

GRAY, J. S. (1952). *Psychology in industry.* New York: McGraw-Hill.

GRAY, L. N., RICHARDSON, J. T., & MAYHEW, B. H. (1968). Influence attempts and effective power: A re-examination of the unsubstantiated hypothesis. *Sociometry, 31*, 245–258.

GREEN, S. G., & MITCHELL, T. R. (1979). Attributional processes of leaders in leader–member interactions. *Organizational Behavior and Human Performance, 23*, 429–458.

GREENBERG, C. I., THOMAS, J. M., DOSSETT, D. L., ROBINSON, R., DEMEUSE, K. P., & PENDERGRASS, M. (1981). Perceptions of industrial/organizational doctoral programs: A survey of APA Division 14 members. *Professional Psychology, 12*, 540–548.

GREENBERG, J., & ORNSTEIN, S. (1983). High status job title as compensation for underpayment: A test of equity theory. *Journal of Applied Psychology, 68*, 285–297.

GREENE, C. N. (1976, August). *Causal connections among cohesion, drive, goal acceptance, and productivity in work groups.* Paper presented at the meeting of the Academy of Management, Kansas City, MO.

GREENE, C. N., & PODSAKOFF, P. M. (1981). Effects of withdrawal of a performance-contingent reward on supervisory influence and power. *Academy of Management Journal, 24*, 527–542.

GRIFFIN, R. W. (1983). Objective and social sources of information in task redesign: A field experiment. *Administrative Science Quarterly, 28*, 184–200.

GRIGSBY, D. W., & BIGONESS, W. J. (1982). Effects of mediation and alternative forms of arbitration on bargaining behavior: A laboratory study. *Journal of Applied Psychology, 67*, 549–554.

GUILFORD, J. P. (1954). *Psychometric methods* (2nd ed.). New York: McGraw-Hill.

GUION, R. M. (1961). Criterion measurement and personnel judgments. *Personnel Psychology, 14*, 141–149.

GUION, R. M. (1965a). Industrial psychology as an academic discipline. *American Psychologist, 20*, 815–821.

GUION, R. M. (1965b). *Personnel testing.* New York: McGraw-Hill.

GUION, R. M. (1973). A note on organizational climate. *Organizational Behavior and Human Performance, 9*, 120–125.

GUION, R. M., & CRANNY, C. J. (1982). A note on concurrent and predictive validity designs: A critical reanalysis. *Journal of Applied Psychology, 67*, 239–244.

GUION, R. M., & IRONSON, G. H. (1983). Latent trait theory for organizational research. *Organizational Behavior and Human Performance, 31*, 54–87.

GUTENBERG, R. L., ARVEY, R. D., OSBURN, H. G., & JEANNERET, P. R. (1983). Moderating effects of decision-making/information-processing job dimensions on test validities. *Journal of Applied Psychology, 68*, 602–608.

GUZZO, R. A., JETTE, R. D., & KATZELL, R. A. (1985). The effects of psychologically based intervention programs on worker productivity: A meta-analysis. *Personnel Psychology, 38*, 275–291.

HACKETT, R. D., & GUION, R. M. (1985). A reevaluation of the absenteeism–job satisfaction relationship. *Organizational Behavior and Human Decision Processes, 35*, 340–381.

HACKMAN, J. R., & OLDHAM, G. R. (1975). Development of the Job Diagnostic Survey. *Journal of Applied Psychology, 60*, 159–170.

HACKMAN, J. R., & OLDHAM, G. R. (1976). Motivation through the design of work: Test of a theory. *Organizational Behavior and Human Performance, 16*, 250–279.

HACKMAN, J. R., OLDHAM, G., JANSON, R., & PURDY, K. (1975). A new strategy for job enrichment. *California Management Review, 17*(4), 57–71.

HACKMAN, J. R., & PORTER, L. W. (1968). Expectancy theory predictions of work effectiveness. *Organizational Behavior and Human Performance, 3*, 417–426.

HAKEL, M. D. (1986). Personnel selection and placement. *Annual Review of Psychology, 37*, 351–380.

HALL, D. T., & NOUGAIM, K. E. (1968). An examination of Maslow's need hierarchy in an organizational setting. *Organizational Behavior and Human Performance, 3*, 12–35.

HALPIN, A. W., & WINER, B. J. (1957). A factorial study of the leader behavior description. In R. M. Stogdill & A. E. Coons (eds.), *Leader behavior: Its description and measurement.* Columbus, OH: Bureau of Business Research, Ohio State University.

HAMMER, T. H., & BERMAN, M. (1981). The role of noneconomic factors in faculty union voting. *Journal of Applied Psychology, 66*, 415–421.

HAMMER, T. H., & DACHLER, P. (1973). *The process of supervision in the context of motivation theory.* (Tech. Rep. No. 3). College Park, MD: Department of Psychology, University of Maryland.

HAMNER, W. C., & SMITH, F. J. (1978) Work attitudes as predictors of unionization activity. *Journal of Applied Psychology, 63*, 415–421.

HANSER, L. M., & MUCHINSKY, P. M. (1980). Performance feedback information and organizational communication: Evidence of conceptual convergence. *Human Communication Research, 7,* 68–73.

HARVEY, B. H., & LUTHANS, F. (1979, Summer). Flexitime: An empirical analysis of its real meaning and impact. *MSU Business Topics,* 31–36.

HARVEY, J. H., & WEARY, G. (1984). Current issues in attribution theory and research. *Annual Review of Psychology, 35,* 427–459.

HARVEY, R. J., BILLINGS, R. S., & NILAN, K. J. (1985). Confirmatory factor analysis of the Job Diagnostic Survey: Good news and bad news. *Journal of Applied Psychology, 70,* 461–468.

HATFIELD, J. D., & HUSEMAN, R. C. (1982). Perceptual congruence about communication as related to satisfaction: Moderating effects of individual characteristics. *Academy of Management Journal, 25,* 349–358.

HAYNES, R. S., PINE, R. C., & FITCH, H. G. (1982). Reducing accident rates with organizational behavior modification. *Academy of Management Journal, 25,* 407–416.

HEILMAN, M. E. (1984). Information as a deterrent against sex discrimination: The effects of applicant sex and information type on preliminary employment decisions. *Organizational Behavior and Human Performance, 33,* 174–186.

HEILMAN, M. E., & HERLIHY, J. M. (1984). Affirmative action, negative reaction? Some moderating conditions. *Organizational Behavior and Human Performance, 33,* 204–213.

HEILMAN, M. E., HORNSTEIN, H. A., CAGE, J. H., & HERSCHLAG, J. K. (1984). Reactions to prescribed leader behavior as a function of role perspective: The case of the Vroom–Yetton model. *Journal of Applied Psychology, 69,* 50–60.

HEILMAN, M. E., & SARUWATARI, L. R. (1979). When beauty is beastly: The effects of appearance and sex on evaluations of job applicants for managerial and nonmanagerial jobs. *Organizational Behavior and Human Performance, 23,* 360–372.

HEILMAN, M. E., & STOPECK, M. H. (1985). Being attractive, advantage or disadvantage? Performance-based evaluations and recommended personnel actions as a function of appearance, sex, and job type. *Organizational Behavior and Human Decision Processes, 35,* 202–215.

HEMPHILL, J. K. (1949). The leader and his group. *Journal of Educational Research, 28,* 225–229, 245–246.

HEMPHILL, J. K., & COONS, A. E. (1957). Development of the Leader Behavior Description Questionnaire. In. R. M. Stogdill & A. E. Coons (eds.), *Leaders behavior: Its description and measurement.* Columbus, OH: Bureau of Business Research, Ohio State University.

HENEMAN, H. G., JR. (1973). Work and nonwork: Historical perspectives. In M. D. Dunnette (ed.), *Work and nonwork in the year 2001.* Pacific Grove, CA: Brooks/Cole.

HENEMAN, H. G., III. (1974). Comparisons of self- and superior ratings of managerial performance. *Journal of Applied Psychology, 59,* 638–642.

HENNIG, M., & JARDIM, A. (1977). *The managerial woman.* Garden City, NY: Anchor Press/ Doubleday.

HEROLD, D. M., & PARSONS, C. K. (1985). Assessing the feedback environment in work organizations: Development of the Job Feedback Survey. *Journal of Applied Psychology, 70,* 290–305.

HERZBERG, F. (1964). The motivation-hygiene concept and problems of manpower. *Personnel Administrator, 27,* 3–7.

HERZBERG, F. (1966). *Work and the nature of man.* Cleveland, OH: World.

HERZBERG, F., MAUSNER, B., PETERSON, R. O., & CAPWELL, D. F. (1957). *Job attitudes: Review of research and opinion.* Pittsburgh, PA: Psychological Service of Pittsburgh.

HERZBERG, F., MAUSNER, B., & SNYDERMAN, B. (1959). *The motivation to work.* New York: Wiley.

HICKS, W. D., & KLIMOSKI, R. J. (1981). The impact of flexitime on employee attitudes. *Academy of Management Journal, 24,* 333–341.

HILGARD, E. R., & BOWER, G. H. (1966). *Theories of learning* (3rd ed.). New York: Appleton-Century-Crofts.

HINRICHS, J. R. (1976). Personnel training. In M. D. Dunnette (ed.), *Handbook of industrial and organizational psychology.* Chicago: Rand McNally.

HINTON, B. L., & BARROW, J. C. (1975). The superior's reinforcing behavior as a function of reinforcements received. *Organizational Behavior and Human Performance, 14,* 123–149.

HOBERT, R. D., & DUNNETTE, M. D. (1967). Development of moderator variables to enhance the prediction of managerial effectiveness. *Journal of Applied Psychology, 51,* 50–64.

HOCKEY, G. (1978). Effects of noise on human work efficiency. In D. May (ed.), *Handbook of noise assessment.* New York: Van Nostrand Reinhold.

HOGAN, J. (1985). Tests for success in diver training. *Journal of Applied Psychology, 70,* 219–224.

HOGAN, J. C., & FLEISHMAN, E. A. (1979). An index of the physical effort required in human task performance. *Journal of Applied Psychology, 64,* 197–204.

HOGAN, J., HOGAN, R., & BUSCH, C. M. (1984). How to measure service orientation. *Journal of Applied Psychology, 69,* 167–173.

HOGAN, J. C., OGDEN, G. D., GEBHARDT, D. L., & FLEISHMAN, E. A. (1980). Reliability and validity of methods for evaluating perceived physical effort. *Journal of Applied Psychology, 65,* 672–679.

HOLLANDER, E. P., FALLON, B. J., & EDWARDS, M. T. (1977). Some aspects of influence and acceptability for appointed and elected group leaders. *Journal of Psychology, 95,* 289–296.

HOLLANDER, E. P., & JULIAN, J. W. (1970). Studies in leader legitimacy, influence, and innovation. In L. Berkowitz (ed.), *Advances in experimental social psychology* (vol. 5). New York: Academic Press.

HOPPOCK, R. (1935). *Job satisfaction.* New York: Harper and Brothers.

HOUGH, L. M. (1984). Development and evaluation of the "accomplishment record" method of selecting and promoting professionals. *Journal of Applied Psychology, 69,* 135–146.

HOUGH, L. M., KEYES, M. A., & DUNNETTE, M. D. (1983). An evaluation of three "alternative" selection procedures. *Personnel Psychology, 36,* 261–276.

HOUSE, R. J. (1971). A path goal theory of leader effectiveness. *Administrative Science Quarterly, 16,* 321–338.

HOUSE, R. J. (1977). A 1976 theory of charismatic leadership. In J. G. Hunt & L. L. Larson (eds.), *Leadership: The cutting edge.* Carbondale, IL: Southern Illinois University Press.

HOUSE, R. J., & BAETZ, M. L. (1979). Leadership: Some empirical generalizations and new research directions. In B. M. Staw (ed.), *Research in organizational behavior* (vol. 1). Greenwich, CT: JAI Press.

HOUSE, R. J., & DESSLER, G. (1974). The path goal theory of leadership: Some post hoc and a priori tests. In J. G. Hunt & L. L. Larson (eds.), *Contingency approaches to leadership.* Carbondale, IL: Southern Illinois University Press.

HOUSE, R. J., & FILLEY, A. C. (1971). Leadership style, hierarchical influence, and the satisfaction of subordinate role expectations: A test of Likert's influence proposition. *Journal of Applied Psychology, 55,* 422–432.

HOUSE, R. J., & MITCHELL, T. R. (1974). Path-goal theory of leadership. *Journal of Contemporary Business, 3,* 81–97.

HOWAT, G., & LONDON, M. (1980). Attributions of conflict management strategies in supervisor-subordinate dyads. *Journal of Applied Psychology, 65,* 172–175.

HOWELL, J. P., & DORFMAN, P. W. (1981). Substitutes for leadership: Test of a construct. *Academy of Management Journal, 24,* 714–728.

HOWELL, W. C., & DIPBOYE, R. L. (1986). *Essentials of industrial and organizational psychology* (3rd ed.). Chicago: Dorsey Press.

HOYT, C. (1941). Test reliability estimated by analysis of variance. *Psychometrika, 6,* 153–160.

HUGHES, J. L., & MCNAMARA, W. J. (1959). *Manual for the revised Programmer Aptitude Test.* New York: Psychological Corporation.

HULIN, C. L., DRASGOW, F., & KOMOCAR, J. (1982). Applications of item response theory to analysis of attitude scale translations. *Journal of Applied Psychology, 67,* 818–825.

HULIN, C. L., DRASGOW, F., & PARSONS, C. K. (1983). *Item response theory: Application to psychological measurement.* Homewood, IL: Dow Jones-Irwin.

HULIN, C. L., & SMITH, P. C. (1964). Sex differences in job satisfaction. *Journal of Applied Psychology, 48,* 88–92.

HULIN, C. L., & SMITH, P. C. (1965). A linear model of job satisfaction. *Journal of Applied Psychology, 49,* 209–216.

HULL, C. L. (1928). *Aptitude testing.* New York: Harcourt, Brace and World.

HUNT, D. M., & MICHAEL, C. (1983). Mentorship: A career training and development tool. *Academy of Management Review, 8,* 475–485.

HUNT, J. G., SEKARAN, U., & SCHRIESHEIM, C. A. (1982). Beyond establishment views of leadership: An introduction. In J. G. Hunt, U. Sekaran, & C. A. Schriesheim (eds.), *Leadership: Beyond establishment views.* Carbondale, IL: Southern Illinois University Press.

HUNTER, J. E., & HUNTER, R. F. (1984). Validity and utility of alternative predictors of job performance. *Psychological Bulletin, 96,* 72–98.

HUNTER, J. E., SCHMIDT, F. L., & PEARLMAN, K. (1982). History and accuracy of validity generalization equations: A response to the Callender and Osburn reply. *Journal of Applied Psychology, 67,* 853–858.

IAFFALDANO, M. T., & MUCHINSKY, P. M. (1985). Job satisfaction and job performance: A meta-analysis. *Psychological Bulletin, 97,* 251–273.

IES lighting fundamentals course. (1976). New York: Illuminating Engineering Society.

IES lighting handbook, application volume. (1981a). New York: Illuminating Engineering Society of North America.

IES lighting handbook, reference volume. (1981*b*). New York: Illuminating Engineering Society of North America.

ILGEN, D. R., FISHER, C. D., & TAYLOR, M. S. (1979). Consequences of individual feedback on behavior in organizations. *Journal of Applied Psychology, 64,* 349–371.

INDUSTRIAL USE OF ERGONOMICS. (1969). *Applied Ergonomics, 1,* 26–32.

IRONSON, G. H., GUION, R. M., & OSTRANDER, M. (1982). Adverse impact from a psychometric perspective. *Journal of Applied Psychology, 67,* 419–432.

IVANCEVICH, J. M. (1979). Longitudinal study of the effects of rater training on psychometric error in ratings. *Journal of Applied Psychology, 64,* 502–508.

IVANCEVICH, J. M., & DONNELLY, J. H., JR. (1975). Relation of organizational structure to job satisfaction, anxiety–stress, and performance. *Administrative Science Quarterly, 20,* 272–280.

IVANCEVICH, J. M., & MCMAHON, J. T. (1982). The effects of goal setting, external feedback, and self-generated feedback on outcome variables: a field experiment. *Academy of Management Journal, 25,* 359–372.

JACKOFSKY, E. F. (1984). Turnover and job performance: An integrated process model. *Academy of Management Review, 9,* 74–83.

JACKSON, P. R., STAFFORD, E. M., BANKS, M. H., & WARR, P. B. (1983). Unemployment and psychological distress in young people: The moderating role of employment commitment. *Journal of Applied Psychology, 68,* 525–535.

JACOBS, R., KAFRY, D., & ZEDECK, S. (1980). Expectations of behaviorally anchored rating scales. *Personnel Psychology, 33,* 595–640.

JACOBS, R., & SOLOMON, T. (1977). Strategies for enhancing the prediction of job performance from job satisfaction. *Journal of Applied Psychology, 62,* 417–421.

JACOBY, J., MAZURSKY, D., TROUTMAN, T., & KUSS, A. (1984). When feedback is ignored: Disutility of outcome feedback. *Journal of Applied Psychology, 69,* 531–545.

JAGO, A. G., & VROOM, V. H. (1980). An evaluation of two alternatives to the Vroom/Yetton model. *Academy of Management Journal, 23,* 347–355.

JAGO, A. G., & VROOM, V. H. (1982). Sex differences in the incidence and evaluation of participative leader behavior. *Journal of Applied Psychology, 67,* 776–783.

JAMAL, M. (1981). Shift work related to job attitudes, social participation and withdrawal behavior: A study of nurses and industrial workers. *Personnel Psychology, 34,* 535–547.

JAMAL, M. (1984). Job stress and job performance controversy: An empirical assessment. *Organizational Behavior and Human Performance, 33,* 1–21.

JAMES, L. R., & BRETT, J. M. (1984). Mediators, moderators, and tests for mediation. *Journal of Applied Psychology, 69,* 307–321.

JAMES, L. R., & TETRICK, L. E. (1986). Confirmatory analytic tests of three causal models relating job perceptions to job satisfaction. *Journal of Applied Psychology, 71,* 77–82.

JAMES, S. P., CAMPBELL, I. M., & LOVEGROVE, S. A. (1984). Personality differentiation in a police-selection interview. *Journal of Applied Psychology, 69,* 129–134.

JANZ, T. (1982). Initial comparisons of patterned behavior description interviews versus unstructured interviews. *Journal of Applied Psychology, 67,* 577–580.

JENKINS, G. D., JR., & TABER, T. D. (1977). A Monte Carlo study of factors affecting three indices of composite scale reliability. *Journal of Applied Psychology, 62,* 392–398.

JENKINS, W. O. (1947). A review of leadership studies with particular reference to military problems. *Psychological Bulletin, 44,* 54–79.

JOHNSON, C. D., MESSÉ, L. A., & CRANO, W. D. (1984). Predicting job performance of low income workers: The Work Opinion Questionnaire. *Personnel Psychology, 37,* 291–299.

JOHNSON, S. M., SMITH, P. C., & TUCKER, S. M. (1982). Response format of the Job Descriptive Index: Assessment of reliability and validity by the multi-trait, multi-method matrix. *Journal of Applied Psychology, 67,* 500–505.

JONES, A. P., MAIN, D. S., BUTLER, M. C., & JOHNSON, L. A. (1982). Narrative job descriptions as potential sources of job analysis ratings. *Personnel Psychology, 35,* 813–828.

JORDAN, P. (Producer, Director). (1972). *Business, behaviorism and the bottom line.* [Film]. New York: McGraw-Hill.

JOYNSON, R. B. (1974). *Psychology and common sense.* London: Routledge & Kegan Paul.

JULIAN, J. W., HOLLANDER, E. P., & REGULA, C. R. (1969). Endorsement of the group spokesman as a function of his source of authority, competence, and success. *Journal of Personality and Social Psychology, 11,* 42–49.

KABANOFF, B. (1980). Work and nonwork: A review of models, methods, and findings. *Psychological Bulletin, 88,* 60–77.

KABANOFF, B. (1981). A critique of Leader Match and its implications for leadership research. *Personnel Psychology, 34,* 749–764.

KABANOFF, B., & O'BRIEN, G. E. (1980). Work and leisure: A task attributes analysis. *Journal of Applied Psychology, 65,* 596–609.

KANE, J. S., & LAWLER, E. E., III. (1978). Methods of peer assessment. *Psychological Bulletin, 85,* 555–586.

KANE, J. S., & LAWLER, E. E., III. (1979). Performance appraisal effectiveness: Its assessment and determinants. In B. M. Staw (ed.), *Research in organizational behavior* (vol. 1). Greenwich, CT: JAI Press.

KANTER, R. M. (1977). *Men and women of the corporation.* New York: Basic Books.

KANTOWITZ, B. H., & SORKIN, R. D. (1983). *Human factors: Understanding people–system relationships.* New York: Wiley.

KAPLAN, R. M., & SACCUZZO, D. P. (1982). *Psychological testing: Principles, applications, and issues.* Pacific Grove, CA: Brooks/Cole.

KATERBERG, R., & HOM, P. W. (1981). Effects of within-group and between-groups variation in leadership. *Journal of Applied Psychology, 66,* 218–223.

KATZ, D., & KAHN, R. L. (1978). *The social psychology of organizations* (2nd ed.). New York: Wiley.

KAVANAGH, M. J. (1971). The content issue in performance appraisal: A review. *Personnel Psychology, 24,* 653–668.

KEELEY, M. (1984). Impartiality and participant-interest theories of organizational effectiveness. *Administrative Science Quarterly, 29,* 1–25.

KEINAN, G., FRIEDLAND, N., YITZHAKY, J., & MORAN, A. (1981). Biographical, physiological, and personality variables as predictors of performance under sickness-inducing motion. *Journal of Applied Psychology, 66,* 233–241.

KELLER, R. T. (1983). Predicting absenteeism from prior absenteeism, attitudinal factors, and non-attitudinal factors. *Journal of Applied Psychology, 68,* 536–540.

KELLER, R. T., & HOLLAND, W. E. (1983). Communicators and innovators in research and development organizations. *Academy of Management Journal, 26,* 742–749.

KENNEDY, J. K., JR. (1982). Middle LPC leaders and the contingency model of leadership effectiveness. *Organizational Behavior and Human Performance, 30,* 1–14.

KEPHART, N. C., & TIFFIN, J. (1950). Vision and accident experience. *National Safety News, 62,* 90–91.

KERR, S., & JERMIER, J. M. (1978). Substitutes for leadership: Their meaning and measurement. *Organizational Behavior and Human Performance, 22,* 375–403.

KIM, J. S., & CAMPAGNA, A. F. (1981). Effects of flexitime on employee attendance and performance: A field experiment. *Academy of Management Journal, 24,* 729–741.

KING, N. (1970). Clarification and evaluation of the two-factor theory of job satisfaction. *Psychological Bulletin, 74,* 18–31.

KINGSTROM, P. O., & BASS, A. R. (1981). A critical analysis of studies comparing behaviorally anchored rating scales (BARS) and other rating formats. *Personnel Psychology, 34,* 263–289.

KINKEAD, R. (1975). Typing speed, keying rates, and optimal keyboard layout. *Proceedings of the Human Factors Society.* Dallas, TX.

KIPNIS, D. (1972). Does power corrupt? *Journal of Personality and Social Psychology, 24,* 33–41.

KIRCHNER, W. K. (1965). Relationships between supervisory and subordinate ratings for technical personnel. *Journal of Industrial Psychology, 3,* 57–60.

KIRKPATRICK, D. L. (1967). Evaluation of training. In R. L. Craig & L. R. Bittel (eds.), *Training and development handbook.* New York: McGraw-Hill.

KLAUSS, R., & BASS, B. M. (1981). *Impact of communication.* New York: Academic Press.

KLEIMAN, L. S., & FALEY, R. H. (1985). The implications of professional and legal guidelines for court decisions involving criterion-related validity: A review and analysis. *Personnel Psychology, 38,* 803–833.

KLIEGER, W. A., & MOSEL, J. N. (1953). The effect of opportunity to observe and rater status on the reliability of performance ratings. *Personnel Psychology, 6,* 57–64.

KLIMOSKI, R. J., & LONDON, M. (1974). Role of the rater in performance appraisal. *Journal of Applied Psychology, 59,* 445–451.

KLIMOSKI, R. J., & STRICKLAND, W. J. (1977). Assessment centers—Valid or merely prescient. *Personnel Psychology, 30,* 353–361.

KNIGHT, P. A., & SAAL, F. E. (1983, August). *Gender bias in managerial performance ratings.* Paper presented at the meeting of the American Psychological Association, Anaheim, CA.

KNIGHT, P. A., & SAAL, F. E. (1984). Effects of gender differences and selection agent expertise on leader influence and performance evaluations. *Organizational Behavior and Human Performance, 34,* 225–243.

KNIGHT, P. A., & WEISS, H. M. (1980). Effects of selection agent and leader origin on leader influence and group member perceptions. *Organizational Behavior and Human Performance, 26*, 7–21.

KNOUSE, S. B. (1983). The letter of recommendation: Specificity and favorability of information. *Personnel Psychology, 36*, 331–341.

KOCHAN, T. A. (1980). *Collective bargaining and industrial relations.* Homewood, IL: Irwin.

KOCHAN, T. A., & HELFMAN, D. E. (1981). The effects of collective bargaining on economic and behavioral outcomes. In R. G. Ehrenberg (ed.), *Research in labor economics.* Greenwich, CT: JAI Press.

KOHLBERG, L. (1968). The child as moral philosopher. *Psychology Today, 2*(4), 24–30.

KOMAKI, J., BARWICK, K. D., & SCOTT, L. R. (1978). A behavioral approach to occupational safety: Pinpointing and reinforcing safe performance in a food manufacturing plant. *Journal of Applied Psychology, 63*, 434–445.

KOMAKI, J. L., COLLINS, R. L., & PENN, P. (1982). The role of performance antecedents and consequences in work motivation. *Journal of Applied Psychology, 67*, 334–340.

KOMAKI, J., HEINZMANN, A. T., & LAWSON, L. (1980). Effect of training and feedback: Component analysis of a behavioral safety program. *Journal of Applied Psychology, 65*, 261–270.

KOPELMAN, R. E. (1976). Organizational control system responsiveness, expectancy theory constructs, and work motivation: Some interrelations and causal connections. *Personnel Psychology, 29*, 205–220.

KOPELMAN, R. E., GREENHAUS, J. H., & CONNOLLY, T. F. (1983). A model of work, family, and interrole conflict: A construct validation study. *Organizational Behavior and Human Performance, 32*, 198–215.

KOPROWSKI, E. J. (1983). Cultural myths: Clues to effective management. *Organizational Dynamics, 12*, 39–51.

KORMAN, A. K. (1971). *Industrial and organizational psychology.* Englewood Cliffs, NJ: Prentice-Hall.

KORMAN, A. K. (1977). *Organizational behavior.* Englewood Cliffs, NJ: Prentice-Hall.

KORMAN, A. K., GREENHAUS, J. H., & BADIN, I. J. (1977). Personnel attitudes and motivation. *Annual Review of Psychology, 28*, 175–196.

KRAIGER, K., & FORD, J. K. (1985). A meta-analysis of ratee race effects in performance ratings. *Journal of Applied Psychology, 70*, 56–65.

KRAJEWSKI, J. T., KAMON, E., & AVELLINI, B. (1979). Scheduling rest for consecutive light and heavy workloads under hot ambient conditions. *Ergonomics, 22*, 975–987.

KRAUT, A. I. (1976). Developing managerial skills via modeling techniques: Some positive research findings—A symposium. *Personnel Psychology, 29*, 325–328.

KROECK, K. G., BARRETT, G. V., & ALEXANDER, R. A. (1983). Imposed quotas and personnel selection: A computer simulation study. *Journal of Applied Psychology, 68*, 123–136.

KUDER, G. F., & RICHARDSON, M. (1937). The theory of the estimation of test reliability. *Psychometrika, 2*, 151–160.

KUNIN, T. (1955). The construction of a new type of job satisfaction measure. *Personnel Psychology, 8*, 65–77.

LADD, R. T., GORDON, M. E., BEAUVAIS, L. L., & MORGAN, R. L. (1982). Union commitment: Replication and extension. *Journal of Applied Psychology, 67*, 640–644.

LAHEY, M. A., & SAAL, F. E. (1981). Evidence incompatible with a cognitive compatibility theory of rating behavior. *Journal of Applied Psychology, 66*, 706–715.

LANDSBERGER, H. A. (1958). *Hawthorne revisited: Management and the worker, its critics and developments in human relations in industry.* Ithaca, NY: New York State School of Industrial and Labor Relations.

LANDY, F. J. (1976). The validity of the interview in police officer selection. *Journal of Applied Psychology, 61*, 193–198.

LANDY, F. J. (1978). An opponent process theory of job satisfaction. *Journal of Applied Psychology, 63*, 533–547.

LANDY, F. J. (1985). *Psychology of work behavior* (3rd ed.). Homewood, IL: Dorsey Press.

LANDY, F. J., & FARR, J. L. (1975). *Police performance appraisal.* University Park, PA: Department of Psychology, Pennsylvania State University.

LANDY, F. J., & FARR, J. L. (1980). Performance rating. *Psychological Bulletin, 87*, 72–107.

LANDY, F. J., & FARR, J. L. (1983). *The measurement of work performance: Methods, theory, and applications.* New York: Academic Press.

LANDY, F. J., FARR, J. L., & JACOBS, R. R. (1982). Utility concepts in performance measurement. *Organizational Behavior and Human Performance, 30*, 15–40.

LANDY, F. J., FARR, J. L., SAAL, F. E., & FREYTAG, W. R. (1976). Behaviorally anchored scales for rating the performance of police officers. *Journal of Applied Psychology, 61*, 750–758.

LANDY, F. J., & GUION, R. M. (1970). Development of scales for the measurement of work motivation. *Organizational Behavior and Human Performance, 5,* 93–103.

LARSON, J. R., JR. (1984). The performance feedback process: A preliminary model. *Organizational Behavior and Human Performance, 33,* 42–76.

LARSON, J. R., JR., LINGLE, J. H., & SCERBO, M. M. (1984). The impact of performance cues on leader-behavior ratings: The role of selective information availability and probabilistic response bias. *Organizational Behavior and Human Performance, 33,* 323–349.

LATHAM, G. P., FAY, C., & SAARI, L. (1979). The development of behavioral observation scales for appraising the performance of foremen. *Personnel Psychology, 32,* 299–311.

LATHAM, G. P., & MARSHALL, H. A. (1982). The effects of self-set, participatively set and assigned goals on the performance of government employees. *Personnel Psychology, 35,* 399–404.

LATHAM, G. P., MITCHELL, T. R., & DOSSETT, D. L. (1978). Importance of participative goal setting and anticipated rewards on goal difficulty and job performance. *Journal of Applied Psychology, 63,* 163–171.

LATHAM, G. P., & SAARI, L. M. (1979). The application of social-learning theory to training supervisors through behavioral modeling. *Journal of Applied Psychology, 64,* 239–246.

LATHAM, G. P., & SAARI, L. M. (1984). Do people do what they say? Further studies on the situational interview. *Journal of Applied Psychology, 69,* 569–573.

LATHAM, G. P., & STEELE, T. P. (1983). The motivational effects of participation versus goal setting on performance. *Academy of Management Journal, 26,* 406–417.

LATHAM, G. P., & WEXLEY, K. N. (1977). Behavioral observation scales for performance appraisal purposes. *Personnel Psychology, 30,* 255–268.

LATHAM, G. P., & WEXLEY, K. N. (1981). *Increasing productivity through performance appraisal.* Reading, MA: Addison-Wesley.

LATHAM, G. P., WEXLEY, K. N., & PURSELL, E. D. (1975). Training managers to minimize rating errors in the observation of behavior. *Journal of Applied Psychology, 60,* 550–555.

LAWLER, E. E., III. (1967). The multitrait–multirater approach to measuring managerial job performance. *Journal of Applied Psychology, 51,* 369–381.

LAWLER, E. E., III. (1973). *Motivation in work organizations.* Pacific Grove, CA: Brooks/Cole.

LAWLER, E. E., & SUTTLE, J. L. (1972). A causal correlation test of the need hierarchy concept. *Organizational Behavior and Human Performance, 7,* 265–287.

LAWRENCE, P. R., & LORSCH, J. W. (1967). *Organization and environment: Managing differentiation and integration.* Boston: Division of Research, Harvard Business School.

LAWSHE, C. H. (1952). Employee selection. *Personnel Psychology, 5,* 31–34.

LAWSHE, C. H. (1975). A quantitative approach to content validity. *Personnel Psychology, 28,* 563–575.

LAWSHE, C. H. (1983). A simplified approach to the evaluation of fairness in employee selection procedures. *Personnel Psychology, 36,* 601–608.

LAWSHE, C. H. (1985). Inferences from personnel tests and their validity. *Journal of Applied Psychology, 70,* 237–238.

LAWSHE, C. H., & NAGLE, B. F. (1953). Productivity and attitude toward supervisor. *Journal of Applied Psychology, 37,* 159–162.

LEDVINKA, J., MARKOS, V. H., & LADD, R. T. (1982). Long-range impact of "fair selection" standards on minority employment. *Journal of Applied Psychology, 67,* 18–36.

LEE, R., & KLEIN, A. R. (1982). Structure of the Job Diagnostic Survey for public sector occupations. *Journal of Applied Psychology, 67,* 515–519.

LEE, R., MILLER, K. J., & GRAHAM, W. K. (1982). Corrections for restriction of range and attenuation in criterion-related validation studies. *Journal of Applied Psychology, 67,* 637–639.

LEIB, J. W., CUSACK, J., HUGHES, D., PILETTE, S., WERTHER, J., & KINTZ, B. L. (1967). Teaching machines and programmed instruction: Areas of application. *Psychological Bulletin, 67,* 12–26.

LEITHEAD, C. S., & LIND, A. R. (1964). *Heat stress and heat disorders.* London: Cassell and Co.

LEMKE, E., & WIERSMA, W. (1976). *Principles of psychological measurement.* Chicago: Rand McNally.

LEPPER, M. R., & GREENE, D. (1975). Turning play into work: Effects of adult surveillance and extrinsic rewards on children's intrinsic motivation. *Journal of Personality and Social Psychology, 31,* 479–486.

LEVI, M. A. (1954). A comparison of two methods of conducting critiques. San Antonio, TX: AFPTRC-TR-54-108.

LEVINE, E. L. (1980). Introductory remarks for the symposium "Organizational applications of self-appraisal and self-assessment: Another look." *Personnel Psychology, 33,* 259–262.

LEVINE, E. L., ASH, R. A., & BENNETT, N. (1980). Exploratory comparative study of four job analysis methods. *Journal of Applied Psychology, 65,* 524–535.

LEVINE, E. L., ASH, R. A., HALL, H., & SISTRUNK, F. (1983). Evaluation of job analysis methods by experienced job analysts. *Academy of Management Journal, 26,* 339–348.

LEWIN, K. (1958). Group decision and social change. In E. E. Maccoby, T. M. Newcomb, & E. L. Hartley (eds.), *Readings in social psychology.* New York: Holt, Rinehart & Winston.

LEWIN, K., LIPPETT, R., & WHITE, R. K. (1939). Patterns of aggressive behavior in experimentally created "social climates." *Journal of Social Psychology, 10,* 271–299.

LIDEN, R. C., & GRAEN, G. B. (1980). Generalizability of the vertical dyad linkage model of leadership. *Academy of Management Journal, 23,* 451–465.

LINN, R. L., HARNISCH, D. L., & DUNBAR, S. B. (1981). Corrections for range restriction: An empirical investigation of conditions resulting in conservative corrections. *Journal of Applied Psychology, 66,* 655–663.

LISSITZ, R. W., & GREEN, S. B. (1975). Effect of the number of scale points on reliability: A Monte Carlo approach. *Journal of Applied Psychology, 60,* 10–13.

LITWIN, G. H., & STRINGER, R. A. (1968). *Motivation and organization climate.* Boston: Division of Research, Harvard Business School.

LOCKE, E. A. (1968). Toward a theory of task motivation and incentives. *Organizational Behavior and Human Performance, 3,* 157–189.

LOCKE, E. A. (1969). What is job satisfaction? *Organizational Behavior and Human Performance, 4,* 309–336.

LOCKE, E. A. (1976). The nature and causes of job satisfaction. In M. D. Dunnette (ed.), *Handbook of industrial and organizational psychology.* Chicago: Rand McNally.

LOCKE, E. A. (1978). The ubiquity of the technique of goal setting in theories and approaches to employee motivation. *Academy of Mangement Review, 3,* 594–601.

LOCKE, E. A. (1980). Latham versus Komaki: A tale of two paradigms. *Journal of Applied Psychology, 65,* 16–23.

LOCKE, E. A. (1982a). Critique of Bramel and Friend. *American Psychologist, 37,* 858–859.

LOCKE, E. A. (1982b). Licensing. *American Psychologist, 37,* 239.

LOCKE, E. A. (1982c). Relation of goal level to performance with a short work period and multiple goal levels. *Journal of Applied Psychology, 67,* 512–514.

LOCKE, E. A., CARTLEDGE, N., & KNERR, C. S. (1970). Studies of the relationship between satisfaction, goal setting, and performance. *Organizational Behavior and Human Performance, 5,* 135–158.

LOCKE, E. A., & SCHWEIGER, D. M. (1979). Participation in decision making: One more look. In B. M. Staw (ed.), *Research in Organizational Behavior* (vol. 1). Greenwich, CT: JAI Press.

LOCKE, E. A., SHAW, K. N., SAARI, L. M., & LATHAM, G. P. (1981). Goal setting and task performance: 1969–1980. *Psychological Bulletin, 90,* 125–152.

LOFQUIST, L. H., & DAWIS, R. V. (1969). *Adjustment to work: A psychological view of man's problems in a work-oriented society.* New York: Appleton-Century-Crofts.

LOHER, B. T., NOE, R. A., MOELLER, N. L., & FITZGERALD, M. P. (1985). A meta-analysis of the relation of job characteristics to job satisfaction. *Journal of Applied Psychology, 70,* 280–289.

LOMBARDO, M. M., & MCCALL, M. W., JR. (1982). Leaders on line: Observations from a simulation of managerial work. In J. G. Hunt, U. Sekaran, & C. A. Schriesheim (eds.), *Leadership: Beyond establishment views.* Carbondale, IL: Southern Illinois University Press.

LONDON, M., & BRAY, D. W. (1980). Ethical issues in testing and evaluation for personnel decisions. *American Psychologist, 35,* 890–901.

LONDON, M., CRANDALL, R., & SEALS, G. W. (1977). The contribution of job and leisure satisfaction to quality of life. *Journal of Applied Psychology, 62,* 328–334.

LONDON, M., & STUMPF, S. A. (1983). Effects of candidate characteristics on management promotion decisions: An experimental study. *Personnel Psychology, 36,* 241–259.

LOPEZ, F. M., KESSELMAN, G. A., & LOPEZ, F. E. (1981). An empirical test of a trait-oriented job analysis technique. *Personnel Psychology, 34,* 479–502.

LORD, F. M. (1953). On the statistical treatment of football numbers. *American Psychologist, 8,* 750–751.

LORD, R. G. (1977). Functional leadership behavior: Measurement and relation to social power and leadership perceptions. *Administrative Science Quarterly, 22,* 114–133.

LORD, R. G. (1985). Accuracy in behavioral measurement: An alternative definition based on raters' cognitive schema and signal detection theory. *Journal of Applied Psychology, 70,* 66–71.

LORD, R. G., DEVADER, C. L., & ALLIGER, G. M. (1986). A meta-analysis of the relation between personality traits and leadership perceptions: An application of validity generalization procedures. *Journal of Applied Psychology, 71,* 402–410.

LORD, R. G., FOTI, R. J., & PHILLIPS, J. S. (1982). A theory of leadership categorization. In J. G. Hunt, U. Sekaran, & C. A. Schriesheim (eds.), *Leadership: Beyond establishment views.* Carbondale, IL: Southern Illinois University Press.

LORD, R. G., PHILLIPS, J. S., & RUSH, M. C. (1980). Effects of sex and personality on perceptions of emergent leadership, influence, and social power. *Journal of Applied Psychology, 65,* 176–182.

LORENZO, R. V. (1984). Effects of assessorship on managers' proficiency in acquiring, evaluating, and communicating information about people. *Personnel Psychology, 37,* 617–634.

LUMSDEN, J. (1976). Test theory. *Annual Review of Psychology, 27,* 251–280.

LUTHANS, F., & KREITNER, R. (1975). *Organizational behavior modification.* Glenview, IL: Scott, Foresman.

LUTHANS, F., & KREITNER, R. (1985). *Organizational behavior modification and beyond: An operant and social learning approach.* Glenview, IL: Scott, Foresman.

LYNTON, R. P., & PAREEK, U. (1967). *Training for development.* Homewood, IL: Irwin.

LYSAUGHT, J. P., & WILLIAMS, C. M. (1963). *A guide to programmed instruction.* New York: Wiley.

MAAS, J. B. (1965). Patterned scaled expectation interview: Reliability studies on a new technique. *Journal of Applied Psychology, 59,* 431–433.

MABE, P. A., III, & WEST, S. G. (1982). Validity of self-evaluation of ability: A review and meta-analysis. *Journal of Applied Psychology, 67,* 280–296.

MACHLE, W. (1945). The effect of gun blast on hearing. *Archives of Otolaryngology, 42,* 164–168.

MACHUNGWA, P. D., & SCHMITT, N. (1983). Work motivation in a developing country. *Journal of Applied Psychology, 68,* 31–42.

MADIGAN, R. M. (1985). Comparable worth judgments: A measurement properties analysis. *Journal of Applied Psychology, 70,* 137–147.

MAHER, J. R., & OVERBAGH, W. B. (1971). Better inspection performance through job enrichment. In J. R. Maher (ed.), *New perspectives in job enrichment.* New York: Van Nostrand Reinhold.

MALAVIYA, P., & GANESH K. (1976). Shift work and individual differences in the productivity of weavers in an Indian textile mill. *Journal of Applied Psychology, 61,* 774–776.

MALAVIYA, P., & GANESH K. (1977). Individual differences in productivity across type of work shift. *Journal of Applied Psychology, 62,* 527–528.

MANN, R. D. (1959). A review of the relationships between personality and performance in small groups. *Psychological Bulletin, 56,* 241–270.

MANN, R. B., & DECKER, P. J. (1984). The effect of key behavior distinctiveness on generalization and recall in behavior modeling training. *Academy of Mangement Journal, 27,* 900–910.

MARKHAM, S. E., DANSEREAU, F., JR., & ALUTTO, J. A. (1982). Group size and absenteeism rates: A longitudinal analysis. *Academy of Management Journal, 25,* 921–927.

MASLOW, A. H. (1943). A theory of human motivation. *Psychological Review, 50,* 370–396.

MASLOW, A. H. (1965). *Eupsychian management: A journal.* Homewood, IL: Irwin.

MASLOW, A. H. (1970). *Motivation and personality* (2nd ed.). New York: Harper & Row.

MATSUI, T., OKADA, A., & INOSHITA, O. (1983). Mechanism of feedback affecting task performance. *Organizational Behavior and Human Performance, 31,* 114–122.

MATSUI, T., OKADA, A., & KAKUYAMA, T. (1982). Influence of achievement need on goal setting, performance, and feedback effectiveness. *Journal of Applied Psychology, 67,* 645–648.

MATSUI, T., OKADA, A., & MIZUGUCHI, R. (1981). Expectancy theory prediction of the goal theory postulate "the harder the goals, the higher the performance." *Journal of Applied Psychology, 66,* 54–58.

MAUSNER, B. (1953). Studies in social interaction. III. Effect of variation in one partner's prestige on the interaction of observer pairs. *Journal of Applied Psychology, 37,* 391–393.

MAUSNER, B. (1954). The effects of one partner's success in a relevant task on the interaction of observer pairs. *Journal of Abnormal and Social Psychology, 49,* 557–560.

MAXWELL, S. E., & DELANEY, H. D. (1985). Measurement and statistics: An examination of construct validity. *Psychological Bulletin, 97,* 85–93.

MAYFIELD, E. C. (1964). The selection interview: A reevaluation of published research. *Personnel Psychology, 17,* 239–260.

MCCAULEY, R., & PARKINSON, R. (1971). The new popularity of the Dvorak simplified keyboard. *Computers and Automation, 20*(11), 31–32.

MCCLELLAND, D. C. (1961). *The achieving society.* Princeton, NJ: Van Nostrand.

MCCLELLAND, D. C. (1965). Toward a theory of motive acquisition. *American Psychologist, 20,* 321–333.

McClelland, D. C. (1975). *Power: The inner experience.* New York: Irvington.

McClelland, D. C. (1976). Power is the great motivation. *Harvard Business Review, 54,* 100–110.

McClelland, D. C., Atkinson, J. W., Clark, R. A., & Lowell, E. L. (1953). *The achievement motive.* New York: Appleton-Century-Crofts.

McClelland, D. C., & Boyatzis, R. E. (1982). Leadership motive pattern and long-term success in management. *Journal of Applied Psychology, 67,* 737–743.

McClelland, D. C., & Winter, D. (1969). *Motivating economic achievement.* New York: Free Press.

McCormick, E. J. (1976). Job and task analysis. In M. D. Dunnette (ed.), *Handbook of industrial and organizational psychology.* Chicago: Rand McNally.

McCormick, E. J., & Bachus, J. A. (1952). Paired comparison ratings: I. The effect on ratings of reductions in the number of pairs. *Journal of Applied Psychology, 36,* 123–127.

McCormick, E. J., & Ilgen, D. R. (1980). *Industrial psychology* (7th ed.). Englewood Cliffs, NJ: Prentice-Hall.

McCormick, E. J., & Ilgen, D. R. (1985). *Industrial and organizational psychology* (8th ed.). Englewood Cliffs, NJ: Prentice-Hall.

McCormick, E. J., Jeanneret, P. R., & Mecham, R. C. (1969). *Position Analysis Questionnaire.* West Lafayette, IN: Purdue Research Foundation.

McCormick, E. J., Jeanneret, P. R., & Mecham, R. C. (1972). A study of job characteristics and job dimensions as based on the Position Analysis Questionnaire (PAQ) [Monograph]. *Journal of Applied Psychology, 56,* 347–368.

McCormick, E. J., & Roberts, W. K. (1952). Paired compairson ratings: II. The reliability of ratings based on partial pairings. *Journal of Applied Psychology, 36,* 188–192.

McCormick, E. J., & Sanders, M. S. (1982). *Human factors in engineering and design.* (5th ed.). New York: McGraw-Hill.

McCormick, E. J., & Tiffin, J. (1974). *Industrial psychology* (6th ed.). Englewood Cliffs, NJ: Prentice-Hall.

McDonald, T., & Hakel, M. D. (1985). Effects of applicant race, sex, suitability, and answers on interviewer's questioning strategy and ratings. *Personnel Psychology, 38,* 321–334.

McEvoy, G. M., & Cascio, W. F. (1985). Strategies for reducing employee turnover: A meta-analysis. *Journal of Applied Psychology, 70,* 342–353.

McGehee, W., & Thayer, P. W. (1961). *Training in business and industry.* New York: Wiley.

McGregor, D. (1960). *The human side of enterprise.* New York: McGraw-Hill.

McGregor, D. (1967). *The professional manager.* New York: McGraw-Hill.

McIntyre, R. M., Smith, D. E., & Hassett, C. E. (1984). Accuracy of performance ratings as affected by rater training and perceived purpose of rating. *Journal of Applied Psychology, 69,* 147–156.

Mecham, R. C., Jeanneret, P. R., & McCormick, E. J. (1983). *The applicability of job component validity based on the PAQ to the Uniform Guidelines' validation requirements—A reply to Trattner.* Unpublished manuscript, Department of Business Administration, Utah State University, Logan, UT.

Meehl, P. E. (1954). *Clinical versus statistical prediction.* Minneapolis, MN: University of Minnesota Press.

Meehl, P. E. (1957). When shall we use our heads instead of a formula? *Journal of Counseling Psychology, 4,* 268–273.

Meehl, P. E. (1965). Seer over sign: The first good example. *Journal of Experimental Research in Personality, 1,* 27–32.

Megargee, E. I. (1969). Influence of sex roles on the manifestation of leadership. *Journal of Applied Psychology, 53,* 377–382.

Megargee, E. I., Bogart, P., & Anderson, B. J. (1966). Prediction of leadership in a simulated industrial task. *Journal of Applied Psychology, 50,* 292–295.

Meltzer, H., & Stagner, R. (eds.). (1980). Industrial/organizational psychology: 1980 overview. [Special issue]. *Professional Psychology, 11*(3).

Meritt-Haston, R., & Wexley, K. N. (1983). Educational requirements: Legality and validity. *Personnel Psychology, 36,* 743–753.

Messick, S. (1980). Test validity and the ethics of assessment. *American Psychologist, 35,* 1012–1027.

Meyer, H. H. (1980). Self-appraisal of job performance. *Personnel Psychology, 33,* 291–295.

Meyer, H., Kay, E., & French, J. R. (1965). Split roles in performance appraisal. *Harvard Business Review, 43,* 123–129.

Michaels, C. E., & Spector, P. E. (1982). Causes of employee turnover: A test of the Mobley, Griffeth, Hand, and Meglino model. *Journal of Applied Psychology, 67,* 53–59.

Mihal, W. L., & Barrett, G. V. (1976). Individual differences in perceptual information processing and their relation to automobile accident involvement. *Journal of Applied Psychology, 61,* 229–233.

MILLER, H., KATERBERG, R., & HULIN, C. L. (1979). Evaluation of the Mobley, Horner, and Hollingsworth model of employee turnover. *Journal of Applied Psychology, 64,* 509–517.

MILLER, R. W., & ZELLER, F. A. (1967). *Social psychological factors associated with responses to retraining.* Final Report, Office of Research and Development, Appalachian Center, West Virginia University (Research Grant No. 91-52-66-56), U.S. Department of Labor.

MILLS, C. J., & BOHANNON, W. E. (1980). Personality characteristics of effective state police officers. *Journal of Applied Psychology, 65,* 680–684.

MINER, J. B. (1965). *Studies in management education.* Altanta, GA: Organizational Measurement Systems Press.

MINER, J. B. (1967). *The school administrator and organizational character.* Eugene, OR: Center for the Advanced Study of Educational Administration, University of Oregon.

MINER, J. B. (1968a). The early identification of managerial talent. *Personnel and Guidance Journal, 46,* 586–591.

MINER, J. B. (1968b). The managerial motivation of school administrators. *Educational Administration Quarterly, 4,* 55–71.

MINER, J. B. (1974a). Motivation to manage among women: Studies of business managers and educational administrators. *Journal of Vocational Behavior, 5,* 197–208.

MINER, J. B. (1974b). Motivation to manage among women: Studies of college students. *Journal of Vocational Behavior, 5,* 241–250.

MINER, J. B. (1975). *The challenge of managing.* Philadelphia: W. B. Saunders.

MINER, J. B. (1977a). Motivational potential for upgrading among minority and female managers. *Journal of Applied Psychology, 62,* 691–697.

MINER, J. B. (1977b). *Motivation to manage: A ten-year update of the "studies in management education" research.* Atlanta, GA: Organizational Measurement Systems Press.

MINER, J. B. (1978a). The Miner sentence completion scale: A re-appraisal. *Academy of Management Journal, 21,* 283–294.

MINER, J. B. (1978b). Twenty years of research on role-motivation theory of managerial effectiveness. *Personnel Psychology, 31,* 739–760.

MINER, J. B., & CRANE, D. P. (1981). Motivation to manage and the manifestation of a managerial orientation in career planning. *Academy of Management Journal, 24,* 626–633.

MINER, J. B., & SMITH, N. R. (1969). Managerial talent among undergraduate and graduate business students. *Personnel and Guidance Journal, 47,* 995–1000.

MINTON, H. L., & SCHNEIDER, F. W. (1980). *Differential psychology.* Pacific Grove, CA: Brooks/Cole.

MINTZBERG, H. (1980). *The nature of managerial work.* Englewood Cliffs, NJ: Prentice-Hall.

MIRVIS, P. H., & SEASHORE, S. E. (1979). Being ethical in organizational research. *American Psychologist, 34,* 766–780.

MIRVIS, P. H., & SEASHORE, S. E. (1980). Reply to Walter and Pinder. *American Psychologist, 35,* 937–938.

MITCHELL, T. R. (1974). Expectancy models of job satisfaction, occupational preference, and effort: A theoretical, methodological, and empirical appraisal. *Psychological Bulletin, 81,* 1096–1112.

MITCHELL, T. R. (1979). Organizational behavior. *Annual Review of Psychology, 30,* 243–281.

MITCHELL, T. R., & WOOD, R. E. (1980). Supervisor's responses to subordinate poor performance: A test of an attributional model. *Organizational Behavior and Human Performance, 25,* 123–138.

MITCHELL, T. W., & KLIMOSKI, R. J. (1982). Is it rational to be empirical? A test of methods for scoring biographical data. *Journal of Applied Psychology, 67,* 411–418.

MITROFF, I. I. (1983). Archetypal social systems analysis: On the deeper structure of human systems. *Academy of Management Review, 8,* 387–397.

MOBLEY, W. H. (1977). Intermediate linkages in the relationship between job satisfaction and employee turnover. *Journal of Applied Psychology, 62,* 237–240.

MOBLEY, W. H. (1982). Supervisor and employee race and sex effects on performance appraisals: A field study of adverse impact and generalizability. *Academy of Management Journal, 25,* 598–606.

MOBLEY, W. H., GRIFFETH, R. W., HAND, H. H., & MEGLINO, B. M. (1979). Review and conceptual analysis of the employee turnover process. *Psychological Bulletin, 86,* 493–522.

MOBLEY, W. H., HORNER, S. O., & HOLLINGSWORTH, A. T. (1978). An evaluation of precursors of hospital employee turnover. *Journal of Applied Psychology, 63,* 408–414.

MOBLEY, W. H., & LOCKE, E. A. (1970). The relationship of value importance to satisfaction. *Organizational Behavior and Human Performance, 5,* 463–483.

MOCH, M. K. (1980). Job involvement, internal motivation, and employees' integration into networks of work relationships. *Organizational Behavior and Human Performance, 25,* 15–31.

MOOK, D. G. (1983). In defense of external invalidity. *American Psychologist, 38,* 379–387.

MOORE, B. V. (1962). Some beginnings of industrial psychology. In B. v. H. Gilmer (ed.), *Walter*

Van Dyke Bingham. Pittsburgh, PA: Carnegie Institute of Technology.

MORSH, J. E. (1964). Job analysis in the United States Air Force. *Personnel Psychology, 17,* 7–17.

MOSSHOLDER, K. W. (1980). Effects of externally mediated goal setting on intrinsic motivation: A laboratory experiment. *Journal of Applied Psychology, 65,* 202–210.

MOSSHOLDER, K. W., & ARVEY, R. D. (1984). Synthetic validity: A conceptual and comparative review. *Journal of Applied Psychology, 69,* 322–333.

MOTT, P. E., MANN, F. C., MCLOUGHLIN, Q., & WARWICK, D. P. (1965). *Shift work.* Ann Arbor, MI: University of Michigan Press.

MOUNT, M. K. (1984). Psychometric properties of subordinate ratings of managerial performance. *Personnel Psychology, 37,* 687–702.

MOWDAY, R. T. (1983). Equity theory predictions of behavior in organizations. In R. M. Steers & L. W. Porter (eds.), *Motivation and work behavior* (3rd ed.). New York: McGraw-Hill.

MOWDAY, R. T., KOBERG, C. S., & MCARTHUR, A. W. (1984). The psychology of the withdrawal process: A cross-validational test of Mobley's intermediate linkages model of turnover in two samples. *Academy of Management Journal, 27,* 79–94.

MOWDAY, R. T., PORTER, L. W., & STEERS, R. M. (1982). *Employee–organization linkages: The psychology of commitment, absenteeism, and turnover.* New York: Academic Press.

MOWDAY, R. T., STEERS, R. M., & PORTER, L. W. (1979). The measurement of organizational commitment. *Journal of Vocational Behavior, 14,* 224–247.

MUCHINSKY, P. M. (1976). An assessment of the Litwin and Stringer organization climate questionnaire: An empirical and theoretical extension of the Sims and LaFollette study. *Personnel Psychology, 29,* 371–392.

MUCHINSKY, P. M. (1977a). A comparison of within and across subjects analyses of the expectancy valence model for predicting effort. *Academy of Management Journal, 20,* 154–158.

MUCHINSKY, P. M. (1977b). Employee absenteeism: A review of the literature. *Journal of Vocational Behavior, 10,* 316–340.

MUCHINSKY, P. M. (1983). *Psychology applied to work: An introduction to industrial and organizational psychology.* Homewood, IL: Dorsey Press.

MUELLER, C. G. (1979). Some origins of psychology as science. *Annual Review of Psychology, 30,* 9–29.

MÜNSTERBERG, H. (1913). *Psychology and industrial efficiency.* New York: Houghton Mifflin.

MURPHY, K. R. (1983). Fooling yourself with cross-validation: Single sample designs. *Personnel Psychology, 36,* 111–118.

MURPHY, K. R. (1984). Cost–benefit considerations in choosing among cross-validation methods. *Personnel Psychology, 37,* 15–22.

MURPHY, K. R., BALZER, W. K., LOCKHART, M. C., & EISENMAN, E. J. (1985). Effects of previous performance on evaluations of present performance. *Journal of Applied Psychology, 70,* 72–84.

MURPHY, K. R., MARTIN, C., & GARCIA, M. (1982). Do behavioral observation scales measure observation? *Journal of Applied Psychology, 67,* 562–567.

MURRAY, H. A. (1938). *Explorations in personality.* New York: Oxford University Press.

MURRAY, H. A., & MACKINNON, D. W. (1946). Assessment of OSS personnel. *Journal of Consulting Psychology, 10,* 76–80.

NARAYANAN, V. K., & NATH, R. (1982). A field test of some attitudinal and behavioral consequences of flexitime. *Journal of Applied Psychology, 67,* 214–218.

NASH, A. N., & CARROLL, S. J., JR. (1975). *The management of compensation.* Pacific Grove, CA: Brooks/Cole.

NATHAN, B. R., & ALEXANDER, R. A. (1985). The role of inferential accuracy in performance rating. *Academy of Management Review, 10,* 109–115.

NATHAN, B. R., & LORD, R. G. (1983). Cognitive categorization and dimensional schemata: A process approach to the study of halo in performance ratings. *Journal of Applied Psychology, 68,* 102–114.

NATIONAL LEAGUE FOR NURSING, RESEARCH AND STUDIES SERVICE. (1964). *A method for rating the proficiency of the hospital general staff nurse: Manual of directions.* New York.

NAYLOR, J. C., PRITCHARD, R. D., & ILGEN, D. R. (1980). *A theory of behavior in organizations.* New York: Academic Press.

NAYLOR, J. C., & SHINE, L. C. (1965). A table for determining the increase in mean criterion score obtained by using a selection device. *Journal of Industrial Psychology, 3,* 33–42.

NEAR, J. P., SMITH, C. A., RICE, R. W., & HUNT, R. G. (1984). A comparison of work and nonwork predictors of life satisfaction. *Academy of Management Journal, 27,* 184–190.

NEFF, W. S. (1968). *Work and human behavior.* New York: Atherton.

NEIDIG, R. D., & NEIDIG, P. J. (1984). Multiple assessment center exercises and job relatedness. *Journal of Applied Psychology, 69,* 182–186.

NICHOLSON, N., BROWN, C. A., & CHADWICK-JONES, J. K. (1976). Absence from work and job satisfaction. *Journal of Applied Psychology, 61,* 728–737.

NOLLEN, S. (1979). *New patterns of work.* New York: Work in America Institute.

NORBORG, J. M. (1984). A warning regarding the simplified approach to the evaluation of test fairness in employee selection procedures. *Personnel Psychology, 37,* 483–486.

NORD, W. R. (1980). Toward an organizational psychology for organizational psychology. *Professional Psychology, 11,* 531–542.

NORD, W. R. (1982). Continuity and change in industrial/organizational psychology: Learning from previous mistakes. *Professional Psychology, 13,* 942–953.

NOSSEL, N. (1982). The InterFace Project: Background. *Personnel Psychology, 35,* 553–555.

NUNNALLY, J. C. (1978). *Psychometric theory* (2nd ed.). New York: McGraw-Hill.

O'BRIEN, G. E. (1982). Evaluation of the job characteristics theory of work attitudes and performance. *Australian Journal of Psychology, 34,* 383–401.

O'CONNOR, E. J., PETERS, L. H., POOYAN, A., WEEKLEY, J., FRANK, B., & ERENKRANTZ, B. (1984). Situational constraint effects on performance, affective reactions, and turnover: A field replication and extension. *Journal of Applied Psychology, 69,* 663–672.

ODEWAHN, C. A., & PETTY, M. M. (1980). A comparison of levels of job satisfaction, role stress, and personal competence between union members and nonmembers. *Academy of Management Journal, 23,* 150–155.

OLDHAM, G. R. (1976). Organizational choice and some correlates of individual expectancies. *Decision Science, 7,* 873–874.

OLIAN, J. D. (1984). Genetic screening for employment purposes. *Personnel Psychology, 37,* 423–438.

OLIAN, J. D., & WILCOX, J. C. (1982). The controversy over PACE: An examination of the evidence and implications of the Luevano consent decree for employment testing. *Personnel Psychology, 35,* 659–676.

OLSON, C. A., & BECKER, B. E. (1983). A proposed technique for the treatment of restriction of range in selection validation. *Psychological Bulletin, 93,* 137–148.

OLSON, H. C., FINE, S. A., MYERS, D. C., & JENNINGS, M. C. (1981). The use of functional job analysis in establishing performance standards for heavy equipment operators. *Personnel Psychology, 34,* 351–364.

O'REILLY, C. A., III. (1978). The intentional distortion of information in organizational communi-

cation: A laboratory and field approach. *Human Relations, 31,* 173–193.

O'REILLY, C. A., III. (1980). Individuals and information overload in organizations: Is more necessarily better? *Academy of Management Journal, 23,* 684–696.

O'REILLY, C. A., III, & CALDWELL, D. F. (1979). Informational influence as a determinant of perceived task characteristics and job satisfaction. *Journal of Applied Psychology, 64,* 157–165.

O'REILLY, C. A., III, & ROBERTS, K. H. (1976). Relationships among components of credibility and communication behaviors in work units. *Journal of Applied Psychology, 61,* 99–102.

ORGAN, D. W. (1977). A reappraisal and reinterpretation of the satisfaction-causes-performance hypothesis. *Academy of Management Review, 2,* 46–53.

ORPEN, C. (1978). Work and nonwork satisfaction: A causal-correlational analysis. *Journal of Applied Psychology, 63,* 530–532.

ORPEN, C. (1981). Effect of flexible working hours on employee satisfaction and performance: A field experiment. *Journal of Applied Psychology, 66,* 113–115.

ORPEN, C. (1985). Patterned behavior description interviews versus unstructured interviews: A comparative validity study. *Journal of Applied Psychology, 70,* 774–776.

OSBORN, R. N., & VICARS, W. M. (1976). Sex stereotypes: An artifact in leader behavior and subordinate satisfaction analysis? *Academy of Management Journal, 19,* 439–449.

OSBURN, H. G., CALLENDER, J. C., GREENER, J. M., & ASHWORTH, S. (1983). Statistical power of tests of the situational specificity hypothesis in validity generalization studies: A cautionary note. *Journal of Applied Psychology, 68,* 115–122.

OSBURN, H. G., TIMMRECK, C., & BIGBY, D. (1981). Effect of dimensional relevance on accuracy of simulated hiring decisions by employment interviewers. *Journal of Applied Psychology, 66,* 159–165.

OUCHI, W. G. (1981). *Theory Z: How American business can meet the Japanese challenge.* Reading, MA: Addison-Wesley.

OWENS, W. A. (1968). Toward one discipline of scientific psychology. *American Psychologist, 23,* 782–785.

OWENS, W. A. (1976). Background data. In M. D. Dunnette (ed.), *Handbook of industrial and organizational psychology.* Chicago: Rand McNally.

PANNONE, R. D. (1984). Predicting test performance: A content valid approach to screening applicants. *Personnel Psychology, 37,* 507–514.

PAOLILLO, J. G. (1981). Role profiles for managers at

different hierarchical levels. *Proceedings of the annual meeting of the Academy of Managment, 91–94.*

PARKER, J. W., TAYLOR, E. K., BARRETT, R. S., & MARTENS, L. (1959). Rating scale content: 3. Relationship between supervisory and self-ratings. *Personnel Psychology, 12,* 49–63.

PARSONS, C. K., & HULIN, C. L. (1982). An empirical comparison of item response theory and hierarchical factor analysis in applications to the measurement of job satisfaction. *Journal of Applied Psychology, 67,* 826–834.

PARSONS, C. K., & LIDEN, R. C. (1984). Interviewer perceptions of applicant qualifications: A multivariate field study of demographic characteristics and nonverbal cues. *Journal of Applied Psychology, 69,* 557–568.

PARSONS, H. M. (1982). More on the Hawthorne effect. *American Psychologist, 37,* 856–857.

PARTRIDGE, B. E. (1973). Notes on the impact of flextime in a large insurance company: II. Reactions of supervisors and managers. *Occupational Psychology, 47,* 241–242.

PAVETT, C. M., & LAU, A. W. (1983). Managerial work: The influence of hierarchical level and functional specialty. *Academy of Management Journal, 26,* 170–177.

PEDHAZUR, E. J. (1982). *Multiple regression in behavioral research* (2nd ed.). New York: Holt, Rinehart & Winston.

PENNER, D. D., MALONE, D. M., COUGHLIN, T. M., & HERZ, J. A. (1973). Satisfaction with U.S. Army leadership. *U.S. Army War College, Leadership Monograph Series,* No. 2.

PETER, L. J., & HULL, R. (1969). *The Peter principle.* New York: Morrow.

PETERS, D. L., & McCORMICK, E. J. (1966). Comparative reliability of numerically anchored versus job-task anchored rating scales. *Journal of Applied Psychology, 50,* 92–96.

PETERS, L. H., FISHER, C. D., & O'CONNOR, E. J. (1982). The moderating effect of situational control of performance variance on the relationship between individual differences and performance. *Personnel Psychology, 35,* 609–621.

PETERS, L. H., O'CONNOR, E. J., WEEKLEY, J., POOYAN, A., FRANK, B., & ERENKRANTZ, B. (1984). Sex bias and managerial evaluations: A replication and extension. *Journal of Applied Psychology, 69,* 349–352.

PETTY, M. M., & BRUNING, N. S. (1980). A comparison of the relationships between subordinates' perceptions of supervisory behavior and measures of subordinates' job satisfaction for male and female leaders. *Academy of Management Journal, 23,* 717–725.

PFEFFER, J. (1977). The ambiguity of leadership. *Academy of Management Review, 2,* 104–112.

PFEFFER, J. (1981). Management as symbolic action: The creation and maintenance of organizational paradigms. In L. L. Cummings & B. M. Staw (eds.), *Research in organizational behavior* (vol. 3). Greenwich, CT: JAI Press.

PHILLIPS, J. S. (1984). The accuracy of leadership ratings: A cognitive categorization perspective. *Organizational Behavior and Human Performance, 33,* 125–138.

PHILLIPS, J. S., & LORD, R. G. (1982). Schematic information processing and perceptions of leadership in problem-solving groups. *Journal of Applied Psychology, 67,* 486–492.

PIMBLE, J., & O'TOOLE, S. (1982). Analysis of accident reports. *Ergonomics, 25,* 967–974.

PLOVNICK, M.S., & CHAISON, G. N. (1985). Relationships between concession bargaining and labor–management cooperation. *Academy of Management Journal, 28,* 697–704.

PODSAKOFF, P. M., TODOR, W. D., & SKOV, R. (1982). Effects of leader contingent and noncontingent reward and punishment behaviors on subordinate performance and satisfaction. *Academy of Management Journal, 25,* 810–821.

POKORNEY, J. J., GILMORE, D. C., & BEEHR, T. A. (1980). Job Diagnostic Survey dimensions: Moderating effect of growth needs and correspondence with dimensions of job rating form. *Organizational Behavior and Human Performance, 26,* 222–237.

PORRAS, J. I., & ANDERSON, B. (1981). Improving managerial effectiveness through modeling-based training. *Organizational Dynamics, 9*(4), 60–77.

PORRAS, J. I., & BERG, P. O. (1978). The impact of organizational development. *Academy of Management Review, 3,* 249–266.

PORTER, L. W., & LAWLER, E. E., III (1968). *Managerial attitudes and performance.* Homewood, IL: Irwin.

POSNER, B. Z. (1981). Comparing recruiter, student, and faculty perceptions of important applicant and job characteristics. *Personnel Psychology, 34,* 329–339.

POTTER, E. H., III, & FIEDLER, F. E. (1981). The utilization of staff member intelligence and experience under high and low stress. *Academy of Management Journal, 24,* 361–376.

POWELL, G. N. (1984). Effects of job attributes and recruiting practices on applicant decisions: A comparison. *Personnel Psychology, 37,* 721–732.

PREMACK, S. L. & WANOUS, J. P. (1985). A meta-anlaysis of realistic job preview experiments. *Journal of Applied Psychology, 70,* 706–719.

PRESSEY, S. L. (1950). Development and appraisal of devices providing immediate automatic scoring of objective tests and concomitant self-instruction. *Journal of Psychology, 29,* 417–447.

PRICE, K. H., & GARLAND, H. (1981). Compliance with a leader's suggestions as a function of perceived leader/member competence and potential reciprocity. *Journal of Applied Psychology, 66,* 329–336.

PRIMOFF, E. S. (1975). *How to prepare and conduct job element examinations.* Washington, DC: U.S. Government Printing Office.

PRITCHARD, R. D., DUNNETTE, M. D., & JORGENSON, D. O. (1972). Effects of perceptions of equity and inequity on worker performance and satisfaction. *Journal of Applied Psychology, 56,* 75–94.

PRITCHARD, R. D., HOLLENBACK, J., & DELEO, P. J. (1980). The effects of continuous and partial schedules of reinforcement on effort, performance, and satisfaction. *Organizational Behavior and Human Performance, 25,* 336–353.

PRITCHARD, R. D., LEONARD, D. W., VONBERGEN, C. W., & KIRK, R. J. (1976). The effects of varying schedules of reinforcement on human task performance. *Organizational Behavior and Human Performance, 16,* 205–230.

PRITCHARD, R. D., MAXWELL, S. E., & JORDAN, W. C. (1984). Interpreting relationships between age and promotion in age-discrimination cases. *Journal of Applied Psychology, 69,* 199–206.

PULAKOS, E. D. (1984). A comparison of rater training programs: Error training and accuracy training. *Journal of Applied Psychology, 69,* 581–588.

PULAKOS, E. D., & SCHMITT, N. (1983). A longitudinal study of a valence model approach for the prediction of job satisfaction of new employees. *Journal of Applied Psychology, 68,* 307–312.

QUAYLE, D. (1983). American productivity: The devastating effect of alcoholism and drug abuse. *American Psychologist, 38,* 454–458.

RAFAELI, A., & KLIMOSKI, R. J. (1983). Predicting sales success through handwriting analysis: An evaluation of the effects of training and handwriting sample content. *Journal of Applied Psychology, 68,* 212–217.

RAJU, N. S., & BURKE, M. J. (1983). Two new procedures for studying validity generalization. *Journal of Applied Psychology, 68,* 382–395.

RAJU, N. S., & EDWARDS, J. E. (1984). Note on "Adverse impact from a psychometric perspective." *Journal of Applied Psychology, 69,* 191–193.

RAMBO, W. W., CHOMIAK, A. M., & PRICE, J. M. (1983). Consistency of performance under stable conditions of work. *Journal of Applied Psychology, 68,* 78–87.

RAMOS, R. A. (1981). Employment battery performance of Hispanic applicants as a function of English or Spanish test instructions. *Journal of Applied Psychology, 66,* 291–295.

RANDOLPH, W. A. (1981). Cross-lagged correlational analysis in dynamic settings. *Journal of Applied Psychology, 66,* 431–436.

RASMUSSEN, K. G., JR. (1984). Nonverbal behavior, verbal behavior, resumé credentials, and selection interview outcomes. *Journal of Applied Psychology, 69,* 551–556.

RAUSCHENBERGER, J., SCHMITT, N., & HUNTER, J. E. (1980). A test of the need hierarchy concept by a Markov model of change in need strength. *Administrative Science Quarterly, 25,* 654–670.

RAVEN, B. H., & FRENCH, J. R. P. (1958a). Group support, legitimate power, and social influence. *Journal of Personality, 26,* 400–409.

RAVEN, B. H., & FRENCH, J. R. P. (1958b). Legitimate power, coercive power, and observability in social influence. *Sociometry, 21,* 83–97.

READ, P. B. (1974). Source of authority and the legitimation of leadership in small groups. *Sociometry, 37,* 180–204.

REESE, H. W., & FREMOUW, W. J. (1984). Normal and normative ethics in behavioral sciences. *American Psychologist, 39,* 863–876.

REILLY, R. R., BROWN, B., BLOOD, M. R., & MALATESTA, C. Z. (1981). The effects of realistic previews: A study and discussion of the literature. *Personnel Psychology, 34,* 823–834.

REILLY, R. R., & CHAO, G. T. (1982). Validity and fairness of some alternative employee selection procedures. *Personnel Psychology, 35,* 1–62.

REILLY, R. R., & SMITHER, J. W. (1985). An examination of two alternative techniques to estimate the standard deviation of job performance in dollars. *Journal of Applied Psychology, 70,* 651–661.

REILLY, R. R., ZEDECK, S., & TENOPYR, M. L. (1979). Validity and fairness of physical ability tests for predicting performance in craft jobs. *Journal of Applied Psychology, 64,* 262–274.

RICE, R. W. (1978). Construct validity of the least preferred co-worker score. *Psychological Bulletin, 85,* 1199–1237.

RICE, R. W., INSTONE, D., & ADAMS, J. (1984). Leader sex, leader success, and leadership process: Two field studies. *Journal of Applied Psychology, 69,* 12–31.

RITCHIE, R. J., & MOSES, J. L. (1983). Assessment center correlates of women's advancement into middle management: A 7-year longitudinal analysis. *Journal of Applied Psychology, 68,* 227–231.

ROBERTS, K. H., & GLICK, W. (1981). The job characteristics approach to task design: A critical review. *Journal of Applied Psychology, 66,* 193–217.

ROBEY, D. (1974). Task design, work values, and worker response: An experimental test. *Organizational Behavior and Human Performance, 12,* 264–273.

ROBINSON, D. D. (1981). Content-oriented personnel selection in a small business setting. *Personnel Psychology, 34,* 77–87.

ROETHLISBERGER, F. J., & DICKSON, W. J. (1939). *Management and the worker.* Cambridge, MA: Harvard University Press.

ROGOSA, D. (1980). A critique of cross-lagged correlation. *Psychological Bulletin, 88,* 245–258.

RONAN, W. W. (1980). Some ethical considerations in worker control. *American Psychologist, 35,* 1150–1151.

RONEN, S. (1980). The image of I/O psychology: A cross-national perspective by personnel executives. *Professional Psychology, 11,* 399–406.

RONEN, S. (1981). Arrival and departure patterns of public sector employees before and after implementation of flexitime. *Personnel Psychology, 34,* 817–822.

RONEN, S., & PRIMPS, S. B. (1981). Organizational change: Behavioral and attitudinal outcomes. *Academy of Management Review, 6,* 61–74.

ROSCOE, S. N. (1968). Airborne displays for flight and navigation. *Human Factors, 10,* 321–332.

ROSE, R. L., & VEIGA, J. F. (1984). Assessing the sustained effects of a stress management intervention on anxiety and locus of control. *Academy of Management Journal, 27,* 190–198.

ROSEN, B., & JERDEE, T. H. (1973). The influence of sex-role stereotypes on evaluation of male and female supervisory behavior. *Journal of Applied Psychology, 57,* 44–48.

ROSEN, B., & MERICLE, M. F. (1979). Influence of strong versus weak fair employment policies and applicant's sex on selection decisions and salary recommendations in a management simulation. *Journal of Applied Psychology, 64,* 435–439.

ROSENTHAL, R. (1978). Combining results of independent studies. *Psychological Bulletin, 85,* 185–193.

ROSENTHAL, R., & JACOBSON, L. (1968). *Pygmalion in the classroom.* New York: Holt, Rinehart & Winston.

ROTHAUS, P., MORTON, R. B., & HANSON, P. G. (1965). Performance appraisal and psychological distance. *Journal of Applied Psychology, 49,* 48–54.

ROTTER, G. S., & TINKLEMAN, V. (1970). Anchor effects in the development of behavior rating scales. *Educational and Psychological Measurement, 30,* 311–318.

ROZELLE, R. M., & BAXTER, J. C. (1981). Influence of role pressures on the perceiver: Judgments of videotaped interviews varying judge accountability and responsibility. *Journal of Applied Psychology, 66,* 437–441.

RUBIN-RABSON, G. (1982). The place of women in psychology. *American Psychologist, 37,* 866–867.

RUCCI, A. J., & TWENEY, R. D. (1980). Analysis of variance and the "second discipline" of scientific psychology: A historical account. *Psychological Bulletin, 87,* 166–184.

RUSH, M. C., THOMAS, J. C., & LORD, R. G. (1977). Implicit leadership theory: A potential threat to the internal validity of leader behavior questionnaires. *Organizational Behavior and Human Performance, 20,* 93–110.

RUSSELL, C. J. (1985). Individual decision processes in an assessment center. *Journal of Applied Psychology, 70,* 737–746.

RUSSELL, J. S. (1984). A review of fair employment cases in the field of training. *Personnel Psychology, 37,* 261–276.

RUSSELL, J. S., TERBORG, J. R., & POWERS, M. L. (1985). Organizational performance and organizational level training and support. *Personnel Psychology, 38,* 849–863.

RUSSO, N. F., & O'CONNELL, A. N. (1980). Models from our past: Psychology's foremothers. *Psychology of Women Quarterly, 5,* 11–54.

RYNES, S. L., & MILLER, H. E. (1983). Recruiter and job influences on candidates for employment. *Journal of Applied Psychology, 68,* 147–154.

SAAL, F. E. (1979). Mixed standard rating scale: A consistent system for numerically coding inconsistent response combinations. *Journal of Applied Psychology, 64,* 422–428.

SAAL, F. E., DOWNEY, R. G., & LAHEY, M. A. (1980). Rating the ratings: Assessing the psychometric quality of rating data. *Psychological Bulletin, 88,* 413–428.

SAAL, F. E., & LANDY, F. J. (1977). The mixed standard rating scale: An evaluation. *Organizational Behavior and Human Performance, 18,* 19–35.

SAARI, L. M., & LATHAM, G. P. (1982). Employee reactions to continuous and variable ratio reinforcement schedules involving a monetary incentive. *Journal of Applied Psychology, 67,* 506–508.

SACKETT, P. R. (1982). The interviewer as hypothesis tester: The effects of impressions of an applicant on interviewer questioning strategy. *Personnel Psychology, 35,* 789–804.

SACKETT, P. R., CORNELIUS, E. T., III, & CARRON, T. J. (1981). A comparison of global judgment vs. task oriented approaches to job classification. *Personnel Psychology, 34,* 791–804.

SACKETT, P. R., & DREHER, G. F. (1982). Constructs and assessment center dimensions: Some troubling empirical findings. *Journal of Applied Psychology, 67,* 401–410.

SACKETT, P. R., & DREHER, G. F. (1984). Situation specificity of behavior and assessment center validation strategies: A rejoinder to Neidig and Neidig. *Journal of Applied Psychology, 69,* 187–190.

SACKETT, P. R., & HARRIS, M. M. (1984). Honesty testing for personnel selection: A review and critique. *Personnel Psychology, 37,* 221–245.

SACKETT, P. R., SCHMITT, N., TENOPYR, M. L., KEHOE, J., & ZEDECK, S. (1985). Commentary on Forty questions about validity generalization and meta-analysis. *Personnel Psychology, 38,* 697–798.

SACKETT, P. R., & WADE, B. E. (1983). On the feasibility of criterion-related validity: The effects of range restriction assumptions on needed sample size. *Journal of Applied Psychology, 68,* 374–381.

SACKETT, P. R., & WILSON, M. A. (1982). Factors affecting the consensus judgment process in managerial assessment centers. *Journal of Applied Psychology, 67,* 10–17.

SALANCIK, G. R., & PFEFFER, J. (1977a). An examination of need satisfaction models of job satisfaction. *Administrative Science Quarterly, 22,* 427–456.

SALANCIK, G. R., & PFEFFER, J. (1977b). Constraints on administrator discretion: The limited influence of mayors on city budgets. *Urban Affairs Quarterly, 12,* 475–498.

SALANCIK, G. R., & PFEFFER, J. (1978). A social information processing approach to job attitudes and task design. *Administrative Science Quarterly, 23,* 224–253.

SALINGER, R. D. (1973). *Disincentives to effective employee training and development.* U.S. Civil Service Commission, Bureau of Training.

SAMELSON, F. (1977). World War I intelligence testing and the development of psychology. *Journal of the History of the Behavioral Sciences, 13,* 274–282.

SANDERS, G. S., & MALKIS, F. S. (1982). Type A behavior, need for control, and reactions to group participation. *Organizational Behavior and Human Performance, 30,* 71–86.

SAUSER, W. I., JR., & YORK, C. M. (1978). Sex differences in job satisfaction: A re-examination. *Personnel Psychology, 31,* 537–547.

SCHACHTER, S., & SINGER, J. E. (1962). Cognitive, social, and physiological determinants of emotional state. *Psychological Review, 69,* 379–399.

SCHEIN, E. H. (1981). Does Japanese management style have a message for American managers? *Sloan Management Review, 23,* 55–68.

SCHEIN, V. E. (1973). The relationship between sex role stereotypes and requisite management characteristics. *Journal of Applied Psychology, 57,* 95–100.

SCHEIN, V. E. (1975). Relationships between sex role stereotypes and requisite management characteristics among female managers. *Journal of Applied Psychology, 60,* 340–344.

SCHEIN, V. E., MAURER, E. H., & NOVAK, J. F. (1977). Impact of flexible working hours on productivity. *Journal of Applied Psychology, 62,* 463–465.

SCHMIDT, F. L. (1973). Implications of a measurement problem for expectancy theory research. *Organizational Behavior and Human Performance, 10,* 243–251.

SCHMIDT, F. L., & HUNTER, J. E. (1977). Development of a general solution to the problem of validity generalization. *Journal of Applied Psychology, 62,* 529–540.

SCHMIDT, F. L., & HUNTER, J. E. (1980). The future of criterion-related validity. *Personnel Psychology, 33,* 41–60.

SCHMIDT, F. L., & HUNTER, J. E. (1982). Two pitfalls in assessing fairness of selection tests using the regression model. *Personnel Psychology, 35,* 601–607.

SCHMIDT, F. L., & HUNTER, J. E. (1983). Individual differences in productivity: An empirical test of estimates derived from studies of selection procedure utility. *Journal of Applied Psychology, 68,* 407–414.

SCHMIDT, F. L., & HUNTER, J. E. (1984). A within setting empirical test of the situational specificity hypothesis in personnel selection. *Personnel Psychology, 37,* 317–326.

SCHMIDT, F. L., HUNTER, J. E., & CAPLAN, J. R. (1981). Validity generalization results for two job groups in the petroleum industry. *Journal of Applied Psychology, 66,* 261–273.

SCHMIDT, F. L., HUNTER, J. E., MCKENZIE, R. C., & MULDROW, T. W. (1979). Impact of valid selection procedures on work-force productivity. *Journal of Applied Psychology, 64,* 609–626.

SCHMIDT, F. L., HUNTER, J. E., & PEARLMAN, K. (1981). Task differences as moderators of aptitude test validity in selection: A red herring. *Journal of Applied Psychology, 66,* 166–185.

SCHMIDT, F. L., HUNTER, J. E., & PEARLMAN, K. (1982). Progress in validity generalization: Comments on Callender and Osburn and further developments. *Journal of Applied Psychology, 67,* 835–845.

SCHMIDT, F. L., HUNTER, J. E., PEARLMAN, K., & HIRSH, H. R. (1985). Forty questions about validity generalization and meta-analysis. *Personnel Psychology, 38,* 697–798.

SCHMIDT, F. L., & KAPLAN, L. B. (1971). Composite vs. multiple criteria: A review and resolution of the controversy. *Personnel Psychology, 24,* 419–434.

SCHMIDT, F. L., MACK, M. J., & HUNTER, J. E. (1984). Selection utility in the occupation of U.S. park ranger for three modes of test use. *Journal of Applied Psychology, 69,* 490–497.

SCHMIDT, F. L., OCASIO, B. P., HILLERY, J. M., & HUNTER, J. E. (1985). Further within-setting empirical tests of the situational specificity hypothesis in personnel selection. *Personnel Psychology, 38,* 509–524.

SCHMITT, N. (1976). Social and situational determinants of interview decisions: Implications for the employment interview. *Personnel Psychology, 29,* 79–101.

SCHMITT, N., & BEDEIAN, A. G. (1982). A comparison of LISREL and two-stage least squares analysis of a hypothesized life–job satisfaction reciprocal relationship. *Journal of Applied Psychology, 67,* 806–817.

SCHMITT, N., GOODING, R. Z., NOE, R. A., & KIRSCH, M. (1984). Metaanalyses of validity studies published between 1964 and 1982 and the investigation of study characteristics. *Personnel Psychology, 37,* 407–422.

SCHMITT, N., & MELLON, P. M. (1980). Life and job satisfaction. Is the job central? *Journal of Vocational Behavior, 16,* 51–58.

SCHMITT, N., NOE, R. A., MERITT, R., & FITZGERALD, M. P. (1984). Validity of assessment center ratings for the prediction of performance ratings and school climate of school administrators. *Journal of Applied Psychology, 69,* 207–213.

SCHMITT, N., & SON, L. (1981). An evaluation of valence models of motivation to pursue various post high school alternatives. *Organizational Behavior and Human Performance, 27,* 135–150.

SCHNEIDER, B. (1985). Organizational behavior. *Annual Review of Psychology, 36,* 573–611.

SCHNEIDER, D. J. (1973). Implicit personality theory: A review. *Psychological Bulletin, 79,* 294–309.

SCHNEIDER, J., & MITCHEL, J. O. (1980). Functions of life insurance agency managers and relationships with agency characteristics and managerial

tenure. *Personnel Psychology, 33,* 795–808.

SCHNEIER, C. E., & BARTOL, K. M. (1980). Sex effects in emergent leadership. *Journal of Applied Psychology, 65,* 341–345.

SCHRIESHEIM, C. A. (1978). Job satisfaction, attitudes toward unions, and voting in a union representation election. *Journal of Applied Psychology, 63,* 548–552.

SCHRIESHEIM, C. A., & DeNISI, A. S. (1979). Task dimensions as moderators of the effects of instrumental leader behavior: A path-goal approach. *Proceedings of the annual meeting of the Academy of Management,* 103–106.

SCHRIESHEIM, C. A., & DeNISI, A. S. (1981). Task dimensions as moderators of the effects of instrumental leadership: A two-sample replicated test of path-goal leadership theory. *Journal of Applied Psychology, 66,* 589–597.

SCHRIESHEIM, C. A., & HOSKING, D. (1978). Review essay of Fiedler, F. E., Chemers, M. M., & Mahar, L. Improving leadership effectiveness: The leader match concept. *Administrative Science Quarterly, 23,* 496–505.

SCHRIESHEIM, C. A., & KERR, S. (1974). Psychometric properties of the Ohio State leadership scales. *Psychological Bulletin, 81,* 756–765.

SCHRIESHEIM, C. A., & STOGDILL, R. M. (1975). Differences in factor structure across three versions of the Ohio State leadership scales. *Personnel Psychology, 28,* 189–206.

SCHRIESHEIM, J. F. (1980). The social context of leader–subordinate relations: An investigation of the effects of group cohesiveness. *Journal of Applied Psychology, 65,* 183–194.

SCHRIESHEIM, J. F., & SCHRIESHEIM, C. A. (1980). A test of the path-goal theory of leadership and some suggested directions for future research. *Personnel Psychology, 33,* 349–370.

SCHULTZ, D. P. (1982). *Psychology and industry today: An introduction to industrial and organizational psychology* (3rd ed.). New York: Macmillan.

SCHWAB, D. P., & CUMMINGS, L. L. (1976). A theoretical analysis of the impact of task scope on employee performance. *Academy of Management Review, 1,* 23–35.

SCHWAB, D. P., HENEMAN, H. G., III, & DeCOTIIS, T. A. (1975). Behaviorally anchored rating scales: A review of the literature. *Personnel Psychology, 28,* 549–562.

SCHWAB, D. P., & WICHERN, D. W. (1983). Systematic bias in job evaluation and market wages: Implications for the comparable worth debate. *Journal of Applied Psychology, 68,* 60–69.

SCHWARTZ, B. (1984). *Psychology of learning and behavior* (2nd ed.). New York: Norton.

SCOTT, W. D. (1903). *The theory of advertising.* Boston: Small, Maynard.

SCOTT, W. D. (1908). *The psychology of advertising.* New York: Arno.

SCOTT, W. E., JR. (1977). Leadership: A functional analysis. In J. G. Hunt & L. L. Larson (eds.), *Leadership: The cutting edge.* Carbondale, IL: Southern Illinois University Press.

SCOTT, W. E., JR., & ERSKINE, J. A. (1980). The effects of variations in task design and monetary reinforcers on task behavior. *Organizational Behavior and Human Performance, 25,* 311–335.

SCOTT, W. G., & MITCHELL, T. R. (1976). *Organizational theory: A structural and behavioral analysis.* Homewood, IL: Irwin.

SEERS, A., McGEE, G. W., SEREY, T. T., & GRAEN, G. B. (1983). The interaction of job stress and social support: A strong inference investigation. *Academy of Management Journal, 26,* 273–284.

SEKIMOTO, M. (1983). Performance appraisal in Japan: Past and future. *The Industrial-Organizational Psychologist, 20(4),* 52–58.

SHAFFER, D. R., & TOMARELLI, M. (1981). Bias in the ivory tower: An unintended consequence of the Buckley Amendment for graduate admissions? *Journal of Applied Psychology, 66,* 7–11.

SHANNON, C., & WEAVER, W. (1948). *The mathematical theory of communication.* Urbana, IL: University of Illinois Press.

SHAW, J. B., & RISKIND, J. H. (1983). Predicting job stress using data from the Position Analysis Questionnaire. *Journal of Applied Psychology, 68,* 253–261.

SHAW, M. E. (1964). Communication networks. In L. Berkowitz (ed.), *Advances in experimental social psychology.* New York: Academic Press.

SHERIDAN, J. E., VREDENBURGH, D. J., & ABELSON, M. A. (1984). Contextual model of leadership influence in hospital units. *Academy of Management Journal, 27,* 57–78.

SHIMBERG, B. (1981). Testing for licensure and certification. *American Psychologist, 36,* 1138–1146.

SHRANK, R. (1974). Work in America: What do workers really want? *Industrial Relations, 13,* 124–129.

SIEGEL, A. I. (1983). The miniature job training and evaluation approach: Additional findings. *Personnel Psychology, 36,* 41–56.

SIGELMAN, L., MILWARD, H. B., & SHEPARD, J. M. (1982). The salary differential between male and female administrators: Equal pay for equal work? *Academy of Management Journal, 25,* 664–671.

SILVERMAN, S. B., & WEXLEY, K. N. (1984). Reaction of employees to performance appraisal interviews as a function of their participation in rating scale development. *Personnel Psychology, 37,* 703–710.

SIMON, C. W., & ROSCOE, S. N. (1956). *Altimetry studies: II. A comparison of integrated versus separated, linear versus circular, and spatial versus numerical displays* (Technical Memorandum 435). Culver City, CA: Hughes Aircraft Co.

SIMS, H. P., JR. (1977). The leader as a manager of reinforcement contingencies: An empirical example and a model. In J. G. Hunt & L. L. Larson (eds.), *Leadership: The cutting edge.* Carbondale, IL: Southern Illinois University Press.

SIMS, H. P., JR. (1980). Further thoughts on punishment in organizations. *Academy of Management Review, 5,* 133–138.

SIMS, H. P., JR., & SZILAGYI, A. D. (1975). Leader reward behavior and subordinate satisfaction and performance. *Organizational Behavior and Human Performance, 14,* 426–437.

SINGH, R. (1983). Leadership style and reward allocation: Does Least Preferred Co-worker Scale measure task and relation orientation? *Organizational Behavior and Human Performance, 32,* 178–197.

SKINNER, B. F. (1953). *Science and human behavior.* New York: Macmillan.

SKINNER, B. F. (1959). *Cumulative record.* New York: Appleton-Century-Crofts.

SKINNER, B. F. (1969). *Contingencies of reinforcement.* New York: Appleton-Century-Crofts.

SLOVIC, P., FISCHHOFF, B., & LICHTENSTEIN, S. (1977). Behavioral decision theory. *Annual Review of Psychology, 28,* 1–39.

SMITH, D. B., & PLANT, W. T. (1982). Sex differences in the job satisfaction of university professors. *Journal of Applied Psychology, 67,* 249–251.

SMITH, D. E. (1986). Training programs for performance appraisal: A review. *Academy of Management Review, 11,* 22–40.

SMITH, J. E., & HAKEL, M. D. (1979). Convergence among data sources, response bias, and reliability and validity of a structured job analysis questionnaire. *Personnel Psychology, 32,* 677–692.

SMITH, P. C. (1976). Behaviors, results, and organizational effectiveness: The problem of criteria. In M. D. Dunnette (ed.), *Handbook of industrial and organizational psychology.* Chicago: Rand McNally.

SMITH, P. C., & KENDALL, L. M. (1963). Retranslation of expectations: An approach to the construction of unambiguous anchors for rating scales. *Journal of Applied Psychology, 47,* 149–155.

SMITH, P. C., KENDALL, L. M., & HULIN, C. L. (1969). *The measurement of satisfaction in work and retirement: A strategy for the study of attitudes.* Chicago: Rand McNally.

SNELGAR, R. J. (1983). The comparability of job evaluation methods in supplying approximately similar classifications in rating one job series. *Personnel Psychology, 36,* 371–380.

SNIZEK, W. E., & BULLARD, J. H. (1983). Perception of bureaucracy and changing job satisfaction: A longitudinal analysis. *Organizational Behavior and Human Performance, 32,* 275–287.

SOCIETY FOR INDUSTRIAL AND ORGANIZATIONAL PSYCHOLOGY, INC. (1986). *Graduate training programs in industrial/organizational psychology and organizational behavior.* College Park, MD: Author.

SOCIETY FOR INDUSTRIAL AND ORGANIZATIONAL PSYCHOLOGY, INC. (1987). *Principles for the validation and use of personnel selection procedures* (3rd ed.). College Park, MD: Author.

SONNENFELD, J. (1982). Clarifying critical confusion in the Hawthorne hysteria. *American Psychologist, 37,* 1397–1399.

SORCHER, M., & SPENCE, R. (1982). The InterFace Project: Behavior modeling as social technology in South Africa. *Personnel Psychology, 35,* 557–581.

SORENSON, W. W. (1966). Test of mechanical principles as a suppressor variable for the prediction of effectiveness on a mechanical repair job. *Journal of Applied Psychology, 50,* 348–352.

Specialty guidelines for the delivery of services by industrial/organizational psychologists. (1981). *American Psychologist, 36,* 664–669.

SPECTOR, P. E. (1982). Behavior in organizations as a function of employee's locus of control. *Psychological Bulletin, 91,* 482–497.

SPRINGER, D. (1953). Ratings of candidates for promotion by co-workers and supervisors. *Journal of Applied Psychology, 37,* 347–351.

STAGNER, R. (1982). Past and future of industrial/organizational psychology. *Professional Psychology, 13,* 892–903.

STAGNER, R., & EFLAL, B. (1982). Internal union dynamics during a strike: A quasi-experimental study. *Journal of Applied Psychology, 67,* 37–44.

STAGNER, R., & ROSEN, H. (1965). *Psychology of union–management relations.* Belmont, CA: Wadsworth.

STAHL, M. J. (1983). Achievement, power and managerial motivation: Selecting managerial talent with the Job Choice Exercise. *Personnel Psychology, 36,* 775–789.

STAHL, M. J., & HARRELL, A. M. (1981). Modeling effort decisions with behavioral decision theory: Toward an individual differences model of expectancy theory. *Organizational Behavior and Human Performance, 27,* 303–325.

Standards for educational and psychological testing. (1985). Washington, DC: American Psychological Association.

Standards for providers of psychological services. (1977). Washington, DC: American Psychological Association.

STARKE, F. A., & NOTZ, W. W. (1981). Pre- and post-intervention effects of conventional versus final offer arbitration. *Academy of Management Journal, 24,* 832–850.

STAW, B. M. (1981). The escalation of commitment to a course of action. *Academy of Management Review, 6,* 577–587.

STAW, B. M. (1984). Organizational behavior: A review and reformulation of the field's outcome variables. *Annual Review of Psychology, 35,* 627–666.

STEEL, R. P., & OVALLE, N. K., 2ND. (1984). Self-appraisal based upon supervisory feedback. *Personnel Psychology, 37,* 667–685.

STEERS, R. M. (1983). Murray's manifest needs theory. In R. M. Steers & L. W. Porter (eds.), *Motivation and work behavior* (3rd ed.). New York: McGraw-Hill.

STEERS, R. M., & PORTER, L. W. (1983). *Motivation and work behavior* (3rd ed.). New York: McGraw-Hill.

STEERS, R. M., & RHODES, S. R. (1978). Major influences on employee attendance: A process model. *Journal of Applied Psychology, 63,* 391–407.

STEIN, R. T., & HELLER, T. (1979). An empirical analysis of the correlations between leadership status and participation rates reported in the literature. *Journal of Personality and Social Psychology, 37,* 1993–2002.

STERRETT, J. H. (1978). The job interview: Body language and perceptions of potential effectiveness. *Journal of Applied Psychology, 63,* 388–390.

STEVENS, S. S. (1946). On the theory of scales of measurement. *Science, 103,* 670–680.

STEVENS, S. S. (1951). *Handbook of experimental psychology.* New York: Wiley.

STEWART, R. (1982). The relevance of some studies of managerial work and behavior to leadership research. In J. G. Hunt, U. Sekaran, & C. A. Schriesheim (eds.), *Leadership: Beyond establishment views.* Carbondale, IL: Southern Illinois University Press.

STOGDILL, R. M. (1948). Personal factors associated with leadership: A survey of the literature. *Journal of Psychology, 25*, 35–71.

STOGDILL, R. M. (1959). *Individual behavior and group achievement.* New York: Oxford University Press.

STOGDILL, R. M. (1963). *Manual for the Leader Behavior Description Questionnaire—Form XII.* Columbus, OH: Bureau of Business Research, Ohio State University.

STOGDILL, R. M. (1974). *Handbook of leadership.* New York: Free Press.

STONE, D. L., GUEUTAL, H. G., & MCINTOSH, B. (1984). The effects of feedback sequence and expertise of the rater on perceived feedback accuracy. *Personnel Psychology, 37*, 487–506.

STONE, E. F. (1974). *The moderating effect of work related values on the job scope–job satisfaction relationship.* Unpublished doctoral dissertation, University of California, Irvine.

STONE, E. F., & GUEUTAL, H. G. (1985). An empirical derivation of the dimensions along which characteristics of jobs are perceived. *Academy of Management Journal, 28*, 376–396.

STONE, E. F., GUEUTAL, H. G., GARDNER, D. G., & MCCLURE, S. (1983). A field experiment comparing information-privacy values, beliefs, and attitudes across several types of organizations. *Journal of Applied Psychology, 68*, 459–468.

STONE, E. F., & HOLLENBECK, J. R. (1984). Some issues associated with the use of moderated regression. *Organizational Behavior and Human Performance, 34*, 195–213.

STRASSER, S., & BATEMAN, T. S. (1984). What we should study, problems we should solve: Perspectives of two constituencies. *Personnel Psychology, 37*, 77–92.

STRUBE, M. J., & GARCIA, J. E. (1981). A meta-analytic investigation of Fiedler's contingency model of leadership effectiveness. *Psychological Bulletin, 90*, 307–321.

STRUBE, M. J., & GARCIA, J. E. (1983). On the proper interpretation of empirical findings: Strube and Garcia (1981) revisited. *Psychological Bulletin, 93*, 600–603.

STUMPF, S. A., & LONDON, M. (1981). Management promotions: Individual and organizational factors influencing the decision process. *Academy of Management Review, 6*, 539–549.

STURGIS, S. P., PULLING, N. H., & VAILLANCOURT, D. R. (1981). Measuring drivers' glare sensitivity: Evaluation of an automated technique. *Journal of Applied Psychology, 66*, 97–101.

SUMMERS, L. S. (1984). When in Cairo…: Applying I/O psychology in the Middle East. *The Industrial-Organizational Psychologist, 22*(1), 26–30.

SWAROFF, P. G., BARCLAY, L. A., & BASS, A. R. (1985). Recruiting sources: Another look. *Journal of Applied Psychology, 70*, 720–728.

SZILAGYI, A. D., & SIMS, H. P. (1974). An exploration of the path-goal theory of leadership in a health care environment. *Academy of Management Journal, 17*, 622–634.

SZILAGYI, A. D., JR., & WALLACE, M. J., JR. (1983). *Organizational behavior and performance* (3rd ed.). Glenview, IL: Scott, Foresman.

TABER, T. D., BEEHR, T. A., & WALSH, J. T. (1985). Relationships between job evaluation ratings and self-ratings of job characteristics. *Organizational Behavior and Human Decision Processes, 35*, 27–45.

TASTO, D. L., & COLLIGAN, M. J. (1977). *Shift work practices in the United States* (DHEW Publication No. 77–148). Washington, DC: U.S. Government Printing Office.

TAYLOR, F. W. (1911). *The principles of scientific management.* New York: Harper and Brothers.

TAYLOR, H. C., & RUSSELL, J. T. (1939). The relationship of validity coefficients to the practical effectiveness of tests in selection: Discussion and tables. *Journal of Applied Psychology, 23*, 565–578.

TAYLOR, M. S., & SCHMIDT, D. W. (1983). A process-oriented investigation of recruitment source effectiveness. *Personnel Psychology, 36*, 343–354.

TAYLOR, P. J. (1967). Shift and day work: A comparison of sickness, absence, illness, lateness, and other absence behavior at an oil refinery from 1962 to 1965. *British Journal of Industrial Medicine, 24*, 93–102.

TENOPYR, M. L. (1977). Content-construct confusion. *Personnel Psychology, 30*, 47–54.

TENOPYR, M. L. (1981). Trifling he stands. *Personnel Psychology, 34*, 1–17.

TENOPYR, M. L., & OELTJEN, P. D. (1982). Personnel selection and classification. *Annual Review of Psychology, 33*, 581–618.

TERPSTRA, D. E. (1981). Relationship between methodological rigor and reported outcomes in organization development evaluation research. *Journal of Applied Psychology, 66*, 541–543.

THAYER, P. W., & MCGEHEE, W. (1977). On the effectiveness of not holding a formal training course. *Personnel Psychology, 30*, 455–456.

THOMPSON, D. E., & THOMPSON, T. A. (1982). Court standards for job analysis in test validation. *Personnel Psychology, 35*, 865–874.

THORNDIKE, R. L. (1949). *Personnel selection: Test and measurement techniques.* New York: Wiley.

Thornton, G. C., III. (1980). Psychometric properties of self-appraisals of job performance. *Personnel Psychology, 33*, 263–271.

Tiffin, J. (1942). *Industrial psychology*. New York: Prentice-Hall.

Tilgher, A. (1930). *Work: What it has meant to men through the ages*. New York: Harcourt, Brace and World.

Tjosvold, D. (1982). Effects of approach to controversy on superiors' incorporation of subordinates' information in decision making. *Journal of Applied Psychology, 67*, 189–193.

Toch, H. (1982). Sed qui dicit, non qui negat? *American Psychologist, 37*, 855.

Tolchinsky, P. D., McCuddy, M. K., Adams, J., Ganster, D. C., Woodman, R. W., & Fromkin, H. L. (1981). Employee perceptions of invasion of privacy: A field simulation experiment. *Journal of Applied Psychology, 66*, 308–313.

Torrance, E. P. (1953). Methods of conducting critiques of group problem-solving performance. *Journal of Applied Psychology, 37*, 394–398.

Townsend, J. T., & Ashby, F. G. (1984). Measurement scales and statistics: The misconception misconceived. *Psychological Bulletin, 96*, 394–401.

Trattner, M. H. (1982). Synthetic validity and its application to the Uniform Guidelines validation requirements. *Personnel Psychology, 35*, 383–397.

Travers, R. M. W. (1951). A critical review of the validity and rationale of the forced-choice technique. *Psychological Bulletin, 48*, 62–70.

Tsui, A. S. (1984). A role set analysis of mangerial reputation. *Organizational Behavior and Human Performance, 34*, 64–96.

Tubiana, J. H., & Ben-Shakhar, G. (1982). An objective group questionnaire as a substitute for a personal interview in the prediction of success in military training in Israel. *Personnel Psychology, 35*, 349–357.

Turnage, J. J., & Muchinsky, P. M. (1982). Trans-situational variability in human performance within assessment centers. *Organizational Behavior and Human Performance, 30*, 174–200.

Turnage, J. J., & Muchinsky, P. M. (1984). A comparison of the predictive validity of assessment center evaluations versus traditional measures in forecasting supervisory job performance: Interpretive implications of criterion distortion for the assessment paradigm. *Journal of Applied Psychology, 69*, 595–602.

Turner, A. N., & Lawrence, P. R. (1965). *Industrial jobs and the worker: An investigation of response to task attributes*. Boston, MA: Division

of Research, Graduate School of Business Administration, Harvard University.

Tushman, M. L., & Scanlan, T. J. (1981). Boundary spanning individuals: Their role in information transfer and their antecedents. *Academy of Management Journal, 24*, 289–305.

Tversky, A. (1969). Intransitivity of preferences. *Psychological Review, 76*, 31–48.

Tziner, A., & Dolan, S. (1982). Validity of an assessment center for identifying future female officers in the military. *Journal of Applied Psychology, 67*, 728–736.

Tziner, A., & Vardi, Y. (1982). Effects of command style and group cohesiveness on the performance effectiveness of self-selected tank crews. *Journal of Applied Psychology, 67*, 769–775.

Ulrich, L., & Trumbo, D. (1965). The selection interview since 1949. *Psychological Bulletin, 63*, 100–116.

Umstot, D. D., Bell, C. H., Jr., & Mitchell, T. R. (1976). Effects of job enrichment and task goals on satisfaction and productivity: Implications for job design. *Journal of Applied Psychology, 61*, 379–394.

Umstot, D., Mitchell, T. R., & Bell, C. H., Jr. (1978). Goal setting and job enrichment: An integrated approach to job design. *Academy of Management Review, 3*, 867–879.

U.S. Bureau of the Census. (1975). *Historical statistics of the United States, colonial times to 1970, Bicentennial edition, Part 1*. Washington, DC: U.S. Government Printing Office.

U.S. Bureau of the Census. (1984). *Money income of households, families, and persons in the United States: 1982* (Current Population Report, Series P-60, No. 142). Washington, DC: U.S. Government Printing Office.

U.S. Civil Service Commission. (1970). *Programmed instruction: A brief of its development and current status*. Washington, DC: U.S. Government Printing Office.

U.S. Department of Labor. (1986). *Employment and earnings, 33*(1). Washington, DC: U.S. Government Printing Office.

U.S. Department of Labor, Employment and Training Administration. (1977). *Dictionary of occupational titles* (4th ed.). Washington, DC: U.S. Government Printing Office.

Using the managerial grid to ensure MBO. (1974). *Organizational Dynamics, 2*(4), 54–65.

Valenzi, E. R., & Andrews, I. R. (1971). Effect of hourly overpay and underpay inequity when tested with a new induction procedure. *Journal of Applied Psychology, 55*, 22–27.

VARDI, Y., SHIROM, A., & JACOBSON, D. (1980). A study of the leadership beliefs of Israeli managers. *Academy of Management Journal, 23*, 367–374.

VECCHIO, R. P. (1977). An empirical examination of the validity of Fiedler's model of leadership effectiveness. *Organizational Behavior and Human Performance, 19*, 180–206.

VECCHIO, R. P. (1981). An individual-differences interpretation on the conflicting predictions generated by equity theory and expectancy theory. *Journal of Applied Psychology, 66*, 470–481.

VECCHIO, R. P. (1982). A further test of leadership effects due to between-group variation and within-group variation. *Journal of Applied Psychology, 67*, 200–208.

VECCHIO, R. P. (1983). Assessing the validity of Fiedler's contingency model of leadership effectiveness: A closer look at Strube and Garcia. *Psychological Bulletin, 93*, 404–408.

VINEBERG, R., & JOYNER, J. N. (1982). *Prediction of job performance: Review of military studies.* Alexandria, VA: Human Resources Research Organization.

VITELES, M. S. (1932). *Industrial psychology.* New York: Norton.

VITELES, M. S. (1934). *The science of work.* New York: Norton.

VOGEL, W. (1982). A Judeo-Christian rejoinder to Bramel and Friend's Marxist critique of the capitalist "Hawthorne effect." *American Psychologist, 37*, 859–860.

VROOM, V. H. (1964). *Work and motivation.* New York: Wiley.

VROOM, V. H. (1976). Leadership. In M. D. Dunnette (ed.), *Handbook of industrial and organizational psychology.* Chicago: Rand McNally.

VROOM, V. H., & JAGO, A. G. (1978). On the validity of the Vroom–Yetton model. *Journal of Applied Psychology, 63*, 151–162.

VROOM, V. H., & YETTON, P. W. (1973). *Leadership and decision-making.* Pittsburgh, PA: University of Pittsburgh Press.

WAGNER, R. (1949). The employment interview: A critical summary. *Personnel Psychology, 2*, 17–46.

WAHBA, M. A., & BRIDWELL, L. B. (1976). Maslow reconsidered: A review of research on the need hierarchy theory. *Organizational Behavior and Human Performance, 15*, 212–240.

WAKABAYASHI, M., & GRAEN, G. B. (1984). The Japanese career progress study: A 7-year follow-up. *Journal of Applied Psychology, 69*, 603–614.

WALBERG, H. J., & HAERTEL, E. H. (eds.). (1980). Research integration: The state of the art. [Special issue]. *Evaluation in Education: An International Review Service, 4*, 1–135.

WALL, T. D., & PAYNE, R. (1973). Are deficiency scores deficient? *Journal of Applied Psychology, 58*, 322–326.

WALTER, G. A., & PINDER, C. C. (1980). Ethical ascendance or backsliding? *American Psychologist, 35*, 936–937.

WALTON, R. E. (1975). The diffusion of new work structures: Explaining why success didn't take. *Organizational Dynamics, 3*(3), 2–22.

WANOUS, J. P. (1974a). A causal-correlational analysis of the job satisfaction and performance relationship. *Journal of Applied Psychology, 59*, 138–144.

WANOUS, J. P. (1974b). Individual differences and reactions to job characteristics. *Journal of Applied Psychology, 59*, 616–622.

WANOUS, J. P., KEON, T. L., & LATACK, J. C. (1983). Expectancy theory and occupational/organizational choices: A review and test. *Organizational Behavior and Human Performance, 32*, 66–86.

WANOUS, J. P., & LAWLER, E. E., III (1972). Measurement and meaning of job satisfaction. *Journal of Applied Psychology, 56*, 95–105.

WANOUS, J. P., & ZWANY, A. (1977). A cross-sectional test of need hierarchy theory. *Organizational Behavior and Human Performance, 18*, 78–97.

WATSON, C. J. (1981). An evaluation of some aspects of the Steers and Rhodes model of employee attendance. *Journal of Applied Psychology, 66*, 385–389.

WATSON, K. M. (1982). An analysis of communication patterns: A method for discriminating leader and subordinate roles. *Academy of Management Journal, 25*, 107–120.

WEAVER, C. N. (1977). Relationships among pay, race, sex, occupational prestige, supervision, work autonomy, and job satisfaction in a national sample. *Personnel Psychology, 30*, 437–445.

WEAVER, C. N. (1978a). Black-white correlates of job satisfaction. *Journal of Applied Psychology, 63*, 255–258.

WEAVER, C. N. (1978b). Sex differences in the determinants of job satisfaction. *Academy of Management Journal, 21*, 265–274.

WEAVER, C. N. (1980). Job satisfaction in the United States in the 1970s. *Journal of Applied Psychology, 65*, 364–367.

WEBER, M. (1947). *The theory of social and economic organization.* (A. M. Henderson & T. Parsons, trans.). New York: Oxford University Press.

WEDDERBURN, A. A. I. (1978). Some suggestions for increasing the usefulness of psychological and sociological studies of shiftwork. *Ergonomics, 21,* 827–833.

WEED, S. E., & MITCHELL, T. R. (1980). The role of environment and behavioral uncertainty as a mediator of situation–performance relationships. *Academy of Management Journal, 23,* 38–60.

WEEKLEY, J. A., FRANK, B., O'CONNOR, E. J., & PETERS, L. H. (1985). A comparison of three methods of estimating the standard deviation of performance in dollars. *Journal of Applied Psychology, 70,* 122–126.

WEINER, B., FRIEZE, I., KUKLA, A., REED, L., REST, S., & ROSENBAUM, R. M. (1972). Perceiving the causes of success and failure. In E. E. Jones, D. E. Kanouse, H. H. Kelley, R. E. Nisbett, S. Valins, & B. Weiner (eds.), *Attribution: Perceiving the causes of behavior.* Morristown, NJ: General Learning Press.

WEINER, N. (1980). Determinants and behavioral consequences of pay satisfaction: A comparison of two models. *Personnel Psychology, 33,* 741–757.

WEISS, D. J., DAWIS, R. V., ENGLAND, G. W., & LOFQUIST, L. H. (1967). *Manual for the Minnesota Satisfaction Questionnaire* (Minnesota Studies on Vocational Rehabilitation, vol. 22). Minneapolis, MN: Industrial Relations Center, Work Adjustment Project, University of Minnesota.

WEISS, H. M. (1977). Subordinate imitation of supervisor behavior: The role of modeling in organizational socialization. *Organizational Behavior and Human Performance, 19,* 89–105.

WEISS, H. M. (1978). Social learning of work values in organizations. *Journal of Applied Psychology, 63,* 711–718.

WEISS, H. M., & SHAW, J. B. (1979). Social influences on judgments about tasks. *Organizational Behavior and Human Performance, 24,* 126–140.

WELLS, D. L., & MUCHINSKY, P. M. (1985). Performance antecedents of voluntary and involuntary managerial turnover. *Journal of Applied Psychology, 70,* 329–336.

WELLS, W. D., & SMITH, G. (1960). Four semantic rating scales compared. *Journal of Applied Psychology, 44,* 393–397.

WEXLEY, K. N. (1984). Personnel training. *Annual Review of Psychology, 35,* 519–551.

WEXLEY, K. N., & LATHAM, G. P. (1981). *Developing and training human resources in organizations.* Glenview, IL: Scott, Foresman.

WEXLEY, K. N., & PULAKOS, E. D. (1982). Sex effects on performance ratings in manager–subordinate dyads: A field study. *Journal of Applied Psychology, 67,* 433–439.

WEXLEY, K. N., & YUKL, G. A. (1984). *Organizational behavior and personnel psychology* (rev. ed.). Homewood, IL: Irwin.

Where Skinner's theories work. (1972, December 2). *Business Week,* 64–65.

WHERRY, R. J. (1950). *The control of bias in rating: Survey of the literature* (Tech. Rep. DA-49-0853 OSA 69). Washington, DC: Department of the Army, Personnel Research Section.

WHITE, J. K. (1978). Individual differences and the job quality–worker response relationship: Review, integration, and comments. *Academy of Management Review, 3,* 267–280.

WHITE, M. C., CRINO, M. D., & DeSANCTIS, G. L. (1981). A critical review of female performance, performance training and organizational initiatives designed to aid women in the work-role environment. *Personnel Psychology, 34,* 227–248.

WHITEHEAD, T. N. (1938). *The industrial worker.* Cambridge, MA: Harvard University.

WIARD, H. (1972, Summer). Why manage behavior? A case for positive reinforcement. *Human Resource Management, 11,* 15–20.

WIENER, Y. (1970). The effects of "task-" and "ego-oriented" performance on 2 kinds of overcompensation inequity. *Organizational Behavior and Human Performance, 5,* 191–208.

WILEY, M. G., & ESKILSON, A. (1982). The interaction of sex and power base on perceptions of managerial effectiveness. *Academy of Management Journal, 25,* 671–677.

WILLIAMS, K. J., DeNISI, A. S., BLENCOE, A. G., & CAFFERTY, T. P. (1985). The role of appraisal purpose: Effects of purpose on information acquisition and utilization. *Organizational Behavior and Human Decision Processes, 35,* 314–339.

WILLIAMS, R. (1961). *The long revolution.* London: Chatto and Windus.

WILPERT, B. (1982). Various paths beyond establishment views. In J. G. Hunt, U. Sekaran, & C. A. Schriesheim (eds.), *Leadership: Beyond establishment views.* Carbondale, IL: Southern Illinois University Press.

WILPERT, B. (1983). I/O psychology in Germany: Recent developments and trends. *The Industrial-Organizational Psychologist, 20(3),* 38–42.

WING, H. (1981). Estimation of the adverse impact of a police promotion examination. *Personnel Psychology, 34,* 503–510.

WING, H. (1982). Statistical hazards in the determination of adverse impact with small samples. *Personnel Psychology, 35,* 153–162.

WING, J. F. (1965). *A review of the effects of high ambient temperature on mental performance* (TR 65-102). U.S. Air Force, AMRL.

WINTER, D. G. (1978). *Navy leadership and management competencies: Convergence among tests, interviews, and performance ratings.* Boston: McBer.

WOODMAN, R. W., & SHERWOOD, J. J. (1980). The role of team development in organizational effectiveness: A critical review. *Psychological Bulletin, 88,* 166–186.

WRIGHT, O. R. (1969). Summary of research on the selection interview since 1964. *Personnel Psychology, 22,* 341–413.

WRIGHT, R. L. D. (1976). *Understanding statistics: An informal introduction for the behavioral sciences.* New York: Harcourt Brace Jovanovich.

YEAGER, S. J. (1981). Dimensionality of the Job Descriptive Index. *Academy of Management Journal, 24,* 205–212.

YOUNG, F. W. (1984). Scaling. *Annual Review of Psychology, 35,* 55–81.

YOUNGBLOOD, S. A., MOBLEY, W. H., & MEGLINO, B. M. (1983). A longitudinal analysis of the turnover process. *Journal of Applied Psychology, 68,* 507–516.

YUKL, G. A. (1981). *Leadership in organizations.* Englewood Cliffs, NJ: Prentice-Hall.

YUKL, G. A., & LATHAM, G. P. (1975). Consequences of reinforcement schedules and incentive magnitudes for employee performance: Problems encountered in an industrial setting. *Journal of Applied Psychology, 60,* 294–298.

YUKL, G. A., LATHAM, G. P., & PURSELL, E. D. (1976). The effectiveness of performance incentives under continuous and variable ratio schedules of reinforcement. *Personnel Psychology, 29,* 221–231.

ZAHARIA, E. S., & BAUMEISTER, A. A. (1981). Job preview effects during the critical initial employ-ment period. *Journal of Applied Psychology, 66,* 19–22.

ZALESNY, M. D. (1985). Comparison of economic and noneconomic factors in predicting faculty vote preference in a union representation election. *Journal of Applied Psychology, 70,* 243–256.

ZALEZNIK, A. (1970, May-June). Power and politics in organizational life. *Harvard Business Review, 48,* 47–60.

ZAVALA, A. (1965). Development of the forced-choice rating scale technique. *Psychological Bulletin, 63,* 117–124.

ZEDECK, S., & CASCIO, W. F. (1984). Psychological issues in personnel decisions. *Annual Review of Psychology, 35,* 461–518.

ZEDECK, S., IMPARATO, N., KRAUSZ, M., & OLENO, T. (1974). Development of behaviorally anchored rating scales as a function of organizational level. *Journal of Applied Psychology, 59,* 249–252.

ZEDECK, S., JACKSON, S. E., & SUMMERS, E. (1983). Shift work schedules and their relationship to health, adaptation, satisfaction, and turnover intention. *Academy of Management Journal, 26,* 297–310.

ZEDECK, S., TZINER, A., & MIDDLESTADT, S. E. (1983). Interviewer validity and reliability: An individual analysis approach. *Personnel Psychology, 36,* 355–370.

ZELKO, H. P. (1967). The lecture. In R. L. Craig & L. R. Bittel (eds.), *Training and development handbook.* New York: McGraw-Hill.

ZIMBARDO, P. G. (1979). *Psychology and life* (10th ed.). Glenview, IL: Scott, Foresman.

ZOHAR, D. (1980). Safety climate in industrial organizations: Theoretical and applied implications. *Journal of Applied Psychology, 65,* 96–102.

NAME INDEX

SUBJECT INDEX

Absenteeism:
  and job design, 457, 459
  and job satisfaction, 296, 297,
    305, 313–315, 322,
    449
  and job stress, 439
  and leader behavior, 352
  and organizational theory, 417
  as performance data, 102–104,
    258
  and physical working
    conditions, 503
  social-exchange model of,
    314–315
  and work schedules, 487, 489,
    491–493
Academy of Management Journal,
  145
Accident proneness, 505–507
Accidents, 482, 504–511
  actuarial prediction of, 507
  and job design, 464
  job-related causes of, 504–505,
    507
  as performance data, 102, 104
  prevention of, 286, 507–510
  worker-related causes of,
    505–507
Accomplishment record, 163, 164
Adverse impact, 209–213
Affirmative action, 209, 211–212
AFL-CIO, 377, 379
Agent Orange, 503
Alpha change, 239, 476–477
American Federation of Labor
  (AFL), 376–377
American Psychological
  Association (APA), 3–5,
    7, 8, 10, 12, 15, 20, 58, 72

American Psychological
  Association *(continued)*
  Division 14 (Society for
    Industrial and
    Organizational
    Psychology), 3, 9, 22
  ethical guidelines, 59–61
  *Standards for Educational and
    Psychological Testing,* 148
  women in, 5
American Psychologist, 59
Analysis of variance (ANOVA),
  53–54, 124
Application blanks, 141, 159,
  162–163 *(see also*
    Biographical data)
Apprenticeships, 248–249
Asbestos, 503
Assessment centers, 19, 22, 159,
  173–175, 192
Attitudes:
  definition of, 296–297
  importance of, 328
  and job design, 449–450,
    452–453, 455, 457, 460,
    463–464
  and job satisfaction theories,
    303, 305–306, 308–312
  and labor unions, 378,
    380–384, 394, 396–399
  and leadership theories, 366
  measurement of, 322–323,
    325–327
  and organizational
    communication, 429, 431
  and organizational
    development, 466
  and organizational theories,
    412–413, 418

Attitudes *(continued)*
  and physical working
    conditions, 494, 502
  research on, 298–300
  and work schedules, 483, 485,
    487–490, 493
Attributions:
  for job performance, 127,
    349–350
  and job satisfaction, 310–312
  and leadership, 336–337,
    349–350, 367–368, 369
Authority:
  and collective bargaining, 387
  definition of, 338, 339
  hierarchy of, 408, 410–413,
    415, 421, 450
  and job design, 450–451
  and leadership, 366, 368
  and organizational
    communication, 428–429
  and organizational
    development, 473
  and organizational theories,
    406–408, 410–413, 415,
    419, 421
  and power, 340–343
  and safety, 508, 510
  and women, 344
  and work schedules, 491
Autonomy, 453, 455–457, 459–460

Bargaining:
  collective, 277, 376–377, 383,
    385–392, 395
  concession, 395, 400
  positions, 385–387, 389
    tolerance limits of, 386–387
  zone, 386–387

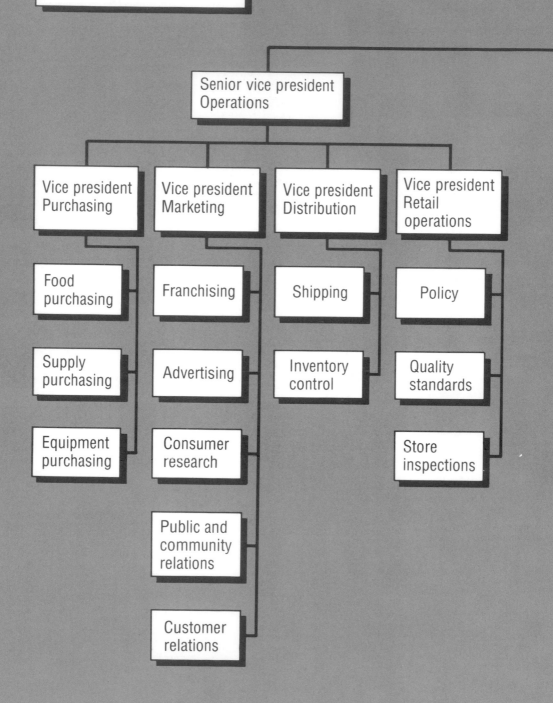